ALSO BY ALVIN TOFFLER AND HEIDI TOFFLER

Future Shock

The Third Wave

Powershift

War and Anti-War

Creating a New Civilization

The Adaptive Corporation

Previews and Premises

The Eco-Spasm Report

The Culture Consumers

Learning for Tomorrow (editors)

The Futurists (editors)

The Schoolhouse in the City (editors)

Revolutionary
Wealth

Revolutionary Wealth

ALVIN TOFFLER
and
HEIDI TOFFLER

ALFRED A. KNOPF   NEW YORK   2006

THIS IS A BORZOI BOOK
PUBLISHED BY ALFRED A. KNOPF

Knopf, Borzoi Books, and the colophon are registered trademarks
of Random House, Inc.

This title may be purchased for business or promotional use or for special sales.
For information, please write to Special Markets Department,
Random House, Inc.,
1745 Broadway, MD 6-3, New York, NY 10019 or e-mail
specialmarkets@randomhouse.com.

Library of Congress Cataloging-in-Publication Data

Toffler, Alvin.
Revolutionary wealth / by Alvin and Heidi Toffler.
p. cm.
ISBN 0-375-40174-1
1. Economic forecasting. 2. Wealth. 3. Social change. 4. Social prediction.
5. Economic history—1945– 6. Social history—1945– 7. Civilization,
Modern,—1950– 8. Twenty-first century—Forecasts. I. Toffler, Heidi, [date].
II. Title.

HB3730.T64 2006
339—dc22   2005044493

Manufactured in the United States of America
First Edition

CONTENTS

Introduction   xiii

PART ONE / REVOLUTION

1. SPEARHEADING WEALTH   3

   Fad of the Month • Loosened Constraints • Guitars and Anti-Heroes • Giggle News • Embedding Intelligence • Capital Tools for Knowledge • The Wilder Shores • Converging Possibilities

2. THE CHILD OF DESIRE   13

   The Meaning of Wealth • Managers of Desire

PART TWO / DEEP FUNDAMENTALS

3. WAVES OF WEALTH   19

   The Pre-Historic Einstein • The Man Who Ate Himself • Beyond Fantasy • Today's Wealth Wave • Three Lives, Three Worlds

4. DEEP FUNDAMENTALS   24

   The Inerrantists • Obsolete Fundamentals • The Future of the Job • Interplay

PART THREE / REARRANGING TIME

5. THE CLASH OF SPEEDS   31

   Trains on Time? • Ready with the Radar • Leaders and Laggards • When Elephants Stand Pat • Inertia Vs. Hyper-Speed

6. THE SYNCHRONIZATION INDUSTRY   41

Dancing Toward Productivity • No More Cold Eggs • No Last-Minute Scramble

7. THE ARRHYTHMIC ECONOMY   46

The Ecology of Time • Casualties of Time • Post-merger Blues • The Time Tax • The Technology Ballet • Supper Without Sushi

8. THE NEW TIMESCAPE   52

The Chains of Time • Love at High Speed • Customizing Time • When Good Ideas Arrive • Media Time • Family, Friends and Face Time • The Americanization of Time? • The 24/7 Future • Whizzing Toward Where?

PART FOUR / STRETCHING SPACE

9. THE GREAT CIRCLE   63

Asia, Ho! • Opening the Floodgates

10. HIGHER-VALUE-ADDED PLACES   66

Yesterday's Places • Dissolving Borders • The Cheap-Labor Derby • Tomorrow's Real Estate

11. SPATIAL REACH   73

Personal Geography • Mobile Money • Invaders and Invaded

12. AN UNREADY WORLD   78

More Capitalist Than Thou • The Evian and Ketchup Test • Yellow Dust • True Believers

13. THRUST REVERSERS   84

The New Titanic • Export Overload • The Nano-Teaspoon • Mad Max Scenarios

14. THE SPACE DRIVE   90

From Dialysis to Heart Pumps • Pilots, Planes and Packages • Unexplored Wealth Frontiers

PART FIVE / TRUSTING KNOWLEDGE

15. THE EDGE OF KNOWLEDGE   99

    Kicking Tires

16. TOMORROW'S "OIL"   104

    The More We Use . . . ? • Steel Mills and Shoes • Our Inner "Warehouse" • Just ASK • Forget Alzheimer's

17. THE OBSOLEDGE TRAP   111

    Yesterday's Truths • Emily's Attic

18. THE QUESNAY FACTOR   115

    Blooper Economics • Estimates of Estimates • Piecemeal Papers • The Missing Framework • The Mistress's Doctor

19. FILTERING TRUTH   122

    Truth on Trial • Six Filters • Consensus • Consistency • Authority • Revelation • Durability • Science • Truth Shifts

20. TRASHING THE LAB   130

    Razor Blades and Rights • Flip-Flop Politics • Patriarchy and Palmistry • Las Vegas as Role Model • The Eco-Missionaries • Secret Science

21. THE TRUTH MANAGERS   139

    Persuading the Boss

22. CODA: CONVERGENCE   143

    Tortoise Time • Once-True Analogies • Mapping the Knowable

PART SIX / PROSUMING

23. THE HIDDEN HALF   151

    The Prosumer Economy • A Mum in a Million • The Potty Test • What Price Disintegration? • Grossly Distorted Product (GDP)

24.   THE HEALTH PROSUMERS   160

      Betting on One Hundred? • *The Panic Zone* • *Besieged by
      Breakthroughs* • *The Diabetes Game*

25.   OUR THIRD JOB   168

      Beyond the Buffet • *The Supermarket Shove*

26.   THE COMING PROSUMER EXPLOSION   172

      Guitars and Golf Bags • *Rampant Consumerism?* • *Cookies
      and Simulations* • *Dwarfing Hollywood* • *Collective Prosuming*
      • *Busting the Hierarchies*

27.   MORE "FREE LUNCH"   180

      Teachers, Nurses and Horses • *Amateurs Matter* • *Uncooking
      the Books* • *Down-to-Earth* • *Attacking Anthrax*

28.   THE MUSIC STORM   187

      Estonian Geeks • *Prosumer Power* • *Baby Prosumers* •
      Liposuction Without Surgery

29.   THE "PRODUCIVITY" HORMONE   194

      Beyond Education • *Rajender's Game*

30.   CODA: INVISIBLE CHANNELS   198

      The Prosumer Impact • *Unnoticed Therapy*

      PART SEVEN / DECADENCE

31.   THE GOSPEL OF CHANGE   205

      The Third Source • *Teen Trash* • *Paul's Story* • *Hollywood
      Hedonism* • *One Step in the River*

32.   IMPLOSION   211

      Pandemic Loneliness • *Post-Kindergarten Factories* • *Creative
      Accounting* • *Intensive Care* • *The Golden Years* • *Politics of
      the Surreal* • *Systemic Breakdown* • *An Epidemic of Failure* •
      Stars on Strike

33. CORRODING THE WIRES   220

FBI Time • Global Space • An Overload of Obsoledge

34. COMPLEXORAMA   225

What Bill Gates Knows • 12,203 Problems

35. THE SEPULVEDA SOLUTION   230

Every American Woman • Fake Transformation • Shifting Chairs • Cameras and Cops • Creating New Institutions • Innovations That Breed Innovations • Inventing the Think Tank

36. CODA: AFTER DECADENCE   240

The Values War • Extreme Extremes • Anti-Decadence • Mingling with Moguls • Inventing New Models • "Satanic Mills" • Post-Cassandra?

PART EIGHT / CAPITALISM'S FUTURE

37. CAPITALISM'S END GAME   253

Cars and Cameras • The Untouchables • The Fetish of Touch • The Horse and the Song

38. CONVERTING CAPITAL   259

Ranges of Risk • Democratic Doorways • Growth in Econo-Land • Flattening the Down

39. IMPOSSIBLE MARKETS   265

Rare Money • Mass + Mass = Mass+ • Flash-Markets • Personal Pricing • Approaching the Limits? • Whispered Secrets • The Virtual Twin

40. RUNNING TOMORROW'S MONEY   273

The Hidden Tax • Blips on Chips • The Closing Bell • Wildcat Currency • Para-Money • The Anti-Obesity Card • Streaming Money • Pepsi Vodka • Prosumer Pay?

PART NINE / POVERTY

41. THE OLD FUTURE OF POVERTY   287

*Hitting the Limit • A Poverty of Strategies • Typical Japanese
"Muck" • The Spillover Effect • Asia Can't Wait*

42. TWIN TRACKS TO TOMORROW   295

*India Awakened • Bangalore Central • The Greatest
Generation? • Yes, but No*

43. CRACKING POVERTY'S CORE   303

*Instead of Trial and Error • Bring on the Bananas • Bio-
Economies • Help from the Heavens • Secret Prices • The
Smartest Agronomist • Smart Dust • Bill Gates's Echo •
What Worked Best Won't • Distributing Energy • Hyper-
agriculture*

PART TEN / THE NEW TECTONICS

44. CHINA'S NEXT SURPRISE?   319

*Looming over the World • Accelerating Acceleration • Global
Space • Mining Knowledge • Wave Politics • Three Chinas •
Mercedes, Malls and Militia • Wave War • The Bloody Thread •
Meet Mao II*

45. JAPAN'S NEXT BAMBOO RING   332

*Latte, Anyone? • Japan's Lopsided Leap • Flex-Nations •
Decision Delay • No More Christmas Cakes • The Silver Wave
• A Filipina or a Robot? • Awaiting the Ring*

46. EUROPE'S LOST MESSAGE   344

*The All-Time Low • The Widening Split • Speeding in Slow
Motion • Yesterday's Heartland • The Lisbon Dream*

47. INSIDE AMERICA   354

*More Wave Warfare • 24 Billion Hours • Stealing the Future •
The Nameless Coalition • Forces for Change • The Next Step*

48. OUTSIDE AMERICA   363

*The Old Game • An "Unsordid Act" • Backlash and
Bewilderment • Reversing Homogeneity*

49. THE UNSEEN GAME OF GAMES   369

*Neo-games • No Longer Human? • Tomorrow's NGOs •
Religio-Economics • God on the Move • The End of Petro-
power • Utopia Past • The Fragility of Power • The Nano-Now*

50. EPILOGUE: THE PROLOGUE IS PAST   380

*The Nostalgia Brigade • A Prosumer Pathway? • Pessimist-in-
Chief • Moon Power • Hope for the Human Race? • From
Picos to Yoctos*

Notes   393

Bibliography   457

Acknowledgments   467

Index   471

INTRODUCTION

All books are written over a span of time—that interval between conception in the author's mind and birth in print. And just as an embryo in a mother's womb is affected by what happens outside the womb, a book in process is necessarily affected by events that make an impression on the writer during gestation. To that degree, even a book about the future is inescapably a product of its own slice of history.

The "slice" it took to write this book was the twelve years bracketing the arrival of the twenty-first century, and no reasonably alert person interested in the world could have escaped the dramatic headlines during that period. An obscure cult's murderous sarin attack on the Tokyo subway; the cloning of Dolly the sheep; the impeachment of Bill Clinton; the decoding of the human genome; the nonoccurrence of a dreaded millennial attack on our computers; the spread of AIDS, SARS and other diseases; the 9/11 attack; the war in Iraq; the great tsunami of 2004, followed by Hurricane Katrina in 2005.

These news stories were matched by economic and business drama as well—the Asian crisis of 1997–98; the dot-com rise, crash and stock market comeback; the introduction of the euro; runaway oil prices; a succession of corporate scandals; out-of-sight U.S. fiscal and trade deficits; and, above all, the ascent of China.

Yet even with all the reportage on business and economics bombarding us in print, online, on TV and on our mobile phones, the biggest story of all—a historic transformation of wealth—was missed or buried in an avalanche of less important factoids. Our task in these pages is to tell that missing story.

Wealth does not arise only from fields, factories, offices and machines. And revolutionary wealth is not just about money.

By now even the dimmest observers recognize that the United States and numerous other countries are transitioning to brain-driven "knowledge economies." But the full impact of this change—on individuals and on whole countries and continents—has yet to be felt. The past half century has merely been prologue.

The importance of knowledge in wealth creation has steadily grown and is now about to leap to a much higher level and cross additional borders as more and more parts of the world plug in to an ever growing, ever changing, ever more accessible planetary brain bank. As a result, we will all, rich or poor, be living and working with revolutionary wealth or its consequences.

The term *revolution* is tossed around so casually these days, attached to new diets and political upheavals alike, that much of its meaning has drained away. In this book, we use the word in its broadest meaning. Compared with the scale of revolution we now face, a collapse of the stock market or a change of regime, the introduction of new technologies, even wars and the breakup of nations don't qualify.

The revolutionary change we focus on in these pages is an upheaval similar to but even more sweeping than the industrial revolution—when thousands of seemingly unrelated changes came together to form a new economic system, accompanied by nothing less than a new way of life, a new civilization, called "modernity."

For wealth to be regarded as truly revolutionary, it has to be transformed not just in quantity, but in how it is created, allocated, circulated, spent, saved and invested. In addition, as we'll explain later, the degree to which it is tangible or intangible must be altered. Only when changes happen at all these levels can we justifiably call wealth "revolutionary."

Today, as we'll show, all that is in fact happening—at unprecedented speed and on a global scale.

As to the other word in the title—*wealth:* While almost all of us live in a money economy, wealth, in these pages, refers not just to money. We also live in a fascinating, largely unexplored, parallel economy. In it, we fulfill many vital needs or wants without pay. It is the combination of these two—the money and the non-money economies—that together form what we will call in these pages the "wealth system."

By simultaneously revolutionizing both of these interacting economies, we are creating a powerful, historically unprecedented wealth system.

To grasp the significance of this, we need to recognize that no wealth system exists in isolation. A wealth system is only one component, although a very powerful one, of a still larger macrosystem whose other components— social, cultural, religious, political—are in constant feedback with it and with one another. Together they form a civilization or way of life roughly compatible with the wealth system.

For this reason, when we speak here about revolutionary wealth, we constantly bear in mind its links with all these other subsystems. To revolutionize wealth, then, as we are doing, is to introduce change—and resistance from vested interests—in all these and many other spheres of life as well.

Revolutionary wealth rests on these core ideas which, once grasped, can help us make sense of the colliding, seemingly senseless changes and conflicts raging around us.

While not economists by profession, we have spent the better part of our careers writing about economic and social policy, development strategy and business issues. Along the way, we have lectured at innumerable universities, testified before the Joint Economic Committee of the U.S. Congress, met with corporate leaders around the globe, and advised presidents and prime ministers on the transition from an industrial to a high-tech, knowledge-based economy.

But economics, even more than other disciplines, needs a grounding in real life. For each of us, "real life" in our youth included five unforgettable years working in factories, on punch presses and assembly lines; making automobiles, aircraft engines, lightbulbs, engine blocks and other products; crawling through ducts in a steel foundry, jackhammering and performing other forms of physical labor. We learned about manufacturing as seen from the bottom. We also know, firsthand, what it feels like to be unemployed.

Since the appearance of *Future Shock,* the first of our books about change and the future, its publication in approximately one hundred countries has given us extraordinary face-to-face access to people in every walk of life—children in Venezuelan slums, Brazilian *favelas* and Argentinean *villas miserias;* billionaires in Mexico, Japan, India and Indonesia; imprisoned female murderers in California; finance ministers and central bankers; and Nobel Prize winners—not to mention kings and queens. In all, they represent many personality types, every religion (and none), every political ideology, every degree of greed or social concern, idealism and cynicism. These varied experiences have provided a real-life context for all economic abstractions.

Of course, no one knows the future—especially *when* something will happen—with certainty. That is why throughout these pages the term *will,* as in "will happen," should always be recognized as a shorthand version of "probably will" or "in our opinion will." That saves us from continually repeating these reservations and qualifications and putting the reader to sleep.

It is also worth bearing in mind that facts have shorter and shorter life spans these days and people move up, down and around, so that an executive identified with corporation A or a professor with university B may already have transferred to corporation or college C by the time this book is read. In addition, readers should not forget one inescapable reality: All explanations are simplifications.

It is important to know two more facts about the writing of this work.

The twelve years it took to write this book would have been even longer if chance hadn't made Steve Christensen available to help speed things up. I

asked Steve, at one point, if he could recommend a good editor to assist us as
we finished the book. To my delight, he recommended himself. An experienced journalist, formerly Western Division editor for United Press International, then one of world's main news agencies, and later editor and general
manager of the Los Angeles Times Syndicate, Steve came on board three
years ago. He proved to be a first-class in-house editor. More important, he
brought with him discipline, brains, warmth, good nature and a delightful, sar-
donic sense of humor. It made finishing this book a pleasure. In the process, it
made a friendship.

Finally, because of the lingering, ultimately fatal illness of Karen, our only
child, which commanded our attention and slowed the writing of this book,
Heidi spent countless round-the-clock years at Karen's bedside, fighting the
disease, hospital bureaucracies and medical ignorance. Her day-to-day contributions to this work were necessarily sporadic. Even so, many of the assumptions, ideas and models behind *Revolutionary Wealth* are the result of our
shared travels, joint interviews and a lifetime of discussion and stimulating
argument.

There were times when Heidi, for a variety of reasons, did not want her
byline on the cover of a book, relenting only in 1993 with the publication of
War and Anti-War, and again in 1995 with the appearance of *Creating a New
Civilization.* But readers should consider all the Toffler books joint products
of our loving life together.

—Alvin Toffler

PART ONE

Revolution

CHAPTER 1

SPEARHEADING WEALTH

This book is about the future of wealth, visible and invisible—a revolutionary form of wealth that will redesign our lives, our companies and the world in the years now speeding toward us.

To explain what that means, the pages ahead will deal with everything from family life and jobs to time pressures and the mounting complexity of everyday life. They will grapple with truth, lies, markets and money. They will cast surprising light on the collision of change and anti-change in the world around us—and inside ourselves.

Today's wealth revolution will unlock countless opportunities and new life trajectories, not only for creative business entrepreneurs but for social, cultural and educational entrepreneurs as well. It will open fresh possibilities for slashing poverty both at home and around the globe. But it will accompany this invitation to a glowing future with a warning: Risks are not merely multiplying but escalating. The future is not for the fainthearted.

Today e-mails and blogs bombard us. EBay makes marketers of us all. Corporate megascandals burst into the headlines. Drugs are belatedly pronounced too dangerous and yanked off the market. Robots go to Mars and land with exquisite precision. But computers, software, cell phones and networks constantly fail. Warming warms. Fuel cells beckon. Genes and stem cells trigger bitter controversy. Nano is the new techno-grail.

Meanwhile, criminal street gangs from Los Angeles roam across Central America and build a quasi-army, and thirteen-year-old aspiring terrorists depart France for the Middle East. In London, Prince Harry dresses as a Nazi even as anti-Semitism re-rears its disgusting head. AIDS wipes out a generation in Africa, while strange new diseases in Asia threaten to sweep across the world.

To escape—or at least forget—what appears like chaos, millions turn to television, where "reality TV" fakes reality. Thousands form "flash mobs" and gather to beat one another with pillows. Elsewhere, players of online games pay thousands of dollars in real money for nonexistent, virtual swords that their virtual selves can use to win virtual castles or maidens. Irreality spreads.

More important, institutions that once lent coherence, order and stability to society—schools, hospitals, families, courts, regulatory agencies, trade unions—flail about in crisis.

And it is against this background that America's trade deficit soars to unprecedented levels. Its national budget staggers drunkenly. The world's finance ministers wonder out loud if they should risk triggering a global depression by recalling the billions they have lent to Washington. Europe celebrates itself for expanding the European Union—but German unemployment hits a fifty-year high and the French and Dutch overwhelmingly reject the proposed E.U. constitution. Meanwhile, China, we're told—again and again—is certain to become the next superpower.

The combination of economic high-wire acts and institutional failures leaves individuals back home face-to-face with potentially devastating personal problems. They question if they will ever receive the pensions for which they have worked, or whether they can afford the rocketing costs of gasoline and health care. They agonize about appalling schools. They worry about whether crime, drugs and an anything-goes morality will destroy civil life. How, everyone wants to know, will this seeming chaos affect our wallets? Will we even have a wallet?

FAD OF THE MONTH

Not only do ordinary mortals find it hard to answer these questions, so do the experts. Corporate CEOs succeed one another like passengers pushing through a rush-hour turnstile: merging, divesting, kowtowing to the stock market; pursuing core competence one month, synergy the next, the latest management fad a month later. They study the most recent economic forecasts, but many economists themselves are befuddled as they wander around in a cemetery of dead ideas.

To decode this new world we need to cut through the chatter of rear-window economists and business pundits who prattle about "business fundamentals." We need to probe below the obsolete obvious. In these pages, therefore, we will focus on the unexplored "deep fundamentals" on which the so-called fundamentals themselves depend.

Once we do, things look different, less crazy, and previously unnoticed opportunities pop out of the shadows. Chaos, it turns out, is only part of the story. And chaos itself generates new ideas.

Tomorrow's economy, for example, will present significant business opportunities in fields like hyper-agriculture, neurostimulation, customized health care, nanoceuticals, bizarre new energy sources, streaming payment systems, smart transportation, flash markets, new forms of education, non-lethal weapons, desktop manufacturing, programmable money, risk management, privacy-invasion sensors that tell us when we're being observed—indeed, sensors of all kinds—plus a bewildering myriad of other goods, services and experiences.

We can't be sure when these will or will not turn profitable or how they will converge. But understanding the deep fundamentals will reveal the existence, even now, of new needs and previously unidentified industries and sectors—a huge "synchronization industry," for example, and a "loneliness industry."

To forecast the future of wealth, we also need to look not just at the work we do for money but at the unpaid work all of us also do as "prosumers." (We'll explain later, but it might shock most people to learn just how much unpaid output we all produce every day.) We'll look, as well, at the invisible "third job" that many of us hold without even knowing it.

Because prosuming is set to explode, the future of the money economy can no longer be understood, let alone forecast, apart from that of the prosumer economy. The two, in fact, are inseparable. Together they form a wealth system. And once we understand this—and the channels by which the two feed each other—we gain piercing insights into our private lives now and into the future.

LOOSENED CONSTRAINTS

New wealth systems don't come often, and they don't travel alone. Each carries with it a new way of life, a civilization. Not just new business structures but new family formats; new kinds of music and art; new foods, fashions and standards of physical beauty; new values; and new attitudes toward religion and personal freedom—all of which interact with and shape the emerging new wealth system.

America today is spearheading just such a new civilization built around a revolutionary way of creating wealth. For better and worse, billions of lives around the world are already being changed by this revolution. Nations and whole regions of the globe are rising or declining as they feel its impact.

Today millions of people around the world dislike or even hate America.

Some fanatics wish to incinerate the United States and everyone in it. The reasons they give range from its Middle East policies and its refusal to sign various international treaties to what they regard as its imperial ambitions.

Yet even if peace reigned in the Middle East, even if all the world's terrorists turned pacifist and democracies flowered like dandelions, the rest of the world would still view the United States with trepidation at best.

This is because the new wealth system the United States is developing, by its very nature, threatens old, embedded financial and political interests around the world. Moreover, in the United States the rise of the new wealth system has been accompanied by controversial changes in the roles of women, racial and ethnic minorities, gays and other groups.

Because America's emergent culture promotes greater individuality, it is seen as a threat to community. Worse yet, because it has loosened some of the traditional sexual, moral, political, religious and lifestyle constraints placed on the individual during earlier economic eras, it is seen as dangerously seducing the young into nihilism, license and decadence.

In short, the combination of revolutionary wealth and the social and cultural changes so far associated with it may have more to do with global anti-Americanism than the usual litany of reasons cited by the media.

The revolutionary wealth system, however, as we'll see, is no longer an American monopoly. Other nations are racing to catch up. And it is not clear how long the United States will retain its lead.

GUITARS AND ANTI-HEROES

The roots of revolutionary wealth can be traced to 1956—the year when, for the first time, white-collar and service workers outnumbered blue-collar workers in the United States. This sea change in the composition of the labor force was arguably the kickoff point for the transition from an industrial economy based on manual labor to one based on knowledge or mind work.

The knowledge-based wealth system is still called the "new economy"—and for convenience we will at times continue to call it that here—but the first computers, still huge and expensive, actually were migrating from government offices into the business world by the mid-1950s. And Princeton economist Fritz Machlup, as early as 1962, showed that in the 1950s knowledge production in the United States was already growing faster than the gross national product.

The 1950s are often pictured as a deadly dull decade. But on October 4, 1957, Russia launched *Sputnik,* the first artificial satellite to orbit the earth, triggering a great space race with the United States that radically accelerated the development of systems theory, information science, software programming and training in project-management skills. It also promoted an emphasis on science and mathematics in U.S. schools. All this began pumping new, wealth-relevant knowledge into the economy.

Culture and politics began to change as well. Just as the industrial revolution centuries ago brought new ideas, art forms, values and political movements, along with new technology, so did the knowledge economy in the United States.

Thus the 1950s saw the universalization of television and the introduction of Elvis Presley, the Fender Stratocaster electric guitar, and rock 'n' roll. Hollywood shifted from heroes and happy endings to surly anti-heroes played by actors like James Dean and Marlon Brando. The literary Beats and their hippie followers glorified "doing your own thing"—a precision attack on the conformity valued in industrial mass societies.

The 1960s were marked by Vietnam War protests and the rise of movements for civil rights, gay rights and equality for women. By 1966 the National Organization for Women was pointing out that "today's technology has . . . virtually eliminated the quality of muscular strength as a criterion for filling most jobs, while intensifying American industry's need for creative intelligence." NOW demanded the right of women to participate on fair terms in the "revolution created by automation" and in the economy generally.

While the world's media focused on these dramatic events, almost no attention was paid to the work of top scientists, funded by the Pentagon, on an obscure new technology called ARPANET—a forerunner of what became the world-changing Internet.

Given this history, the common belief that the "new" economy was the product of a 1990s stock-market bubble, and that it is going to go away, is ridiculous.

GIGGLE NEWS

History records endless examples of "revolutions" that replaced old technologies and even governments without significantly altering society itself and the people in it. By contrast, real revolutions replace institutions as well as technologies. And they do more: They break down and reorganize what social psychologists call the role structure of society.

Today traditional roles are changing at high speed in many countries transitioning to knowledge economies. The roles of husbands and wives, parents and children, professors and students, bosses and workers, in-laws and activists, executives and team leaders all have psychological as well as economic implications. At issue are not merely a person's tasks or functions but the social expectations that come with them.

On and off the job, the result is rising ambiguity, high uncertainty, complexity and conflict as tasks and titles are continuously renegotiated. We see stress and burnout as the roles of doctors and nurse practitioners, lawyers and paralegals, police and community workers are challenged and redefined to a degree not seen since the advent of the industrial revolution.

Revolutions also smash boundaries. Industrial society set a clear border between life at home and life on the job. Today, for the growing millions who work from home, the line is blurred. Even who works for whom is becoming unclear. Robert Reich, former U.S. secretary of labor, points out that a significant part of the labor force consists of independent contractors, free agents and others who work in company A but are actually employees of company B. "In a few years," says Reich, "a company may be best defined by who has access to what data and who gets what portion of a particular stream of revenues over what period of time. There may be no 'employees' at all, strictly speaking."

Academic boundaries are eroding, too. Against enormous resistance, more and more work on the campus is becoming transdisciplinary.

In pop music, borderlines between grime, garage, rock, Eastern, hip-hop, techno, retro, disco, big band, Tejano and a variety of other genres disappear in "fusion" and "hybridization." Consumers turn into producers by remixing or "sampling" sounds from different bands, different instruments and different vocals into "mash-ups"—the musical equivalent of collages.

On TV in the United States, the once-clear line between news and entertainment is being erased as "giggle anchors" joke between headlines and studio audiences applaud. Advertisers insert their messages and products into the story lines of dramas or sitcoms, thus vaporizing the border between entertainment and marketing.

Even sexual boundaries are no longer fixed, as homosexuality and bisexuality blast out of the closet and the small population of transsexuals grows. Just ask Riki Anne Wilchins, a Wall Street computer expert who also happens to be what *The New York Times* described as a "post-operative male-to-female transsexual." Wilchin heads GenderPAC, a group that lobbies Washington on issues pertaining to gender rights and argues that categorizing people as "he" or "she" is itself oppressive, force-fitting into one of those two roles all those who more accurately fit into neither.

Not all the new roles and rights will survive, as still more economic, technological and social changes bombard us. But anyone who underestimates the revolutionary character of today's changes is living an illusion.

The world is being transformed, dramatically and irrevocably.

EMBEDDING INTELLIGENCE

Today there are more than 800 million PCs on the planet—one for every seven or eight human beings.

Today there are more than 500 billion computer chips. Many contain more than 100 million transistors—on-off switches—and Hewlett-Packard has found a way to put billions or even trillions of "molecular-size" transistors on a single, tiny chip.

Today there are something like four billion digital switches clicking on and off for every human being alive on the planet.

Today an estimated 100 billion ever-more-powerful chips deluge the market per year.

In 2002 the Japanese built a computer called the Earth Simulator, designed to help forecast global climate changes. It performed 4 trillion calculations per second—faster than its seven closest rivals combined. By 2005, a computer at Lawrence Livermore National Laboratory was capable of 136 trillion operations per second. And scientists predict that computers may reach petaflop speeds—a thousand trillion mathematical operations a second—by the end of the decade.

Meanwhile, the number of Internet users worldwide is estimated at between 800 million and one billion.

Does anyone really think all these chips, computers, companies and Internet connections are going to vanish? Or that the world's 1.7 billion mobile-phone users are going to throw their phones away? In fact, these, too, are daily morphing into more and more advanced and versatile digital devices.

What we see, therefore, in parallel with the transformation of roles and boundaries in society, is the even more rapid transformation in its knowledge infrastructure. Compared with the changes it makes possible, everything done so far will seem trifling. And not just in a few "developed" countries. For while the United States has spearheaded these developments, they are no longer an "American" phenomenon.

Chinese will soon be the mostly widely used language on the Internet. Korean boys and girls now date in thousands of Internet cafés where they play multi-user computer games against counterparts in Denmark and Canada. Costa Rica, Iceland and Egypt export software. Vietnam hopes its software sales will top $500 million in five years.

Brazil counts more than 22 million Internet users, and the city of Recife has attracted a cluster of foreign information-technology firms, including Microsoft and Motorola, and hundreds of local companies. In addition, according to a U.N. task force, "The last five years in Africa have seen a mobile phone explosion," and while the digital divide is still huge, "tele-centers, cyber cafés and other forms of public Internet access are growing rapidly in urban areas."

In total, according to Digital Planet 2004, the world information-technology market exceeds $2.5 trillion a year. It is served by 750,000 companies around the globe. And change is so rapid that all these numbers are already obsolete by the time you read them.

CAPITAL TOOLS FOR KNOWLEDGE

The digital revolution is not the only source of fundamental change heading in our direction. Our scientific knowledge base is exploding in all directions.

Astronomers are studying "dark matter." Scientists probing anti-matter have created anti-hydrogen. We are making breakthroughs in fields as diverse as conductive polymers, composite materials, energy, medicine, micro-fluidics, cloning, supramolecular chemistry, optics, memory research, nano-technology and scores of others.

U.S. scientists are rightly lamenting recent cutbacks in spending for research in many fields—and especially for basic research. But largely over-looked are advances being made in a special class of technology—the tools use research scientists.

The industrial revolution clicked into high gear and vaulted to a whole new level when, beyond merely building machines to make products, our ancestors began inventing machines to make more—and better—machines. Today we call them capital tools.

This same process on a vastly larger scale is now happening to what might be termed "K-tools"—the instruments we use to generate knowledge, the most important form of capital in advanced economies.

Armed with supercomputers and supersoftware, the Internet and the Web, scientists now also have access to powerful tools that facilitate rapid collabo-ration. They are forming more and more multinational teams, pooling insights, methods and tools across multiple time zones.

Another cluster of K-tools consists of fabulous instruments for visualiza-tion in the laboratory. In principle, researchers can—or soon will be able to—"walk around" inside a single grain of rice to visually observe how its internal structures morph as it grows, then continue to watch as the rice is stored, processed, shipped and cooked. Researchers will be able, as it were, to stroll through an intestine as it digests the rice.

Scientific periodicals and Web sites are filled with advertisements for bet-ter, faster, time-saving lab technologies. "Automate your research," reads one from Roche Applied Science. "Process virtually any sample material to iso-late DNA, RNA, mRNA, and viral nucleic acids in less than two hours. . . .

Perform real-time PCR analysis . . . in less than 40 minutes." Another, from AB Applied Biosystems, announces that "whatever your path of discovery," its DNA analyzer "will get you there faster."

But faster is astonishingly slow when it comes to nuclear physics. To study the erratic motion of individual electrons surrounding the nucleus of an atom, researchers need to fire extremely short bursts of electromagnetic radiation. The briefer the better.

Recently Dutch and French laser scientists broke records by creating pulses of strobe light lasting no more than 250 attoseconds—that is, 250 billion billionths of a second. But to study what happens inside the nucleus, even that is too slow. So American researchers have been working on a "lasetron" designed to create flashes measured in zeptoseconds—billionths of a trillionth of a second.

In all these widely different fields, the next step is clear. We are likely to see, before long, not only more and more potent capital tools for knowledge acquisition but capital tools for making those capital tools.

THE WILDER SHORES

The combination of more scientists, more powerful K-tools, instant communication, widespread collaboration and an ever-broader base of knowledge on which to draw is changing the borders of science itself, reopening questions that were once regarded as B-movie science fiction.

Serious scientists today are no longer afraid of damaging their reputations by talking about time-travel, cyborgs, near-immortality, anti-gravity devices that could transform medicine and provide an endless source of non-fossil-fuel energy, and many other possibilities once found only on the wilder shores of unbelievability.

Discussions of topics like these are not dismissed, as they were when we wrote about them in *Future Shock* in 1970. Nor is it only shaggy-haired scientists who are investing effort in these fields. Some of the biggest corporations in the world—and some armies—are spending huge sums to investigate them.

Day after day, our labs offer fresh discoveries. Many will present us with profound moral issues—witness the conflict over stem-cell research and cloning. We now have clues to the genetic manipulation of certain forms of intelligence. Imagine what that might mean to knowledge-based economies and parents who want biologically smartened children. But also imagine what social and political dangers might arise from such manipulation.

CONVERGING POSSIBILITIES

No one can know for sure where all these breakthroughs will lead. And which will result in practical, profitable products and services that people will want and businesses or governments will supply. Most of today's leads will, no doubt, prove to be dead ends.

But if even one of these fields proves fruitful, its effects on wealth and on society could be explosive. Remember all the experts who swore that airplanes would never fly. Or the London *Times* that assured its readers that the newfangled device called a telephone was just "the latest example of American humbug."

Now add to more powerful capital tools and online collaboration among scientists yet another accelerative factor.

It is a mistake to regard advances in science and technology as stand-alone events. The truly big intellectual—and financial—payoffs occur when two or more breakthroughs converge or are plugged together. The more diverse the projects, the more scientists involved and the more advances made, the greater the potential for novel juxtapositions that yield huge results. We will see many such convergences in the years ahead.

The developments in capital tools for knowledge expansion are like a rocket in the fueling stage, preparing to launch us toward the next phase of wealth creation. That next phase will spread the new wealth system more widely around the world.

A revolution is under way. And the civilization arising with it will challenge everything we thought we knew about wealth.

CHAPTER 2

THE CHILD OF DESIRE

Wealth has a future. Despite all today's profound upsets and reversals, chances are the world will create more, not less, wealth in the years to come. But that is not universally regarded as a good thing.

From the ancients like Aristotle who regarded the pursuit of wealth beyond barest self-sufficiency as unnatural, to nineteenth-century socialists and anarchists who saw wealth as misappropriated property, to many of today's environmental fundamentalists who preach "voluntary simplicity" and regard "consumerism" as a curse, wealth has had a bad name.

Unlike a defendant in an American courtroom, wealth does not enjoy a presumption of innocence. Yet wealth, in itself, is neutral. Which is why, in these pages, wealth is innocent until proven guilty.

What matters is who has and hasn't got it and what purposes it serves. As the Mexican author Gabriel Zaid has written, "Wealth is above all an accumulation of possibilities."

Of course, certain forms of wealth are more or less universally regarded as "good." Health. A strong and loving family. Respect from those we respect. Few would deny that these are wealth, even if they don't easily fit into the calculations of economists.

In everyday usage, however, the term usually refers, all too narrowly, to financial assets, and often carries a connotation of excess. For some, wealth may mean having a bit more than their subjectively perceived need, whatever that is. For others no amount suffices. Among the poor, matters are less subjective. For the mother whose child is starving, a daily handful of rice may be wealth beyond measure. Whatever else it means, therefore, wealth, at least as used here, doesn't just mean a second Ferrari.

Nor is wealth synonymous with money, as popular misconception might have it. Money is only one of many tokens or symbolic expressions of wealth. In fact, wealth can sometimes buy things money cannot.

To understand the future of wealth—our own or anybody else's—in the fullest sense, we need to start with its very origin: Desire.

THE MEANING OF WEALTH

Desire may reflect anything from a desperate need to a transitory want. In either case, wealth is anything that satisfies the craving. It applies balm to the itch. It may, in fact, gratify more than one desire at a time. We may want a touch of beauty on our living room wall. A painting, even an inexpensive reproduction, may provide a small surge of pleasure every time we pause to look at it. The same work of art may simultaneously fulfill our desire to impress visitors with our splendid good taste or our social importance. But wealth can also be a bank account, a bicycle, a hoard of food or a health-insurance policy.

In fact, we can roughly define wealth as any possession, shared or not, that has what economists call "utility"—it provides us with some form of well-being or can be traded for some other form of wealth that does. In any case, wealth is the child of desire. Which is yet another reason some people detest the very thought of it.

MANAGERS OF DESIRE

Some religions, for example, stigmatize desire. Ascetic beliefs propagate passivity in the face of poverty and tell us to seek happiness by reducing, rather than fulfilling, our desires. Want less. Live without. For eons, India did just that—in the midst of unbelievable poverty and misery.

By contrast, Protestantism, when it arose in the West, sent, if anything, the opposite message. Instead of suppressing material desire, it preached hard work, thrift and virtue, promising that if you followed those guidelines, God would help you help yourself to fulfill your desires. The West very largely adopted those values and grew wealthy. It also invented that perpetual desire machine—advertising—to keep generating more and still more desire.

More recently, in the 1970s in Asia, a wizened, tough old Chinese Communist, Deng Xiaoping, was quoted as saying that "to get rich is glorious"—thereby unleashing the pent-up desire of a fifth of the world's population and jolting China out of its age-old poverty.

In the United States, TV screens blare financial advice. Ads for stockbrokers and publications like *Money* and *The Wall Street Journal* erupt from the screen. Infomercials promise ways to save on taxes, make a stock-market killing, strike it rich in real estate and retire to your own sunny island. An enormous barrage of messages legitimizes and promotes desire.

In 2004 alone, U.S. companies paid $264 billion for advertising in newspapers, magazines, TV, radio, direct mail, business publications, telephone books and on the Internet. That same year, advertisers spent $125 billion in Europe and $56 billion in Japan.

In short, whether through asceticism, ideology, religion, advertising or other means, whether consciously or not, the elites in all societies manage desire—the starting point of wealth creation.

Obviously, just pumping up the desire level—or, for that matter, extolling greed, which is different from either wealth or desire—won't necessarily make anyone rich. Cultures that promote desire and pursue wealth do not necessarily attain it. On the other hand, cultures that preach the virtues of poverty usually get precisely what they pray for.

PART TWO

Deep Fundamentals

CHAPTER 3

WAVES OF WEALTH

Human beings have been producing wealth for millennia, and despite all the poverty on the face of the planet, the long-term reality is that we, as a species, have been getting better at it. If we hadn't, the planet would not now be able to support nearly 6.5 billion of us. We wouldn't live as long as we do. And, for better or worse, we wouldn't have more over-weight people than undernourished people on earth—as we do.

We've achieved all this, if we want to call it an achievement, by doing more than inventing plows, chariots, steam engines and Big Macs. We did it by collectively inventing a succession of what we have here been calling wealth systems. In fact, these are among the most important inventions in history.

THE PRE-HISTORIC EINSTEIN

Wealth, in its most general sense, is anything that fulfills needs or wants. And a wealth system is the way wealth is created, whether as money or not.

Long before the first true wealth system arose, we humans apparently began as nomadic hunters, killing or foraging for the barest necessities. With the domestication of animals, hunting and gathering gradually merged with, or gave way to, herding or pastoralism. But thousands of years ago these were little better than survival systems, hardly deserving the term *wealth system.*

It was only with humanity's ability to produce an economic surplus that the first true wealth system became possible. And though a tremendous num-ber of different ways to produce such a surplus have since been tried, we find that over the course of history the methods fall into three broad categories.

The first true wealth system probably emerged ten millennia ago when some prehistoric Einstein (probably a woman) planted the first seed some-where near the Karacadag mountains in what is now Turkey, and thereby introduced a way to create wealth. Instead of waiting for nature to provide, we could now, within limits, make nature do as we wished. (The world should create an annual holiday to honor this unknown inventor whose innovation has affected more lives than any other in human history.)

The invention of agriculture meant that in good years peasant labor might produce a tiny surplus over bare subsistence. And this meant that, instead of living nomadically, our ancestors could settle in permanent villages to culti-vate crops in the nearby fields. Agriculture, in short, brought an entirely new way of life as it spread slowly around the world.

The occasional tiny surplus made it possible to store a bit for the bad days to come. But over time it also enabled governing elites—warlords, nobles and kings, supported by soldiers, priests and tax-and-tribute collectors—to seize control of all or part of the surplus—wealth with which to create a dynastic state and to finance their own luxurious lifestyles.

They could build grand palaces and cathedrals. They could hunt for sport. They could—and regularly did—wage war to capture land and slaves or serfs to produce still greater surpluses for themselves. These surpluses allowed their court to support artists and musicians, architects and magicians, even as the peasants hungered and died.

In short, the First Wave of wealth, as it moved across the map, created what we came to call agrarian civilization.

THE MAN WHO ATE HIMSELF

Across the millennia, agriculture was the most advanced form of production, far more fruitful than hunting and gathering. By AD 1100, writes historian Lynn White, "the heavy plough, the open fields, the new integration of agri-culture and herding, three field rotation, modern horse harness, nailed horse-shoes and the whippletree had combined into a total system of agrarian exploitation." White refers to a "zone of peasant prosperity stretching across Northern Europe from the Atlantic to the Dnieper."

This first wealth wave also brought with it a greater division of labor—hence the need for exchange in the forms of trade, barter, buying and selling.

But hunger and extreme poverty remained the norm. According to histo-rian Teofilo Ruiz, as late as the 1300s in parts of Europe famine might still strike every three or five years. In the words of Piero Camporesi of the Univer-sity of Bologna, "Famine constituted an almost structural feature" of reality down through the seventeenth century. Says historian Richard S. Dunn: "Hamburg lost one quarter of its population in 1565, Venice one-third in 1575–1577, Naples nearly half in 1656."

In a satirical play performed during a famine in 1528, a character declares,

"I shall kill myself. . . . And it will be even better, because I myself shall eat me, and so I shall die well-nourished." Grim humor in an even grimmer era.

Camporesi's unforgettable book *Bread of Dreams* quotes original, vivid sources on the ravages of hunger on the skin and organs of its victims, the putrid smells, the filth and feces, the heaped bodies on piles of dung, and the cannibalism that saw mothers eating their own babies. He writes of the "almost tactile association and intimacy with the products of death—corpse, bones, the diseased and dying." Starving peasants periodically flooded the towns, creating "semi-marginalized" populations and mass mendicancy.

Today First Wave populations predominate in many countries. And while cannibalism may be rare, many of the other horrors described by Camporesi can still be found in backward agrarian regions where peasants even now work and live the way their ancestors did so many centuries ago.

BEYOND FANTASY

A second revolutionary wealth system and society—industrialism—began to emerge in the late 1600s and sent a Second Wave of transformation and upheaval across much of the planet.

Historians still debate the dating and the multiple underlying causes of the industrial revolution. But we know that during that period a remarkable group of Western European intellectuals, philosophers, scientists, political radicals and entrepreneurs, drawing on the ideas of Descartes, Newton and the Enlightenment, changed the world again.

The Second Wave wealth system that sprang up along with these new ideas eventually brought factories, urbanization and secularism. It combined fossil-fuel energy and brute-force technologies requiring rote and repetitive muscle work. It brought mass production, mass education, mass media and mass culture.

Colliding with traditional work ways, values, family structure and increasingly decadent political and religious institutions of the agrarian age, it pitted the interests of a rising commercial, urban-industrial elite against entrenched rural-agricultural elites. Eventually, Second Wave "modernizers" came to power in all of what we now call the "developed" economies.

Industrialism polluted the earth. It was accompanied by colonialism, wars and plenty of misery. But it also gave rise to a vast, expanding urban-industrial civilization that created riches beyond the wildest dreams of our peasant ancestors.

Built on common principles of standardization, specialization, synchronization, concentration, centralization and maximization of scale, industrial economies took various forms. They ranged from Anglo-American capitalism to Stalinist communism, from Sweden's "middle way" to Japan's hierarchical and heavily bureaucratic variant, Korea's variant of that variant, and many other versions. All focused heavily on production in their early stages and consumption later on.

Today, the Organization for Economic Cooperation and Development classes its thirty member nations with a total population of 1.2 billion as "developed" or industrialized. These, along with Russia and several other countries, are products of modernity—the second wealth wave to sweep across the planet.

TODAY'S WEALTH WAVE

The third and latest wealth wave, still explosively spreading as we write, challenges all the principles of industrialism as it substitutes ever-more-refined knowledge for the traditional factors of industrial production—land, labor and capital.

Where the Second Wave wealth system brought massification, the Third Wave de-massifies production, markets and society.

Where Second Wave societies substituted the one-size-fits-all nuclear family for the large extended family of most First Wave agrarian societies, the Third Wave recognizes and accepts a diversity of family formats.

Where the Second Wave built ever-more-towering vertical hierarchies, the Third Wave tends to flatten organizations and brings a shift to networks and many alternative structures.

And these only begin the lengthy list of radical changes. Thus, manufacturing things we can touch—the core function of Second Wave economies—has increasingly become an easily commoditized, comparatively simple, low-value-added activity.

By contrast, such intangible functions as financing, designing, planning, researching, marketing, advertising, distributing, managing, servicing and recycling are frequently more difficult and costly. They often add more value and generate more profit than metal bending and muscle work. The result is a profound change in the relations of different sectors in the economy.

As each wealth wave swelled, it moved unevenly across the world, so that today in countries such as China, Brazil and India we can find all three waves overlapping and moving at the same time—vestigial hunters and gatherers dying away as First Wave peasants take over their land; peasants moving to cities for jobs in Second Wave factories; and Internet cafés and software start-ups cropping up as the Third Wave arrives.

With these shifts comes a combination of decadence, innovation and experiment as old institutions become dysfunctional and people try out new ways of life, new values, new belief systems, new family structures, new polit-ical forms; new types of art, literature and music; new relations between the genders.

No wealth system can sustain itself without a host society and culture. And the host and culture themselves are shaken up as two or more wealth systems collide.

These crude sketches only begin to hint at the differences in the world's three wealth systems and the three great civilizations that come with them. But they are enough to suggest their main themes: If the First Wave wealth system was chiefly based on growing things, and the Second Wave on making things, the Third Wave wealth system is increasingly based on serving, think-ing, knowing and experiencing.

THREE LIVES, THREE WORLDS

It is clear that, just as industrialism usually created more wealth and bigger surpluses per capita than peasant economies ever could, today's emergent, still-incomplete Third Wave wealth system promises to make the amount of wealth produced by all its forerunner systems look minute by comparison. It could increase not only money wealth but human wealth as well—the non-money wealth we make for ourselves and our loved ones.

Each of these three wealth systems imposes different imperatives on soci-eties and the lives of ordinary people. They produce very different forms and amounts of wealth. They have utterly different ecological and cultural conse-quences. And they produce three radically different lifeways.

Compare the lives of a peasant in rural Bangladesh, a Ford assembly-line worker in Cologne and a software writer in Seattle or Singapore. Even within the same country, India, say, compare the peasant in Bihar, the factory worker in Mumbai and the programmer in Bangalore. Operating within different wealth systems, they live in different worlds.

To understand these differences and where they are carrying us, we now need to go where economists and financial pundits seldom take us—to the subterranean fundamentals on which the future of wealth depends.

CHAPTER 4

DEEP FUNDAMENTALS

E very morning, millions of people around the world blink their eyes open and immediately check the Web for stock-market prices, scan the business pages of their newspaper, tune in to the latest business news on TV—or do all three. Only then do they worry about breakfast.

Some, no doubt, would be willing to embed a microchip in their brain if it would automatically alert them to the latest twitch in interest rates or changes in their stock portfolio. Before long, some will.

Until then, housewives in Shanghai, cabdrivers in New York, and currency traders in Frankfurt will have to make do with the close-to-real-time information pumped out, 86,400 seconds a day, by Reuters, Bloomberg, CNBC, CNN, BBC, and their partners and rivals around the world. Providing all this news, online and off, has itself become a global industry.

No one can pretend to understand how the media and its unprecedented output of information (and misinformation) influence and distort stock markets and the world money economy. Nonetheless, amid all the clamor, experts confidently attribute an astonishing variety of stock-market swings, business shifts and economic ups and downs to changes in what they call "fundamentals."

General Motors' chief economist allows that "mainstream economic fundamentals remain strong." The chairman of Time Warner Telecom attributes its success in a weak economy to its "sound business fundamentals" despite the odd fact that its stock price had plummeted 90 percent in the previous twelve months.

A top economist at Credit Suisse First Boston urges investors to look at Russia's "economic fundamentals, rather than its recent history." A high-level Chinese official ascribes the strong export market to "economic fundamentals."

What exactly we mean by that term, however, remains extremely hazy. Depending on who does the talking, it includes factors like "low inflation," "sound credit quality" and "world prices for gold and copper." Or maybe not.

During the wild run-up of the U.S. stock market in the 1990s, economists threw into the definitional gumbo such supposedly fundamental variables as a balanced government budget, a strong manufacturing sector, the presence or absence of a global central bank, the disparity between stock prices and profits, levels of personal borrowing and the percentage of low-wage jobs, not to mention increased bankruptcies.

No doubt some of these variables are important—sometimes. But what if, in fact, by focusing on them we miss some things that are even more important? What if all such factors depend, directly or not, on a deeper set of forces—"deep fundamentals," so to speak, that shape the more superficial fundamentals themselves?

What if the fundamentals tell us one thing and the deep fundamentals another? And what if these more basic, more potent factors are themselves changing at high speed?

THE INERRANTISTS

Christian theologians use the term *inerrantists* for those who insist that, even after two thousand years of problematic interpretations and mistranslations, the Bible is error-free, and that, moreover, its every word must be understood in its most literal sense.

Economics has its own inerrantists who maintain, in the face of all sorts of anomalous, puzzling and contradictory evidence, that nothing has really changed. At the "fundamental" level, they claim the economy has been only minimally affected by the digital upheaval and the shift to a knowledge-based economy.

The manager of one of America's biggest mutual funds reassures an audience of European petrochemical executives that, in finance, things always go up and down, so what's new? Brent Moulton, then an official of the U.S. Bureau of Economic Analysis—a government agency that measures with greater and greater precision variables that mean less and less—advises us that "the economy is still the same as it was before."

This illusion, however, becomes unsustainable the minute we shift our gaze from the everyday fundamentals to the deeper ones. For it is at this deeper level that we find the most compelling evidence that the economy is not "as it was before"—that, in fact, today's entire structure of wealth creation is quaking and rocking, suggesting even bigger changes to come.

OBSOLETE FUNDAMENTALS

Not only are there such sub-surface fundamentals, but there is a coherent way of determining what they are.

Across the planet today, as we've just seen, we find three markedly different wealth-making systems, crudely symbolized by the plow, the assembly line and the computer. The first thing we need to know is that much of what today passes for "fundamental" is not present in all of them. For example, while "a strong manufacturing sector" virtually defines the industrial wealth system, it was vestigial in pre-industrial peasant economies—and still is in many parts of the world.

Again, while the Federal Reserve and central banks in general have played a key role throughout the industrial age, they did not exist as such in pre-industrial societies, and they may not in the future. No less a worthy than the governor of the Bank of England, Mervyn King, has suggested that they may disappear, since many of their functions will no longer be needed or will be carried out automatically by the electronic infrastructure. Among the many so-called fundamentals, in short, some are relevant only for societies at one stage of development and not another.

By contrast, some fundamentals are so vital to wealth creation that they matter in *all* economies, at *all* stages of development, in *all* cultures and every civilization, past or present.

These are the deep fundamentals.

THE FUTURE OF THE JOB

Some of the deep fundamentals are obvious. For example, work.

It may come as a surprise to many that, until field labor was replaced by factory work, few of our ancestors ever held a job. This surely wasn't because they were rich. Most were wretchedly poor. They didn't hold jobs because the "job," in today's sense of formally committed work in return for stipulated pay, had not yet been invented. Like the steam engine and other industrial innovations, jobs and wage labor became widespread only during the last three centuries.

Work itself was transferred from outdoors to indoors, on schedules set no longer by sunrise and sunset but by the punch clock. Most payment came in the form of wages based on hours worked. Indeed, these arrangements essentially defined the term *job*.

But the job is only one way of packaging work. And as the latest, knowledge-based wealth system unfolds, we are moving toward a future in which, as we'll see, more people "work" but fewer hold "jobs." It will drastically alter labor relations, human resource departments, legislation and the overall labor market. It is bad news for trade unions as we know them. The deep fundamental of work is changing more profoundly than at any time since the industrial revolution.

Division of labor, like work itself, traces back to hunting and gathering, when the division was mainly based on gender. But here, too, we are approaching a turning point.

Ever hear of a "metallurgy and failure analysis litigation consultant" or a "post-harvest horticulturalist"? Neither have most of us. (The latter is the superspecialist who determines such things as how many microscopic holes are needed to admit oxygen into the plastic bags that hold vegetables in the supermarket.)

Adam Smith in 1776 called the division of labor the source of "the greatest improvement in the productive powers of labour." And this has been true ever since. But the more refined and specialized tasks become, the harder and more expensive it becomes to integrate them—especially in an innovation-driven competitive economy.

At some point, the costs of integration may exceed the value of such super-specialization. Moreover, narrowly focused specialists may be good at incremental innovation. But breakthrough innovation is often the product of temporary teams whose members cross disciplinary boundaries—at a time when breakthroughs in every field are, in fact, blurring those very boundaries. And this is not just a matter for scientists and researchers.

The new wealth system demands a complete shake-up in the way increasingly temporary skill sets are organized for increasingly temporary purposes throughout the economy. Nothing is more deeply fundamental to the creation of wealth.

Not only are work and the division of labor changing, but income distribution itself—the "who gets what?"—may be heading, over the long term, toward truly revolutionary change.

INTERPLAY

These are just a few examples of fundamentals that lie beneath the "fundamentals." And they are even more important than they may seem because they form a system. Thus, changes in the deep fundamentals interact with one another. Moreover, the limited examples cited so far are just that—limited. A fuller list would surely include others—energy, the environment and family structure, for example—all changing at high speed, all shaking the ground under the more superficial, everyday fundamentals.

Many of the deep fundamentals have received scrutiny from time to time.

For example, since the 1970s, the relationship between the biosphere and wealth creation has become the center of global concern and controversy.

By contrast, several of the deep fundamentals most relevant to revolutionary wealth have, in fact, received scant attention.

That, therefore, takes us on a journey to strange, largely unknown territory to probe three of the fastest-changing, most powerful and most fascinating of all the deep fundamentals today—three that will without question shape the future of wealth.

PART THREE

Rearranging Time

CHAPTER 5

THE CLASH OF SPEEDS

The countries with the key economies in today's world—the United States, Japan, China and the European Union—are all heading for a crisis that none of them wants, that few political leaders are ready for and that will set limits on future economic advance. This looming crisis is a direct result of the "de-synchronization effect," an example of how we mindlessly deal with one of the deepest of all the deep fundamentals: Time.

Nations all over the world today are struggling at different rates of speed to build advanced economies. What most business, political and civil leaders have not yet clearly understood is a simple fact: An advanced economy needs an advanced society, for every economy is a product of the society in which it is embedded and is dependent on its key institutions.

If a country manages to speed up its economic advance but leaves its key institutions behind, it will eventually limit its potential to create wealth. Call it the Law of Congruence. Feudal institutions everywhere obstructed industrial advance. In the same way, today's industrial-age bureaucracies are slowing the move toward a more advanced, knowledge-based system for creating wealth.

This is true of Japan's Okurasho (its Ministry of Finance) and other government bureaucracies. It is true of China's state-owned enterprises and of France's ingrown, elitist ministries and universities. It is also true of the United States. In all these countries, key public institutions are out of step with the whirlwind of change that surrounds them.

Nowhere has this been more evident than in the inability of the U.S. Securities and Exchange Commission to cope with the skyrocketing speed and complexity of the private-sector financial institutions it is supposed to regulate. In the great Enron scandal, in the illegal mutual-fund machinations that directly involved time and timing, and in case after case of overcreative accounting, regulators were left in the dust by the accelerated manipulations of sleazy companies. This was matched elsewhere by the striking failure of U.S. intelligence agencies to shift quickly enough from a focus on Cold-War targets to anti-terrorism capabilities—leaving the door open to the horror of 9/11. More recently, the impact of de-synchronization was dramatized by the embarrassing, tragic ineptitude of governmental responses to Hurricane Katrina in 2005.

Everywhere, as we'll see later, attempts to change or replace an industrial-era agency spark resistance from its traditional beneficiaries and their allies. This resistance creates, or at least contributes to, drastically uneven rates of change. Which helps explain why so many of our primary institutions are dysfunctional—out of sync with the accelerative pace that a knowledge-based economy demands. Today's governments, in brief, have a severe problem with time itself.

TRAINS ON TIME?

The dream of a perfectly synchronized, machinelike society tantalized many of the "modernizers" who influenced the industrial age. Thus, what Taylorism was to the factory, Leninism was to the Soviet Union. The object was to create a state and a society that ran with the efficiency of a machine: every bureaucracy acting as one, every individual moving in lockstep.

But human beings and human societies are, in fact, open systems. Messy and imperfect. In our lives and in our societies, regions of chaos and chance alternate with, and give rise to, regions of temporary stability. We need both.

Stability and synchronization provide the degree of predictability we need to function as individuals in social groups and especially in the economy. Without some stability and time coordination, life is reduced to oppression by anarchy and chance. But what happens when instability and de-synchronization take over?

Despite decades of bloodshed and internal suppression, the Soviet regime (1917–1991) never completed the industrialization that its founders promised. And the synchronization and effectiveness envisioned by the Communist Party never materialized in the formal economy—which worked only because a corrupt underground ran a parallel subterranean economy where, if payoffs were sufficient, the goods just might appear on time.

In 1976, nearly sixty years after Lenin's revolution, coffee was nonexistent and oranges were rare in our Moscow hotel. Bread was measured out and paid for by the gram. Ten years later, even the favored Muscovite middle class was frequently reduced to eating nothing but potatoes and cabbage.

Then came the collapse of the Soviet system and economy. In 1991 in Moscow, we wandered through ghostly supermarkets with virtually empty shelves. We can still see in our mind's eye the few jars of gray, moldy pasta that were on sale. And the freezing old women standing on the steps of public buildings trying to sell a single ballpoint pen or a potholder—their only possessions.

Not only did the Russian economy approach total breakdown, the very social order on which it depended dissolved, and along with it any pretense of synchronized efficiency. No one knew when, or even if, promised products would arrive. Instead of just-in-time, Russian enterprises ran on not-on-time. During one trip, we were prevented from flying to Kiev from Moscow as scheduled, forced to take a midnight train instead because, we were told, no one was sure whether aviation gas would arrive in time for the flight.

People hungered for things to work, for predictability, for someone—as the Italian dictator Mussolini once put it—"to make the trains to run on time." Hoping he could do the job, Russians elected Vladimir Putin.

But societies need more than just trains that run on time. They need institutions that run on time. What happens, however, when one institution runs at such high speeds that it leaves society's other vital institutions miles behind?

READY WITH THE RADAR

No one can answer this question scientifically. The hard data aren't there. Nevertheless, it is revealing to see what's happening to key institutions in America, where the race to a twenty-first-century economy is, at least for now, most advanced.

What follows, then, is a first sketch, purely conjectural and surely controversial, that may help not just business leaders and government policymakers, but all of us as we try to cope with rapid change. And while we use the United States as the example, the implications are international.

Let us focus, then, on rates of change. Start with a mind's-eye image of a freeway. At its side a cop sits astride a motorcycle, pointing a radar gun at the road. On the highway are nine cars, each representing a major institution in America. Each car travels at a speed that matches that institution's actual rate of change.

We'll start with the fastest car on the road.

LEADERS AND LAGGARDS

• One hundred miles per hour: Zooming along at a hundred miles per hour on our figurative freeway is a car representing the fastest-changing major institution in America today—the company, or business. It is, in fact, the driver of many transformations in the rest of society. Companies are not only moving rapidly, they force suppliers and distributors to change in parallel, all driven by intense competition.

As a result, we find firms speeding to alter their mission, functions, assets, products, size, technology, workforce, customer relations, internal culture and just about everything else. Each of these spheres changes at a different rate.

In the business world, technology blasts ahead—at a pace very often faster than managers and employees can handle. Finance, too, is transforming itself at eye-popping speeds in response not just to technology but to new scandals, new regulations, diversifying markets and financial volatility. Meanwhile, accounting and other systems scramble to keep up.

• Ninety miles per hour: There's a car speeding right behind business, and its occupants may surprise you, as they did us. Institution number two, we have concluded, is civil society considered collectively, and packed like circus clowns into that second speeding car.

The civil society is a burgeoning hothouse sector made up of thousands of churning and changing nongovernmental grassroots organizations (NGOs)—pro-business and anti-business coalitions, professional groups, sports federations, Catholic orders and Buddhist nunneries, plastics-manufacturing associations, anti-plastic activists, cults, tax haters, whale lovers and everyone in between.

Most such groups are in the business of demanding change—in the environment, government regulations, defense spending, local zoning, disease-research funding, food standards, human rights and thousands of other causes. But others are dead set against certain changes and do everything they can to prevent or at least slow such change.

Using lawsuits, pickets, and other means, environmentalists have slowed the building of nuclear plants in the United States by delaying their construction and driving legal costs up to the point at which they are potentially unprofitable. Whether one agrees with the anti-nuke movement's position or not, it illustrates the use of time and timing as an economic weapon.

Because NGO-led movements tend to be made up of small, fast, flexible units, organized in networks, they can run rings around huge corporate and government institutions. Overall, a case can be made that none of the other key institutions in American society comes close to the rates of change we see in these two sectors: business and the civil society.

• Sixty miles per hour: The third car, too, has surprising occupants. In it, we find the American family.

For thousands of years, the typical household in most parts of the world was large and multigenerational. Significant change began only when countries industrialized and urbanized, at which point family size shrank. The nuclear-family model, more suitable to industrial and urban conditions, became dominant.

As late as the mid-1960s, experts insisted that the nuclear family—officially defined as a working father, a stay-at-home-mom, and two children under the age of eighteen—would never lose its dominance. Today fewer than 25 percent of American homes fit the designation.

Single parents, unmarried couples, once-, twice- (or more) remarried couples with children from previous alliances, geriatric marriages, and, recently, legalized gay civil unions, if not marriages, have all sprung up or gone public. In a few short decades, therefore, the family system—once among the slowest of all social institutions to change—has been transformed. And another rapid change is on the way.

During the long agrarian millennia, the family unit had many important functions. It worked as a production team in the fields or cottage. It educated its children, tended the sick and took care of the elderly.

As one country after another industrialized, however, work shifted from home to factory. Education was outsourced to the schools. Health care moved to the doctor or hospital. Care of the elderly became a state obligation.

Today, while corporations are outsourcing functions, the American family is insourcing them. For tens of millions of American families, work has already moved back into the home part- or full-time. The same digital revolution that facilitates work-at-home also moves shopping, investing, trading stocks and many other functions into the house.

Education remains locked in the schoolroom but, paralleling work, is likely to migrate at least partially back into the home and to other locations as Internet access, WiFi and cellular communications spread through society. More and more elder care, too, will likely return to the home, spurred by government and private insurance plans that seek to reduce the high costs of nursing homes and hospitalization.

Family formats, frequency of divorce, sexual activity, intergenerational relations, dating patterns, child rearing and other dimensions of family life are all changing rapidly.

• Thirty miles per hour: If companies, NGOs and family arrangements are changing at high speed, what about labor unions?

For half a century, as we've seen, the United States has been shifting from muscle work to mind work, from interchangeable to non-interchangeable skills, and from blindly repetitive to innovational tasks. Work is increasingly mobile, taking place on airplanes, in cars, at hotels and restaurants. Instead of staying in one organization with the same co-workers for years, individuals are moving from project team to task force and work group, continually losing and gaining teammates. Many are "free agents" on contract, rather than employees as such. Yet while corporations are changing at a hundred miles per hour. American unions remain frozen in amber, saddled with legacy organizations, methods and models left over from the 1930s and the mass-production era.

In 1955 U.S. labor unions represented 33 percent of the total workforce. Today that number is 12.5 percent.

The proliferation of NGOs reflects the rapid de-massification of interests and lifeways in a largely Third Wave America. The parallel decline of unions reflects the decay of Second Wave mass society. Unions have a residual role to play, but to survive they will need a new road map and a faster vehicle.

WHEN ELEPHANTS STAND PAT

• Twenty-five miles per hour: Sputtering along in the slow lane, government bureaucracies and regulatory agencies.

Skilled at deflecting criticism and delaying change for decades at a time, pyramidal bureaucracies run the day-to-day affairs of governments all over the world. Politicians know that it is far easier to start a new bureaucracy than to close down an old one, no matter how obsolete or purposeless. Not only do they themselves change slowly; they slow the pace at which business can respond to fast-moving market conditions.

A case in point is the excruciatingly long time it takes the U.S. Food and Drug Administration to test and approve new drugs while desperate victims of disease wait—and sometimes die. Government decision-making is so sluggish that it typically takes a decade or more to gain approval for building a new airport runway and often seven or more years to okay a highway project.

• Ten miles per hour: But even bureaucrats, as they look out their rear-view mirror, can glimpse a car far behind them. This one shudders along with a flat tire and steam coming out of its radiator, slowing down all the traffic behind it. Is it possible it costs $400 billion to maintain this broken heap? The answer is yes, every year. It is the American school system.

Designed for mass production, operated like factories, managed bureaucratically, protected by powerful trade unions and politicians dependent on teachers' votes, America's schools are perfect reflections of the early twentieth-century economy. The best that can be said of them is that they are no worse than schools in most other advanced countries.

While businesses are driven to change by high-speed competition, public-school systems are protected monopolies. Parents, innovative teachers and the media clamor for change. Yet, despite a growing number of educational experiments, the core of U.S. public education remains the factory-style school designed for the industrial age.

Can a ten-mile-per-hour education system prepare students for jobs in companies moving at a hundred miles per hour?

• Five miles per hour: Not all dysfunctional institutions that affect the world economy are national. The economy of every country in the world is substantially influenced, whether directly or not, by global governance—a collection of intergovernmental organizations, or IGOs, such as the United Nations, the International Monetary Fund, the World Trade Organization and scores of less visible entities that set rules for cross-boundary activities.

Some, like the Universal Postal Union, are over a century old. Others sprang up roughly seventy-five years ago during the League of Nations era. Most of the remainder—the WTO and the World Intellectual Property Organization are exceptions—were created after World War II, half a century ago.

Today national sovereignty is being challenged by new forces. New players and new problems are arriving on the international stage. But the bureaucratic structures and practices of the IGOs remain largely in place.

When the 184 nations that form the IMF chose a new head recently, the United States and Germany disagreed sharply over the choice. In the end the German candidate was selected because, according to *The New York Times,* President Clinton and his secretary of the Treasury, Larry Summers, concluded that "they could not violate the 50-year-old rule that allows Europe to fill the IMF post."

• Three miles per hour: Even slower changing, however, are political structures in the rich countries. U.S. political institutions, from Congress and the White House to the political parties themselves, are being bombarded by demands from more and more different groups, all of which expect faster reaction times from systems built for leisurely debate and bureaucratic indolence. As a then-leading member of the U.S. Senate, Connie Mack, once complained to us:

We never have more than two and a half uninterrupted minutes for anything on Capitol Hill. There's no time to stop and think or to have anything approaching an intellectual conversation. . . .

We have to spend two thirds of our time doing public relations, campaigning or raising campaign funds. I'm on this committee, that task force, the other working group, and who knows what else. Do you think I can possibly know enough to make intelligent decisions about all the different things I'm supposed to know about? It's impossible. There's no time. So my staff makes more and more decisions.

We thanked him for his honesty. And then asked: "And who exactly elected your staff?"

The current political system was never designed to deal with the high complexity and frenetic pace of a knowledge-based economy. Parties and elections may come and go. New methods for fund-raising and campaigning are emerging, but in the United States, where the knowledge economy is most advanced and the Internet allows new political constituencies to form almost instantly, significant change in political structure comes so slowly as to be almost imperceptible.

One hardly needs to defend the economic and social importance of political stability. But immobility is another matter. The U.S. political system, two centuries old, changed fundamentally after the Civil War of 1861–1865 and again in the 1930s after the Great Depression, when it adapted itself more fully to the industrial era.

Since then the government has certainly grown. But as far as basic, institutional reform is involved, the U.S. political structure will continue crawling along at three miles per hour, with frequent rest stops at the side of the road, until a constitutional crisis strikes. That could happen sooner than the world thinks. The election of 2000—when the president of the United States was essentially elected by one vote in the Supreme Court—came dangerously close.

• One mile per hour: Which brings us, finally, to the slowest of all our slow-changing institutions: the law. The law has two parts. One is organizational—courts, bar associations, law schools and law firms. The other is the actual body of law these organizations interpret and defend.

While American law firms are changing rapidly—merging, advertising, developing new specialties such as intellectual-property law, teleconferencing, globalizing and struggling to adapt to new competitive realities—American courts and law schools remain basically unaltered. And the pace at which the system operates has remained glacial, with important cases dragging listlessly through the courts for years.

During the landmark antitrust case against Microsoft, widespread speculation arose that the U.S. government might attempt to break up the company. That, however, would take years to accomplish, by which time technological advances would have rendered the entire case irrelevant. It was, wrote Silicon Valley chronicler Robert X. Cringley, a collision between "hyper-accelerated Internet time" and "judicial time."

The body of law is said to be "living"—but only barely so. It changes every day as Congress writes new laws and courts add new interpretations to existing law. But the additions represent a minute, if not infinitesimal, percentage of the total. They inflate the volume and sheer mass of law without significantly recodifying or in any way restructuring the system as a whole.

Of course, law *should* change slowly. It provides a needed degree of predictability to society and the economy, applying brakes in times of overly rapid economic and social change. But how slow is slow?

Until 2000, a law reduced the benefits paid to U.S. Social Security recipients aged sixty-five to sixty-nine by one dollar for every three they earned over a set amount. Written at a time of massive unemployment, its original purpose was to discourage oldsters from working so that more jobs would be available for young people. The law stayed on the books for almost seventy years, prompting *Forbes,* tongue in cheek, to hail the change under the headline, "Flash! The Great Depression Is Over."

The U.S. Congress, after decades of debate, also rewrote two of the fundamental laws governing the knowledge economy. Until 1996, one of the fastest-changing industries in the world—telecommunications—was regulated by a sixty-two-year-old law passed in 1934. In finance, the Glass-Steagall Act, which supervised banking in the United States, also went unchanged for sixty years. Basic rules for the issuance of stocks and other securities in the United States today were written into law in 1933.

Today there are more than 8,300 mutual funds representing nearly 250 million accounts and assets of nearly $7 trillion. Yet these massive investments are still basically subject to a law written in 1940, when there were fewer than 300,000 accounts, managed in only 68 funds, with assets amounting to 1/146,000 of today's total.

In yet another field, when a blackout swept across America's Northeast in 2003, technicians struggling to restore electricity were crippled because, according to Thomas Homer-Dixon of Toronto University, they were forced to use "rules developed decades earlier when most power was generated reasonably close to consumers."

Critical laws directly affecting the advanced economy in fields such as copyright, patents and privacy remain hopelessly out of date. The knowledge economy has emerged not because of these laws but in spite of them. This is neither stability nor immobility. It is legal rigor mortis.

Lawyers may be changing how they work. But law itself is barely in motion.

INERTIA VS. HYPERSPEED

As we look at these institutions and how they interact, it becomes clear that what America confronts today is not simply a runaway acceleration of change but a significant mismatch between the demands of the fast-growing new economy and the inertial institutional structure of the old society.

Can a hyperspeed, twenty-first-century info-biological economy continue to advance? Or will society's slow-paced, malfunctioning, obsolete institutions grind its progress to a halt?

Bureaucracy, clogged courts, legislative myopia, regulatory gridlock and pathological incrementalism cannot but take their toll. Something, it would appear, will have to give.

Few problems will prove more challenging than the growing systemic dysfunctionality of so many related but desynchronized institutions. If Americans want the enormous benefits of a world-leading economy, the United States will have to root out, replace or radically restructure its legacy institutions that stand in the way.

As change accelerates still further, institutional crises will not be limited to the United States. Every country in the twenty-first-century world economy—including China, India, Japan and the E.U. nations—will need to invent new-style institutions and adjust the balance between synchronization and de-synchronization. Some countries may find that more difficult than the United States, whose culture, at least, smiles on change-makers.

In any case, while our partially tongue-in-cheek speed rankings are certainly debatable, one central reality is not: All across the board—at the level of families, firms, industries, national economies and the global system itself—we are now making the most sweeping transformation ever in the links between wealth creation and the deep fundamental of time itself.

CHAPTER 6

THE SYNCHRONIZATION INDUSTRY

Nowhere is a failure to achieve perfect synchronization more lamented than in the bedroom—unless it's when the U.S. Federal Reserve or the Bank of Japan raises or lowers interest rates and gets the timing wrong. Timing, as any comedian can tell us, is everything. But we are, for the most part unwittingly, changing our links to time, and that is no joke.

As interested as investors and economists may be about exact timing in finance, they are remarkably uninformed about the role of synchronization—and, even more so de-synchronization—in the creation of wealth and poverty. Yet understanding these can give us a wholly new way of thinking about wealth creation.

DANCING TOWARD PRODUCTIVITY

Some degree of synchronization has been needed ever since hunters and gatherers began working in groups. Historian William McNeill argues that mass rhythmic activities have been used throughout history to promote synchrony, which in turn improved economic productivity. Tribal dancing, he suggests, strengthened teamwork and made hunting more efficient. For thousands of years fishermen have chanted in unison as they hauled in their nets, the musical beats indicating when to pull and when to breathe.

Agrarian economies also reflected *seasonal* change. According to anthropologist John Omohundro, writing about the Philippine island of Panay, "Through the dry season . . . and into the rainy season . . . businessmen are in their slowest season. All aspects of the distribution system slow down. By September or October the rice crop begins to arrive in town. . . . Because the wealth of the province is regulated by agrarian cycles, city business activity rises and falls by these cycles."

Economic anthropologist Willem Wolters adds: "Purely local banks have never been viable in the semi-arid tropics because of seasonality and synchronic timing."

Early industrial economies operated under completely different temporal conditions. Assembly-line work required a different rhythm. Thus, the factory whistle and the time clock were invented to coordinate work schedules.

By contrast, today, as we will see, business activities are speeding toward real time. In addition, the uses of time are becoming increasingly personalized and irregular, if not erratic. More different tasks need to be integrated, and the acceleration effect truncates the time available for each task. All this makes synchronization harder to achieve. And that's only the beginning.

If we look deeper, we find that every economy throbs and vibrates with unnoticed rhythms. We may buy a newspaper daily, pick up soap or milk at the supermarket weekly, gas up the car every ten days or so, cash a paycheck every two weeks and pay credit card bills monthly. We might call a broker sporadically according to what's happening in the stock market, buy a movie ticket or a book on a whim a few times a year, pay taxes quarterly or annually, go to the dentist when a toothache strikes and purchase a gift for a relative who is getting married in June. These and countless other transactions create rhythms that flow through banks, markets and lives.

With the very first slap on our infant behind, every one of us becomes part of this ongoing economic music. Even our biorhythms are affected (and in turn influence) the marvelously complex, orchestrated processes that pulse around us as people work—making things, providing services, managing others, caring for one another, financing companies or processing data and information into knowledge.

At every moment, some tempos speed up, others slow down. New melodies and harmonies are introduced, then fade out. There are choruses, counterpoints and crescendos. Beyond these, throughout the entire society and economy, there is a generalized pulse of life that is itself the average, as it were, of all its subordinate tempos. The "economic music" never stops.

The result is not patternless chaos because, within every wealth system, various components or subsystems are continually adapting their speeds, phases and periodicities to one another. In biology this process is called "entrainment."

Neurons, it turns out, don't work alone. They form temporary teams—much as businesses increasingly do today. In the words of *Science* magazine, "Neurons frequently fall into step with one another, forming ensembles that play the same tune, as it were, firing in relative synchrony for brief periods, before some neurons drop out of synch, perhaps to join another ensemble."

Firing in sync, moreover, apparently predisposes the neurons to "joint processing" at higher levels of the system. Today's breakup of monolithic corporations into congeries of short-lived project teams, alliances, partnerships and joint ventures parallels these ephemeral "ensembles" in the neural system.

NO MORE COLD EGGS

In a perfectly timed world, friends would never show up late, breakfast eggs would never be cold and kids would always come home on schedule. Better yet, inventories would be reduced to zero, eliminating their various costs, including storage, maintenance, management and warehousing. Best of all, meetings would always begin and end on time.

But what kind of economy would result?

In economics, the term *balanced growth* has been loosely used to mean many things. For some, it suggests that environmental factors are taken into account. For others, it signifies the inclusion of transportation or take your pick of other factors in the definition of "growth." It can mean growth that occurs when capital and labor inputs (adjusted for productivity) increase at the same rate. Alternatively, it can imply an equal emphasis on agriculture and industry in development policy.

In the 1960s and '70s, a school of "balanced growth" economists argued that the best way for an economy to develop was for all sectors to grow at the same rate, with the relations of all inputs and outputs held steady. This was, in fact, a call for perfectly synchronized development—a belief that the path to ever-growing wealth was through ever-greater synchrony. But things are not that simple.

These theorists brushed aside something important. Perfect synchronization, holding key variables in fixed relationships, makes any system inflexible, inert and slow to innovate. It creates an all-or-nothing game in which you have to change everything at once or change nothing at all. And changing everything at once, still less proportionally, is extremely difficult.

By contrast, as economist Joseph Schumpeter showed, economic development also requires "gales of creative destruction"—winds of change that annihilate old, backward technologies and industries to make way for the new and disruptive ones. And the first thing creative destruction tears up is yesterday's timetable.

Every firm, every financial system, every national economy needs, therefore, both synchronization and some degree of de-synchronization. Unfortunately, at present we lack both the data and the metrics that would help us know when we are about to crash the limits of either. What might be called "chronomics"—the study of timing in the economy—is still primitive at best.

NO LAST-MINUTE SCRAMBLE

What is clear, however, is that time adjustment is now so complex and important that a big, booming synchronization industry has grown up around it. This industry experienced three "great leaps forward" between the mid-1980s and the beginning of the new century. Today it is a giant. Tomorrow it will be even bigger.

In 1985, when the Institute of Industrial Engineers published a book called *Innovations in Management: The Japanese Corporation,* the term *kanban*— what the West came to call the "just-in-time" principle or JIT—hardly rated mention. Manufacturing in the United States was still dominated by something called material requirements planning or MRP, a mainframe-based system for scheduling factory resource requirements.

MRP's purpose was to produce parts and products according to a preset schedule. The JIT system, by contrast, first developed by Toyota, allowed the customers' changing needs to set the schedule. It made flexible timing practical.

By 1990, when the National Center for Manufacturing Sciences in the United States published its *Competing in World-Class Manufacturing* report, JIT had already become a buzzword in America and was spreading throughout manufacturing.

Soon management consultants jumped on board the JIT express and sped its implementation. IBM, Motorola, Harley-Davidson and scores of other leading firms adopted it. A study of 291 diverse manufacturing facilities in the United States and 128 in thirty other countries found that, as the NCMS summarized it, "of the many potential means of improving productivity, only JIT-related ones were statistically shown to be consistently effective." What JIT did, however, was shave time tolerances even more closely. And that required far more sophisticated synchronization than ever before.

Another burst of change in business began when consultants Jim Champy and Michael Hammer, in their best-selling book *Reengineering the Corporation,* told managers to "reengineer" their firms when "leading competitors achieve significantly shorter development cycles," when the organization responds to markets too slowly, when orders are late or when work is marked by "last-minute scrambles."

Synchronization blasted into hyperdrive in its next phase. This went beyond a single supplier and required the restructuring of entire long supply chains in the 1990s and early 2000s. Not only did first-tier makers of components have to deliver them as needed, but second-tier suppliers did as well, in order to accelerate through-put and reduce inventories. The goal was tighter synchronization at every level.

Huge companies such as Oracle, SAP, PeopleSoft and scores of others offering enterprise resource planning (ERP) and related software owe their very existence, in substantial measure, to the mounting demand for smarter and closer timing in business. Hundreds of consulting firms by now were heavily into the synchronization business. SAP or Oracle, say, would sell the software. Then I.T. consultants would be called in to implement it.

Anderson Consulting (now Accenture), one of the largest consulting firms in the world, owed much of its remarkable growth to the new synchronization systems. In the words of David L. Anderson, an Accenture consultant, and Professor Hau Lee of Stanford University, "The greater the synchronization, the greater the value added to the entire supply chain's performance." No wonder some UPS delivery trucks bear the slogan: "Synchronizing the World of Commerce."

The synchronization industry still has a long way to go—and grow. First, many small firms that have not yet restructured their supply and/or value chains will increasingly be compelled to do so. Second, synchronizing supply and distribution chains is only one step toward tomorrow's deeper and more comprehensive temporal integration. Now the synchronizers want to do more than sell just the initial software. They also want to service their direct customers and tier after tier of downstream customers stretching all the way to the end user.

Indeed, it may even extend beyond that someday because more and more products may be returned to the manufacturer for recycling, as is already the case with autos in Europe and printer ink cartridges in the United States. All these changes multiply layer after layer of suppliers, distributors, servicers and users needing synchronization. Last, the synchronization industry will expand because rising competition requires innovation after innovation, each of which, in turn, changes timing requirements and requires re-synchronization.

But the hidden paradox of the law of de-synchronization is that the more you synchronize at one level in a system, the more you de-synchronize at another.

CHAPTER 7

THE ARRHYTHMIC
ECONOMY

Until recently, a mindless cult of acceleration led by numerous business "gurus" in the United States urged companies to "Be first! Be agile! Shoot now, aim later!" This simplistic advice led to the launch of many low-quality, poorly tested products; angry customers; unhappy investors; a loss of strategic focus; and a high turnover of CEOs. It ignored the problems of synchronization and de-synchronization. It was a superficial way of dealing with the deep fundamental of time.

Mismatched timing can damage—even kill—individual companies. But that isn't just a problem of particular enterprises. It can upset relations among multiple firms. Moreover, anecdotal evidence at least suggests that it can impact whole industries, entire sectors of a country's economy, and even the global economy.

THE ECOLOGY OF TIME

Study a small lake or pond and you are likely to find many intertwined life-forms, including host and parasite species, some reproducing quickly, others slowly, all changing at different speeds as they interact with one another in a kind of ecological ballet.

Inside every business, too—and every hospital, school, government agency or city hall—there is what might be called an "ecology of time," with different subunits and processes all interacting and running at different speeds. Though truly perfect synchronization is never attainable, under ordinary conditions the lack of synchrony may be maintained at a tolerable degree.

But conditions today are far from ordinary. The gurus' advice was unrealistic, but the acceleration they sought to address was—and is—very real.

Never have the pressures been greater for companies—and other organizations as well—to speed up their operations. Cascading technological innovations and consumer or client demands for instant gratification, added to the competition, all conspire to drive up the pace of change. If one department or division falls behind, multiplier effects ricochet throughout the entire organization.

One often-overlooked cost reflects the diversion of energy and attention from other needed tasks as time becomes increasingly politicized. Often, organization leaders find themselves clashing bitterly over conflicting schedules and time horizons, and I.T. departments become battle zones.

CASUALTIES OF TIME

The time needed for software development or for a major system overhaul is notoriously difficult to estimate. It can even be hard to estimate how long it will take to make the estimate. But that is what I.T. executives are often compelled to do.

Software managers who insist they need a long time to complete a project catch flak from bosses and from department chieftains whose work might be slowed or disrupted. On the other hand, I.T. managers who promise quick results are frequently fired when subsequent glitches impede progress.

As various business units are de-synchronized and schedules need revision, budgets, power and egos come into play and a lot of emotional artillery is called up. Time itself, in the form of deliberate delays or imposed deadlines, may be used as an internecine weapon.

Battles over timing are even more common in connection with research and development. Pressed by investors demanding faster returns, CEOs often feel compelled to slash spending on R&D. Or they shift funding away from research to development and reallocate whatever is left from basic to applied research. The result slows major innovation when it is most needed.

Time battles inside a fast-changing firm take many other forms as well. They can kill important deals and, ironically, can actually waste so much management attention and energy that they slow down the firm's overall capacity to adapt to change.

POST-MERGER BLUES

Things become even more complicated when they involve two or more companies, each with its own internal ecology of time. Fights over synchronization greatly complicate partnerships, joint ventures and other alliances and are particularly stressful before and after mergers.

Even when the main hurdles are overcome, trying to sync up the internal rhythms of two firms after their marriage takes time, costs money, sucks attention from other matters, disrupts operations—and upsets already upset people. People hate to be speeded up—or slowed down—by others. Though little is written about it, many partnerships and mergers founder precisely because synchronization turns out to be so painful. Witness AOL Time Warner. Nor are technological issues necessarily the most difficult.

Within any firm, de-synchronization can occur among divisions, functions, hierarchical levels, regional offices and in other dimensions as well. Often it is culture that is the breaking point.

When a new CEO took over Siemens Nixdorf some years back, he seemed, according to the *Financial Times,* "more worried about units of time" than dollars. Siemens, the German electronics giant, had acquired Nixdorf, a PC firm, to supplement its mainframe-computer business.

The CEO knew that part of the firm needed to "have a major technical feature change every six months." The parent firm, however, was older, more hierarchical and slower to react. Changing a product is one thing. But, as he complained at a press conference, "changing a corporation's mentality usually takes three to five years, and we don't have it." The CEO is no longer at Siemens—and neither is Nixdorf.

Scaling up from companies, we find even bigger examples of costly de-synchronization at the level of whole industries. Some, indeed, are infamous for being out of sync.

THE TIME TAX

Ask any American who has ever hired a contractor to build or remodel a house. Chances are the estimated completion date is a fairy tale. Delays may run to months. Needed parts—everything from flush toilets to drawer pulls—rarely seem to arrive on schedule. The only experience even more frustrating is dealing with the municipal zoning and building bureaucrats who must issue various permits or variances along the way.

We asked a prominent California developer to look closely at the issue of construction delays in his project to build hundreds of homes in a high-tech center. "I was shocked," the not-easily-shockable contractor told us on the promise of anonymity.

> *Including land, our houses cost us $228,000 to build. They should take 120 days to complete. But we've had houses take as much as 180 days. That means 60 days of extra interest on a $110,000 loan. So that's going to be an extra $1,741 per house—more, of course, if interest*

rates go up. And that's just in actual construction—it doesn't begin to include costs of delays in permitting, environmental approvals, failure of the utilities to install the electrical, gas and water lines on schedule.

Subcontractors don't show up on time. Sinks arrive that are defective—they have to go back and we wait for replacements. If the subs are delayed, they want more money on the next contract to build in protection against lost time. Add up all the other expenses. How about property taxes? How about management fees? I pay a management firm to oversee the project. Their bill runs up. What if buyers cancel because of the delay?

I had my accountant quantify the known cost of construction time glitches. I run an extremely tight ship. And yet, at least on this project, they add up to almost 4 percent of the cost of a house. Bigger firms might be able to cut that somewhat. But if I were just a private person, building one house, just for myself, delays are even more expensive percentagewise. All that lost time adds up to a penalty—a kind of time tax on every project.

With the United States spending some $544 billion a year on new residential construction, a 3 to 5 percent "time tax"—the overall cost of wasteful, never-on-time, de-synchronized operations—would run into the $16–27 billion range annually.

At, say, $150,000 a unit, that is roughly what it might cost to provide more than 1.4 million homes or apartments for low-income Americans every decade. That could make a dent in the problem of homelessness.

But that's only the amount for the residential end of the housing industry. Its erratic, costly performance in turn reflects (or causes) de-synchronization among its supplier industries and labor pool as well. Shortages of drywall, insulation, skilled carpenters and the like are common. Track this all the way down the chain, and the costs must swell significantly.

If housing is a sinkhole of unsynchronized operations, what needs to be said about a very different example—America's giant defense industry?

Here are major firms making everything from the highest of high-tech communications gear, satellites and weapons systems to relatively simple products like shirts and boots. It is an industry perennially attacked by Congress for cost overruns, waste and inefficiency. Its seven-hundred-dollar hammer or toilet seat—whether apocryphal or not—has become a national symbol of scandalous waste.

But it is worth noting that de-synchronization in an industry may sometimes be partially imposed on it from outside. And that is the case here. Thus, to prevent corruption and maximize efficiency, the U.S. Defense Department's

procurement processes, many of them mandated by Congress, are so byzantine, so complex and aggravating, that many sensible firms refuse even to bid
for a Pentagon contract. Worse yet, those firms that do undertake defense
work often find themselves caught in a steel cage largely constructed by Congress itself.

An editor of *Armed Forces Journal International* once summed it up in a
single, hard-to-forget sentence: "Faced with a twenty-year threat," he wrote,
"government responds with a fifteen-year program in a five-year defense plan,
managed by three-year personnel funded with single-year appropriations."

We've seen the de-synchronization effect within individual firms, groups
of firms and whole industries. But de-synchronization occurs on an even
larger scale when two related industries develop at different speeds.

THE TECHNOLOGY BALLET

The rise of the personal computer from the 1970s on was marked by a kind of
technological pas de deux as Microsoft launched bigger and more powerful
versions of its Windows software for PCs, and Intel successively developed
the faster and more powerful chips needed to support them.

For years, the two symbiotic companies were referred to in the media as
though they were a single firm called "Wintel." The synchronization, imperfect as it was at times, powered the phenomenal spread of the PC worldwide.
In sharp contrast, however, the closely linked computer and communications
industries have more than once found themselves without a dance partner. No
ballet here.

In the United States, the rise of the computer industry throughout the last
half century has been wild, wooly and unregulated. Computer makers were
frequently frustrated by far slower rates of change in the tightly and confus-
ingly overregulated telecom industry. As the basic technologies of these two
industries converged, their rates of change diverged. According to many analysts, advances in chips, computers and related fields could have come even
faster but for this discrepancy. Similarly—and more interestingly—in recent
years the development of networks trailed far behind increases in the speed of
computer chips. By 2005, however, this de-synchronization went into reverse.

We simply don't know the aggregate costs of the de-synchronization effect
at the level of firms and industries, but we can only imagine how much greater
the effects are when we look at de-synchronization in whole sectors of an
economy in the age of revolutionary wealth.

SUPPER WITHOUT SUSHI

When Minoru Naito, a small-business owner, decided to celebrate his daughter's birthday at a posh sushi restaurant in Tokyo, it was on a Saturday. He went to a nearby ATM to withdraw some cash. But it was 6:00 p.m. and the machine had shut down at 5:00. Hence, no sushi that evening.

The fact that banks closed their ATMs so early was, in the words of *Nihon Keizai Shimbun,* Japan's *Wall Street Journal,* "particularly striking because more retail stores in Japan are operating around the clock." In short, the banking sector was out of sync with developments in the retail sector of Japan's economy.

Faced with competition from foreign banks and securities firms that did offer twenty-four-hour services, the relatively small Tokyo Sowa Bank eventually opened the first "twenty-four-hour" ATMs at a Japanese bank (never mind that they initially closed down at 10:00 p.m.). It wasn't until 2003 that one of Japan's major banks, UFJ, followed suit.

Closing the gap between shopping hours and banking hours requires new I.T. systems. That normally means ditching or upgrading older, so-called legacy I.T., piece by piece, program by program. And that cannot be done without altering the timing of data flows, accounting procedures, work schedules, reports and other matters, speeding some work units up but necessarily leaving others to lag temporarily. Every new computer, software operating system, application or change in a network inescapably changes the tempo, rhythms and synchronization levels in the organization. In Japan, too, one man's synchronization is another's de-synchronization.

Moreover, it can legitimately be argued that disparities in rates of change open countless opportunities for entrepreneurial synchronizers who, by synchronizing some functions or organizations, create new disparities elsewhere.

The problems of synchrony are becoming more, not less, difficult because, as during the industrial revolution, we are once more transforming the way humans work, play and think in the time dimension. We are profoundly altering the way we deal with the deep fundamental of time. Until we understand time's relationships to wealth creation, we will never free ourselves of today's crushing time pressures—or huge unneeded costs.

CHAPTER 8

THE NEW TIMESCAPE

The American Airlines 757 was approaching the Rocky Mountains on a flight from Boston to Los Angeles when passenger Michael Tighe's arm and head suddenly lurched into the aisle. His wife, a nurse, who was sitting alongside him, immediately knew something terrible was about to happen. Tighe's heart had begun beating erratically, failing to send an adequate blood supply to his brain. Tighe, sixty-two, was at the edge of death when flight personnel appeared with a laptop-sized device.

Attaching electrical leads to his body, they shocked him—once, twice, several times—and literally brought him back to life, making him the first person to be saved in-flight by a defibrillator. It had been installed on the plane only two days earlier.

Like the human heart, societies and economies, too, are subject to premature beats, local tachycardias, fibrillations and flutters, as well as "chaotic" irregularities and paroxysms. While this has long been true, the uneven, ever-accelerating pace of change and the continual de-synchronization that comes with it may now be pushing us toward temporal incoherence—without a defibrillator on board.

What happens to us as individuals when our institutions, companies, industries and economy are out of sync with one another? If we are, indeed, running faster and panting harder, where will it end? How did we get chained to time and speed in the first place?

THE CHAINS OF TIME

Start here with a point made earlier that in peasant societies, ancient China or feudal Europe for example, people were not generally paid hourly wages. As slaves, serfs or sharecroppers, they typically received or kept some fraction of what they actually produced. Work time, as such, did not directly translate into money.

Add to that the facts that weather, the limitations of human and animal energy, and extremely primitive technology all set upper limits on human productivity, no matter how many hours a peasant family might work. The result was a relationship to time remarkably different from our own.

As late as the fourteenth century in Europe, according to French historian Jacques Le Goff, clerics were still preaching that time belonged to God alone and therefore must not be sold. Selling work for time was almost as bad as usury—the selling of money for interest. And as far as the fifteenth-century Franciscan monk Bernardino of Siena was concerned, humans were not even supposed to know how to tell time.

The industrial revolution changed all that. Fossil fuels and factories smashed the agrarian limitations on human productivity. Clocks and watches made it possible to monitor and measure time more accurately. And how long or fast you worked did make a difference.

Second Wave employers, in hopes of maximizing output, sped up assembly lines or paid piecework to squeeze additional muscle power from workers. And based on the "time is money" formula, factory workers came to be paid by the hour. Which explains why the U.S. Bureau of Labor Statistics still typically measures "labor productivity" in terms of output per hour.

The early modernizers went further, forging another link in the chain that inextricably bound wealth to time. The West gradually did away with traditional anti-usury laws and legitimized interest payments based on time. This was ultimately followed by a vast expansion of other time-based payments by consumers, corporations and, above all, governments.

In this way, the pricing of labor and the pricing of money both became increasingly based on time. Introduced separately and gradually, these twin changes were momentous. They meant that the same individual as worker, as consumer, as borrower, lender and investor became chained to time as never before.

Workers grumbled about the rat race. Artists, writers and filmmakers satirized it, as did Fritz Lang in his scenes of workers and clocks in his amazing film *Metropolis* (1927) and Charlie Chaplin in his classic *Modern Times* (1936). But the chains of time only tightened over the years as punch clocks and time-based Taylorite management methods spread.

Even today some employers in call centers and factory-style offices equipped with the latest Third Wave technologies continue to use Second Wave methods of management. Counting an employee's keystrokes or calls per hour, they apply the traditional speed-up methods of the old-line textile mill or auto assembly line.

In 1970 our book *Future Shock* forecast that the pace of life—and not just at work—was in for a jolting further acceleration. Since then, acceleration has clicked into ultra-drive and an avalanche of words has been devoted to elaborations by others on the *Future Shock* theme.

An entire new vocabulary of terms—"twitch speed," "hurry sickness," "time deepening," "Internet time," "digital time," "time famine"—reflects the accuracy of that early forecast. Today millions feel harassed, stressed out and "future shocked" by the compression of time. London's *Evening Standard* reports the unsurprising arrival of therapists who specialize in helping "rusha-holics" to slow down.

We hate to wait. The epidemic of attention deficit disorder among American kids may be chemical rather than cultural in origin, but it perfectly symbolizes the growing refusal today to defer gratification as the future speeds by.

LOVE AT HIGH SPEED

Around the world, multi-tasking and multi-focus replace single-minded concentration as an entire generation grows up in a culture and an economy moving from sequential to simultaneous processing. Young Americans, write Ian Jukes and Anita Dosaj of the InfoSavvy Group, "take for granted having access to computers, remote controls, the Internet, e-mail, pagers, cell phones, MP3 players, CDs, DVDs, video games, PalmPilots, and digital cameras. . . . For them, the notion of time and distance . . . means very little." They are processing more and more input at faster and faster rates and are bored with anything they regard as slow.

Twenty-first-century matrimonial services offer "speed dating." One such American company, serving the Jewish community, organizes seven-minute face-to-face meetings among twosomes, after which clients indicate on a form whether they wish to make a (presumably less speedy) follow-up date with the seven-minute partner. Not to be outsped, a service in New Delhi offers three-minute "dates."

Across the globe at a bank in Britain, dozens of customers dash around the room to engage in five-minute conversations with one another in search of new contacts—what the *Financial Times* calls "speed dating for business."

But three minutes might as well be an eon on the Internet, where users now typically click off a site if it takes more than eight seconds for a page to download. Young Chinese have invented what might be called the "micro-novel"—a speedy story of fewer than 350 words that is published on cell-phone screens.

In fact, kids everywhere are speeding up communications by creating their own digital shorthand for text messaging. Thus, "boyfriend" becomes "BF," "keep in touch" becomes "KIT" and "Why doesn't he love me?" becomes "WDHLM."

Visuals on U.S. network TV change every 3.5 seconds—and faster on MTV. NextCard's offer to clear your credit history and approve you for a charge card in thirty-five seconds seems positively leisurely. And when Wall Streeters pontificate about a stock on TV, viewers can almost see the share price rise or fall in direct response to what is being said.

All these pressures for speed explain why a covey of "time management" consultants and shelfloads of books offer advice on how to reschedule our days and relate time to our personal priorities. Yet all this advice scarcely touches on the less obvious reasons for the speed-up of life.

Several forces have been converging to drive the acceleration needle off the gauge. The 1980s and '90s saw a global shift toward liberal economics and hypercompetition. Combine that with the eighteen-month doubling rate of semiconductor-chip power and you get near-instantaneous financial transactions. (Currency traders can find out about a trade within two hundred milliseconds of its completion.) Put differently, behind all of these pressures is the historic move to a wealth system whose chief raw material—knowledge—can now move at nearly real-time speed. We live at a pace so hyper that the old law that "time is money" needs revision. Every interval of time is now worth more money than the last one because, in principle if not in practice, more wealth can be created during it.

In turn, all this changes our personal relationship to the deep fundamental of time.

CUSTOMIZING TIME

In yesterday's work world, time was packaged in standard lengths. "Nine-to-five" became the template for millions of U.S. workers. Half an hour or an hour for lunch were the norm, along with so many days of holiday time. Labor contracts and federal laws made overtime expensive for employers and discouraged deviance from standard time packages.

With metronomic regularity, therefore, masses of people arose, ate breakfast, commuted to office or factory, worked a standard shift, then commuted home at rush hour, had dinner and watched TV—all more or less in sync with one another.

These standard time packages spread from the factory throughout the rest of life as well. Paralleling the factory, virtually all industrial-age offices also set fixed, standardized schedules. Schools, meanwhile, prepared future generations of factory workers by submitting children to a similar time discipline. In America, kids in their conspicuous yellow buses were unwittingly being prepared to commute to work on time. Inside, the school bells rang and the children were (and still are) marched through a sequence of standard-length classes.

By contrast, today's emergent economy, for which those schoolchildren are being misprepared, runs on radically different temporal principles. In it, we are fragmenting yesterday's standard time packages as we shift from collective time to customized time. Put differently, we are moving from impersonalized to personalized time in parallel with the moves toward personalized products and markets.

WHEN GOOD IDEAS ARRIVE

In his book *Free Agent Nation,* Daniel H. Pink pictures a country whose labor force is increasingly composed of "free agents"—that is, workers who are solo professionals, freelancers, independent contractors, consultants and other self-employed workers—many of whom set their own hours.

According to Pink, there are already 33 million free agents or "disorganization" men and women in the United States—more than a quarter of the entire American workforce. This, he points out, is about twice the number of manufacturing workers and twice the number of labor union members.

Although the available statistics don't tell us, according to Pink, "probably more than half" of all free agents are paid by project, by commission or on some other non-temporal basis. Thus another characteristic of industrial capitalism, wage labor, can no longer be taken for granted.

People working at home, as so many millions already do, may stop for a sandwich or go out for a walk when they choose, unlike the assembly-line worker whose absence, even for a moment, can keep large numbers of downstream workers waiting.

The same, of course, is true for other at-home or online economic activities as well—shopping, banking and investing—most of which can also be done asynchronously at any time. More important, because the value of work increasingly depends on knowledge, work time does not lend itself as well to standardized packaging.

As Akio Morita, the late cofounder of Sony, once said to us, "I can tell a factory worker to show up at seven a.m. and be productive. But can I tell an engineer or researcher to have a good idea at seven?"

MEDIA TIME

Because leisure time is usually seen as "non-work" time, it is the flip side of the work calendar. According to Bill Martin and Sandra Mason, writing in

Foresight, "The timing of our free-time periods is becoming more varied as the hours and weeks of paid work become more flexible."

Media time may soon follow suit. An episode of *American Idol, Desperate Housewives, CSI* or *24,* or a news program on BBC, France's Canal Plus or Japan's NHK, lasts a predictable amount of time. So-called "reality shows" in the United States run a half hour or an hour minus time for commercials. Commercials, in turn, typically come in neat sixty-second, thirty-second, fifteen-second or ten-second modules.

The television and online programming of the future, by contrast, may no longer come in such predictable chunks. One of the early indications of this shift arrived when Emmy-winning TV and new-media producer Al Burton was asked to create forty-five short-form "bursts" of entertainment for television. "What was unusual," says Burton, "was that we were not given any fixed, standard length. They could range from ninety seconds to five minutes."

Future entertainment formats may include segments strung together in uneven, variable lengths. NBC experimented with "supersize" half-hour versions of *Friends* that actually ran forty minutes and abbreviated twenty-minute episodes of *Saturday Night Live,* and tinkered with the idea of one-minute "movies" to intersperse among commercials. Then there are the programs made up only of the climactic moments of ball games, eliminating all the intervening play.

Someday viewers may be able to download only the eight minutes when a particular actor is on camera. In due course, the viewer will be able to rewrite the plot, introduce new characters and shorten or lengthen scenes at will.

In the words of Betsy Frank, executive vice president for research and planning at MTV Networks: "This is an audience that wants to make their own schedules." New consumer devices already give viewers the power to cut and paste parts of programs to suit their individual preferences. This shift away from standard time slots will itself accelerate as media audiences equipped with new technology produce their own content. At the same time that viewers are creating their own content, they are also insisting on accessing programs "on demand" rather than at times preset by the media. In the words of William Randolph Hearst, III: "Appointment-based television is dead."

FAMILY, FRIENDS AND FACE TIME

Changes like these are reflected in family life as well. The line between work time and family time is blurring, along with fixed schedules. Says John Moody, an executive with Fox News: "When I was growing up my parents came home from work, had dinner at half-past five, and watched the news at six.... I don't know anybody in my neighborhood who has that regular a life." *BusinessWeek* reports that fewer than a third of Americans now work a nine-to-five schedule and "rituals such as the family dinner are disappearing."

Nor, armed with TiVo, iPod and other time-shifting technologies, do we all watch television shows at the same time. Schedules are so individualized that family members and friends cannot assume they can gather face-to-face. Many could use a database in which family members and friends make their schedules available to one another so that face time can be organized.

The wealth system, in short, is not just accelerating; it is introducing greater irregularity into our relationships with time. In so doing, it liberates the individual from the prisonlike rigidities and regularities of the industrial age. But it increases unpredictability and requires fundamental changes in the way personal relations and wealth creation are coordinated and business is done.

THE AMERICANIZATION OF TIME?

Few things upset people—and whole cultures and economies—more than changes in timing. This, as we wrote in 1970 when fast food started flooding into France, "explains the pathological antagonism toward what many regard as the 'Americanization' of Europe."

Nearly thirty years later in Germany, retailer Günter Biere got a taste of precisely this reaction when he insisted on opening his Kaufhof department store in Berlin on a Sunday, using a loophole in regulations that forbade Sunday sales. He instantly became the storm center of national controversy and was attacked as an upsetter of convention and a "Rambo."

Supporters of Sunday sales came to his defense. Only the "stupid tradition of an old Germany is against this," said one shopper from Schwedt in the former East Germany. "We should accept our Americanization."

What is happening, however, is not Americanization. It is the arrival of an alien rhythm of life associated with the latest wealth system. The changed rhythm is present and, despite opposition, slowly advancing in France, Germany and the United Kingdom. Things already move faster in Tokyo, Seoul and Shanghai than in Paris, London or Berlin.

THE 24/7 FUTURE

Speed and irregularization go hand in hand with another time shift—from intermittent to continuous-flow operations. This is seen in the rapid spread of 24/7 in everything from hotel business centers to newspaper-printing plants. In Japan, beauty parlors, gyms, supermarkets and retail chains are staying open later and later. A growing number of Maruetsu supermarkets and Aeon Maxvalue outlets are operating around the clock. In time, according to marketing professor Tomoo Noguchi of Waseda University, sales at late-night businesses will grow to 50 percent of the ordinary daytime total.

For a glimpse of tomorrow night, visit Curitiba, Brazil. Home to international Linux distributor Conectiva, and with two hundred other software companies operating there, this model "green" city is studied by architects and urban planners from around the world.

One midnight we accompanied its former mayor, Jaime Lerner, an urban planner by training, on a visit to its "24 Hour Street," a block glistening with new coffee shops and restaurants jammed with young couples who smile, wave and call out "Jaime!" The next street was designed to house twenty-four-hour-professional services—doctors, dentists and lawyers. The next one was planned to hold twenty-four-hour municipal offices where individuals can get permits or licenses and take care of other city business at any hour.

Continuous-flow services permit consumption schedules to be designed by each individual, thus further promoting the shift to irregular time. In both production and consumption, then, times and tempos are becoming more complex and "de-massified." This, in turn, has practical consequences for every business, in every sector, and for economies at every level of development.

The shift toward continuous flow is especially conspicuous in finance. Electronic communications networks allow people to buy and sell stocks after the markets are officially closed. And online trading has forced staid stock exchanges to consider increasing their hours. The trading systems of the future will never sleep.

The pressures of time, our ability to slice it into ever tinier, uneven units, the overwhelming power and speed of the electronic infrastructure, the unbundling of products, and the growing granularization of payments all point to the day when money flows no longer predictably peak on certain preset days—Friday nights, for example, or the fifteenth of the month.

These interrelated shifts—acceleration, irregularization and continuous flow—are transforming the entire timescape. But even these changes are only part of a larger story as we replace industrial time with twenty-first-century time.

As we pointed out in *Future Shock,* these self-feeding alternatives will trigger many social consequences: a faster flow of things, people, places, relationships and information through our corporate and personal lives. Throwaway products multiply—cameras today, telephones tomorrow. So do throwaway ideas, business models—and personal relationships.

WHIZZING TOWARD WHERE?

They also push us farther toward ad-hocracy—the shift away from permanent or long-lasting organizational structures in business to one-shot, short-term organizational formats—even temporary stores. Thus a Tokyo-based company formed by designer Rei Kawakubo and her husband, Adrian Joffe, has opened a store in Berlin that, they claim, will exist for only one year, and will be closed down after that, whether profitable or not. The idea is supposed to reflect the ever-shorter shelf life of fashions, movies, music and celebrity.

Companies also engage in continuous-flow internal reorganization as they race to adapt to changes in markets, finance and other variables. Organizational temporariness or transience, which has been on the increase for decades, is now an inescapable feature of advanced economies.

Even more ephemeral are the management fads that pop up, influence these successive reorganizations and whiz into oblivion. Prices, too, change more frequently. Investors demand quicker and quicker payback. Relations to people, places, ideas, technologies and vendors become more and more short-lived.

How far can any society go toward hyperspeed and jangled time relations if part of its population is freeing itself from routine, standardized schedules and the other part remains driven by the clock time of the past? How do employers cope with young workers, products of the new way of life, who regard punctuality as an imposition on their freedom and creativity?

Researchers today suggest that the spread of cell phones has been accompanied by a more relaxed attitude toward punctuality inasmuch as people can call ahead and apologize in advance for lateness. But the deeper reason is the decline of the assembly line. Assembly lines require synchronized work, so that if one worker is late it slows down all the others on the line. It requires a level of punctuality little known in agrarian societies. Today, with more free agents, more individuals working on all different schedules, time is more important, but exact punctuality matters less.

We cannot discuss here the full social, cultural, psychological and economic implications of these shifts. What should be clear by now, however, is that with our key institutions out of sync with one another; with tensions between synchronization and de-synchronization rising; with hyper-acceleration continuing; with the irregularization of time; with productivity less and less linked to time, while each interval of time is potentially worth more than the last; with humans capable of measuring, exploring and controlling shorter and shorter, as well as longer and longer, expanses of time, something truly historic is under way.

We are revolutionizing humanity's links to one of the deep fundamentals of wealth. That alone will transform our lives and those of our children. But even that isn't all.

PART FOUR

Stretching Space

CHAPTER 9

THE GREAT CIRCLE

One of the biggest geographical shifts of wealth in history is now taking place. Wealth, as never before, is on the move.

Just as we are changing our relationships to time, we are also changing our relationships to the deep fundamental of space—the places where wealth is created, the new criteria by which we choose these places and the way we are linking them together.

The result is a period of spatial turbulence. This increasing "wealth mobility" will affect the future of jobs, investment, business opportunities, the structure of companies, the location of markets and the daily lives of ordinary people all over the world. It will determine the fate of cities, countries and whole continents.

ASIA, HO!

Because the West has been so economically dominant for so long, it is often overlooked that five centuries ago China, not Europe, had the most advanced technology, and it was Asia that led the world, turning out fully 65 percent of the globe's measurable economic output.

It is largely forgotten, at least in the West, that in 1405 a fleet of 317 ships manned by some 27,000 sailors and warriors set out on the first of seven extraordinary voyages of exploration. According to historian Louise Levathes, the fleet was commanded by Admiral Zheng He, a Chinese Muslim eunuch and one of the most remarkable men ever to put to sea. It explored the coasts of Africa and the Gulf of Aden in the Middle East, reaching as far west as Jiddah and Dhofar, and laying the naval basis for Chinese trade all across the Indian Ocean.

It wasn't until another two and a half centuries passed that the Enlightenment and the early industrial revolution launched the great Second Wave transition that gradually shifted the locus of economic, political and military power to Europe.

It didn't, however, stay there. By the end of the nineteenth century the center of world wealth creation had begun to move on—pushing farther westward to the United States. Two world wars put an end to what was left of Europe's economic dominance.

By 1941, just before the Japanese attack on Pearl Harbor drew the United States into World War II, Henry Luce, publisher of *Time* magazine, could write that the twentieth century was already "the American Century." The United States, he wrote, "must undertake now to be the Good Samaritan of the entire world, to undertake to feed all the people of the world who as a result of this worldwide collapse of civilization are hungry and destitute."

Indeed, since this time, and especially since the mid-1950s, when the Third Wave and the transition to a knowledge-based economy began, the American economy has been dominant. But the wealth shift toward Asia, starting with a trickle toward Japan and later the so-called newly industrialized countries (NICs) such as South Korea, gathered strength throughout the subsequent decades.

OPENING THE FLOODGATES

The floodgates really began to open when, in the 1980s, China explicitly legitimized and encouraged the not-very-communist pursuit of wealth. They swung fully open in the 1990s, and foreign direct investment (FDI) poured in—an estimated $570 billion in the last twenty-five years.

In 2002 the Xinhua news service called the torrent of FDI "nothing less than miraculous." At the rate of $53.5 billion in 2003, China became the world's biggest FDI recipient, outstripping even the United States. In 2005 FDI to China was estimated to reach $70 billion.

China's remarkable rise is a tribute to the hard work, brains and innovation of its people, once freed from the severe constraints of communism. But, and here the story of Henry Luce resumes, it could not have happened without the assistance of the United States.

Luce was the son of a missionary in China and was himself a committed Christian and anti-communist who never lost his interest in China. And if he were alive to look back at the last few decades, he might take astonished satisfaction in the powerful support given by the United States to China's rapid economic rise, though the suspicion flickers that altruism had little to do with it.

By 2003, Americans had poured $44 billion in investments into China. The United States also provided a gigantic market for Chinese goods, importing more than $150 billion in 2003. By then China's world exports had hit $436.1 billion, and its GDP reached $6.5 trillion.

That year marked an Asian watershed. China, along with Singapore, South Korea and Taiwan, had an aggregate GDP nearly equal to the combined total of Germany, France, the United Kingdom, Italy and Spain—the five biggest economies in Europe. And that calculation did not even include Japan. Or India. If Japan and India are added, the six Asian nations have a combined GDP $3 trillion greater than the entire twenty-five-member European Union—or the United States.

What we have been witnessing, therefore, has been a monumental transfer of wealth and wealth creation across the world map. It can be seen as nothing less than the continuation of the movement begun when economic power first shifted from China to Western Europe and then to the United States—the completion of a great historical circle, returning economic dominance to the Asia it left centuries ago.

"Ponder the world of 2050," Robert Manning of the Council on Foreign Relations has suggested, "an Asia with more than half the world's population; perhaps 40 percent of the global economy; more than half the world's information technology industry; and world class high-tech military capabilities."

But is this really the great circle closing? Will today's changes continue in linear—or should we say circular—fashion? We'll return to the future of China and Asia later. For now, we need to look at some of the other surprising spatial changes that come with revolutionary wealth.

CHAPTER 10

HIGHER-VALUE-ADDED PLACES

I magine a nowhere in which we all live and in which all the riches of the world are made. Exactly such a fantasy took wing during the Internet explosion of the late 1990s. The growth of the Internet was so dramatic that it began to call into question the very meaning of space and spatial relations. Many digerati and Internet enthusiasts spoke glowingly of "placelessness." Author William Knoke, in one of the more extreme statements of this position, asked: "What if location becomes irrelevant? Imagine a world where you could close your eyes and appear in Bombay or Paris as if you had been assisted by a Star Trek transporter. Picture the ability to make passionate love with someone while he or she is in another part of town or in another city. Think of being in two or three spots at once. . . . Such is a world without place. The Placeless Society . . . does not exist. Not yet." However, he argued, convergent technologies were moving us in precisely this direction.

Others described cyberspace as a territory that has no place in the physical world and even as the first instance of a parallel world. For them, the virtual world occupies what might better be called "unspace."

Despite the poetry and hyperbole, however, even electronic bits are stored somewhere, in some actual location, and they move through space, not unspace, as they are transmitted.

Digitization, in short, doesn't dematerialize space. It doesn't substitute "virtual space" for reality. But it does speed up and facilitate the shift of wealth and wealth creation everywhere, not just on the scale of a "great circle" but right down to the local level.

Back here on the ground, the wealth maps of the world are being redrawn as waves of change roll across the Earth, fast-forwarding some cities and regions into the future and sending others into economic oblivion. Around the world tomorrow's higher-value-added places are even now taking form.

YESTERDAY'S PLACES

Cleveland, Ohio, was once an important center of hard-core industry, with its steel mills, foundries and auto plants. Today Cleveland claims one of the nation's top science and engineering universities, Case Western Reserve, and has a huge medical sector led by the Cleveland Clinic. But its housefronts and stores are still blackened by decades of smog and smoke, and Cleveland is listed as the poorest big city in America, a victim of its past industrial success and its failure to move on even as the Third Wave carried other parts of America toward the future.

Cleveland, moreover, is only the most obvious example. Much the same fate has met the other great smokestack cities around the world—yesterday's engines of industrial wealth. It is not just cities, however. Whole regions are declining in economic significance as new ones rise to take their place.

Take Guangdong in southeastern China. A decade ago, as *Industry Week* put it, "water buffalo pulled plows across paddy fields; now there are rows of factories producing computer chips, radios, toys, and clothes. Big-name investors with production bases there include Procter & Gamble, Nestlé, Coca-Cola, and Mitsubishi."

Millions of people have flowed into the area. Millions of jobs have been created, and Guangdong's per capita GDP has quadrupled in the last decade.

Today Guangdong and the Pearl River Delta of which it is a part, along with Hong Kong and Macao, form one of the most powerful manufacturing centers in the world. They have made the transition from agrarian economies to industrial centers, taking over much of the manufacturing earlier done in the West's smokestack cities.

But that isn't all they've accomplished. For instead of setting its sights on a Second Wave future, Guangdong has one eye fixed on what happens after cheap-labor factory jobs run out. It is grabbing all the low-tech work it can get, but it is already going after Third Wave, knowledge-intensive, higher-value-added production.

Thus the China Development Institute notes that Guangdong's growing high-tech sector now includes companies in fields like "information technology, new materials, new energy, biotechnology and laser-machine-electronic integrated systems manufacturing." Apart from research at Case Western Reserve, relatively few of these are found in Cleveland—or in its rust-belt sister cities. All of which need new strategies for survival. And new wealth maps.

DISSOLVING BORDERS

New strategies are needed because new economic realities no longer necessarily align with old borders and existing power relationships.

Kenichi Ohmae has written brilliantly about the rise of what he calls "region-states" in many parts of the world, calling them "engines of prosperity." In China, according to Ohmae, an outdated, centralized Communist government, "whether deliberately or not," is reorganizing itself along corporate lines. "Like many corporations," he writes, "China is moving most decision-making to the 'business unit' level—semi-autonomous, self-governing economic region-states that compete fiercely against each other for capital, technology, and human resources."

Indeed, he writes in his 2005 book, *The Next Global Stage,* "Dalian, along with a dozen other regions in China, has become a de facto regional-state, setting its own economic agenda. While still part of China and, in theory, subject to the rule of Beijing, it is largely autonomous. The reality is that its ties with Beijing are weaker than those with business centers throughout the world."

Many emerging economic zones spill across existing nation-state boundaries. Thus parts of Texas and southern California are merging with stretches of northern Mexico into two big bi-national economic regions, each of which could, in the decades to come, develop its own distinctive bi-national culture—and cross-border political structure as well.

Elsewhere, Jussi Jauhiainen, professor of geography at the University of Helsinki, describes a region that embraces Helsinki in Finland and spills over into Tallinn in Estonia; another that exists on both sides of the border between Finland and Russian Karelia; and a third that includes Narva in Estonia and Ivangorod in Russia. The U.N. has proposed developing the Tumen River region bordering Russia, China and North Korea in Northeast Asia. The *Financial Times* even speculates on a Vladivostok-Vancouver-Sapporo linkage that, for various reasons, "could become a Pacific powerhouse."

Here again we are altering the maps of the past and our various relationships to the deep fundamental of space.

The acceleration of change implies, however, that the new maps will be increasingly temporary, always ready for on-the-ground reversals or relocations. For little is permanent in the revolutionary wealth system. If in doubt, ask Alejandro Bustamante.

THE CHEAP-LABOR DERBY

In 1993 Mexico signed the North American Free Trade Agreement (NAFTA) with the United States and Canada. Within seven years, 3,500 *maquiladora* plants manufacturing everything from furniture to apparel to TV sets had sprung up along Mexico's U.S. border, creating 1.4 million new, mainly assembly-line jobs for workers drawn from all parts of Mexico.

But in the late 1990s, with Guangdong and, indeed, all of China now competing in the cheap-labor derby, an estimated 250,000 to 300,000 of those Mexican jobs followed the great circle route across the Pacific.

That put Bustamante in a spot. When his employer, Plantronics, a leading manufacturer of telephone accessories, received an order, it called Bustamante. Although he ran the firm's three factories in Tijuana, Mexico, he was told he must compete for each contract just like anyone else. But Bustamante paid his workers an average of $2.20 an hour (including benefits) and had to bid against a Chinese manufacturer whose employees average only about 60 cents.

There's nothing unique or new about that. Many *maquiladora* operators in northern Mexico face Chinese competition. But what especially irked Bustamante was that the Chinese rival he faced was, in fact, itself also owned by Plantronics.

This may be a case of serial outsourcing—sending jobs to China that had already been outsourced to Mexico. Outsourcing, while involving a small percentage of all jobs, has aroused fierce condemnation and prompted so much media coverage that there is no reason here to recap the familiar arguments, beyond recognizing that it is part of a much larger pattern of change in the spatial distribution of wealth and wealth creation.

Outsourcing enrages the critics of re-globalization who insist that it creates an unstoppable, brutalizing "race to the bottom." They typically contend that companies go where labor costs are lowest and are ready to pick up and spatially relocate at a moment's notice.

If this were true, it would be easy to forecast where wealth is heading. It would be good news for Africa, which can offer a big pool of available labor at the lowest wages on earth. (Africans should cheer each time workers in Asia join unions and drive wages up.) If labor cost were the sole consideration, why haven't all those factories now in China wound up in Africa instead?

The fact is that even for low-tech work, labor cost is seldom, if ever, the exclusive basis for a company's decision to relocate. Africa's endless violence and war, inadequate infrastructure, stratospheric levels of corruption, ravaging AIDS and shameful regimes may rule out significant investment no matter what the wage level.

The race-to-the-bottom theory, moreover, presupposes that workers are essentially interchangeable—which may largely be true in repetitive, assembly-line operations. The higher up the skill ladder one goes in a knowledge-based economy, however, the less valid it becomes.

As the knowledge components of wealth creation—marketing, finance, research, management, communication, I.T., vendor and distributor relations, regulatory compliance, legal affairs and other nontangibles—all grow in complexity and importance, workers, like the work itself, become less interchangeable and the required skill sets more temporary.

That is why attempts to forecast which cities, regions or, for that matter, countries will become the next Guangdong are doomed to failure if they extrapolate tomorrow's economy from existing or projected wage levels alone.

Any such simplistic analysis becomes even more questionable because, where economies are transitioning from smokestacks and assembly lines to knowledge-based production, we are already radically changing the very criteria by which a location, city, region or country becomes a high-value-added place.

What we are about to see is less racing to the bottom and more of a race to the top.

TOMORROW'S REAL ESTATE

To anticipate tomorrow's surprising geography—including the location of high-pay jobs, prime real estate, business opportunities, wealth and power—another key point needs to be understood: We are changing not merely the where of wealth but the why—the criteria by which we value places. And that further changes the where.

Seeking to woo industry in 1955, the state government of Indiana placed an advertisement in *Fortune* listing its economic advantages. These, it claimed, included low-cost coal, limestone, white clay, aluminum, gypsum, rock asphalt, dolomite, fluospar, water, sand, gravel, wood, corn, soybeans and easy access to the Ohio River. In addition, it promised an "enviable strike and lockout record"—that is, a weak or dormant labor movement.

That was then. Today Indiana's development council boasts of breaking away from "over-reliance on traditional industries."

No limestone here.

Inc. tells American small-business leaders that the "best" place to "start or grow a company" is Phoenix, Arizona, because of its growing high-tech workforce, sunny climate, renovated art museum and "four major sports franchises."

A group called the Small Business Survival Committee concludes that the place to invest is South Dakota because it imposes the fewest costs on business in the form of taxes, minimum-wage laws, number of state employees and the like. Still another rating system bases its conclusions about the future on the age and growth rate of companies in any given location. A contributor to Microsoft's bCentral.com then confects a hybrid index out of these last two methods and concludes that Nevada is the place to pull out your wallet.

Citing the 1955 Indiana ad in a 2002 study called the "State New Economy Index," Robert D. Atkinson and Rick Coduri of the Progressive Policy Institute write: "In an economy in which fewer than 20 percent of economic activity consists of creating, processing, or moving physical goods, access to raw materials, transportation and markets means less. As an increasing share of economic inputs and outputs are in the form of electronic bits, the old locational factors diminish in importance."

Take, for example, nearness—proximity. Some economists today believe that because Mexico is so close to American markets, it can beat Chinese competitors in the long run. They assume that distance still plays the same role it did before the knowledge economy arrived. But, thanks to information-intensive technologies, products are becoming smaller and lighter every day.

To rely on proximity means, to the degree that transportation costs matter, that Mexico's advantage would apply to the older, bigger, bulkier, heavier physical products—precisely those now being replaced. And it means still less to high-value-added intangible services whose transportation costs have little or nothing to do with distance—finance, software, satellite TV, airline reservations, music and the like. Continuing to count on proximity will set Mexico even farther behind—and keep it there.

Today, in their race to the top, competing states boast less about limestone and coal than about their great universities, low communication costs, advanced technology, frequent airline service, low crime, good climate and superior quality of life. The economy has been transformed along with workers' values and way of life.

The very categories with which we describe spatial units and relationships change as new economic networks emerge. We are seeing, for example, the rise of an entire ecology of airports linked to one another more strongly than with their local and national governments. In what Greg Lindsay in *Advertising Age* calls "Airworld," each airport is increasingly surrounded by its own ring of "shopping malls, conference centers, 24/7 gyms, chapels, post offices, dentists and doctors, rooftop pools and luxury hotels."

The result has been a sprint—no longer just in the United States—to create what might be called higher-value-added places that will attract the brightest, most creative workforce capable of producing knowledge-intensive, higher-value-added products and drawing businesses from around the world.

In sum, the historical shift toward Asia, the digitalization of many economic functions, the emergence of cross-national regions and the change in the criteria by which we value place or location are all parts of a larger transformation in our relations with the deep fundamental of space. They merely form the background against which even bigger changes loom.

CHAPTER 11

SPATIAL REACH

When the 2002 world soccer championships were held jointly in Japan and South Korea, Hugo Enciso, a Los Angeles marketing executive, decided to take his son to Tokyo. Enciso, Mexican by birth, American by education and lifestyle, works for *La Opinión,* the biggest Spanish-language daily in the United States. In Japan they met members of the tiny community of Latin Americans who live there and were introduced to Japanese food, manners and its mania for sports. For Enciso it was an experience he would long remember. Hundreds of thousands of other foreigners, from all parts of the globe, poured into Korea and Japan to attend the games.

We later met Enciso in California at the wedding of two young software executives—he born in Pakistan, she in India. His family was Muslim, hers Hindu. When the speaker system blared Pashtun music, Enciso joined the crowd of frenetic, happy dancers, most of whom had never heard a note of Pashtun before that night. Among them were WASP executives, Asian students, American Jews and many with still other ethnic, religious or geographical backgrounds. It was not merely a mixed marriage but a mixed celebration. And it was truly symbolic.

We are not only still shifting the center of world economic gravity toward Asia, including South Asia, where the married couple have their ancestral roots. We are not only altering the criteria that will determine where tomorrow's jobs will be found, where new factories, offices and homes will be built, and where revolutionary wealth will be created. We are expanding something we might call our personal "spatial reach."

Twenty-four hundred years ago in ancient China, where peasants were rooted to the soil, the Chinese philosopher Chuang-tzu declared that people who travel are apt to be "troublesome, false, restless, and engaged in secret plots." Today an estimated 8 percent of the human race—roughly half a billion people—travel across some national boundary in the course of a year. This number is equal to the entire population of the Earth in 1650 at the dawn of the industrial age. Troublesome or not, engaging in secret plots or not, searching for a job or just flying to Milwaukee to visit a customer, we are a species on the move.

PERSONAL GEOGRAPHY

Americans on average drive eleven thousand miles per year. But most car trips are back and forth to one's workplace—an average round-trip journey of twenty-three miles, or to destinations closer to home, like the supermarket or the bank. Vacation travel may take the family farther. We could easily track our car travel on a map. A business traveler can also pinpoint the cities to which she has journeyed in the course of the year and the trips within those places. The result would be a map showing one's "travel reach." But we could also show on the map all the locations to and from which we have sent or received e-mail, snail mail, phone calls and faxes, plus the physical addresses of all the people in our Rolodex and sites visited online.

With considerably more difficulty, we could even track the geographical origin of the products we buy and the destinations of the waste matter and pollution we create. Even these do not exhaust all the geographical locations with which we have, or wish to have, some relationship. But they would give us a rich image of our spatial reach—a continually changing map of our personal geography.

Compare our individual spatial reach today with that of the average European peasant in, say, the twelfth century, who in the course of an entire lifetime was unlikely to ever have traveled more than fifteen miles from his or her village. Except, perhaps, for religious ideas that came over the centuries all the way from Rome, fifteen miles largely bounded his or her life. That was the peasant's personal footprint on the planet.

If we apply this kind of mapping to companies, industries or nations, we promptly discover that the spatial reach of each varies and continually changes. Similarly, different segments of each economy require a different "reach." A country may need to import raw materials or components from many countries in order to sell exports to only a few. Or vice versa. Hollywood uses equipment from Japan and acting talent from Britain, but its films are exported all over the world. But that is just a simple example.

BusinessWeek notes that your PDA or camera phone may include a processor from America, a circuit board from China, chips designed in Taiwan, Austria, Ireland or India, a color display from South Korea and a lens from Germany. It is the combination of these spatial relationships that together define each company's or country's spatial reach.

The Japanese, for example, have had a decades-long debate over whether to focus their economy on ties with Asia or spread them around globally. During Japan's momentary triumphalism in the 1980s and '90s, flag-waving politicians like Shintaro Ishihara, now governor of Tokyo, urged Japan to replace the United States as the dominant power in Asia.

That, however, was before Japan's economic slowdown and China's simultaneous rocketlike rise, not to mention its big military buildup and recent explosions of anti-Japanese sentiment. Since then, Ishihara, sensing Japan's new vulnerabilities in the region, has called for stronger relations with the United States.

The real question has to do with the spatial reach of Japan's economy. Is Japan a regional or a global player? What is its economic and cultural footprint on the world, when *Manga Blast!,* a magazine based on Japanese cartoon art, is published in Milwaukie, Oregon, and sold, as we recently discovered, on a newsstand in Mexico City?

Some countries don't need global reach, just a few partners from nearby. Japan's requirements, by contrast, even during recession, are far too diverse and complex for it to flourish as a merely regional economic power. On the input side, it must import oil from the Middle East, software from the United States, car components from China. Its output—Nissan SUVs, Sony Play-Stations, Matsushita flat-panel TVs, NEC computers—is marketed around the world. Japanese companies operate plants on virtually every continent.

Whether anyone likes it or not, Japan needs resources, markets, opportunities, energy, ideas and information from all over the globe, not just from its nearby neighbors. Whether or not it is dominant in the region, its spatial footprint is global. But Japan is only an example. Today the spatial reach or footprint of every person, company and country is undergoing major change.

And it's not just people and products that are on the move. Money, too, has spatial reach. And that, too, is changing rapidly, with deep implications for the global economy.

MOBILE MONEY

It is common knowledge that trillions of dollars are continually zapping across electronic channels at phenomenal speeds, from nation to nation, bank to bank, and person to person, in a grand unending monetary tango. Most people also know—or should by now know—that international currency trading is a global casino. What most people don't know, however, is that the dollar is not just an American currency.

It is popularly believed that Americans use dollars, Germans use euros, Japanese use yen and Argentineans use pesos. In fact, according to economist

Benjamin J. Cohen of the University of California/Santa Barbara, author of *The Geography of Money,* "nothing could be further from the truth." This idea has become "an outmoded and misleading caricature" because competition has "greatly altered the spatial organization of monetary relations."

Put differently, each currency, like each person, has its own, continually changing spatial reach. At present the dollar, despite its recent plunge, has the longest reach, some countries actually forgoing a currency of their own in favor of "dollarization." They make the U.S. dollar legal tender, and it becomes their own official currency. In other countries, the dollar unofficially supplants local money for many purposes.

As of January 2002, fifteen mostly tiny states ranging from Panama and Ecuador to East Timor officially used the dollar. But unofficially the dollar also served as money in Argentina, Bolivia, Peru and Central America. The same was the case in Russia as well as most of the former Soviet Union, including Armenia, Georgia, Azerbaijan and Ukraine. Also unofficially dollarized were Romania, Turkey and Vietnam. In fact, according to the Federal Reserve, more U.S. dollars are held by foreigners than by Americans—somewhere between 55 and 70 percent, mostly in hundred-dollar bills.

The dollar isn't the only currency that has supplemented or supplanted another. For all practical proposes, before the introduction of the euro, one could use the German mark in the Balkans, the French franc in parts of Africa, the Swiss franc in Liechtenstein, the Indian rupee in Bhutan, the Danish krone in Greenland. In all, a study by the International Monetary Fund found eighteen countries in which foreign currency makes up more than 30 percent of the money supply and another thirty-four in which it averages 16.4 percent or more.

According to Cohen, currencies "increasingly are employed outside their country of origin, penetrating other national monetary spaces. . . . The rapid acceleration of cross-border currency competition . . . has transformed the spatial organization of global monetary relations. National currency domains are more interpenetrated today than at any time since the dawn of the era of territorial money."

In short, money has been unleashed from its former spatial limits.

INVADERS AND INVADED

This shift carries important power consequences. An "invading" currency (our term) doesn't always benefit the nation from which it comes. Many factors play a role, and it can sometimes prove costly. The "invaded" country's government usually loses a degree of control over its domestic monetary policy and is weakened in the eyes of its citizens. It loses a part of what economists call "seigniorage"—the money it makes for making its own money, that is, printing and issuing it. And if it ranks low in the world pecking order of currencies, it can, as a rule, be more easily whipsawed by the action of other economies.

The much bigger change, however, according to Cohen, isn't in the relationship of nations to one another but in the relationship between governments and markets. Thus the use of more than one currency in a country opens more options for companies and financial institutions doing business there. It may offer choices with respect to currency risk, taxes, regulations, accounting rules, transaction and conversion costs, financial instruments and the like. Conversely, it reduces the local government's influence or control.

Finally, it also makes the "invaded" country more sensitive to, and potentially responsive to, world financial markets. Which is why the first stop of many a new president or prime minister is a de rigueur visit to Wall Street to perform a reassurance ritual promising financial prudence during the ensuing term of office.

What we've seen so far—the great wealth shift toward Asia, the creation of cyberspace, the change in criteria by which locations are appraised, the expansion of global reach, and the geographical spread of the currently shaky dollar—are only some of the changes taking place in our relationship to the deep fundamental of space.

We turn next to the most controversial of all today's spatial changes, the one that has set antagonists marching all over the world and beating their drums (literally) in Pôrto Alegre, Brazil, while its defenders, during their annual fish fry in Davos, Switzerland, try to make nice to the marchers. At issue, of course, is the most misunderstood, misleading, and misused term in the entire economic lexicon: *Globalization.*

Does it still have a future?

CHAPTER 12

AN UNREADY WORLD

I n 1900 the turn of a new century was celebrated in Paris with a Grand
Exhibition devoted to progress, and the newspaper *Le Figaro,* barely
able to contain itself, crowed: "How fortunate we are to be living on this
first day of the 20th century!" One source of enthusiasm was the world's
advance, as the rich nations saw it, toward global economic integration—a
rational process that, by changing spatial and political relationships, would
make economies flourish.

Sounding much like the true believers in economic globalization today,
economists spoke enthusiastically of how more and more of the world was
being stitched or bolted together. Foreign trade as a percentage of world output had risen nearly ninefold between 1800 and 1900—some of it going into
colonies in Asia and Africa. Anyone projecting these trends forward could
have concluded that the process of economic globalization would complete
itself long before the year 2000. But trends don't continue indefinitely, the
future doesn't arrive in straight lines, and the world wasn't ready for what happened next.

Within fourteen years of the Grand Exhibition, the "stitches" or "bolts"
broke and the slaughter of World War I violently disrupted flows of trade
and capital. The Bolshevik Revolution followed in 1917, the Great Depression
in the 1930s, World War II in 1939–45, the Communist takeover of China
in 1949 and from the 1940s and into the '60s, and successive decolonizations
in India, Africa and Asia.

Together, these events and countless smaller, less visible ones shattered
long-established trade arrangements, encouraged tit-for-tat protectionism and
touched off violence and instability—all discouraging border-crossing trade,
investment and economic integration. In short, the world went through half a
century of *de-globalization.*

MORE CAPITALIST THAN THOU

In the post–World War II years, America, its industrial base intact and, if anything, strengthened by the war, needed export markets for its goods and, above all, its capital. The world was hungry for American products, often the only products available.

Moreover, advancing technology made it cheaper and easier to serve larger-than-national markets. Thus, convinced that global economic reintegration would serve their own purposes while generally advancing world economic growth, American elites undertook to create cross-border markets through which goods, capital, information and skills could once more flow with minimal friction. This, then, took on the form of an ideological crusade for *re-globalization.*

As late as 1990, vast areas of the world were still essentially closed to the trouble-free exchange of goods, currencies, people and information. Only a billion people lived in any form of open economy. But by the year 2000, that number had, by some counts, leaped to four billion.

China alone, with well over a billion people, became committed to "market socialism," perhaps better described as "social capitalism," and opened its doors to foreign plants, products and money. Postcommunist Russia invited investment from outside. Eastern Europe and former Soviet republics in the Caucasus and Central Asia followed suit. Much of South America, urged on by the United States and led by Chile and Argentina, deregulated, privatized, invited Wall Street capital and became for a time "more capitalist than thou."

Currencies, too, as we've seen, were increasingly unleashed from their countries of origin. We expanded the spatial reach not only of giant, globe-girdling corporations but of tiny firms, even Internet-connected, micro-financed village enterprises in remote regions, encouraging once more the dream of a fully integrated world economy—one in which no part of the 510 million square meters of the Earth's surface is beyond reach.

The re-globalizers were on a roll.

THE EVIAN AND KETCHUP TEST

It is true this drive toward re-globalization has not gone quite as far as many of its friends and enemies assume. According to R. I. Weingarten, chairman of the Whitehall Financial Group, even within the financial sector the loose term *globalization* "masks sharply different rates of change. While currency markets are truly global, bond markets lag, and stock markets, in the main, continue to list largely domestic securities."

In Europe, where intense pressures for economic integration have led to a single currency and central bank, the *Financial Times* finds that "equity markets remain highly fragmented, with a mosaic of different rules and regulations." Despite hundreds of frequently questionable new laws and regulations intended to produce uniformity, the same bottle of Evian water that in 2003 cost .44 euro in France went for 1.89 euros in Finland; the same bottle of Heinz ketchup priced at .66 in Germany cost 1.38 in Italy—not exactly the uniformity the autocrats in Brussels hoped to see.

Far more significant on a global scale, as Zanny Minton Beddoes has pointed out in *Foreign Policy,* "only 18 developing countries have regular access to private capital," and even if more countries did, "it would not mean that a unified global capital market existed." At yet another level, accounting methods still differ around the world, despite a drive to adopt a universal standard.

Nonetheless, as early as the 1990s, thirty-five thousand to forty thousand multinational corporations operated two hundred thousand subsidiaries or affiliates around the world. Worldwide foreign-currency deposits soared from $1 billion in 1961 to $1.5 trillion by the end of the century. World foreign direct investment had grown to $1.3 trillion. Cross-border debt reached $1.7 trillion by 2001. And world trade had hit $6.3 trillion.

One of the most comprehensive recent attempts to determine the extent of globalization today is an index developed by A. T. Kearney and *Foreign Policy.* It measures such things as trade, foreign direct investment, the flow of portfolio investments, technology, travel and tourism, then compares countries. It also treats a broad set of other variables ranging from culture and communications to the number of foreign embassies a country maintains and the number of intergovernmental agencies to which it belongs.

On the basis of all these, the 2003 Kearney study ranked sixty-two countries and found that small ones topped the list of the most globalized—Ireland, Switzerland, Sweden, Singapore and the Netherlands. The United States was number 11, France 12, Germany 17 and South Korea 28, ahead of Japan at 35.

The level of cross-border economic integration actually declined in 2002 because of a slowdown in the U.S. economy and a drop in FDI in 2001. But the total amount was still above that for any year before 1999. In spite of these figures, *Foreign Policy* expressed little doubt that re-globalization would continue. And if to these measures we add the growing cross-fertilization of currencies already described, the reasons for that optimism are strengthened.

YELLOW DUST

Ironically, still another reason lies hidden in the remark of Harriet Babbitt, former deputy administrator of the U.S. Agency for International Development, who has noted, "We are . . . globalizing our vices more quickly than we're globalizing our virtues."

Illegal drugs, for example, are a $400 billion business, according to the United Nations, and add up to about 8 percent of the world economy. The narco industry, using the latest technologies, forms a giant *unter-economy* that actually overshadows the aboveground or formal economy in many countries and reaches from one end of the Earth to the other. From Afghanistan and Colombia to the schoolrooms and slums of Rio de Janeiro to the sidewalks of Chicago, narco-traffickers operate one of the most globalized industries in the world. No one government can control it even if it has the will to do so.

The sex business is similarly global. In an Albanian refugee camp, young women kidnapped in Romania await shipment to Italy to serve as sex slaves. In Bucharest so-called "agencies" peddle "dancers" to the sex trade in Greece, Turkey, Israel and as far away as Japan. According to UNICEF, an estimated one million impoverished young people, mostly girls, are caught up in the sex trade every year.

A striking article by Moisés Naím, editor of *Foreign Policy,* explains: "Drugs, arms, intellectual property, people and money are not the only commodities traded illegally for huge profits by international networks. They also trade in human organs, endangered species, stolen art and toxic waste." Precisely because these activities are illegal and need to escape detection, traffickers constantly change the routes they take to deliver their "products."

Smugglers, armed with fake papers and aided by bribed officials, slip easily past frontier guards. But police in hot pursuit of them are often stopped at the border. As Naím explains, governments will huffily protect their "sovereign" space from one another. Yet that same spatial sovereignty "is compromised daily, not by nation-states, but by stateless networks that break laws and cross borders in pursuit of trade." Venezuela, for example, would not allow U.S. planes in its airspace to hunt for drug traffickers from Colombia—who regularly violate the same so-called sovereignty with impunity.

Naím concludes that our efforts to control these illegal and antisocial activities in the under-economy will fail because government strategies are rooted in "wrong ideas, false assumptions and obsolete institutions." His message is clear: It will take a global—or at least multilateral—effort to stop them.

Then there is the rain of "yellow dust" from China's deserts that periodically blankets Seoul, Korea. And there are the fires in Indonesia that unleash choking smog that sends thousands gasping and coughing in Malaysia and Singapore. And the cyanide spill in Romania that poisoned rivers in Hungary and Serbia. Global warming, air pollution, ozone depletion, desertification and water-supply shortages, like the drug trade and sexual slavery, are all problems that demand organized regional or even global effort. Whether any-one wants it or not.

TRUE BELIEVERS

Today a widespread—indeed, global—controversy rages over the benefits and costs of further cross-border integration. One thing is clear. Life is unfair. Eco-nomic integration and its spatial consequences do not deliver anything like a "level playing field"—a metaphysical concept with no existence in reality.

We need not replay all the arguments about the benefits and costs of extending spatial reach and globalizing economies. Even identifying the pros and cons accurately is more complex than it seems. Thus the Hungarian econ-omist András Inotai, director-general of the Institute for World Economics in Budapest, has analyzed the pluses and minuses for countries joining the European Union. His words apply to economic integration at the global level as well.

Referring to the two deep fundamentals so far discussed in these pages, he points out that "benefits and losses do not spread evenly in space" and that results "differ in time as well." Short-term gains or losses, he notes, can turn into their opposites in the long term. Some payoffs or losses are here and now. Others are spatially here but not now. Still others are now but not here.

Both sides reduce these complexities to bumper-sticker slogans.

Pro- and anti-globalization literature threatens to swamp us, with Google's search engine alone pointing to over 1.5 million relevant documents. A *News-week* survey of forty major newspapers and magazines found only 158 articles on globalization in 1991. In 2000 it reported 17,638.

Given all this attention, it's easy to point out globalization's evils—though many of them have more to do with corruption, environmental degradation and brute enforcement than with economic integration as such.

Nevertheless, reality shouts. China has been—and still is—guilty of all these evils—corruption up to the nostrils, massive ecological damage, unashamed suppression of social unrest.

Yet these negatives must be weighed against the facts that China has sys-tematically integrated itself into the global economy and, according to *The Economist,* had by 2001 used global capital to help raise as many as 270 mil-lion people out of extreme peasant misery.

Pro-globalization forces, their enthusiasm slightly dimmed by criticism and by the current weakness of the world economy, nevertheless remain optimistic for the long term. Some religiously believe that complete globalization is our destiny—that whatever the backward steps and stumbles, it will triumph in the end, linking not only every person but every place.

These true believers argue that (1) no country will indefinitely turn its back on globalization's "breathtaking" potential for raising living standards; (2) we face new problems that cannot be solved without it; and (3) new technologies will increasingly facilitate it.

To which skeptics might reply that (1) the benefits of peace could also be breathtaking, yet they have been passed up repeatedly; (2) not all problems get solved; and (3) history is full of counter-technologies developed to "in-facilitate" what earlier technologies facilitated.

Re-globalization could also screech to a halt at some point if oil prices continue to soar as reserves decline; if stabilizing alliances fall apart; if renewed trade protectionism spreads; or if every container, every package and every person crossing a border must be closely inspected because of terrorism, fear of epidemic or for other reasons.

So the real question looming over us is this: Is the decades-long drive toward re-globalization pausing briefly for breath? Or is it about to suddenly go into reverse once more? Are we, in fact—despite the increased mobility of factories and FDI, despite the Internet and cyberspace, and despite the massive movements of people—about to undergo another historic shift from re-globalization to de-globalization. But that isn't the whole—or real—story.

CHAPTER 13

THRUST REVERSERS

F ew words in recent years have fueled as much hatred and controversy around the world as *globalization*—and few have been used more hypocritically—and naïvely—by all sides.

For many anti-globalists, the real target of their wrath is the United States, world headquarters of free-market economics.

The U.S. drive over past decades to globalize (or, more accurately, to re-globalize) the world economy also flew a false flag. Successive administrations, especially that of President Bill Clinton, preached a mantra to the world. The so-called Washington Consensus held that globalization plus liberalization in the form of privatization, deregulation and free trade would alleviate poverty and create democracy and a better world for all.

Both pro- and anti-globalist ideologues typically lump globalization with liberalization, as though they were inseparable. Yet countries can integrate economies without liberalizing. Liberalizing countries, by contrast, can sell off their state enterprises, deregulate and privatize their economies, without necessarily globalizing. None of this guarantees that long-term benefits will flow from the macroeconomy to the microeconomy in which people actually live. And none of it guarantees democracy.

It is now perfectly clear that both sides in the ideological war over re-globalization have been perfectly and deliberately unclear.

Thus the Web site of a protest movement that has waged a ceaseless campaign against globalism listed "actions" in Hyderabad, India; Davos, Switzerland; Pôrto Alegre, Brazil; Buenos Aires, Argentina; Washington, D.C.; and Barcelona, Spain, as well as others in New Zealand, Greece, Mexico and France. Demonstrators surrounded world leaders in their luxury hotels at numerous international meetings from Seattle to Genoa or forced them to seek refuge in remote locations—and to call up security forces to maintain the peace. Now protesters are invited to meet with these leaders and much of the fizz has gone out of the movement.

It hardly escapes notice, however, that much of this purportedly anti-globalist activity is coordinated by interlinked Web sites on the Internet, itself an inherently global technology. The political impact of the movement comes largely from television coverage delivered by global satellite systems. Many of the demands of these groups—for lower-cost AIDS drugs, for example—can be met only by global corporations the protesters excoriate, using computers built by yet other global corporations. Most protesters could not fly to their demonstrations without globally linked airlines dependent on global reservation systems. And the goal of many of the protesters is to create a movement with global impact.

In fact, the movement has split into many different, often short-lived groups with dizzyingly diverse goals, from eliminating child labor to outlawing tobacco to protecting the rights of transgender prison inmates. A few are dewy-eyed anarcho-localists, glorifying the supposed authenticity of face-to-face life in pre-industrial villages—conveniently forgetting the lack of privacy, the sexism, and the narrow-minded local tyrants and bigots so often found in real villages. Others are back-to-nature romantics. Still others are United States– and European Union–hating supernationalists identified with neofascist anti-immigrant political movements. But many others are, in fact, not "anti-global" at all but "counter-global."

These counter-globalists, for example, strongly support the United Nations and other international agencies. Many long to see something approximating a single world government, or at least better, stronger global governance financed, perhaps, by a global tax. What many of them do want, however, is a world crackdown on global corporations and global finance, which they blame for exploiting workers, damaging the environment, supporting undemocratic governments and an infinity of other ills.

The antis make the most noise. But even if all the chanting, marching anti- and counter-globalization protesters were to steal away in the night, the advance of economic re-globalization might still slow or stop in the years immediately ahead.

Powerful factors now loom before us that could halt the continued extension of spatial reach and make even the anti-globalists sorry to see that happen.

THE NEW *TITANIC*

The re-globalization period has seen the world economy suffer one devastating regional or national crisis after another—in Asia, in Russia, in Mexico, in

Argentina. In each case, investors, business decision-makers and governments all over the world worried about financial "contagion." Would Argentina's collapse destroy the Brazilian economy? Could the 1997–1998 Asian crash cause a worldwide meltdown? (It came close.)

Because economic integration today is far more dense, multilayered and complicated, linking so many diverse economies at so many different levels, it requires systemically designed fail-safes, redundancies and other safety devices. Unfortunately, overenthusiastic re-globalizers are constructing a gigantic financial cruise ship lacking the watertight compartments that even the *Titanic* had.

U.S. stock markets have "circuit breakers" intended to stop a crash in its tracks. For example, the New York Stock Exchange will call a one-hour halt in trading if the Dow Jones index falls 10 percent before 2:00 p.m. on a trading day. So-called collars are imposed on certain trades if prices move too far above or below a preset limit.

Similar measures are in place or under discussion in many countries from India to Taiwan. These may or may not be adequate locally or nationally. But trade, currency and capital markets at the global level lack equivalents of even these cautionary measures, let alone a comprehensive system of firewalls, compartments, backups and the like.

By integrating faster than we are inoculating ourselves against contagion, two processes are out of sync—setting us up for a global epidemic that could send individual nations rushing back, head over heels, into their protective financial shells. Their frenzied responses could include yanking foreign investments back home, restoring trade barriers, drastically reshuffling import-export patterns and relocating businesses, jobs and capital around the planet—in short, reversing the recent direction of change.

EXPORT OVERLOAD

What other events or conditions could limit or reverse re-globalization? Plenty.

We have entered the age of export overload—or, if not the age, at least the interval. Starting in the 1970s, Japan soared to prosperity by combining computerized design and manufacture, relatively closed domestic markets and aggressive exports.

That strategy was soon emulated by South Korea, Taiwan, Hong Kong, Singapore and later by Malaysia and Indonesia. All pumped their products into American and European markets, and more "things" than ever in history moved across the Pacific by containership, tanker and cargo planes. Exports—

a spatial phenomenon by definition—came to be regarded as the magic bullet for development.

In all these Asian countries, exports grew faster than domestic demand—another example of large-scale de-synchronization. At that point, China roared into the fray, cramming even cheaper products into the crowded global market and especially into the United States. Suddenly America was awash with Chinese hair dryers, hoses, handbags, clocks and calculators, tools and toys. Overcapacity and rapacity marched hand-in-hand.

It hardly needs noting that if the U.S. economy, which alone accounts for more than 30 percent of world demand, were at any time to lurch into free fall, the relocations of wealth in the world would be shattering for many other countries—including some of the very poorest.

Among those hardest hit would be countries whose governments are dangerously overdependent on a single export for their day-to-day revenue. This could be copper, as in Zambia. It could be bauxite, sugar, coffee, cocoa or cobalt. Or it could be oil.

With crude-oil prices at record highs, it may seem unlikely. Yet the unlikely happens again and again, and a severe slowdown in the United States or a crash in China could, despite producers' efforts to control supply, send oil prices plummeting again. Even if the decline is temporary, the results could shake many governments out of power.

Fully 80 percent of Nigeria's government revenue comes from oil, as does 75 percent of Saudi Arabia's. Much the same can be said of Kuwait, Oman, the United Arab Emirates and Angola. For Venezuela the number is 50 percent, for Russia close to 30 percent. Unstable or politically fragile at best, oil-funded governments could be forced to cut domestic subsidies and social benefits at the risk of triggering upheaval in their streets. More bad news for re-globalization.

The decades ahead may also see a further formation of supranational blocs and trade groups following in the wake of the European Union.

Ranging from Mercosur in South America to emergent groupings in Asia, these blocs, since they create larger-than-national markets, can be seen as half steps toward global integration and more open trade. That is how they are usually portrayed. However, despite protestations to the contrary, they can also, under extreme pressures, flip the protectionist switch and become large-scale deterrents to further openness and globalization. With respect to global integration, area-wide supranational blocs could prove to be a double-edged switchblade.

THE NANO-TEASPOON

And so could the next explosion of scientific and technological break-throughs. Propelled by the fusion of information and biological technologies, it could reduce the need for some previously imported raw materials and other goods. Radical miniaturization, customization and the partial substitution of knowledge content for raw material mean that tomorrow's economies may no longer need as many of the bulk commodities that now form so large a part of the global market. Teaspoons of a nanoproduct tomorrow could replace tons of material that today needs to be shipped across the world. This may be long in coming, but its impact will be felt in major port cities around the world, from Qingdao to Los Angeles to Rotterdam. Again, all this points to more do-it-at-home processes and less reliance on a globalized marketplace.

Furthermore, we can't rule out war and its partner, terror, the most obvious de-globalizers. Both can physically destroy energy and transportation infra-structures needed for the movement or relocation of oil, gas, raw materials, finished products and other goods. Both can also unleash capital flight and unstoppable tidal waves of cross-border refugees. Both will target critical information infrastructures in knowledge-intensive economies.

Unfortunately, the period ahead is likely to see high geopolitical instability and frequent outbreaks of military conflict—leaving not only dead and wounded on the field but, as in the past, the disintegration of what has already been integrated.

MAD MAX SCENARIOS

Beyond these potential de-globalizers are what futurists call wild cards, sce-narios that, though highly improbable, cannot be ruled out: strange new pan-demics and quarantines, asteroid strikes and ecological catastrophes that could knock the entire economic firmament off its current course and reduce it to Mad Max conditions. It is useful to reserve at least a speck of mind space for thinking the unthinkable, for history is little more than a sequence of high-impact events that began as utterly improbable and exploded into actuality.

We cannot know with certainty which of these thrust-reversers might come into play, or how they might converge. But any one of them could prove a far more potent force for turning back re-globalization than all the headline-grabbing protest movements put together. Moreover, it is easy to imagine two or more of these de-globalizing events coming into play simultaneously—and in the not-so-far-off future. It is a lot harder to imagine a future in which none of them occurs.

The most likely scenario is a split—a possible slowdown in further economic integration as such, even as world pressures rise for globally coordinated action on such issues as terror, crime, environmental issues, human rights, slavery and genocide.

This should put to bed any dream of linear progress toward a fully integrated, truly global economy—and any illusions about a world government in the foreseeable decades. It points, instead, to more not fewer, faster not slower, bigger not smaller, spatial jolts to job markets, technologies, money and people around the planet. It points to an age of accelerating spatial turbulence.

What we've seen so far, therefore, is not only a massive shift of wealth toward Asia, a growing importance of region-states and a change in spatial criteria in advanced economies, but a gigantic—though reversible—process of re-globalization. Any of these, by itself, represents an important change in the way revolutionary wealth is related to the deep fundamental of space. Yet, as we will see, one final spatial change may, some distant day, dwarf all these put together.

CHAPTER 14

THE SPACE DRIVE

O urs is the first civilization to plant human-made objects far beyond the surface of our home planet and use them to help us create wealth. That by itself would mark our time as a revolutionary moment in history.

Yet little is known about the impact of this fact on our daily lives and our economy. Few are aware that every time they use an ATM or a telephone they are relying on technology twelve thousand miles from Earth. Or that every patient receiving dialysis or wearing a pacemaker owes some thanks to technologies and, in some cases, people who have left the surface of the planet we call home.

Communication satellites, the Global Positioning System (GPS)—developed by the U.S. Defense Department over four decades at a cost estimated at $14 billion—and commercial remote imaging are parts of an emerging space infrastructure that will be greatly elaborated over the decades and centuries to come, with increasing impact on how we create economic value. Nothing more clearly symbolizes today's changes in the relationship of wealth to the deep fundamentals.

In its present, still-primitive form—often myopically derided as a wasteful luxury—the drive into space has already transformed many aspects of daily life. One result is a $100 billion worldwide satellite industry composed of manufacturers such as Boeing, EADS/Astrium and Alcatel Space; launch firms like China Great Wall Industry Corporation; operators and coordinators such as Intersputnik in Russia; plus myriad service firms, space-image distributors and ground-equipment suppliers.

During the 1990s, business pages reported that investors had lost billions in space-industry stocks and that many space firms were in terminal trouble. But a recent survey by the Satellite Industry Association tells a quite different story—a steady, year-after-year revenue-growth rate of 15 percent from the mid-1990s on. What's more, despite temporary overcapacity, more and more commercial start-ups and countries are racing to join the space "club." Brazil and Ukraine, for example, are partnering to launch Ukrainian Cyclone-4 rockets from Brazil's Alcantara Launch Center—regarded as one of the world's best launch sites. And, as of 2005, equity firms were buying up stakes in such satellite operators as Intelsat, PanAmSat and New Skies.

Similarly, while $100 billion may seem trivial in a multi-trillion-dollar world economy, that number does not begin to tell the whole story. It doesn't include the hidden increases in value generated by the many industries that directly or indirectly rely on space—big television networks, medical technology, sports teams, advertising agencies, telephone and Internet companies and financial-data suppliers, to cite a few.

FROM DIALYSIS TO HEART PUMPS

A little-known consortium of commercial space firms called the Mapping Alliance Program now offers remote sensing, images from space and software for use in computer-aided design, surveying, automated mapping and other services. MAP customers include oil and gas companies, water, gas and electric utilities, agriculture, mining, and transportation, as well as natural-resource managers.

Knowledge derived from space operations is also helping companies anticipate, reduce and hedge their risks. Thus space data play a key role in financial markets in which "weather futures" are traded.

Says Ian Dudden of the London International Financial Futures and Options Exchange (LIFFE), variations in weather can have "a major impact on productivity, turnover and overall profitability" in fields as diverse as "insurance and agriculture as well as [for] the manufacturers and retailers of everything from soft drinks to cold remedies," not to mention the organizers of "pop festivals and package holidays." In the United States, according to the Department of Commerce, one seventh of the entire $10 trillion economy in 2001 was subject to weather risk. Weather futures, traded on the LIFFE and other exchanges, offer a way of hedging against that risk.

The health industry is another largely unacknowledged beneficiary of space activity. The 250,000 U.S. victims of kidney failure who today survive because of dialysis owe their treatment, in some measure, to NASA and its astronauts. A chemical process developed by the space agency to remove toxic waste from dialysis fluids is now helping patients stay alive.

Meanwhile, a company called StelSys, using technology or ideas licensed from the U.S. space agency, is working to develop the equivalent of a dialysis system for patients with liver failure. Additional space research holds promise for improving the treatment of brain tumors, blindness, osteoporosis and other diseases responsible for megabillions of dollars in the ever-swelling health-care budget.

Today Europeans are clinically testing a heart pump based on space-shuttle fuel-pump technology. With the annual cost of heart disease and stroke in the United States alone estimated to exceed $350 billion, how much might such a heart pump save? How much economic value should be assigned to the "bioreactor" designed for growing cells in space—a tool now used by tissue-engineering labs developing methods to grow human hearts?

Parallel questions could be asked about the blindness, limb loss and kidney failure associated with diabetes—a disease that now costs the United States at least $132 billion annually and that is forecast to soar as the population ages.

Meanwhile, space plays a crucial role in environmental monitoring as well. France's SPOT-4 spacecraft, for example, carries an American POAM III instrument for measuring polar ozone and aerosol. According to the U.S. Naval Research Laboratory's 2001 Review, "Every year huge tracts of forest in Alaska, Northern Canada, Scandinavia, Russia and China are racked by forest fires from May through October. Enormous quantities of smoke billow into the atmosphere, where high-altitude winds sometimes carry the smoke thousands of kilometers from the original fires." SPOT-4/POAM III tracks it.

Similarly, a joint Brazil-NASA space project is studying the global effects of ecological changes in the Amazon region. A NASA "bird" measures the rate at which ice is melting at the North and South Poles. Other space-based environmental projects focus on everything from water utilization and fisheries to the ecology of estuaries and El Niño weat er effects.

Never before has the human race had as detai l and accurate an image of the earth's surface. Space shuttles such as *Endeavor* have produced massive data needed for making high-resolution images of desolate tundras and deserts, of jungles where endangered gorillas live and of ancient ruins such as Angkor Wat and Ubar. The same amazingly precise data can, among many other uses, help us locate cell-phone towers, identify flight hazards for aircraft and forecast floods.

PILOTS, PLANES AND PACKAGES

Twenty-four hours a day, at Schriever Air Force Base in Colorado, a handful of U.S. Air Force men and women—some little more than eighteen or nineteen years old—sit at computer consoles and control satellites orbiting the earth twelve thousand nautical miles away. They operate more than twenty satellites that together form the NAVSTAR Global Positioning System that can tell anyone with a small, inexpensive receiver his or her precise location on earth.

Used by online services, hikers, drivers, truckers, boaters, ships and shippers, banks and telecom companies, not to mention the military, GPS is one of the marvels of our era.

So far-reaching are its implications for both security and business that Europe is belatedly planning to launch its own system, called Galileo.

A little-known fact about GPS is that it helps locate us in time as well as space. Thus, in addition to positioning us spatially, the system also operates as a key synchronizer. In the words of Glen Gibbons of Advanstar Communications, "Every time we get cash from an ATM or make a phone call (whether wireless or wire-line), the synchronization of the voice and data streams in those . . . communications networks is almost certainly based on GPS timing . . . it has made nanosecond-level timing readily available throughout the world, courtesy of the cesium and rubidium atomic clocks on board the GPS satellites." The productivity benefit of precision timing and synchronization in the economy has yet to be calculated. And more is on the way.

Since the attack on the World Trade Center in New York, anti-terror experts have devoted increasing attention to the 200 million shipping containers that move by sea each year. Any one of these can contain a hidden biological weapon, a smuggled terrorist, illegal drugs or arms or other dangerous contraband. Today only about 2 percent are inspected as they enter the United States. Add to that the additional containers that arrive by land and air.

GPS satellites, in principle, can track the coordinates of these containers as they move from place to place. In the future, not just the containers but every product in them will be continually followed as it moves through the supply chain from the plant to the wholesaler, the retailer, onto the shelves and into the customer's home. Prototype tracking systems are already being studied or tested by such companies as Wal-Mart, Target, Sears and Kmart.

Furthermore, the day will come when many packages carrying food, for example, will have embedded chips that continuously report to the shipper the changing condition of the food as it moves.

Other "smart" packages will actually process their contents en route. Linking these to GPS or similar satellite systems will transform large sectors of both the transportation and the food industry, ensure fresher and higher-quality packaged food and other products, change the economics of both production and distribution in these and many other fields—and improve security.

Like all technologies, of course, GPS has both positive and negative potentials. It can make our lives far more secure. It can track a car full of Al Qaeda terrorists across the Yemeni desert. It can also make a visit to a bordello or a

Swiss bank less private than it might once have been. But, then, so can "cookies" in a computer—or a gossipy neighbor. Benefits and sacrifices need to be weighed against one another.

One of the biggest economic payoffs from GPS, however, will come when today's ground-based world air traffic control system becomes essentially a backup to a space-based alternative. Today flight plans require most aircraft to fly from one ground-based radio beacon to the next over heavily congested airways. Capacity near many big cities is limited. A GPS control system can increase capacity along with precision. It can also permit landings under conditions now regarded as prohibitive, including at remote and small airports, and improve over-the-ocean navigation. All at far less cost than the ground-based system.

Even more remarkable, NASA's Global Differential GPS, recently developed at its Jet Propulsion Lab in Pasadena, California, has been tested in Greenland and the United States. It is now capable of positioning aircraft to within 3.9 inches horizontally and 7.9 inches vertically anywhere in the world. JPL proudly boasts that this is a "factor of ten improvement" over the accuracy of current systems.

UNEXPLORED WEALTH FRONTIERS

Across the board, then, space activity is paying off for the emergent economy—often in unseen ways—and promises even more in days to come. A Midwest Research Institute study has estimated that every dollar invested in NASA adds nine dollars to U.S. gross domestic product. Another analysis, by Chase Econometrics, has suggested that space-related research yields productivity increases that translate into a 43 percent return on investment. All such numbers are relatively old, shaky and incomplete. Nevertheless, even if we arbitrarily slash them, they would still strongly suggest that space activity already pays off handsomely for the economy. And we are still using only a tiny fraction of its potential.

Looming on the horizon are thousands upon thousands more satellites in the heavens. Algeria, Pakistan and Nigeria have already purchased microsatellites weighing little more than a hundred pounds, capable of carrying cameras and being propelled into orbit for a fraction of what it now costs for conventional satellites. Professor Martin Sweeting of the company supplying them, Surrey Satellite Technology in Britain, claims that within a decade we will launch satellites no bigger than a credit card. As size and costs plummet they will become cheaper, making it possible for medium-sized businesses, NGOs, private groups and even individuals—good and bad alike—to afford them.

It is time, in short, to recognize that even in purely economic terms the drive into space is anything but trivial. Humanity's baby steps into space are already creating significant value on earth in ways about which earlier civilizations could only fantasize. And it is only the beginning.

Today more than fifty nations claim to have space programs. But governments are not alone in space. In 2004, twenty-six companies competed to win the Ansari X Prize for the first private firm in the world to build a ship capable of carrying three people into suborbital space and repeat the test in the same vehicle within two weeks. The purpose: To hasten the development of commercial space tourism.

On October 4, 2004—exactly forty-seven years to the day after *Sputnik* was launched—*SpaceShipOne* flew into suborbital space and won the prize. It was funded not by government billions, but by $20 million provided by Paul Allen, cofounder of Microsoft. Its pilot, Brian Binnie, was the 434th human to leave planet Earth and venture into space.

Just months earlier, when *Spirit* and *Opportunity*, two NASA spacecraft, landed safely on Mars, the Jet Propulsion Laboratory's deputy director, Eugene Tattini, estimated that the event drew ten billion hits on the Internet from people around the world who wanted to follow the news and share in the meaning of the moment.

Even if we were making no other changes in the "where" of wealth—if we were not shifting it toward Asia and forming region-states, if there were no search for higher-value-added places, if we were not re-globalizing and de-globalizing the world economy, the leap beyond our planet would, by itself, mark a revolutionary turning point in wealth creation.

The combined evidence, therefore, is overwhelming. We are simultaneously transforming the relationship of wealth to both time and space—two of the deep fundamentals that have underpinned all economic activity since we were hunter-gatherers.

Wealth today is not merely revolutionary but is becoming more so. Nor is this just a matter of technology. It is, as we will next make clear, a revolution of the mind as well.

PART FIVE

Trusting Knowledge

CHAPTER 15

THE EDGE
OF KNOWLEDGE

Nguyen Thi Binh, a peasant in her fifties, grows rice on a small paddy sixty miles south of Hanoi in Vietnam. When she is growing rice in her paddy, we cannot.

Tatiana Raseikina, a twenty-something, screws door handles onto Avto-VAZ cars as they whiz by on an assembly line in Togliatti, an industrial city south of Moscow. And, like that rice paddy in Vietnam, when Tatiana's clattering assembly line is racing along, we cannot use it.

The lives and cultures of these two women are very different. One symbolizes agrarian production; the other, industrial production. Yet both live in economies in which the central assets, resources and products are what economists call "rival"—meaning that their use by one party denies their simultaneous use by anyone else.

Since most economies are still agrarian or industrial, it is no surprise that most economists have spent their careers collecting data and analyzing and theorizing about rival means of wealth creation.

Suddenly, so to speak, a different wealth system has arrived that is driven not only by dramatic changes in our relationships with time and space but with a third deep fundamental: Knowledge.

The response of rearguard economists has been to either deny its importance, continue working as though it made no difference, or probe it with inappropriate tools. One reason is that, unlike rice and car handles, knowledge is intangible and attempts to define it usually lead into a maze from which there is no graceful exit.

Fortunately, for our purposes, we don't need a mind-numbing, comprehensive review of the endless competing definitions. Nor are extreme precision and specificity necessary. Unsatisfying as it may seem, for our purposes we require only a working definition that helps reveal the way in which our global knowledge base is being transformed—and how today's changes will affect wealth in the future.

One commonly used approach sets knowledge apart from data and information. Data are usually described as consisting of discrete items devoid of context—for example, "three hundred shares." When those data are placed in context, they become information—for example, "We have three hundred shares of pharmaceutical company X."

Only when information is configured into broader, higher-level patterns and linked to other patterns do we arrive at something we might call knowledge—for example, "We have three hundred shares of pharmaceutical company X up two points in a rising market, but volume is low and it's likely the Fed will raise interest rates."

We'll use the terms this way, but to avoid the annoying repetition of the phrase "data, information and knowledge" we will, where specificity doesn't matter, use the words *knowledge* or *information* to mean any or all of the above.

Together these distinctions provide, at best, only a gross definition of *knowledge*. But it's adequate for us right now in describing what might be called the revolutionary wealth system's "knowledge supply."

Billions of words about the knowledge economy have been written, uttered, digitized and disputed in just about every language on earth. Yet few of those words make clear just how profoundly different knowledge is from any of the other resources or assets that go into the creation of wealth. Let us look at some of those ways.

1. **Knowledge is inherently non-rival.** You and a million other people can use the same chunk of knowledge without diminishing it. In fact, the greater the number of people who use it, the greater the likelihood that someone will generate more knowledge with it.

The fact that knowledge is non-rival has nothing to do with whether or not we pay for using it. Patents, copyrights, anti-pirating technology may protect a particular piece of knowledge and exclude its use by those who don't pay for access to it. But these are artifacts of law, not the inherent character of knowledge itself, which is essentially undepletable. Arithmetic doesn't get used up when we apply it.

In advanced economies today, the vast majority of workers are busy creating or exchanging non-rival data, information and knowledge. Yet we know of no theory that systematically maps the interaction of rival and non-rival sectors in a whole economy, and what happens when the balance between them shifts.

2. Knowledge is intangible. We can't touch, fondle or slap it. But we can—and do—manipulate it.

3. Knowledge is non-linear. Tiny insights can yield huge outputs. Stanford students Jerry Yang and David Filo started Yahoo! by simply categorizing their favorite Web sites. Fred Smith, also while still a student, flashed on the idea that in an accelerative economy people would pay extra for speed—and went on to found Federal Express, the world's best-known package-delivery firm.

4. Knowledge is relational. Any individual piece of knowledge attains meaning only when juxtaposed with other pieces that provide its context. Sometimes that context can be communicated with a wordless smile or scowl.

5. Knowledge mates with other knowledge. The more there is, the more promiscuous and the more numerous and varied the possible useful combinations.

6. Knowledge is more portable than any other product. Once converted to zeros and ones, it can be distributed instantaneously to one person next door or to ten million people from Hong Kong to Hamburg—at the same near-zero price.

7. Knowledge can be compressed into symbols or abstractions. Try compressing a "tangible" toaster.

8. Knowledge can be stored in smaller and smaller spaces. Toshiba entered Guinness World Records in 2004 with a computer hard drive smaller than a postage stamp. Coming soon is storage at the nano scale—that is, measured in billionths of a meter. And even tinier—if the knowledge available to us is correct.

9. Knowledge can be explicit or implicit, expressed or not expressed, shared or tacit. There is no tacit table, truck or other tangible.

10. Knowledge is hard to bottle up. It spreads.

Putting all these characteristics together, we wind up with something so unlike the tangibles with which economists have traditionally been concerned that many of them just shake their heads and, like most people, seek comfort in the world they know—the familiar world of rival tangibility.

Even all these differences, however, do not complete the ways in which knowledge refuses to fit into existing economic categories.

KICKING TIRES

Knowledge assets have strange, paradoxical characteristics. Take the difference between buying a car and buying proprietary knowledge.

Owners or originators of some very valuable knowledge are protected by trade-secret laws. Not long ago the Lockheed Martin Corporation sued Boeing, alleging that a Lockheed engineer had made off with thousands of pages of rocket-launch data and cost estimates and made them available to Boeing. The suit claimed the documents were then used by Boeing to win a multibillion-dollar contract.

That takes us to what Professor Max Boisot of ESADE (La Escuela Superior de Administración y Dirección de Empresas) in Barcelona has called a paradox. "The value of physical goods is established by comparing them with each other." A car buyer kicks tires, looks under hoods, asks friends for advice, test-drives the Toyota, the Ford, the Volkswagen. That doesn't reduce the value of the car.

By contrast, in the Lockheed-Boeing case, let's hypothetically say that another aerospace company, Northrop, had wanted to buy Lockheed's secret document. To establish their value, Northrop has to know what's in them. But the minute we know what's in them, they are no longer completely secret, and at least some of their value may well be gone.

In Boisot's words, "Information about information goods . . . cannot be so diffused without compromising their scarcity"—the very scarcity on which their value is partly based. That would be like looking under the car's hood and making off with its fuel system.

In an economy based more and more on knowledge and innovation, this creates a challenging problem not just for economists but for economics. Thus, Boisot writes, "when information ceases to play merely a supporting role in economic transactions, when it becomes instead their central focus, the logic that regulates the production and exchange of physical goods ceases to apply."

The rise of knowledge intensivity is not just a minor bump in the road. Economists, having hoped to turn economics into a science with the precision and predictability of Newton's physics, once pictured economies as deterministic, equilibrial and machine-like. Even today much in economics, including the legacies of Adam Smith, David Ricardo and later Karl Marx, John Maynard Keynes and Milton Friedman is still based, at least partly, on Newtonian mechanics and Cartesian logic.

Almost a century ago, however, quantum theory, relativity and the uncertainty principle produced a crisis in physics that led first physicists, and then non-physicists as well, to a clearer understanding of the limitations of the machine model. It turns out that not everything in the universe behaves, at all times, with the regularity, predictability and lawfulness of a machine. In Boisot's words: "The message . . . is a disconcerting one for those who believe that economics is or should be an exact science: it is that information goods are indeterminate with respect to value. And just as the discovery of indeterminacy in physical processes entailed a shift in paradigm from classical physics to quantum physics, so the indeterminacy of information goods calls for a distinct political economy of information."

Now combine the unanswered questions about knowledge with those posed by the simultaneous sweeping changes in our relations with time and space, and we begin to glimpse just how little we know about the revolutionary wealth system now transforming America and spreading around the world.

For starters, just how much knowledge is there?

CHAPTER 16

TOMORROW'S "OIL"

Amazing as it may seem, fully half a century after the knowledge economy began, we know embarrassingly little about the "knowing" that lies behind it.

If, for example, knowledge is the oil of tomorrow's economy, as many have suggested, then how much of this intangible "oil" exists? Petroleum companies, armies, Wall Street traders and Middle East sheikhs spend fortunes trying to estimate the real—as distinct from claimed—size of global oil reserves. But does anyone know how much the world *knows*? Or how the world's knowledge supply is changing? How much of it is worth knowing? And what's it worth?

To answer questions like these, we'll need to blaze some surprising pathways, exploring bizarre beliefs about everything from the Bible and the Koran to science, the behavior of beavers and toxic tomatoes.

THE MORE WE USE . . . ?

Our starting point is a single critical fact: Knowledge—another of the deep fundamentals of revolutionary wealth—has become one of the fastest-changing components of our economic and social environment. This is why any comparison of knowledge to oil is misleading.

The ways in which we store and deliver petroleum have changed only modestly in the past century—we still rely on pipes, tanks and tankers. By contrast, with the spread of computers, satellites, cell phones, the Internet and other digital technologies, we are drastically altering the ways in which we create and store knowledge, the speed at which it decays, how we judge its validity, the tools we use to make more of it, the languages in which it is expressed, the degree of specialization and abstraction in which it is organized, the analogies we rely on, the amount that is quantified and the media that disseminate it.

Moreover, all these dimensions of knowledge are changing simultaneously, at speeds never before encountered—and opening up countless new ways to create wealth.

Another basic difference between oil and knowledge is that the more oil we use, the less we have left. By contrast, as we've suggested, the more knowledge we use, the more we create. This difference alone makes much of mainstream economics obsolete. Economics can no longer be defined—as it often was—as the science of the allocation of scarce resources. Knowledge is essentially inexhaustible.

These changes in the way we relate to knowledge have powerful effects on real-world wealth—who gets it and how. They send lawyers, accountants and legislators scurrying to rewrite existing rules about taxes, accounting, privacy and intellectual property. They intensify competition and accelerate innovation. They make old regulatory rules obsolete. They create continuous turbulence and turnover in methods, markets and management.

They allow whole industries and sectors to move beyond mass production and mass consumption to higher-value-added, more personalized products, services and experiences. Above all, these changes in knowledge demand much faster, smarter decision-making under more and more complex, if not chaotic, conditions.

Yet, for all the thousands of analyses and studies of emerging knowledge economies, the impact of knowledge on creating wealth has been, and remains, misleadingly undervalued.

STEEL MILLS AND SHOES

Though the United States is still a great manufacturing power, fewer than 20 percent of its labor force works in this sector. Fully 56 percent performs work that is managerial, financial, sales-related, clerical or professional. The category growing most rapidly of all is professional—the most knowledge-intensive.

Such much-quoted numbers, however, underestimate the new reality. Far more than 56 percent are engaged in knowledge work. That is because today many machine operators, whether in leading-edge American steel mills or, for that matter, South Korean consumer-product plants, spend at least part of their time monitoring computers, much like pilots in a 747 cockpit. Truck drivers rely on computers in their cabs. They may not be categorized as knowledge workers, but they, too, are generating, processing and transmitting knowledge or the data and information that underlie it. They are, in effect, part-time knowledge workers, but aren't counted as such.

And that isn't all that goes uncounted. The knowledge we all use to create wealth includes hard-to-measure tacit or implicit knowledge stored inside our heads. What makes us "knowledgeable," for example, is an everyday understanding of the people around us. It includes knowing whom to trust, how a boss will react to bad news, how teams work. It includes job skills and behavior we may have learned by simply watching others. It includes knowing about our own bodies and brains, how they perform and when they let us do our best work.

Some of this tacit knowledge is trivial. But some is vital to everyday life and to productive endeavors. It is that back-of-the-mind knowledge on which we all depend—knowledge we may not even know we have. And precisely because it is so varied, and so far in the background, it, too, is often ignored by economists.

In short, for these and other reasons, knowledge has long been short-changed by economists—and today more than ever. To peer into the heart of tomorrow's economy, therefore, we need to compensate for this lack of knowledge about knowledge.

OUR INNER "WAREHOUSE"

Every one of us, at any given moment, has an individualized inventory of work- and wealth-related knowledge. Authors presumably know something about the craft of writing and about the book-publishing industry. Dentists know about teeth. Gas station attendants know about steering fluids.

But not all knowledge belongs to individuals. Work teams, companies, industries, institutions and whole economies each, at any given moment, develop their own collective knowledge supply. The same might be said of societies and nations.

All this knowledge is stored in two fundamentally different ways. One part of the knowledge supply is found inside our skulls. In each of us there is a crowded, invisible warehouse full of knowledge and its precursor data and information. But unlike a warehouse, it is also a workshop in which we—or, more accurately, the electrochemicals in our brains—continually shift, add, subtract, combine and rearrange numbers, symbols, words, images and memories, combining them with emotions to form new thoughts.

As they stream by, these thoughts may include everything from Wall Street stats, ideas about our customers, a friend's tip about our golf swing, images of our mother's face, worries about a sick child or a technical formula for improving a product, all interspersed with flashes of last night's basketball game on TV, fragments of an advertising jingle from a car commercial and a half-finished outline for an overdue memo.

Individually, such disparate items may mean little. But rearranged, they take on shape and larger meaning. They often turn into action that alters important decisions about our personal life, work and wealth. Concern for the sick child may make it hard to concentrate on the memo, or to keep tomorrow's golf date with a customer, while the drop in stock-market prices may lead us to defer buying a new car.

Let's inspect that knowledge warehouse and workshop. If we could shrink ourselves down to nanosize and walk around inside this constantly changing mental space, we'd find endless rows and piles of facts and supposed facts. We'd find concepts jumbled together or neatly piled atop other concepts, and linked to still others. Somewhere we'd find all of our assumptions, plausible or not, about people, love, sex, nature, time, space, religion, politics, life, death and causation. Hidden in some dark, remote corner we'd find grammar, the very languages we use and the logic and rules we apply to arrive at and manage our collection of meanings.

It's a busy, churning place, operating without stop, even when we sleep. While some knowledge is continually lost, forgotten, mutated or rendered pointless, new, wealth-relevant knowledge is continually added. We can call all of this put together our personal knowledge supply. We all have one.

There are more than six billion of these personal knowledge supplies currently walking around the planet—more than at any time in human history.

JUST ASK

But by far most of the world's knowledge supply is stored *outside* the brains of living humans. It is the accumulated knowledge of the ages—and of the moment—stored externally on everything from ancient cave walls to the latest hard drives and DVDs.

For millennia humans had extremely limited ways to pass knowledge from one generation to the next. Apart from oral narratives (told and retold with accumulating inaccuracy), most knowledge died with each dying person and each dying generation. The rate of social and technological change in these early human societies was so slow, therefore, that even accurate accounts mainly told the same stories over and over again.

A giant breakthrough occurred thirty-five thousand years ago when some unremembered genius drew the first pictograph or ideograph on a stone or a cave wall to memorialize an event, person or thing—and, in so doing, began storing non-oral memories outside the human brain. Another great advance followed the invention of various forms of writing. Millennia later came additional huge leaps with the successive invention of libraries, indexing and printing, all of which increased the rate at which knowledge grew from generation to generation.

It is sobering to think that without this one factor—growth in our ability to generate and accumulate knowledge—we might still be living little better than our ancestors did more than thirty-five thousand years ago.

Today, with the arrival of ever-more-powerful computers, ever-more Web sites and ever-more new media, we are generating—and accumulating—data, information and knowledge at unprecedented speeds. To accommodate them, we have in recent decades been building what is, in effect, an immense megabrain outside, and in addition to, our six and a half billion individual human brains.

This global megabrain is still that of a baby, incomplete, with adult connections not yet in place. Yet at some unknown, crucial tipping point in human history, the amount of knowledge stored outside our brains became larger than the amount stored inside. If anything proves our ignorance about knowledge, it is the fact that this truly momentous change in the history of our species is either unknown or unnoticed by humanity.

This "outside brain" is expanding at unbelievable speeds. In 2002, researchers at the School of Information Management and Systems at the University of California/Berkeley estimated that the amount of data, information and knowledge stored in print, film, magnetic or optical form in that one year alone was equivalent to that "contained in half a million new libraries the size of the Library of Congress." It was, they said, equal to every word ever uttered by a human being "since the dawn of time." Today, we can assume, the pace is even faster.

It is only when we add this exploding external storage to what is inside our human brains that we arrive at our human species' total supply of knowledge—what might be called the Aggregate Supply of Knowledge, or ASK. This becomes the immense wellspring on which revolutionary wealth can draw.

We are not merely expanding the ASK, but altering the way it is organized, accessed and distributed. Internet search engines permit more and more refined and granular queries, and more and more ways to combine and manipulate contents. Moreover, systems that have until now been dominated by Western approaches to logic and thinking will soon be enriched by alternative epistemologies and more diverse ways to organize thought as we move toward a global knowledge meta-system.

We are, therefore, transforming the entire relationship of wealth, in all forms, to the deep fundamental of knowledge—even as we similarly transform its links to time and space. Only by recognizing this can we appreciate, for the first time, why revolutionary wealth today is so qualitatively different from wealth in any previous era.

FORGET ALZHEIMER'S

Berkeley's study wasn't the only attempt to measure the emerging global brain. Computer scientist Michael E. Lesk of the U.S. National Science Foundation also cast light on it and took a different tack.

Beginning with our six billion-plus brains, and based on the rates at which they absorb information and how fast we forget it, Lesk roughly calculated that the "total memory of all the people now alive" is the equivalent of 1,200 petabytes of data. Since a petabyte is equal to 1,125,899,906,842,624 bytes, 1,200 sounds like a lot. But, Lesk nonchalantly assures us, "we can store digitally everything that everyone remembers. For any single person, this isn't even hard."

After all, he continues, "the average American spends 3,304 hours per year with one or another kind of media." Some 1,578 hours are spent watching TV, another 12 in front of movie screens—which adds up to about 11 million words. Another 354 hours are devoted to newspapers, magazines and books. The result, he suggests, is that "in 70 years of life you would be exposed to around six gigabytes of ASCII." Today you can buy a 400-gigabyte disk drive for your personal computer.

He concluded that combining information stored in human brains with information stored outside our skulls, there are all together approximately 12,000 petabytes of information in the world—or, put in plain language, for every byte in a human's memory, there are about ten stored in what we've just called the planet's baby megabrain.

All this led Lesk, finally, to suggest that the day is not far off when pupils will need to memorize nothing—they will wear a gadget that stores everything for them. And that raises fascinating questions. Might that gadget also help Alzheimer's patients? If Lesk is right, and we won't need internal memory for information, what part of the human brain might become superfluous? And what part will still be needed for knowledge?

One can, of course, quibble with these numbers and far-out speculations. We can talk about multitasking, nonverbal information and other problems with these estimates. Moreover, information is, as we don't need to be reminded, a far cry from knowledge. Neither Berkeley's work nor Lesk's, both of which reduce information to digital bits, tells us about the *meaning* of what is measured. What is it that we actually "know"?

An attempt to answer this question was recently made by Adrian Woolfson, a Darwin Research Fellow at Cambridge University. In his book *Life*

Without Genes, Woolfson writes: "Everything that has, can, or ever will exist, in this or any other world may be fully described by the complete collection of relevant facts and the corresponding set of logical interconnections."

One is immediately tempted to grab him by the collar and say, "Oh, yeah?" But no need. His discussion of the knowability of what is known is dazzling, but ultimately, Woolfson hauls up the white flag and concludes that what he proposes is, in fact, impossible.

So none of these attempts comes close to telling us how much meaningful knowledge there is in all this storage. Or what it's worth. But all of them support our contention that revolutionary changes are taking place in the deep fundamental of knowledge—changes for which even the term *revolution* is an understatement.

We are, in fact, living through the deepest upheaval in the world knowledge system since our species started to think. Until we digest this point, our best-laid plans for the future will misfire.

And that takes us to those toxic tomatoes and . . . the buried head of a child.

CHAPTER 17

THE OBSOLEDGE TRAP

Thinking matters. But many of the facts we think about are false. And much of what we believe is almost certainly stupid.

Despite the floods of data, information and knowledge crashing over us today, a greater and greater percentage of what we know is, in fact, less and less true. And this, as we'll see, would be the case even if we could believe the media, even if every advertiser were truthful, every lawyer honest, every politician sealed his lips, every adulterer confessed and every fast-talking telemarketer went straight.

If this is the case, how should individuals—or, for that matter, companies or countries—turn the deep fundamental of knowledge into wealth?

Some knowledge has always been needed to produce wealth. Hunter-gatherers had to know the migratory patterns of the animals they pursued. Peasants came to know a lot about soil. Normally, however, once learned the same knowledge remained useful generation after generation. Factory workers had to know how to operate their machines quickly and safely for as long as they had the job.

Today work-relevant knowledge changes so rapidly that more and more new knowledge has to be learned both on and off the job. Learning becomes a continuous-flow process. But we can't learn everything fast enough. And that helps explain why, if some of what we think is stupid, there's no need to be embarrassed. We are not alone in believing stupidities.

The reason is that every chunk of knowledge has a limited shelf life. At some point it becomes obsolete knowledge—what might more appropriately be called "obsoledge."

YESTERDAY'S TRUTHS

Does Plato's *Republic* or Aristotle's *Poetics* constitute "knowledge"? Or the ideas of Confucius or Kant? We can, of course, describe their ideas as wisdom. But the wisdom of these authors or philosophers was based on what they knew—their own knowledge base—and much of what they knew was, in fact, false.

Aristotle, whose views held sway across Europe for almost two thousand years, believed that eels were asexual and "originated in . . . the entrails of the earth." He also believed that the Indian Ocean was a landlocked sea—a geographical error that was still shared centuries later by Ptolemy and other European and Islamic scholars.

In the third century AD, Porphyry, the biographer of Pythagoras, assured his readers that if you took a part of a bean plant, put it into an earthenware pot, buried it for three months, then dug it up, you would surely find either the head of a child or female genitalia.

In the seventh century, Saint Isadore of Seville assured contemporaries that "bees are generated from decomposed veal." Half a millennium later no less a genius than Leonardo da Vinci declared that beavers knew their testicles were being used by humans for medicinal purposes. When trapped, he asserted, a beaver bites them off "and leaves them to its enemies."

When tomatoes, native to South America, first reached Europe in the sixteenth century, perfectly intelligent people knew that they were toxic to humans. It was two hundred years before Linnaeus declared otherwise. And as late as 1820 a particularly daring fellow attracted a large crowd when he risked eating two tomatoes to prove Linnaeus was right.

But obsoledge is not always amusing. As late as 1892 it was common knowledge—and scientifically accepted since the time of Galileo—that the planet Jupiter had four satellites. That knowledge became obsolete, however, on September 9 of that year, when astronomer E. E. Barnard of the Lick Observatory discovered a fifth moon. By 2003, astronomers had counted sixty.

Similarly, scientists for decades had assumed that there were only nine planets in our solar system. However, in 2005, a California Institute of Technology astronomer discovered an object he named Xena, which he and other scientists believe may be a tenth planet orbiting our sun.

Then there was London physiologist L. Erskine Hill, who reported in 1912 that experimental evidence showed that "purity of air is of no importance." How many more people around the world would have died of pollution-related causes if, over the last few decades, we hadn't learned otherwise? And how many patients will die today because somewhere an otherwise intelligent doctor is relying on outdated "facts" learned years ago in medical school? How many companies will go belly-up because of a marketing strategy based on yesterday's fad? How many investments are doomed because of out-of-date financial data? And what about tomorrow's deaths or disasters just waiting to happen?

Look, for example, at the minutes of the September 2002 meeting of the Advisory Committee of CERN users. (CERN is the European Organization for Nuclear Research.) Tucked away among references to decisions about providing ashtrays "close to the outside doors of major buildings for smokers" and notification of "changes in mail delivery service" is the following item: "The names of persons to be contacted in case of accident should be restored in the Human Resource database."

Why on earth, one might ask, should the list of persons to be contacted in case of a nuclear accident be missing? The answer: Because "for the majority of people the information became obsolete" and the administration "did not have the resources to ensure systematic updating." It took the chairman of the users' group to point out that "the potential human cost in case of a serious accident is immense, and a solution should be found."

EMILY'S ATTIC

What is clear is that wherever knowledge is stored, whether in digital databases or inside our brains, there is the equivalent of Aunt Emily's attic overstuffed with obsoledge—facts, ideas, theories, images and insights that have been outrun by change or replaced by later, presumably more accurate, truths. Obsoledge is a big part of the knowledge base of every person, business, institution and society.

By accelerating change, we also speed up the rate at which knowledge becomes obsoledge. Unless constantly and ruthlessly updated, experience on the job becomes less valuable. Databases are out of date by the time we finish building them. So, too, are books (including this one) by the time they are published. With every passing semi-second, the accuracy of our knowledge about our investments, our markets, our competition, our technology and our customers' needs diminishes. As a result, whether they are aware of it or not, companies, governments and individuals today base more of their daily decisions on obsoledge—on ideas and assumptions that have been falsified by change—than ever before.

Occasionally, of course, some antique bit of obsoledge comes back to life, as it were, and proves useful today because the context around it has changed and given it powerful new meaning. But more often the reverse is true.

Ironically, in advanced economies, companies brag about "knowledge management," "knowledge assets" and "intellectual property." Yet with all the numbers crunched by financial quants, economists, companies and governments, no one knows what obsoledge costs us in the form of degraded decision-making. What, one might ask, is the drag placed on individual investments, corporate profits, economic development, poverty-reduction programs and wealth creation in general?

Beneath all this, moreover, lies an even more important, hidden epistemological change. It affects not merely what we regard as knowledge but the tools we use to acquire it. Among these instruments of thought, few are remotely as important as analogy, in which we identify similarities in two or more phenomena and then draw conclusions from one to apply to the other.

Humans can barely think or talk without making analogies. The Irish golfer Padraig Harrington tells a sports reporter that "A U.S. Open is one that really tests your ability to hit. . . . you sort of want to be like a machine." Which takes us back to the followers of Newton who said the entire cosmos was "like" a machine.

Then there are all the people described as having "a mind like a computer," or who "sleep like a baby," or who are told to invest "like a pro" or think "like a genius." Implicit analogies are built into language itself. Thus we still rate cars in terms of their "horsepower"—a leftover from the day when they were seen as analogs of horse-drawn coaches and were known as "horseless carriages."

But the thought-tool we call analogy is growing harder to use. Analogies, always tricky, are growing trickier. For as the world changes, old similarities can turn into dissimilarities. Once-legitimate comparisons become strained. As parallels with the past break down, often unnoticed, conclusions based on them become misleading. And the faster the rate of change, the shorter the useful life span of analogies.

In this way, a change in one deep fundamental—time—affects a basic tool we use in the pursuit of another—knowledge.

In sum, then, as we've seen, even among experts on the knowledge economy, few have thought much about what might be called the law of obsoledge: As change accelerates, so does the speed at which still more obsoledge accumulates. All of us carry with us a far bigger burden of obsolete knowledge than our ancestors did in the slower-moving societies of yesterday.

And that is why so many of our most cherished ideas will set our descendants roaring with laughter.

CHAPTER 18

THE QUESNAY FACTOR

Today more than ever we are governed, all over the world, by the students of economics professors. Presidents and politicians, treasury secretaries or ministers of finance and chancellors of the exchequer, central bankers, investment bankers and senior officials of the world's biggest and most powerful corporations have all dutifully sat in their classrooms listening to them, poring over their texts and imbibing their key ideas.

The same goes for brokers, financial advisers and newspaper and television pundits who take these ideas to the public. Unfortunately, many ideas remembered from college days belong in the "obsoledge attic," or better yet, in the cemetery of dead ideas.

BLOOPER ECONOMICS

In February 2004 U.S. president George W. Bush stiff-armed his own Council of Economic Advisers, refusing to publicly back its forecast that the economy would provide 2.6 million new jobs that year. But, as *The Washington Post* reported,

> *That forecast, derided as wildly optimistic, was one of the more modest predictions the administration has made about the economy over the past three years.*
>
> *Two years ago, the administration forecast that there would be 3.4 million more jobs in 2003 than there were in 2000. And it predicted a budget deficit for fiscal 2004 of $14 billion. The economy ended up losing 1.7 million jobs over that period, and the budget deficit [for 2004] . . . is on course to be $521 billion.*

No doubt, some of this is political exaggeration. Any statistic can be tortured into submission. Nor are the torturers just Republicans. The discrepancies between forecasts and subsequent results began to widen under the previous Democratic administration. It was clear that, even allowing for political fact manipulation, something was seriously amiss.

In the words of a Republican White House press spokesman, "The old theories ... proved themselves wildly wrong. . . . Nobody saw this happening—not Wall Street, not Vegas, not Poor Richard, not Nostradamus."

Economists have failed to anticipate more than job numbers and deficits. They have contributed to some of the most publicized, embarrassing financial debacles in recent decades. The fact that two Nobel Prize–winning economists were partners in the Long-Term Capital Management hedge fund did little to prevent its near collapse in 1998. Only emergency action by the U.S. Federal Reserve averted a chain reaction that could have shaken the entire global economy.

Hardly more inspiring was the role economists played in the disintegration of the Russian economy after the fall of the Soviet Union. Or the reluctantly admitted mistakes made during the Asian financial crisis in the late 1990s by the macroeconomists of the International Monetary Fund—errors that helped trigger bloody ethnic clashes in Indonesia.

So frequently off-base are the predictions of economists that the *Financial Times* in 2001 suggested that, along with much-despised Wall Street analysts, they belong in "the hall of forecasting shame." Nor, according to the *Financial Times,* were they just having a bad year. "Nothing is new here. Macroeconomic forecasting rarely has a good year. And its record is particularly poor when accuracy is most desired."

So many disparate projections are issued by economists that they are often bundled together into a "consensus forecast" in hopes that the resulting average will prove more accurate than its individual guesses. Yet over the seventeen-year period ending in 2000, the Blue Chip Consensus Forecast on Economic Growth never once correctly estimated what economists call growth.

In January 2001 *The Wall Street Journal* reported growth predictions made by fifty-four prominent American economists for the next four quarters. Only two even came close.

Economists outside the United States perform no better. Their "record of failure to predict recessions is virtually unblemished," according to the International Monetary Fund. (Here the proverbial pot was calling the kettle black. Just six months before the Thai economy crashed and burned in 1997, the IMF itself had loudly hailed the soundness of its economy and financial system.) Critics of the IMF also charged that its experts had missed anticipating major changes like the "industrial growth slowdown in 1995" and the "hyperinflation in the late 1980s."

ESTIMATES OF ESTIMATES

It is, of course, unfairly easy to take potshots at economists. As long as chance plays a role in human affairs, no one can know the future with the kind of certainty decision-makers want. Economists themselves are right when they complain about the unrealistic expectations of the public, the politicians and the media, each with their demands for partisan interpretations or sound-bite simplifications of complex data.

Economists are plenty smart and hardworking. And they have legitimate reasons for many of their predictive failures. For example, much of the government and business data on which they are forced to rely is incomplete, misleading or flawed. On such issues as technological change, geopolitical upheaval, energy use and oil prices, the data are often preliminary, leaving analysts to grapple with estimates of estimates of estimates. But this is hardly new. Economists of the past had even less data and information to go on.

However, these shortcomings hardly explain the deeper reasons why so much of conventional economics seems irrelevant or misleading today.

First, the economy that economists are trying to understand is enormously more complex than that faced by the great economists of the past. Neither Adam Smith nor Karl Marx, David Ricardo nor Léon Walras, not even John Maynard Keynes or Joseph Schumpeter confronted anything like the density of confusing relationships, interactions and feedback links involved in today's wealth creation and distribution, let alone its global extent.

Second, and more important, is the unprecedented speed of transactions and transformations in the system under study. No sooner do economists map some aspect of the economy or come up with a relevant insight than it changes. Useful numbers and findings—and their interconnections—have the half-life of a firefly.

Third, there is an even bigger problem. Just as economists in the early years of the industrial revolution had to go beyond agrarian thinking and leave behind what was no longer applicable, economists today face a similar challenge. They have to reach beyond industrial thinking to understand the transformatory impact of the latest revolutionary wealth wave.

They confront a wealth system that, in a few decades, has gone from dependence on scarce resources to one in which the main growth factor, knowledge, is essentially inexhaustible; from rival to non-rival inputs and outputs; from predominantly local and national to predominantly national and global production and distribution; from low-skill to high-skill requirements;

from homogeneous mass production to demassified heterogeneous production. And the list goes on.

In addition, economists face changes in the degrees of integration needed in different parts of the economy. They need to factor in changing levels of complexity, rates of innovation and dozens of other variables, not to mention the multiple rhythms of economic activity and their interactions.

Many of the great advances in economic thinking during the last century came with the application of ever-more-sophisticated mathematics to the problems of the time. That meant measuring things. And here the accent was, appropriately enough, on things, in the sense of tangibles.

But to understand revolutionary wealth, which increasingly derives from, and produces, intangibles, we are compelled to cope with the slipperiest and hardest-to-measure of all resources—knowledge.

The leading economists of yesterday were hardly unaware of the importance of intangibles. But economies were never as knowledge-intensive as they are today.

PIECEMEAL PAPERS

To their credit, economists have made many notable breakthroughs in the last half century. They range from the introduction of game theory to a more sophisticated understanding of feedback between economic factors previously thought to be endogenous and exogenous. They include better models for pricing capital assets, options and corporate liabilities. Nobel Prizes have been awarded for the development of powerful new analytic tools.

But for decades, many met the idea of a knowledge-based economy with widespread skepticism. As late as 1987, Nobel Prize–winner Robert Solow's quip that "you can see the computer age everywhere except in the productivity statistics" brought widespread head-nodding in the profession.

Since then, economists have been trying to come to terms with the Third Wave. According to economist Jeffrey Eisenach, co-chairman of CapAnalysis, who once served with the White House Office of Management and Budget, "They certainly missed the Internet and its impact for a long time. . . . But they've got religion now."

He points to four fundamental changes in the last fifty years that have challenged economists and economic analysis—and still do.

The first is the growth of "network industries." These are industries in which, as he puts it, "my use of the product increases its value to you. The more people have phones, the more people I can theoretically reach with mine, which makes all the phones in the network more useful, and therefore valuable. Serious study of such 'network externalities' began in the early nineties."

The second, as we've already noted, is the non-rival, undepleteable character of knowledge products. We don't deplete the alphabet by using it. In the case of software, moreover, once the cost of creating it is met, it can be endlessly replicated at almost no cost. This isn't the way things work with tangible products, and its far-reaching implications are still not fully understood.

A third challenge comes with de-massification and the rapid growth in product customization—pointing toward an economy in which no two products are identical. In theory, each should be priced differently. Arriving at that turns out to be complicated and affects the nature of markets.

Next come the effects that arise from the global portability of capital, which, he says, "have fundamentally changed the way economies work."

Economists are thinking hard about these new problems, but, says Eisenach,

Many economists still underestimate the impact of innovation and dynamism in the knowledge economy—how fluid things are . . . how quickly innovation can change whole industries, reorder terms of trade, and rearrange comparative advantages.

Finally, perhaps, they are missing the potential productivity impact of bringing several billion people who are currently living at subsistence quickly into the world information economy.

THE MISSING FRAMEWORK

To deal with these increasingly complex and novel problems, economists have belatedly begun to call on psychologists, anthropologists and sociologists—whose work they once disdained as insufficiently "hard" or quantitative. Whole new branches of economics have opened up—for instance, behavioral economics, neuroeconomics—and various sub-subspecialties.

Economists are also working on many of the issues attending the rise of revolutionary wealth. For example, according to Eisenach, the cost-of-living index is now statistically corrected to take account of improved quality in successive versions of the same product. Economists have turned out a substantial literature on the costs of acquiring the information needed to make intelligent choices. And they are trying to cope with complex intellectual-property issues, asymmetric information and other aspects of revolutionary wealth.

Yet gaping holes still exist. For all the attention it receives, intellectual property remains inadequately understood, as does the non-rival and essentially inexhaustible character of knowledge. Other glaring questions cry out for answers. The last—and sometimes the first—word has not been written about the value of knowledge that proves valuable only when combined with other knowledge, or about the de-synchronization effect, or about what happens to trade patterns when wealth waves collide.

For all the effort of individual economists or teams, the profession as a whole has yet to fully appreciate the enormousness of today's runaway, revolutionary change. There is no systematic effort to map interdependent changes in our relationships to time, space and knowledge—let alone to the larger, full set of the deep fundamentals—all of which, as we've seen, are occurring at high speed.

Half a century since the revolution began, they have yet to formulate the coherent, overarching theories about this historical stage of economic development to help us understand who we are and where we are going.

THE MISTRESS'S DOCTOR

The failure of many economists to grasp the profundity of today's revolutionary change is ironic. It is not the first time brilliance walked arm in arm with myopia.

François Quesnay was a genius. He was also the official physician of Louis XV's famous mistress, Madame de Pompadour.

Son of a commoner, he didn't learn to read until he was eleven. But once he did, he never stopped. He quickly taught himself Latin and Greek. For a time he worked for an engraver, then enrolled in medical school, became a surgeon and a renowned expert on blood. Over the years, he rose to the pinnacle of French medicine and won his place in the palace of Louis XV.

Quesnay, however, had more than medicine or Madame de Pompadour on his inquisitive mind. In the cramped *entresol* over Madame's quarters, he made a deep study of agricultural economics. He was frequently visited there, we are told, by Turgot, who later became the controller general of finances under Louis XVI, and by other thinkers and doers of the time. He contributed articles to Diderot's great *Encyclopédie* on subjects such as farmers and grains. He wrote about taxes, interest rates and subjects as far afield as the Incas of Peru and despotism in China.

By 1758 Quesnay's ideas about economics had sufficiently crystallized for him to publish *Tableau Économique,* a remarkable precursor of the much more complex input-output tables for which Wassily Leontief won the Nobel Prize in 1973. In the *Tableau,* Quesnay compared the economy to the circulation of blood in the body.

This analogy turned out to have powerful political implications—both in his time and in ours. For if the economy is, in fact, naturelike and homeostatic, he believed, it would naturally seek equilibrium.

And if that were the case, Quesnay argued, the French government's mercantilist policies and its endless regulations of trade and manufacture interfered with the natural balance of the economy. Soon a group calling themselves the Physiocrats sprang up around Quesnay and began to extend and promote these ideas. Quesnay himself came to be regarded as one of the greatest *penseurs* in the West—a thinker some even compared to Socrates and Confucius.

Yet Quesnay made one fateful mistake. He insisted that the sole source of all wealth was agriculture. For him and the Physiocrats, only the rural economy mattered. Indeed, he wrote, there were only three classes of people: peasants, landowners and everybody else. The first two were productive, the very womb of wealth. Everyone else, for Quesnay, was a member of the "sterile class."

Brilliant as Quesnay might have been, he simply could not imagine an industrial society in which most wealth, in fact, would soon be coming from smoke-belching factories in cities, and from the hands and minds of precisely the "sterile class." He missed the big picture.

Today, too, we find many economists suffering from Quesnay's myopia, making brilliant contributions to components of a problem without examining the far larger picture into which they fit—including the social, cultural and political effects that come with revolutionary wealth. The time has come, in short, to inoculate ourselves against the Quesnay factor.

And we won't be able to do that until we can separate true from false.

CHAPTER 19

FILTERING TRUTH

I f, as we saw, Leonardo da Vinci had outlandish ideas about beaver testicles, what should we make of some of the seemingly kooky beliefs floating through the culture today? One trip to the Internet is enough to deluge anyone with conspiracy theories, alien-abduction stories and evidence that Elvis lives.

We're told that Kentucky Fried Chicken is genetically breeding six-legged hens; that if you don't turn your cell phone off at the gas station, it could spark an explosion; that the missing flier Amelia Earhart was a spy; that eelskin wallets erase magnetic credit cards; that waterproof sunscreen can cause blindness in children; that some children born today have received mysterious messages from this generation's sperm and ova warning them of environmental disasters to come. Want more? Just go online and search for "weird theories."

Knowledge may be one of the deep fundamentals of revolutionary wealth, but even if we set aside "obsoledge"—obsolete knowledge—how much of what we know about money, business and wealth—or anything else—is total nonsense? Or pure fiction? How much can we trust what we're being told? How do we decide? And even more important, who decides how we decide?

TRUTH ON TRIAL

Lies and errors abound in job applications, tax returns, contractors' estimates, performance reviews, press releases, studies and statistics and surely in profit statements. Indeed, hyping profits led to the spectacular spate of business scandals that marked the turn of the millennium.

At one level, CEOs, CFOs, accountants, stock analysts and others grew Pinocchio noses on the front pages of the world's press. Hiding from television cameras, a few were marched off to prison in handcuffs for lying about profits, for dumping their own shares of stock while publicly urging others to buy them and for other high crimes and misdemeanors. Authorities accused them of causing investors to lose confidence in stock markets and of shaking global financial markets. Truth, it appeared, was in short supply.

SIX FILTERS

Decisions, sometimes affecting the life or death of a business or even a person, are often based on obsolete, misleading, inaccurate or flat-out false knowledge. Today the computer, the Internet, the new hypermedia environment, special effects and other new tools make online fraud and fabrication easier, while the sheer mass of innocent, but just plain unverified and untrue, knowledge on the Web skyrockets.

In consequence, questions that were once the province of philosophers, theologians and epistemologists will increasingly confront decision-makers in every field. Every estimate of risk, every consumer decision to buy or not to buy, every investor's decision to invest or wait and every executive decision—to outsource or insource, quit or stay, hire or lay off, partner or go it alone—is ultimately based on torrents of data, information and knowledge. How, in the face of all that, can we know what is—or is not—true?

There are at least six rival criteria by which most of us decide whether something is true. While different people and cultures may have used other tests of truth at one time or another, these six filters or screens are surely among the most prevalent.

Ironically, market researchers, political pollsters, advertising agencies, survey firms and others go to great and expensive length to ask people what they believe. Rarely do they ask the more revealing question: *Why* do they believe it? The answer largely depends on which of these six criteria is used for validation.

CONSENSUS

A lot of what we call truth is assumed to be correct because of *consensus*. It is conventional wisdom. Everyone "knows" X to be true, therefore, it must be true. We absorb consensus truth from family, friends, co-workers and the surrounding culture, usually without thinking twice. It forms the *zeitgeist* of the lemmings.

Going along with the crowd requires no thought. Even better, lemming truth is safely uncontroversial. If it turns out to be wrong, you don't look foolish. After all, everyone else believed it, too—even smart people.

We saw lemming behavior in the herd of investors who stampeded into the early dot-coms—and then out again. We see it in the otherwise intelligent business executives who rush to adopt, then jettison, the latest managerial fad. New ideas whip through the ranks of senior management, are taken on, implemented, imposed on people and quickly discarded. They frequently have direct, destructive impacts on the economy, leading, for example, to ill-considered mass layoffs, imitative mergers and the like. Whole industries even now are being restructured or bent out of shape as a result of management reliance on "lemming truth."

Nor are disasters based on lemming truth limited to business and the economy. In 2004, the U.S. Senate Intelligence Committee accused American spy agencies of "groupthink" in concluding that Iraq had, or was about to acquire, weapons of mass destruction. In response to critics, the agencies noted that the friendly intelligence organizations of other nations had confirmed the information on which they based their conclusion. Consensus was doing its persuasive work.

Only much later did the public learn that Iraqi defectors, eager for the United States to overthrow Saddam's regime, had spread the same false information to the spy agencies of France, Germany, England, Spain, Denmark, Italy and Sweden, thus "gaming the system" and helping create the fake consensus on which the U.S. agencies relied. Here lemming truth helped start a war.

CONSISTENCY

This criterion is based on the assumption that if a fact fits with other facts regarded as true, it too must be true. Detectives, lawyers and courts lean heavily on *consistency* as the primary test of a witness's truthfulness. In the world-famous trial of Michael Jackson for child-molestation, millions of TV viewers around the globe were mesmerized for months as each side, prosecution and defense, highlighted discrepancies in the evidence presented by the other. Every bit of evidence was fine-tooth-combed for internal contradictions as though noncontradiction proved truthfulness.

In business, too, consistency wins points, even though it is quite possible to be consistently false. When a SWAT team of auditors descends on a firm to perform what is known as "due diligence" in preparation for a merger or acquisition, the first thing it looks for are inconsistencies. Do accounts receivable, reported in the "control ledger," line up precisely with what the underlying subledgers show? Inconsistencies all raise suspicion that the truth is being massaged. Since the accounting scandals at Enron, WorldCom, Adelphia,

Tyco and a host of other high-flying firms, the consistency criterion has been applied with greater consistency.

AUTHORITY

In our daily lives, a great deal of accepted "truth" is based on *authority*—secular as well as divine. For years in the United States, if the famed investor Warren Buffett murmured so much as a syllable about where Wall Street was heading, it had to be true. For others, if the Bible or the Koran says so, it must assuredly be true. Authority is the test.

Authority may be embodied in a Muslim imam or ayatollah. In the words of the Iraqi Shi'a leader, the Grand Ayatollah Ali al-Sistani, "You do what the [leader's] expert opinion says you should do, and refrain from what his expert opinion says you should refrain from, without any research on your part."

Alternatively, authority can be located in the Vatican where, in 1870, the pope was declared "infallible." Such religious worthies are presumed by their followers to have a profound understanding of the Koran or the Bible, both of which, in turn, are held to contain the views of an ultimate authority.

For some, if leading news sources such as *The New York Times, Le Monde* or CBS News report it, it must be true. Of course, that was before CBS admitted it had broadcast a story about President Bush's National Guard service that was based on forged documents. Before *The Times* publicly revealed that it had printed scores of stories by an up-and-coming staffer who had conned his editors into using lies, fiction and plagiarized material. And before France made a smash best seller out of a book charging that the top editors of *Le Monde* planted stories that served their own private self-interests.

Authority is also (often absurdly) attributed to media celebrities. Actor Richard Gere is taken for an authority on Tibet, singer Barbra Streisand on foreign policy and Charlton Heston on the Bible—after all, he once acted the role of Moses in a movie. Few, however, have been worshipped as blindly by executives as leading CEOs. For years the American businessperson's authority-in-chief was the now retired Jack Welch of General Electric.

Today so much knowledge is needed for good decision-making that the smartest people know what they do not know. Authority is, therefore, frequently shared or passed around. At a corporate board meeting, directors may follow the lead of one member on financial issues, turn to another on questions of executive compensation and to still another on matters of technology.

We seldom in any coherent way test the actual capability of an authority, relying instead on the image of authority conferred by a title, a diploma or an

accreditation agency of some type. In which case we bow to the authority con-
ferring the certification. It becomes the authority on authority.

REVELATION

For some, truth is based on what is presumed to be mystical *revelation.* It can't
be questioned, it just is. Take it from me. (Of course, if you do "take it from
me," and believe it because I say so, I become the trusted authority, and the
criteria you are relying on is that of authority.)

DURABILITY

Here the test of truth is based on age and *durability.* Has the "truth" stood "the
test of time"? Is it "tried and true," or is it new, hence questionable? Here the
authority is not a god, a book or a person but that immense slice of time called
the past.

Maybe chicken soup is good for curing colds, but does the fact that it has
been passed down through a long line of grandmas necessarily make it so?

For most of us today it is hard to appreciate just how important inherited
truth was before the Enlightenment and the industrial revolution. Historian
Alan Kors of the University of Pennsylvania says that "the overturning of the
presumptive authority of the past was one of the most profound developments
in the entire history of the West."

SCIENCE

Science is different from all the other truth-test criteria. It is the only one that
itself depends on rigorous testing.

Yet of all these various criteria, science is probably the one we least rely on
in our daily lives. We don't, as a rule, choose a puppy because he passes some
scientific test; we just fall in love with him. We don't perform lab tests to
decide what movie to watch. Or what friends to make. Among all our daily
personal—and business—decisions, those that are made scientifically are no
more than a trace element. Yet among the six truth criteria, none in recent centuries has had a greater impact on wealth. And none, as we'll see, is more
endangered.

Science is not a collection of facts. It is a process—often messy and non-
sequential—for testing ideas. The ideas must be testable, at least in principle,
and, some would add, falsifiable. The tests involve observation and experiment. Results must be reproducible. Knowledge that hasn't met these tests is
not scientific.

Even the most persuasive scientific findings are, therefore, held to be incomplete and tentative—always subject to further investigation, revision and dismissal in the light of new scientifically tested discoveries.

This makes science the only one of the six truth filters that is inherently opposed to fanaticism of any kind, religious, political, nationalist, racist or otherwise. It is fanatic certainty that breeds persecution, terrorism, inquisitions, suicide bombings and other atrocities. And it is fanatic certainty that science replaces with a recognition that even the most entrenched scientific findings are at best partial or temporary truths and hence uncertain.

This idea—that every scientific finding could and should be improved or thrown out—puts science in a class by itself. Thus among all the other main truth filters, whether consensus, consistency, authority, revelation or durability, only science is self-correcting.

While the other five criteria have been in use since the beginnings of time and reflect the static or change-resistant character of agrarian societies, science swung the door wide open to change.

Joseph Needham, the great historian of Chinese science and a biologist by background, has shown how technologically advanced the Chinese were compared with Europeans, until a certain turning point—at which time science in the West leaped ahead and left China behind. What accounted for the West's *grand jeté* toward the future was not this or that scientific discovery but something infinitely far more powerful. As Needham put it, "During the Renaissance in the West, in the time of Galileo . . . the most effective method of discovery was itself discovered."

Elements of "scientific method" can be traced as far back as early Islam, the Renaissance and to Francis Bacon in the sixteenth and early seventeenth centuries. But not until much later did it exist as a clear, broadly agreed upon method for determining the truth of any assertion or hypothesis.

Canadian historian Ian Johnston of Malaspina University-College explains: "The pursuit of scientific inquiries was by no means always a well-coordinated, disciplined activity, with a clear and shared sense of method. . . . Science was still sorting out what the activity really involved, and there were many competing methods, theories and systems in almost all areas" right on down through the eighteenth and even early-nineteenth centuries.

Only gradually, then, did the elements of empirical observation, experiment, quantification, dissemination of results, replication or disconfirmation, come together, along with randomized blind controls and other techniques so widely used today.

The invention of scientific method was the gift to humanity of a new truth filter or test, a powerful meta-tool for probing the unknown and—it turned out—for spurring technological change and economic progress.

As we've noted, among all the decisions made in the economy on any given day, only a minute amount can be said to have been made scientifically. Yet that tiniest trace has transformed the world's capacity to make and expand wealth. It will continue to do so in the future—if we let it.

TRUTH SHIFTS

In reality, of course, we all rely on more than one form of truth validation. We may turn to science for medical help, to revelatory religion for moral advice, and to face-to-face or remote validating authorities on other issues. We shift among these criteria or use combinations of them.

Many companies, political parties, religious movements, governments and other groups attempt to manipulate us by stressing one or another of the truth filters. Watch, for example, how TV commercials use real doctors to peddle pharmaceuticals, implying that the message is true because it is based on science. Other ads feature celebrities—Bob Dole for Viagra or Lance Armstrong for Bristol-Myers Squibb—as though they are relevant authorities. Dell Computer's message is delivered by a casually dressed young man roughly the same age as the consumers Dell wishes to reach—suggesting to viewers that, by buying from Dell, they would be joining the consensus of that age group.

Products like Quaker oats or Aunt Jemima pancake mix—and the vast number whose name begins with "Old-Fashioned"—imply that being old makes the product good, just as Grandma believed. In these ways, the different truth criteria are themselves exploited commercially. The next step will come when marketing experts segment, then target consumers according to the specific truth filter most persuasive to each.

But it isn't just individuals who make up their minds about what is or isn't true. Whole cultures and societies have what might be called a "truth profile"—a characteristic preference for one or several truth criteria.

One society may be dominated by a reliance on authority and religious revelation—Iran, say, after the theocratic revolution of 1979. Another may emphasize science and its proxy, technology—Japan, from 1960 on.

A society's truth profile profoundly affects the amount and type of wealth it will produce. It will influence how much money it allocates to building mosques and churches as opposed to research and development or how much it basks in post-imperial nostalgia (as France and England have done). It affects the extent of its litigiousness, the nature of its justice system, the weight of tradition, its levels of resistance to change.

Ultimately, its choice of truth filters speeds up or slows down the rate of what the late Czech economist Eugen Loebl called "gain"—the pace at which human beings accumulate the additional knowledge needed to keep raising their living standards.

The shape of tomorrow's economies will be heavily based on which truth filters we use to validate knowledge. Once again, we are changing our relations to a deep fundamental of wealth without anticipating the consequences—and putting at risk one of the key sources of economic progress.

The future of science is at stake.

CHAPTER 20

TRASHING THE LAB

Of everything found in the entire human knowledge base, including both current knowledge and obsoledge, nothing in recent centuries has increased the life span, nutrition, health and wealth of our species more than that trace element we call science. Yet among the many signs that we are changing the deep fundamentals of wealth is today's mounting guerrilla war against science.

This war is an attempt not just to challenge scientific facts but to devalue science itself. Its goal is to change how science is conducted and to dictate what scientists may or may not investigate. At the deepest level, it aims to force a worldwide truth-shift—to reduce reliance on science as a way of validating truth. If successful, it could sidetrack the future of the knowledge economy and the chances for reducing global misery and poverty, darkening the century to come.

On the surface, it would appear that, on a global basis, science is flourishing. Worldwide, the number of scientists and engineers is growing, as are R&D expenditures—$284 billion in 2003 in the United States alone.

A significant amount of that R&D funding has gone to foreign researchers and immigrants who have flooded into the U.S. science community from all parts of the world. The United States has also been the training ground for legions of scientists now working around the globe, from China and India to the Middle East and Mexico.

In the business sector, IBM alone spent $5 billion on R&D in 2004. Its researchers, headed by Paul Horn, patented a total of 3,248 innovations—about one every 2.6 hours, 24 hours a day, times 365 days. It received 68 percent more U.S. patents that year than the number-two company, Matsushita.

These innovations not only improved IBM's physical products but, more important, represent salable intellectual property of the kind that brought in $1.2 billion in licensing profit that year—roughly 15 percent of the firm's

2004 net income. IBM's main products are no longer just physical—they are services and knowledge.

The precise pathways by which science translates into generalized economic growth are extremely complex and a matter of lively debate. But in the words of Gary Bachula, former U.S. undersecretary of commerce, "Leading economists now identify technical progress as a major, if not the single most important, factor in sustained economic growth, accounting for as much as one half U.S. economic growth in the past 50 years."

In recent years, according to a National Science Foundation report, "other nations are increasing their R&D investments, focusing on areas such as physical sciences and engineering, which receive comparably less funding in the United States."

It is, of course, a cliché to say that scientific knowledge is a two-edged sword because some of its findings are exploited in destructive ways. The same is true, however, for religion and non-scientific knowledge—neither of which has unleashed a comparable flood of discoveries that have contributed to global health, nutrition, safety and other social benefits.

RAZOR BLADES AND RIGHTS

In light of these contributions, one might imagine that scientists, not just in the United States but around the world, would be held in high regard, as they once were.

Instead, when medical researchers at U.S. universities opened their mail a few years ago they found bare razor blades taped inside the envelope flaps—a warning from extremists in the animal rights movement to stop animal experimentation—or else. The "else" implied car bombs, arson and other forms of intimidation or violence. More recently, aging pop singer Stephen Patrick Morrissey made headlines in 2006 when he said he endorsed the actions of the Animal Rights Militia because laboratory scientists themselves deal in violence "and it's the only language they understand."

Animal-rights fanatics are merely one branch of a broad anti-science coalition whose members are recruited from the farthest fringes of feminism, environmentalism, Marxism and other supposedly progressive activist groups. Backed by sympathizers in academia, in politics and among media celebrities, they indict science and scientists for a lengthy list of what some of them regard as hypocrisy at best, cruelty and criminality at worst.

They claim, for example, that pharmaceutical scientists sell their objectivity to the highest corporate bidder. (Some, no doubt, do, but lack of principle is hardly limited to a single profession.)

Zooming in from another direction, neofeminists charge (all too accurately) that, in many countries, girls suffer from gender discrimination in education and women scientists face sexist barriers in hiring and promotion. This is certainly a worthy fight—such practices are stupid and unfair and deprive us all of half the human race's brainpower. But again, gender discrimination is not inherent in science, as such, and unfortunately it prevails in countless other professions as well.

Science, meanwhile, is simultaneously besieged by radical environmentalists. Scientists, we're told, threaten to destroy entire populations with genetically modified foods.

There is clearly cause, as we were among the very first to suggest more than thirty years ago, to be cautious in the application of genetic engineering. But panic-stricken, irrational opposition is hardly warranted.

Eco-extremists in Europe fed the media sensational stories about "Franken-foods" and joined forces with protectionist European governments seeking to block American agricultural imports. In turn, despite a crisis threatening mass starvation in Zimbabwe, some European nations pressured its government, under threat of trade sanctions, to reject food aid sent by the United States on grounds that it had been genetically modified.

This in the face of opposition by James Morris, executive director of the U.N. World Food Program, who told African governments that "the genetically modified maize in question has been consumed literally billions of times with no ill effect. So if the concern is food safety, there is no scientific evidence to support that."

The raging campaign in Europe against genetically modified organisms (GMOs) severely damaged the Monsanto Corporation, a leader in the creation of genetically modified seeds. In Lodi, Italy, activists set fire to maize and soybean seeds in a Monsanto warehouse and painted "Monsanto Killers" and "No GMOs" on its walls.

Campaigns like these have other companies, too, worrying about the dry-up of markets for science-linked products, over rigorous or ill-thought-through regulation, a switch of investment to other sectors and a decline in smart young people entering the field.

Hostility to science slides truly strange partners under the same rumpled bedclothes, from left-wing social activists to Britain's Prince Charles, who, in a BBC Reith Lecture on "Respect for the Earth," attacked what he termed "impenetrable layers of scientific rationalism." He had on an earlier occasion referred to science as trying to impose "a tyranny over our understanding." In doing so, he echoed those environmentalists, New Agers and others who seek a return to the supposedly "sacral."

Which takes us to yet another source of anti-science agitation—this from the hard-line, never-tiring religious creationists whose ferocious hostility to

Darwin leads to campaigns against science textbooks, litigation over educational curricula and standards, and attacks on secularism in general, which they associate with science.

To all these anti-science combatants, we must add the occasional freelance warrior, sane or otherwise, ready to commit murder for the cause.

The Unabomber, Ted Kaczynski, killed three and wounded twenty-three in a bombing spree in the 1990s. He blackmailed major newspapers into publishing his lengthy anti-science and anti-technology diatribe by threatening more killings if they did not. The popular reaction was outrage. But some academics leaped to praise the manifesto, and the Internet came alive with fan sites such as Chuck's Unabomb page and alt.fan.unabomber.

Overall, then, we find a loose, diverse anti-science guerrilla movement that merges, at its outer reaches, with legions of believers in the paranormal and in little green men from outer space, not to mention practitioners of various forms of "alternative" medical quackery and Falun Gong levitators.

The voices of this movement are amplified by Hollywood's persistent presentation of the scientist as villain and by television's endless exploitation of shows such as *Crossing Over* (offering to help you communicate with your dead) or *Pet Psychic* (offering to help you communicate with your iguana).

So shrill has the anti-science chorus become in the United Kingdom that when a leading British reproductive biologist, Richard Gosden, left for a post in Canada, the British Royal Society feared that his going might unleash a flood of departures. Meanwhile, in France, the Sorbonne, after much protest, awarded a Ph.D. in astrology to a former Miss France who was the astrologer for a weekly TV magazine. Ironically, her defense of her dissertation took place before a crowd of glitterati in—where else?—the Université René Descartes in Paris.

FLIP-FLOP POLITICS

In the past in Europe and the United States hostility to science typically came from right-wing, sometimes protofascist and Nazi, sources. (Even now many American scientists complain of a "Republican war on science"—charging that the party and particularly the George W. Bush White House have been guilty of politically manipulating or distorting scientific findings about issues as diverse as global warming, birth control, acid rain and stem-cell research.) The left, by contrast, typically supported science. Marxism, indeed, claimed for itself the mantle of "scientific" socialism.

Today, in a startling reversal, the anti-science banner is flapped most frenetically by elements of the left. It is chiefly found in departments of literature, social science, women's studies and the humanities in American and European universities. Indeed, while the left in America hotly opposes the religious right on such emotionally charged social issues as abortion or public subvention of religious schools, the same left links arms with the right in today's guerrilla war on science.

None of this is to suggest that scientists are above reproach, that fraud never happens in a laboratory, that irresponsible, even dangerous experiments never occur, or that the benefits of science are shared equally by rich and poor. Moreover, the rapid global expansion of scientific research has outpaced the ability of governments, universities and the profession itself to monitor fraudulent projects—another example of de-synchronization.

Correcting these faults is surely necessary. But the anti-science war has far wider goals.

It arrives at a moment when scientific breakthroughs are coming faster and faster in field after field. With the decoding of the human genome alone, the world's knowledge base is dramatically expanded and the rate of likely "gain" or accumulation of knowledge is hastened. But, as biogeographer Philip Stott of the University of London puts it, "we are standing on a great peak and a new country lies at our feet. But not everyone wants to explore it." Instead, he writes, "they are desperate to cabin, crib and confine the new science."

PATRIARCHY AND PALMISTRY

Most critics of science do not shoot to kill: They do not challenge the method that is its essence. Instead, they complain that only 3 percent of drug research, for example, is directed at diseases among the world's poor. Or that too much funding goes toward diseases of men, rather than women. Or that animals are mistreated in research for non-life-and-death products such as cosmetics. Or that too much science is directed to weaponry—all charges that have the ring of uncomfortable truth. Changing these conditions would not injure science and might well improve it.

Critics also correctly complain that, despite its image, science is not and cannot be entirely value-free. Some feminists insist that it is by its very nature androcentric and masculinist. Other critics contend that it is too positivist and quantitative or short on intuition. Some debate whether there couldn't be an alternative, feminist science not based on scientific method.

Another challenge comes from religion, New Age pop spiritualism and other peddlers of the occult. A stroll through any commercial district will likely lead past a retail shop offering New Age books, incense and gewgaws. Anyone interested in opening such a shop can go online and instantly locate twelve hundred wholesalers hawking four thousand New Age and witchcraft-related products. A single online promoter offers more than nine hundred posters in "40 New Age categories: Astrology, Chakras, Goddess, Witchcraft, Palmistry, Tarot, Ancient Places, Shamanism, Angels, Yoga, Whales, Dolphins, Gypsies, Egyptian, Zen and much more."

The culture is so awash in the paranormal, occult and irrational that *New York* magazine devotes a cover to "Psychic New York" and "The City's Supernatural Superstars." It pictures an open human palm surrounded by the words "clairvoyants . . . mediums . . . telepaths . . . mystics . . . shamans."

The New Age realm encompasses a bewildering variety of practices and beliefs, but the movement, generally speaking, shares a schizophrenic attitude toward both science and religion.

As defined by Wouter Hanegraaff in his magisterial work *New Age Religion and Western Culture,* the New Age is a belief system that "rejects neither religion and spirituality nor science and rationality," claiming to combine them in a "higher synthesis." Yet with its continual invocation of "higher level beings," and reality as an immaterial projection of our beliefs, and its jumble of paganism, channeling, past-life experiences and promises of unadulterated bliss, it asks us to believe claims that are scientifically untestable and unfalsifiable.

LAS VEGAS AS ROLE MODEL

Yet another attack on science as a truth filter comes from residual postmodernism, the murky French philosophy that decades ago began infiltrating university departments of literature and social science—and even business schools—worldwide. Businesses have been told to adopt "postmodern management." They are offered data communications systems for "Post-Modern SMEs [small business enterprises]." Students can study "postmodern business ethics" at Brunel University in London or Simon Fraser University in Canada and are urged to go to Las Vegas to see a postmodern "business role model."

Postmodernism, or POMO, would not be very important today—much of it is being supplanted by other obscurantisms—but for its attack on truth itself. In their offensive against science as a test of truth, POMOs tell us that scientific truths are not universal. And that makes sense. Many scientists might even agree. Since we do not know the limits of the universe(s) we inhabit, and maybe cannot do so, we cannot logically prove the universality of anything.

They—along with feminist critics and others—also have a point when they say scientific truths are not entirely neutral. After all, money often determines what research is done, and values help determine the very questions that scientists choose to study, the hypotheses they frame and even the language they use to convey results.

But this is where their arguments go from half-right to half-cocked. We are told that all truths are relative, so that no one's explanation of anything is better than anyone else's. The real question, however, is "Better for what?" If we want to fly to Munich or Maui, do we want a competent, knowledgeable pilot at the controls—or the world's best flower arranger?

It is when the POMOs tell us that all truths, scientific or not, are subjective and only exist inside people's heads, that they go fully around the bend and lapse into sophomoric solipsism. By their own theory, their own assertions are inherently unverifiable. Even if they were true, we would still need to lead our lives as though they were not. Try paying a credit-card bill with money that exists only in your mind.

At its heart, POMO theory not only attempts to discredit science; taken to its extreme, it actually undermines all the truth criteria because it calls into question the very concept of truth. And it is here that postmodernists merge with snake-oil salesmen, cult leaders, hoaxers and others who stretch our gullibility to the max, and who, when asked "Why should I believe you?" have no better answer than "Because."

THE ECO-MISSIONARIES

Science, as we've already seen, is simultaneously under attack by elements of the environmental movement—a movement that itself is increasingly taking on a religious character.

Professor Robert N. Nelson of the University of Maryland writes: "As the end of the 20th Century approached, a religious vacuum in Western society existed. . . . In this circumstance, the contemporary environmental movement emerged as one way to fill the vacuum. . . . For many of its followers today, environmentalism has been a substitute for fading mainline Christian and progressive faiths."

While environmentalists do, of course, rely on scientific data, environmentalism, Nelson points out, is "possessed of a strong missionary spirit." Moreover, its very language is "overtly religious: 'saving' the earth from rape and pillage; building 'cathedrals' in the wilderness; creating a new 'Noah's Ark' with laws such as the Endangered Species Act; pursuing a new 'calling' to preserve the remaining wild areas; and taking steps to protect what is left of 'The Creation' on earth."

At the "heart of the environmental message," he points out, "is a new story of the fall of mankind from a previous, happier, and more natural and innocent time—a secular vision of the biblical fall from the Garden of Eden."

In short, says Nelson, "despite its modern appearance, environmentalism is closer to an old-fashioned form of religious fundamentalism."

SECRET SCIENCE

If these were the only threats to science—a key pillar of the knowledge economy—concern would be justified. But a new, far more threatening attack is brewing that could give powerful ammunition to every science-hater in society. Again, this attack is aimed not at the scientific method as such but on two elements of the ethic associated with it—the ideas that knowledge produced by science should be freely circulated and that scientists should be free to explore everything.

The free circulation of scientific findings is under withering fire from both business and government. More and more scientific research is either funded or conducted by corporations that, for high-stakes commercial reasons, are racing to patent their findings or cloak them in secrecy. Simultaneously, governments, reacting to the genuine threat of terrorism, are demanding that more and more scientific findings be kept secret for security reasons.

The age of the "Super-Empowered Individual"—the terrorist, criminal or psychotic armed with weapons of mass destruction—is fast approaching. While it is clear that the media and the Internet cannot continue to offer instruction manuals for bomb building and the manipulation of toxic materials, disquieting debates are under way about how much of science needs to be withheld from public view.

On the one hand, in the light of terrorism, registration of laboratories and surveillance of research activity may now be necessary, according to Nobel Prize–winner David Baltimore, head of the California Institute of Technology. But on the other, he says, "the most dangerous thing is secrecy," noting that biological weaponry itself was developed behind walls of secrecy.

Baltimore heads a roundtable at the U.S. National Academy of Science that is devoted to the topic of freedom of scientific communication. "Making the distinction about which knowledge is dangerous and ought to be censored is very hard." For example, he says, "the distinction between offensive and defensive uses of biological agents is really a matter of how information is utilized rather than the information itself. You have to know how to defend against bioterrorism, but in knowing that you also know how to inflict bioterrorism."

Preventing disclosure of new findings is one thing. But even more disturbing are proposals to make whole broad categories of knowledge off-limits to research. Some are even coming from scientists themselves, who conjure up apocalyptic scenarios to support their theses.

Bill Joy, chief scientist at Sun Microsystems, raised a furor when he called for science to "relinquish" research that might lead, as he saw it, to the domination of the human species by the runaway "destructive self-replication" of technologies now made possible by advances in genetics, robotics and nano-technology. By 2030, he forecast, computers might be smarter than humans—smart enough to reproduce themselves and essentially take over.

Even more frightening scenarios come from Martin Rees, England's Astronomer Royal. In his book *Our Final Hour,* Rees describes various doomsday experiments actually under discussion among physicists that, he believes, could—if something went wrong—wipe out not only the human race but Earth and the cosmos as well. Other scientists regard this claim as nonsensical.

Arguing that we do not know enough even to assess the levels of risk, Rees proposes various steps that should precede the undertaking of dangerous experiments in any field, not just physics. He cites a sensible suggestion by physicist Francesco Calogero that would pit two teams of scientists against each other—a "red team" to offer reasons why such an experiment would not be safe and a "blue team" that would make the case for going forward. Rees calls for involving representatives of the public in authorizing such experiments.

Yet, as Rees himself points out, the attempt to avoid risk carries risks of its own—thus "the most extreme precautionary policy . . . would utterly paralyze science." And with it, one might add, the knowledge economy of the future.

Self-criticism is at the very heart of science. And science and scientists should never be above criticism from the public. Science is itself a social activity, dependent, to a degree many scientists underestimate, on the ideas, epistemologies and built-in assumptions of the surrounding culture. Nor should scientists alone police science, since, like everyone else, they have their own self-interests.

What we are seeing, however, is not just a series of unrelated, disparate attacks on science but a convergent conviction that science needs to be reduced in influence, stripped of the respect it has earned—in short, devalued as a key test of truth.

But the battle over truth is not confined to science. Different groups in society are, for different reasons, actively trying to manage our minds by shifting the truth filters through which we, in our turn, see the world—the tests we use to separate true from false.

This battle has no name. But it will have a profound effect on the revolutionary wealth system now superseding that of the industrial age.

CHAPTER 21

THE TRUTH MANAGERS

I n the movie *The Manchurian Candidate,* an American soldier is captured by the enemy and subjected to mind-control procedures that turn
him into an assassin. The same theme—the brainwashing of the individual—forms the basis for the study of everything from consumer behavior and
cults to suicide bombers.

In brainwashing, it is far more effective to change *why* a person thinks the
way he does than *what* he thinks. This means altering the filters he uses to
determine truth. This applies not just to individual brainwashing, but to social
and cultural brainwashing, as well.

A large body of research examines the way advertisers and the media
attempt to manipulate us all. A sizable literature also exists describing the way
dominant elites manipulated colonial populations psychologically and culturally to ensure their political passivity. What has been less noticed and studied,
however, are the ways in which entire economies and cultures are affected by
changes in their definitions of truth.

One reason for this omission is that these changes occur over long
stretches of time and often beneath awareness at the individual level. What we
can say, however, is that each revolutionary wave was accompanied by significant changes in the filters people relied on to determine truth or falsity—and
that these influenced the amount and types of wealth produced.

During the Enlightenment and the early days of the industrial revolution,
people in the West stopped believing in the divine right of kings and pro-
ceeded to topple their monarchs. The subsequent rise of democracy, with its
reliance on voting and majority rule, made large-scale consensus a more
important truth-filter than ever before, and not just in politics. Later the introduction of mass education, sending uniform messages to the young, further
favored consensus as a test of truth.

As living standards gradually improved and wealth spread, industrialization led to useful new products, from clocks and sewing machines to automobiles, and people came to value the new, not just the durable old. Beliefs were no longer necessarily true because they were ancient. They could, therefore, be challenged.

The most important of these changes was the relative devaluation of religious authority that followed the rise of science. People didn't easily or completely cast off their reliance on religious authority, but they increasingly turned elsewhere for answers when new problems arose. The priest or minister was no longer the only, or best, source of knowledge.

Changes like these didn't happen without conflict.

It was a battle that science gradually won, not by eradicating religious authority but by overthrowing its claims to be the sole basis of universal, ultimate truth. This shift—narrowing the range of religious authority and widening that of science—contributed to the rise and predominance of secularism wherever the Second Wave brought an industrial economy, society and culture.

PERSUADING THE BOSS

Today once again a subtle battle over truth is taking place. As we move farther into the twenty-first century, and more societies develop economies based on ideas, culture and wealth-relevant knowledge, *why* we believe what we believe becomes more critical than ever.

Every culture, at every moment, has a truth profile—the weights people assign to the different truth filters. As these weights shift, they influence decision-making at every level from the most personal to the political and corporate. Try talking a consensus-oriented CEO out of pursuing synergy when he or she sees competitors chasing the same greyhound around the track. Or try selling a new idea, no matter how good, to a boss impressed by authority if you lack the paper credentials or plaque on the wall that supposedly make you one.

The revolutionary economy will carry many products and services beyond mass customization to full personalization—that is, even greater diversity. Similarly, jobs and work will follow a greater diversity of schedules in more dispersed locations. These changes will be paralleled by the growing diversity of family formats, implying that more individualized children, with different growing-up experiences, will have less in common.

Such changes point to further de-massification of industrial mass society—making it harder for elites, or anyone else, to engineer consensus.

Under these conditions, the belief that consensus validates truth seems likely to lose some of its validity.

What about age or durability as a truth test—the conviction that any idea that has lasted for centuries or millennia must be true? The acceleration of change may induce nostalgia in many, and mind manipulators take advantage of it. But the invasion of newness into the economy is inescapable, and the current generation, at least, wants not only what is new but the very latest.

In earlier, relatively unchanging societies, the old were respected not, as we are so often told, because they knew the past but because they knew the future—which, when it arrived, was little more than a replication of the past.

Today, given the rate of change, a vast amount of old knowledge is obsoledge, unlikely to help the young make their way. And they treat it as such. The chicken-soup formula for testing truth may work. But don't count on it.

What about authority, then? Will generations to come slavishly genuflect to authorities? And, if so, what kind? Today wherever the knowledge-based economy spreads, expertise-based authority is being challenged as never before.

Patients now question and sometimes contradict their doctors. Bloggers challenge the authority of professional journalists. Amateurs take on professionals—and not just on television shows. Celebrities run against, and increasingly beat, professional politicians. And amateurs with computers can now direct, produce and act in their own movies.

At the same time, a long list of institutional failures, disasters and corporate scandals, along with sexual abuse in Catholic churches, all undermine confidence in established authority—and the truths that it supposedly validates.

It is in light of this generalized revolt against industrial-era authority that today's attack on the authority of science needs to be seen. The difference is that science remains the most potent mind tool we have for increasing prosperity and well-being.

Science is key to designing better, smarter, safer technology, to mapping and solving environmental crises and to stopping epidemics like SARS. We will need science to lower our reliance on fossil fuels, to provide better security, to advance medicine and to reduce wealth disparities between city and country, nation and nation.

Problems like these will be solved by decisions based not on lemming-like consensus, or religious revelation, or blind acceptance of authority but on truths observed, subjected to experiment and open to continual challenge and revision as additional knowledge is acquired. In short, the future of revolutionary wealth will depend more and more on how science is used—and respected—in society.

Science and the basic method on which it relies will change as its practitioners tackle strange new and recalcitrant problems and profound ethical issues in genetics, biology and other fields, as they reach down beyond nanoscience to ever smaller phenomena and up to the expanding cosmos. But those who wish to blindfold or silence science would not merely shrink tomorrow's wealth and indirectly slow the alleviation of poverty but return humanity to the physical and mental poverty of the Dark Ages.

We must not allow the end of the Enlightenment to be followed by an anti-science darkening.

CHAPTER 22

CODA: CONVERGENCE

T he past is drifting away at a faster and faster rate. When we look back at, say, the last half of the twentieth century we realize that many of its defining episodes no longer grip us as strongly as they once did. For the generation now coming into power, events like the first moon landing, the assassination of John F. Kennedy, the Vietnam War, the Cultural Revolution in China seem increasingly remote and irrelevant.

Yet much of what will happen in our lifetimes will consist of adaptation to and further development of a process that began half a century ago—the most revolutionary wave of change in wealth creation since at least the eighteenth century.

Let's pause briefly, then, to summarize and draw together the key themes sketched in the preceding pages.

First, this revolution is a matter not just of technology, stock-market swings, inflation or deflation but of profound social, cultural, political and geopolitical changes as well. Failure to recognize the connections between these and economics leads us to seriously underestimate the oncoming challenges we face.

Second, while headlines and business chatter continually refer to improving or declining "fundamentals," we suggest that that these ups and downs are largely superficial responses to far more important shifts in what we've termed "deep fundamentals"—those factors and forces that have governed all economic activity since our days as nomadic hunter-gatherers.

Economists have long studied some of these essentials—things like work, the division of labor, exchange and the sharing of rewards. They have also filled libraries with studies on technology, energy and the environment. Business gurus drawing on these studies pour out advice about everything from human-resource management to network organization, insourcing and outsourcing, leadership and strategy.

Yet how good can advice and proposed strategies be if they ignore three key forces driving today's wealth revolution—dramatic changes in our relations to time, space and, above all, knowledge? It is, we've contended, only by recognizing the centrality of these wealth drivers that we can prepare for tomorrow.

TORTOISE TIME

For this reason, we've looked closely at each of these deep fundamentals and their impacts on wealth.

Take, for instance, the de-synchronization effect. As we saw earlier, companies are compelled to shift and re-shift their products and relationships incessantly. Customer demands, financial imperatives and market forces all change at accelerating, but very different, rates. In doing so, they impose destabilizing cross-pressures on firms whose managers struggle to come to terms with time. In response, a big synchronization industry has grown up to help firms cope with clashing speeds.

At the same time, a backward, tortoise-paced public sector—itself badly de-synchronized—imposes a huge "time-tax" on companies by slowing them down with delays in court decisions, procurement processes, regulatory rulings, permit procedures and in a thousand other ways. In short, one part of the system is flooring the gas pedal while the other is slamming on the brakes.

Nowhere, as we have noted, is this more frustratingly evident than in the contradiction between the fast-changing skill requirements of an advanced, accelerative economy and the glacial immobility of its schools.

We've seen also that some degree of de-synchronization is essential to keep competition and innovation going. But it is equally clear that excessive de-synchronization can throw companies, industries and entire economies into chaos. Indeed, one can look at the great stock market shakeouts as desperate attempts by the wealth system to re-synchronize itself.

But time is only part of the story. To understand tomorrow's oncoming changes, the cumulative effects of time conflicts need to be seen against the equally powerful transformations in the spatial landscape. Thus the world today holds its breath while watching the massive relocation of wealth and wealth creation toward formerly "third world" countries led by China and India—surely one of the biggest and fastest such transfers in history and possibly the completion of a great circle of wealth movement that began some five hundred years ago.

Moreover, we've suggested that, instead of asking whether globalization will continue, we recognize a coming split—possible *de-globalization* on the economic level and *re-globalization* of campaigns against such problems as pollution, terrorism, drugs, sexual slavery and genocide. Here, too, gas pedal and brake are applied at the same time.

Out of this collision will come the accelerated relocation of the globe's wealth creation to new high-value-added hot spots—leaving behind new pockets of poverty.

But the most dramatic spatial shift of all has little to do with these terrestrial concerns. Though millions brush it aside, we actually stand at the historical edge of humanity's serious thrust into outer space. For historians of tomorrow looking back at the twenty-first century, one of most important economic events of all may prove to be the colonization of space and wealth creation beyond our home planet.

None of these changes would occur without even more potent transformations in the deep fundamental of knowledge and our relations with it.

While shifts in the use of time and space will be easy to recognize, today's revolution in knowledge—the defining deep fundamental of our time—is far harder to grasp. These changes are, by their very nature, intangible, invisible, abstract, epistemological and seemingly remote from daily life. Yet no attempt to forecast the future of wealth can succeed without a thorough appreciation of the new role of knowledge.

In several chapters, therefore, we have provided an admittedly simplified primer on the scope, nature and role of knowledge as the central resource of advanced economies. But here again we don't just need to analyze, but to synthesize—to see these deeply fundamental changes in interaction with one another.

When we alter our relationship to time, for example, by speeding things up, we inevitably make some knowledge obsolete. We thereby increase the backlog of obsoledge that we lug around with us.

ONCE-TRUE ANALOGIES

Acceleration not only makes facts obsolete but blunts some of the key tools we use when we think. Analogy provides a case in point. It is virtually impossible for us to think without relying on analogies. This "thought-tool" is based on identifying similarities in two or more phenomena and then drawing conclusions from one to apply to the other.

Doctors, we noted, will often say "the heart is like a pump" and then describe its "valves" and other components in mechanical terms. This model helps them conceptualize and treat the heart. Often this process yields powerful results.

But once similarities are identified, it is typically taken for granted that the similarities continue. And in slow-change eras, they may do so for long periods. In today's hyper-change environment, however, once-similar things also change and very often become markedly dissimilar, often making conclusions based on the analogy false and misleading. To deal with today, therefore, we need not only new knowledge but new ways to think about it.

Yet too many economists, consciously or otherwise, cling to the belief that economics is analogous to physics. This notion arose centuries ago, when Newtonian ideas about equilibrium, causation and determinism dominated that science. Since then, of course, physicists have drastically revised their views about these matters. But many economists still base their findings on crude Newtonian assumptions.

Trained to think in industrial terms, many find it difficult to grapple with the odd character of knowledge—the fact that it is non-rival and non-depletable, that it is intangible and thus hard to measure.

It is only when we set today's failures of economics alongside the looming crisis in science that we begin to gauge their true significance. For together these two fields have the greatest—or at least the most direct—impact on how we create wealth. And both are heading for transformation.

MAPPING THE KNOWABLE

Yet even these crises are only part of a vastly larger intellectual drama. Economics and science are, for all their importance, only interacting parts of the world's far larger knowledge system. And that entire system is caught up in a history-making upheaval.

We are slicing and dicing knowledge in new ways, crashing out of industrial-age disciplinary boundaries and reorganizing the deep structure of our knowledge system. Knowledge without organization loses accessibility and context. Thus scholars throughout time have divided knowledge into distinct categories.

When twelfth-century Europeans translated the works of Arab philosopher Abu Nasr al-Farabi (AD 870–950), they found what has been called a "map of the knowable"—a systematic, hierarchical organization of knowledge into categories. In the medieval West, later on, universities mapped knowledge differently. Every educated person was supposed to master the *trivium* (consisting of grammar, rhetoric and Aristotelian logic) and the *quadrivium* (astronomy, arithmetic, geometry and music).

Today, as knowledge is broken into more and more specialized and sub-subspecialized categories university offerings are still, like al-Farabi's, neatly categorized in hierarchical structures. For example, in terms of both academic status and budget, science typically outranks the social sciences, which are regarded as too "soft." Physics until recently topped the science pyramid but is currently being nudged off its pinnacle by biology. Of all the social sciences, economics pulls top rank because, being highly mathematized, it is (or pretends to be) the most "hard." But these structures are in danger of collapsing under their own weight.

More and more jobs require cross-disciplinary knowledge, so that we find increasing need for hyphenated backgrounds—"Astro-biologist," "bio-physicist," "environmental-engineer," "forensic-accountant." Some tasks require two or more hyphens. Hence, "neuro-psycho-pharmacologist."

Soon, it seems clear, we will run out of hyphens. Seemingly permanent disciplines and hierarchies may disappear altogether as knowledge is organized into ad hoc non-hierarchical configurations determined by the problems at hand. At which point the "map of the knowable" becomes a flickering set of constantly changing patterns.

This alone represents a quake in the knowledge system that will transform work groupings, professions, universities, hospitals and bureaucracies in general. Beneficiaries of the old ways of organizing ever-more-specialized knowledge—tenured professors, bureaucrats, economists and others—will resist such changes. Surely, deep specialization has paid enormous dividends. But it also kills surprise and imagination, and breeds individuals afraid to step, let alone think, outside their disciplinary perimeter.

Conversely, imagination and creativity are fed when previously unrelated ideas, concepts or categories of data, information or knowledge are juxtaposed in fresh ways. By pulling together widely diverse streams of personal experience and know-how, knowledge workers are likely to bring temporary, novel, out of the you-know-what ideas into their thinking and decision-making. As we've seen, what may be lost in knowledge based on long-term, deeper and deeper specialization may thus, in this new system, be compensated for by enhanced creativity and imagination.

Powerful new technologies will help us inject temporary disciplines into fresh plug-in, plug-out modules and models. They already do. We are mining and matching bigger and more diverse databases against one another in search of previously unnoticed patterns and connections. This matching is more than just a convenient tool for finding out how supermarket sales of beer and diapers, or how Pop-Tarts and hurricanes may be related.

Data mining produces sometimes startling "who would have thought" insights. Virginia health officials used it to trace an outbreak of salmonella to fruit produced in a small packing shed on a farm in Brazil. Said an official of the U.S. Centers for Disease Control and Prevention: "We never had an outbreak from mangos that we recognized before." If creativity involves the novel juxtaposition of facts, ideas or insights previously thought to be unconnected, then mining and matching are fundamental parts of the innovation process.

When we put changes like these together and then add the splitting of data, information and knowledge into smaller, more granular chunks—making it more perishable, classifying things differently, proliferating what-if scenarios, introducing new models at a faster and faster rate and operating at ever-higher levels of abstraction—it is clear that we are not simply accumulating more knowledge.

And when we add these to the crises in economic thinking and science, it becomes evident that we are engaged in the fastest and most profound restructuring of knowledge in history, with implications reaching far beyond the economy to culture, religion, politics and social life. At the same time we are making the wealth of individuals and nations alike more dependent than ever on that growing global knowledge base.

We do not know what strange shortcuts and twisted pathways knowledge as an expanding, organic system will take, or where it will ultimately carry us.

Even when we combine all these changes in humanity's relationships to time, space and knowledge—and the other deep fundamentals as well—we only glimpse the truly awesome outlines of today's global revolution. To see beyond, we need to look at the extraordinary changes that lie ahead, not merely in the visible economy but in the "hidden half" of the entire emerging wealth system.

Without taking this next exploratory step, we, as individuals and as societies, will stumble into tomorrow unaware of the amazing potential we hold in our hands.

PART SIX

Prosuming

CHAPTER 23

THE HIDDEN HALF

More than a billion humans, we are frequently told, subsist on the equivalent of less than a dollar a day. Many survive—just barely—on much less. In fact there are still vast numbers who live without any money at all. They have never entered the world money system, scratching by, as our distant ancestors did, basically consuming only what they themselves can produce. A substantial part of this impoverished population would do almost anything to move into the money economy.

To enter that economy, humans have had to go through one of what might be called the "Seven Doorways to Money." Imagine a long hallway with seven locked doors. A tired, dirty, hungry crowd pushes and pulls its desperate way along the hall. Each doorway bears a brief, brusque sign telling what must be done to open the lock. Illiterates eagerly ask others to read the signs to them. The signs read as follows:

Doorway One: CREATE SOMETHING SALABLE. Grow surplus corn. Draw a portrait. Make a pair of sandals. Find a buyer and you're in.

Doorway Two: GET A JOB. Work. Get paid money in return. You are in the money system. As such, you are now a part of the visible economy.

Doorway Three: INHERIT. If your parents or your Uncle Frank bequeaths money to you, this door will swing open. You thereby enter the system. You may never need a job.

Doorway Four: OBTAIN A GIFT. Someone—anyone—could give you money, or something you can sell or translate into money. Whatever its form, once you have it, you, too, are in.

Doorway Five: MARRY. (Or remarry.) Pick a spouse who has already walked through one of the doors and will share his or her money. Then you, too, can walk on in.

Doorway Six: GO ON WELFARE. Money may be grudgingly transferred to you by a government. The amount may be a pittance, but to that degree, you, too, are in the money system.

Doorway Seven: STEAL. Finally, there is always theft, first resort of the criminal and last resort of the desperate poor.

Of course, there are minor variations—bribes, accidental discovery of money and the like. But these seven are the main portals through which humanity over the centuries has marched into the money economy.

Today the total annual output of the world money economy—what we have referred to as the visible economy—is something on the order of $50 trillion. That is, we are told, the total economic value created on the planet each year.

But what if the total we humans produce each year is not $50 trillion a year in goods, services and experiences, but closer to $100 trillion? What if, in addition to the $50 trillion, there were another $50 trillion "off the books," so to speak? We believe there may well be, and the hunt for that missing $50 trillion is the subject of the next several chapters. The hunt will take us from supercomputers to Hollywood and hip-hop music, biological threats, intellectual-property piracy and the search for life in outer space.

THE PROSUMER ECONOMY

In contrast to the seven doorways into the money economy, the hidden or off-the-books economy has a thousand doorways. These are open to everyone, monied and moneyless alike. There are no requirements for entry. We are all born prequalified.

This invisible economy should not be confused with the underground or "black" economies of the world where money is laundered, taxes evaded and terrorists, dictators and drug lords flourish. The very fact that the black economy is used to transmit and conceal money places it within the money economy—and not the non-money economy we are describing here.

The economic map most of us use today—and on which business leaders and politicians heavily rely—is actually a fragment, a detail of a much larger map. It charts only the money economy.

But there is also a massive "hidden" economy in which large amounts of mostly untracked, unmeasured and unpaid economic activity occurs. It is the non-money Prosumer Economy.

When people turn out goods, services or experiences for sale in the money economy, we call them "producers" and the process "production." But there were no counterpart words, at least in English, for what happens in the off-the-books, non-money economy.

In *The Third Wave* (1980), we therefore invented the word *prosumer* for those of us who create goods, services or experiences for our own use or satisfaction, rather than for sale or exchange. When, as individuals or groups, we both *pro*duce and con*sume* our own output, we are "prosuming."

If we bake a pie and also eat it, we are prosumers. But prosuming is not just an individual act. Part of the purpose of baking that pie might be to share it with family, friends or community without expecting money or its equivalent in return. Today, given the shrinkage of the world because of advances in transportation, communications and I.T., the notion of prosuming can include unpaid work to create value to share with strangers half a world away.

We are all prosumers at one time or another, and all economies have a prosumer sector because many of our highly personal needs and wants aren't or can't be supplied in the marketplace, or are too expensive, or because we actually enjoy prosuming or desperately need to.

Once we take our eyes off the money economy and mute all the econobabble, we discover surprising things. First, that this prosumer economy is huge; second, that it encompasses some of the most important things we do; and third, that even though it is given little attention by most economists, the $50 trillion money economy they monitor couldn't survive for ten minutes without it.

No axiom is uttered with more heartfelt conviction by conventional businesspeople and economists than "There's no such thing as a free lunch." Most of us happily mumble the phrase even as we munch the meal. Yet no mantra is more misleading. Prosumer output is the subsidy on which the entire money system depends. Producing and prosuming are inseparable.

Most people, including most economists, would unhesitatingly agree that what we do as prosumers—whether it's caring for a sick father or volunteering at a community organization or firehouse—has social value. But most would also, to the degree that they think about it, accept the common assumption that an impenetrable Iron Curtain or Berlin Wall separates what we do for money and what we do as prosumers.

By contrast, we hope to show—logically but, given the paucity of quantitative data, anecdotally—that this curtain or wall does not exist in reality, that many prosumers regularly move back and forth from one side of it to the other, and that what we do as prosumers profoundly affects the money economy in often overlooked ways.

Moreover, we will show that this is not just an abstract matter for economists to ponder. It is important for parents paying tuition or taxes to educate their children for the future. It is important for marketing executives and managers, advertising agencies and investors, CEOs and venture capitalists, bankers, lobbyists and strategic planners. It is especially important for policy-makers and political leaders who wish to lead us safely into tomorrow.

A MUM IN A MILLION

Prosuming takes myriad forms, from writing shareware or rewiring a lamp to baking brownies for the school fund-raiser. It may include hunting down anthrax, saving earthquake victims, building churches or searching for life in outer space. It can be done with the help of a hammer and nails or with a giant supercomputer and the Internet.

Prosuming is what Sharon Bates of Alvaston, England, does when she cares for her homebound epileptic husband, even though she herself is disabled by arthritis. She receives no paycheck for that—although she was nominated for the "Mum in a Million" award. (She also cares for two children.)

Prosuming is what our close friend Enki Tan did when he suddenly canceled dinner with us in California to fly all night to Aceh, Indonesia, which was devastated by the tsunami of December 2004. A physician by training, Enki bandaged babies, performed surgery, fought to keep victims alive, struggling without adequate instruments, under unimaginable conditions—one of the thousands of volunteers from twenty-eight countries who rushed to help the victims of this tragic disaster.

Then there is Canadian physician Bruce Lampard, who treks through Nigeria or the Sudan helping to set up health clinics in villages lacking electricity and safe water.

Marta Garcia, a single mom with three children, can't roam the world, but in addition to working for pay six hours a day, she volunteers to stamp books in the library of the nearby charter school and serves as secretary of her neighborhood association.

In Yokosuka, Japan, Katsuo Sakakibara, a bank employee, helps out each year at a sports events for the mentally impaired. And in Belo Horizonte, Brazil, Mariana Pimenta Pinheiro, despite warnings about crime and violence, climbs up a narrow stairway one day a week to the top of a *favela*—a shanty-town—to teach children English and how to use a computer—preparing them for an escape from misery.

It is in the invisible prosumer economy that we comfort friends who have lost a child. We collect toys for homeless children, take out the garbage, separate recyclables, drive a neighbor's kid to the playground, organize the church choir and perform countless other unpaid tasks in home and community.

Many of these cooperative activities are what author-activist Hazel Henderson describes as "socially cohesive." They balance equally valuable competitive activities in the paid economy. Both create value. Recognizing this, according to *Daily Yomiuri,* Japan's Ministry of Health, Labor and Welfare noted in 2005 that working means "not only paid labor, but also volunteer work for non-profit organizations and community services."

Focusing on the family, Norwegian sociologist Stein Ringen of Oxford University explains, "When a family sits down to a meal, its members enjoy the product of a range of activities which are carried out in the market and in the household. From the market, they benefit from farming and fishing, processing, packaging, storage, transport and retailing. The family contributes by shopping, preparing ingredients, cooking, setting the table and washing up afterwards."

All these typically unmeasured activities are production, he writes, "every bit as much as when similar activities are provided in the market." They are, in a word, prosumption—production in the non-money economy. And were we to hire and pay others to do such tasks for us, the size of the bill would stagger us.

THE POTTY TEST

The assertion that the money economy could not survive ten minutes without inputs from the prosumer economy is not a wild exaggeration. "Ten minutes" may overstate the case. But the basic point is valid.

Every single day, some part of the workforce retires or dies and has to be replaced. One generation moves in as another exits the ranks of labor. Were this process ever to stop, the paid economy at some point would come to a screeching—or whining—halt. There would be no one left to work for pay, and what Marxist economists call economic "reproduction" would cease. Survivors would have to revert entirely to prosuming necessities, as our remote ancestors did.

This explains why the money economy depends so completely on the most elemental form of prosuming in society: Parenting. Parents (or their surrogates) have always been the primary agents of socialization and acculturation, preparing each new generation to fit into the existing social order and its economy.

Employers rarely recognize how much they owe to the parents of their employees. We have often made this point to corporate managers by asking a simple, if indelicate, question: "How productive would your workforce be if someone hadn't toilet-trained it?" We call it "the potty test."

Employers normally take this for granted, but, in fact, someone did that training. Almost certainly a mom. Of course, parents do more than merely housebreak their children. They spend years—and enormous amounts of caloric energy and brain effort—trying to ready their young for the years of toil that lie ahead. More broadly, they give children tools needed to work with other people, not the least of which is language.

How productive would workers be who could not communicate in words? Language is so basic a human skill that it, too, is taken for granted. It is particularly important in the money economy, doubly so in one based on knowledge.

While we may, as a species, be wired up to learn language, we actually acquire the necessary skills at home as children, by listening to and talking with our family members. Mothers and fathers are the first teachers. They are the primal prosumers—without whose contributions we can barely imagine an economy of paid producers.

More broadly, how productive would an economy be if parents did not transmit culture—the rules of behavior that make it possible for humans to work together in teams, groups and communities?

Young people entering the labor force today typically need far more preparation than their predecessors, who worked mainly with their hands. Employers complain incessantly about the lack of appropriate workforce preparation. They demand more math and science, more standardized tests. Yet the main failure in the workplace is not just a result of inadequate job skills.

It is a more general failure of culture—of confused and self-destructive values, lack of motivation, poor interpersonal skills, inappropriate images of the future. All these problems hamper the development of job skills. How much productivity in the money economy is lost when people fail as parents?

Someday, if the economy ever attains the science-fictional capacity to operate autonomously without people, or humans attain immortality, parenting may become economically unnecessary. Until then, at the deepest level, production is life-and-death dependent on the unpaid exertions of billions of parent prosumers.

WHAT PRICE DISINTEGRATION?

As outsiders, we and many others for decades have repeatedly hectored economists about their failure to adequately credit the crucial role prosuming plays in generating wealth. In doing so, we followed in the pioneering footsteps of Gary Becker and Amartya Sen. From within the economics profession, they made very early, intellectually powerful efforts to persuade their colleagues of the importance of this hidden economy—only to face decades of polite ho-humming before being belatedly awarded their Nobel Prizes.

Among activists, too, Hazel Henderson, in *Paradigms in Progress* and other insightful books; Edgar Cahn in *Time Dollars;* Nona Y. Glazer in *Women's Paid and Unpaid Labor;* and others have attacked the self-imposed blinders of mainstream economists. Finally, and perhaps most important, countless NGOs in many countries have echoed these criticisms.

Yet even today, little has been done to systematically map the vital two-way links that connect the money economy and its huge, off-the-books *doppelgänger.*

When prosumers help glue families, communities and societies together, they do it as part of everyday life without, as a rule, calculating its effects on the nation's visible economy. Yet it would be highly instructive if economists could tell us what social cohesion is worth in dollars, yen, yuan, won or euros—or what social disintegration costs.

So what, then, is all this unpaid work worth?

GROSSLY DISTORTED PRODUCT (GDP)

In a groundbreaking paper as far back as 1965, thirty-four-year-old Gary Becker pointed out that "non-working time may now be more important to economic welfare than working time; yet the attention paid by economists to the latter dwarfs any paid to the former."

Analyzing the allocation of time between the two, he calculated the value of non-work activities such as getting an education. He quantified its value by assuming that each hour spent in the classroom was an hour that might have been devoted to paid work instead, then toted up the earnings forgone.

Far more complicated than this simple description suggests, his work was a brilliant advance in economic theory, presented in mathematical terms that economists could respect. Yet it took twenty-seven years before Becker, in 1992, was awarded the Nobel Prize, in part because of this work. Today, despite many studies, prosuming and unpaid work, especially that of women, remain far outside the main concerns of everyday, conventional economics.

Efforts have also been made by sociologists and social-policy experts to calculate the value of prosuming. By estimating hours spent doing unpaid labor and asking what having it done by paid employees would cost, some have come up with startling conclusions. They echo Becker's assumption that the household is a "small factory" and that actual *paid* working time may be less important to the overall economy than it appears.

Stein Ringen, writing in 1996, concludes, "The material standard of living would be more than halved if it were not for the effects of living in house-holds. In the national economy, households contribute as much as market institutions. This is an astonishing result," he writes, considering that "the family is often believed to have become marginal in economic terms." That family output is almost entirely a result of prosuming.

Even if such numbers are only fractionally correct, we are still looking at an enormous, gaping black hole in standard economics, which partially explains why even top-league economists and scholars have so poor a record in forecasting. By failing to take prosuming adequately into account, they rely heavily, almost cultishly, on measures that mislead them—and us.

Conventional economists and their "true believer" followers tend to brush aside this hidden economic activity as inconsequential, despite the real-life evidence to the contrary. By essentially defining economic "value" as something created only when money changes hands, economists often wind up focusing on easily measured superficialities. Thus, just as the deep fundamentals of time, space and knowledge—those most crucial to advanced economies—are the least studied by economists, so, too, their insistence on the traditional definition of "economic value" blinds them to the approaching drama of tomorrow.

They cling to this core definition in part because money is easy to count and lends itself to mathematization and modeling. Unpaid activity doesn't. And in a profession obsessed with metrics, that puts prosuming outside the perimeter of central concern. Little effort is made to create a parallel metric for prosuming and to systematically track the many pathways through which the paid and unpaid systems interact.

An exception is the work of Rishab Aiyer Ghosh of the University of Maastricht in Holland, who holds that "without money as a tool of measurement, you must find other ways of quantifying value, and you must identify the different systems of ascribing value and exchange rates between them." Ghosh's work in general, however, focuses on unpaid work done by software prosumers as distinct from unpaid contributions in many other fields.

Our ignorance about prosuming might be acceptable if prosuming were, in fact, inconsequential—or if it had little impact on the money economy. But neither is true. The result is that a basic tool like the gross domestic product, on which so many business and government decisions are based, would more accurately be named grossly distorted product.

Given how little attention is still paid to this huge underlying force in wealth creation, and how little data about it are available, we are reduced to speculation. But that is better than ignoring so massive a factor in wealth creation. If the value of prosuming is, in fact, roughly equal to the output of the money economy that economists measure, it is the hidden half. Applied to the world as a whole—taking into account the output of the teeming millions of peasants who live *only* by prosuming—we perhaps do wind up with a missing $50 trillion.

What makes this so important today is that as we move into the next phase of revolutionary wealth, the prosumer sector of our economies is poised for tremendous change, including a striking historical turnabout.

Amazingly, even as millions of peasants in the poor world are being gradually absorbed into the money economy, millions of people in the rich world are doing the exact opposite: They are rapidly expanding their activity in the non-monetized half—the prosumer part—of the world economy.

In fact, as we'll see next, we are laying the base for a veritable explosion of prosuming in the richest countries—and not just of the Home Depot variety. Completely new markets will open before us as others slam shut. The role of the consumer will be transformed as the role of the prosumer expands. Health care, pensions, education, technology, innovation and government budgets will all be heavily impacted.

Don't think of hammers and screwdrivers. Think of biology, nanotools, desktop factories and fantastic new materials that will permit all of us, as prosumers, to do things for ourselves that we could never have imagined.

CHAPTER 24

THE HEALTH PROSUMERS

T he coming explosion in the prosumer economy will make many new millionaires. Not until then will it be "discovered" by stock markets, investors and the media—at which point it will finally lose its invisibility. Countries such as Japan, Korea, India, China and the United States—rich in advanced manufacturing, niche marketing and highly skilled knowledge workers—will be the first beneficiaries. But that isn't all.

Prosuming will shake up markets, alter the role structure in society and change the way we think about wealth. It will also transform the future of health. To understand why, we need to look briefly at rapidly converging changes in demography, the costs of medical care, knowledge and technology.

Health care is where the most spectacular new technologies are matched by the most obsolete, disorganized, counterproductive and often deadly medical institutions. If the term *deadly* seems excessive, think again.

According to the U.S. Centers for Disease Control, as many as 90,000 body bags are filled each year with victims who die of infections contracted in U.S. hospitals. By another count, between 44,000 and 98,000 die of medical errors committed in hospitals—in what is presumed to be the world's best and most heavily financed health-care system. In 2001, our chances of dying in a hospital from a medical mistake or new infection were much greater than our chances of being killed while driving.

Of course, we don't know how many people die for lack of health care, even in the richest nations. We do, however, know that in all the well-off nations, from Japan and the United States to nations of Western Europe, health-care costs are spiraling out of control, populations are rapidly aging and politicians are panicking.

These facts are part of a bigger, deeper crisis. In the late nineteenth and early twentieth centuries, investments in physical infrastructure led to better water and public sanitation, almost wiping out some diseases that had previously devastated whole populations. The reconceptualization of medicine led to medical specialization. Hospitals multiplied and grew into huge, bureaucratic institutions linked to even-more-bureaucratic government agencies, insurance companies and pharmaceutical giants.

These changes did radically improve health conditions, essentially eliminating some of the most prevalent diseases in the modernizing countries of the West.

Today, however, another change in the deep fundamental of space—a new globe-girdling transportation infrastructure—leaves nations largely unprotected against the cross-border transmission of diseases old and new, not to mention global pandemics. Public-health systems are underfunded. And the danger of biological, chemical or nuclear terrorism from religious, political or psychotic fanatics is no longer a comic-book fantasy.

Medical specialization, meanwhile, has reached the point at which communication among specialties is perilously poor. Bureaucracies are on the edge of unmanageability. Hospitals go broke. And patterns of illness in countries with advanced economies have changed dramatically.

Today's main killers in the affluent nations are no longer communicable diseases like pneumonia, tuberculosis or influenza. They are heart disease, lung cancer and other illnesses that are clearly affected by individual behavior with respect to diet, exercise, alcohol, drug use, smoking, stress, sexual activity and international travel.

What hasn't changed, however, is the underlying premise that doctors are "health providers" and patients still their "clients" or "customers." Demography may compel us to rethink this assumption.

BETTING ON ONE HUNDRED?

Demography, some believe, is destiny. If so, destiny is changing along with everything else. We are fast approaching the point at which a billion people on the planet will be over the age of sixty.

Life expectancy at birth is increasing, even in many parts of the poor world, according to the World Health Organization. In the last half century—in spite of all their poverty, misery, disease, water shortages and environmental disasters—developing countries have seen average life expectancy shoot upward from forty-one years in the early 1950s to sixty-two by 1990. It is heading toward seventy by 2020, and already exceeds that age in Costa Rica, Jamaica, Sri Lanka and Malaysia.

Meanwhile, demographers at Cambridge University and the Max Planck

Institute in Germany tell us that a female baby born in France today has a 50 percent chance of living to age one hundred—which would put her into the twenty-second century.

The World Health Organization reports that Europe, as a region, is now the "oldest" part of the world, while Japan, as a nation, has the highest percentage of people over age sixty. By 2020, WHO forecasts, almost a third of the entire Japanese population will have passed its sixtieth birthday. And in Japan, France, Germany and Spain, among people over sixty, one in five will be older than eighty.

No country's health-care system has been designed for this combination of diseases heavily dependent on behavioral and lifestyle factors plus an aging population. It is historically new, and no currently proposed "reform" of health care will be able to deal with it. Nor do we adequately understand the full effects of these changes on taxes, pensions, housing, employment, retirement, finance and other key wealth variables. What is needed is far more drastic than mere reform.

THE PANIC ZONE

According to the Organization for Economic Cooperation and Development, public and private health expenditures in Germany in 2002 already accounted for 10.9 percent of GDP as conventionally measured. Comparable numbers for France were 9.7 percent; the United Kingdom, 7.7; Japan, 7.8; and South Korea, 5.1. The number for the United States exceeded 14 percent. How far can that number grow before the bankruptcy lawyers arrive?

As we have seen, GDP figures are grossly distorted because of their failure to take prosumer output fully into account. If the economists assigned value to it, the total costs of health care would loom immensely larger.

According to the U.S. Congressional Budget Office, long-term health care for the elderly runs to $120 billion annually. But James R. Knickman and Emily K. Snell of the Robert Wood Johnson Foundation assert that this number "underestimates the economic resources devoted to long-term health care . . . because most care is delivered informally by family and friends and is not included in economic statistics. . . . It has been estimated that the economic value of such informal care-giving in the United States reaches $200 billion a year—one and a half times the amount spent on formal care-giving."

Other researchers suggest that in the United States, family care for Alzheimer's patients alone had a value exceeding $100 billion in 2004. And none of these figures includes unpaid caregiving for short-term problems.

Governments and health industry officials worry that an aging population will mean more disease and debility, and therefore even higher costs. In the

United States, according to *Chain Drug Review,* pharmacies on average fill nineteen prescriptions a year for customers over fifty-five, compared with only eight for younger people. The *Journal of the American Dietetic Association* estimates that U.S. "health care costs for those over 65 years are three to five times greater than for those younger than 65."

Finally, add to all this the potential bankruptcy of pension systems as we know them, and the entire high-pitched public discussion plunges into the panic zone.

There are, however, flaws in this overall picture. First, many such numbers are based on straight-line projections of past experience. That may be delusory in times of crisis or revolution. The longer-lived new generation will likely prove healthier than its parents were. Second, the same demographics that are increasing the percentage of elderly will reduce the percentage of young people and could reduce the cost of schools and pediatric care. Other financial offsets may also be possible. Nevertheless, none of these qualifications alters the need for radical reconceptualization of the entire problem of health in the twenty-first century.

Unfortunately, well-intentioned reforms based on industrial-age assumptions only make matters worse. To cut costs, politicians typically seek "efficiencies" that translate into assembly-line health care, a "managed" system offering one-size-fits-all, standardized treatment.

Exactly as in low-tech factories, efforts are made to speed up the medical assembly line, essentially putting doctors into cubicles and allowing them only a few minutes with each patient. This is a self-defeating Second Wave strategy for a situation that desperately needs a Third Wave response.

In a business lagging behind other industries, smart pharmaceutical companies will soon transition toward de-massified, highly targeted, customized products that could reduce side effects and the additional costs they often impose.

Cost-cutting reformers, in the meantime, seek just the opposite—mass-production health care in the form of standardized, cookie-cutter protocols, procedures and drugs.

With costs and inefficiencies continuing to mushroom, the crisis in health economics cannot be resolved—until we look beyond industrial solutions to the extraordinary opportunities opened to us by the arrival of the knowledge economy and the new potentials for prosumer health care.

BESIEGED BY BREAKTHROUGHS

It isn't just the fantastic growth of medical knowledge (and obsoledge) in recent decades that holds revolutionary potential for improving health; it's also the parallel shift in control of that knowledge.

Patients today are inundated with previously unavailable medical information instantly available on the Internet and on news programs, many of which routinely feature segments with a physician as host.

A degree of background knowledge is also conveyed, with varying degrees of accuracy, by popular TV dramas with titles like *Trauma: Life in the E.R.*, *MDs*, *Scrubs* and *Houston Medical*. When *ER* did a show about human papillomavirus (HPV)—which, though barely known by that name, happens to be the most frequently transmitted sexual disease in the United States—more than five million viewers learned something about it in one night.

Health documentaries abound. A prize-winning program about cochlear ear implants in deaf children took a top prize for TV documentaries in Japan. China, as a matter of health policy, aired a twelve-part series on AIDS and broke ancient taboos with *How Can I Tell You This?*, a sex-education series for teenagers.

Since 1997, when the U.S. Food and Drug Administration first allowed big pharmaceutical firms to advertise prescription drugs on television, viewers have been bombarded by commercials touting everything from anti-inflammatories and cholesterol-lowering drugs to antihistamines. Most hurriedly list side effects and urge viewers to ask their physicians for further information. Permitting such advertising no doubt encouraged the creation of the twenty-four-hour cable-TV Discovery Health Channel.

This avalanche of health-related information, misinformation and knowledge hurled at the individual varies in objectivity and credibility. But it directs more and more public attention to health issues—and changes the traditional relationship between doctors and patients, encouraging a more take-charge attitude on the part of the latter.

Ironically, while patients have more access to health information of uneven quality, their doctors, driven by pressures to speed up, have less and less time to peruse the latest medical journals, whether online or off, and to communicate adequately with relevant specialists—and with patients.

Moreover, while doctors need knowledge about different conditions and see streams of patients whose faces are scarcely remembered from one visit to the next, educated, persistent, Internet-savvy patients may actually have read more recent research regarding their specific ailments than the doctor.

Patients come with printouts of Internet material, photocopies of pages from the *Physicians' Desk Reference* or clips from medical journals and health magazines. They ask questions and no longer tug their forelocks in awe of the doctor's white lab coat.

Here, changes in relationships to the deep fundamentals of time and knowledge have radically altered medical reality.

In economic terms, the doctor selling services is still a "producer." The patient, by contrast, is not just a consumer, but a more active "prosumer" capable of making an increasing contribution to the economy's output of well-ness or health. Sometimes producer and prosumer work together; sometimes they work independently of each other; sometimes they work at cross-purposes. Yet conventional health statistics and forecasts, by and large, ignore today's rapid changes in these roles and relationships.

Many of us change our diets, quit smoking or drinking, and adopt exercise regimens. If, then, our health improves, how much should be attributed to the doctor and how much to our own efforts? Put differently, how much of the health-care output is created by producers and how much by prosumers? And why do most economists count one and not the other?

According to Lowell Levin, professor emeritus at the Yale School of Public Health, "85 to 90 percent of all medical care in the United States is provided by ordinary people." Self-treatment remedies, he says, include aspirin for headaches, ice packs for sprains, ointments for burns, and much more. Levin, according to a 1987 interviewer in *The World & I,* "views all doctors and hospitals as necessary but undesirable social evils, like jails."

Whatever the actual percentage now, the combination of demography, cost pressures and knowledge all point toward a radical increase in the prosumer factor. But all this so far ignores what may yet turn out to be the most important change of all: Tomorrow's technology. Add that to the mix and watch what happens.

THE DIABETES GAME

Patients don't prosume health just by exercising more or quitting tobacco. They invest their money in technologies that can help them better care for themselves and their families.

In 1965, according to Tom Antone, then head of what is now the American Association for Homecare, "about the only equipment available in the home were canes, crutches, walkers, and beds." In 1980, when we first called attention to health prosuming in *The Third Wave,* the market for home-use medical instruments was still relatively tiny.

Today, according to Sharon O'Reilly, president of MedTech, a medical market-research firm, patients are responsible for 99 percent of diabetes-management responsibilities, and sales of home-use diabetes products are forecast to reach $15 billion by 2010. But home-care technology is no longer limited to a few basic products such as insulin-infusion kits, blood-pressure machines and pregnancy-test kits. An ever-widening array of technologies are springing up to help prosumers care for themselves or their loved ones.

Anyone going online today can find and buy self-testing equipment for the detection of everything from allergies to HIV, prostate cancer to hepatitis. Trouble with your hand? The FlagHouse catalog for "special populations" offers a "finger goniometer" for measuring range of motion in metacarpophalangeal finger joints. Along with it you can get a hydraulic dynomometer and hydraulic pinch gauge for other measurements of the hand.

Trouble breathing? You can buy an ultrasonic nebulizer, a spirometer, even a lifesaving ventilator unit. You can lay in a neurologist's hammer or your own pediatric stethoscope.

Women can regularly monitor their estradiol, testosterone and progesterone levels. There are new home tests for osteoporosis and colon cancer.

According to the Food and Drug Administration (FDA), home-care systems are already "the fastest growing segment of the medical device industry." But all this empowering self-help technology is still primitive compared with what lies ahead.

An FDA magazine reports that "the list of planned and imagined medical devices reads like a work of science fiction. . . . imagine a toothbrush with a biosensing chip that checks your blood sugar and bacteria levels while you're brushing. . . . computerized eyeglasses with a tiny embedded display that can help those who wear them remember people and things. . . . a smart bandage . . . that could detect bacteria or virus in a wound and tell the wearer if treatment with antibiotics is warranted and which to use."

It cites a "smart T-shirt" that "monitored the vital signs of climbers on a recent expedition to Mount Everest" and a hands-free device that allows disabled persons to operate machines by blinking an eye or by brain activity.

"Imagine home CAT scans in the privacy of your own marble bathroom. Automatic urine analysis with every flush. Computerized life-expectancy projections updated after each meal," speculates *The New York Times Magazine.*

As with any such forecasts, not all of these products will ever see the light of day, or prove cheap, practical and safe. But they represent only the first drops of a technology torrent to come. It will change the economics of both self-care and paid care. And it represents yet another way in which the mostly unmeasured prosumer economy interacts with the money economy.

Prosumers invest money to buy capital goods that will help them perform better in the non-money economy—which will then reduce costs in the money economy.

Wouldn't the overall "output" of health be increased by recognizing the essential role of prosuming and changing the ratio of input by doctor, on one side, and patient on the other?

Whether we look at demographics or costs, changes in the amount and availability of knowledge or coming breakthroughs in technology, it is clear that prosumers will play an even bigger role in the massive health economy of tomorrow.

It is, therefore, time for economists, instead of regarding the non-money economy as irrelevant or unimportant, to systematically track the most significant ways in which both these economies feed each other, and integrate with one another to form an overarching wealth-creating, health-creating system.

If we understood these relationships better, they would cast important light on the global health crisis. At a minimum, they might introduce vital new questions into today's relentlessly predictable political debates about health in many countries.

If prosumers make huge, unpaid contributions to the level of health everywhere, and if they invest their own money to make those contributions, might it not make sense to reduce overall health costs by educating and training prosumers as we now train producers?

Lowell Levin believes that one of the best investments governments could make in health care would be to instruct schoolchildren on how to be better health prosumers. That would include teaching "some of the same things we teach in medical school—basic human anatomy and physiology and the causes and treatment of disease. . . . Teach them to diagnose and treat common minor health problems. We should also teach them which kinds of health problems really require professional help."

Vikram S. Kumar has been working with the Joslin Diabetes Center to design what he calls a "community-based, predictive game" for children with type 1 diabetes. DiaBetNet aims to develop mental models of their physiologies and motivate them to check their glucose levels more frequently. The game encourages diabetic kids, linked together wirelessly, to play on a computer to predict their own and others' glucose levels. The idea is to "leverage untapped social dynamics" rather than relying entirely on doctor-patient instructions or parental nagging.

In a densely cross-connected knowledge-based economy, why continue to think of the health crisis and the educational crisis as separate, rather than as interlinked? Can we not use imagination to revolutionize the ideas and institutions in both fields? Millions of prosumers stand ready to help.

CHAPTER 25

OUR THIRD JOB

O verstressed? Too busy? Wondering where all the time has gone? With the money economy operating at hyperspeeds, time squeeze is now a source of near-universal anger. People rant about receiving two hundred e-mails a day, while the incessant ring of cell phones makes uninterrupted thought all but impossible. Multitaskers combine television, phone calls, online games, stock-market reports and short typed messages in constant, quivering interaction with the outside world.

This acceleration and shift from sequential to simultaneous activity, driven by hypercompetition, represents a major change in the way we relate to the deep fundamental of time—and to our work, friends and family. In more and more homes and companies, acceleration into the fast lane translates into painful conflict between job time and family time.

In addition to hours spent working for pay at our jobs or professions, we all devote unpaid time to performing the everyday personal and familial tasks required of us. The burden is especially heavy for women and for those in the "sandwich generation," who find themselves simultaneously taking care of both children and aging parents.

Today, however, something new has been added to these burdens. On top of Job One (paid work) and Job Two (unpaid household work), many of us now find ourselves holding down Job Three (unpaid as well).

While we were writing this chapter, an e-mail arrived from the company that had recently sold us a copying machine. The curt message rather peremptorily instructed us to read the meter on our machine and e-mail back the results, along with our machine's serial number, so that we could be properly billed. What, we wondered, had happened to the meter reader who used to come to the office?

There was a time when, if a package hadn't arrived, we could telephone FedEx at a toll-free number to find out why it was late and where it was. A helpful employee—usually a woman—sat at a computer terminal in Memphis, Tennessee, or another distant city and traced our package for us.

At some point, hailing it as a grand innovative convenience for the customer, FedEx announced that we customers could now track our own packages by going online and punching in some data. What, we wondered, had happened to the young lady?

But it wasn't only copier manufacturers and delivery services that demanded prosumer participation from their customers. The Bank of America, explaining that it received "a huge number" of requests for canceled checks, requiring some eight hundred employees to locate the checks on microfilm, copy and mail them, introduced technology making it possible for customers to look up canceled checks themselves either online or at an ATM.

Once again, the change was presented as a benefit to the consumer, which it no doubt is, but only after the customer does a little extra work. Even as it touted the new service, the bank announced a 6.7 percent cut in jobs.

BEYOND THE BUFFET

And that's just one bank. In the United States, bank customers in 2002 executed nearly 14 billion ATM transactions—a third of the worldwide total. Customers like ATMs in part because they save waiting on lines. In a hurry-up economy every minute counts.

Assume that, on average, a simple face-to-face transaction at the bank counter might have taken, say, two minutes. That means that customers perform 28 billion minutes of unpaid work that would otherwise have required banks to hire more than 200,000 additional full-time tellers.

This, however, doesn't mean that 28 billion minutes of customer time have been saved. The average ATM transaction still takes a few minutes. Only now the customer punches keys, doing part of the work previously done by the paid teller, and frequently winds up paying an extra fee for the privilege. Ironically, according to banking-industry experts, keeping customers active—punching keys or whatever—gives them the illusion that they have waited less time.

The shift of work to prosumers is spreading. In 2002, 17 million U.S. households made their stock-market trades online and nearly 40 million customers booked their travel via the Web. In all, nearly 360 million online purchases were made in the United States. In each of these transactions, prosumers acted as their own stockbrokers, travel agents and sales clerks, as companies externalized their labor costs.

General Electric, like other home-appliance manufacturers, was bombarded by calls from customers requesting information about GE appliances. Because at one point it cost the company an estimated $5 to answer a phone request and only twenty cents if the customer went online to get the information, the company looked forward to cutting $96 million in expenses—much of which, we might assume, would be reflected in a shrunken workforce. Where, then, do these jobs go?

The answer: To the same place the tellers' jobs go—from paid producers to unpaid prosumers.

Across the board, canny companies everywhere are discovering more clever ways to externalize labor. The award for business innovation along this line may go not to some giant, greedy American corporation but to the Dohton Bori restaurant chain in Japan. Dohton Bori took the serve-yourself buffet-table concept a long leap forward by having its customers do their own cooking on a hot plate on their table.

It's true that some of these changes offer new services and are actively welcomed by customers. And it is theoretically true that perfect competition should drive down the price of such services, thus indirectly repaying customers for their work. Someday part of the savings from the externalization of labor may, indeed, be passed on to the customer. Right now, however, competition is anything but perfect and customers are providing yet another free lunch that companies are eating. More externalized labor is heading our way. Shifting work from producer to prosumer is the next great frontier of outsourcing.

THE SUPERMARKET SHOVE

Shoving work onto the customer is not new. At one time, groceries were kept behind the counter and clerks retrieved them as requested. Self-serve supermarkets were invented in 1916, when Clarence Saunders figured out that he could get customers to work for him and patented the system.

New technologies make further externalization profitable. If Saunders had returned some years ago, he would not have recognized the optical scanners at the checkout counter. But these still required a cashier. Today in the United States and elsewhere some supermarket chains give customers a handheld gadget that scans each can or box they choose and charges it to their credit card. Look, Ma, no clerk.

Big supermarket chains now also offer *self-scan* checkout machines designed to reduce the time customers have to wait in line to pay—and the number of clerks and baggers on the payroll. Of course, protests Donald L. Potter, a Los Angeles advertising man, "the store offers no discount to shoppers who are taking over the job of an employee." One online critic suggests that supermarkets should have "full- and self-service prices like the gas station. It would incentivize me to use the self check-out more often."

What is new these days is the cyberstructure that makes it possible to convert consumers into prosumers across an astonishingly broad range of activities. With it, all kinds of companies are discovering the delicious potentials of the free-lunch economy.

Among all the e-commerce corpses left behind by the turn-of-the-century crash, one big survivor stood out—a firm whose business model took maximum advantage of unpaid prosumer input. Thus Amazon.com's customers feed free content to its site in the form of book and music reviews, personal opinions, lists of favorite books and the like.

But when it comes to reducing expenses by saddling someone else with unpaid work, the prize for chutzpa must surely go to tax agencies that off-load complex record keeping and calculation onto the taxee, who performs unpaid labor for the privilege of paying.

In sum, when we add a third (unpaid) job to our paid work and our prosuming, it's no wonder we're time-frazzled. We are reallocating our time between producing, consuming and prosuming—another transformatory shift in our relationship to time itself.

And when we add competitive pressures in the money economy to demographic forces like aging, the advance and spread of knowledge, and the high-speed expansion of technologies available for prosuming, there are plenty of reasons to expect prosuming to explode.

The drive to externalize labor by increasing prosuming is so strong that a recent *Dilbert* cartoon shows an executive boasting that "over time, with luck, we'll train our customers to do our manufacturing and shipping, too." As we'll see in chapters to come, he might just be right.

CHAPTER 26

THE COMING
PROSUMER EXPLOSION

T he coming prosumer explosion is underestimated not only in the media that cover business and finance but in academia and government as well. Prosumers aren't going to run the world. But they are going to shape the emerging economy. And they're going to challenge the existence of some of the world's biggest companies and industries. In fact, they're already doing so.

We've just seen the free lunch their third job provides to banks, airlines and countless other industries. And we've seen the growing economic value they contribute to the health system. But the prosumer story is just beginning.

GUITARS AND GOLF BAGS

If prosumers today are buying up tools and technologies to increase their "output" of health, they are doing the same in other fields as well. As of 2005, Home Depot had more than eighteen hundred stores in the United States, Canada and Mexico. As the biggest home-improvement retailer in the United States, it employs 300,000 people and racks up about $73 billion in annual sales. Its stores stock up to forty thousand items, mainly for the do-it-yourselfer.

Overall, the do-it-yourself market (D-I-Y) for home improvement in the United States is estimated to run about $200 billion annually. The comparable estimate for Japan, where houses are much smaller and more sparsely furnished, exceeds $30 billion. In Germany, D-I-Y companies, led by Obi, Praktiker and Bauhaus, ring up $33 billion. In 2003, Europe's home-improvement market was estimated at $100 billion a year.

All this activity is spurred by a rapidly growing audience for home-improvement programs on television. In Britain, shows such as *Changing Rooms* and *Ground Force,* which offer hands-on, how-to advice to D-I-Yers, were among the most watched shows on the BBC. And the HGTV and DIY Network channels are seen in more than 80 million U.S. homes and twenty-nine countries from Japan, Australia and Thailand to the Czech Republic and Hungary.

If that isn't enough advice, prosumers can go online to RepairClinic.com, which sells replacement parts for appliances, or to its "RepairGuru" for how-to instructions. A competitor, Point and Click Appliance Repair, offers professional online diagnosis of your problems with everything from freezers and refrigerators to ovens and microwaves. The Sears Web page provides D-I-Yers with access to "over 4.5 million parts for your appliances, lawn equipment, power tools, and home electronics."

Prosumers buy supplies from these companies, then apply their own sweat equity—that is, unpaid labor—to create economic value whether by adding a room to the house, extending the life of a washing machine or beautifying a property.

A parallel investment of unpaid labor can be found in do-it-yourself auto repair, as a visit to any big auto-parts store suggests. According to the Automotive Aftermarket Industry Association, D-I-Y sales in the United States have reached nearly $37 billion a year.

Moreover, "nearly 80 percent of U.S. households participated in some kind of do-it-yourself lawn and garden activity in 2002," according to the National Gardening Association, which estimated total spending at nearly $40 billion. In much smaller England, "gardening-mad Britons," as *Time* magazine calls them, spend up to $5 billion. German green-thumbers spend $7 billion. In Japan, where prosumers manage to create greenery in even the smallest crevices between buildings, a third of the population, some 40 million people, garden, spending about $15 billion a year on tools, plants and nutrients.

And you don't have to like getting your fingernails dirty to buy prosumer supplies. Sewing remains more than just a hobby for 30 million U.S. women, mostly college-educated and young—nearly one-third of America's adult female population. What's more, after you make that dress, you can keep it spotless by using a home dry-cleaning kit as advertised in the upscale catalogs that fill the mailbox to overflowing.

For those who want a real challenge, do-it-yourself kits are now available that allow prosumers to build everything from electric guitars and computers to golf clubs, sailboats, four-bedroom log cabins and even airplanes good enough to compete in flying shows.

RAMPANT CONSUMERISM?

Conventional economics looks at purchases like these as consumption. But there is a completely different way of thinking about them. What they really represent is a large-scale investment in capital goods that increase the still largely unmeasured value of their prosumer output.

Today, in advanced economies, an inventory of capital goods found in an ordinary worker's home might include a washer, dryer, dishwasher, microwave, refrigerator, gas or electric range, air conditioner, toaster, coffeemaker and possibly a blender or juicer, plus tools for making simple repairs, extra electrical extensions for new wiring and the like.

To which we must now add computers, videocams, PDAs and a vast array of other digital tools that enable D-I-Yers to invest in the stock market, buy a home, trace a long-lost relative or make customized greeting cards. In the words of *Time,* digital tools make it possible "for anyone with minimal geek skills . . . to make his own movies, TV shows, albums, books and even radio programs. . . . It has suddenly become cheap to create your own entertainment. . . . It's the do-it-yourself dream. . . . And this digital-entertainment thing is only getting bigger and bigger."

Critics of "rampant consumerism" who deride the purchase of such items (although their own homes are likely to include many of them) fail to grasp their significance. These are not material expressions of greed but rather investments in prosumer power—the ability to do more for oneself and one's family, while in fact *withdrawing,* at least partially, from the marketplace. In that sense, they are the opposite of consumerism. They allow us to accomplish many tasks outside the marketplace that we would otherwise have to pay others to perform, and to do things that are, in fact, unpurchasable.

If the money spent on all this do-it-yourself technology—in home improvement, auto repair, gardening, computing and digital creation—were aggregated rather than toted up piecemeal, we would find an enormous sum that, at least in part, represents not consumption but investment—the capital investment prosumers make to add value to the wealth system.

And if we now add up the hours spent using all these tools, kits and supplies, and hypothetically assign to each of our unpaid hours some minimal hourly wage—we arrive at even larger totals that might well stagger the statisticians—and our conventional assumptions about how wealth systems operate.

The boundary between paid and unpaid work, between measured value turned out by producers and the mostly unmeasured value turned out by prosumers, is a misleading definitional fiction. On one side we have the money economy, on the other the non-money economy. But it takes both to make a contemporary wealth system—and it is the wealth system as a whole that needs to be understood by anyone planning for the future.

COOKIES AND SIMULATIONS

Prosumers move back and forth across this fictional line as though it weren't there. Thousands of small businesses around the world actually originate when prosuming hobbyists begin to sell what they have previously made only for themselves or for their friends and neighbors.

When Don Davidson of Wilton, Connecticut, was in his mid-fifties, he began thinking about what to do after he turned sixty and retired from his job as associate publisher of *Ladies' Home Journal* and *Woman's Day*. He had always maintained a well-equipped workshop and spent weekends doing woodwork. So it was natural to think of turning his woodworking skills into a part-time post-retirement business.

The only thing wrong with the plan was that the business grew into a successful full-time family enterprise, employing his two grandsons as well.

Across the country in Plano, Texas, Neil Planick raced slot cars as a hobby. With help from the city's small-business development center, his hobby morphed into Neil's Wheels Model Car Speedway.

What we see here are prosumers developing and testing skills and interests that, after a time, are converted into marketed goods and small businesses—another input of value into the money economy.

Prosumer-initiated companies aren't always quite so small and specialized. Consider the Hollywood agent—a high school dropout—who grew up, became a theatrical agent and wound up in the 1960s discovering Simon and Garfunkel and representing them and other top musical stars like Diana Ross and Marvin Gaye.

Inspired by his Aunt Della, he began baking as a hobby, handing out cookies to friends and family. "It reached a point," he says, "where people wouldn't say 'hello' when they saw me. They'd say, 'Where are my cookies?'"

"Everybody told me I should go into the cookie business," he recalls, "but I didn't take it seriously at the time."

When he finally did take the idea of a business seriously, Wally Amos launched Famous Amos chocolate chip cookies, now one of the best-known brands in the United States and a pioneering force in the gourmet-cookie business. And even that is "small potatoes."

DWARFING HOLLYWOOD

Prosumers have not only turned hobbies into businesses. They have also launched or helped launch entire industries. Twenty-five years ago, sophisticated computer games and simulations were primarily made and used by the military. According to J. C. Herz and Michael R. Macedonia, writing in *Defense Horizons,* they "evolved in a focused, formal, hierarchical environment as contractors built specific, costly applications on powerful workstations." By contrast, commercially available computer games at the time "were fly-by-night affairs—floppy disks in Ziploc bags, peddled by enthusiasts."

But, as the article explains, civilian gamers employing small, cheap computers rather than military supercomputers soon formed online communities and began collectively modifying, adapting and improving the commercial games, many devoted to military strategy. By the end of the 1990s, we learn, "nearly every strategy and combat game on the market came with a built-in level editor and tools to create custom characters or scenarios."

In short, the commercial games encouraged prosumers to customize, complexify and enrich them. The result today: "In terms of innovation, the commercial game industry remains leagues ahead [of the military] because of . . . the player base, a highly motivated, globally networked, self-organizing population of millions, all striving to outdo one another."

Prosumer innovation in the non-money economy thus helped spawn today's $20 billion computer gaming industry—an industry bigger, it might surprise many to learn, than Hollywood's movie business.

COLLECTIVE PROSUMING

No act of contemporary prosuming, however, has had as explosive an effect on business and international relations as the pet project of a twenty-one-year-old college student that has shaken the software industry—and some would say world capitalism itself.

While studying at Helsinki University, Linus Torvalds worked with Minix, an offshoot of the UNIX operating system used in giant computers. Dissatisfied with it, he set out to build a new version for PCs. After working on this for three years as a pet project without pay, he succeeded in 1994 in releasing the core of what is now the Linux operating system.

Linux has been called "free-to-share" software because, unlike proprietary products from Microsoft and other companies, it uses an underlying source code that is public and free. This makes it possible for others to adapt Linux to their own needs or to base new commercial products on it, so long as access to the source code remains open.

The Linux operating system today is supported by many computer manufacturers and is used by millions around the world. According to *The New York Times,* "it is being used in about 40 percent of American companies."

But Linux's impact goes far beyond that of U.S. business. As of 2005, governments around the world, eager to save money and develop their own software industries, have promoted the use of Linux. In China, Linux is the operating system in the state postal bureau, the Ministry of Foreign Trade and China Central Television, and the government is strongly pushing public officials at all levels to adopt it. The Brazilian government has directed its agencies to shift to Linux or other open-source software. India has installed Linux at its central bank and local Treasury departments. According to United Press International, "Governments worldwide have invested more than $2 billion in Linux" and "more than 160 different governments worldwide use Linux programs."

The Linux bandwagon has leaped beyond individual nations and companies to the regional level. Thus officials from China, Japan and South Korea have met recently to discuss using Linux under a common information-technology policy.

Nor does the enthusiasm for Linux end there. At a U.N. conference on I.T., major nations urged delegates to endorse open-source software as a key to reducing the digital divide.

All this originated from the unpaid work of Torvalds and a large, spatially dispersed network of prosumer-programmers, connected through the Internet and freely volunteering their time and effort to enhance the product collectively.

What Torvalds and the Linux programmers did, therefore, has had powerful effects within the money economy. Linux does not mean the end of capitalism as some of its enthusiasts have suggested. But it shows, once more, how strongly prosumer activity can impact the money economy.

And even Linux is only a fraction of a still-larger story.

BUSTING THE HIERARCHIES

If knowledge is one of the deep fundamentals on which revolutionary wealth increasingly depends, then how we access and organize knowledge relates directly to growth in the money economy. Today it has become almost impossible to think of the world without the Internet and the Internet without the World Wide Web—two of the most powerful knowledge tools ever invented.

The Web—that ubiquitous "www"—combines the Internet with the ability to cross-connect data, information and knowledge of every kind in new ways. It is hard to remember what things were like in 1980, when a young software engineer at CERN, the Center for European Nuclear Research in Geneva, began thinking about how to access disparate, non-hierarchical bits and pieces of knowledge and link them together.

Often called the father of the World Wide Web, Tim Berners-Lee, in his book *Weaving the Web,* recalls his days at CERN: "I wrote Enquire, my first web-like program . . . in my spare time and for my personal use, and for no loftier reason than to help me remember the connections among the various people, computers and projects at the lab." In short, the Web itself was a result of prosumption.

The result was a knowledge tool that transformed not only the way our culture thinks and young people learn but, increasingly, the way money is made, business is done, economies operate and wealth is created.

Further, if the examples of Torvalds and Berners-Lee are not enough, what should one make of the Internet itself and the three billion sites on the Web— a significant share of which are the product of prosuming? Tens, if not hundreds, of thousands of prosuming professors and students, often on their own time, are pouring out their brains, filling the net with academic papers and research on every conceivable topic from medieval history to mathematics.

Using the Internet—which revolutionizes our relationships to the deep fundamentals of space and knowledge—scientists, again often on unpaid time, commune to debate the latest findings in every field from proteomics to plastics. Metallurgists and managers, magazine writers and military experts dig through the billions of pages of information on the net and freely add to them. And hundreds of thousands of "do-it-yourself journalists" report or comment on the news of the day in their online Web logs, or blogs.

Assume we ruthlessly subtract, say, 95 percent of all these Net and Web sites as baldly commercial or else irrelevant, silly, inaccurate or of interest to only a few. We are still left with 150 million sites with content that can be searched, connected and juxtaposed in countless patterns to produce fresh, imaginative ways of thinking about almost every aspect of wealth creation and life.

This ever-expanding Internet content results in part from one of the biggest volunteer projects in human history. Prosumers, through their contributions to its structure and content, accelerate innovation in the visible marketplace. They are partly responsible for changes in how, when and where we work, how companies are linked to customers and suppliers and just about every other aspect of the visible economy.

Economists may continue to argue over the Net and/or Web's contribution to what they regard as "growth." They may persist in ignoring growth created by prosumers. But they will not begin to understand its relevance so long as they ignore the fascinating, complex interplay between the visible and hidden economies—whether in the form of parenting, improving health, engaging in do-it-yourself endeavors, creating new businesses, identifying new needs, foreshadowing new products, writing free software or helping to access and organize vast volumes of knowledge for the knowledge economy.

It is when we put the two together—the money economy and its non-money counterpart—that we form what we call the wealth-creation system. And once we do, a new fact becomes clear: The money system is going to expand dramatically. But what we do *without* money will have a bigger and bigger impact on what we do with money. Prosumers are the unsung heroes of the economy to come.

CHAPTER 27

MORE "FREE LUNCH"

W hen Rosalyn Bettiford, a forty-seven-year-old editor, arrived at her weekend house in Washington, Connecticut—a two-hour drive from Manhattan—the July night had turned chilly. Her teenage son was asleep in his bedroom. The living room was dark. As her eyes adjusted, she noticed that one of the big sliding-glass windows was wide open. She reached for its handle and—as the heavy window suddenly slipped out of its track—she plunged, screaming, glass and all, to a flagstone terrace twelve feet below.

In that fall, Rosalyn (her name has been changed here for privacy reasons, but the story is true) fractured her skull, cracked a number of vertebrae, broke an arm and smashed all her toes. Her terrified son found her moaning and semi-conscious, with colorless fluid seeping out of her ears.

The young men who arrived only minutes later quickly splinted her arm and drove her madly over country roads to the nearest hospital. They saved her life and vanished quietly into the night when doctors came to her side. The next day they turned up at her bedside in the hospital to see how she was doing. They were volunteers at the local firehouse. Rosalyn and her family did not need the horrors of 9/11 to remind them of the range of emergency services volunteer firefighters provide—and not just in the United States.

Japan in 2001 counted 951,069 men as members of *shobodan*—local volunteer firefighter associations. Similar groups exist in Austria, Canada, Finland, Germany, Italy, Portugal, South Africa and other countries. Their members risk—and all too often lose—their lives.

In economic terms, volunteers are prosumers, delivering valuable services without remuneration for their time, skills and risks.

The scale of volunteer work in the United States, is huge, with something like 110 million people devoting at least a few hours a week to unpaid volunteer work. A 2001 report of Independent Sector, an association of donors and nonprofits, estimated that in the previous year Americans totaled 15.5 billion hours of volunteer work, whether serving food, caring for the sick, fund-raising, running errands for others or filling posts in churches and other non-governmental organizations. The report estimated the aggregate money value of these unpaid efforts at some $239 billion—additional "free lunch" for the visible economy.

In 2005 hurricanes Katrina and Rita devastated America's Gulf Coast, destroying hundreds of thousands of homes and jobs, and led to an almost total breakdown of government emergency aid efforts. By contrast, volunteers all over the South opened their homes and offered food, medical care and other necessities to the stricken population.

In Japan, domestic emergency services were seriously underdeveloped until the Great Hanshin Earthquake struck the Kobe area on January 17, 1995. That catastrophe galvanized the nation, and 1.35 million volunteers rushed to help with construction, medical care, food and water supplies and counseling services. What was the monetary equivalent of their services to the Japanese economy? Was any of it counted as part of Japan's GDP? More important, what is its human value?

In South Korea, an estimated 6.5 million residents serve as volunteers. They provide relief after typhoon flooding. They help build homes for Habitat for Humanity. They teach refugees from North Korea how to adapt to life in the south.

In Italy, volunteers help care for cancer patients and work in hospices. And when unprecedented floods struck Germany in 2002, tens of thousands of volunteers traveled cross-country to battle the rising waters.

All these activities are part of the hidden half—the largely off-the-books part—of each country's wealth system. If their full value were properly calculated, it would change many of the decisions now made by business leaders and politicians.

TEACHERS, NURSES AND HORSES

When economies were local and decentralized, prosuming, too, remained a strictly local phenomenon. With the rise of national markets and the nation-state, helping hands reached beyond the village or neighborhood. Recently, as economies have globalized or re-globalized, many volunteer organizations have gone global as well—expanding their definition of community to embrace the entire human race and extending their operations accordingly in every field.

Examples of international volunteering abound. In 1989, after the San Francisco earthquake, the Japan Emergency Team flew student volunteers across the Pacific to help the victims. When thousands of horses were left to starve in Zimbabwe in 2002 as farmers were ordered off the land, volunteers from as far away as Scotland, Switzerland and South Africa rushed in to rescue the emaciated animals.

On a far larger scale, the Red Cross and Red Crescent operate worldwide. They claim 105 million volunteers in 178 countries and, like other global NGOs, send doctors, nurses, teachers, agronomists and other specialists all over the planet to perform professional services. Almost invariably, these volunteers are aided by local "amateurs" who pitch in during crises or emergencies.

Nothing compared with the outpouring of volunteer aid after the great tsunami of December 2004. Governments and organizations publicly pledged huge amounts of emergency aid money—much of which took a long time to materialize, if it ever did. By contrast, volunteers quickly came from everywhere. The government of Australia closed down an overloaded hotline for volunteers after ten thousand calls "exceeded all expectations." Aid organizations around the world found themselves so flooded with volunteers they had to turn them away. Amateur radio operators, pilots, nurses, teachers, construction workers and truck drivers freely applied their skills to the common good.

Here we saw invisible wealth, over and above monetary contributions, being transferred from one country to another, from one end of the earth to another.

AMATEURS MATTER

In today's highly professionalized world, the term *amateur* invites a brush-off from business executives and economists. Yet throughout history, unpaid amateurs, working for themselves, their families or their communities, have made remarkable achievements in a wide variety of fields, including science and technology.

Because science had not yet become a paying profession, early scientists were almost all amateurs. Many gained a living as paid professionals in one field but made their greatest contributions to history as part-time prosumers. Joseph Priestley, who in 1774 discovered oxygen, was a minister. Pierre de Fermat, whose "last theorem" puzzled mathematicians for centuries, was a lawyer. And Benjamin Franklin, paid as a printer, media mogul and politician, studied ocean currents on the side, inventing bifocals along the way and demonstrating that lightning was a form of electricity. He, too, was a prosumer.

Today prosuming amateurs are collecting huge amounts of valuable environmental information—for example, seismological data in the Philippines.

But it is in astronomy and space that, often in collaboration with profession-als, amateurs are making really important finds. They started early.

When the world's first artificial satellite, *Sputnik,* blasted into orbit in 1957, amateurs all over the globe who had been organized by astronomer Fred Whipple, director of the Smithsonian Astrophysical Observatory, were wait-ing to track it across the heavens. Their effort was dubbed Moonwatch. In his book *Trackers of the Skies,* E. Nelson Hayes writes, "Moonwatch demon-strated what amateurs could do when properly inspired and led." Today ama-teur astronomers are, among other things, charting asteroids and other potentially dangerous objects in space.

Brigadier General Simon "Pete" Worden, a former astronaut, not long ago told the U.S. House Committee on Science that small objects "at the nuclear weapons scale" smash into Earth's upper atmosphere at a rate of once about every two weeks. In June 2002 one such event occurred over the Mediter-ranean and released twenty to thirty kilotons of energy—more than that of the Hiroshima blast.

"Had this occurred over India or Pakistan," Worden suggested, "it could have triggered a nuclear war." Urging more attention to such low-probability, but potentially devastating, dangers, he paid tribute to amateur monitors, pointing out that "some of them are not so amateur."

According to Richard Nugent, himself an amateur asteroid hunter and a contributor to *Starscan,* a newsletter of the Johnson Space Center Astronomi-cal Society, "Amateurs are catching up with the pros in certain fields, and sur-passing them in others [such as] asteroid discoveries, novae, supernovae, variable stars, occultation events, fireballs, meteors, planetary observations, satellite passes, and other unique events."

As research tools become smaller, cheaper, smarter and more powerful, making possible further changes in our relationships to the deep fundamental of knowledge, amateurs will no doubt enter new fields. And this takes us to another overlooked contribution made by prosumers.

UNCOOKING THE BOOKS

Every single day around the world, countless volunteers get behind the wheel of their cars and drive to schools, churches, mosques, synagogues, hospitals, playgrounds or community centers to provide free services. Or they add to their odometers by picking up groceries for neighbors or taking a sick relative to a doctor. Nobody knows how many millions of miles they drive in aggre-gate over the course of a year, or how much gas they use, or how much wear and tear they add to their autos in the course of creating unpaid value.

In addition, therefore, to delivering free lunch to the money economy by donating their unpaid time and labor, they are also contributing what amounts to a prosumer capital asset—the use of a vehicle—that makes possible or increases the value they create for others. That's more free lunch. (It is true that, in the United States, if they go to the trouble, they may be able to reclaim some small part of their expenses as a tax deduction, but it's doubtful that in practice most volunteers do.)

Car use, however, is not the only example of prosumer capital at work. As we've already seen, prosumers, as a group, spend large sums buying machines and tools—or, more accurately, investing in capital goods for use in prosuming. These tools range from telescopes, sewing machines and digital cholesterol testers all the way up to automobiles and other vehicles. And, in a new, fast-spreading practice, another pattern is emerging: Busy prosumers now sometimes volunteer their machines, instead of their labor. Only by taking account of practices like these can we uncook the economic books.

DOWN TO EARTH

The best-known case is that of SETI, the Search for Extraterrestrial Intelligence. While the likelihood of our discovering life elsewhere, let alone "intelligent" life, may be minute, the scientific, philosophical and cultural implications of such a finding can hardly be overestimated. So volunteers have stepped forward to help.

The search required the collection of huge quantities of radio telescope data. But analyzing it required far more supercomputer power than any individual machine at that time could provide. That led two Seattle computer scientists, Craig Kasnoff and David Gedye, to ask whether, if they couldn't gain access to supercomputers, they could create a virtual supercomputer to do the job.

They could build one, they believed, if they could get PC users linked via the Internet to allow free access to their computers and permit the SETI searchers to use the machines when these were otherwise idle.

Optimistically, Kasnoff and Gedye hoped they might link up a few hundred thousand machines. By spring of 2002, more than 3.5 million PC owners had contributed more than a million years of processing time to the SETI venture. The result is a project headquartered at the University of California/ Berkeley, which sends out six hundred thousand packets of data daily for processing on these privately owned computers. According to the Planetary Society, "The sheer power of millions of computers worldwide has made SETI@home the most sensitive deep-sky survey ever done."

ATTACKING ANTHRAX

The SETI model has since been replicated elsewhere. Oxford University scientists and others have turned to Internet users around the world for help in researching smallpox, cancer, AIDS, climate change and other significant problems.

When envelopes bearing anthrax turned up on Capitol Hill in Washington and other sites after the 9/11 terror attacks, they touched off a national panic. In rapid response, three companies—Microsoft, Intel and United Devices—plus Oxford University and the National Foundation for Cancer Research, launched a joint project to search for molecules that could block the deadly action of anthrax. In twenty-four days they screened 3.5 billion different compounds. That helped scientists eliminate as irrelevant all but 300,000 compounds, among which they identified 12,000 priority targets. The project also uncovered a number of potentially useful compounds that conventional methods would have, in all likelihood, overlooked.

Even with the backing of such giants as Microsoft and Intel, this breakthrough would have been impossible without the contribution of prosumer/volunteers. The anthrax research partly piggybacked on the machines already recruited for cancer research and added some more. In all, more than 1.35 million people, from Mexico and China to Equatorial Guinea and Azerbaijan, participated. In the United States more than 100,000 machines were volunteered; in Germany, 14,000; in France, 4,400; and in South Korea, 1,593. There were even four in Afghanistan—which, considering the hunt for Al Qaeda's bioweapons, presumably raised some eyebrows.

The computer innovations exploited by SETI, anthrax and cancer researchers have since exploded into what has come to be called grid or distributed computing. Imitating the prosumer projects, hundreds of big companies have created their own internal grids to take advantage of the unused capacity of their own networked machines.

What we see here is yet another form of free lunch delivered to the money economy by a prosumer project—in this case early testing of a powerful innovation—that has turned into a multibillion-dollar market in the money economy. Again we see that the wall separating the commercial world from the prosumer world is nonexistent.

We see evidence, too, that business and government decision-makers need to understand and take far smarter advantage of the free-lunch phenomenon. Underscoring that statement is the likelihood that prosuming, already far larger than most suspect, is about to become bigger than ever, propelled by mutually reinforcing changes in social, cultural and demographic factors that, in turn, will promote an explosion of new prosumer technologies. Thus, along with a "graying" of the population in the United States has come a different kind of retiree.

Like so many other boundaries, the line between work and retirement is also blurring, with many more senior citizens falling into a semi-retired category and using unpaid time to volunteer and engage in other prosumer activities. According to AARP, the organization of Americans over fifty, this age group forms the backbone of volunteerism in the United States. It forecasts that volunteering will increase as populations live longer and healthier and refuse to live in idleness. The same pattern is evident in Japan.

Similarly, the continuing acceleration of change points to relatively high levels of frictional unemployment—temporary joblessness as people change jobs, switch careers or move to new locations. Today "frictional volunteers" working free for nonprofit organizations include people with a wide range of specialized skills—lawyers, accountants, marketing experts, Web designers and the like.

Beyond all this, the Internet will bring into being temporary groupings of all kinds for as-yet-unheard-of prosumer activities—and with them, very often, temporary new markets—including markets for new technologies. These technologies, in turn, will further diversify and empower prosumers.

This self-feeding process has just begun. As it gains force, it will compel us to recognize the hidden half of the emerging revolutionary wealth system—and the serious risks and fantastic opportunities that come with it.

If you are still in doubt, listen next to the sound of music.

CHAPTER 28

THE MUSIC STORM

In 1970, the heyday of druggy, long-haired hippiedom in the United States, a treatise by Abbie Hoffman called *Steal This Book* appeared in many bookstores—though some outraged owners refused to carry it. The message of its title, that property or ownership was inherently evil, was itself a rip-off of nineteenth-century anarchist rhetoric. But it found an enthusiastic audience.

So enthusiastic that one morning when our recently released book *Future Shock* was displayed up front in the Eighth Street Bookshop in Greenwich Village, a famous literary site at the time, we witnessed a young customer take a copy off the shelf, show it to the equally young clerk behind the counter and ask its price.

"$8.95," replied the clerk.

The customer, crestfallen, put the book back and said he didn't have enough money.

To which the clerk cheerfully replied, "Oh, there's another bookstore down the block, why don't you go there and steal a copy." It would have cheered Hoffman's heart.

But that was in the Paleolithic era of intellectual-property theft. If Hoffman were alive today, his title would no doubt be *Steal This Book and Distribute It Free over the Internet to 80,000,000 People.*

A worldwide controversy is raging over the future of intellectual property. While it may seem like an abstract side issue to those faced with earning a steady paycheck and trying to prepare our children for tomorrow, billions upon billions of dollars are already at stake, along with the fate of many of our jobs and our most important industries. We'll explore these issues in more depth shortly.

What is more important here, however, is to recognize the crucial role that prosumers and prosuming will play in this global battle. Once we understand that, an amazing vision of tomorrow's wealth creation comes into focus.

ESTONIAN GEEKS

When a music-loving, bullet-headed eighteen-year-old with a baseball cap began tinkering with a new computer program, neither he nor anyone else anticipated the hurricane he would unleash.

For those who are wearing earplugs or who may have slept through the first years of the twenty-first century, Napster—the company founded by that eighteen-year-old—offered software that made it possible for an estimated eighty million kids to freely swap copyrighted songs by their favorite bands. The teenager who launched it all was Shawn Fanning, who was soon deified and demonized on front pages worldwide.

What he had done was make available a powerful new technology that shifted "for-sale" products out of the money economy and into the non-money economy—the prosumer half of the wealth system.

In no time, fans were making nearly 2.8 billion highly compressed downloads of music a month, free of charge, as a result of dipping into one another's computers and transferring the songs they liked to their own machines, and then very often changing as well as just exchanging them.

In the words of David Benveniste, a prominent music-group manager, "The kids are so smart these days, they can find, retrieve, disseminate, produce any piece of music or technology now on the Internet. They can take a song, send it to a friend in North Africa, remix it how they want, make their own video for it and make it their own. . . . All that technology makes them so powerful." And they can do it all in no time.

Napster, as we now know, was ultimately sued by the music industry, shut down by a U.S. federal court and resurrected as a for-pay service—that is, shoved back into the money economy. But the battle over free file sharing was not over. Napster was only the first warning shot. And the storm it released was not just musical.

Before long, Kazaa, created by two Scandanavians and a team of Estonian geeks (in Estonia, not Silicon Valley) picked up where Napster left off. Kazaa disseminated a file-sharing program that wound up on an estimated 315 million PCs, allowing their users to freely exchange not only music but movies, porn and much more. Next, from the same group of young programmers came Skype, a program that makes possible no-cost telephone calls from one PC to another.

As Michael Powell, former chairman of the U.S. Federal Communications Commission, told *Fortune,* this and other applications of Voice over Internet Protocol (VoIP) mean nothing less than doom for the existing telecom industry.

Convergent changes in the deep fundamentals—time speeded up, space now global and techie knowledge instantly empowering even the young—have led to what some have called "weapons of market destruction." And these developments are only precursors to other ingenious ways by which goods and services will move out of the pay-for marketplace.

These cases, if nothing else, show that it is now possible for a tiny company or a Linux-like informal group of programmers with a smidgen of creative software to transfer significant volumes of activity from the money economy to the non-money or prosumer economy. And vice versa. Legally or not.

Napster, in effect, "de-marketized"—or attempted to de-marketize—music, but in many cases the exact reverse occurs. As we saw earlier in the Famous Amos cookie example, people create products by prosuming—and then decide to marketize them. Or more generally, they convert prosumer value into money value.

If, as we've seen, excess computing power is valuable and can be donated to SETI or cancer researchers and other worthy causes, why can't it also be marketized—that is, sold through a broker to some corporation that temporarily needs a virtual supercomputer? The same technologies can sometimes help us to either marketize or de-marketize at will.

PROSUMER POWER

From here the implications explode outward and we ask: If computer power can, at least in principle, be sold back by customers, why not power in the sense of energy?

Today a trickle of excess energy from wind power already flows from the homes of customers and is sold to local utility companies. According to the U.S. Department of Energy, under the Public Utilities Regulatory Policy Act of 1978, electric-power utilities must buy this excess power from home owners whose wind generators meet certain requirements.

While the actual amount of energy flowing may be small, it illustrates again the complexity and reversibility of roles. Take a hypothetical case in which Tracy and Bill Parker, being good environmentalists, buy a windmill for their home. The firm selling it to them no doubt regards them as customers or consumers. But their purchase is actually a capital investment.

To the degree that the Parkers generate their own energy and use it, they are energy prosumers. Since they do not pay themselves, money doesn't change hands and, apart from the purchase of the equipment itself, there is no transaction for economists to track. The value the Parkers create is part of the hidden economy.

If, however, they sell the output (or part of it) to the local power company, they are not only prosumers but also energy producers. And they trigger a monetary transaction, which then gets tracked and added to the GDP statistics.

Now imagine advanced technologies of the future in the hands of millions of families who use them both to prosume and to produce. What might make that happen? Cheaper, more powerful solar units could. But if many energy experts are correct, the next great advance will be excess energy flowing back to the utilities from cars and homes powered by fuel-cell technology. The big auto firms have already invested two billion dollars in fuel-cell research and development.

Energy visionaries (in the positive sense) Amory and Hunter Lovins of the Rocky Mountain Institute have long pictured a "soft-energy" economy. According to Amory Lovins, "Once you put a fuel cell in an ultralight car, then you have a 20–25 kilowatt power station on wheels, which is driven 4 percent of the time and parked 96 percent of the time. So why not lease those fuel cell cars to people who work in buildings?"

In this scenario, your car, while parked, is plugged in to the building. The car generates electricity, which you sell back to the grid at a time of peak power demand. Eventually, the conversion from gas-guzzling heavy cars to fuel-cell-driven lightweight cars could, Lovins says, add up to "five to six times" the generating capacity of the national grid.

Whatever form the specifics might take, they open at least the possibility of a highly decentralized energy system—with homes, factories, offices and other buildings networked together and exchanging energy, with less energy coming from huge, highly polluting centralized power plants.

This is not the place to explore the plausibility of this scenario or the impressive potential of fuel-cell technology. The point here is that interactions between the visible and hidden parts of the wealth system are multiplying and growing more complex. And some are even more far-reaching than the Lovinses' scenario suggests.

BABY PROSUMERS

What follows may sound ridiculous, and it is . . . today. But if, as prosumers, we can already make our own mix-and-match music and movies, greeting cards, digital photos and numerous other things, and if we can conceive of both producing and prosuming our own energy, why stop there?

That takes us to the scenario conjured up not merely by Hollywood science-fiction writers but by executives of 3D Systems of Valencia, California, whose founder, Charles Hull, invented something called stereolithography in 1984. It goes by various names, from rapid prototyping and 3D printing to solid imaging, desktop manufacturing, holoforming, hyperduplication and fabbing. The field is still embryonic and has not yet settled on its own jargon. But that hasn't stopped its early innovations from being put to practical use.

Fabbers are based on the assumption that manufacturing largely consists of twisting or bending things, joining things or cutting, slicing, sanding or otherwise separating pieces of material from one another. Users make a three-dimensional digital model of the desired product, then program tools to add, subtract or join material, rather like a printer adding ink or skipping a spot.

When engineers for Penske Racing needed prototype engine parts for cars to be driven by Ryan Newman and Rusty Wallace in the Winston Cup series, they turned to Hull's company to make them quickly—faster than possible by traditional model-makers.

These technologies have been used elsewhere to prototype everything from zippers to lightbulbs and heart valves, drainpipes to dinnerware and dentures. They have been employed by architects, sculptors, Hollywood prop makers, dental labs and an array of the world's biggest companies—including Airbus and Boeing, Mattel and Motorola, Tupperware and Texas Instruments. In fact, according to *Discover* magazine, "Virtually every home in America now contains products prototyped by stereolithographic machines."

But prototyping is only a first step. If inkjet printers can spray ink on pre-designated points on paper, why not spray other substances according to computer-aided design programs? And do it in three dimensions? Why not build a desired shape by using a tiny laser to shave away layer after layer of unwanted material? Why not join components by squirting a bonding agent on their joints?

Clunky and expensive today, these technologies foreshadow smaller, cheaper, more versatile models fed from cartridges holding various powders or chemicals instead of ink. That would make it possible, in principle, for anyone to download instructions from the Net and turn on what amounts to a "desktop factory." Says Mervyn Rudgley of 3D Systems, "Your children's children will print their own toys." Baby prosumers of the future?

Nor, we are told, will desktop manufacture stop there. According to Marshall Burns and James Howison of the Los Angeles–based Ennex Corporation, desktop fabrication will "provide a whole new purpose for peer-to-peer exchanges" as users exchange files that can be used to turn out "toys, clothing, furniture, sports equipment, consumer electronics and even, one day, automobiles." Users of this fabrication technology will someday make "almost any product you can imagine (and maybe some you can't imagine)!"

"What if you could download instructions for making . . . a toaster that prints pictures on toast . . . as easily as you now download music files?" asked *Forbes* in 2005, suggesting that the price of your own private tabletop factory could soon drop to one thousand dollars.

Everyone in the field freely admits that these technologies are still primitive and have limited uses at present. But at MIT's famed Media Lab, Neil Gershenfeld regards the spread of the personal fabricator as "inevitable" and draws on the mainframe-computer analogy. In 1943 the chairman of IBM, Thomas Watson, declared that "there is a world market for maybe five computers." Gershenfeld points out that at that time computers, too, were "large machines . . . housed in specialized rooms . . . used by skilled operators . . . for fixed industrial operations . . . with a limited market." Today there are more than 800 million personal computers in use worldwide. Says Gershenfeld, the fabricator will proliferate because it is the "missing mate to the PC."

Burns and Howison point out that "hundreds of university, corporate, and government laboratories around the world" are working on fab tech today, and small numbers of users are already swapping home-fabricator files. No doubt chortling, they add: "If record companies had a fit over Napster, wait 'til manufacturers find out you can download Rolex.fab or Ferrari.fab and make them yourself."

Long before fabbers turn up in millions of homes, we can expect to see the same process of dispersal by which printing and developing film moved from centralized Kodak or Fuji film-processing factories to street-corner one-hour photo shops and, ultimately, by way of the digital camera, into the hands of the prosumer. An intermediate stage before actual home fabrication may be neighborhood workshops where do-it-yourselfers go to use machines the way they now go to Kinko's for copying.

LIPOSUCTION WITHOUT SURGERY

This step-by-step developmental process could make a giant nonlinear jump, however, by its convergence with advances in nanotechnology—the manipulation of matter at a molecular scale, so tiny it is measured in billionths of a meter. If we learn to do this well, the possibilities point to self-assembling products with endless potential applications.

Many of these are described in *Unbounding the Future* by K. Eric Drexler, founder of the Foresight Institute and the man who coined the term *nanotechnology*. Others are described and debated by scientists and science-fiction writers, technophiles and technophobes, medical researchers and business leaders.

They speak of everything from self-repairing teeth and self-cleaning dishes to computers a thousand times faster, more energy-efficient and cheaper than those based on silicon. The list includes clothes that automatically adjust their size, texture, fit and fashion; solar cells so tiny they can be painted onto a house or embedded in pavement; medical microrobots small enough to "roto-root" arteries and eliminate dangerous plaque; and materials with trillions of submicroscopic motors, computers, fibers and struts built into them. The day may come when we perform nonsurgical liposuction and reshape our bodies with nanotools.

Intercommunicating nano-sized sensors could provide military intelligence. Nanotech could also reduce manufacturing waste, generate energy and give us new materials "lighter than balsa but stronger than steel." But, like nuclear energy and genetic engineering, nanotechnology has also raised serious safety concerns, especially when the word *self-replication* is added to it.

This is not the place to discuss these issues. Our point here is that with or without nanotechnology, we face the possibility of a dramatically changed future economy, one that is far more decentralized, with millions of file-swapping people both prosuming goods for themselves and also producing goods for others. It suggests millions of small businesses built on advanced tools for custom production and prosumption—and a vast growth of high-tech artisans of the kind seen today in northern Italy.

Of course, all this remains speculative. Trends are moving in this direction, but trends get derailed, twisted, reversed or neutralized by countertrends.

What is nevertheless clear is that we are developing ever more dense and complicated interactions between the money and the non-money economy present in all three of the world's dominant wealth systems—those based on peasant agriculture, industrial mass production and advanced knowledge.

The history of the future will surprise us. As more and more of the world's poor are drawn into the money system, we are likely to see a relative decline in First Wave, poverty-based prosuming. But we will also experience a relative *increase* in Third Wave, high-tech prosuming based on the diffusion of ever more powerful and versatile new tools into the hands of ordinary individuals in the most advanced economies. The failure of most economists as yet to recognize this historic shift subverts their best efforts to understand revolutionary wealth and how it will affect us and our children.

CHAPTER 29

THE "PRODUCIVITY" HORMONE

Producivity (def.) *The contribution to productivity made by prosumers.*

One of the most extraordinary examples of prosumer power in modern history has literally changed how people around the world work, play, live and think. And almost no one has noticed it.

So far we have shown how prosumers feed free lunch to the money economy by creating wealth in the non-money economy. But prosumers sometimes do more than that. They pump growth hormone into the money economy so it grows faster. Put more formally, they add not only to production but to productivity.

There is scarcely a mainstream economist who wouldn't agree that increased productivity is good medicine for most economic ills. Few, however, have traced the impact of prosuming on productivity.

In fact, because almost no one pays attention to it, there is, in this most jargon-laden of professions, no adequate word for this phenomenon. So, to coin one, we can call it "producivity"—the extra kick prosumers provide when, beyond creating unpaid value and channeling it into the money economy, they actually increase its growth rate as well.

BEYOND EDUCATION

Most businesspeople and economists would agree that improving the education of the workforce is likely to increase its productivity. Yet, as we've seen, no supposedly "modern" institution is more dysfunctional and obsolete than what passes for public education even in countries with advanced economies.

Moreover, most so-called reforms accept the hidden assumption that factory-style mass education is the only way to go. Most are still unconsciously designed to make the school/factory run more efficiently—rather than to replace it with a post-factory model. And most share the built-in assumption that only teachers teach.

Thus one of the most extraordinary events in the recent history of education has been virtually overlooked.

That event began in 1977 in a most unlikely way. At that time there were, for all practical purposes, zero personal computers on the planet. By the year 2003, however, there were 190 million in use in the United States alone. That was surprising. But more surprising is the fact that more than 150 million Americans knew how to use them. Even more astounding is how they learned.

PCs, from the time the first Altair 8800s and Sol-20s appeared, have been cantankerous little devices, much more balky and complicated to use than any previous household appliance. They had buttons and diskettes, and software (a concept only a relative handful of Americans had ever encountered) and manuals and a strange vocabulary of DOS commands.

So how did so many millions of people—half the entire nation—master these complexities? How did they learn?

We know what they did not do. The overwhelming majority, especially in the early days, did not go to computer school. In fact, with minimal exceptions, they had little or no formal instruction at all.

Their learning began when they walked into a Radio Shack store, one of the first retail chains to begin selling PCs. Radio Shacks at the time were tiny shops jammed with jangles of wires and electronic gadgets and a sales force of enthusiastic sixteen-year-old boys with pimples on their cheeks. The kind who read science fiction and became "geeks."

When a customer showed interest in the TRS-80, one of the primordial PCs, a clerk would show him (rarely a her in those days) how to turn it on and hit a few keys. The purchaser would hurry home to unwrap the $599 machine and plug it in. He would then follow the instructions—and soon discovered that at best he could do very little with his computer. Not surprisingly, he went back to the store and asked the clerk a few more questions. But soon it became apparent that he needed more than the clerk. What he needed was a computer guru. But who was a guru?

What followed was a frantic search for someone—neighbor, friend, colleague, happy-hour acquaintance—who might help. Anyone would do who knew even a bit more than he did about how to use a computer. A guru, it turned out, was anybody who had bought a computer a week earlier.

Next came a cascade of information exchange about PCs, spilling, sloshing, splashing through American society, creating a learning experience in which millions participated.

Today some might term it peer-to-peer learning. But, in fact, it was more complicated than Napster-like trading of music. For the guru and the learner were not peers. One had more knowledge to impart than the other did. It was precisely the knowledge edge, not the equivalence, that brought them together. That in itself is interesting, but even more so is the fact that, in time, the roles might reverse. The late learner often became the guru and the original guru the learner, as they traded experiences and information back and forth.

Since those days, prosumers have become more and more sophisticated about computers. As W. Keith Edwards and Rebecca E. Grinter of the famed Palo Alto Research Center write, the average PC user today deals with chores that would only "seem familiar to a mainframe systems operator from the days of the high priesthood: upgrading hardware, performing software installation and removal, and so on."

This progressive learning process was controlled by nobody, led by nobody. Organized by nobody. With almost nobody getting paid, an immense social process got under way that, largely unnoticed by educators and economists alike, changed the American money economy, radically altered corporate organization and affected everything from language to lifestyle. Only much later did corporations train large numbers of users. Guru prosumers were the indispensable, yet unrecognized, drivers of the PC revolution.

RAJENDER'S GAME

This process is still going on, accelerated and dwarfed by the learning exchanged among Internet users and their gurus. Around the world, people are teaching one another to use the most complex personal appliance in history. And often it is kids teaching grown-ups.

Take a PC with a touch pad and a fast Internet connection and embed it in a stone wall near a slum. Mount a camera opposite it so you can observe it from your office, and watch what happens.

That is exactly what physicist Sugata Mitra of NIIT, a New Delhi–based software maker and computer school, did. There were no instructions and no adults to turn to.

It wasn't long before it was discovered by kids from the Sarvodaya Camp, the adjoining slum. Instead of looting it, Guddu, Satish, Rajender and the others—mostly six- to twelve-year-olds—began playing with it. Within a day or two, they had learned and taught one another to drag, drop, create files and folders, perform other tasks and to navigate the Internet. Again, no classrooms. No tests. No teachers.

In three months they had created more than a thousand folders, accessed Disney cartoons, played online games, drawn digital pictures and watched cricket matches. At first individually, then sharing what they learned, they developed what Mitra, who dreamed up the experiment and has repeated it elsewhere, calls "basic computer literacy."

He believes that making use of the curiosity and learning ability of kids could drastically reduce the cost of crossing the digital divide. In turn, that could help lift millions out of misery—and dramatically increase the growth rate and potential of the Indian economy by applying the principle of producivity.

In defense of obsolete formulas and definitions, some economists and statisticians may continue to quibble. But only perverse dogma would deny that the free sharing of PC skills was (and still is) *producive*—that it improves productivity in the everyday operations of the money economy.

Of course, education should be more than occupational. But if increasing the skill base of an economy can, along with other changes, expand both its output and productivity, and we pay teachers to teach those skills, why do we not equally value the contribution of the gurus? Assuming the same set of skills is transferred by the teacher and the guru, why is one worth more than the other?

Pushed still further, what if the same set of skills is self-taught—as in fact is the way legions of Web-page designers, programmers, video-game developers and others mastered the talents they later marketed.

Self-teaching and guru teaching are especially producive when the skills they develop are at the leading edge of new technologies, before formal, paid courses become widely available. If PC beginners had had to wait for schools to buy computers, develop curricula, reorganize schedules, train teachers and raise funds for all this, the entire process by which this technology diffused through business and the economy would have been significantly delayed. What they did, therefore, was truly producive: By voluntarily spreading knowledge and short-circuiting the delay, they greatly sped technological advance in the paid economy.

This wave of people-to-people learning changed our relationships to many of the deep fundamentals of wealth. It changed when and how people spend their time. It changed our relationship to space, shifting the locations where work is done. It changed the nature of shared knowledge in the society.

Prosumers are not merely productive. They are producive. And they are driving the growth of the revolutionary wealth system of tomorrow.

CHAPTER 30

CODA: INVISIBLE
CHANNELS

The time has now come once again to pull together into a coherent summary and overview the many strands we have so far uncoiled. Thus far, this book has presented three key ideas.

First, that the world is going through a historic change in the way wealth is made and that this is part of the birth of a new way of life or civilization of which, at least for now, the United States is the spearhead.

Second, that far below the surface fundamentals watched closely by businesses, investors and economists, there are deep fundamentals, and that we are changing our relationships to them in revolutionary ways—especially those involving time, space and knowledge.

Today's accelerating changes, as we've shown, are de-synchronizing more and more parts of the economy. They point to a period of possible de-globalization in the economy and increased re-globalization in other fields. Above all, they transform the knowledge base on which wealth creation depends, reducing much of it to obsoledge and irrelevance, while challenging not only science but our very definitions of truth.

Third, we've seen that the money economy is only part of a much larger wealth system and is dependent on largely unnoticed infusions of value from a massive, worldwide *non-money* economy based on what we have called prosuming.

Understanding this concept of a two-part wealth system should help us, among other things, see money for what it is—and to see more clearly how it fits into tomorrow's revolutionary wealth system.

The overwhelming power of money in our lives is attested to by the richness of commentary about it. Willie Sutton, asked why he robbed banks, wondered why anyone would ask so stupid a question and gave his famous answer: "That's where the money is!" More recently, actor Cuba Gooding, Jr., added another line to monetary literature with his outraged shout in the film *Jerry Maguire,* "Show me the money!" And novelist Tom Robbins, lapsing into theological exegesis, allowed that "there is a certain Buddhist calm that comes from having money in the bank." Money has been all but deified. But deification is also mystification.

We've argued, therefore, that the time has come to ditch the false assumption that wealth derives only from what economists generally measure. Or that value is created only when money changes hands. We need, instead, to turn our attention to the larger wealth system—in which the money economy is fed a free lunch and kept alive by prosumers who also pose powerful challenges to it.

THE PROSUMER IMPACT

As we've seen, there are at least a dozen important channels through which prosumers and prosuming interact with the money economy, shifting value back and forth. They will be more and more important in the days ahead. It helps, therefore, to recap them here, starting with the simplest.

1. Prosumers perform unpaid work through "third jobs" and self-service activities.

By using an ATM or checking themselves out in a supermarket, they reduce labor cost—and the number of entry-level jobs—in the money economy. The same, with minor adjustment, is true when they personally care for the ill or elderly or when they cook, clean house, home-school and perform other tasks themselves, instead of paying others to do them.

2. Prosumers buy capital goods from the money economy.

They purchase everything from chain saws to computers and digital cameras that help them create value for themselves and others in the non-money economy. In doing so, they themselves constitute a market within the money economy.

3. Prosumers lend their tools and capital to users in the money economy—another dish of free lunch.

Examples, as we've seen, include allowing others the free use of excess computer capacity for medical and environmental research, astronomical observation and many other socially important purposes.

4. Prosumers improve the housing stock.

They raise its value in the national money economy. They do this every time they paint, reshingle their roof, add rooms or plant trees, substituting their own labor for jobs in the construction industry. The value of the housing stock, in turn, affects mortgages, interest rates and other variables in the money economy.

5. Prosumers "marketize" products, services and skills.

They do this when, having developed a skill, a product or a service for their personal use, they put it up for sale—sometimes creating new companies and business sectors in the process. Linux, created by prosumers outside the market, generates important commercial piggyback products inside the for-pay marketplace.

6. Prosumers also "de-marketize" products or services.

They drive existing goods and services out of the marketplace by offering users all-but-free alternatives. The very threat from outside the money economy leads to new, often cheaper, products inside it. Check VoIP calling, iPods and the like. Prosuming can accelerate the cycle of de-marketization and marketization.

7. Prosumers create value as volunteers.

They offer free help in emergencies. Less dramatically, on a day-to-day basis they work in senior centers, provide medical care and many other services to society. They fight youth gangs, form or maintain neighborhood associations, churches and other groupings that contribute to social cohesion—the absence of which imposes huge money costs for additional police, prisons and the like.

8. Prosumers provide valuable free information to for-profit companies.

Prosumers do this by beta-testing new products, by filling out surveys, by helping businesses identify new customer needs, by "viral marketing" and by performing other unremunerated services for them.

9. Prosumers increase the power of consumers in the money economy.

They do this by sharing information about what to buy or not buy. They share experiences with respect to various health problems and medications, for example, often empowering patients in their relationships with doctors.

10. Prosumers accelerate innovation.

Serving as unpaid gurus, guides, teachers and consultants, prosumers train one another to use the latest technologies as quickly as they appear, thus increasing the rate of technological change and raising productivity in the paid economy. They are not merely productive but producive.

11. Prosumers rapidly create knowledge, disseminate it and store it in the cybersphere for use in the knowledge-based economy.

Much of the data, information and knowledge available in cyberspace has been contributed for free by software writers, financial experts, sociologists, anthropologists, scientists, technicians and others in all walks of life. The accuracy of this content varies widely, and much of it may someday be marketized, but it is routinely drawn upon by investors, businesspeople, managers and others at work in the money economy—another free input.

12. Prosumers raise children and reproduce the labor force.

Prosumers provide monumental contributions as parents and caregivers, dwarfing all these other interactions. By socializing their children, giving them the gift of language and by inculcating values consonant with those demanded by the dominant economy, they prepare generation after generation to create wealth. Without the free lunch they provide, there would soon be no paid economy.

UNNOTICED THERAPY

These, then, are only a dozen of the ways in which the two parts of the wealth system interact. Multiply these by their possible cross-impacts, and they generate new questions about the revolutionary wealth of tomorrow.

Can we still mouth the notion that there is no such thing as a free lunch in the money economy? What, then, is the net value of all the free lunch flowing into and out of the money economy? How might knowing more about those interactions change our business and personal strategies?

Which of our current assumptions about savings, investment, growth, labor, taxes and other key variables still make sense? How might changing those assumptions influence the future of wealth and poverty on the globe?

And if what we have written is essentially correct, what does it do to the oft-stated claim that various classes of people are "unproductive"?

Are people without jobs necessarily unproductive? Are all the people on welfare unproductive? Are all the elderly and retired unproductive? Is a quadriplegic unproductive? Or is the insightful, but unpaid, telephone advice one such quadriplegic offered to friends the equivalent of the therapy psychologists provide for a hundred dollars an hour? And what value should be ascribed to the life her advice actually saved when the person at the other end of the line was preparing for suicide? Was that worth two hundred dollars an hour?

Revolutionary wealth is not just about money.

PART SEVEN

Decadence

CHAPTER 31

THE GOSPEL OF CHANGE

*C*ivilization is one of those big, stuffy words that may intrigue philosophers and historians but puts most people to sleep. Unless it is used
in a sentence like "Our civilization is threatened"—at which point
large numbers of people prepare to load their AK-47s.

Today many people do, in fact, believe that their civilization is threatened—and that the United States is doing the threatening. And it is.

But not in the way most of us think.

THE THIRD SOURCE

Around the world, critics of the United States point to its military and its economy as the main sources of its predominance. It is, however, knowledge in the
broadest sense and new technologies based on it that integrate America's military and financial power and propel both forward.

It is true that America's technological lead is threatened. According to the
National Science Board, foreign students earn nearly 50 percent of all U.S.
doctorates in mathematics, computer sciences and engineering. And American youth are showing less and less interest in these fields. NASA officials
complain that there are three times as many scientists over sixty as there are
under thirty in the space agency.

Shirley Ann Jackson, then president of the American Association for the
Advancement of Science, has cautioned that "centers of technology-based
activity, training, and entrepreneurialism are rapidly spreading throughout the
globe. Thus even the status quo for the U.S. represents a declining share of the
global marketplace for innovation and ideas."

Nevertheless, America still leads in most fields of digital technology, in
microbiology and in science generally. It spends 44 percent of the world
budget for research and development. And, of the thirty-eight Nobel Prize

winners in chemistry, physics and medicine from 1999 to 2003, nearly two-thirds were either Americans or were working at American institutions when they received the award. At least for now, the United States remains the world's scientific powerhouse.

Perhaps even more important is the speed with which scientific and technical findings from everywhere are converted into marketable applications or products and widely dispersed into manufacturing, finance, agriculture, defense, biotech and other sectors. All of which boosts economic productivity, further accelerates change, and increases the U.S. ability to compete at the global level.

But knowledge is not only a matter of bits and bytes or science and technology.

TEEN TRASH

Part of the knowledge economy is the production of art and entertainment, and America is the world's biggest exporter of popular culture. That culture includes fashion, music, TV programming, books, movies and computer games.

Americans have always been told that their most important message to the world is one of democracy, individual freedom, tolerance, concern for "the rights of man" and—more recently—the rights of women. In the last three decades, however, as U.S. media spread into formerly closed or nonexistent foreign markets, a very different set of messages has been communicated. Much of it targeted at young people.

Certainly not all, but a considerable amount of this material has disgustingly glorified pimps, gangsters, drug lords, drug pushers and hollow-eyed drug users. It has celebrated extremes of violence marked by unending car chases, over-the-top special effects and songs dripping with sexist venom. The impact of all this has been further intensified in the hard-sell, over-the-edge advertising used to promote these products.

Hollywood, for example, has painted a fantasy America in which adolescent hedonism reigns supreme and authority figures—police, teachers, politicians, business leaders—are routinely satirized.

Film after film, and TV shows one after another, tell young viewers what many of them hunger to hear: that adults are bumbling fools; that being "dumb and dumber" is okay; that "we don't need no education"; that to be "bad" is really to be good; and that sex, in infinite variety, is or should be nonstop.

In this fantasy world, women are readily available, but they can also leap over giant buildings in a single bound (like Superman), shoot and kill (like James Bond) and practice martial arts (like Bruce Lee).

Extremes, we are repeatedly told, are good and restraint is bad; and, by the way, America is so rich that even its secretaries, cops, clerks and other ordinary working people live in high-rise penthouse apartments or Malibu mansions—images that set adolescent glands tingling from Taipei to Timbuktu.

What few foreign critics of America's pop culture seem to know is that, ironically enough, many of the ostensibly American firms producing and disseminating the worst of this sludge either are, or were, actually financed not by American, but by European and Japanese capital.

Nor is it widely understood that shows are often made by, say, a European director with an Australian star, a Chinese martial-arts consultant, an anime cartoonist from Japan or other foreign contributors.

In the meantime, however, the influence of this trash is so powerful that other societies fear for the survival of their own cultures.

PAUL'S STORY

For centuries, the word *Timbuktu* has been used in the West as shorthand for the remotest possible place. Not long ago our Australian friend, the renowned author/adventurer Paul Raffaele, visited Timbuktu after a two-day drive north from Bamako, the capital of Mali in West Africa. He later e-mailed us an account.

> *Little has changed in Timbuktu for centuries. . . . Nomads herd donkey trains to market, while turbaned Tuareg men in robes and veils, hiding all but their eyes, stride through the alleys and past the fourteenth-century mud mosque. . . . But ahead I see something that looks like a mirage.*
>
> *Scores of teenagers, black, white and brown, clad in American ghetto-style clothing, are streaming along the street. The boys wear dark gym pants, high-tech sneakers, and long, loose basketball shirts boasting the names of teams like the Lakers. . . . The girls wear tight jeans, sneakers and T-shirts.*

They are heading toward City Hall, and Paul joins them. "We're having a rap competition," a boy explains. Timbuktu's young people, he tells Paul, "discovered rap a couple of years ago, but now it's their favorite music. . . . Timbuktu now has cable TV, and we see rap all the time on MTV." Inside the hall, hundreds of similarly dressed kids—Arab, Tuareg, Fulani and Songhai—are screaming and foot-stomping as four young men clutch the mikes.

Over the next two weeks, however, Paul seldom saw anything but traditional garb in the streets of Timbuktu and in the desert. "On that one afternoon," he wrote, "when the kids of Timbuktu flaunted their addiction to modern garb and music, did I get a glimpse of the future?"

Raffaele's question echoes that of millions of parents around the world who see their cultures under attack. The United States, they feel, is seducing their kids.

But, it might be asked, away from what? Paul offers one powerful clue: "I ask [a boy] why there seem to be no girls older than sixteen in the audience. 'That's when their parents marry them off and they spend most of their time inside the house.' I ask whether the girls choose whom they marry. 'Of course not,' he replies. 'Marriage is too important for the girl or boy to make the choice. Our parents always decide.'"

So, as Paul's account makes clear, there are strict limits on Timbuktu's conversion to the American Way.

HOLLYWOOD HEDONISM

While Hollywood sent its message that freedom means unrestrained hedonism, Wall Street was sending a parallel message contending that unrestrained business and trade offer the best path to wealth.

Washington, echoing this theme, chanted the mantra that unrestrained free trade and a "level playing field" benefit everyone. This, as we've seen, was combined with a magic formula: liberalization + globalization = democracy.

For several decades America thus told the whole world—and itself—that laissez-faire (especially privatization and deregulation) would deliver democracy—as though any mechanistic, one-size-fits-all formula would work everywhere, overriding all differences in religion, culture, history and levels of economic and institutional development.

If what America represents to the world is an across-the-board lack of restraint—and if that is its definition of freedom—it is hardly surprising that adults in other cultures see it not as freedom but as chaos.

Unrestrained hedonism and free-marketism are not, however, inherent or inevitable accompaniments of Third Wave economic development.

Instead, they reflect the fact that the process of moving from an industrial economy and society to a knowledge-based economy and society is unprecedented. No previous generation has undergone, let alone completed, a similar transition. No model exists.

America, therefore, arrogant though it often seems, is shaken and uncertain as it experiments with novel ideas, social structures and values. It may well jettison some of today's lack of restraint as unworkable models of behavior are tried and abandoned.

When critics around the world complain that the United States is attempting to dominate and homogenize their culture, they fail to understand that the thrust toward homogeneity comes not from the advanced Third Wave sectors of America's economy and society but from Second Wave holdovers.

The mass-media, mass-marketing and mass-distribution methods that lie behind America's export of mass culture and values are perfect expressions of yesterday's industrial mass society, not tomorrow's knowledge economy based, if anything, on customization and de-massification.

In fact, the very variety that comes with knowledge-based development ensures that other countries will adopt quite different economic, social and political pathways to the future. They will not look like America. But, then, neither will tomorrow's America.

ONE STEP IN THE RIVER

The real message that America sends, more important than its ideological and commercial rhetoric, is the Gospel of Change.

It is the dominant message now being delivered to billions of people in rigid societies around the world: Change is possible—and not just in some blue-sky future but soon, in your own lifetime or that of your child.

This gospel doesn't specify whether change will be good or bad. That will be interpreted differently and fought over. But the very idea that change is possible is still revolutionary for many populations on this planet—especially for the world's poorest young people. And, as innumerable examples show, when people regard change as impossible, they seldom take the future in their hands.

If the emergent generation is inspired by the Gospel of Change, the changes to come will not necessarily please America and Americans. In the Middle East, it could take the form of popularly elected theocratic-fascist regimes duly voted into power. In Africa and Latin America, it might take completely different forms.

The Gospel of Change is most dangerous to established institutions and order precisely because it is not inherently right-wing or left-wing, democratic or authoritarian. Its implicit meta-message is that all our societies, all our current ways of life and even our beliefs are inherently temporary.

It is not the message of Adam Smith or Karl Marx. It is not the message of the French or American revolutionists. It is the message of that most revolutionary of all philosophers, Heraclitus—whose best-known statement still sums it up: "You cannot step in the same river twice, because by the second step it will already have changed." All is process. All is change.

Heraclitus implies that all ideologies, and all religions, like all institutions, are historically transient. That is the real message emanating from the United

States. And that is what, at the deepest level, disturbs the dreams—and triggers the nightmares—of billions of human beings.

The United States cannot help but transmit that message because it itself exemplifies change.

Many countries today have begun the transition from an industrial wealth system and civilization to a knowledge-based wealth system—without appreciating that a new wealth system is impossible without a correspondingly new way of life. America is on the razor edge of that all-encompassing change. And change is its most important export.

That is why even present and former allies are increasingly troubled by America's role in the world. Even as they, too, undergo significant transformation—the recent enlargement of the European Union and the rejection by some countries of its proposed constitution, for example—their overall pace is slower and less revolutionary. As they struggle to build their own future, they see the United States pulling away, speeding into the unknown—and pulling other cultures and countries in its turbulent wake.

But if everything is in fact temporary, so is American power.

CHAPTER 32

IMPLOSION

illions of increasingly anxious, often angry people around the
globe worry about American domination, but how long can any
society, superpower or not, retain external power if its domestic
institutions are in crisis?

So far we have mostly referred to the deterioration of American Second
Wave or industrial-age institutions piecemeal, one at a time. But it is only
when we expand our analysis and see them in relation to one another that the
real picture becomes clear.

If the United States is so powerful, why is there a crisis in its health system? Why a crisis in its pension system? Its education system, its legal system,
and even its politics—all at the same time? Is America facing implosion?

PANDEMIC LONELINESS

Why, too, is the American nuclear family—supposedly the bedrock institution
of society—acknowledged to be in such distress? In America, fewer than 25
percent of the population now live in homes in which the father goes to work
and the wife stays home with one or more children under the age of eighteen—a radical change since the 1960s. Thirty-one percent of U.S. children
now live in single-parent or no-parent homes. Some 30 percent of Americans
over age sixty-five live alone. Why do 50 percent of marriages end in divorce?
Young Americans now talk about what might be called a formalized "rehearsal marriage"—a childless first marriage before the real show goes on the
road. Little wonder loneliness is pandemic in the United States.

Bitter conflict rages over all these issues. But the changes are typically
debated and fought over in fragmentary fashion without recognition that the
crisis in any one institution may be linked to that in others. The nuclear-family
crisis is part of something much, much bigger.

POST-KINDERGARTEN FACTORIES

Reared in a splintered family system that is changing rapidly, but is barely adapted to twenty-first century requirements, fifty million American kids each day are marched into an education system that is also broken.

As we've noted, the United States spends nearly $400 billion a year on public education from preschool through secondary school, with a median of approximately $7,000 per student. Yet 60 percent of high school students cannot read well enough to get through their textbooks, a third of graduates cannot do the basic math required of a beginning carpenter and nearly a third of young adults cannot locate the Pacific Ocean on a map.

The capital of the United States, Washington, D.C., spends over $10,000 per student each year—more than 49 of the 50 states in America. Yet Washington schools have some of the worst academic results in the nation. Its 2002 test results, according to *The Washington Post,* "scored lower than counterparts in any of the 50 states."

Shootings, violence and drugs in the schools make news whenever a Columbine-style massacre takes place. But these are merely symptoms of a factory-style education system that, with only a few exceptions, has not been reconceptualized, let alone restructured, to prepare young people for the knowledge-based economy.

And just as the broken family system sends the children into broken schools, the schools, in turn, send them on to yet another set of broken institutions.

CREATIVE ACCOUNTING

If institutions as basic as family and school are in deep trouble in the United States, why should it come as a shock to discover that key parts of its economy, too, are malfunctioning? Employers throughout America lament the failure of parents to inculcate good work values in their children, and of schools to teach them twenty-first-century skills. The failure of one institution affects the operations of another.

For generations, Americans prided themselves on possessing the world's cleanest, most efficient financial system in the world, the one most capable of allocating capital to its most productive uses.

Having grown up in broken homes and gone through a broken education system, America's baby boom workers—many of them also investors—should not have been stunned by the chain reaction of scandals that followed the spectacular crash of Enron in the late 1990s.

Caught up in an unprecedented flurry of corporate or executive scandals, failures, excesses, number-juggling and lies were WorldCom, Tyco, Rite Aid, Adelphia Communications, Qwest, Xerox and a lengthy list of other giant American firms, together with their ever-obliging investment bankers. All followed by more layoffs.

Meanwhile, America's main accounting firms, supposedly there to audit companies' books and keep them clean, were themselves soon sweating under investigative spotlights. Arthur Andersen, Enron's auditor, quickly perished, and as *Fortune* put it, "the Big Four—which together audit a staggering 78 percent of the nation's 15,000 publicly traded companies—continue to career from one humiliating headline to the next."

Satirists pictured ten thousand chief executive officers fleeing across the border into Mexico. Duped investors screamed. Trust in American stock markets and the American business system as a whole sluiced down the sewer. And with it went the jobs and retirement savings of hundreds of thousands of employees.

Slowly changing regulatory and enforcement methods, along with legal and social norms, were left in the dust by accelerating changes in business, creating turbulence, confusion—and, for some, irresistible new opportunities at the blurred edges of once-clear boundaries, in yet another manifestation of the de-synchronization effect.

INTENSIVE CARE

At the same time, an additional crack has been widening in the sole superpower's institutional infrastructure as its companies and their employees struggle to pay the skyrocketing costs of health insurance.

How, one might ask, can the American health system be in dire need of intensive care when in 2000 it spent the equivalent of $4,499 per person on health compared with, say, $56 spent in Haiti?

Definitions of a crisis vary, of course, but the facts are that some forty million Americans lack health insurance, deadly errors are daily occurrences in the world's most heavily funded hospitals and recurrent health manias spread viruslike through society—anti-tobacco first, then anti-obesity and low-carb diets. What next?

On top of that, a health-care executive warns a congressional subcommittee that "the U.S. health care system is about to implode, and Alzheimer's disease will be the detonator" because the baby boomer generation is reaching the age of the onset of that terrible illness.

The fact that health conditions in most other countries are worse does not change the reality. The world's most expensive health-care system is deeply dysfunctional—and getting more so.

THE GOLDEN YEARS

After wrestling throughout their lives with malfunctioning homes, schools and medical institutions; after being fleeced by corrupt financial institutions and finally reaching retirement, American workers look ahead to their "golden years"—the long-awaited time to take a breath, stroll to the mailbox and pick up one's pension check.

But here Americans young and old face yet another institutional disaster—this one in the pension system. Critics of the current pension arrangements warn of a coming "financial meltdown." Once considered heresy, such doubts have been attributed to no less an authority than a U.S. secretary of the Treasury.

According to *BusinessWeek,* "Damage from corporate pension-plan losses has been piling up like a slow-motion train wreck." One recent three-year period saw assets of U.S. private pension funds shrink by 15 percent, while liabilities soared nearly 60 percent.

"The mother of under-funded pensions," the magazine reported, is no less a behemoth then General Motors, with other automakers, airlines and paper industries not far behind. All told, American corporate pension plans owed workers $350 billion more in 2003 than they had set aside for the purpose.

To assure 45 million workers and pensioners that they wouldn't be left high and dry, the U.S. government undertook to insure their pensions through the Pension Benefit Guaranty Corporation. By 2003, however, the PBGC had a deficit of $11.2 billion and, according to its director, Steven A. Kandarian, was itself racing toward implosion.

Faced with a rapidly aging population and underfunded pensions, an intergenerational war is brewing among pensioners on one side and young workers on the other, who fear there will be nothing left for them by the time they retire.

Confronted by failing institutions on all sides, many Americans seek help from charitable organizations, long regarded as ethically cleaner than the profit-making sector. That, however, was before some of the most prestigious nonprofits such as the United Way and the American Red Cross came under investigation for false accounting or misapplication of contributed funds.

Meanwhile, where did many Americans go to find out more about all these crises? The Internet, of course. But, as newspapers take pains to point out, much of what appears on the Net is unverified, biased or mistaken. What is needed, publishers say, is credible, accurate, carefully checked and rechecked information.

Yes. But the print and broadcast media are themselves facing a credibility crisis that threatens their future, as journalistic scandals recently erupted at

The New York Times, USA Today, CBS News, *Newsweek* and other media outlets.

These scandals take place against a background of declining readership and dwindling network audiences. As the *Los Angeles Times,* holding its breath, noted in 2005: "Daily newspaper circulation has fallen nearly 9 million from its 1984 peak of 63.3 million, while the U.S. population has grown by about 58 million." Between 1960 and 2004, it added, 306 daily newspapers disappeared.

POLITICS OF THE SURREAL

The list of institutional breakdowns in superpower America could be extended to include the failure of U.S. intelligence and counterintelligence agencies—in combination with the White House under both Bill Clinton and George W. Bush—to prevent the 9/11 disaster despite various early warnings or to correctly assess the threat of weapons of mass destruction in Iraq.

Finally, after this litany of failures in institution after American institution, we come to what may yet turn out to be the most important of all. Historians of the future may note that the twenty-first century began with an impeached president in the White House, followed by a president effectively put into office by five out of nine Supreme Court justices. Twice in two years the country swerved within millimeters of a severe crisis in its most basic political institutions.

That point was driven home soon afterward by the surrealistic drive to oust Gray Davis, the governor of California—a campaign that attracted 135 candidates for his replacement, including a porn publisher, a retired meatpacker, a sumo wrestler, a used-car salesman and an elderly woman known solely for putting her name and chest on giant billboards. In the end, Davis was dumped and replaced by actor-muscleman Arnold Schwarzenegger.

SYSTEMIC BREAKDOWN

Crisis, it may be said, is in the eye of the beholder—or in the rhetoric of self-interested parties demanding dramatic change. But even allowing for statistical inadequacy, simplistic trend extrapolation and exaggerated rhetoric, or for differences in their importance, intensity or immediacy, the very multiplicity of these cases tells us something important: The whole adds up to more than its parts.

Until recently, most observers, American or not, have viewed all these institutional crises in the United States as unrelated. But that view is no longer tenable. America's seemingly separate and distinct crises are increasingly interconnected. Health care and pensions. Pensions and the corporate crisis. Family and education. The political crisis and all the rest feed into one another.

What is developing, therefore, inside the United States is a *systemic* breakdown of its vital institutional infrastructure at the very time when many believe its power in the world is diminishing.

AN EPIDEMIC OF FAILURE

To grasp the full meaning of this looming implosion, however, it is not enough to look inside America. For the United States, it turns out, is hardly alone. In fact, from Germany, France and Britain to South Korea and Japan, we find a similar epidemic of failure—widening cracks in key institutions, starting, as in the United States, with the nuclear family.

In Japan, divorce rates, especially among couples married for twenty years or more, are soaring to unprecedented highs. Far more arresting, however, are results of a survey by Japan's Youth Research Institute. According to *Business 2.0,* it showed that 75 percent of American schoolgirls agreed with the statement "Everyone should get married"—but that "a staggering 88 percent of Japanese girls disagreed."

South Korea's divorce rate, traditionally low, has become one of the highest in the world. In the United Kingdom, *The Times* of London reports "a steady decline in the nuclear family." In fact, it notes, "the number of households headed by married couples has fallen below 50 percent for the first time, reflecting sweeping social changes in British family life."

Educational crises, too, are no U.S. monopoly. "CLASSROOM COLLAPSE" GRIPPING SCHOOLS NATIONWIDE, screams a headline in the *Japan Times. The New York Times* reports: EDUCATORS TRY TO TAME JAPAN'S BLACKBOARD JUNGLES.

Simultaneously, as in the United States, Japan's once highly admired corporate giants have been hit by scandal after scandal—"Enronitis" Japanese-style. Even as its banking system teeters under loads of nonperforming loans, Tokyo Electric Power Co. sees its president and chairman resign in disgrace because the company falsified safety data at its nuclear-power plants. Soon following TEPCO into ignominy were leaders of Mitsui, Snow Brand Food, Nippon Meat Packers, Mitsubishi Motors, Nissho Iwai and other top corporations.

All these were followed by crises that beset the Tokyo Stock Exchange in 2005. First a computer crash shut down all trading for the first time in the exchange's fifty-six-year history. A few weeks later, observers repressed laughter when a trader from Mizuho Securities Co. mistakenly sold 610,000 shares of a stock for one yen apiece rather than one share for 610,000 yen—a minor glitch that cost his firm $340 million.

Recent corporate crises have been even more dramatic in South Korea, where scandals have led to the flight of the founder of Daewoo, the suicide of one of the sons of Hyundai's founder and the imprisonment of the head of SK, another of the great *chaebol*—the country's megafirms.

In Europe, the recent scandal list includes Volkswagen in Germany, Parmalat in Italy, Crédit Lyonnais in France, Skandia in Sweden and the oil companies Elf and Royal Dutch/Shell.

If that were not enough to keep the headline writers busy, all these were paralleled, as in the United States, by upsets and upheavals in the health sectors of many countries. In the United States, some politicians routinely point to the British health service as a model to be emulated. Yet, the British Council complains, "not a day goes by without another story about the 'crisis' in the National Health Service." The German health service is described in the press as "collapsing," and Sweden's system as in "acute financial crisis." The *Mainichi Daily News* in Japan reports that the country's "health insurance system could collapse within five years."

As for pensions, France's prime minister claims its impending pension disaster threatens "the survival of the republic." Nor is France alone. "Europe faces a retiree crisis," according to *BusinessWeek. Daily Yomiuri* in Japan reports "shocking figures revealed [in] a report on . . . the nation's pension system." NATIONAL PENSION CRISIS blares a headline in *Korea Times*. Underfunded corporate pensions just in America? Try Siemens in Germany, with its $5 billion pension-fund deficit.

STARS ON STRIKE

The same pattern continues right on down the line. Thus the American media's critical loss of credibility is mirrored, albeit for different reasons, by crises at *Le Monde* and *Le Figaro,* France's top daily newspapers; and at *Asahi Shimbun* in Japan.

How about charities? Scandals at the American Red Cross and United Way were paralleled rather spectacularly not long ago in Britain, where tenor Luciano Pavarotti, rock star David Bowie and playwright Tom Stoppard made headlines by publicly ending their support of War Child UK, a charity set up to help children in war-torn countries. Having discovered that its cofounder and a consultant had taken bribes from a contractor employed by the organization, Pavarotti led the walkout to disassociate himself, as a spokeswoman put it, from "anything that was corrupt."

History, it goes without saying, is replete with scandals, failures and crises. Our generation did not invent them. But today's outbreaks in country after country are qualitatively different. Never—with the possible exception of the worst days of World War II—has a generation seen so many institutional breakdowns in so many countries, occurring within the same brief time frame and coming at so rapid a pace.

Never have so many institutional crises been as tightly interrelated—with powerful feedback flows linking family, education, work, health, retirement, politics and media—all affecting the wealth system. And never has re-globalization sent the financial effects of these crises so quickly across so many borders.

What is happening, therefore, is not a series of isolated upsets but a truly systemic breakdown—a challenge to the survival of whole societies that depend on these shaking and rattling institutions.

Today's institutional upheaval is historically unique for yet another crucial reason.

All these crises at national levels are taking place at a pivotal moment for global institutions, too, starting with the United Nations. Even as the U.N. rocked in 2005 with allegations of large-scale corruption in its oil-for-food program in Iraq, and as Secretary-General Kofi Annan came under fire for his son's involvement with a company seeking contracts in Iraq, another scandal hit the headlines. This one centered on charges of pedophilia and sexual abuse of women by U.N. peacekeepers in Africa. Earlier, Annan had warned that the entire U.N. as an institution is in a potentially terminal crisis owing to its obsolete organizational structure.

Meanwhile, an internal war is raging inside the World Bank even as outside analysts slam it for "incompetence, inefficiency and irrelevance." The über-arrogant International Monetary Fund grudgingly admits that it, too, faces a crisis. The World Trade Organization, meanwhile, is losing ground, along with many other intergovernmental agencies. At the global level, too, we are moving rapidly toward systemic crisis.

And when institutional crises in the major nations converge with the equally systemic breakdown of institutions at the global level, as they are likely to do, the combined, self-reinforcing impact will affect not just Americans.

Affluent young latte sippers on Omotesando in Tokyo will feel the effects, as will coffee farmers in Central America, women on assembly lines in China, and small-business people in Germany's Mittelstand, along with financial analysts and investors from Wall Street, London and Frankfurt to Singapore and Seoul.

What happens will naturally be influenced by other powerful factors—war, terrorism, immigration, ecological disasters, geopolitical shifts. But even without these, the mutually reinforcing convergence of national and global crises could trigger something far bigger and more dangerous than the failure of any single institution or an infrastructural implosion in any one country.

This concatenation of breakdowns and scandals may cheer those who hate America and the West, or who hate rich nations in general. But it would be wise for them to defer any celebration.

For, as the Chinese have long known, crisis and opportunity walk together. Instead of a historical disaster, these interlinked crises can be turned to massive advantage. And not just for the countries experiencing them.

To make that happen, we need to understand why in so many countries, and at the level of the global order itself, so many of our most important, interlinked institutions teeter on the brink of collective implosion.

CHAPTER 33

CORRODING THE WIRES

*The world which is arising is still half-buried in the ruins of the
world falling into decay . . . and no one can know which of the old
institutions . . . will continue to hold up their heads and which in
the end will go under.*

—Alexis de Tocqueville

On October 14, 2002, in a suburb of Washington, D.C., Linda Franklin
and her husband, Ted, were outside a home-remodeling store placing
their packages in their car when the shot rang out. The bullet that
killed her came from the sniper who had terrorized the area for twenty-two
eerie days. As the random killings took nine other victims in the Washington
outskirts, America's premier police agency, the Federal Bureau of Investigation, moved into action.

Tips pouring in to the authorities over a hotline were manually entered by
FBI agents into a computerized database called Rapid Start. But a deluge of
67,000 calls all but overwhelmed the system.

Rapid Start, it turned out, was set up because the agency's Automated
Case Support System did not permit information to be shared among agents in
different offices. Worse yet, it was said to have lost more than four thousand
documents pertaining to the trial of Timothy McVeigh, who had killed 168
people when he blew up the Alfred P. Murrah Federal Office Building in Okla-
homa City in 1995.

Franklin's murder came just three months after FBI director Robert
Mueller predicted that restructuring the bureau's information technology
would take nearly two years. This overhaul was needed because, as FBI technology experts said, most people had better computers at home than FBI

agents had at work. In 2005 the FBI was hauled over the political coals when it was learned that it might have to scrap a key element of the upgrade and delay the project another four years.

A key source of the problem was said to be Louis Freeh, Mueller's predecessor. Reputed to hate computers, Freeh allowed the bureau to fall farther and farther behind the sniper with a laptop in his car and the FBI's own Robert Hanssen, a computer geek who just happened to be spying for the KGB.

Ironically, Linda Franklin had worked for the FBI assessing, among other things, threats to its cybernetworks.

In the United States, the FBI is more than an organization. It is an institution, and it, too, is in crisis. But its crisis, like that of other institutions, has roots that trace back to profound changes in the way society deals with the deep fundamentals of revolutionary wealth.

FBI TIME

To begin with, in a world in which business transactions (and criminal transactions) are accelerating, the FBI's response time, like that of most bureaucracies, is too slow. When traces of anthrax turned up in the Hamilton, New Jersey, postal facility and left five people dead, it took the FBI nearly a year to test all the mailboxes. When the Slammer virus rocketed out of nowhere to contaminate hundreds of thousands of computer systems, the FBI took thirteen hours to publicly acknowledge the threat, by which time private antivirus companies had already issued alerts. FBI experts were at home, a White House official explained, and it was hard to get "the right personnel" to respond.

However, this is not a story about the FBI, which, in fact, is little different from, and in many ways better than, other government bureaucracies. Nothing it did in the sniper case matches, for example, the brilliance of the U.S. Immigration and Naturalization Service, which—six months after they crashed two airliners into the World Trade Center—issued student visas to the decidedly dead terrorists Mohamed Atta and Marwan al-Shehhi.

Meanwhile, referring to his agency's general response to crisis, State Department official Marc Grossman lamented in 2005 that "decision cycles sped up so much that the way we do business at the State Department was now too slow. . . . If we don't change . . . then we're going to go out of business."

New Orleans did, in fact, go "out of business" after the devastation of Hurricane Katrina in 2005 and the breakdown of the city's levee system. Bureaucracies at the level of nation, state and town were hopelessly unable to work together. The Federal Emergency Management Agency proved feckless, leaving hundreds of thousands of victims to fend for themselves.

Would today's bureaucracies, not just in the United States, but in Europe and Asia, be any more effective in the event of a new flu pandemic?

Everywhere today we find slow-moving and slow-thinking bureaucracies struggling unsuccessfully to keep up with the acceleration of the acceleration of change. And given the many powerful, converging forces driving us in this direction, it will become worse.

Extreme economic competition, the cumulative nature of scientific research, the increasing number of minds committed to innovation and the instantaneity of communication are just some of the pressures pushing and shoving transitioning societies toward real-time response rates—and leaving bureaucracies behind. Many are reeling from the "acceleration effect."

Worse yet, today's high-speed changes in the economy and society come unevenly and, by their very nature, magnify the de-synchronization effect. At the level of the firm, as we noted earlier, when one department shifts to precisely calibrated "just-in-time" operations, another is forced to re-synchronize, causing de-synchronization in still other departments, not to mention their suppliers (and their suppliers). Much the same happens in government agencies. But something far more basic is happening at a higher level.

Across the board, a time wedge is being driven between the private sector and the public sector—one racing faster and faster, the other falling farther and farther behind. This worsens relations between the two as companies and governments inadvertently bang into each other, interfering with each other's schedules, obstructing each other, wasting everyone's time and money. Political hostilities intensify. Bureaucrats are demonized as inept, lazy or corrupt. Businesspeople are stigmatized as greedy. Politics becomes even more polarized.

And the dysfunctionality of our institutions grows—driven, at least in part, by today's transformatory changes in our relationships to the deep fundamental of time.

GLOBAL SPACE

Time, however, is only one of the deep fundamentals on which our institutions depend. Growing disparities in our treatment of time are matched by growing disparities in space.

Today a company may manufacture in one country, locate its accounting and back-office operations in another, write its software somewhere else, put its customer-service call centers in still another country, maintain sales offices all around the world, put certain tax-avoiding financial operations on a remote Caribbean island and still nominally call itself an American firm. It may be

Japanese like Sony—70 percent of whose stock was actually owned outside Japan in 2005. The NGOs Greenpeace and Oxfam operate in forty and seventy countries respectively.

But while private-sector institutions and NGOs alike are increasingly global, most public-sector organizations operate only nationally or locally.

In short, as faster communication connects the world, goods, services, people, ideas, crime, disease, pollution and terrorists all spill beyond national boundaries. Eroding traditional notions of sovereignty, they outflank and outrun public-sector institutions designed for purely local or national purposes.

These changes with respect to the deep fundamental of space amplify the disruptions in time. No wonder so many institutions—designed for slow-tempo operations in a pre-global world—find it almost impossible to carry out their assigned functions effectively.

AN OVERLOAD OF OBSOLEDGE

The looming institutional implosion is brought still closer by changes with respect to the deep fundamental of knowledge. And here, again, managers and workers in the public sector are often at a disadvantage.

Rapid change reduces more and more of what all of us know—or think we know—to obsoledge. But the speed at which obsolete knowledge is replaced, updated and reformulated is frequently faster in the private sector, where competitive pressures force quick response and better technology makes that possible.

Thus, by the time much of the data, information and knowledge that public employees need to do their jobs reaches them in useful form, it has already been acted on by private-sector players. Public-sector workers can't keep up.

Worse yet, bureaucratic institutions in both sectors break up knowledge and its components, storing and processing them in separate compartments, or "stovepipes." Over time, these stovepipes multiply as ever-more-narrow specialization increases the number of such uncrossable boundaries. This makes it extremely difficult to cope with fast-changing new problems requiring knowledge that falls beyond artificial departmental borders.

On top of that, guarding each stovepipe is an executive whose power is enhanced by control over data, information and knowledge, with little incentive to share it.

Yet today, as industrial-age boundaries break down, it is only by sharing that important problems can be solved.

The reluctance to share within an organization is even more pronounced with respect to outsiders. Thus the CIA and FBI have historically refused to cooperate with each other, as post-9/11 investigations have shown. Local cops hate sharing crime information with national police agencies. Sales organizations, political parties, even, increasingly, scientists, try to hold their cards close to the chest—sometimes at horrific cost.

What we see, therefore, melting the bolts and corroding the wires holding our industrial-age institutions together, are interconnected changes in our relations to the deep fundamentals.

Each change has its own effects. Each increases the likely implosion of institutions in country after country and at the global level as well. But it is the combination of changes in all three—time, space and knowledge—that is likely to topple our familiar institutions and hurl us, unprepared, into a strange new economic and social tomorrow.

Say hello, then, to Complexorama.

And if that sounds like the name of a theme park, it's because tomorrow will be filled with thrills, surprises and, for those brought up in the middle of the twentieth century, a definite sense of unreality.

CHAPTER 34

COMPLEXORAMA

H as anyone noticed how complicated sports have become? Once upon a time, recreational and even professional sports formed a relatively simple part of a modern economy.

Today we see more and more teams, more leagues, more rules and many multifaceted relations between teams and leagues. Moreover, the sports world finds itself entangled in everything from drug laws, television, politics, labor unions and gender conflict to urban planning and intellectual-property issues.

And sports, as a business, is increasingly linked to other industries, new technologies and audiences, forming a far more complex mesh of constantly changing relationships.

Ohio University notes that its graduates now work in "intercollegiate athletics, professional sports, public assembly facilities, sports tours, motor sports, corporate sports organizations, sports media, and the entertainment industries."

The engineering department of the University of Cape Town in South Africa offers studies in "hardness testing of cricket bats, the drag of bicycle wheels, mountain bike tire aerodynamics, . . . and the heat transfer of cycling helmets." A software company advertises that, "the increased attention that the big sports events draw has resulted in complex scheduling problems" that its customizing software can handle.

The greater the variety and number of interacting components in any system, and the faster the changes among them, the greater its complexity. And this is not just a matter of soccer and skating.

Each of history's three great wealth systems—agrarian, industrial and knowledge-based—differs in its level of complexity. Today we are experiencing a historic, system-wide leap toward greater economic and social complexity. And it affects everything from business to politics, and from child rearing to shopping.

Malls are filled with more and more styles of flashy sneakers. Pizza comes with more exotic toppings. Bottled water is available in multiple flavors. Pharmaceutical houses move toward drugs customized for each patient.

Not surprisingly, everything in daily life now seems more complex and interdependent: Choosing a mobile phone, a credit card or an Internet provider—even, in fact, the way our kids choose their friends.

For young people, the choice of a portable digital gizmo affects the games you play and the group you hang out with. The social group, in turn, affects the clothes you wear, the music you listen to, who is "in" and who is "out."

According to Joseph Epstein, author of a book about snobbery, the very criteria that snobs apply have become more complicated. It is this combination of diversity and interdependence that makes life so complex.

WHAT BILL GATES KNOWS

One reason is the "surplus complexity" imposed on consumers when companies bundle too many functions into a single product in hopes of widening its market, a holdover from the era of mass merchandising.

The result is cell phones that play music, take pictures, screen videos, offer games, track appointments, identify location, store memos and—if you're lucky—place and receive phone calls. Or a Volkswagen Passat that boasts of 120 different features, including a refrigerated glove compartment that can keep sushi cool. But the more multi-functional a product, the more suboptimized its functions are, the more costly it is, and the more difficult it is to use. Since few customers want or need all the functions, the rest of us are victims of this surplus complexity.

Complexity at the personal level is immensely amplified at the level of business, finance, the economy and society. In America, Bill Gates, who ought to know, speaks of "astronomically rising complexity." In Germany, the Federal Financial Supervisory Board speaks of the "growing complexity of banking."

In Basel, Switzerland, the powerful Bank for International Settlements, which sets rules for banks all over the world and tells them how much capital they need to keep on hand, drafted a new set of proposed regulations called Basel II. These rules can shake up the world's biggest banks, and governments everywhere are battling over them.

Yet they were so obfuscating and complex that, according to banking consultant Emmanuel Pitsilis of McKinsey & Co., "Nobody understands 100 percent of Basel II or its implications."

Similarly, the United Nations Conference on Trade and Development is pulling together a collection of the financial and business instruments used in foreign direct investment and in deals among multinational corporations. Designed to be "conveniently available" to its users, the compendium runs to a mere fourteen volumes as of 2005.

Welcome to "Complexorama"—the new everyday reality.

Computers are supposed to help us cope with complexity, but software, according to MIT's *Technology Review,* has "outrun our ability to comprehend it. It's next to impossible to understand what's going on . . . whenever a program runs longer than a few hundred lines of code—and today's desktop software contains millions of lines." Microsoft's ubiquitous Windows software contains fifty million lines of code and its Vista product even more. Says Ron S. Ross of the National Information Assurance Partnership, the complexity of I.T. systems themselves has "outstripped our ability to protect them," making "complexity . . . the No. 1 enemy of security."

We see mounting complexity in every aspect of business, from scheduling and marketing to calculating taxes. Especially taxes.

The Cato Institute in Washington reports that the American tax code has been changed no fewer than seven thousand times in the past two decades, requiring a 74 percent increase in the number of pages needed to print it. The complexity of the system costs Americans an estimated six billion hours each year spent filling out forms, trying to understand the rules and collecting and storing records of transactions.

Then there is the complaint, by *USA Today,* that the perennially low American savings rate is being further depressed by complexity. With seven different types of individual retirement accounts and many others offered by employers, each with its own rules and constraints, "a once simple savings concept has grown into an incomprehensible thicket that can be sorted out only by high-priced accountants."

Exactly as one might therefore expect, the U.S. Bureau of Labor Statistics reports that positions for accountants are multiplying rapidly. As one job-search firm puts it, the growing demand reflects the "increasing complexity of corporate transactions and growth in government."

Yet another measure of skyrocketing complexity is the increase in sub- and sub-sub-specialties in many fields.

Half a century ago, before the shift to a knowledge economy began, the health-care profession was divided into about ten specializations. Today there are more than 220 categories of medical professionals, says Dr. David M. Lawrence of the Kaiser Permanente health network. In the 1970s they had to stay abreast of approximately one hundred randomized, controlled clinical research trials a year. Today the annual number is ten thousand.

12,203 PROBLEMS

Outside the United States we see a slower but similar process of complexification at work. The European Union agency devoted to R&D speaks of the "growing complexity of all our societies," adding that "companies' ability to manage this complexity will be a determining factor for Europe's future innovation capacity."

An official of the British prime minister's Office of Public Reform reports that "more complex personal and social problems are presented for state solution" and that "national objectives for better education, health and other outcomes can only be successful by engaging with this complexity."

Meanwhile, Karola Kampf of the University of Mainz in Germany describes the escalating complexity of higher education. Kampf speaks of the "increasing number of system levels," the multiplying types of "corporative actors" involved with the university, the rising importance of NGOs and "intermediary actors," the "growing number of policy fields concerned with higher education" and a rise in "different modes of coordination."

The mounting complexity of universities, however, whether in Europe or elsewhere, is nothing compared with the dizzying complexity of health-care systems dependent on fast-diversifying medical specializations, tests and forms of medical treatment, equipment, schedules, government regulations, financial and accounting arrangements—all constantly interacting at high speed.

These are just a few examples. But lay over these the additional intricate complexities of local, national and now global environmental regulations; financial and trade rules; disease controls; anti-terror constraints; negotiations over water and other resources; and an endless list of other interrelated functions, processes and laws. Then lay on top of that the complexities introduced by tens of thousands of NGOs each proposing or demanding its *own* new complexities.

A decade ago, the Union of International Associations in Brussels published the two-volume *Encyclopedia of World Problems and Human Potential*. Its ambitious compendium listed no fewer than 12,203 "world problems," each one cross-referenced to others that are "more general, more specific, related, aggravating, aggravated, alleviating [or] alleviated." The index to the section had no fewer than 53,825 entries, backed by a bibliography of 4,650 sources. And that was then.

We are moving beyond the relative simplicity of an industrial era that everywhere emphasized uniformity, standardization and one-size-fits-all massification. And the United States is not alone in generating the new complexity. Add the byzantine complexities imposed by the European Union in an attempt to "harmonize" everything from education to cheese. Only computers can keep track.

What we see, then, are changes in the deep fundamentals that are creating the revolutionary wealth system and a corresponding way of life, both based on unprecedented levels of economic and social complexity.

Together, the convergence of acceleration, de-synchronization and re-globalization, along with a tsunami of new knowledge, is overwhelming our rust-belt institutions and driving us ever closer to implosion.

Fortunately, there is a way out.

CHAPTER 35

THE SEPULVEDA SOLUTION

L os Angeles is famous for its freeways, one of which, the 405, is notorious for its bumper-to-bumper traffic, so jammed that much of it spills over to the street that parallels it for many miles, Sepulveda Boulevard.

It is on Sepulveda that one finds what is surely one of the world's most unusual business enterprises: A car wash. What makes this particular car wash unique is not the gas pumps and autos you see when you pull up but the surprise that awaits you when you go inside to pay your bill. For what you've entered just could be the world's only combination car wash and bookstore.

And as we'll see, it is the spirit that led to that strange juxtaposition that will be needed to overcome—or better yet prevent—the systemic breakdown of the institutions we rely on every day of our lives.

EVERY AMERICAN WOMAN

From its start in the early 1900s until the 1980s, American Telephone and Telegraph grew into the world's biggest company. It is hard today to appreciate just how dominating an institutional presence AT&T was in American life for the better part of a century.

"Ma Bell," as it was known, was a part of every community. Its black rotary telephone was present in virtually every American home. It had enormous political influence, not only in Washington but in communities all over the nation. Its Bell Labs, bedecked with Nobel Prizes, was commonly regarded as the greatest industrial research and development organization in the world.

By the 1970s, AT&T employed almost a million workers. In that age of pre-digital telephones, a tremendous number of these employees were female phone operators, and their number was rising year after year. Broken up by Uncle Sam in 1984, AT&T eventually shrank to a bare wisp of what it once was. And in 2005 its remnants were acquired by SBC Communications. If that can happen to AT&T, it can happen, and a lot faster, to even the most seemingly solid of institutions.

FAKE TRANSFORMATION

Although institutions in Europe, Japan and other economies are also being shaken by changes in their deep fundamentals, it is in the United States—precisely because it has advanced farther than others beyond the industrial age—that the need to create a new institutional infrastructure is most pressing. And nowhere, therefore, is there more loose talk of "transformation"—and so little understanding of what it implies.

Take the case of education. All recent U.S. presidents have wanted to be known as the "education president," and George W. Bush is no exception.

The absolute key to any real improvement in education in the United States is recognition of the changes required by an economy primarily based on knowledge production and distribution. Education is more than occupational preparation, but it surely cheats students if it seeks to ready them for jobs that won't be there. Yet today's mass-production schools—out of sync with the real economy—still mainly emphasize rote, repetitive, factory-like learning.

The supposedly radical Bush plan, instead of emphasizing curiosity, thought, creativity, individuality and self-starting entrepreneurialism—traits needed in knowledge-based economies—calls for yet more routine, standardized testing of students, teachers and schools—tools to make obsolete schools run more efficiently.

An equally striking example of what might be called fake "transformation" can be found in Washington's bureaucratic response to the 9/11 attack—the creation of a Department of Homeland Security. This big-budget, cabinet-level department crunched together twenty-two preexisting pyramidal bureaucracies into a single mega-pyramid.

Washington, in short, did what it knows how to do best: Construct industrial-style bureaucracies. The resultant institution is massive, vertical and hierarchical, with countless competing units, and is supposed to plug into and support tens of thousands of smaller municipal and state bureaucracies.

By contrast, terrorist organizations are designed to run rings around bureaucracies. Comprising tiny, loosely networked cells whose members know the identity of only one or two other people, most can make decisions quickly, are trained to hit, run and vanish—or to blow themselves up. Compared with the Department of Homeland Security, Al Qaeda is flat as a pancake. And its members don't belong to civil-service unions.

Sham transformation is not uniquely American. It is widespread in Europe, where companies and public-sector institutions at the national level are being forced to submit to growing, rigidifying constraints imposed by the E.U., itself a prime example of industrial-age bureaucratic organization.

SHIFTING CHAIRS

An even more striking case of sham transformation, this time at the global level, can be found in the halls of the United Nations.

Facing a severe crisis in the U.N., Secretary-General Kofi Annan announced in 2003 the "urgent need" to restructure the Security Council to reflect the new "geopolitical realities" of the twenty-first century.

The Security Council today reflects power as it was half a century ago, just after the United States, Britain, Russia, France, China and their allies defeated the attempt by Nazi Germany, Italy and Japan to jointly take over the world. Each of the main victors was rewarded with a permanent Security Council seat and the right to veto any proposed action by the full council.

Since then, some of the Big Five have lost power while such countries as Japan, India, Brazil and Germany have gained in global economic and diplomatic importance, yet lack permanent seats and vetoes. Annan wants to fix this problem. But it will take much more than a redistribution of seats among nation-states to save the United Nations.

The U.N.'s influence in the world today is bleeding away because, as a group, nations and/or states are themselves losing power. As we'll see shortly, other forces are gaining clout—global corporations, bond and currency markets, resurgent world religions, tens of thousands of NGOs, sub- and supranational regional units. All these vitiate the dominance of individual nations and states. Collectively, to an even greater extent, they dilute the U.N.'s power.

If the United Nations, therefore, really wants to represent the new realities in the twenty-first century, it must bring these newly powerful global players into its fold, giving them, and not just nations and/or states, voting power as well.

We see, then, in these very different examples involving very different institutions, the same underestimation of the revolutionary character of the knowledge-based wealth system, the same ignorance about the deep fundamentals, and the same forlorn hope that fake transformation can save them.

CAMERAS AND COPS

Real transformation in a corporation, a school or any institution implies significant changes in its main functions, its technology, financial structure, culture, people and organization.

A good example is IBM's strategic shift from a corporation whose chief activity was manufacturing "things" to one whose first priority has become the sale of services. Service revenues reached $46 billion in 2004—48 percent of IBM's total revenue, and the service division, with 175,000 employees, is now the biggest part of the firm.

At Kodak, too, the belated decision to enter the digital-camera field was transformational. For nearly a century, one of Kodak's main functions was to manufacture, develop and print silver-halide film—processes largely eliminated by digital photography. By 2004 it was well on its way to dominating the new field.

Real transformation is possible in the public sector, too, as William J. Bratton showed when he took command of New York's 37,000-person police force in 1994. Its function, he declared, was no longer just to catch criminals but to focus on the future and prevent crime as well.

Until Bratton arrived, the NYPD measured its performance vis-à-vis other police departments on the basis of FBI data supplied only once every six months. Bratton forced unwilling, overworked and sometimes angry police captains to prepare weekly reports for his new CompStat database showing which particular types of crime were increasing or diminishing in their districts. Then they were asked—once a week—to explain what they were doing about it. The better, faster feedback from the field quickly improved performance.

His most publicized innovation was implementation of the "broken window" policy, which directed police to crack down even on minor crimes like breaking windows, scrawling graffiti or bothering motorists by wiping their windshields and demanding money. Catching small fry in these "quality of life" offenses discouraged the commission of more serious felonies and demonstrated to the city that the police meant business.

Organizationally, Bratton shifted power downward toward the local precincts, and culturally he raised police morale by vigorously rooting out corruption and talking tough about crime. He gave his force new respect and a conviction that he would fight politicians and the public on its behalf.

With innovations at all these levels, Bratton turned the NYPD around. Crime statistics even now are tricky at best. Nevertheless, Bratton is widely credited with reducing homicides in New York by 44 percent and "serious crime" by 25 percent in the twenty-seven months of his tenure there. He transformed the department, and is well on his way to doing the same for the Los Angeles police.

CREATING NEW INSTITUTIONS

IBM, Kodak and the NYPD are all large, old organizations. But preventing the oncoming implosion requires more than changing in-place institutions. It also necessitates creating new types of companies, organizations and institutions, large and small, at every level of society. And that calls for social inventors prepared to face inadequate resources, rivalry, suspicion, cynicism and just plain *über*-stupidity.

Daunting as all that sounds, it helps to remember that none of today's familiar institutions—not IBM, not Kodak, not the United Nations, not the IMF, not police forces or post offices—dropped full-blown out of the heavens.

All our institutions, from central banks to blood banks, factories to firehouses, art museums to airports, were in fact originally conceived by business innovators and social inventors who faced far more entrenched resistance to change than we find in the advanced economies today. And many of their innovations in business and society have been at least as important as those in technology.

We know the names of many of history's great technological innovators— Savery and Newcomen and the steam engine, Whitney and the cotton gin, Edison and electric lighting, Morse and the telegraph, Daguerre and photography, Marconi and the radio, Bell and the telephone. And we justly celebrate their immense contributions.

Unfortunately, few—other than specialists and historians, if indeed they— can name the social inventor who first came up with the concept of a limited-liability corporation. Or the person who wrote it into *Gesellschaft mit beschrankter Haftung,* the 1892 German law that was the first to embody it. Can anyone imagine what today's world economy and financial system would look like minus limited liability for investors? Was that any less an achievement than, say, the telegraph?

Not many investors today would build a home, apartment house, office building, shopping center, cinema or factory without buying fire insurance. But who was the innovator inside the Phoenix Assurance Company who, in the 1790s, hired cartographer Richard Horwood to draw the first map of London designed to help a company assess the value of properties and make fire insurance available?

Who was imaginative and brave enough to form the first mutual fund, the first symphony orchestra, the first auto club or any number of other companies and institutions whose existence is taken for granted today? And where is the Nobel Prize for social invention?

If just a tiny fraction of the sums spent on scientific and technological research and innovation were devoted to labs for designing and testing new organizational and institutional structures, we might have a much broader range of options to head off the looming implosion.

INNOVATIONS THAT BREED INNOVATIONS

It required a leap of imagination on the part of Muhammad Yunus to create a bank that lends money to some of the world's most desperately impoverished people—village entrepreneurs who might need as little as thirty or fifty dollars to start a tiny business. Conventional banks couldn't afford to make and service such minute loans, and borrowers didn't have collateral or credit histories.

In 1976 Yunus, a Bangladeshi economist, created the Grameen Bank. Instead of requiring collateral, it asked borrowers to recruit a group of cosigners in their own community to guarantee repayment. The group would have a collective interest in the success of the borrower's small business and could exert social pressure or provide help if payments fell behind. Its members might themselves qualify for loans, in turn, if the debt was repaid.

By 2005, Grameen had made loans to 4.3 million people in tiny amounts totaling $4.7 billion, almost entirely to women—who turn out to be more apt to succeed in their enterprises and also more likely to make full repayment. Grameen has sparked similar operations in at least thirty-four countries and has set up a foundation to help NGOs and others replicate the Grameen model.

Today microfinance is a sizable global industry. Two keys to its success are its interest rates on these loans—very high by U.S. or European standards—and the remarkable 98 percent repayment rate it claims. In truth, Grameen has had collection difficulties. Yet, says Nancy Barry, president of Women's World Banking, "these borrowers are less risky than the Donald Trumps of the world."

What is even more interesting about this social invention is the transformative impact it is having on other institutions. To begin with, Grameen has had many imitators of the model it launched in Bangladesh. By 2001, according to *The Wall Street Journal,* "shopkeepers playing cards in the village of Bagil Bazar can cite from memory the terms being offered by seven competing microlenders."

Because Grameen's profits are unusually strong, some twenty-six NGOs working in poor countries have created microloan banks of their own to help fund their nonprofit activities.

In turn, the spread of microfinance has led to the creation of MicroRate, a rating agency for microfinance banks—itself a novelty. According to its founder, Damian von Stauffenberg, more and more NGO banks will transform themselves into conventional banks in the decade to come, because that would greatly increase their ability to both borrow and lend. As many as two hundred have already taken the preliminary steps.

Some will become competitive with conventional banks, and that, he suggests, will bring big global retail banks and local commercial banks into the microloan business.

In a word, one new organization, Grameen, has had a transformatory impact—not just on the lives of the poor entrepreneurs it has helped but on the way NGOs raise money for their activities. It could alter conventional banking as well, as it blurs the boundaries between the profit and nonprofit worlds.

Grameen is not the only example of high-impact social invention. Amazon.com has created the bookstore without a store. EBay has developed an auction bureau in which the customers do the auctioneering. Google, Yahoo! and other search engines process 600 million queries a day, altering what libraries do and compelling changes—perhaps transformation—in the staid book-publishing industry.

Attacking the industrial-age social welfare model, Vern Hughes in Australia charges that "politicians are still able to get away with promising more schools, more hospitals, more nurses and more police," as if pouring more money into them will cure the crises they face.

In this model, the many social agencies deliver one-size-fits-all services to "disconnected, passive and disempowered 'clients.'"

As an alternative, Hughes cites a program in Melbourne called Person to Person, made up of families of kids with disabilities. These families were "sick of standardized services for their children," all of whom had different needs.

The families persuaded Australia's Department of Human Services to provide cash instead of services, and pay it to a group "support coordinator" the families selected. The coordinator would then buy and allocate "a mix of services chosen by the families (education, home help, day care, etc.)."

As Hughes puts it, the emerging paradigm in human services "shifts focus away from supply-side delivery to demand-side personalization." This demassification is the welfare-service equivalent of product customization in the marketplace.

INVENTING THE THINK TANK

These are only a few examples of social imagination and transformative models. They are important not because all of them necessarily will work as planned but precisely because they exhibit social inventiveness at a time when so many industrial-age institutions are racing toward implosion.

Leaders who attempt to redesign old institutions face denial, stubborn resistance and conflict. Innovators who seek to create new institutions or organizations face skepticism. Both need guts, political skill, tenacity, a sense of timing and commitment. They need allies.

External crisis—and even internal recognition of it—is not enough to bring about transformation in the absence of a persuasive, plausible, non-utopian vision of an alternative. And it is precisely here that social imagination is called for.

Fortunately, there are tested tools that can help unleash it. One of these is the addition or subtraction of functions. For example, the university was originally a place to teach students. In the nineteenth century, the University of Berlin added research to its core functions and became a model for other universities around the world. In the twentieth century, innovators did the reverse, subtracting students from the model of a research university, leaving only the research. The result was a new type of institution called a think tank.

Recently, a wave of adding and subtracting functions has swept through American industry under the rubric of outsourcing and insourcing.

A corporate transformation also occurs when existent functions are either radically expanded or reduced. Big-enough changes in scale can add up to qualitative transformation.

In a world in which borders have become more porous, the distinction between foreign and domestic affairs has broken down. Should each country continue to have a foreign ministry? In universities, should neatly bounded academic disciplines be permanent? Or should disciplinary departments be replaced by temporary, problem-oriented teams comprising students and professors with diverse specialties?

In all sectors of society—private, public and civil—we will need completely new models of organization—strange combinations of networks within bureaucracies, bureaucracies within networks, checkerboard organizations, organizations flexible enough to double or halve their capacity overnight, organizations that survive by forming temporary "coalitions of the willing" to accomplish specified goals.

Preventing systemic institutional implosion will require transforming not just big corporations and governmental departments but every level of the economy and society, from small business to churches, local unions and local NGOs.

On a smaller, slower scale this happened before, when the industrial revolution was still young and needed new, post-agrarian institutions, from department stores and police forces to central banks and think tanks. Innovators arose from the most unexpected places and created them against far greater resistance and odds than those posed in today's societies transitioning beyond industrialism.

And it is here that the United States is perhaps strongest. It has fewer lengthy traditions to protect. It has ethnic and cultural diasporas that bring ideas to America from all over the world. Its people are among the most entrepreneurial in the world—and not just in business.

It has intellectual entrepreneurs, activist entrepreneurs, online entrepreneurs, religious entrepreneurs, academic entrepreneurs. And, unlike societies that suppress individual entrepreneurialism, it preaches a gospel of change that celebrates it.

But America is not alone in innovational resources. Never in history have there existed more educated people committed to making change. Never have there been so many different kinds of institutions, or more powerful tools for matching, mixing, simulating, designing and testing new institutional models.

Fortunately, we are beginning to see a new "meta-institution" appear—a handful of laboratories for social invention and entrepreneurship—mainly focused on the civil-society sector, which is bubbling with energy and imagination.

Some universities now teach courses in social invention. Some foundations offer modest awards for the best ideas. The U.S. Patent Office has approved patents for new business models. But shouldn't there be an imaginative new form of patent for equally creative social models?

Innovation will either be sparked by topside leadership ready to transform existing institutions or it will explode from the bottom, as more and more industrial-age institutions collapse and systemic implosion nears.

Advanced economies are honeycombed with millions of social inventors, innovators, organizational risk-takers, dreamers and practical men and women, better educated, with access to more knowledge from everywhere, armed with the most powerful knowledge tools known to the human race and bursting for the chance to invent a better tomorrow. They are all over the world, ready to remake it.

As for the United States, it is especially rich with innovative, ever-inventive, try-it-out, go-for-it people eager to test new ideas and new models. Even the Sepulveda Solution—the crazy, wonderful juxtaposition of a car wash offering the latest best sellers, how-to books and the works of Cervantes and García Márquez; Dante, Darwin and Du Bois; Whitman and Woll-stonecraft; Aristotle and Plato; Machiavelli and Rousseau; John Locke; and Thomas Paine's ever-inspiring *Rights of Man*.

A car wash, even with a bookstore, won't change America, let alone the world. But thousands, indeed millions, of creative adaptations to the emerging markets, culture and conditions of the knowledge economy will.

If a car wash can also be a bookstore, the range of options for preventing an institutional implosion may be limited only by our social imagination. The time has come to free it.

CHAPTER 36

CODA: AFTER DECADENCE

B y any material standard, most Americans today are far better off than, say, their grandparents were in the 1950s, when the "new" economy began. At that time the ordinary American family paid out nearly a fifth of its disposable personal income just to feed itself. By 2002, only a tenth was needed. Clothing in those long-ago days ate up 11 percent of personal spending. By 2003, despite all the razzle-dazzle about fashion, the number was down to 6 percent.

Back then, only 55 percent of Americans owned their homes. Today it is about 70 percent, and the homes are much larger. Indeed, by 2000, 13 percent of housing sales were for second homes. As far as health is concerned, despite all the problems, average life expectancy has risen from 68.2 years in 1950 to 76.9 years in 2000.

But if all this is true—and a mountain of evidence confirms that it is—why are Americans so seemingly unhappy?

The key is found in the word *material*—which is the opposite of *intangible*. Thus, as both the money economy and its non-money counterpart shift from muscles and metal-bending toward knowledge-based wealth creation and the intangibility it brings, we see yet another historic change: The resurrection of values as a central concern.

THE VALUES WAR

If we listen closely to what ordinary Americans today are saying to one another, we hear countless gripes about the rising inequality of incomes, about too much traffic and too little time, about computers that freeze up and mobile-phone conversations that break up.

Listen longer, though, and a pattern emerges. We hear complaints about the growing inefficiency, greed, corruption, fecklessness or stupidity they encounter daily in the school, the office, the hospital, the media, the airport, the police station and the polling booth—in almost all their day-to-day interactions with America's imploding institutions.

Emotions rise, however, when talk turns to values. In private conversation and in political rhetoric, we hear deafening diatribes about the death of "family values," "moral values," "traditional values," "religious values" and personal and corporate ethics.

What few seem to have noticed, however, is the direct linkage between the implosion of institutions and the implosion of yesterday's value system.

Values arise from many sources. But in any society institutions reflect the values of their builders, and those serving the institution justify its existence by promoting values that do so. If our key institutions can't survive in their present form, neither can the values and norms these institutions embody and promote. We should expect some values to break down and new ones to arise.

However one may define vice or virtue, why should one expect a family system that now encompasses a wide variety of formats to inculcate or express precisely the same set of values that the one-size-fits-all nuclear-family system did when America was still an industrial society? Or the values of large multigenerational families common in pre-industrial agrarian societies?

Why should we expect corporations that no longer depend on muscle power to reflect the macho values of those companies or industries that do? Writing in the *Financial Times,* Richard Tomkins, tongue only partly in cheek, suggests that "these days, most big companies in the west want to be loved. . . . The whole vocabulary of business has changed. Bosses who were once gruff, tough, macho, dominant and bold are now expected to be open, approachable, caring, persuasive and kind. Command and control systems of management, with their rigid hierarchies and strict rules have given way to flexibility, collaboration and teamwork." He describes this as the "feminization" of management.

Tomkins attributes the shift in values to the declining need for physical labor and the new importance of such intangibles as brands. What more and more companies are really selling these days, he says, is "the set of emotions, ideas and beliefs that their brands convey." One may quibble, but he has an important point. So, however, do those who see more sinister implications in the implosion of the value system.

EXTREME EXTREMES

Take institutionalized sports, for example. Once played by amateurs for their own amusement, and later organized more formally into clubs and leagues, it is only in recent decades that sports have become a truly global institution, a multibillion-dollar marketing industry busy selling all kinds of products—and itself largely subordinated to the needs of the television industry.

Corruption in sports, of course, is hardly new. Boxers "throwing" a match and the Black Sox scandal in baseball? Ancient history. The use of drugs by Olympic athletes? Old hat. Even bribery in the megabusiness known as the Olympics has made headlines for years. But corruption in the Little League? Among boys too young to shave? Or the chain of arrests among top athletes for drugs, rape, violence, even murder—all loudly decried by officialdom but recognized by at least one club owner as marvelous for TV ratings and financial returns? If the institution is sick, what kind of values does it propagate?

Much of the seemingly bizarre behavior around us reflects the battle raging in society today between decay and revolutionary rebirth. Throughout history, the search for extremes has been a feature of both decadence and renaissance. Today it is reflected in the application of the adjective *extreme* to every imaginable noun. Thus we are offered "extreme sports," "extreme software," "extreme fashion," "extreme makeovers," "extreme pumpkin carving" and, of course, "extreme Elvis" online, where you can learn more than you want to know about him.

All this is the prelude, as it were, to "extreme fetish porn sites." In sex, diversity and experiment are made more and more publicly visible. Thus television programs feature gays, sadomasochists, cross-dressers and transgender characters. In print, a Completely Bare Spa ad offering "Cucci Couture" is illustrated by a nude girl adorned with a Gucci logo on her pudendum. An Abercrombie & Fitch catalog aimed at teenagers subtly identifies its brand of clothing with group sex. And the *Los Angeles Times* appears on the doorstep in a plastic bag advertising a Vegas.com sweepstakes whose winners get to fly to Las Vegas on a flight on which "clothing can be removed, but your seatbelt must remain fastened."

All this, in turn, arouses predictably extreme reactions from outraged religious groups and other bluestockings eager to restore Victorian virtue—which, as historians pull back the sheets, turns out to have been not so virtuous after all.

Sex is one thing, violence another. What should one make of the hit online game called *Grand Theft Auto: Vice City,* in which players win points for killing cops, selling cocaine and beating prostitutes to death on the screen? Or of "gangsta" rappers who record for companies with charming names like Murder, Inc., or Death Row and rose to fame by singing about killing police or abusing women?

And what about the German cannibal who, on the Internet, recruited a partner supposedly willing to be eaten alive so one or both of them could share a truly extreme experience? Bon appétit! (German legal institutions found themselves unprepared for this novelty, since there was no law actually banning cannibalism.)

One doesn't need a Ph.D. to recognize that a lot of extreme behavior is intended to jolt parents, society in general and any remaining rubes among us. Rubes, however, are increasingly hard to find. They form a tiny, dwindling group, having been replaced by a growing middle class immunized to shock through overexposure. The French used the term *épater le bourgeois*—meaning "to shock the middle classes." What's different today is that the middle class now spits on itself and laughs uproariously about it.

These examples are part of a much broader testing of all the behavioral limits imposed by industrial-era institutions. And not just by the usual bohemians and activists. In the words of *BlackBook* magazine, "Movements in culture point to many people living the life of a misfit. It's not just the rebels and outcasts anymore, now it is the bankers, the Wall Streets, the suits and the blue collars. Where will it all lead?"

What is reflected here is the decay or breakdown not just of yesterday's institutional infrastructure but of the dying culture, value system and social character that grew up with it.

The stench in the air is the smell of decadence.

ANTI-DECADENCE

But there is also a faint scent of renewal.

Revolutions always wear two faces. And today's is no exception. One is the angry face of disintegration. Old things tear apart and crash. The second is the smiling face of reintegration. Things, both old and new, are plugged together in novel ways.

Today change is so rapid that both processes occur almost simultaneously. Along with anti-social trash and decadence, countless positive innovations are appearing as well—pro-social adaptations to the emergent knowledge economy.

Even rap groups are having second thoughts. Having become big commercial enterprises that now peddle fashions, deodorants and numerous other products, some rappers have begun changing their names and image. Or as Anonymous put it:

> *Now we let our diplomas show*
> *Instead of pushin' guns and blow.*
> *It may just be a temp'rary blip*
> *but rap is on a clean-up trip.*

Several rap groups have recently launched innovative campaigns to offer college scholarships and to register young voters—a far cry from urging them to kill cops.

Some innovators reach into the distant pre-industrial past for models, then revolutionize them so that any resemblance to yesterday is more cosmetic than real. Matchmaking provides a case in point.

In village life, couples are often brought together by a local matchmaker. Under urban-industrial conditions, daily life is more anonymous and contacts are more impersonal. Lonely young people make the bar scene in search of Mr. or Ms. Right. Millions are reduced to desperately searching classified ads to find a potential life partner.

Today the village matchmaker is back in electronic form, as growing millions search for mates on the Web and online matchmaking becomes more sophisticated. Instead of throwing Kevin and Stacy together based on a handful of supposedly common traits, eHarmony requires a user to answer 480 questions designed to profile twenty-nine characteristics that its psychologists regard as crucial to long-term success in marriage.

This very process would seem, at least in theory, to help individuals clarify and prioritize their own values. In a society torn between the values of the past and the uncertainties of a fast-arriving future, such self-examination can itself prove useful to the individual. Matchmakers of the future may go farther and ask clients to play specially designed Sims-like online games to identify their thinking style and unconscious behavioral biases before introducing them to other clients. And they may charge a bonus if marriage results, or arrange the wedding for an extra fee.

Online services that help people locate friends or friends of friends may develop similar games to bring like-minded people together. Still others, perhaps marketed by travel agents, may introduce an individual prescreened traveler arriving in a new city to a family of equally prescreened "welcomers" for a home-cooked dinner and an evening of bowling or chamber music. Multiple online sites such as meetup.com are already bringing together, face-to-face, all sorts of people, from political activists to poker players, foreign-language students to film buffs.

Meanwhile, recognizing the widespread hunger for community and social contact, companies such as Starbucks and Borders promote themselves as places where people can come together. This is the old Mitteleuropa coffee shop of the past—only now providing a WiFi hot spot for your laptop so that you can communicate with the world while sipping your frappuccino.

All these are efforts to heal the pain of loneliness caused in good measure by the breakdown of familiar institutions that, until recent decades, provided places, contacts and a sense of community for lonely hearts.

MINGLING WITH MOGULS

Elsewhere, we find imaginative efforts to compensate for the failures of the mass society's mass educational system.

When mass education was widely introduced, teachers were usually the most literate and educated people in the neighborhood. Today parents are frequently far better educated than the teachers to whom they entrust their kids.

Recognizing the role that parents can play in promoting literacy by reading to their children, singer Dolly Parton's Imagination Library sends parents a free book every month from the birth of a baby to age five—sixty books in all. The program, active in thirty-nine states, delivered nearly one million books in 2004 alone.

Meanwhile, more and more disaffected parents in the United States are pulling their kids out of school and teaching them at home. They are supported by a growing variety of up-to-date online services and tools.

One objection to keeping kids home is that they won't learn to get along with other kids. But as public schools decay, and in many places become drug-infested and dangerous, parents wonder if the socialization the schools provide is healthy. If parents keep their children at home, they can develop socialization skills by encouraging the kids to play soccer, or, when a bit older, do volunteer work at an NGO where they can meet other young people engaged in community service.

Here, once more, we find a pre-industrial practice—most children were educated at home before the industrial era—being transformed to meet post-industrial needs.

Charter schools are an attempt to innovate within the system. These are public schools granted a limited degree of freedom to experiment. In the United States they still enroll less than 2 percent of American students, and their results are, no doubt, uneven. But among them we also find many potentially useful innovations.

At the Center for Advanced Research and Technology in Clovis, California, twelve hundred high school students use information technology to help solve real-world community problems. Mentors include local business leaders. Students are encouraged to take part-time jobs and to carry out research projects working with adults in business, industry, trade or the services. A key mission of the center is to demonstrate to young people the relevance of academic subjects to practical problems, on-the-job expectations and work behavior.

Students thus are invited to invent marketable new products that help solve real problems. CART students have invented an ultrasonic cane for the blind and other devices for the disabled. But the school's main output consists of smart young people prepared for twenty-first-century realities.

Institutional invention and experimentation are growing in other fields as well. Across the continent in New York, physician Seth Berkley, who had worked as an epidemiologist in both Uganda and Brazil, created the International AIDS Vaccine Initiative. By 2001 he had raised $230 million to fund the search for an AIDS vaccine.

The sum was equal to annual U.S. government spending on all vaccine research that year and is being used to finance several different lines of research in various countries. What makes the IAVA model noteworthy is that any AIDS drugs resulting from its research grants must be sold at cost in poor countries.

Such social entrepreneurs are rapidly multiplying. Today, more than thirty U.S. business schools, including Stanford, Harvard, Yale, Columbia and Duke, offer courses in pro-social entrepreneurship. Santa Clara University in Silicon Valley has created a Global Social Benefit Incubator to help innovators apply technology to urgent social needs and to assist them in scaling up their efforts.

And, in what many regard as the ideological workshop of contemporary capitalism—the annual World Economic Forum held in Davos, Switzerland—NGO leaders and social entrepreneurs are now peppered in among moguls and magnates, to mingle with presidents, prime ministers and other top-level policy-makers.

Some social entrepreneurs seek to improve the work of existing nonprofits and NGOs by applying businesslike methods to them. Others start new organizations to deal with social problems as they emerge. Both typically rely on volunteers. To that degree, at least, they form part of the non-money or prosumer economy that, as we've seen, creates the social capital and "free lunch" on which the money system depends.

The remarkable growth of social entrepreneurship reflects cuts in government-provided, one-size-fits-all safety nets designed for fast-fading industrial conditions. It reflects the incapacity of smokestack institutions to generate imaginative, customized solutions to new social problems. And it reflects the impatience of millions around the world who have given up waiting for governments and formal institutions to solve problems.

But in the rich societies it reflects something else. In the past, very few people had the luxury of time, energy and education to devote themselves to imagining and inventing—or fighting for—new institutions for the future. Today vast and growing numbers of men and women, including the best-educated and most creative among us, have time, money and access to one another through that empowering global change-maker called the Internet.

INVENTING NEW MODELS

Not all social innovators share a taste for democracy, civility and nonviolence. Fanatics—religious, political and just plain psychotic—can also set up shop as social entrepreneurs. Indeed, some terrorist organizations run schools and hospitals on the side to justify and disguise their fund-raising. And of course, as with all human behavior, even the best-intentioned entrepreneurialism can produce unanticipated negative effects.

Nevertheless, while we should not overestimate what social entrepreneurs can accomplish, even in democracies, it would be an even more egregious mistake to underestimate them. For it is through their experiments—successful and otherwise—that models for new types of institutions can arise. They are a key R&D lab in the battle to design a better future.

However, their value in any society, indeed their very existence, depends on the degree of tolerance by a state and society for internal debate, dissent and deviation from convention. Social entrepreneuring and innovation in general cannot thrive where they are suppressed by government, as in North Korea; by religious police, as in Iran or Saudi Arabia; or simply by the overweening force of tradition. In the United States, by contrast, they have found a receptive host.

American social critics and religious leaders may bridle at the breakdown of traditional values and the emergence of an "anything goes" ethic that may, in fact, verge on decadence.

But such fears are counterbalanced by America's openness, its celebration of experiment and innovation and its willingness to risk investing in new technologies, products, organizational forms and ideas—traits that have fueled the development of the knowledge-based economy since the 1950s.

It is easy to discredit or diminish this rise by pointing out that it now takes two breadwinners in a family to maintain a middle-class standard. Skeptics point to inequalities of income and call attention to America's deficits, debt, job exportation, homelessness and other economic weaknesses. Foreign policy aside, one could continue to list America's shortcomings ad nauseam.

Nevertheless, despite Cassandra-like forecasts repeatedly made since the first arrival of computers in business, the new technologies were never accompanied by massive 1930s-style unemployment. In fact, the predominantly knowledge-based economy in the United States today employs more than twice as many people as the industrial economy employed after World War II. And unemployment rates in recent years have been consistently lower in the United States than in Europe, which has moved forward more slowly.

A close look at America's problems will reveal that many, if not most, of these shortcomings arise from the fact that, while the nation's old industrial economy and social structure are vanishing, their replacements are only half-built.

"SATANIC MILLS"

The material improvements noted earlier were matched to a degree by marked achievements in quality of life. According to the U.S. Environmental Protection Agency, "Pollution from industrial sources and municipal sewage treatment plants has plummeted. By any measure—pounds of pollution prevented, stream segments improved, fisheries restored—tremendous reductions of pollution from point sources have occurred, resulting in substantial improvements in water quality from coast to coast." Since 1970, moreover, "aggregate emissions of the six principal pollutants have been cut by 48 percent." In addition, 45 percent of all paper used in the United States is now recycled, as are 62.6 billion aluminum cans.

Again, any data can be tortured to confess what the issuer wishes them to say, and the struggle against the destruction of nature is still in its infancy in a country in which powerful industrial lobbies successfully resist needed changes. America's refusal to sign the Kyoto Protocol outraged millions around the world.

Nevertheless, here, too, the greatest environmental challenges to the United States—and to the world in general—come from low-tech assembly lines, furnaces and smokestacks, the "satanic mills" of the industrial age, and not from the less tangible activities on which the knowledge-based wealth system is founded.

Finally, the dramatic economic and environmental changes in the United States have been accompanied by important social changes as well. Despite its many problems, America today is less racist, less sexist and more aware of the immense contributions brought to its shores in earlier generations by immigrants from Europe, Asia and Latin America, not to mention by black slaves and their descendants.

American television, whatever its shortcomings, now as never before stars people of color. American supermarkets are filled with ethnic foods from all over the world that are enjoyed by shoppers of every national origin. All this represents the growing internal diversification of its culture, products and people and the social acceptance of these changes.

This is the good news for and from the country leading the world toward a new civilization based on revolutionary wealth.

POST-CASSANDRA?

The story this book has told to this point, then, is the story of the rise of a new knowledge-based wealth system and the new civilization of which it is a part. It has been about the deep fundamentals that underlie economic and civilizational change. It is about the role of time, space and knowledge in our lives and in tomorrow's world. It is about the obsolescence of industrial-age economics and the looming threats to truth and science. It is not just about wealth but about how wealth fits within, and changes, the very civilization of which it and we are a part.

These developments, taken together, require nothing less than a complete rethinking of the role and nature of wealth in the world. And that presents us with three inescapable questions.

Can capitalism, as we know it, survive the transition to revolutionary wealth?

Can we, in fact—and not just in U.N. blah-blah resolutions—actually break the back of global poverty?

Finally, how will the spread of the knowledge-based economies redraw the map of world power?

We turn next to these inflammatory questions.

PART EIGHT

Capitalism's Future

CHAPTER 37

CAPITALISM'S END GAME

Like Broadway theater, capitalism has been pronounced dead countless times—usually in the depths of a depression or at the peak of runaway inflation. Indeed, there are those who say that if capitalism could survive the repeated financial upheavals of the nineteenth century and the Great Depression of the 1930s, its regenerative ability will keep it going no matter what. Capitalism, they tell us, is here to stay.

But what if they're wrong? No other human creation lasts forever. So why suppose that capitalism is eternal? And what if regeneration runs away with itself? In fact, today every key feature of capitalism, from property, capital and markets to money itself, is becoming nearly unrecognizable.

The results of their transformation will directly impact who owns what, the work we'll do, how we'll be paid, our role as consumers, the stocks we'll invest in, how capital will be allocated, the struggle between CEOs, employees and shareowners, and ultimately the rise and fall of countries across the world.

In our 1990 book *Powershift,* we examined the role of all four of these factors—property, capital, markets and money—in relationship to power. Here we focus on the changes since then in each of these, changes that pose critical challenges not just to our personal welfare but to capitalism's very survival. The picture that emerges should shake up its friends and enemies alike.

CARS AND CAMERAS

Property is the place to start because property is the origin of the capital on which capitalism itself is based. And both are now morphing into something new and strange.

Property has often been described, as it still is in one leading English-language dictionary, as "a thing or things belonging to someone." But dictionaries can be wrong, and property never was just a thing or things.

In his groundbreaking book *The Mystery of Capital,* the brilliant Peruvian economist Hernando de Soto has shown that no matter how thing-like or tangible, property has always had an intangible aspect as well.

A house, a car or a camera isn't property if it is unprotected by laws and social norms, and if anyone can snatch it away from you at any time and use it for any purpose. In capital-rich countries there is, in addition to protected legal rights and rules of ownership, an immense system in place that helps convert property to investable capital, which, in turn, stimulates economic development and wealth creation.

This system consists of a vast, ever-changing knowledge base that lists who owns what, tracks transactions, helps hold people accountable for contracts, provides credit information and is integrated nationally so that users are not limited to doing business locally. This adds to the value of property. No such highly developed information systems are found in capital-poor countries, according to de Soto.

It is, in short, the intangible aspects—not just the physical aspects alone—that define property and give it value. Thus de Soto proposes important policy changes to help the world's most economically backward countries while spreading and strengthening capitalism.

When we take this seminal insight one step farther, however, to see how it applies to the most advanced economies, we begin to see how today's knowledge-based wealth system calls the very concept of property into doubt—and capitalism along with it.

THE UNTOUCHABLES

The intangibles we attach to tangible property are still rapidly multiplying. Every day there are more legal precedents, more real-estate records, more transactional data and the like. Each piece of tangible property, therefore, contains a higher component of untouchability. In advanced economies the degree of intangibility in society's property base is spiraling upward.

What's more, even industrial-age manufacturing giants now depend on ever-growing inputs of skill, R&D findings, smart management, market intelligence, et cetera. Their upgraded assembly lines are loaded with digital components busily communicating data back and forth. Their labor force is increasingly peopled with individuals who think for a living. All this changes the tangibility ratio in the economy's property base, further reducing the role of touchables.

Now add to this the rapid rise of what should properly be called "double intangibility"—that is, intangibles attached to property that is intangible to begin with.

The hordes who clamored to purchase shares of Google in 2004 were prepared to buy into a company whose property and operations are almost entirely intangible, in turn protected and enhanced by other intangibles. Investors in Oracle software or in information markets, online auction sites, business models or billing systems don't worry about not owning physical raw materials, furnaces, coal, railroad sidings or smokestacks.

Property thus comes in two distinct forms. In one, the intangibility is wrapped around a tangible core. In double intangibility, it is wrapped around a core that is itself intangible.

Today we don't even have a word that differentiates property according to these two classes. Combine the two, however—and their rapid rates of growth—and we gain fresh insight into the massive "intangibilization" that accompanies the advance to a knowledge-based wealth system.

THE FETISH OF TOUCH

Property in today's U.S. economy is already surprisingly less touchable than most people imagine.

A Brookings Institution study found that, as early as 1982, intangible assets even in mining and manufacturing companies accounted for 38 percent of their total market value. Ten years later—still long before the dot-com climb and crash—the intangible component represented fully 62 percent—nearly two thirds of their value.

These remarkable numbers, however, hardly hint at what lies ahead. In the wake of the late-1990s stock-market dive, investors were told to seek safety in tangibility. But no matter what Wall Street's "back to fundamentals" stock pitchers may say, all advanced economies will relentlessly resume their march toward the untouchable.

A key reason for this is acceleration—a change, as we've seen, in our relationship to the deep fundamental of time. As it reduces product life, hastens technical obsolescence and makes markets more temporary, today's speed-up of change requires companies to innovate. As Baruch Lev, author of *Intangibles* and professor of finance and accounting at New York University, puts it, "The life and death of corporations is now based on innovation," and that means "a huge growth in intangibles."

What's more, innovation is contagious. Leading-edge firms force others to keep up. Even small low-tech supplier companies are compelled by their customers to adopt and redesign I.T. systems, communicate by e-mail, get on the

Internet to connect with their networks, transact business electronically and do more research. In other words: Intangibilize or die.

To survive today, smart companies systematically shift toward higher and higher value-added production. That strategy, too, almost always increases the need for more data, information, knowledge and other intangibles.

Further, managers trained to deal with familiar business matters increasingly find themselves confronted by unfamiliar social, political, cultural, legal, environmental and technological issues of ever-increasing transience and complexity. And the first step in making decisions about novel or unusual circumstances is the call for yet more intangible data, information and knowledge.

Then note the fact that in all the advanced economies, according to Stanford economist Robert E. Hall, "produced goods . . . account for declining fractions of spending." By contrast, "spending is shifting toward the services that are becoming more expensive." These clearly include high-intangibility fields like health and education, media, entertainment and financial services.

Finally, there is an even more powerful reason why we should expect both kinds of intangibility—single and double alike—to become a larger and larger part of the society's property base. That reason is simple: As we've previously seen, fast-breeding intangibles are essentially limitless. And that fact alone puts a dagger at capitalism's throat.

The assumption of limited supply, after all, is at the very heart of capitalist economics. No capitalist "law" is more sacred than the law of supply and demand. Yet if intangibles of both kinds are, for all practical purposes, in inexhaustible supply, can a maximally intangible economy coexist with capitalism? How intangible can the property base of an economy become—and still be capitalist?

THE HORSE AND THE SONG

As the entire property base grows more intangible, hence more inexhaustible, a bigger and bigger part of it also becomes non-rival. Knowledge products, as we've seen, can be exploited by millions of people at the same time without being depleted. All those music swapper-swipers downloading songs for free don't consume the notes.

This change, too, has system-shaking implications. Whole industries confront death staring them in the face as new technologies make it possible to end-run the traditional intellectual-property protections—copyrights, patents and trademarks—on which they have based their very existence.

Media corporations watch their movies and music instantly bootlegged around the world and circulated freely on the Internet. Pharmaceutical firms, having spent hundreds of millions to research and test a new drug, see it pirated by others, who, having spent nothing to create it, peddle it at peanut prices. Other companies have their heavily promoted products copied right down to the brand name and huckstered cut-rate in street carts and at swap meets. They argue that failure to police and protect their rights will dry up incentives for innovation and even destroy their industries.

Their armies of well-tailored lawyers and lobbyists flail about in a revolutionary environment, but their proposals so far are anything but revolutionary. They are instead incremental attempts to stretch yesterday's Second Wave legal codes to meet the challenges posed by an endless, fast-arriving succession of explosive new Third Wave technologies.

"Incremental stretching of old models is what lawyers do," says Eugene Volokh, of the University of California/Los Angeles Law School, with a chortle. But one thing is clear, he says: "However the battle comes out, property is going to become more, not less, intangible—and that means less easily protected."

Which perfectly suits John Perry Barlow, once a lyricist for the Grateful Dead and now a leader in the fight against the further extension of intellectual-property protection. "Otherwise intelligent people," Barlow says, "think that there's no difference between stealing my horse and stealing my song."

As property, the horse is both tangible and rival. The song is neither. Millions can't saddle and ride the same horse. By contrast, Barlow has argued, songs, as it were, "want" to be free, and composers should not depend on copyright royalties to earn a living.

Further, Barlow and others regard extending copyright and other protections as part of a larger, indeed sinister, strategy of giant firms to impose or extend content control over the Internet and other media. They argue that the new media demand radical change.

On the intellectual-property issue, both sides claim they wish to preserve imagination and innovation—though the debate has reflected neither.

The war over intellectual property shows no signs of reaching a truce. It has not yet reached its climax, because it does not yet include coming battles over the ownership of age-old ideas or concepts developed by non-Western cultures.

Digital computation depends on switching between ones and zeros. If we can patent new life-forms—an idea until recently utterly unthinkable—how long before some fanatic ethnic, national or religious group shows up at WIPO, the World Intellectual Property Organization of the United Nations, to claim it "owns" the zero? Or, for that matter, the alphabet? (Think of the royalties!)

Whether we measure intangibles well or poorly, whether we protect them or not, nothing like this has ever been seen in the history of capitalism. And nothing challenges the very concept of property as deeply. But the shift toward revolutionary intangibility is only step one in the extreme makeover of capitalism that is now under way—a makeover it might not survive.

CHAPTER 38

CONVERTING CAPITAL

Q uestion: How does an unemployed heating salesman, scraping by in
the midst of the greatest economic depression the world has ever
seen, become a millionaire?

Answer: By finding a way for millions of others to get rich—with
play money in a game called Monopoly.

Since Charles Darrow sold his game to Parker Brothers in 1935, an estimated 500 million people in eighty countries have moved tokens across
Monopoly boards printed in twenty-six languages including Czech, Portu-
guese, Icelandic and Arabic. In playing the game, they were introduced to a
white-mustached, tubby figure in top hat and tux, seen hauling a huge sack of
money to the nearest bank.

That cartoon figure and the acquisitive nature of the game itself commented wryly on reality in yesterday's industrial America—a country shaped
by the concentrated wealth and power of a few families with names like Morgan, Rockefeller, Carnegie, Harriman, Vanderbilt and Mellon. Pro-business
Americans called them captains of industry—the great personages who built
the American economy. Anti-business Americans called them robber
barons—criminals who bilked, rather than built, the country. The one word on
which both sides could agree was *capitalist*.

During most of the industrial era, capital in the world's most capitalist
country was correctly seen as tightly concentrated. "Before the 1920's," writes
Ron Chernow in *The Death of the Banker,* "Wall Street spurned the small
investor as too trivial to consider."

In the mid-1950s, as white-collar and service workers began outnumbering blue-collar workers, about 7 million Americans owned stock. By 1970, the
number had soared to 31 million—mostly small accounts, perhaps, but no
longer trivial in aggregate. And in the years since then, as the transition to a

knowledge economy continued, direct and indirect ownership of financial assets by the public skyrocketed.

Company after company, starting out in private hands, reached out to a broader and broader public for financing. The Ford Motor Company is typical. Wholly owned by Henry and Edsel Ford as of 1919, Ford went public in 1956 and now boasts 950,000 shareowners.

Today, writes veteran business analyst James Flanigan, the owners of America are the "more than 100,000,000 Americans who hold more than $5 trillion worth of company stock through their pension funds, retirement plans and individual retirement accounts. . . . American workers own more than 60 percent of the stock in all U.S. public companies." That averages out to $50,000 each, not counting equity in the houses owned by nearly 70 percent of them, plus additional assets in the form of health, life and property insurance.

But these ownership statistics tell only half the story. Americans, including a huge percentage of that 100 million, also carry on their backs, like the capitalist's money bag, an immense, ever-ballooning burden of household debt that can all too often outweigh these assets.

In 2005, according to the Federal Reserve, U.S. home owners owed $8 trillion on their mortgages. They owed another $2 trillion on their credit cards, car loans and other consumer debt.

Even so, wide distribution of company stock and other assets makes American workers "owners" to a degree unique in a major capitalist country, including Western European nations under social democratic governments. To those in the poor world, these numbers may be unimaginable.

Ironically, if even 10 percent of China's population bought shares in publicly traded stock of non-state-owned companies, its Communist Party could boast of extraordinary success in transferring ownership of what Marx called "the means of production" to the working class. At present, that number is more like 1 percent.

RANGES OF RISK

Not only the ownership of capital but the way it is collected, allocated and transferred from pocket to pocket is also undergoing unprecedented change. The financial infrastructure in the United States—the beating heart, as it were, of world capitalism—is being revolutionized, its operations altered to adapt to changes in the deep fundamentals of knowledge, time and space. Investments can be made within milliseconds. Spatially, they can reach around the globe. And investors have easier access to ever-faster, more diverse, more customized, more accessible data, information and knowledge.

The main function of this fast-growing infrastructure is to make it easier to convert property into capital and, theoretically, to allocate the resultant capital to those who can make the most efficient use of it—with efficiency measured by profits returned.

The new infrastructure offers a dizzying range of risk-reward choices, including high-yield bonds, venture capital, mutual funds and funds that parallel the performance of stock-market indices. Investors are offered derivatives, securitized mortgages, and financial packages with evocative names like Spyders, Vipers, Qubes and Cocos, as well as funds that offer "socially responsible" investment vehicles, environmental portfolios, microfinance and countless other options.

DEMOCRATIC DOORWAYS

This increased diversity of financial products and instruments is matched by increased access to them.

Thus the United States has seen what John C. Duca, a research vice president in the Federal Reserve Bank of Dallas, refers to as "the democratization of America's capital markets."

In the past, entrepreneurs and even long-established firms had few doors to knock on if they needed capital to expand a company or start a new one. At the top end, a few moguls fared better or used their own money when investing in a railroad in Argentina, a meatpacking plant in Chicago or some company claiming it knew how to cash in on "oil for the lamps of China." For everyone else the doors slammed shut.

As for bonds, even healthy mid-sized firms were regarded as "below investment grade," and many institutional lenders were prohibited, either by law or regulations, from investing in them.

But, writes Duca in the bank's *Economic and Financial Review,* several factors helped free up investment. One was the development of a market for high-yield bonds. Another was the introduction of advanced I.T., which not only cut back-office expenses but radically increased the information available to investors.

At the level of small or mid-sized business, entrepreneurs once had to rely on their own savings or go hat in hand to some wealthy person or family member for capital. Today, according to Duca, "the increased openness, or democratization, of U.S. capital markets means that households have a wider array of investment choices and small businesses have more sources of capital."

Most investments are still made through intermediaries—institutional investors, investment bankers, stockbrokers and others—who either allocate it according to the owner's wishes or who make choices for the investor. But today's investors large and small can end-run the middleman, using the Internet to trade on their own account, directly allocating capital to companies of their own choosing.

When Google, the search engine started by two Stanford University students, decided to sell shares to the public in 2004, it announced to surprised observers that it would let a public auction, rather than an investment bank, set the share price. It would, moreover, give average investors the same opportunity to acquire shares as major investment banks and insiders. So intense was the public interest that, reversing common practice, Google actually took steps to prevent its stock price from opening on an unsustainable high.

Wall Street investment bankers and stock exchanges, having suffered blow after blow, scandal after scandal, in the previous ten years, pooh-poohed Google's end run around them—but worried in private about other companies' raising capital directly, without signing up for their expensive services.

These cumulative and interrelated developments in the way capital is raised and allocated do not take place in a vacuum. They closely parallel changes in other sectors of the economy. Manufacturers, too, as we've seen, are moving toward greater diversity and customization of their products. And retailers are multiplying the pathways by which customers can access them—including shopping online.

All these are part of a societywide conversion to a knowledge-based wealth system. So, too, is the marriage of finance and the media—and its impact on capital flows.

GROWTH IN ECONO-LAND

The U.S. media have become, inadvertently, a vital part of the country's financial infrastructure.

As investor hunger for information has grown, so, too, has Econo-Land—the pseudointellectual agora where economists, business pundits and politicians expound daily on finance and economics. They help fill the ravening hunger of television and the Net for twenty-four-hour programming with chatter about institutional and personal finance.

Round-the-clock stock-market reports, interviews with CEOs, discussions of mergers and acquisitions, with stock prices crawling continuously across the bottom of TVs and computer screens, are now all but unavoidable—along with a carnival of competing commercials for banks, mutual funds, insurance companies, mortgage brokers and other financial services.

The combination of broadcast, satellite and cable television and, even more important, the Internet, makes millions of ordinary Americans aware of financial alternatives never before available to anyone but the super-rich.

Much of this media coverage in Econo-Land is superficial, misleading and highly conventional. But its glaring presence changes the field of play in unanticipated and unanalyzed ways, influencing the amount, forms and directions of capital investment.

In the words of Robert Thompson, director of Syracuse University's Center for the Study of Popular Television, cable TV is capable of whipping "amateur investors" into a frenzy and has essentially put "a ticker tape into every American home."

If nothing else, this bombardment of financial facts and pseudofacts aimed at the American middle class focuses unprecedented public attention on the economy. Every word spoken by Alan Greenspan, as chairman of the Federal Reserve, became countertop conversation in highway truck stops and hospital waiting rooms. Warren Buffett's slightest mumblings about the stock market are passed along by schoolteachers and taxi drivers like biblical wisdom.

The increasing public mind-share devoted to economics in general and capital investment in particular impacts everything from consumer confidence to outsourcing, trade policy and daily politics. Thus the campaign waged by CNN against outsourcing work from the United States to India and other countries fueled Democratic Party attacks on the White House. And at one point the White House protested to two cable news channels for showing stock-market prices plummeting even as President George W. Bush held forth on the economy.

Like other changes in the financial infrastructure, the kudzu-like growth of Econo-Land also reflects change at the level of deep fundamentals. Its near-instantaneous effects on capital market behavior are part of the acceleration of all economic activity—changes in the dimension of time.

Constant reports on global capital markets—Japan's Nikkei, Hong Kong's Hang Seng, Britain's FTSE, Germany's DAX or Mexico's Bolsa—alongside the latest numbers on NASDAQ and the New York Stock Exchange—reflect the incomplete, but growing spatial integration of capital markets. And the fire-hose flow of data, knowledge, information and misinformation about capital markets is a clear reaction to the rise of the knowledge-dependent wealth system.

FLATTENING THE DOWN

We are only beginning to see the effects of this transformation. One of the most significant is the foot-tapping impatience of capital. With capital more mobile, it doesn't stay locked up in bad investments for as long as it once did. Capital commitments are becoming increasingly transient.

According to economist Glenn Yago, a pioneer in the movement to democratize capital access and co-author with Susanne Trimbath of a book on expanding high-yield markets, the increased mobility of capital and the dispersal of risk may have prevented the U.S. economic recession of the early 2000s from spiraling downward and lasting longer.

Another effect of the shift to the new capital infrastructure is less positive and more problematic. It can de-synchronize high-speed finance from the operations of the lower-speed "real" economy.

In the 1997–98 Asian crisis, the Indonesian exchange rate plunged about 70 percent almost overnight. "Hot money" zipped out of the country almost as though 70 percent of its workforce had gone on strike and 70 percent of its stores had closed. Nothing of the sort occurred. It was the speed and hyperactivity of finance that brought the economy down rather than the reverse.

Clearly, more side effects—both good and bad—of the revolution in capital and the financial infrastructure lie in wait. Where, then, are we headed?

Straight-line continuation of these changes could, at least in theory, lead to a single, completely integrated worldwide capital marketplace. One can imagine, at some point in the future, 20 million or, for that matter, 100 million Indian investors suddenly pouring into a British stock on Monday and out again on Tuesday. Or frenzied overnight global auctions that would dwarf the Google experience. But trend projection is a poor tool for forecasting, especially in the midst of a transformation like the one we are living through. Neither history nor the future moves in straight lines.

An alternative, more complicated scenario would alter the very meaning of capital by recognizing and perhaps in some way monetizing other forms of it—knowledge capital, social capital, human capital, cultural capital, moral capital, environmental capital and especially contributions now made by unpaid prosumers. Creating para-currencies and markets for them, all linked to existing financial markets, would transform world economics and further integrate the money and non-money components of the future wealth system.

Even short of this, however, we have already changed capital to the point of near unrecognizability. We have changed who provides it, how it is allocated, the way it is packaged, the speed with which it flows, the places it goes, the amounts and kinds of information and misinformation about it and the ratio of tangiblity to intangibility in the property from which capital is derived.

As both property and capital morph into something drastically new, however, even more wide-reaching changes are remaking capitalism's other crucial features: markets and money.

CHAPTER 39

IMPOSSIBLE MARKETS

T he word *wealth*—the last time we checked—turned up in 52 million documents on the Internet, clearly outranked by the 142 million references to God. Mammon, it seemed, was kept firmly in place. Or was it?

The problem, it turned out, was that one other term turned up 405 million times—twice as often as *God* and *wealth* combined. That term was *market*. Regarded with reverence by mainstream business leaders, executives, economists and politicians in the West, and with hostility verging on disgust by critics of capitalism, markets—like property and capital—are being transformed by revolutionary wealth.

To appreciate how truly striking these changes are—and especially those still to come—it helps to glance briefly backward.

RARE MONEY

The colorful history of ancient markets includes camel caravans on the Silk Road between China and the West, piracy at sea, bazaars in Baghdad and bloody banking rivalries between Venice and Genoa. These stories have been told many times over, and trade surely had political, military and economic effects out of all proportion to its size.

Yet the single most important fact about markets, throughout thousands of years of human history, is not how important they were but how tiny and relatively rare they were.

Until recent centuries, the overwhelming majority of our ancestors lived in a pre-market world. Pockets of commerce existed, but most humans never bought or sold anything during their lives.

As we've seen in earlier chapters, our forerunners—with the exception of a minute minority—were peasant prosumers who subsisted by growing, building, sewing or otherwise producing most of what they consumed. As historian Patricia Crone of the Institute for Advanced Study in Princeton writes, "Every village or manor was more or less autarkic (self-sufficient); money was rare and trade extremely limited."

Even markets for land in the countryside, so central to agriculture, were few and far between. Most land was owned by kings or the state and only granted to noble families under terms that restricted their rights to dispose of it. Land tended to pass slowly from father to son, generation after generation.

Nor, except for slavery, was there anything approximating a developed market for labor. Crone reminds us that "labour was more commonly forced than hired" and that along with slavery there were various forms of feudal serfdom. Wage work was uncommon at best.

Even more remote from the life of the average person were financial markets. At least two cities in China, Chengdu and Pingyao, claim to have invented the world's first bank roughly a thousand years ago. Italians claim that the Banca Monte dei Paschi in Siena is "the world's oldest," having been founded in 1472. Other claims, no doubt, abound, but regardless of which bank was the first, financial transactions basically took place only among elites, beyond the reach of 98 or 99 percent of the total population, if that. In this sense, most humans lived in a world that was essentially not only pre-capitalist, but pre-market.

MASS + MASS = MASS+

It was the industrial revolution—bringing the Second Wave of revolutionary wealth—that transformed the relationship among markets, marketers and ordinary people all over the world.

Industrialization transferred millions of peasants who had until then lived primarily as prosumers outside the money economy into producers and consumers inside the money economy—thereby making them dependent on the marketplace.

Wage labor replaced slavery and feudal relations in the labor sector of the marketplace, and a large labor force sprang up. This meant that workers for the first time were paid in money, minimal though it was.

And as industrial mass production spread, it eventually brought with it the corresponding development of mass markets spurred by three converging forces.

The first was urbanization, as peasants flooded into cities. Between 1800 and 1900 the population in London exploded from 860,000 to 6.5 million; in Paris from 550,000 to 3.3 million; and in Berlin, from 170,000 to 1.9 million.

As city populations mushroomed, urban markets for mass-produced goods expanded; and they expanded yet again when the first railroads made possible a huge leap from local to national markets.

Mass markets and mass production were, in turn, supported by mass media. Thus the early nineteenth century in England also saw the beginnings of the so-called penny press—publications carrying ads aimed at "the masses" as markets sprang up for factory-made clocks, home furnishings, eyeglasses, wallpaper, pewter, apparel and countless other goods.

Innovations in technology and production were followed by innovations in markets and marketing. By 1852 Parisians could shop at Bon Marché, the first big store divided into many departments. Ten years later, the eight-story Cast Iron Palace was built in Manhattan. Downtown department stores soon became a routine feature of cities everywhere.

To sell mass-produced goods to rural customers as well, Aaron Montgomery Ward invented the paper counterpart of a department store in 1872. Taking advantage of advances in postal service and transportation, he created a sell-by-mail business that by 1904 was sending three million potential buyers around the United States a fat, four-pound catalog divided into the equivalent of departments.

Eventually, as mass production, mass media and mass markets continued to fuel one another, innovative retailers and land developers invented those cathedrals of consumerism—shopping malls—spreading these, too, across America, Europe, Latin America and Asia.

In short, the wave of interlaced changes we call the industrial revolution tremendously expanded the role of markets in the everyday lives of most people.

FLASH-MARKETS

Today's transition to a knowledge-based wealth system is once more transforming markets in response to changes at the level of deep fundamentals. Once we understand this, we can catch a glimpse of the future.

In high-turnover economies, markets are continually flooded with new products that are often interrelated in as yet unsuspected ways. As speeds continue to accelerate, with currency and securities markets already operating at blinding, blistering, blitzing rates, the market life of products (and products related to them) will continue to shorten. Synchronizing multiple markets, fed by seemingly unrelated companies, will become an urgent necessity. We are already seeing corporate collaborations along this line.

The attempt, meanwhile, by some marketers to create enduring links between a customer and a brand or a product is likely to prove more and more difficult, if not impossible. Speed will shorten, not lengthen, temporal relationships—including customers' loyalty to brands.

Meanwhile, the spatial shift to global markets adds foreign to domestic competition, not just in fixed or familiar products or in prices but in rates of innovation. Companies on different sides of the world wind up racing one another in arenas so transient they could appropriately be termed "flash-markets."

Simultaneously, rising levels of intangibility and complexity demand vast increases in flows of data, information and know-how. Marketers will increasingly face consumers who are armed with their own arsenal of facts. Many will demand the right to participate in the design of their own products—and to be paid for the data, information or knowledge they supply.

Marketers will also face the opposite—customers in a hurry who revolt against time-wasting surplus complexity and demand the unbundling of unwanted functions.

Smarter and smarter technologies will reduce the cost advantages of mass production, making the halfway step called mass customization obsolete, and true product personalization available at close to zero additional cost.

Markets will thus continue to splinter into ever narrower, more temporary and more knowledge-intensive slivers. De-massification will continue to spread wherever there is a middle class or a culture that favors individuality over herd uniformity.

PERSONAL PRICING

One little-noticed consequence of this growing customization of products is a parallel customization of prices in the marketplace—that is, a shift from standard fixed prices for standard products to tiered or negotiable prices for the same item.

In pre-industrial markets, buyers and sellers typically haggled over price, as they still do in much of the poor world today. By contrast, in mass-production economies, "one size fits all" was paralleled by "one price fits all." Today, in yet another Hegelian flip-flop, we are moving back toward flexible, personal pricing.

As any traveler knows, U.S. airline-ticket prices for the same seat on the same flight can vary madly. In one not-surprising case, the same seat was offered for fifteen different amounts. Using "alternative" or "dynamic" pricing models, sellers now manipulate price according to distribution channel, time and individual customer characteristics.

The growing personalization of pricing is underscored by the phenomenal success of eBay and other online sites in which prices are set by auction. In fact, in everything from hotel bookings to hardware, Beanie Babies, boats, cars, computers and clothing, we see a proliferation of specialized auction markets.

Priceline went a step farther with the so-called reverse auction, in which brand-indifferent buyers post the price they are willing to pay and let the sellers come to them. Other specialized variations quickly followed.

Auctions, in turn, give rise to yet another niche market—a specialized "payments service" for their participants. An ad from Western Union shows a pleased-as-punch online payment-service customer—clearly not a Metropolitan Museum curator—next to the headline: "Bought a velvet matador painting."

Customized pricing will continue to spread for several convergent reasons. For sellers, customized or semi-customized products don't all cost the same amount to make or provide. Computers can handle the added complexity of multiple pricing schemes. And sellers can now collect more and more detailed information about individual customers.

For buyers, the much-delayed day will come when individualized online "bots" or "agents" will crawl the Web, armed with the power to match the most complex and individualized specs against the lowest price.

There is a deeper reason as well. Fixed pricing—ideal for industrial mass production—works best in relatively stable or slowly changing markets. And that is the last thing to expect in the years to come.

APPROACHING THE LIMITS?

Further hastening the retreat from mass markets is today's upheaval in media and advertising—tools without which capitalist markets as we know them could barely exist.

Yesterday's dominant mass media have been giving way to de-massified media capable of targeting ever smaller micromarkets. This process began as far back as 1961 and rapidly spread, as we forecast at the time in an IBM publication. By 2004 it was so hard to miss that the *Financial Times* belatedly announced the coming of "The Audience of One" and "The End of the Mass Market."

Companies that have failed to make the transition to the new marketplace complain about "fragmentation." Those that are thriving in the new environment hail the choices offered to customers who themselves are increasingly individuated.

The speed at which individual markets and entire market sectors rise and fall is unprecedented. The metabolism of capitalism is racing, raising the question of what happens when it breaks far past its normal limits.

Take, for example, rates of marketization and de-marketization.

No market can exist unless it has something to sell. Thus markets, by definition, need inputs—items put up for sale, otherwise known as commodities. Those commodities can be Btu's of energy, hours of labor, a pair of gloves, a DVD, a patent, a Toyota Camry or, for that matter, a ticket to *Tosca*. Today the number and variety of buyable items available for purchase around the world is astronomical and growing every minute. The sum of all these on-sale items is not known.

It is, after all, a prime feature of competitive capitalism to commodify—that is, to put up for sale—as many things, services and experiences, as much data, information and knowledge, and as many hours of available labor, as are thought to be salable.

The spread of market capitalism, hypercompetition, faster rates of innovation and population growth are simultaneously pushing toward further commoditization. Put differently, more "things" are being put up for sale.

But more things are also being withdrawn from sale. Old models and their parts, for example. Even as Toyota shoved additional millions of Camrys into the marketplace, DaimlerChrysler shut down its entire line of Plymouths, and new Prowlers thus disappeared from the marketplace.

In every market at any moment, therefore, we find these same two basic processes at work—marketization and de-marketization. Yet little attention is paid to the speeds at which these processes occur. These rates differ from industry to industry and from country to country as though each operates at a different metabolic speed.

What happens if these speeds become too disparate? Conversely, what happens if both these processes slow down or accelerate in sync? Is there a maximum or optimum rate at which markets can operate? And how do the rates in one country affect other countries? Does anyone know?

WHISPERED SECRETS

Knowledge has always been a factor in the creation of wealth. But in no previous wealth system has the knowledge sector played so dominant a role. Today we are seeing an explosive growth in the amount, variety and complexity of knowledge needed to design, produce and deliver value in every market. As a result, the market for data, information and knowledge is itself growing exponentially.

Consumers devour endless amounts of information, misinformation and disinformation on every conceivable subject, from business and finance to news and entertainment, health and religion, sex and sports. Companies burn through nonstop flows of data about their customers, competitors and suppliers. Scientists and researchers collect findings and formulas from all over the world.

Knowledge has always been hard to define, but as we use it here, it includes not just printed texts or computer data but whispered secrets, visual images, stock tips and other intangibles. No one today knows precisely how large the knowledge sector is, and controversy rages over what to include or exclude. But never before has so much money passed from hand to hand in exchange for knowledge, its component data and information—or for obsoledge.

The knowledge market, however, is not merely expanding. It is simultaneously morphing, owing once more to changes at the deep-fundamental level of the wealth system.

Never has the collection, organization and dissemination of everything from the rawest of data to the most abstract and sophisticated knowledge moved through society and the marketplace at such click speeds. This parallels and even exceeds the accelerative processes we see in every sector of the economy. Time is compressed to nanoseconds. Simultaneously, dissemination crosses all boundaries, expanding the spatial reach of knowledge in all its forms.

Even more important are changes in our knowledge *about* knowledge and in the way knowledge is organized, with long-standing disciplinary divisions going up in flames.

In earlier wealth systems, access to economically valuable knowledge was severely limited. Today much of it flashes nonstop across hundreds of millions of screens and monitors in offices, kitchens and dorm rooms from Manhattan to Mumbai.

In agrarian societies for thousands of years, peasants needed to know about planting a patch of land, predicting bad weather, storing harvested crops. This knowledge was local, spread by word of mouth and basically unchanging.

In industrial economies, workers and managers alike required non-local knowledge from more sources about more things. But economically valuable knowledge—about, say, advances in metallurgy—needed relatively infrequent updating.

Today, by contrast, much knowledge becomes obsoledge almost before it is delivered. The range of subject matter is constantly broadening. The sources are multiplying. And they may originate in any part of the world.

What we are seeing, then, are self-reinforcing, interacting changes that transform the relationships among not only products but whole market sectors. Yet even the cumulative impact of all of these is dwarfed in long-term significance by the emergence of an entirely new, previously impossible marketplace.

THE VIRTUAL TWIN

As noted earlier, virtually every traditional market sector—whether for land, labor, capital, things, services, experiences or knowledge—now has a virtual twin. In effect, the great, global cybermart adds a second layer on top of every conventional marketplace. Nothing like this has ever happened before.

At the turn of the last century, the dot-com collapse briefly made *e-commerce* a dirty word among investors as headlines proclaimed the death of online business: DOT-COMS FLAME OUT . . . THE PARTY'S OVER . . . DOT.COM DISASTER . . . BOOM TO BUST IN SECONDS FLAT . . . THE CRAZE COLLAPSES . . . THE END OF INTERNET TIME.

But, as with the Idaho baby revived an hour after being pronounced dead, eager naysayers buried e-commerce too soon. In 2003, consumers around the world were buying some $250 billion worth of products through e-markets that did not, and could not, exist even twenty years ago—something like $40 worth a year for every person on the planet.

Even that figure may drastically underestimate the total if online retail sales in 2003 in the United States alone ran to $55 billion—and this Commerce Department number did not include such nongoods as travel purchases, financial services, entertainment-ticket sales and online dating-site fees.

Further, they offer no clue to the real size, power and potential of online markets or exchanges for direct business-to-business transactions.

Thirteen airlines, ranging from All Nippon and KLM Royal Dutch to Lufthansa, Air New Zealand and Northwest, created Aeroxchange, the virtual equivalent of a medieval fair, to display their wares and make deals. Today's thirty-three members buy parts from four hundred online vendors in thirty countries. Similar electronic exchanges now exist for many industries, including automotive, utilities, chemicals, defense, health care, restaurants, all kinds of repair services and spare parts.

In 2003, business to business e-commerce was already estimated to top $1.4 trillion a year. That's not $50 per human—it's more like $230. And that number will soar in the years ahead and account for a bigger and bigger percentage of all commerce.

This global move to a knowledge-based wealth system should not be measured merely in terms of stock-market prices and the diffusion of technology. It is much more profound, and threatens capitalism as it has, until now, been described.

As the Third Wave, knowledge-intensive wealth system spreads to Asia and other parts of the world, they, too, will see revolutionary changes in their property bases, capital formation, markets and—as we'll see next—in money itself.

CHAPTER 40

RUNNING TOMORROW'S MONEY

T he economics of the future are somewhat different. You see, money doesn't exist in the twenty-fourth century."

So said Captain Jean-Luc Picard of the starship *Enterprise* in the science-fiction movie *Star Trek: First Contact*. Neither, perhaps, will capitalism exist by then—and its demise may arrive long before AD 2300.

It is a strange new world we are entering as revolutionary wealth continues to unfold here on Earth, yet both enemies and defenders of capitalism still hurl centuries-old clichés at one another. If changes in the nature of property, capital and markets aren't enough to shake their minds free of the past, perhaps a look at the future of money will.

Like the other key elements of capitalism, money is undergoing the fastest, deepest revolution in centuries—one that will create radically new forms, new ways to pay and be paid, and more and more business opportunities that use no money at all.

THE HIDDEN TAX

The invention of money clearly was one of the great world-changing events in human history, and all capitalist economies run on it.

That invention, despite all its subsequent misuse, opened the path to tremendous advances in human well-being. But running money, or more properly, the money system, imposes a heavy cost on society—and on each of our pocketbooks.

We hardly notice this cost because it is usually embedded or bundled into the price we pay for goods, services and other marketed items. Go to a movie theater or a sports stadium. Part of the price you pay covers the cost of the person who takes your money and hands you the ticket. The same is true for the 3.5 million cashiers behind U.S. checkout counters at Wal-Mart, Home Depot, 7-Eleven, Office Depot and Office Max outlets; at supermarkets, department stores and railroad stations. And this doesn't include the total number outside America.

Then, too, at McDonald's, Burger King and other fast-food emporia, the person at the counter takes both your order and your money. It is true that taking your order and passing it to the kitchen is technically distinct from cashiering. That means that only part, rather than all, of his or her wages is attributable to time spent collecting money. But collecting money is similarly part of the job for many other occupations—millions upon millions of waiters, barbers and salesclerks. All these costs, too, are passed along to the customer.

And this is only the most visible expense of operating the world's money system. Someone has to keep track of all the transactions. And that, too, costs money. So add at least part of the fees paid to bookkeepers and the world's 2.5 million accountants. And someone has to actually print, store and transport the cash we use; protect it from theft and counterfeiting; authenticate documentation and so forth. These functions, too, cost money.

Ultimately transferred to the customer, these costs are, in effect, part of a hidden "tax" we pay for the convenience of employing money. And they are only a small part.

Which raises some important, mind-sparking questions. What if we could reduce or even eliminate this hidden "tax"? Is that possible? In fact, do we need money at all to run a knowledge-based wealth system?

BLIPS ON CHIPS

Ever since brokers began congregating at Jonathan's Coffee House in the eighteenth century and gave birth to what became the London Stock Exchange, the money system in each country in the West has had within it a financial-services industry handling the needs of borrowers and investors. This industry has relied on the most advanced data storage and communications available in each period. But, as late as the 1950s, that still meant file cabinets, the post office, rotary telephones and ticker tapes to manage money-relevant knowledge.

The rise since then of the knowledge-based economy has been attended not merely by the extremely rapid expansion of constantly changing data, information and knowledge but by the brisk growth of the middle class, burgeoning pension funds and insurance coverage, a vast increase in customers for financial services—and the need for an entirely new financial infrastructure.

By 2002, financial services employed fully 5.5 percent of the entire U.S. workforce. Put differently, more than one out of every twenty American workers was engaged in banking, insurance, pension management, mortgage companies, real estate investment trusts and the securities industry.

These businesses manage the flow of money through the money system, providing liquidity, assembling and allocating investments, rating and furnishing credit, maintaining secondary markets for stocks and bonds and grading and managing risk.

In the United Kingdom, where the City of London is home to some of the world's largest traders in Eurobonds, derivatives and insurance, more than one million people are employed in finance. Concentrations in financial services are also found in Zurich, Frankfurt (sometimes labeled "Bankfurt"), Tokyo, Hong Kong and Singapore. And new regional centers are springing up from Shanghai to Dubai. Linking all these and other nodes together are high-powered computers and high-speed networks that aggregate and disperse money for investment and credit, not to mention speculation.

In 2001 alone, financial firms in the United States, where the network is most dense and most advanced, spent $195 billion on I.T.—more than any other industry and more than the total gross domestic product that year of such technology-hungry countries as Singapore or Finland. Yet the demand for even more instantly available information, data and knowledge is growing constantly.

The effects of this shift from the industrial-age financial infrastructure to its near-instantaneous, almost global digital form are by no means understood as yet, either by its users or by its customers—and least of all by policymakers and the public.

THE CLOSING BELL

Only a small fraction of the sums exchanged each day on the world's stock markets is actually channeled to companies on the basis of their needs and long-term prospects. Instead, pre-programmed computers simultaneously scan thousands of firms to identify the most minute variations in their stock prices and frequently "invest" funds not for months or years but for minutes or even seconds. The result in large part is no longer investment but mathematically based, hyperspeed electronic poker.

And it is no secret that within these markets, one in particular has grown so fast and furiously that the *Financial Times* describes it as "virtually unrecognizable from ten years ago." This is the global currency market—swollen to the point that $1.2 trillion is bought and sold in it every single day, more than thirty times the entire amount traded daily on the New York Stock Exchange.

In it, the *Financial Times* adds, trades are often multibillion-dollar transactions that take less than a second.

But little if any attention has gone to an even more troubling issue. For here once more we see change at the level of the deep fundamental of time—and yet another case of de-synchronization.

Theoretically, the value of a country's currency reflects, in great measure, the strength of its underlying economy. The de-synchronization, however, between high-speed currency trading and the slower pace at which a country's "real" economy operates has grown so pronounced that the polarities—at least in some countries—are reversed.

That's why, as noted earlier, it was not bad economies that destroyed Asian financial markets in 1997–98 but bad currency markets that tore down one economy after another.

Similarly, near-instantaneous currency markets have left not only real economies but financial regulators in the dust. The result of this lack of synchrony is a system regarded by many as a threat not merely to individual countries but to the world economy. Super-slow national authorities with different and conflicting rules cannot regulate superfast global networks.

Many economies and economists still have trouble coming to terms with immense sums of "money" that exist only as temporary ones and zeros continually zipping from node to node in digital trading networks, with minimal human interaction. The effects are abstract, seemingly impersonal. Yet once in a while a poignant image encapsulates the revolutionary shift from the old money infrastructure to the still-emergent new structure.

World-renowned photographer Robert Weingarten recently decided to shoot a series of pictures of the world's stock exchanges. Assuming that their trading floors would someday all be replaced by electronic markets, he wanted to record their twilight in a series called "The Closing Bell." It would capture frantic traders shouting and rushing about to close sales while telephones ring endlessly and changing prices blink across overhead light boards. He would then shoot the rooms as they look after closing: empty and desolate.

Because he is a Californian, his first stop was the Pacific Stock Exchange in San Francisco. But when he arrived to scout the location, he found the former stock-trading floor under reconstruction. The exchange had already converted equity trading to an electronic auction system called Archipelago, increasing the volume of its business twentyfold. The specialists and traders were already gone.

The floor was on its way to becoming a gymnasium. And Archipelago was on its way to merging with the New York Stock Exchange.

WILDCAT CURRENCY

On its surface, today's revolution in money—much of it still to come—seems chaotic. Yet if we look a bit closer we discover a hidden motif. It is the same pattern of de-massification and diversification that we have already seen in production, markets, media, family structure—indeed, throughout the emergent new civilization. So profound are these changes—and those to come—that they challenge the very definition of money.

Central banks have their own answers to the question "What is money?" The U.S. Federal Reserve definition essentially bundles together actual currency with money in our checking accounts and traveler's checks and calls this "M1" money. Add to M1 the sums in our savings accounts and money-market mutual funds and it's called M2. Add a basket of other, mostly arcane, items and it becomes M3.

For ordinary people going about their daily lives, these distinctions don't exist. The basic unit of money in America is the "almighty dollar." Few of those who use it every day know that until the industrialization of the nation was ramping up, the government-backed dollar was only one among as many as eight thousand different wildcat currencies in the United States issued by states, banks, individual companies, merchants and miners.

The standardization of money imposed by the U.S. government in 1863 paralleled the standardization of products, prices and consumer tastes that came as part of the process of industrialization. And the same was true in other countries as well.

The Japanese yen didn't become the national currency until 1871, as the Meiji restoration was starting the country on the path to industrial modernity. Similarly, the deutschemark did not become Germany's monetary unit until 1873, as Germany raced to overtake Britain as the leading industrial power.

China long suffered from monetary chaos—with warlords, states, revolutionary bases, foreign enclaves and others each issuing their own currencies—right down to December 1948, as the Communists took over and introduced the renminbi yuan. And Europe, of course, has only recently standardized on the euro.

Ironically, this belated standardization—like much else in the European Union—comes just as the knowledge-based wealth system begins to move advanced economies in the opposite direction. In fact, homogeneous currencies are about to be challenged by a dizzying diversity of alternatives.

PARA-MONEY

In 1958—just two years after white-collar and service workers initially out-numbered blue-collar workers in the United States—a prototype for the first nationwide credit card was launched. This was the start of a Third Wave leap away from conventional money and into what today sometimes seems like a wilderness of "para-money"—a jungle of substitutes that have some or all of the characteristics of official currencies but aren't.

Money is fungible, meaning that it can be used in principle to buy just about anything. It can also be transferred to and from just about anyone. That near-universal applicability has made it very handy as a medium of exchange.

But a strange thing is happening. Today, with more than 840 million credit cards in use in the United States, Americans charge one trillion dollars a year on plastic—more than they spend in cash. And every day, it seems, we invent additional substitutes for money.

Our airline tickets are often "free," paid for with frequent-flier points. Originally, these points could be redeemed only for free seats on another flight. They were completely nonfungible—and not transferable to anyone else. They were unmoneylike.

Before long, however, airlines permitted your points to be used by family members, friends—anyone you chose. Beyond airline tickets, the points became redeemable for hotel rooms and rental cars, then an ever-widening range of merchandise—health-club memberships and hockey tickets, barbe-cues and wide-screen TVs, gardenias and garden hoses. What we saw, there-fore, was growing transferability and fungibility. Frequent-flier points were becoming more moneylike.

They become actual money when they are sold to any of the various "mileage brokers" who operate a gray market for points, over the objections of the airlines.

True, given the financial shakiness of some of the issuing airlines, one might worry that the redeemability of all these points is in doubt. But these intangible frequent-flier points may soon be worth more than the currency issued by some of the world's dead-broke governments who still own airlines.

Of course, loyalty programs of various kinds, with greater or lesser degrees of fungibility, are used not just by airlines. They are offered by every-one from InterContinental Hotels and Hilton to Neiman Marcus and Tesco Europe, from CVS drugstores and Chart House restaurants to Kawasaki motorcycles.

In the swirling, changing, milling marketplace they, too, perform some of the functions of plain old garden-variety money. But this is only part of a larger change—the arrival of "flexible fungibility" in the form of program-mable money. And your thirteen-year-old may not like it.

THE ANTI-OBESITY CARD

A torrent of oncoming technologies will make possible endless further vari-eties of para-money. Thus, cards may soon let us decide how much fungibilty we want. The Arab Malaysian Bank in Kuala Lampur has offered a card to Muslim customers that disallows use in massage parlors or nightclubs.

Before long, activist political movements, for example, may issue millions of "boycott cards" that are fully fungible—except that they cannot be used to buy Nikes, Shell gasoline, clothes from the Gap or products of other compa-nies on their hit list. Wives or husbands might program restrictions on a free-spending spouse's card. Or parents may give their children cards that cannot be used to buy candy, alcohol, tobacco—or fast food.

Overweight individuals wishing to avoid fast-food fat-food but finding it hard to resist may get help from a pay card they themselves can program to block any payment to Pizza Hut or Taco Bell—or all fast-food vendors. Make a resolution, quit carrying more than a dollar's worth of cash and let your card help stiffen your resolve.

Even newer technologies are making cards themselves obsolete. In South Korea, cell phones are already the equivalent of electronic wallets. Containing a chip provided by a participating bank, the phone can authorize the retailer to make a withdrawal from your account. Such phones are already used at high-end clothing stores, restaurants, vending machines and train stations, among other locations.

In Europe major banks such as UBS, Barclays, BNP Paribas and Deutsche Bank have joined Visa in exploring the potential of similar technologies. Wax-ing enthusiastic, Liisa Kanniainen, a vice president of the Scandinavian bank Nordea, says, "I don't expect to kill cash by next year, but hopefully eventu-ally." What she didn't add was the parallel death threat these technologies pose to cards as well as cash.

Three new converging forces will provide an even greater variety of pay-ment options.

First are new technologies to verify a user's identity. A rash of increasingly reliable identification methods are coming into use. In Japan, for example, the largest credit-card issuer, JCB, has introduced a system that identifies individ-uals by the unique pattern of blood vessels in a finger. Banks and card issuers, using research accelerated by the fight against terrorism, are also exploring other biometric methods, including retinal scanning and voice and face recognition.

Second are new wireless technologies, too numerous and rapidly changing to detail here.

And third, across the board, are dramatic advances in miniaturization.

Drawing on innovations in all three of these fields, many companies, including Sony, Philips, Sun Microsystems and IBM, are working on striking alternatives to conventional plastic. Says Sun's John Gage: "Credit cards are just a physical variant of identity, so any way you can identify someone can be a way to pay for things."

Blend these technologies together with the Gage principle, and it is not difficult to imagine the eventual implantation in our pinky, say, of a minute chip that would make it possible to purchase anything at any time from any place by simply activating it.

A pinky chip could wirelessly assure a retailer that we are who we claim to be, supply a bank-account number and simultaneously authorize the bank to pay the appropriate amount. The phrase "giving someone the finger" could take on fresh meaning.

This rapid diversification of both payment methods and degrees of fungibility reflects the advanced economy's overall move away from the one-size-fits-all mass society of the industrial past.

Even more radical possibilities, including whole new currencies, are being examined by some of the world's biggest companies. Sony, for instance, has been considering creating a currency of its own for use inside the company. That could permit a Sony unit in China, for instance, to do business with sister units in Japan or elsewhere without first exchanging foreign earnings into yen. The main objective would be to reduce currency risk. A further possibility would be to create a joint currency with other companies such as Honda or Canon.

The dollar may not remain a low-risk haven for foreign investors forever. And unlikely as it may seem today, the day could come when one would rather have an electronic pocketful of Microsoft "Gateses" or Sony "Moritas" than euros or dollars. Or a currency collectively backed by the Fortune 500—or, someday, the Xinhua 500.

STREAMING MONEY

Among their other functions, para-monies are designed to speed up or slow down payment. Thus, credit cards encourage delayed payment (in return for an interest charge, of course). Debit cards, rather than delaying payment, speed it, immediately deducting the purchase price from the cardholder's bank account.

The emerging new wealth system also opens the path to radical changes in how, and especially when, we are paid for work.

In the industrial past, workers were typically paid intermittently, at the end of a week or month. Most still are. This means that employers have a week's or month's free use of money actually owed to the employees. This "float" is the equivalent of an interest-free loan from workers to their employers.

Conversely, utility bills, for example, are usually paid after the customer has already received a month's worth of electricity or gas. In this case, the customer is the beneficiary of float.

In the larger economy, some companies and industries—publishers of subscriber magazines, for example—live on float. But float, regarded by some economists as inefficient for the economy as a whole, may be on its way out.

Once companies and customers are all adequately wired up or wirelessly interconnected and we pay bills electronically, we may see utility providers demand streaming payment—a contract to allow their computer to electronically suck payments out of our equally electronic bank accounts moment by moment as we use their services. They would get their money sooner, would be able to use or invest it earlier and could—theoretically, at least—reduce the price they charge us.

We may also see groups of workers demanding to be paid electronically minute by minute for the work they do, rather than waiting for paydays.

Streaming pay and payments are the natural parallel of the move in advanced knowledge-based economies from batch or intermittent production to continuous-flow, 24/7 operations. And the more instantaneous the in-stream of paychecks and the out-stream of payments, the closer the effects are to direct cash transactions.

These accelerating innovations have given rise to many forecasts suggesting the "death of money." At one time, these may have seemed fanciful. But are they?

PEPSI VODKA

During the worldwide Great Depression in the 1930s, a satirical French movie called *Le Million* showed two farmers sitting at an outdoor bistro savoring glasses of Bordeaux. When the waiter gives them the check, *l'addition,* one farmer reaches into a sack and hands him a chicken. The waiter returns with change, putting two eggs on the table, at which point the farmer picks up the eggs and places one back as the tip, or *pourboire*.

The absurdity perfectly captures the realities of life for millions in economies where money loses its value, as it did not so long ago in Southeast Asia, Russia and Argentina.

However, tomorrow we may not wait for crises to engage in moneyless transactions. Barter, long regarded as impractical in complex markets, is being given new life.

For the average person, the word *barter* calls to mind images of a primitive society or of small-scale personal exchanges. A lawyer writes a will for a friend who gives him a tennis lesson in return. So many of these transactions occur daily and are so natural that they pass for favors. But economically speaking, they are in fact minor forms of barter.

However, barter is also big business.

While reliable global statistics are hard to come by because definitions vary, according to *Forbes,* "it is estimated that more than 60 percent of all Forbes 500 companies use barter. Even heavyweights, including General Electric, Marriott, and Carnival Cruise Lines have been known to barter goods or services." *Fortune* reports that two thirds of all major global companies regularly engage in barter and have set up departments specifically to handle such deals.

In Argentina in 2002, as the economy tanked and auto sales melted away, Toyota and Ford agreed to accept grain in payment for cars. When Ukraine racked up a massive debt for natural gas, Russia took eight Tu-160 Blackjack bombers as partial payment. Russia swapped three billion dollars worth of Stolichnaya vodka for Pepsi-Cola syrup. Other governments have put on the barter block everything from alpaca cloth to zinc.

At the global level, according to Bernard Lietaer, formerly chief planner of the Belgian central bank and one of the architects of the euro, international corporate barter, otherwise known as countertrade, is in "common use among no less than 200 countries around the world, with a volume that now ranges from $800 billion to $1.2 trillion per year." And barter growth is accelerating.

One reason is that we may well be heading into decades of tempestuous economic conditions. Says Lietaer, major currencies today are "exhibiting a volatility that is presently four times higher than in 1971."

High volatility suggests that an increasing number of countries will find themselves facing periodic foreign-exchange shortages. Barter gives governments and businesses a way to trade when no one wants their own nation's currency. It is also a way to reduce risk when currencies oscillate wildly. When countries agree to exchange goods or services in lieu of money, currency risk is essentially eliminated.

Until now, the main objection to barter has been the difficulty of matching what one person wishes to sell with what another has to offer in return—what economists have called a necessary "coincidence of needs."

However, the rise of the Internet radically reduces these impediments, making it almost instantly possible to locate potential trading partners around the world and expanding the variety of barterable items.

Not only is it easier—given today's remarkable financial networks—to find a partner for a two-sided trade, but the ready availability of data and global communications makes it possible to match the simultaneous offerings and needs of multiple participants. This points toward more complex but far bigger barter deals in days to come.

How big? Big enough to replace money within this lifetime?

"There is no reason products and services could not be swapped directly by consumers and producers through a direct exchange—essentially a massive barter economy." That conclusion comes from Mervyn King, formerly deputy governor of the Bank of England.

Combine (1) the rise of para-money; (2) the growth of barter; (3) the increase of intangibility; (4) the spread of ever-more-complex global financial networks; and (5) radical new technologies soon to be deployed. Set these against (6) a world economy that is highly leveraged, rocked by largely unregulated speculation; and (7) the coming decades of seismic changes in the world geopolitical framework, and conventional, industrial-age money may not disappear—but it may become a collector's item.

PROSUMER PAY?

Today, as these forces converge, we also find scattered small-scale experiments with alternate currencies, mostly at a community level, often combined with elements of barter.

A program pioneered in Ithaca, New York, and now copied in dozens of other communities allows consumers and merchants to use chits rather than real currency to exchange goods and services for everything ranging from rent and medical bills to theater tickets.

Another system, created by Edgar Cahn and detailed in his book *Time Dollars,* lets people build up service credits for, say, taking an elderly neighbor shopping, which can then be used to obtain babysitting from another participant in the network.

In their own ways, all of these ventures seek to recognize and give quasi-monetary value to the many economic contributions made by prosumers. Considering the vast new opportunities opened by electronic exchange, it may be possible to expand on such community-based experiments and develop large-scale alternative currencies for certain kinds of prosumer activity described in earlier chapters.

At the opposite end of the spectrum, the Terra Project calls for a supranational currency based not on gold or wildly floating exchange rates but on a basket of internationally traded commodities and services.

The larger questions facing us, however, involve not only the fate of money but, as we've seen, the future of property, capital and markets—and their interactions—as well.

They involve the shift from wage labor toward "portfolio work" and self-employment; from handcraft prosuming to technology-based prosuming; from profit-based production toward open-source contributions to software, medicine and other fields; and from value embedded in machines and raw materials to value based on ideas, images, symbols and models inside billions of brains. They involve completely altered uses of time, space and knowledge—among the deepest fundamentals of wealth.

How might the growing links between unpaid prosumer production in the non-money economy and the paid production in the money economy affect capitalism? What happens to capitalism when its most important input is not scarce, but essentially limitless and non-rival? What happens to capitalism when a growing proportion of property becomes not only intangible, but doubly intangible?

Faced with these changes, as the Third Wave of change supplants industrialism and spreads far beyond its origins in the United States, capitalism faces a crisis of redefinition. When that revolutionary redefinition is completed, will what remains still be capitalism?

PART NINE

Poverty

CHAPTER 41

THE OLD FUTURE
OF POVERTY

R evolutionary wealth brings a new future for impoverishment.
While no future arrives with a guarantee, the arrival of the Third
Wave knowledge-based economy brings with it the best chance yet
of—once and for all—breaking the back of global poverty.

It would be utopian to suggest that we could totally eliminate material
want everywhere on the planet. Poverty has too many sources—from stupid
economic policies and bad political institutions to climatic shifts, epidemics
and war. But it is not utopian to recognize that we now have—or are on the
edge of developing—extremely powerful new anti-poverty tools.

Poverty is supposedly everyone's enemy. Virtually every government in
the world claims to be trying to eliminate it. Thousands of NGOs collect
money to feed hungry children, purify village water supplies and bring medical care to the countryside.

Pious resolutions issue forth from the United Nations, the World Bank, the
International Monetary Fund, the Food and Agriculture Organization and
other international agencies charged, at least in part, with fighting poverty.
And the adjectives applied to global penury run from merely "heartbreaking"
to "disgraceful," "tragic," "shameful," "scandalous," "appalling," "shocking,"
"unspeakable" and "inexcusable."

Thousands of meetings and conferences have been devoted to the problem. Hordes of well-intentioned experts have flown into remote regions to
provide technical assistance, and an enormous multibillion-dollar "aid industry" has grown up around global poverty reduction.

Between 1950 and 2000, more than $1 trillion flowed from the rich world
to the poor in the form of "aid" or "development assistance." Some of these
dollars saved lives and did improve conditions: The smallpox eradication program in the 1960s, child immunization in the 1980s and campaigns against

river blindness, trachoma, leprosy and polio. Yet we are told by the World Bank that nearly 2.8 billion people—almost half the population of the planet—still live on the equivalent of two dollars a day or less. Of these, some 1.1 billion survive in extreme or absolute poverty on less than one dollar.

What is truly amazing about this, however—apart from the failure to wipe out global poverty after half a century of concerted international effort—is the incredible *success* these numbers reveal—once we look at them in reverse.

None of this is intended to minimize the tragedy of twenty-first-century poverty. But a time traveler from the seventeenth century who turned up in the world today would be stunned not by how poor the human race is but by how big and unbelievably rich it has become.

Having left behind a world that barely supported a population of 500 million people ridden by successive famines and plagues, he or she would surely marvel that more than 6 billion humans survive on the planet today, including more than 3.6 billion who live *above* the two-dollar poverty line.

HITTING THE LIMIT

Before the industrial revolution, horrific poverty was not just concentrated in Africa, Asia or Latin America. According to historian Fernand Braudel, in the Beauvaisis region of France in the seventeenth century, over one third of all children died every year. Only about 60 percent reached the age of fifteen.

Braudel describes a Europe swept by plague and recurrent famine. The poor crowded into cities, begging and stealing to stay alive. Children and wives were routinely abandoned, many doomed to perish in poorhouses alongside the elderly and infirm.

Nobel Prize–winning economic historian Robert Fogel points out that "the energy value of the typical diet in France at the start of the 18th Century was as low as that of Rwanda in 1965, the most malnourished nation for that year."

France was not alone. For ten thousand years, only the tiniest fraction of the world's population ever lived above the barest subsistence level. And the world's richest countries were only twice as rich as the poorest.

If this was roughly true around the globe, with all the diversity of agrarian people, cultures, climates, religions and farming methods, it strongly suggests that peasant agriculture had at some point hit its upper limit of productivity.

A POVERTY OF STRATEGIES

It was only after the industrial wealth system began to replace agriculture that the population soared and significant numbers of people crawled out of utter destitution.

This history led economists and policy-makers to a common prescription for what is still called "development" or "modernization"—a strategy for moving a country's workforce and economy from low-productivity, low-value-added farming to more productive, low-tech manufacturing and its support services.

From the early 1950s on, this Second Wave strategy was propagated in endless variants by experts from the United States, Europe, the former Soviet Union, the United Nations and NGO development agencies. Its message was, essentially, that each country had to replay the industrial revolution.

And, indeed, there was no realistic alternative model.

After the 1960s, some critics attacked this strategy and proposed focusing not on factories and the urbanization that came with them but on small-scale "appropriate" or "alternative" technologies that are sustainable and use local resources.

Since then, this movement has broadened, encouraging microfinance and the creation of small business in poor-world countries, reaching out to science, and becoming more sophisticated.

Many imaginative innovations have flowed from this movement. But it is essentially designed to stop or slow further industrialization and to keep peasant populations on the land. Moreover, in their assumption that "small is beautiful," many of the movement's militant adherents still romanticize peasant existence and village life. They demonize all but the most primitive machines and make little distinction between industrial and knowledge-intensive technologies.

Claiming that both these technologies serve only the rich, critics ignore the benefits they have, in fact, brought to millions of the world's destitute. More important, they do not understand that Third Wave technologies have already indirectly raised huge numbers out of misery and offer for the first time in more than three centuries fresh, powerful ways to attack the poverty of the poorest.

TYPICAL JAPANESE "MUCK"

In the past, economic development and poverty reduction depended mainly on a country's domestic factors—the availability of capital, local resources and environment, along with the propensity of the population to save, the drive, energy and work habits of the labor force, and so forth.

Since the mid-1950s, this has been less and less the case. As the world economy has become more integrated, with trade, people, capital and especially knowledge moving across boundaries, external factors have risen in importance.

And that includes indirect, second-order effects all too often unnoticed or ignored. The future of poverty cannot be understood until these spillover implications are taken into account.

A good example can be seen in the amazing chain reaction that helped fuel Asia's economic rise—a rise that has seen more than half a billion Asians climb above the two-dollar-a-day poverty line in just twenty years.

The story actually began in the mid-1950s as the United States started its development of a knowledge-based wealth system.

Across the Pacific, Japan's industrial economy, having been ground into dust during World War II, was still pathetic. Its defeated military was nonexistent and its politics were shaky at best.

At this pivotal moment, the United States, facing an ascendant, nuclear-armed Soviet Union, reached a three-part deal with Japan. Militarily, Japan would ally with the United States against the threat posed by the communist U.S.S.R. In return, politically, the United States would tacitly support the conservative Liberal Democratic Party; economically, it would fling its doors wide open to Japanese exports.

The problem with this last point was that Japan had little to sell that Americans might want. Around the world, Japanese products were a laughingstock. In a British play as late as the 1970s, actor Robert Morley still got a laugh by referring to "typical Japanese muck." But by then Japanese exports were no longer "muck."

Japan solved its muck problem by drawing on two largely American innovations. The first involved statistical quality-control methods spread throughout Japan by Joseph M. Juran and W. Edwards Deming during the 1950s and '60s. Assembly-line perfection became a national passion. (For their contributions, the emperor awarded both men the Order of the Sacred Treasure.)

Quality did not become a catchword in U.S. manufacturing for another decade or two. Even today Japanese Toyotas, Hondas and Nissans routinely outrank the cars of Detroit and Europe in J. D. Power quality surveys.

The other American contribution was the industrial robot, about which a similar story can be told. In 1956, engineer Joseph F. Engelberger and entrepreneur George C. Devol met one evening over cocktails and discussed *I, Robot,* Isaac Asimov's classic science-fiction novel.

Together they set up a company, named it Unimation (for "universal automation"), and, five years later, delivered the world's first working industrial robot. General Motors installed it in its plant outside Trenton, New Jersey, but other American companies showed little enthusiasm for the new computer-driven technology.

"I had a hard time with American industrialist[s]," Engelberger later said.

By contrast, he continued, "the Japanese caught on right away. That's why robotics is a $7 billion industry and it's dominated by Japan."

In 1965, according to the Japan Automobile Manufacturers Association, "new technologies . . . became a top priority." More specifically, by 1970, digital technology, much of it imported from the United States, led "in a short while to computerization of the entire manufacturing process," while robots "gradually eliminated the need for humans to perform dangerous work."

By the late 1970s, according to John A. Kukowski and William R. Bolton in a Japanese Evaluation Center report, "Japan was the world leader in industrial assembly robots, and in 1992 it operated 69 percent of all installed industrial robots in the world, compared with 15 percent operated by Europe and 12 percent by the United States."

Armed with these and other knowledge-based tools, Japan, in little more than a decade, began astounding the world not only with high-quality products but with products no one had ever seen before.

Soon names like Sony, Fujitsu, Hitachi, Toshiba and Mitsubishi started popping up on billboards all over the world. In 1957 Toyota sold exactly 288 cars in the United States. In 1975 it brushed aside the Europeans to become the best-selling foreign car brand in the United States. In 2002 Americans bought 1.7 million Japanese cars, including many turned out in Japanese-run plants in the United States.

The combination of U.S. technological knowledge and an American hunger for Japanese products, plus Japan's own technological savvy and underestimated innovativeness, shot adrenaline into its economy.

While its factories poured out such consumer products as VCRs, TVs, cameras and stereos, Japan also moved aggressively into semiconductor chips and computer components for the American market, bringing itself farther toward knowledge-based production.

By 1979, Japan was IBM's chief rival in the manufacture of computers, and a book entitled *Japan as No. 1* attracted attention on both sides of the Pacific. The author attributed much of the Japanese corporation's success to its ravenous hunger for knowledge and its emphasis on training—bringing in foreign consultants and sending countless teams out to visit world centers where the most advanced knowledge was being pursued.

The first secret of Japanese success was "learning, learning, learning." The second was creative commercial application of new knowledge. The third was speed.

Thus, by the 1980s, Japanese chip technology was advancing so rapidly that Washington slapped trade limits on the importation of Japanese semiconductors.

Cars, consumer electronics, computers, chips, copiers—none of these, on the surface, seemed relevant to the lives of Asian peasants. Or to the attack on poverty.

But they were.

THE SPILLOVER EFFECT

Japan's high-tech manufacturing miracle brought in such immense amounts of money and sent the yen spiraling so high that Japanese companies began investing heavily in factories in Taiwan, South Korea and, in time, Malaysia, Indonesia and the Philippines—helping to kick-start the development process in what soon were called the Newly Industrialized Countries, or NICs.

In effect, Japan had begun off-loading its low-tech, low-value production to neighboring cheap-labor countries, while it upshifted more and more to knowledge-based operations.

Japan was not the only spigot from which direct investment flowed into Asia. Nonetheless, by the 1980s, according to the Library of Congress Country Studies, Japan had, in fact, "displaced the United States as the largest provider of investment and economic aid" in the Asia-Pacific region. In all, Japan poured more than $123 billion into its Asian neighbors between 1980 and 2000.

It is difficult to determine precisely how many new manufacturing and related service jobs in these Asian countries are specifically attributable to the influx of investment from Japan, America and Europe. Or to the next step, when South Korea and Taiwan themselves began investing in their poorer neighbors—setting in motion a developmental chain reaction spilling over from the United States to Japan to these other countries.

The result was the flow of billions of dollars into agrarian economies in the region where some of the world's worst poverty existed.

In each of these recipient countries, we saw the same classic process at work—the shift of the workforce from agriculture to industry. In South Korea as late as 1970, 51 percent of the labor force was still in agriculture. By 2000, the number was down to 9 percent, while manufacturing employment had risen to 22 percent.

In Taiwan during the same period, the shift went down from 37 percent rural to 7 percent, as the industrial workforce swelled to 35 percent. Malaysia went from more than 50 percent in agriculture to 16 percent, with manufacturing jumping to 27 percent. Similar, though less dramatic, shifts occurred in Thailand, Indonesia and the Philippines.

In each case, too, it was not just money that was transferred. With it came what economist William Easterly, formerly of the World Bank, has called "leakage"—a diffusion of knowledge, not just about technologies, but about finance, about markets and marketing, about import-export rules and business in general.

The net effect of this massive transfer of industrial-age activities and know-how has been to raise multitudes of the world's poorest people out of the most extreme poverty. Ending up struggling in urban slums may hardly seem like progress to people with full bellies. But for most of the Asian millions driven off the land by drought, hunger and disease, going back would be worse. And they know it.

This process, during which countries transitioning toward knowledge economies transferred some of their manufacturing to poor, mainly agrarian countries from Asia to Latin America, had important corollaries.

The recipient countries saw lengthened life expectancy, a general decline in infant mortality and reduced rates of population growth, the latter a key factor in the poverty equation. Between 1960 and 1999, per capita food production in the world grew by nearly 25 percent, and the number of those surviving on less than 2,100 calories a day—the threshold used to define malnutrition—plunged by 75 percent.

Not incidentally, during roughly the same period, East Asians, starting from an admittedly low base, saw a 400 percent increase in average real incomes.

The gains made by these and other poor countries, and not merely in Asia but in Latin America and elsewhere, are not the result of the softhearted benevolence of the rich world. These external inputs of capital—accompanied by hand-me-down relevant knowledge—would have had little impact without the brains, energy, hard work, ideas, entrepreneurialism and struggle of leaders and ordinary people in the poor countries themselves.

Overall, however, what we find is a remarkable case of trickle-down economics—which for reasons that were unanticipated and unintentional actually worked, and not just in Asia.

Yet an important question remains: How much of this anti-poverty progress in recent decades would have happened had the computer never been invented and the latest revolutionary wealth system never arrived?

The story, moreover, doesn't end with this question hanging in the air. For none of what we've seen here so far fully explains the turbo-powered rise of Asia—or tells us what happens next as China and India burst onto the world scene.

ASIA CAN'T WAIT

Much has been written about the Dickensian horrors of early industrial society, and much of it could still apply to the lives of the poor today, including those who migrated to the overburdened cities of the world. Many on the left attacked industrial capitalism on economic grounds and urged national planning and social progress to eliminate the terrible "booms and busts" that came with it. Some bemoaned its atrocious environmental effects, often on aesthetic grounds. From the right, others, for cultural and religious reasons, romanticized the past and attacked industrial modernity. Often, as among the Luddites, technology became the *bête noire.*

Today many of the same arguments are directed at proponents of the knowledge-based wealth system and the civilization that accompanies it—often in the very same words, as though nothing has changed in the last half century—the period marked, in fact, by the most accelerated, deepest global transformations in the history of poverty.

To this point we've seen linear change. Wave One, then Wave Two—exactly matching the traditional claim that the only pathway out of poverty is sequential. But now change comes faster. To adapt, leading companies now replace sequential steps in decision-making and production with new systems based on simultaneity. You don't finish one part before starting the next. You make the parts simultaneously and integrate them faster.

And that is exactly what China and India are doing today. They are no longer content to complete Second Wave industrialization before beginning their Third Wave development.

The result is a strategy for parallel development. And they may even be able to skip certain steps in the process.

What we are really seeing in these countries—whose combined peasant populations form the core of global poverty—is nothing less than the greatest experiment in poverty reduction since the beginning of time.

CHAPTER 42

TWIN TRACKS TO TOMORROW

In October 1983, just four years after Deng Xiaoping began to release China from the iron grip of anti-capitalism, a conference of policy leaders was held in Beijing under the wing of the reformist premier Zhao Ziyang, who called on China to study the concept of the Third Wave as introduced in our book of that name.

Some, still fearful of stepping outside the perimeter of Marxist theory, reportedly went over Zhao's head to the then general secretary of the Communist Party, Hu Yaobang, and asked what he thought of the conference proposal. Himself a liberal in the Chinese context at the time, Hu responded with words to the effect that "too many people in the party are afraid of new ideas."

Since then, top Chinese leaders—and tens of millions of their followers—have strongly supported the idea that China should not merely focus on industrialization. It should simultaneously, and as rapidly as possible, try to build a knowledge-intensive economy, skipping wherever possible the traditional stages of industrialization.

This is why China shoots an astronaut into space, why it sets out to become a biotech superpower, and why in just a few years it has more than 377 million mobile-phone subscribers and more than 111 million Internet users.

It is why China is attempting to set its own technical standards for DVD players, chips and computers, not merely for protectionist reasons but to influence future technological advance around the globe, as the British did in the nineteenth century and the Americans did in the twentieth.

It is why the Beijing Genomics Center impressed the world by breaking the genetic code for rice in record time. It is why—while the Bush White House slowed medical research by severely restricting government money for embryonic stem-cell research—China is moving aggressively forward in this field.

It is why, according to *New York Times* columnist Thomas Friedman, the Chinese city of Dalian is becoming a knowledge center rather than a manufacturing base. "No," he writes, "they are not just making tennis shoes here. Try GE, Microsoft, Dell, SAP, HP, Sony and Accenture, which are setting up backroom operations here for Asian companies and software R&D centers."

It is why China graduates 465,000 engineers and scientists a year and is making a concerted effort to bring home thousands of Chinese scientists working in the United States.

It is why hundreds of multinationals have rushed to set up R&D labs in China—with an estimated two hundred labs arriving each year. Says Harry Shum, chief of Microsoft's Beijing lab, "Nowhere in this universe has a higher concentration of I.Q. power."

And it is why, in 2003, China passed Japan and Europe in exports of digital equipment, then overtook the United States in 2004, according to the Organization for Economic Cooperation and Development.

China's twin-track strategy—selling cheap industrial labor while racing to build its knowledge sector—is set against a background of less central planning, a downshift of power to regions and local governments, expansion of market activities and, if anything, an overemphasis on exports.

These changes are accompanied by widespread pain, social disruption and unrest, all of which may well get much worse. Chinese leaders are right to put stability at the top of their agenda.

As we'll see in more detail later, they need to worry also about AIDS, SARS and disease outbreaks yet to come; protests not merely on a manageable local level but on a national level; financial panics; environmental crises; out-of-control energy costs and looming shortages; and generational cleavages—not to mention greater instability in relations with Taiwan. Even worse, two or more of these crises could converge. Only the naïve think revolutionary changes follow straight trend lines.

But they also know their historic mission—to end the mass poverty that has characterized China for the past five thousand years. And according to *The Economist,* China has raised 270 million people above the extreme-poverty line since 1979.

The glass may be half empty, but before this, for these people, there was no glass. And no future.

Nor is the twin-track strategy applied only in China. The other vast pool of poverty is in India.

INDIA AWAKENED

A short man with a friendly face and a helmet of long silver hair falling over his ears climbed a few steps onto the stage, clipped a microphone to his gray Nehru jacket, and began speaking in a voice so soft and gentle that one strained to hear it even over the loudspeakers as he called up slide after slide in his presentation. We were in New Delhi in 2003 at a conference entitled "India—Giant or Pygmy?"

Although his name is little known outside India, A. P. J. Abdul Kalam, son of an impoverished boatbuilder, is a Muslim in a predominantly Hindu nation and the former chief scientist/engineer behind India's satellite, missile and nuclear programs. He is also president of India.

Kalam doesn't govern the nation—politicians do that. But he is a widely admired symbol of up-from-poverty success and a commitment to interreligious harmony. He is also coauthor of *India 2020—A Vision for the New Millennium.*

Kalam's priority project, when we spoke with him later in the presidential palace, was connectivity. Not among technologies but among villages—tiny, remote villages distant from one another. Kalam has developed a program to slow urbanization by linking villages physically, electronically, economically—and in terms of access to knowledge.

Counter to the belief that advanced technologies do nothing for the poor, it is the knowledge economy and the technologies associated with it that have awakened India from a half century of postcolonial slumber, helping to lift more than 100 million Indians out of poverty and placing it, according to some estimates, ten or fifteen years behind China.

That lag, according to some, may be offset by three advantages that India brings to the race. First, the wide prevalence of English makes contact and communication with the Anglophone world easier. Second, India is less export-dependent than China, thus less vulnerable to currency and other risks. And third, its less authoritarian, relatively open society is more likely to promote innovation.

BANGALORE CENTRAL

The world media today focus on the striking changes wrought by the outsourcing of jobs to India from the United States and elsewhere. Indeed, the story of I.T. jobs flowing to Bangalore, Hyderabad, Pune, Gurgaon and Jaipur has made front-page headlines around the world. By 2004 India was earning $12.5 billion a year by manning call centers, writing software, performing back-office work, accounting and even financial analysis for American and other foreign firms.

But the charge that outsourcing takes jobs away from Americans overlooks a reverse effect. As the *Los Angeles Times* found, "Bangalore . . . is full of evidence that outsourcing directly benefits the United States. The city's well-paid workers are taking their wages and giving them right back to U.S. as well as European companies." They do so at places like Bangalore Central, a new shopping mall offering such imported brands as Levi's, Polo, Lacoste and Jockey.

The outsourcing boom—insourcing from India's point of view—is unlikely to continue at its present pace of growth, but it has helped create a segment of nouveaux riches who are young, middle-class, focused on the "now" and too smart-ass for its elders.

The 2004 election in India resurrected the Congress Party, whose roots in quasi-socialism led it to view development conventionally as a matter of factories and smokestacks rather than the transition to a knowledge-based wealth system. But even longtime holdouts are coming around, including Communists, who are theoretically farther to the left than the Congress Party.

A reporter not long ago chided the Communist chief minister of the state of West Bengal, where Calcutta is located, pointing out that "your party helped protest the advent of computers."

The chief minister's response: "That was in the 1970s—that was foolish, foolish. It started when they were going to introduce computers in banks and [insurance companies]. Their employees protested and we supported it. . . . Nowadays they have understood. . . . We have entered a century where industries will be talent-based." Now even Calcutta, once the world symbol of urban misery, has reached out and attracted IBM.

Article after article has pictured India's talented young I.T. workers as a greedy, socially irresponsible, yuppiesque middle class. Less attention has been paid to the fact that, because of computers, 6.7 million peasants in the state of Karnataka can now, for the equivalent of thirty cents, get a printout of land records securing their property from takeover by corrupt, farm-grabbing landlords.

On a wider scale, in 2005, a consortium of Indian and U.S. corporations, along with the World Bank, announced a plan to set up Internet kiosks in five thousand Karnataka villages to allow rural residents access to banking, education and government services. Karnataka is held up as a model for the rest of the nation.

I.T. and telecommunications, however, are not the only advanced technologies that can contribute to a real war on poverty. Thanks in part to President Kalam, India has "one of the most successful operational space programs running in the developing world, with capabilities to design, develop, fabricate and launch its own communication and remote sensing satellites," according to science writer Dinesh C. Sharma in the journal *Futures*. "It is also planning to send a scientific payload to go around the moon using its own rocket."

Once more, this may seem irrelevant to the poor—unless, as Sharma points out, your land is subject to sudden flooding or you are among the thousands saved from drowning with the help of satellite-based disaster-warning systems and remote sensing technologies.

Or if you are among the 100,000 patients of the Regional Cancer Center in Thiruvananthapuram who once had to travel extremely long distances, often more than once, and at high cost, for treatment or follow-up care.

The RCC has now set up six peripheral centers. All six are teleclinics linked to the main facility by the Internet—and the number of necessary follow-up visits has fallen by more than 30 percent.

The Indian Space Research Organisation has also created satellite links between big, multi-specialty hospitals and eight remote health centers to allow the exchange of patients' records, images and data from medical instruments, along with live video and audio contact. All this means that doctors in central locations can help guide medics in the remote rural villages.

In biotechnology, according to Ernst & Young, India could generate $5 billion and up to a million new jobs in the coming five years. India's Insurance Regulatory and Development Authority has agreed to allow insurance firms to put money into biotech, and the government has made it easier for foreign venture capitalists to invest. It is in this sector, as we'll see shortly, that some of the most important tools for the reduction of poverty may well be found. And not just in India.

Many of the advances we see in India are still either experimental or limited. They are patchy and not yet systemically integrated.

But as more pieces of the knowledge-based wealth system are laid in place and begin to interact and reinforce one another, their payoffs will increase combinatorially, if not exponentially, as happened in the past when different components of the industrial wealth system—social, institutional, political and cultural—came together.

India faces many of the same social, political and cultural challenges we find in China—corruptionitis, AIDS, massive environmental problems, the need for institutional reinvention and generational conflict, to name a few. Externally, while China worries about Taiwan, India worries about a shaky, nuclear-armed Pakistan and the ever-bloody struggle against Muslim secessionists in Kashmir. What's more, and unlike China at present, India faces caste conflict and intermittent murderous battles between Hindu and Muslim fanatics.

Despite all this, India knows it cannot delay a fresh assault on poverty—and it cannot win that attack with smokestacks alone. It also cannot win so long as most of its population remains doomed to a low-productivity peasant existence, no matter how much small-scale "appropriate technology" is introduced. Neither a Second Wave strategy nor a First Wave strategy is enough.

THE GREATEST GENERATION?

This, indeed, is true not merely for China and India but for Asia in general and the rest of the world. It is a reality grasped by a remarkable generation of Asian leaders long before their counterparts elsewhere.

Lee Kwan Yew, the founder of independent Singapore, propelled a once sleepy colonial port into a world leader in high technology and services. In 2002 it became Asia's top investor in biotech.

Mahathir Mohamad, Malaysia's controversial former prime minister, set high-tech goals for Malaysia 2020 and attracted investment from Microsoft, Intel, Japan's NTT, British Telecom and others. When Malaysia gained independence in 1957, its key exports were rubber and tin. Today it is a leading exporter of semiconductors and electrical goods.

President Kim Dae-jung in South Korea, who served on the National Committee on Science and Technology before his election, approved $1.1 billion in funds for nanotechology research. Once in the Blue House, he campaigned successfully to make his country a world leader in the application of I.T. and broadband communications—which it is today.

Our talks with these and other Asian leaders make it clear that for them low-wage manufacturing jobs—and even routine call-center jobs like those outsourced to India—are just baby steps toward something far more dramatic: The leap to an advanced knowledge-based economy and society.

As we scan the rest of the world, we can only ask, Where are the Lee Kwan Yews or Kim Dae-jungs of Latin America or Africa? In the Arab world, hopefully, we see the first glimmerings of awakening in some of the Gulf States and in Jordan under young, computer-literate King Abdullah.

What is it that has kept these various regions so mired in poverty? The hangover of colonialism? Religion? Culture? Corruption? Climate? Unstable politics? Tribalism? Or combinations of these? Why do these regions lag so far behind the United States, Europe and fast-rising Asia? The answers differ by time and place. But one thing is clear: It is in Asia—in rural China and rural India—that the true core of world poverty is found, and it is in these regions that the knowledge-based wealth system can have its greatest success.

YES, BUT NO

It would be naïve to assume that India or China can wipe out poverty with technology alone. No country can. We have repeated throughout that the wealth revolution involves more than computers and hardware—more, in fact, than economics. It is clearly a social, institutional, educational, cultural and political revolution as well.

But it is also true that no country can eradicate its age-old rural poverty without drastically increasing agricultural productivity, and that can't be done on a wide scale just by building better hoes and plows.

Nor can it be accomplished by eliminating the agricultural subsidies paid by Europe and the United States to their minute handful of farmers.

The effects of these subsidies are far more complex than their opponents suggest. A controversial case can even be made that, while they severely hurt subsistence peasants, they can indirectly spur industrial development. But there is no doubt about the immediate short-term devastation they create in many poor countries.

Yes, European and American subsidies—mainly payoffs to favored political constituencies—should be slashed. But no one should imagine that even their total and immediate elimination would actually solve the problem of rural poverty.

Yes, the rich world, if only for moral reasons, should drastically increase funds for humanitarian aid and disaster relief. But feeding people during an emergency or digging out corpses and helping re-house displaced victims after an earthquake or tsunami will not, in and of themselves, transform the economics of world poverty.

Yes, hunger must be addressed. Immediate, emergency aid must be provided for the world's hungriest people. Among the benefits, it will save the brains of children from the effects of malnutrition—brains needed in a future in which knowledge assumes increasing importance. But hit-and-run food supplies for the worst-off will not break the back of global poverty.

The same goes for AIDS and other country-ravaging diseases that are killing millions each year in Africa and Asia. No one can be anything but horrified and heartsick at the immense human tragedy they represent. We must save every life we can. Yet stopping the spread of these diseases without making other fundamental changes will not break the cycle of rural destitution.

Economic advance, as everyone by now should know, demands saving women from degradation and inequality. It demands that we reduce, if not wipe out, corruption—and that we do the best we can, for now, with what passes for education.

But all of these measures, even all of them together, will not ultimately liberate the billions of rural poor whose lives are severely limited by the earth's stingy response to their unending, bitterly hard, sweaty labor.

For that stingy response is the core reason for core poverty.

Subsistence-level poverty cannot be conquered unless peasant agriculture is replaced by more productive activities. Any other plan is illusory.

There is an upper limit, even under the best of circumstances, to how much First Wave peasants can make the earth produce with the tools they now use.

There are limits, as well, to how much Second Wave mechanized agribusiness can produce without severely damaging the environment. (Once the cost of rehabilitation is included, the productivity is less than it seems.)

For all practical purposes, however, there are no limits to what Third Wave knowledge-based agriculture can produce. And that is why we are on the edge of the biggest change in rural life since our ancestors first began to till the soil.

CHAPTER 43

CRACKING
POVERTY'S CORE

Behind every strategy there is a dream, an image of what should be. A Third Wave strategy for breaking the back of poverty begins with what may, to some, seem like a dream—but could well become a reality, and soon.

Indeed, it is the old anti-poverty strategies, not the new one, that are unrealistic. Incremental microchanges at the village level are not enough to bring about the massive progress that is needed.

Nor can China or India, or those who follow their course, hope to succeed by turning themselves into megafactories polluting their air, land and water to degrees never before seen and jam-cramming hundreds of millions more peasants into cities already at the breaking point.

We will keep people from fleeing the countryside into urban *favelas, villas miserias,* shantytowns and squatter villages only when the productivity gap is closed between what brute labor on the soil can accomplish and what advanced technology makes possible today—and will make possible tomorrow. It will also take far greater clarity of purpose.

The entire public discussion of global poverty is muddied by a failure to decide whether the goal is to minimize absolute poverty—or to close the much-discussed "gap" between rich and poor.

Closing the gap can be accomplished by impoverishing the affluent without necessarily raising the living standards of the poor one iota. By contrast, the industrial revolution radically widened the gap—but also reduced poverty. Attempts to move everyone forward equally have repeatedly proved a disaster. The prime goal should be to raise the living conditions above absolute poverty, whether or not the relative gap widens.

Only after every baby is fed, after everyone's drinking water is safe, after average life expectancy in poor countries reaches at least seventy and after basic education targets are met should closing the gap be a priority.

What is needed is a strategy aimed at nothing less than the transformation of today's impoverished rural areas into centers of advanced, highly productive enterprise—regions no longer dependent on the muscle power of emaciated, old-before-their-time parents but on the brainpower of their children.

To be realistic, this strategy must look beyond the immediate—at what is emerging, even embryonic. Fortunately, powerful tools now being developed can help us. They begin with the fiercely contested issue of genetically modified food.

INSTEAD OF TRIAL AND ERROR

Public pressure to improve safety and prevent accidental cross-contamination of crops is valid and socially helpful. But attempts to ban genetically modified (GM) foods altogether are irresponsible and potentially deadly. Even the cofounder of Greenpeace, Patrick Moore, has charged that the campaign against these foods is based on "fantasy and a complete lack of respect for science and logic."

Despite Luddite opposition, the world is going to move toward the production and use of environmentally safe genetically modified foods and other products of biotechnology. And that, combined with innovations brewing in a dozen other fields, can help crack once and for all the core of poverty on Earth.

We know by now that genetic modification and other biotech methods can increase a crop's nutritional content. They can reduce the need for fertilizers, irrigation and pesticides. They can help plants grow on arid land or in cold climates. They can radically boost per-acre yield. They can slash costs and increase the value of agricultural output.

Until now, GM food crops have been widely grown in only six countries and have been largely limited to soybeans, canola, corn and cotton because these crops are popular in the West and are commercially profitable. But this is changing.

The Indian Department of Biotechnology sees in the near future large-scale production of transgenically improved cabbage, tomato and potato crops. According to India's former minister of agriculture, Rajnath Singh, the country also plans genetic research into twelve major poor-world crops, including maize, cassava and papaya.

China has recently approved the importation of Monsanto's genetically modified corn and soybeans, having, according to some, delayed until now in order to give its own scientists more time to catch up with the technology. But some farmers don't want to wait.

According to the Science and Development Network, "Strict measures adopted in recent years to tighten control over imports of GM soybean have failed to stop the growth rate of GM imports. In 2003, China imported more than 20,000,000 tons of soybean worth U.S. $4.8 billion—a rise of 100 percent over the previous year. More than 70 percent of China's imported soybeans are genetically modified."

This underlines the difficulty of regulating or policing the new tools, especially in regions where governments have little control. But it hardly invalidates the crying need for them. Recognizing this reality, according to *Science,* "China is developing the largest plant biotechnology capacity outside North America."

Richard Manning, author of *Against the Grain,* a study of the historical rise and impact of agriculture, reminds us that farmers have been crossbreeding and raising hybrids for centuries—all based on trial, error and luck. "Now," he writes, "replace those fuzzy factors with precise information about the role each gene plays in a plant's makeup. Today, scientists can tease out desired traits on the fly—something that used to take a decade or more to accomplish."

BRING ON THE BANANAS

With the help of biotechnology, more and more foods will also be enhanced with disease-fighting properties—including illnesses widely prevalent in poor countries.

Hepatitis B kills more than half a million people a year, a third of them in Asia. Four hundred million of us around the world are carriers. In the United States, hepatitis inoculations consist of three shots that together cost about two hundred dollars—a sum far beyond the reach of millions of peasants. Researchers at Cornell University are trying to drive the cost down to about ten cents a dose by implanting hepatitis vaccine in bananas. Before long, we may also see tomatoes and potatoes fortified with vaccines to prevent hepatitis B.

Or take a strain of "golden rice" fortified with vitamin A to help prevent the blindness now common among children in poor regions. In India, scientists are also working on vaccine-laden foods to fight cholera and rabies.

Tomatoes that may protect against diarrhea (one of the worst baby killers), corn enhanced to combat cystic fibrosis and vitamin-loaded fruits and vegetables—are all being studied.

Moreover, it should surprise no one if, as we learn more about the genetic and proteomic makeup of individuals, other high-value-added foods are designed not merely for medical purposes but for cosmetic reasons or to enhance personal performance.

As biotech companies continue to turn out new strains of seeds, "pharmers" will be able to customize output for smaller and smaller high-value markets, and eventually even for individuals.

In fields where everyone is still, so to speak, at the starting gate, there is no inherent reason why poor countries cannot "catch up" with leading nations and not only feed their own populations better but profitably export high-value-added agricultural products. All these, however, are just the start of the possibilities.

BIO-ECONOMIES

In a striking document that has received too little attention, the Center for Technology and National Security Policy, a branch of the National Defense University in Washington, D.C., pictures a world in which "agricultural fields will assume the same significance as oil fields."

Even oil-company executives have begun talking about the "last days of the Age of Oil." Dr. Robert E. Armstrong, author of the NDU paper, takes this idea one step further, suggesting that we are moving toward a "biobased" economy in which "genes will replace petroleum" as a key source not only of many types of raw material and products but of energy.

American farmers at the start of this century were generating 280 million tons of waste leaves, stalks and other plant parts a year. Some of that biomass is already converted into chemicals, electricity, lubricants, plastics, adhesives and above all, fuel.

This, however, is only the beginning. Armstrong foresees the countryside dotted with small "biorefineries" that would turn waste biomass into foods, feeds, fibers, bioplastics and other goods. He cites a 1999 National Research Council report estimating that a domestic bio-based economy in the United States could ultimately fulfill "90 percent of U.S. organic chemical consumption and 50 percent of our liquid fuel needs."

Nor is this just an American matter. In such an economy, Armstrong continues, "the basic raw material will be genes, and these, unlike oil, are found all over the world." He thus forecasts a huge geopolitical shift of power from desert-bare oil countries toward tropical regions richly endowed with biodiversity.

"In a biobased world," he writes, "our relations with Ecuador (to use a representative country . . .) will be more important than those with Saudi Arabia." The reason: Ecuador has far greater biodiversity—hence gene diversity—of potential value to the world. And if that is true for Ecuador, what might it mean for Brazil? Or central Africa?

At the Eden Project in Cornwall, England, Tim Smit directs what *Fast*

Company calls "the world's largest greenhouse." "We are on the verge of a revolution that is greater than any in the 20th century," according to Smit. "There are now composite materials that you can make from plants that are stronger than steel and Kevlar. The implications are phenomenal. Every country in the world could have access to advanced materials created from their own plants."

Moreover, he continues, "biorefineries will have to be built close to the source of their raw materials. A regionalized agriculture will likely develop, with certain areas growing specific crops to supply regional biorefineries. . . . The significance is the likely creation of nonfarming jobs in rural areas."

Armstong concludes, "A biobased economy ultimately could help stem the flow of urbanization."

HELP FROM THE HEAVENS

Peasants aren't stupid. They couldn't survive if they were. They know their tiny patch of earth. They know the smell of an oncoming storm. They know when the dry season is due. But what they know is a minute fraction of what they could know. And that delta—that difference—helps keep them poor.

Even smart farmers in rich countries waste labor, energy, water, fertilizers and pesticides; cause serious ecological damage; and grow less product than is possible because of what they don't know in detail about their land. Help, however, is on the way, from twelve thousand miles in space.

Until now farmers—including agribusiness companies—have usually applied the same treatment to an entire field—a one-size-fits-all strategy.

But we are approaching the point at which a handheld Global Positioning System receiver in a village—or one shared by several villages—will receive increasingly detailed information from currently orbiting satellites about the specific fertilizer, nutrients, water and other needs of every individual plot, if not plant.

This will customize farming, allowing a grower to apply fertilizer, say, only where, when and in the least amount needed. It can also transform current water systems by improving irrigation and recycling methods and even make possible higher-value-added water for specialized uses.

In fact, according to a National Research Council study, "improvements in irrigation technology alone can reduce the anticipated worldwide demand for additional water resources by one half during the next 25 years."

Good for farmers and good for the environment, "precision agriculture" and customized purification methods bring de-massification to the field.

And this points to a larger, indeed, transformatory change. We know that industrial-style agriculture leads to environmentally dangerous monocrops and monoculture. By contrast, what we see here is a first hint of potential movement in the opposite direction, not by a reversion to pre-industrial methods but by an advance far beyond them.

As markets, at least in the rich world, call for increasingly customized foods and health products, we can expect to see new, varied methods and technologies that will ultimately draw on more varied crops from around the world—something that environmentalists should anticipate and welcome.

Today precision agriculture and many of these other new methods are still nascent—and expensive. But costs will plummet.

SECRET PRICES

Wang Shiwu, a peddler in rural Anhui Province in China, used to haul his wares in a basket hoping to find customers in nearby villages and markets. It was a way of life not too different from that of peddlers or peasants a thousand years ago.

Wang's life changed in 1999.

He realized then, he says, that "a wonderful opportunity had arrived." And today Wang's customers come to him. The wonderful opportunity was the Internet.

Wang was not a geek. And, at fifty-two, he wasn't a kid. But he was entrepreneurial, and before long he was surfing the Net in his home, collecting market information and offering it to fellow villagers free of charge.

Every farmer knows the importance of timely price information. Traditionally, sellers had to take their crop or herd to market on the bare chance that it would sell. Only then would they learn what prices were being offered—a system that severely limited their bargaining power. By supplying current price information, Wang changed all that.

Wang then also offered to sell their products online. He sold the first 2 million kilograms of sweet potatoes at a higher price than that available in the local market. Before long, e-mail began pouring in, and Wang was in business.

Wang's story is told by Xinhua, the official Chinese news agency, which reported enthusiastically that, as of 2001, most farmers in Anhui had access to a computer and that 1,634 towns in the province—90 percent of the total—could obtain free market information online. The province also sponsored online "trade fairs" that saw more than 100 million kilograms of grain change hands in one year alone.

Xinhua has more recently reported that more than 17,000 Chinese villages—41 percent of the total—now have access to the Net. But China still has a long way to go. Its Ministry of Science and Technology paints a less glowing picture of rural reality, estimating that rural residents make up less than 1 percent of the country's Internet users, and these are concentrated in a relatively few provinces.

THE SMARTEST AGRONOMIST

Twenty-five hundred miles away, Shashank Joshi, who raises soy on two acres in India's Madhya Pradesh state, is also providing online price information to farmers—but as part of a business-cum-social innovation called e-*choupal.*

ITC, one of India's biggest corporations, needed a better system for procuring the soy, tobacco, coffee, wheat and other crops it exports. Which was why it set up its own I.T. network for thousands of growers in rural India. It provided computers to Joshi and others like him. In return, the recipient agreed to turn his home into a *choupal,* or gathering place, where peasants could come to meet, chat, drink tea—and find out the latest prices for their crops in local, government-mandated markets. Or, for that matter, on the Chicago Board of Trade.

According to Kuttayan Annamalai and Sachin Rao of the World Resources Institute, each *choupal* computer serves "an average of 600 farmers in 10 surrounding villages."

In addition to tracking prices, the grower can learn about new farming techniques—either directly from the screen or, because many farmers are illiterate, with help from the host farmer, or *sanchalak.* Some online information is rewritten by the farmers themselves to make it more reader-friendly.

The *sanchalak* receives a commission from ITC for purchases made through him but "is obligated by public oath to serve the entire community."

The bottom line: When ITC buys from the farmers, it is at the previous day's closing price. Only then does the farmer transport his crop to an ITC processing center. And prices average 2.5 percent higher than those available to him in the government market system.

The basement line: Despite India's success in attracting outsourced high-tech business from the United States and elsewhere, and despite e-*choupals* and many other innovations and experiments, the country has an even longer way to go than China in closing the digital divide.

Price information and a few tips on how to improve a crop are the least of the Internet's potential for the rural poor. The Web is, in fact, the world's smartest agronomist, offering no fewer than 21 million agriculture sites, accessible by plant, region, climate, ecology, chemistry, biology and just about every other topic of relevance to a farmer.

Rural villagers can teach outsiders plenty about courage, grit, humor in the face of hardship, and about coming to terms with bitter reality. And arrogant, ignorant outsiders traipsing into a village to "help" deserve the scorn they often receive.

But as the price of computers continues to tumble toward one hundred dollars, along with the cost of cell phones and other tools that put isolated minds in contact with one another, nothing is more important than opening villages to the rich (and enriching) flow of outside knowledge.

In a world in which knowledge and its component information and data are more and more inextricably linked to wealth creation, villagers need to know about matters that never seemed to matter. About the dangers of new plant and animal diseases from distant sources, about the changing value not merely of crops but of land and supplies, about looming environmental dangers (and opportunities), about new ways to fight corrupt local officials, about breakthroughs in medical care, and about other ways of life—including the lives of the children they have sorrowfully sent to the cities.

Today's best knowledge tools, including the Internet, are still rudimentary, still maldistributed across the world, still clunky to use and still difficult for illiterates—no matter how intelligent—to navigate without help from intermediaries. (It may seem odd at first glance, but cracking the remaining barriers to cheap, simple speech-recognition technology could have a dramatic effect on village life and oral cultures by making it possible for millions to use the Net without first having to become literate. Few advances could do more to close the digital divide.)

Yet the Internet, mobile phones and cam-phones, handheld monitors and their successor technologies will be as fundamental a part of tomorrow's agriculture as the shovel and the hoe have been throughout history.

SMART DUST

Changes in biotechnology, space and the Internet do not even begin to suggest the full range of technologies pouring out of rich-world laboratories around the globe. These include thousands developed for other purposes but that may, with modification, turn out to have important agriculture-related uses in the poor world.

Cloning technologies—such as those used to clone Dolly the sheep in Scotland, Snuppy the dog in South Korea, and those used by University of Georgia scientists to clone a cow that had been dead for forty-eight hours—are steadily advancing. Whatever one's ethical position on cloning, its potential implications for agriculture and livestock production can hardly be overestimated.

Water is the lifeblood of agriculture. A pen-sized device that can purify up to three hundred liters of filthy water more effectively than chlorine or iodine has been developed for the U.S. Department of Defense. Could it—or something like it—be scaled up for use in village water?

Sensor technology is emerging as one of the most important industries of the future. New car models are populated by sensors. Sensors are now being embedded in clothing. Why not in land and crops?

Sensors that tell farmers when to irrigate wine grapes are already being tested. Some scientists even envision the day when each individual plant will have a tiny built-in biosensor and clock that signal its exact needs at exactly the right time.

Others forecast sensors so tiny that they can form "smart dust" and be seeded across a field to report on soil temperature, moisture and other variables.

Researchers are also testing the use of liver tissue, lung tissue, and neural and cardiac cells as sensors that can identify threats from agents such as anthrax. Can these or others like them be useful in identifying threats to a crop?

Then there is the nanodevice—smaller, that is, than a billionth of a meter—that can monitor a living cell's function by sensing minute changes in electrical charges on its surface. Plants are living cells. How do changes in electric charges alter their nature or output?

Or Controlled Biological and Biomimetic Systems now being studied that collect information from insect populations? Some insects accumulate airborne bacterial spores on their bodies as they fly. Can that tell us how to protect crops?

And what about magnetism that switches intracellular activities like protein synthesis or color change on and off? If current work succeeds, what impact might this have on plants? Will farmers be able to boost the vitamin content—and economic value—of a vegetable overnight with a tiny jolt of magnetism?

These are just a random handful of thousands of ongoing studies that may well, directly or indirectly, impact the future of agriculture. Many of these ideas will no doubt prove silly, unworkable, useless or too expensive. But others won't. And the truly big changes will come not from any individual technology, no matter how powerful, but from the explosive convergences of two of more of them. Sensors and wireless technology are already being combined to measure heat buildup in stored sugar beets.

Or how about the combination of nanotechnology and magnetism? Scientists are studying the use of magnetism at the nano scale to monitor and control biological activity at the cellular and even the single-molecule level.

BILL GATES'S ECHO

Again and again we are told that advanced technology cannot solve the problem of poverty. "Let's get real!" declares a typical article: "There is little evidence to indicate that information and communications technologies are poised for a 'frontal attack' to improve the lot of the world's poor." Even Bill Gates has echoed this thought.

But this litany is based on three questionable premises. First, it narrowly refers to I.T., rather than the full range of technological changes sweeping across our moment of time—or the effect of I.T. on these other technologies.

Second, it is too short-term. Nobody has suggested that poverty can be eliminated within the time frame most such statements reflect. Even with today's acceleration and the shift toward simultaneity, technologies typically arrive in overlapping phases.

In the first phase, a new technology begins to be used by early adopters. By then, it is already being improved, and technologies in seemingly unrelated fields converge with it. Thus, computers, printers, communications and other tools are integrated to form self-reinforcing multifunctional systems.

Finally, at a slower pace, users of the systemic technology alter their organizational structures to take fullest advantage of it. And it is here, but not necessarily in the next stock-market quarter, that the greatest payoffs arrive.

The derogation of technology is also historically naïve. At the time the steam engine became practical, few imagined that the "newfangled" device for use in mining would have any impact on agriculture. And it didn't—for many years. Then came steam-powered textile factories that benefited cotton farmers and steam-powered trains that widened markets for farm products. Steam transformed the place of agriculture in the economy.

What is proposed in these pages, therefore, is not a quick technological fix but something more complex, realistic and far-reaching.

However, we should not underestimate the potential impact of technology. "It is easy to dismiss the suggestion that technology can save the day. . . . Nevertheless . . . new ways are needed to ensure that science and technology are given the prominence needed to address a wide range of increasingly urgent global problems," says economist Jeffrey D. Sachs, director of the U.N. Millennium Project.

WHAT WORKED BEST WON'T

Making the needed technology happen is the easy part. Far more complicated and difficult is overcoming the list of non-technological obstacles.

The first is heavy-handed tradition—and the powerful feedback loop that maintains it. In traditional peasant communities, for decades or even centuries, each generation has lived much as its distant ancestors did. The governing assumption is that the future will replicate the past.

This implies that what worked best in the past will continue to work best in the future. And, since life is lived close to the margin of survival, peasants around the world have plenty of cause to be rationally risk-averse. Their very resistance to the new, however, slows the rate of change, further reinforcing the anachronistic conviction that the future will resemble the past.

A second obstacle is education—and its absence.

Everyone, of course, is in favor of education. Except.

Except desperate parents who, to keep the family from starving, need their children to slave in the field, to care for younger kids or to beg at the roadside. Except all those who think women should be kept ignorant and obedient. Except governments with other priorities.

In villages across the world, the family is often the *de facto* school, passing down yesterday's suspicion of the new, further reinforced in some places by religious instruction. Where state schools do exist, teachers are underpaid and undereducated themselves. Schools frequently lack even pencils and paper.

Critics attack this global disgrace. But the alternative typically offered resembles the factory-style education systems found in industrial societies. Classrooms. Desks. Age-segregated classes. Rote work. Standardized tests. Enforced punctuality. Uniformity in the name of democracy. A system, in short, that promotes what employers used to call "industrial discipline." Can this ever be successfully replicated in every village? Should it?

Mass education designed for the industrial age meets the needs of neither the pre-industrial village nor the post-industrial future.

Rural education—indeed, all education—has to be totally reconceptualized. Today technology offers educators a tool for customizing education to the diverse cultures and needs of small groups and even individuals.

We are approaching a time when we will be able—inexpensively—to put in every village some kind of computer connected in some way to the outside world. A time when children, given the chance, can, as we saw in India, teach themselves to access the Internet. A time when multiplayer games can educate. A time when local teachers can advance their own learning through distant online mentors. A time of "reverse home schooling," when children teach their parents—and help reduce the parents' suspicion of the new.

Here, too, technology alone offers no remedy for ignorance. Political, economic and social forces must be mobilized to educate the coming generation.

DISTRIBUTING ENERGY

Yet another critical obstacle is the paucity of energy in rural areas. Unless the poor of the world gain access to sources of energy more powerful than their own muscles and those of their farm animals, they will remain forever trapped in destitution.

In a world where 1.3 billion rural people still lack electricity, it is impractical, in the face of massive poverty and today's realities, to dogmatically oppose any and every extension of coal, gas and even nuclear power, despite their well-known dangers and environmental costs.

China's twin-track development strategy, calling for the simultaneous development of its Second and Third Wave sectors, includes the planned construction of two new reactors a year for the next sixteen years. Its controversial Three Gorges Dam is the biggest in the world. Similarly, other governments around the globe, in Africa, Asia and Latin America, are also spending huge sums to bring electricity to their rural poor.

But, as in education, these plans usually reflect the solutions of the industrial era—mass energy systems designed mainly to serve urban centers where factories and population are densely concentrated.

The cost of applying the same solutions to highly dispersed rural populations is enormous. According to a 2002 report by India's planning commission, "Traditional grid connection would be uneconomical in villages. . . . [At] the cost and pace at which rural electrification is taking place, it would be technically and financially impractical to expect the non-electrified villages to be covered even in two decades."

By contrast, the report continues, "decentralizing power generation will be possible with renewable energy sources such as solar energy, biomass, small hydro power and wind energy."

Few planners take seriously into account the likelihood that, over the next generation or two, in energy as in so many other fields, convergences of old and new technologies will produce powerful hybrid results and completely new breakthroughs that will surprise us all.

HYPER-AGRICULTURE

The day is coming when peasant farming and industrial-style agribusiness are both made obsolete, increasingly replaced by a form of "hyper-agriculture" that can ultimately have a far greater long-term impact on global poverty than all the subsidies, tariffs and aid packages combined.

A transformed world awaits tomorrow's rural children. Our task is to bring it closer.

Emergency aid, debt relief, elimination of rich-world subsidies and other onetime or short-term measures will, no doubt, continue to be needed. But incremental changes like these can no more lift rural billions out of poverty than Band-Aids can cure a chronic disease.

What the world needs to recognize is that the countries whose peasants form the massive core of global poverty, China and India, by rejecting sequential change and embracing twin-track development, are testing the path for the rest of the poor world.

To understand their significance, we need to look beyond momentary matters such as interest rates, trade relations and finance, as important as these may be. For China and India are doing something at a far deeper level than even their leaders may recognize.

They are accelerating change and challenging the slow pace of peasant life—resetting their relationship to the deep fundamental of time.

They are simultaneously shifting the axis of global economic power across the Pacific—a function of the deep fundamental of space.

Above all, China understands (India is still learning) the central importance of knowledge to its economy. It increasingly relies on data, information and knowledge—self-generated, leaked, purchased or pirated and put to work—to transform its economy, altering its relationship to the deep fundamental of knowledge.

For millennia, peasants have lived in virtual isolation—informationally cut off from the larger world and even, very often, from the nearest village. It took months, sometimes many years, for even the most useful knowledge to reach them. Knowledge that might save a child from illness or death. Knowledge about farming. Knowledge about prices. Knowledge, the denial of which let them fall farther and farther behind urban populations in standards of living.

That silence is now being broken by technologies that bring them images, ideas and information, giving them the right to adopt or reject them—and shortening the catch-up time needed to eliminate poverty.

The strategy broadly sketched in these pages is aimed not merely at transforming rural life but at radically reducing the rising, dangerous pressures placed on cities by tidal waves of peasants fleeing the unbearable—pressures that could explode at any time.

By opening minds to new possibilities, today's changes bring with them a trace of hope. And that may be the most important, most motivating advance of all.

Everywhere and every day we are bombarded by endless, repetitive, numbing descriptions of the plight of the world's poor. Pictures of starving babies. Manifestos from well-intentioned groups and governments. U.N. resolutions. Behind seemingly positive official rhetoric and NGO calls to help one baby at a time lies a terrible sense of hopelessness. And helplessness.

The poor do not need outsiders to tell them the costs of poverty. And if the outside world wants to help, it needs to replace failing strategies, speed the development of revolutionary new tools and replace morbid pessimism with a culture of hope.

As industrialism rolled across parts of the Earth in the eighteenth and nineteenth centuries, it changed the entire distribution of wealth and well-being on the planet. Revolutionary wealth, as we'll see next, is about to do that once again. In ways that will astound us.

PART TEN

The New Tectonics

CHAPTER 44

CHINA'S NEXT SURPRISE?

T hree tragic conflicts in the twentieth century—World War I, World War II and the Cold War—represented the terminal climax of the industrial era and gave rise to the unique collision of wealth waves that we see on the planet today.

The Second Wave wealth system is in retreat. By contrast, the Third Wave wealth system, starting in the United States, has already—in a few short decades—crossed the Pacific and transformed Asia. In the years ahead, we will see the wave overrun the shores of Latin America and Africa as well. The signs are already apparent.

Behind this world transformation, as we've shown, are unprecedented changes at the level of the deep fundamentals of wealth. Nowhere is this clearer or more revealing than in Asia's historic rise and China's great awakening.

While much mentioned in financial news, Asia remains insufficiently understood on both Wall Street and in Washington—which, because of history and geography, face more toward the Atlantic than the Pacific.

Between 2001 and 2005, when the United States opened free-trade negotiations with twenty nations, just one was in Asia.

Citing this critically, one U.S. senator reminded Washington that Asia "is home to six of the past decade's ten fastest growing economies, five of the top ten U.S. trading partners and more than half the world's population." He might have added that it is also home to the overriding majority of the world's Muslims and is the region most surrounded by nuclear weaponry.

Above all, Asia is home to China. And unless the United States, Europe and the rest of the world understand what is really happening in China—the China that lies hidden behind the flood of unreliable economic and financial statistics—it will be difficult to make sense of what lies ahead. For what happens there—one way or the other—will radically reallocate wealth and shake the planet.

LOOMING OVER THE WORLD

By 2004, China had edged past Japan to become the world's third-biggest trading nation after the United States and Germany. That same year saw China sitting on more than $500 billion of the world's $3.5 trillion in foreign-currency reserves. It owned nearly $175 billion worth of U.S. Treasuries—an amount exceeded only by Japan—putting it in a position to jolt the entire global economy if it chose to replace dollars with euros or a basket of other currencies. In little more than two decades, China had become a giant force looming over the world economy.

But can China's spectacular growth continue? Will China actually become the global superpower of the year 2020, as so many forecasters predict?

To answer these questions, we need to challenge the clichés about that country that pass for wisdom among the lemmings. And we need to understand what made China's rise possible in the first place.

Conventional wisdom attributes China's startling progress to its break with communism and its transition toward a market economy. But that is hardly a sufficient explanation. Other nations have tried shifting in the same direction, and none has experienced anything like China's success. Moreover, China even now cannot yet be described as a fully developed market economy.

That market cliché also overlooks the trickle-down effect set in motion when, as we've seen, Silicon Valley transferred progressively higher-level computer-manufacturing operations to Japan, South Korea and Taiwan—each of which then set up plants and mainlined capital into China—all this before Beijing's shift toward market economics had gone very far.

Another equally important reason for China's spectacular performance can be found in the way it has applied its novel twin-track development strategy.

ACCELERATING ACCELERATION

Intent on catching up with the West, China's leaders knew this would be impossible if China focused exclusively on low-tech development while the United States shed Second Wave industries and raced to build a high-tech Third Wave economy. China, they therefore decided, needed more than sweatshops. It also needed its own world-beating, high-value-adding, knowledge-intensive sector.

To make this twin-track policy work, China had to compress time—to accomplish in decades what took others one or more centuries. It would also have to extend its spatial reach. And, most important, it would need advanced

I.T., telecom, digitalization and access to the latest economically relevant knowledge.

This explains why China's strategy since then has focused—whether deliberately or inadvertently—on precisely the three deep fundamentals emphasized in these pages: Time, space and knowledge.

Thus China has become remarkably skillful in the use of speed as a competitive weapon in international trade. According to Robert B. Cassidy, a U.S. government trade official cited in *BusinessWeek,* Japanese, South Korean and European exporters often took "four or five years to develop their place in the market. . . . China overwhelms a market so quickly you don't see it coming." So fast, in fact, "that it's nearly impossible [for companies] to adjust through the usual strategies, such as automating or squeezing suppliers," the magazine adds. By the time they do, it's too late.

And when China sets a strategic priority, it can break domestic speed records as well.

"What happened in the 1990s in China was nothing short of a social miracle," writes Robert C. Fonow, former president of Sprint Japan and general manager of Scientific-Atlanta in Shanghai. "In the space of 10 years, China has developed one the most advanced telecommunications infrastructures in the world. Within a few years, it is likely to have the single most advanced telecommunications infrastructure in the world."

To reach this point, Fonow explains, China would first "bring in new technology as quickly as possible, study it, imitate it, and improve it." Next, it would "develop indigenous technology capabilities equal to the West's and use them as a base to develop a greater capacity for technological innovation."

Nor is acceleration in China limited to business tactics and technology. It is part of the country's new culture. When author Alexander Stille went to Xian to write about historic artifacts like its third-century BC army of terracotta warriors, he wondered if ordinary people were troubled by the rush forward.

"Most Chinese," he writes, "many of whom have known famine and extraordinary hardships in their own lifetimes, are surprisingly unsentimental about these changes. . . . For most younger Chinese [change] cannot come fast enough." That wasn't the case during thousands of years of China's past.

GLOBAL SPACE

While its neighbors try to figure out where they may fit in a new Asia they assume will be dominated by China, China no longer sees itself as merely an Asian power. It talks about creating an Asian free-trade zone, but its ambitions—economic and otherwise—are global. It is changing its relations not only to time but to the deep fundamental of space as well.

Starting with the reforms in the 1980s and '90s, its opening to foreign investment, its entry into the World Trade Organization and its immense expansion of imports and exports, China has, with every passing day, been deepening and diffusing its links to the outside world. And here, too, the twin-track strategy is evident.

At one level, floods of cheap Chinese goods blanket the world, undercutting the makers of Mexican electronic components, Indonesian garments or Colombian copper wire. These are now turned out in China's industrial-age sweatshops.

But China is also encouraging its high-tech companies to move out and conquer the world. Thus Lenovo, its top PC maker, buys IBM's PC manufacturing division. Huawei, its big I.T. company, boasts of having ten thousand R&D workers and of maintaining labs in India, Britain, Sweden and the United States. It partners with Intel, Microsoft, Siemens and Qualcom to produce communications equipment.

China's expanding spatial reach will soon be more evident in finance as well. By the end of 2003, China had launched more than 3,400 businesses in 139 countries. Indeed, according to the U.N. Conference on Trade and Development, by the end of 2004 China was expected to become the world's fifth-largest provider of foreign direct investment to other countries, eclipsing even Japan.

On a recent visit to South America, President Hu Jintao zipped across the continent promising significant investment spanning the regional map from Brazil to Cuba—$20 billion to Argentina alone.

While the economics of this tour drew widespread attention, few noticed its geographic implications. Like a master of the game Go, China was thrusting itself, big-time, as it were, into a region long regarded as America's backyard—counterbalancing America's strong presence in China's backyard, Taiwan.

This economic foray into South America took place at a time of especially strained relations between Beijing and Taipei, with Taiwan emphasizing its American-backed independence and China threatening to take it over, even by military force if necessary.

China's highly focused drive toward economic expansion should, in theory, keep it too busy for foreign military adventures. Nevertheless, its Asian neighbors watch with gathering concern China's soaring military budget, estimated to have shot up at least sixfold between 1991 and 2004. And here, too, we see a widening of its geographical interests.

China is acquiring long-range unmanned aircraft and air-refueling equipment that extend the range of its air force. It now has nuclear missiles that can reach targets all across the United States. And it seeks to transform its navy—once designed to protect coastal waters—into a "blue water" nuclear-armed fleet capable of ever-more-distant operations.

China is pursuing a bold maritime program that, according to retired Japanese admiral Hideaki Kaneda in 2005, includes building "a series of military and diplomatic strategic bases—a so-called 'string of pearls'—along the major sea lanes from the South China Sea to the oil-rich Middle East."

Other military projects, according to Kaneda, include constructing a port in Pakistan to "guard the throat of the Persian Gulf"; installing intelligence-gathering facilities on islands belonging to Myanmar; building a $20 billion canal in Thailand to provide an alternative oil-import route that avoids the Strait of Malacca; and constructing runways capable of handling long-range bombers on the contested Spratley and Paracel islands.

Thus, as China compresses time, it also expands its influence spatially, profoundly altering its traditional economic—and military—relations to these deep fundamentals.

MINING KNOWLEDGE

Even these changes, however, are dwarfed by China's ravenous pursuit of wealth-relevant know-how. China has become a world leader in the creation, purchase—and theft—of data, information and knowledge.

As far back as the winter of 1983, soon after Deng Xiaoping shut the door on the Maoist past, we personally witnessed Chinese scientists in Beijing reverse-engineering computers and carrying out the country's earliest experiments with fiber optics in Shanghai. The available facilities were primitive, dirty and freezing. China was still wretchedly poor. But its leaders, even then, understood the importance of technology—and piracy.

Today the picture is dramatically different. Up-to-date research labs are proliferating, and R&D expenditures in 2003 jumped 19.6 percent over the previous year. In the same period, funds for basic research rose 18.8 percent—three times greater than the U.S. increase. And, as we've noted, thousands of United States–trained Chinese scientists are heading home.

In five years, America will still be the world center of corporate research, according to Maximilian von Zedtwitz, who teaches management at Qinghua University. But by then, he says, China will outrank Britain, Germany and Japan.

Add China's sharklike appetite for data, information and ideas from the outside world. To do business in China, foreign companies usually have had to transfer technology—and many agreed to do so in return for even limited access to the huge Chinese market.

Nor is this hunger for know-how narrowly restricted to technology. As formerly Communist China entered into broader economic relationships with the West, it also sought practical knowledge about capitalist management, finance and business in general. Thus by 2004 there were more than sixty MBA programs offered by Chinese universities—many in partnership with leading American schools such as MIT, UC/Berkeley and Northwestern.

Less formally, knowledge is transferred by the more than 600,000 foreigners who now live and work in China—in sharp contrast to the days when foreigners were likely to be labeled spies or allowed to enter only as part of closely monitored tourist groups.

Behind China's amazing drive, therefore, we find radically changed attitudes toward all three of the deep fundamentals central to economies of the future—further evidence of its intention to create the world's leading knowledge-based economy.

Taken together, facts like these suggest an unstoppable China on a short, double-quick march to superpowerdom.

Beijing, however, knows better.

WAVE POLITICS

Recently, China watchers have begun to spin dark scenarios. These include the possibility that China could suffer a financial crisis like the one that hit the rest of Asia in 1997–98, for example. Or that it will go through a series of ups and downs that it will attempt to mitigate with Keynesian measures. Alternatively, worriers point to a possible convergence of other troubles—an energy breakdown, an environmental crisis or a far more serious SARS-like outbreak of disease. Or, worse yet, a war with Taiwan in which both sides hurl missiles at each other, destabilizing the new Asia. Any or all of these could hammer the global economy in the years immediately ahead.

One of the most pessimistic assessments of China's future can be found in Gordon G. Chang's book *The Coming Collapse of China,* whose table of contents tells us that "The Revolution Has Grown Old," "The Discontent of the People Is Explosive," "State-Owned Enterprises Are Dying," "Chinese Banks Will Fail" and "Ideology and Politics Restrain Progress"—and that's only part of the list.

If Chang's thesis is even half-right, the global financial system might have to be wheeled into the intensive-care ward. Investors, corporations and central banks around the world could all be traumatized. The price of T-shirts and toys might drop still further in the corner Wal-Mart. But hundreds of millions of workers around the world—from iron-ore miners in Brazil to bankers in Manhattan or Tokyo—would be looking for jobs.

These scenarios are dire enough. But they overlook far more startling possibilities.

THREE CHINAS

So long as Mao Zedong was alive, China's economy was divided in two. One part was the rural China of desperately poor peasants. The other was the urban China of smokestacks and assembly lines. What Mao's successors have done is add a fast-growing knowledge-based sector. Unlike the bisected China of the past, China is now trisected.

It isn't the only trisected country in the world today. Three distinctly different wealth systems can be found in other nations as well—in India, Mexico and Brazil, for example. But the very existence of trisected countries is new to world history. And here, too, China is pioneering new territory.

As we've seen, China's twin-track development strategy has helped it lift vast numbers out of the worst poverty and to raise its stature and influence among nations. But all this comes with a hidden price. Each wealth wave in a country has its own constituency, so to speak—a population defined not simply by the nature of its work but by its needs and demands. The result is "wave conflict."

When China's leaders allocate resources to cutting-edge labs, they face stubborn opposition from those who want the money to support manufacturing industries and social welfare. This conflict, however, is just a skirmish.

On a far larger scale, at the national level, the replacement of President Jiang Zemin by Hu Jintao reflected a major shift of "wave policy." The Jiang government was seen by many as following a "city-first" strategy. By contrast, as soon as Hu took office, he made a symbolic tour of the interior, promising increased aid to the hard-pressed peasantry. No sooner was this tour over, however, than the wave battle was renewed. Opponents attacked aid to the interior as a giant waste of money and proposed, instead, to relocate additional millions of peasants from the west to the northeast's rust belt.

This would be on top of the seventy million impoverished rural souls who, having already lost their land, were compelled to stream into the cities in search of sweatshop jobs.

This process is classic, closely resembling the forced migration of British peasants to the cities in the late 1700s and early 1800s, spurred by legislation

known as the Enclosure Acts. The consequence was the continual enlargement of the pool of extremely low-wage factory labor—and the consequent
speedup of England's conversion from an agrarian to an industrial economy.

In China's own past, as in the former Soviet Union, fierce ideological
battles were waged over so-called "industry bias"—the policy that raised capital for industrial development by squeezing and starving even those peasants
who stayed on the land. Wave conflict led to gulags and the death of tens of
millions. Between 1953 and 1983, according to *China Today,* peasants contributed more than $72 billion to the country's industrialization program.

Despite promised reforms, even today, according to *The New York Times,*
Beijing "enforces a two-class system, denying peasants the medical, pension
and welfare benefits that many urban residents have, while often denying
them the right to become urban residents." Add to that the fact that, according
to Yasheng Huang of MIT, "a huge portion of China's urban boom has been
financed by massive, yet indirect taxation on peasantry, including fees for
education in rural areas."

There remains in China today strong support for Second Wave industrialization. However, Wu Jinglian, a senior development researcher under China's
State Council, noted in 2005 that this strategy "increases the risk of a financial
crisis." Further, he adds, it would tax already scarce natural resources, damage
China's fragile ecosystems and "undermine efforts at technology innovation
and upgrading of products." Under "policies that prioritize heavy industries . . . enterprises are satisfied with merely increasing their production of
low-value-added and low-profit products. . . . This will cause severe harm . . .
over time."

These top-level wave policy struggles take place against a background of
mushrooming unrest. China is racked with protests by both peasants and
workers. Police and security forces are putting down militant marches and rallies from one end of the country to the other. The issues range from unemployment, nonpayment of wages, local corruption and forced relocation to high
taxes, fees and other impositions, with new demonstrations breaking out
seemingly every day.

According to Zhou Yongkang, a senior police official in China, there were
approximately 74,000 protests across the country in 2004, involving 3.7 million participants, widespread violence and numerous deaths. In 2005, Chinese
officials reported 87,000 protests.

Many protests occur in rural communities where peasants have been
cheated by local officials or fight to hold on to their land. A single rally in
Sichuan drew ninety thousand angry farmers facing eviction from their
homes. Other protests are among industrial laborers—textile workers in
Shaanxi, metal workers in Liaoyang, laid-off oil workers in Daqing and min-

ers in Fushun. In December 2005, Chinese police opened fire on protesting farmers in Dongzhou in the deadliest confrontation since the massacre in Tiananmen Square in June 1989. The list goes on and is growing longer still.

MERCEDES, MALLS AND MILITIA

Now add to this the growth of a Third Wave population, young, educated, self-confident, middle-class, impatient, increasingly nationalist and sure that it—not parents, not workers, and certainly not peasants—is the wave of the future. Surrounded by glittering shopping malls, these young people either have or hunger for a Mercedes or BMW. And they have something China values highly—computer and Internet skills.

So highly, indeed, that the People's Liberation Army has made a deep study of information warfare. It has organized and trained "information militias" and developed doctrines for attacks not merely on enemy military targets, but on foreign business networks, research centers and communication systems.

One theory holds that information technology makes possible a war waged not by the military alone but by hundreds of millions of citizens—joined, perhaps, by large numbers of sympathizers in other countries. Together they might use their laptops—sharing unused capacity to create supercomputers—to assault an adversary's critical infrastructure, including financial networks and other civilian targets. Such an attack would be most effective against the United States, since it is the country most heavily dependent on information technology and electronic communications.

This, as some have written, would be a striking new version of what Mao called a "People's War." What may be overlooked, however, by Chinese information-war enthusiasts is that Mao's People's War was waged not in defense of an existing government but in an effort to overthrow it. And it is just as conceivable that millions of Chinese who engage in information combat might someday turn their know-how against the reigning Communist Party in defense of their own Third Wave self-interests. In a civil war, they might turn their laptops against the People's Liberation Army itself.

WAVE WAR

Protests may start small, but history shows just how dangerous wave conflicts can become when they escalate. It was the clash between an industrializing North and a backward, slave-based agrarian South that led to the Civil War in the United States in 1861–65. It was wave conflict that lay behind Japan's Meiji Restoration a few years later. Wave conflict was reflected in the Russian

Revolution of 1917. And conflicting wave interests in Asia—usually disguised as urban-versus-rural, ethnic or religious in nature—underlie violence today in India, Thailand and other nearby countries as well.

But these conflicts all counterposed two wealth systems. In emergent China there are three, each with sharply different needs and interests—confronting its government with unprecedented tensions.

China's economic advance cannot continue in a straight line, unperturbed. It cannot avoid wave conflict. It will no doubt crash and recover more than once in the decades to come, sending successive jolts through the global economy.

The country is not quite at the edge of calamity, but to many Beijing seems increasingly out of touch and out of control in whole swaths of the country. As an editorial in Xinhua, the official Chinese news agency, put it, China will either enjoy a "golden age of development" or enter a "contradictions-stricken age" of chaos.

This does not imply that its long-term twin-track strategy will fail. But technology and economics are the easy part of any revolution.

THE BLOODY THREAD

Beijing is skilled at dealing with protests by farmers fighting the corruption of local government or industrial workers demanding jobs. But it is more worried about escalation than it lets on.

This helps explain its seemingly extreme response to the cultist quasi-religious Falun Gong movement, whose members have been imprisoned and, according to some reports, brutalized and even killed.

Falun Gong insists it is not a political movement at all. But when it brought as many as thirty thousand members from all over China to the very walls of Zhongnanhai, the government compound in Beijing, to protest repression, it called up still-fresh memories of the Tiananmen Square tragedy.

What rocked China's leaders may not have been the movement's religio-mystical ideology, replete with demons and aliens from other planets, or its exercise regimen, but the mere fact that it was not restricted to a single locality or region. Falun Gong was big. And its reach was national. Even more worrisome, many of its followers were in the police and military.

Historically, Beijing has tried to block large-scale organization by any group other than the Communist Party itself. But its ability to do so is rapidly declining as widespread cell phones, the Internet and other technologies make it easier for protesters to organize.

That raises a threat for the Communist leadership—something that runs like a bloody thread throughout the history of communism: the concept of a worker-peasant coalition. This was precisely what the Chinese Communist

Party itself attempted to create until Mao split with his Soviet advisers and built his revolutionary force around peasants, rather than harder-to-recruit workers.

Because of their competing needs, today's First Wave peasants, Second Wave workers and Third Wave advocates would be hard to unite in opposition to the government—unless . . .

MEET MAO II

Busy people often focus on the immediate future and pay attention only to what they regard as the most likely of scenarios. Yet if history teaches us anything, it is that extremely unlikely events often shake the world. What, for example, was more unlikely than two commercial jetliners destroying the World Trade Center? China, too, may surprise us.

What follows is, admittedly, most unlikely. But a convergence of high-probability events such as those cited above—a financial collapse, for example, coming at the same time as an epidemic outbreak and war with Taiwan—can easily trigger a far more serious low-probability crisis.

Imagine, as some in Beijing no doubt do, the ultimate nightmare vision in which a future Mao—a Mao II—arises: A charismatic leader who, given enough unrest and upheaval, could sweep aside the current leadership and introduce something beyond the West's imagination. Not a Communist Mao or even a capitalist Mao but, in a country hungry for something to replace the near religion of Marxism, a Mao who gathers workers and peasants and young Third Wave elements together under a religious flag.

That religion could be Christianity, which is growing rapidly across China. More likely, it would be some bizarre new religion growing out of one of the countless cults that now abound in the nation. *The New York Times* reports a seething cauldron of religious and quasi-religious activity and competition, especially in the countryside, and conservatively estimates that 200 million Chinese are regular or casual followers of various religious faiths in the country. "Christian sects form and mutate . . . , vying to attract the same disadvantaged classes. . . . There are the Shouters and the Spirit Church, the Disciples Association and White Sun, the Holistic Church and the Crying Faction. Many are apocalyptic. A few are strongly anti-Communist. Three Grades of Servants and Eastern Lightning are among the largest, each claiming memberships in the millions."

Now imagine Zhongnanhai in the hands of new, potentially fanatic management—and in control of China's nuclear weapons and its missiles. Or imagine competing warlord cult leaders in charge of different provinces.

So extreme a scenario may seem impossible, even inconceivable to Western readers and leaders. But it would not be the first time in China that a cultish religious mass movement ignited large-scale bloodshed, tried to overthrow the government and tore parts of China into shreds.

That is precisely what happened when Hong Xiuquan, having convinced himself he was Jesus' brother, and therefore a son of God, recruited followers, built an army, stormed north out of Guangxi Province and set out in 1851 to overthrow the Manchu Dynasty.

His troops—including ferocious all-female combat units—took Yongan, moved into Hunan and captured Yuezhou, Hankou, Wuchang and Nanjing, which he then ruled for eleven years until, at last, his Taiping Rebellion was put down, having claimed at least 20 million lives.

Of course, a religious Mao II scenario is unlikely, but the Chinese remember this history all too well, and this explains why something like the Mao II scenario may seem less improbable to them than to the outside world. That excruciating memory may be another reason for the government's vicious crackdown on Falun Gong.

When the West prods China to speed its transition to democracy, the almost certain response echoes what Zhao Ziyang, then general secretary of the Communist Party, told us in Beijing in 1988. When we pressed him about the need for democracy, Zhao told us: "Stability is necessary to make democratic advances."

Westerners may ho-hum about *stability*. The Chinese cannot—not when the deaths of tens of millions during the so-called Great Leap Forward and the Cultural Revolution are still so fresh, so painful—and so personal.

China went through its own version of hell during those periods, and the West stood by, unaffected, because China was cut off from economic relations at that time. Today, by contrast, foreigners—Americans, Europeans, Japanese, South Koreans, Singaporeans and others—own billions of dollars' worth of Chinese factories, real estate and other fixed assets.

Were violence in China to escalate, the central government would have a hard time keeping it secret from its own people, now armed with the Web and cell phones. If protesters begin demanding regional secession (already an issue in China's Muslim northwest), and social breakdown converges with other crises into what Kenneth Courtis, vice chairman of Goldman Sachs Asia, has suggested to us could become a "volcanic explosion," it is unlikely that the outside world will just stand by passively with its assets at risk.

Given runaway escalation, outsiders might not only yank their financial investments but meddle covertly inside China in an effort to protect their factories and other physical assets—even, perhaps, by making deals with corrupt local officials and rebel military commanders. That happened during the chaotic 1930s, when China was under attack by Japan and torn by revolution. It must not happen again.

China's development into a contemporary, affluent world power can be detoured, blunted, reversed for years. China may be beset by tragedy. But it is in the interest of the human race as a whole that its shaky, corrupt, frightening, painful experiment in the twin-track reduction of poverty not be allowed to fail. For how it deals with its collision of wealth waves will affect jobs, portfolios and products, right on down to the clothes our children wear and the computers they use.

China is now a part of us all.

CHAPTER 45

JAPAN'S NEXT BAMBOO RING

When Japanese prime minister Hayato Ikeda visited France in the 1960s, Charles de Gaulle is said to have asked, "Who is that transistor salesman?" The *faux pas* has rattled down through history, but for its economic size and significance no country was more underestimated by the rest of the world than Japan in the 1960s and '70s. (Even more underestimated was the transistor, but that is another story.)

In the 1980s and early 1990s, the reverse was true. Suddenly the yen threatened to displace the dollar, Japanese money was taking over Hollywood and Rockefeller Center, and Japan was being hailed as "No. 1." Fears of a Japanese superstate rippled across the world's financial pages.

As the new century arrived, Econo-Land's lemmings, marching in step, assured the world that China would soon be No. 1 and that Japan was about to become its economic and political "poodle." Yet Japan could surprise the world once more.

The basic changes it makes—or refuses to make—in the decade ahead will impact not only the cars we drive, the energy we use, the games we play and the music we enjoy but quite possibly the way we treat our elderly, the price of a retirement condo and the future of the dollar.

What Japan does will be especially relevant to a whole class of nations that, like the United States, members of the European Union and South Korea, are transitioning toward knowledge-intensivity. Unburdened by a large-scale peasant population, they are not trisected, like China, India, Mexico or Brazil, but bisected—internally divided between a shrinking smokestack sector and a growing knowledge sector.

LATTE, ANYONE?

Countless analyses purport to explain why the Japanese miracle came to a screeching standstill in the 1990s. What occurred was a strange crash, as crashes go.

One could stroll along Omotesando in Tokyo, where foreigners and teenage fashionistas stop for a Grande Soy Hazelnut Vanilla Latte, and see little evidence of distress. As Kenichi Ohmae later wrote in his book *The Invisible Continent*, "Where are the beggars? . . . Where were the double-digit unemployment rates?" Sales of fancy bottled water were zooming. Cruise ships were fully booked. And hordes of young Japanese women were buying "enough Hermes, Prada, Gucci, Louis Vuitton and similar products to make Japan the number one purchasing nation for most luxury brands."

Yet even now Japan's economy feels the after-effects of a real estate bubble that sent property prices plummeting 60 percent between 1990 and 2003. In Tokyo, prices fell almost 80 percent.

And real estate alone doesn't explain why Japan's banks as late as 2003 still carried nonperforming loans amounting, according to whom you believe, to around $400 billion. Worse yet, manufacturing output in 2003 was 10 percent below its 1991 level and, according to a Council on Foreign Relations report, Japan's share of both global output and exports "was shrinking for the first time in a century."

What happened? Why did the superstate shrivel up? (Could China make the same mistakes? Its real estate bubble already seems to parallel Japan's experience.) But it takes more than real estate fizz—or bad bank loans—to explain what happened to Japan. The long-ticking bomb that blew Japan's economy apart was, in fact, failure at the level of the deep fundamental of time.

JAPAN'S LOPSIDED LEAP

We've already seen how Japan, early on, used advanced information technology to revolutionize its manufacturing base, to dramatically improve the quality of its exports and, above all, to usher wholly novel products into world markets. Along with these changes, it also introduced powerful new management tools like just-in-time delivery. The world had never seen anything quite like this high-speed Japanese success story.

And even today, after the long slump of recent years, Japan is still a world leader in many scientific and technological fields. In automotive fuel cells and alternative energy generally, in industrial and humanoid robots, in research into artificial blood and glycobiology, in digital electronics, in game devices and many other fields, Japan is at or near the forefront. In 2004 its government invested \$900 million—more than all of Europe combined—in nano-technology research. And Japan's researchers, scientists and engineers are accustomed to pushing frontiers forward.

But, as stressed throughout these pages, science and technology alone do not add up to an advanced economy. And a successful knowledge-intensive economy cannot base itself on manufacturing alone. It requires an advanced service sector as well. Yet Japan, even as it accelerated manufacturing and helped speed up supply chains around the world, was much slower to apply computers and I.T. or new business models and management concepts to its service sector. Indeed, from 1995 to 2003, Japan had to import \$456 billion more in services than it exported.

In short, its lopsided development created a degree of de-synchronization that distorts the whole Japanese economy right down to today: Manufacturing and services are still out of sync.

In the words of *The Economist,* "It is hard to think of a single nonmanufac-turing sector in which Japan excels. High domestic transport costs hinder dis-tribution travel and tourism. A lack of competition in energy and telecoms keeps business costs high. Professional services, such as law and accountancy, remain hidebound. Health care, a crucial sector for a country that is ageing rapidly, has shamefully low levels of productivity by international standards."

Bringing service industries up to the level of manufacturing requires a leap toward smarter, more knowledge-intensive operations and new forms of orga-nization. But the heavy emphasis on manufacture has another effect as well.

Exports are particularly important for Japan because, lacking significant domestic sources of food and energy, it depends on imports and needs export income to help pay for them. But Japan went overboard. The result, according to the Council on Foreign Relations report cited above, is that Japan is "a dys-functional hybrid of super-efficient exporting industries and super-inefficient domestic sectors."

This, it turns out, is a particularly worrisome position to find oneself in today because the world has changed. When Japan built its "miracle" on exports, South Korea, Taiwan, Malaysia and other Asian economies offered little competition in world markets. China was not a factor. Today export mar-kets are highly competitive, if not, indeed, overloaded.

Exports, therefore, while important, can no longer be the main strategic path to Japan's future. Japan has to build a domestic economy as advanced as its export sector. It cannot cling to what made it successful yesterday.

FLEX-NATIONS

If there is anything an accelerative economy now requires, it is the organizational flexibility needed to deal with transient conditions. This applies to every society moving toward a knowledge-based economy. But it is especially important for Japan, whose rigid industrial rules have made flexibility all but impossible.

Until these residua of the industrial age are subdued or replaced, Japan will continue to lag in the race toward tomorrow. But whether we look at Second Wave critics of de-industrialization, or the over-representation of old agricultural regions in politics or bureaucratic resistance to restructure, we see, beneath the surface, the same counterrevolutionary resistance to tomorrow's Third Wave knowledge economy found in other countries.

Efforts to change Japan's industrial-age rules and institutions are stubbornly resisted by those with an investment in them, whether they be gray-haired leaders of yesterday's corporate giants, long-serving bureaucrats in the ministry of finance or educators who have been teaching the same course material for twenty-five years. Polite and understated but bitter nevertheless, a guerrilla war is being waged against tomorrow—wave conflict, Japanese-style.

Despite this opposition, some change is taking place. For instance, Japan's famous lifetime employment system is now breaking down. Under this arrangement, the biggest corporations would annually hire a cohort of students right out of school with the expectation that they would stay until retirement. That provided security to the individual but radically proscribed his opportunities. Employers would rarely hire an employee who had quit a rival firm—meaning that if he left, his opportunities for another job were limited. Better stay put. In fact, at one time, labor regulations actually banned skilled workers from leaving without the boss's okay. The system fostered inflexibility.

Locked-in relationships were paralleled at the level of companies. Thus, while manufacturers in the West normally were free to choose suppliers of materials, components or services from any subcontractors, giant Japanese firms were frequently part of, or linked to, a *keiretsu*—a family of financially intertwined, mutually supportive firms grouped around a big trading company and a single major bank.

The *keiretsu* system gave big firms far more power over small suppliers than is typically the case in the West, often requiring their corporate offspring to buy from within the family even if better or cheaper parts were available elsewhere. The *keiretsu,* too, limited flexibility.

In this matter, Japan has made previously unimaginable progress. In five years, according to the Japan External Trade Organization, contracts placed among members of the same *kereitsu* fell from 70 percent to 20 percent. But even here, vacillation prevails. Mitsubishi auto shut down its *keiretsu* organization in 2002, only to re-create it in 2004.

Japanese managers and officials also cling to another obsolete remnant of industrialism. This is the idea that bigger is (almost) always better. And it derives from the theory of economies of scale in mass production.

It overlooks, however, the diseconomies of sheer size—as, for example, when in large organizations the left hand doesn't know—or care—what the right hand is doing. It also overlooks the difference between traditional industries and new ones in which, once an intangible product is created by a tiny firm, it can be replicated and disseminated to a world market at next-to-zero cost.

More important, however, is the inflexibility that accompanies giantism. Small craft can turn around faster than battleships, and in today's accelerating environment, high-speed turns are essential for survival.

If one lesson has been learned from experience with the Third Wave so far, it is that small businesses can, as Silicon Valley proved, change the world. But like any small new organisms, small companies, and especially technological start-ups, need a friendly host environment. That means a comeback culture in which failure is regarded less as the end of a career than as a useful learning experience—as in the story, perhaps apocryphal, about Thomas Watson, former chairman of IBM.

Asked if he were going to fire an executive who had lost several million dollars on a failed project, Watson reportedly replied: "Fire him? Hell, no. I've just paid his tuition!"

Technological start-ups need venture capital—in short supply in Japan. A friendly host culture means democratized finance—finance that can be accessed through many different, competitive channels. In Japan, apart from one's family, banks have been the main source of funding for small business. But this money comes with demands for heavy collateral. As a result of this and other traditional rules and cultural norms, Japan's efforts to create anything like Silicon Valley never got very far. When the gray-haired gentlemen of Keidanren, the top business organization in Japan, finally got around to promoting the "Digital New Deal," not much came of it.

A resurgence occurred later in the telecom industry, with the widespread adoption of mobile phones and other technologies by Japan's young people. But how much of this will translate into entrepreneurialism? In the United States, one out of every ten people is engaged in some entrepreneurial activity. In Japan the number is one in a hundred.

As Henry S. Rowen and A. Maria Toyoda write in a report for the Asia-Pacific Research Center at Stanford University, "Japanese firms do not lack ideas. Japan was the world leader in the growth in absolute numbers of patents from 1992 to 1999 (with the United States coming in second), and was among the top countries in IT patents. . . . But in the IT sector, and despite the country's strengths in physical capital, educated work force, and deep reservoir of technology, this has not translated into global market share or into many valuable new products."

Industrial societies separate institutions into bureaucratic stovepipes. Japanese law actually at one time banned joint enterprises between universities and companies. The breakdown of these rigid boundaries is critical to the development of a knowledge economy. In the United States, Silicon Valley would never have arisen if the boundary between universities and businesses had not been crossed—if Stanford University, the California Institute of Technology, MIT and others hadn't linked up with venture capitalists to start new high-tech businesses.

According to *Nikkei Weekly,* 2,624 start-ups were launched by universities in the United States between 1980 and 2000. By contrast, the number for Japan was a mere 240.

In 2004, however, Japan finally broke through the cast-iron wall that separated academic innovators from the business community by enacting laws to encourage university start-ups. The result, according to Tokyo University, will be the formation of two hundred new businesses not every two decades but every year.

DECISION DELAY

To create a positive host culture for a flexible knowledge-intensive economy, Japan will also have to reexamine the social rules that contribute to inflexibility—including the way decisions are made.

Much has been written about Japan's emphasis on group decision-making, especially about the fact that once a consensus decision has been reached, its implementation is rapid because all relevant parties have by then bought into the goal and understand what needs to be done.

The reverse side of this, however, is the length of time needed to reach a decision, and the difficulty of changing quickly in response to new information or conditions. We saw this at work once during a television shoot with a crew of Japanese, Canadians and Americans. The Japanese team was extremely professional and, during the many months of working together, formed warm relations with the westerners. Each side had an opportunity to observe and learn from the other.

Typically, the night before shooting at a new location, the Japanese team would stay up late debating every aspect of the task—who would do what, exactly when and where. By morning the team was fully prepared.

By contrast, the Americans and Canadians were more likely to spend the evening hours chatting, downing a beer or two and going to bed.

But Wally Longul, the Canadian director, would get up very early and go, by himself, to look the location over again. One morning he discovered a nearby location that he believed would provide a better background for the shoot. When he suggested to the Japanese that they switch to the alternate location, he faced a wall of stubborn refusal—even though none of the them had seen the place he proposed.

The reason for this seemingly blind resistance was clear. The Japanese had invested a great deal of time and energy in arriving at their decision in the first place. Switching to a better location—which, under the circumstances, might have been a better decision—was ruled out. Yet in today's increasingly accelerated and complex economy and society, the ability to change plans rapidly, to arrive at decisions quickly, is a vital survival mechanism.

We can expect to see a decline in collective decision-making in Japan under the pressure of high-speed change and the rise of a new generation that is increasingly individuated.

NO MORE CHRISTMAS CAKES

For its economy to advance in a period of rapid, often confusing and complex change, Japan will also have to loosen its rigid role structure—not merely in the professions and the workplace generally but at the deeper level of family life and gender.

Old assumptions about marriage and family—and their relationship to the economy—are falling away. In 1972, according to a white paper issued by Japan's Cabinet Office, 80 percent of Japanese men and women agreed that only men should hold jobs. Wives should be full-time homemakers. By 2002, 42 percent of men and 51 percent of women no longer agreed with that division of labor.

Young women are marrying later and attach less stigma to staying single. Among those between thirty and thirty-four, 27 percent have never married— a remarkable doubling over a single decade. Today's more assertive unmarried women refuse to be classified as "Christmas Cakes," a disparaging term that compares them to leftovers tossed in the garbage bin the day after the holiday.

Those who do marry are having fewer babies. The national birthrate is at a sixty-year low: 1.29 per couple. In addition, a higher percentage of women work, 13 percent more in 2003 than in 1985. But equal treatment is still a long way off.

Thus, while promotional opportunities for women are better in I.T. and

Internet-related companies, *The Japan Times* reports that in 2003, women accounted for only 9.9 percent of management staff in Japan, compared with 45.9 percent in the United States and over 30 percent in Britain, France, Germany and Sweden. And women's earned income in Japan was still only 46 percent that of males.

Meanwhile, the government, hoping to stem the decline in the birthrate, has called on business to offer paternity leave to fathers, hoping they would help their wives and bond with their newborns. So few men, however, have taken advantage of this that the city of Ota decided sterner, more creative (and procreative) measures were needed.

In 2004 it ruled that all males working for the city would henceforth be compelled to take forty days off in the year after a birth, to keep notes and to report back on what they had learned from the experience. The idea, said one city official, was to "get men involved in raising children" and to counteract the notion that doing so was effeminate.

Ota proves that even a city hall can, on occasion, think outside the proverbial box. Or that, faced with these birth numbers, Japan's leaders are desperate. But are they desperate enough?

This doesn't mean that all women should enter the workforce. Caring for children and managing a home are critical prosumer functions that, as we've seen, create economic value and keep the money economy alive. But the old division of labor based on gender is another structural rigidity standing in the way of Japan's economic advance toward revolutionary wealth.

In today's worldwide race to create knowledge-based money economies, Japan, once a leader, is using only half of its available brainpower. And that's not smart.

THE SILVER WAVE

Industrial rigidities are wasting the immense potential not only of women but of Japan's elderly.

Japan isn't the only major power facing the possible collapse of an industrial-age social-security program. The same is true all across Europe and in the United States. But the risk is perhaps greatest in Japan. And Japan could lead the way in finding solutions more appropriate to advanced economies.

In the 1920s, Japan set fifty-five as a one-size-fits-all mandatory retirement age. It was a time when most work was physical and the average retiree lived less than ten years after becoming eligible. It wasn't until 2000 that the mandatory age was raised to sixty-five.

With an average life span of 81.9 years, the Japanese are, in the words of Julian Chapple of Kyoto Sangyo University, "fast becoming the world's oldest-ever population." Its typical elderly are also among the world's healthiest, racking up seventy-five years of more or less good health—as compared with sixty-nine years for Americans.

The result, in the eyes of most people, is an overwhelming crisis that will heavily burden the younger generation and leave Japan smaller and poorer.

In the swirling debate about how to deal with this crisis, many of the ideas flung around raise troubling questions. Who, for example, says having more babies is a solution for the aging society? Who says having a smaller population necessarily makes a nation poorer? Switzerland? Singapore? Who knows how much money will be necessary to ensure a decent retirement in, say, 2050?

We can reasonably assume, for example, that within the next twenty years or so, at least partial cures will be found for high-cost diseases like Alzheimer's, diabetes, osteoporosis and rheumatoid arthritis, which are especially common among the elderly. Or at least ways to reduce their prevalence. Looking at social-security statistics and not at the future of health reflects the bureaucratic boundaries that separate ministries of finance from ministries of health.

Moreover, isn't it possible that rising expenses for the elderly might be accompanied by declining costs for other population groups? Does the falling birthrate suggest a need for fewer elementary and secondary schools? Or lower costs for pediatric wards and services?

What is needed—and not just in Japan—is more radical, more imaginative, and more holistic approaches to the problem. Japan will have to invent multiple new ways to deal with the "silver wave," as it has been called.

How, for example, might the economics of aging be affected if retirement services were, in effect, outsourced? Today an estimated two million American retirees live outside the United States, according to University of Texas professor David Warner. They are scattered around the world, but 600,000 live in Mexico alone, where a three-bedroom home near Guadalajara can be rented for seven hundred dollars a month.

As many as one million British retirees live abroad—a figure set to hit five million by 2020, according to a report by Alliance & Leicester International. By 2012, the report suggests, poor-country governments will compete for rich-country retirees.

Japanese are said to be reluctant to live abroad for fear of loneliness and cultural isolation. But two who do are Akira Nihei and his wife, who moved in 2003 from Hokkaido in the north of Japan to Penang in much-warmer Malaysia. They report that their new three-bedroom apartment costs five hundred dollars a month—instead of the twelve hundred needed in Hokkaido.

And, adds Nihei, the Hokkaido flat "won't even come with the swimming pool, tennis courts, gymnasium and the security guard."

Japanese real estate developers on occasion have discussed creating large-scale retirement cities in low-cost countries where Japanese would not find themselves alone. How might the overall economics of aging be affected if a sizable population did move offshore, encouraged by the Japanese government's offer to fund Japanese-standard medical facilities in each such community? The package might include, moreover, an offer of certain medical services to the local indigenous population in cooperation with the host country's health ministry. Some costs might come out of Official Development Assistance funds.

A FILIPINA OR A ROBOT?

What are needed, in short, are far more innovative approaches to the problem of the silver wave—solutions that may have to cross the boundaries of multiple existing bureaucracies.

A key slander of retirees holds that they are unproductive. But older people do not have to be unproductive, and most are not, once we recognize, in addition to their paid production, the economic value they create by prosuming.

We needn't replay the discussion of prosuming in earlier chapters. But Japan could lead the world toward solutions of the aging problem by increasing the productivity and producivity of elderly prosumers.

We know that prosumers create social capital by volunteering. Japan might envision large-scale ways to facilitate that. Or it might consider modest loans to some retirees for tools or materials with which to test their long-held ideas for new kinds of products or services that might sell in the money economy. Or for woodworking tools a retiree might use to make furniture he could barter to a friend for driving him to the doctor on Wednesday afternoons. As we've seen, there are many ways in which prosumer output can be increased, and alternative forms of money that can be used in lieu of a regular paycheck.

The choice for retirees requiring care does not have to be, as science-fiction writer Sakyo Komatsu once rather insensitively put it to us, "between a Filipina and a robot."

Admittedly, some of the specific ideas sketched here may be impractical. But to solve many twenty-first-century problems it will be necessary to explore ideas outside the many boxes stuffed with obsolete industrial-age assumptions.

Japan has repeatedly shown that it is a highly creative country, capable of finding tiny, fascinating, novel solutions to problems. To solve the problems now piling up, it will have to apply the same creativity and willingness to explore and experiment on a large scale as well.

AWAITING THE RING

Across the board, then, at almost every level, Japan faces structural rigidities that, taken together, are even more difficult to eliminate than nonperforming loans in its banks or technical and organizational backwardness in the service sector. Indeed, it is structural rigidity itself that threatens Japan as the fast-arriving future confronts it with unprecedented challenges. In Japan as elsewhere, there is a point at which rigidity becomes rigor mortis.

But in 2005, Prime Minister Junichiro Koizumi of the Liberal Democratic Party broke the long-standing rigor mortis by performing a remarkable act of political jujitsu. Turning his back on rural voters—for fifty years the LDP's most reliable and conservative voting bloc—he won widespread urban support instead and was reelected.

Urban-rural wave conflict has long been a fact of life in Japan and the government "has used public debt to suppress this internal conflict for the past few decades," says Goldman Sachs' Courtis. "Wave conflict has been softened by massive spending, which made it possible, in effect, to buy off different sectors of the economy.

"For Japan, however, this game is approaching an end. It faces a weakened yen, higher energy prices, increasingly powerful competition from China and India. If China faces a 'volcano,' Japan faces an explosion of its own."

Fortunately, Japan is beginning to recognize the need for profoundly rethinking the system that served it so well for nearly half a century after World War II. One indication is the growing discussion about changing its constitution. The most immediately controversial issue—whether and how to redefine the role of the military—has been on the agenda for decades. But the constitutional discussion now goes far beyond this. Some proposed provisions that could affect the future of wealth would deal with the environment, bioethics and—clearly central to a knowledge-based economy—intellectual property.

Perhaps also needed is a clause that calls for periodic review of the power, role and structure of the bureaucracy. A clause advancing the rights of women. And a clause that reconsiders the roles and rights of immigrants and ethnic minorities—not merely for the bodies they add to the labor force but for the diversity of ideas and cultures they can bring to fuel innovation and enrich Japan.

Finally, Japan is painfully rethinking its entire role in the world economy in light of the rise of China. Japanese investment in China now equals that in the United States, and China in 2002 bypassed the United States in the export of goods to Japan—a third coming from Japanese plants in China.

This isn't the place for a discourse on Asian geopolitics or the rising nationalism in both China and Japan. But decisions Japan must make in the decade to come will have a powerful effect on the economy and security of the United States and the rest of the world.

On the one hand, Japan is racing to take advantage of low-cost production in China and access to its internal market. At the same time, it is strengthening its military ties with the United States. The economic significance of the existing United States–Japanese security arrangement is often overlooked. Yet much of Asia's spectacular rise might never have happened without it.

Their bilateral Treaty of Mutual Cooperation and Security has played a key role in stabilizing the Asia Pacific region during its recent decades of rapid and widespread economic growth.

Without this stability factor, Asia—including even China—would have had a much harder time attracting investment from Europe and the United States, not to mention Taiwan and South Korea. It is part of the reason companies such as GM, Intel and Anheuser-Busch from the United States as well as BMW, Siemens and BASF from Europe have risked dotting the region with factories, call centers, research laboratories and other investments.

Today, as Japan simultaneously tightens its security links with the United States and its economic links with China, it could make Japan an even more pivotal force in a region with a high potential for military conflict, pandemics, environmental damage, religious collision and terrorism. But it could, alternatively, reduce its bargaining power with both.

While many Japanese companies are rushing to put their plants in China, the very same companies may find themselves losing global markets to low-cost Chinese goods. In the period ahead, Japan, too, needs a twin-track policy. It must reduce its reliance on exports—especially of mass-produced, low-end, impersonal consumer products. At the same time it must rapidly complete its transition to a knowledge-based economy and society—even if that requires drastic changes at home. Either that or its new generation, busy with *anime, manga* and games, will see Japan's affluence and influence shrink in an increasingly unstable Asia.

It is sometimes said that Japan is like bamboo. Bamboo grows in long, straight sections of green trunk periodically marked by a narrow gray-brown ring. The straight sections, we are told, symbolize Japan's long resistance to change. The rings, by contrast, represent sudden, revolutionary upheaval.

The future of wealth everywhere—from the United States and Europe to China and East Asia—will in considerable measure depend on whether Japan is approaching its next bamboo ring.

CHAPTER 46

EUROPE'S
LOST MESSAGE

X avier de C*** (his last name is secret) is a spy. He is also an adven-
turer, scholar and adviser to governments. And he is the author of a
startling proposal for Europe to help create "the United States of the
West" by hitching its own wagon directly "to the American star," forming one
new supernation and jointly policing the various barbarians in the rest of the
world.

Making this case in a witty essay, Xavier scathingly punctures what he
regards as France's oversized ego and explains why he has actually given up
his French passport to become an American citizen.

In listing the many advantages that would accrue to an enlarged West,
Xavier writes about culture, military cooperation and expansion of the American tax base by bringing in the Europeans. What's more, it would give Europe
the right to vote in U.S. elections—in Xavier's view, the only ones that matter.

The essay drew bitter protests from French nationalists and left-wingers
who took its proposal at face value—even though Xavier, as it turned out, was
a fictional character. He was created by Régis Debray, the intellectual stormy
petrel best known for his friendships in the 1960s with Che Guevera and Fidel
Castro.

What Xavier doesn't offer, however, is any half-serious analysis of the
economics of the imagined unification. What could Europe bring to the marriage? What could Europe count on getting in return? Where are the
economies of each heading in the decades ahead? Which way would wealth
flow between them?

THE ALL-TIME LOW

Whatever the theoretical virtues of this fictional fusion, the unfortunate reality is that the United States and Europe are growing apart, not closer together.

While it is true that re-globalization has caused both to adopt some common rules of the financial ; .me and to speak in a common vocabulary about corporate issues such as "tr: nsparency," far more profound forces are driving them apart. The rise of China, having thrown a giant rock into the global pool, is sending out powerful riptides that affect all the major currencies and trade relationships and disrupt long-standing alliances.

Historically, Europe and the United States have been each other's chief trading partner. Since 1985, however, as each increased its trade with China and other emerging countries, the flow of imports and exports between the two has been declining as a percentage of their total trade. If you don't believe it, go buy a Vuitton bag. Chances are it was manufactured in China, legally or otherwise.

The reduction in transatlantic economic interdependency has been accompanied by increasingly contentious trade disputes as the European Union banned the import of genetically modified food and raised tariffs on American goods ranging from honey, bananas and roller skates to nuclear reactors.

In addition, as William A. Reinsch of the National Foreign Trade Council points out, the European Union killed a proposed merger of Honeywell and General Electric in 2001 and fined Microsoft $613 million for anti-competitive behavior, ordering it to unbundle its media player from its Windows software. On its side, the United States imposed duties or suspended imports on European steel, cold cuts, ball bearings and pasta.

By 2004, *CFO* was reporting that "even on traditional trade issues, relations between the United States and the EU are at an all-time low."

All this was further fraught by the controversy raised in 2005 by Europe's plan to lift its embargo on arms sales to China. This confronted the United States with an unlikely but dangerous possibility: If China were to attack Taiwan, which the United States is obligated to defend, American troops could face weapons supplied by its European "partners." As 2005 drew to a close, the Europeans had put the plan on hold.

All these conflicts, however, can be seen as early skirmishes pointing to larger transatlantic conflicts to come.

THE WIDENING SPLIT

The latest erosion of United States–Europe ties was typically attributed to their sharp differences over the Iraq war. But far deeper forces are at work.

The alliance can be said to have cracked the day Western Europeans stopped fearing an attack by the Soviet Union—and concluded they no longer needed U.S. troops and taxpayers to defend them. But while true, even this doesn't explain what is happening.

For today's widening split actually began decades earlier when the United States started to change its relationship to the deep fundamentals and began building a knowledge economy. Europe's core countries, by contrast, focused on reconstruction after World War II and subsequent expansion of their smokestack economies.

Rich with talent, top-notch scientists, I.T. engineers, futurists and thinkers, Europe for a time seemed poised to embrace the new technological potentials. But it was largely led by rear-mirror business and political leaders steeped in the guiding doctrines of the industrial age and incapable of thinking beyond them.

It is true that in recent years Europe has moved faster than the United States in several advanced sectors, including mobile-phone use. Its Airbus for a time did well competing against an under-the-weather Boeing. It may lead the United States in grid computing. The French are strong competitors in the satellite-launch business, and Europe is planning to loft a rival to the American Global Positioning System. Tim Berners-Lee, who is British, gave us the World Wide Web. Linus Torvalds, a Finn, gave us Linux. And the European Space Agency led the project that, in collaboration with NASA, put a probe on Titan, Saturn's moon. This list could easily be extended. But all these successes need to be set against a larger, much darker picture.

To this day, key industrial principles such as standardization, concentration, maximization of scale and centralization still dominate European Union thinking. Thus, as knowledge-based economies move from massification toward de-massification of products and markets—accompanied by growing social and cultural diversity—the European Union has been homogenizing national differences. Giving lip service to the concept of diversity, it has, in fact, kept busy attempting to "harmonize" everything from taxes to cosmetics, job résumés to motorcycle laws. In applying one-size-fits-all rules, moreover, as *The Economist* points out, it usually opts for the most stringent and least flexible of the available versions.

As in Japan and elsewhere, success in advanced knowledge economies requires increasingly flexible business and governmental organizations. But the European Union specializes in imposing inflexible, top-down industrial-style controls—even on the budgets and financial decisions of its member nations.

Under the Maastricht Treaty each nation using the euro as currency was bound to limit government deficits to no more than 3 percent of its GDP. This was done largely at the imperial insistence of Germany, which eventually found the limits so restrictive that it, itself, repeatedly violated the inflexible standard it helped impose on everyone else. In 2004, the *International Herald Tribune* noted that "around 6 of the 12 euro-zone members are in violation of the pact."

In 2005, French and Dutch voters rejected the proposed E.U. constitution, a four-hundred-page masterwork of bureaucratic overkill. Critics noted that the authors of the U.S. Constitution required fewer than ten pages, including the Bill of Rights.

SPEEDING IN SLOW MOTION

The widening gulf between Western Europe and the United States also reflects two contrasting attitudes toward the deep fundamental of time.

Europe and America operate at different speeds. Europe is well behind the United States in work-at-home arrangements that typically allow employees to adjust their work hours. Even in the shop or office, Europe lags in flexible scheduling, 24/7 operations and other departures from traditional industrial routines.

Workforce flexibility is needed for firms to compete successfully in today's global markets. But European workers and employers alike remain trapped in inflexible temporal arrangements.

This situation is not merely reflected in the longer vacations, generally shorter workweek and overall slower pace of life on which Europeans, and especially the French, pride themselves. It is even seen in attitudes toward meals. In response to the American-born fast-food industry spreading across the globe, Europe has originated the "slow food" movement aimed at fighting it.

Started almost as a joke in Italy in 1986, this movement now claims as many as eighty thousand members in one hundred countries, including 145 chapters in the United States. Its organizers stage events, publish books about food and celebrate good (and slow) eating.

The slow-food movement has (slowly) spawned a counterpart called *cittàslow* devoted to maintaining slow life in small cities. It promotes local products and sustainability and is so committed to slowness that, as of 2002, of the thirty Italian towns that helped found the movement, none had as yet qualified for membership. "They're not supposed to qualify quickly," explained one of the movement's organizers. "It could take years."

Whether a new organization ever springs up for those who enjoy both a fast and a slow pace of life at different times, both a burger on the run and a languorous lobster, remains to be seen.

Meanwhile, Britons are flocking to villages like Agincourt in northern France in search of greater tranquillity and a still-slower-paced lifestyle.

The surge is helped, no doubt, by lower house prices and just possibly by the Channel Tunnel and additional airline flights that—forfend the thought—speed up travel. All of which led one Agincourt real estate agent, Maggie Kelly, to exclaim, "These days I hardly have five minutes to turn around!" Apparently, no irony intended.

But amusement shouldn't deceive us. Whatever the virtues of slow versus fast, how a society deals with time has important implications for how it creates wealth—for both de-synchronization at home and integration into the world economy.

European headlines are dotted, in fact, with the word *slow*, as in CORE EUROPE COUNTRIES SLOW TO IMPLEMENT . . . , EU "TOO SLOW" ON ECONOMIC REFORMS and GENDER EQUALITY: SLOW PROGRESS. But it's not just the European Union that's slow. Business transactions in Europe must confront layer after impenetrable layer of regulations.

Writing in *Parliament Magazine,* Professor Viktor Mayer-Schoenberger of Harvard says, "In Europe things move slower and take more time and energy." So it is no surprise to learn from the European Commission itself that "in the USA, it takes just six hours to establish a business, and while differences remain between member states . . . in Europe, it takes much longer in all of them."

Try, for example, obtaining a patent in Europe. According to Trevor Cook of the European law firm Bird & Bird, "It takes much longer to secure patents in Europe than it does in the U.S., typically at least four, sometimes as many as ten years, and this is a real problem for fast-moving high-tech businesses."

Or talk to Rita Villa, an American certified public accountant who operates on both sides of the Atlantic. "Things just take longer in Europe. Transactions have many more steps. For example, if a U.S. company wants to move its headquarters from, say, Chicago to Dallas, no problem. But if a German firm wants to move from Berlin to Frankfurt, it requires a whole time-consuming, multi-step process of 'registration.'"

Or, she says, try changing the legal form of a company, something smaller firms often need to do.

If I have a limited liability corporation, or LLC, in the U.S. and want to convert it to an ordinary corporation with "Inc." at the end of its name, I can do that rapidly. But in Germany when we wanted to change a GMBH to an AG—a comparable change—it took over a year.

Say the company wants to issue a dividend to its shareholders. In the U.S., the board of directors meets and, if it thinks it's a good idea, it votes and that's it. Not in Germany. There the auditors first have to approve it. Then it goes to the management board. After that it has to go to the supervisory board. Then it has to go to the notary who can demand last-minute alterations even after all the parties have reached an agreement. Then it has to be registered.

The transatlantic differences in time and pace even affect Europe's defense industries and military. American military technology and capabilities are aimed at enabling faster and faster responses to crisis. European forces in NATO can't keep up, making integrated joint action more difficult. The European Union, meanwhile, is moving—slowly—to create its own "rapid reaction" military force.

At all these levels, therefore, from lifestyle and culture to military matters and, above all, business and the economy, the speed gap between Europe and the United States is, if anything, widening. Each is responding to the accelerative economy and the deep fundamental of time at its own, very different pace.

YESTERDAY'S HEARTLAND

The United States and Europe have very different approaches to the deep fundamental of space as well.

Deriving from the industrial belief that bigger is almost always better, the European Union continues to push its spatial boundaries ever eastward by incorporating more and more member countries. The bigger its population, its leaders believe, the richer.

However, in pursuing sheer size, Europe sees space through the lens of a previous era.

The European Union's leaders would be quite justifiably horrified to be compared in any way to Nazis. The E.U.'s peaceful expansion to the east, with the incorporation of additional countries and murmured speculation about someday even bringing Russia into the E.U. fold, is the opposite of Nazi Germany's *Drang nach Osten*—the drive to the east—that sent its troops and death legions all the way to the gates of Moscow.

But both recall the once popular geopolitical theory that held that whoever controls the "heartland" will command the world. The heartland, originally defined by Halford Mackinder in 1904, was the entire landmass from Eastern Europe across Russia to Siberia. Of course, his theories have been shattered by, among other things, the invention of airplanes, missiles and global communication. However, some apparently see a "Europe" stretching eastward all the way to the Sea of Japan as, in effect, a new heartland.

Also shattered are many of today's taken-for-granted assumptions. Timothy Garton Ash of St. Antony's College, Oxford, argues that the European Union is a "transnational organization based on supra-national law" rather than an "old-fashioned . . . classical nation-state." But Ash himself hangs onto the obsolete assumption that scale necessarily translates into economic power.

Thus he writes that the European Union's future is more promising than that of the United States because "put very simply, the European Union is getting bigger" while "Haiti cannot hope to follow Hawaii into the American union."

Hidden here, in addition to the bigger-is-better assumption, is a further spatial premise: That if a group of nations wishes to form a "transnational organization," the countries need to be next door to one another—that contiguity, that is, geographical proximity, is what counts. Yet, we are racing into a world when nearness matters less and less, thanks to speedy transportation, lighter and lighter products and the growing trade in intangible services.

If, indeed, landmass mattered, Ash might consider that Russia alone is more than four times the size of the expanded European Union. Brazil is more than twice its size. And then there is prosperous Singapore, with not quite seven hundred square kilometers all told. If, indeed, the United States wished to create a "transnational organization based on supra-national law," what would prevent such an organization from including noncontiguous South Korea, Singapore or Israel as members? Or, for that matter, Japan? Total GDP of this group in 2004: $15.7 trillion—$4.7 trillion more than the European Union.

A noncontiguous supranational organization consisting of America and Japan alone—we call it Jamerica—would exceed the combined GDP of all twenty-five members of the European Union by $3.6 trillion.

Ironically, while the European Union has been busy expanding its scale and territorial limits, its member nations that have advanced the most in the direction of revolutionary wealth are the smaller ones on its periphery. Finland with Nokia and Sweden with Ericsson shine in telecommunications, as Ireland does in software—although much of its output is turned out by American firms such as Microsoft, Oracle, Novell, Symantec and Computer Associates.

THE LISBON DREAM

The United States and Europe increasingly differ in their relationships not only to the deep economic fundamentals of time and space but to knowledge as well—including knowledge-intensive technologies.

In 1997, the European Union's then membership of fifteen countries produced $53.5 billion worth of computers as against $82.4 billion by the United States and $67.7 billion by Japan. Europe's $40.1 billion output of electronic components was barely half that of the United States or Japan. Of the top ten I.T. companies in the world in 1998—including IBM, Hitachi, Matshushita, Hewlett-Packard, Toshiba, Fujitsu, NEC, Compaq and Motorola—only Siemens was European. Only thirty European producers make it onto the list of the world's three hundred biggest software companies, and only two— Misys and SAP—are in the top ten.

In 2000 Europe's leaders finally gathered in Lisbon and bravely announced their intention to make Europe "the most competitive and dynamic knowledge-based economy in the world" by 2010.

"I hadn't laughed so hard and so much since the Communist Politburo used to announce totally unrealistic production targets. It was the same kind of thing," Radek Sikorski, the former deputy foreign minister of Poland, said when the goal was adopted.

In a 2001 study the European Commission concluded that "overall living standards in Europe are falling behind those in the United States, with under-performance in innovation and the use of information and communication technologies pinpointed as major factors behind the widening gap. . . . The gap in living standards between the European Union and the U.S. is now wider than it has ever been in the past 25 years."

In 2003 the commission also warned that Europe—which, as we saw earlier, has set up a number of bioresearch centers—may be about to "miss the boat" on the biotech revolution.

Ditto for nanotechnology. In May 2004 the commission found that both the United States and Japan invest more per capita in nanotechnology R&D than the European Union, and that "the gap is expected to widen."

In 2004, in yet another *cri de coeur,* the commission declared that "innovation is a key to economic success, but it is an area where Europe lags badly behind the U.S."

By the end of that year, then German Chancellor Gerhard Schröder concluded that Europe could not meet the "unrealistic" goal for 2010, and outgoing Commission president Romano Prodi lamented that the European Union's attempts to catch up with America economically had been "a big failure."

In 2005, as the European Union considered yet another relaunch of the Lisbon Agenda, the European business group Eurochambres published a study concluding that the union's economy now matched that of the United States circa the late 1970s.

In sum, by 2005, the 2010 program was fast becoming a corpse—and Europe's leaders were still shortchanging research and development, science and science education, still brushing off the "new economy" and complaining about de-industrialization.

In his 2004 book *After the Empire,* the French geopolitical analyst

Emmanuel Todd refers to Europe as "the planet's leading industrial power." He is right. It is. But the United States is the planet's leading "no-longer-industrial power." And Europe, with some important exceptions, has still not adequately altered its relationship to the deep fundamental of knowledge—and to revolutionary wealth.

In the years ahead, the big countries of Western Europe could see many of their low-tech manufacturing jobs migrate to lower-cost E.U. member states in the former Soviet bloc or elsewhere. Failure to replace these jobs through a faster transition to services and knowledge-based, innovation-intensive, higher-value-added production will increase unemployment levels—already significantly higher than those in the United States and Japan. In turn, this will further increase anti-immigrant tensions—and the potential for escalating militancy and terrorism in Europe's large Muslim underclass. The car-burning riots in France in 2005 may only be a foreshadow of things to come.

Part of Western Europe's problem is a deep-seated hostility toward technology. Its trade unions fear job losses. Its NGOs offer knee-jerk opposition to new technologies often because of imagined dangers. While a technophiliac Asia races to adopt the latest advances, technophobic Western Europeans create obstacles to their development and application.

This technophobia is somewhat less apparent as one moves eastward to the former Communist countries. The Czech Republic, with one of the world's highest percentages of science and engineering graduates compared with all degrees awarded there, has attracted projects by IBM, Accenture, Logica and Olympus. Slovenia, writes the *Financial Times,* has "all the attributes of a top destination for smaller knowledge-economy projects, high-tech centers, distribution and logistic hubs and call centres."

Hungary already claims Nokia's largest R&D center outside Finland, and ExxonMobil has opened a new headquarters in Budapest to consolidate its European I.T. and accounting support operations. In fact, in 2001, according to the European Union itself, the value of Hungary's high-tech exports already rivaled those of Denmark or Spain.

Eastern European members may soon be scouting high-tech, value-added niches ignored by slower-moving Western Europeans—and pondering the possibility of actually leaping ahead of some of their neighbors.

With respect, therefore, to all three of the deep fundamentals we have explored—time, space and knowledge—the United States and Europe are moving apart. And that would be happening even if differences over the war in Iraq had never been an issue.

To reverse that process, the United States would need to stall or drive in reverse as Europe, with a new map, accelerates its transition to a Third Wave wealth system.

Someday, if one listens to its triumphalists, Europe could become a global counterweight to what many see as excessive American power. But the geopolitical power of nations presupposes economic and military might—both of which now increasingly depend on that softest of all resources: Knowledge.

Regrettably, it would appear, Europe has still not received that lost-in-the-snail-mail message.

CHAPTER 47

INSIDE AMERICA

A new way of life based on revolutionary wealth is still taking form in America—plug-in/plug-out jobs, glitter and hype, speed, commercialism, 24/7 entertainment, speed, cleaner air, dirtier television, rotten schools, speed, a broken health system and longer life, speed again, perfect landings on Mars, information overload, surplus complexity, reduced racism, hyper-diets and hyper-kids. Oh, yes, and still more speed.

Add to this kaleidoscope the multiplying contradictions in American life today. Viagra commercials and anti-abortion marchers. Free markets—but tariffs and subsidies that favor U.S. firms. Americans who are provincials—bad at languages, uninterested in other cultures. But hooray for globalization!

Outsiders don't know what to make of all this noisy disarray. In the words of Dominique Moïsi, the French foreign-affairs expert, "It's not that we are so much against America, it is that we cannot understand the evolution of that country." But neither do most Americans. And outsiders don't know that the Americans don't know.

It might help to think about America not simply as the world's most powerful nation-state, which it currently is, but as the world's greatest social and economic laboratory.

It is the main place in the world where new ideas and new ways of life are eagerly tried—and sometimes pushed to stupid, even cruel extremes—before they are rejected. Experiments are under way in this lab not merely with technologies but with culture and the arts, sexual patterns, family structure, fashion, diets and sports, start-up religions and brand-new business models.

Simultaneously, the United States is experimenting with all three of the deep fundamentals of wealth. That's what all the speed is about—and it's why so many people yearn for a less frenzied time. It is why machines may need to work faster and people more slowly. America is experimenting as well with space and how it is divided up—witness the growing permeability of economic boundaries. And above all, of course, it is experimenting with countless new ways of turning data, information and knowledge into wealth.

The United States is the place where mistakes are allowed to happen—and sometimes lead to economically or socially valuable breakthroughs. It is where almost any failure is redeemable and where "comeback kids" are admired rather than shunned (sometimes when they shouldn't be).

Great laboratories are free to make mistakes. If they don't risk error, they aren't reaching out for the future. And America is.

The trouble is that not everyone likes to live in a laboratory—or next door to one. Lab mistakes can cost people jobs, influence, power—even lives. Many Americans fear change and yearn for a return to the so-called good old days of the early 1950s, when America was a Second Wave country and the Third Wave was barely visible.

Conveniently forgetting the backbreaking physical labor, racial hatred and subjugation of women that still characterized the U.S. economy and society during those supposedly "good" times, and legitimately afraid of losing their jobs, position, prestige or prominence, they derogate the present and fear—and resist—the future. The result, therefore, inside America, no less than in China, Japan, Europe and elsewhere, is wave conflict.

When a revolutionary wealth-creation system arises, one of the first things it does is create counter-revolutionaries. The late banker Walter Wriston, head of the White House Economic Advisory Policy Board under President Reagan, put it bluntly: "Whenever there is a shift in how wealth is created, the old elites give up their position and a new group of people arise and control society. We're in the middle of that right now." What he did not point out is that "old elites" don't give up without a fight.

MORE WAVE WARFARE

In the United States and most rich democracies, wave conflict is usually subtler than in the poor world. But it is there nonetheless. It appears at many different levels, ranging from energy policy and transportation to corporate regulation and, above all, education.

Industrial America was built on the back of cheap fossil fuels and an immense infrastructure for distributing energy around the country. Costly and overdependent on imported oil and gas, the American energy-distribution system includes 158,000 miles of electrical transmission lines and 2 million miles of oil pipelines that, because they are heavy fixed assets, are hard to alter in response to rapid change.

The United States is rushing to build an advanced knowledge-based economy but remains saddled with an industrial-age, legacy energy system politically defended by some of the world's biggest and most influential corporations against a growing, growling public demand for fundamental change in the system. The conflict is not usually posed in these terms, but it is, in fact, an example of Second Wave vs. Third Wave warfare.

24 BILLION HOURS

A parallel, related conflict is occurring over America's transportation system, starting with its nearly 4 million miles of public highways, roads and streets. These are traveled by 23 million commercial trucks operated by more than 500,000 companies that carry more than three quarters of all goods moved within the United States. Together they make up a nearly $600 billion industry that, along with other means of transportation, equals fully 11 percent of the nation's GDP. However, it isn't just goods that are moved. People are, too.

This huge infrastructure was a response to the mass society that grew up with mass production, urbanization and work patterns that required masses of workers to commute back and forth over the same pathways on uniform schedules.

In 2000, some 119 million Americans wasted approximately 24 billion hours getting to and from their jobs—surely one of most counterproductive things Americans do. Today, as mass production has given way to increasingly customized, de-massified and decentralized knowledge production, large numbers of people no longer work in city cores. Work patterns shift from fixed schedules to anytime, anyplace, including home, again altering the way time and space are used.

Between 1991 and 1997, the U.S. Department of Transportation looked into a Third Wave alternative. Termed "intelligent transportation," it called for the use of smart technology to increase the safety and capacity of existing highways. According to *Government Technology,* the DoT concluded that intelligent "freeway management systems" could "reduce accidents by 17 percent while permitting highways to handle as much as 22 percent more traffic at greater speeds." Just computerizing traffic signals could decrease travel times by 14 percent and delays by 37 percent.

But pressure from pour-more-concrete lobbies greatly outmatched the political influence of the nascent information-technology sector. When President Clinton in 1998 signed an act allocating $203 billion for repairing and "building roads, bridges, transit systems and railways," the amount set aside for intelligent systems was approximately one tenth of 1 percent—this from an administration that touted its support for the "information superhighway."

The U.S. transportation system, on which most business enterprises directly or indirectly depend, is still gridlocked by a politically powerful triad of oil companies, car manufacturers and often corrupt highway-construction firms.

Thus, while America's communications system has introduced a dazzling succession of innovations, making it possible to distribute knowledge in ways never before possible, Americans are still denied energy and transport systems that would be more efficient, safer and cleaner. These key elements of America's infrastructure—and their component subsystems—are de-synchronized and fought over by vested industrial-age interests and breakthrough innovators advancing the knowledge-based wealth system. Wave conflict again.

A similar pattern can be seen in many struggles over business practices. For example, a battle over the way stock options are accounted has pitted the influential Financial Accounting Standards Board, or Fazbee—which has traditionally favored tangible over intangible assets—against fledgling knowledge-based firms, making it harder for the latter to attract both capital and talented employees.

These are just snapshots of the low-intensity wave warfare now found in almost all American institutions as they attempt to come to terms with high-speed technological and social change. Nowhere is the outcome of this conflict more important than in America's schools.

STEALING THE FUTURE

The United States will not maintain its spearhead role in the world wealth revolution, it will not hold on to global power and it will not reduce poverty without replacing—not merely reforming—its factory-focused education system.

Wave conflict over public education—and the $400 billion the present system costs every year (not counting the societal costs of its failure and its indirect costs to business in terms of an ill-prepared workforce)—will escalate in personal and political passion in the years ahead.

Perhaps the greatest cost of wave conflict in America will be paid by nearly fifty million children currently compulsorily enrolled in schools that are attempting to prepare them—and not very successfully at that—for jobs that won't exist. Call that stealing the future.

Education is about far more than jobs. But the schools, with minute exceptions, also fail to prepare students for their roles as consumers and prosumers. Nor does this system, by and large, help kids cope with the rising complexity and new life options they face in sex, marriage, ethics and other dimensions of the emerging society. Least of all does it succeed in introducing more than a tiny fraction of them to the enormous pleasure of learning itself.

THE NAMELESS COALITION

Negative as it sounds today, however, the mass education system, in its time, was in fact a progressive advance over pre-industrial reality where, by and large, only a small percentage of children ever went to school, and where literacy and numeracy were almost non-existent among the poor. It took generations, even after the rise of industrialism, to put children in school rather than in cheap-labor factories from the earliest possible age.

Today we still keep all these millions of children in factory-style schools because that is where an unlikely, nameless coalition of special interests has wanted them to be.

To understand this coalition, we need to glance back to its origins in the late 1800s. At that time, while many parents opposed sending their children to school because they needed them to work in the fields or factories, an increasingly vocal number fought for free public education. But it was only when business interests concluded that schools could contribute to productivity by helping to impose "industrial discipline" on young workers fresh off the farm that the pro-education coalition gained real power.

"The values and attitudes associated with industrial discipline," writes Lawrence A. Cremin in *American Education,* "were . . . inner discipline, hard work, punctuality, frugality, sobriety, orderliness and prudence." Schools taught these "not only through text book preachments, but also through the very character of their organization—the grouping, periodizing and objective impersonality were not unlike those of the factory."

In addition, the arrival of millions of immigrants speaking diverse languages brought cheap labor to U.S. shores from many different countries and cultures. But to be productive in the factory economy, they needed to be assimilated or homogenized into the dominant American culture of the time, and from about 1875 to 1925, one of the dominant functions of the schools was the Americanization of the foreign-born.

Business, in short, now had a crucial stake in massifying armies of the young to help build the mass-production economy of the industrial age.

As industrialism developed further in the twentieth century, big labor arose to protect the interests of workers. Unions as a rule strongly supported public education—not just because its members wanted a better life for their children, but because unions, too, had a hidden, or unnoticed, stake in the system. The smaller the available workforce, the less competition for jobs and the higher the wages. Unions not only fought the good fight against child labor but also campaigned to extend the years of compulsory education, thus keeping millions of young people out of the labor market for longer and longer periods.

The subsequent unionization of teachers, moreover, created a large membership with an even stronger, personal reason to support the mass-education system designed for the industrial age.

In addition to parents, business and labor, government, too, had reason to support big education. Public agencies recognized the economic advantages of the system but had secondary, less obvious reasons to support it. For example, when compulsory education worked, it kept many millions of high-testosterone teenagers off the streets, improving public order and reducing crime and the costs of policing and prison.

What we saw, therefore, throughout the industrial era, was an unbreakable coalition that has preserved the factory-school model—a mass education system that fit neatly into the matrix of mass production, mass media, mass culture, mass sports, mass entertainment and mass politics.

In the words of Sir Ken Robinson, senior adviser on education policy to the president of the famed Getty Foundation in Los Angeles and author of *Out of Our Minds: Learning to Be Creative,* "The whole apparatus of public education has largely been shaped by the needs and ideologies of industrialism . . . predicated on old assumptions about the supply and demand for labour. The keywords of this system are linearity, conformity and standardisation."

FORCES FOR CHANGE

Today a new wave conflict looms on the horizon, and not just in the United States. The coming clash will set defenders of our existing education factories against a growing movement committed to replacing them—a movement comprising four key elements.

Teachers: The existing system typically reduces teaching to mechanical, by-the-book instruction and standardized testing, draining the last creativity out of both teacher and student. Within the schools today are millions of burned-out teachers resigned to serving their time until retirement as passive supporters of this status quo.

Yet within these same schools are legions of heroic, miserably underpaid teachers who struggle against the system from within. Despite the constraints imposed on them, some manage to do remarkable things for children and burst with ideas that could help propel education out of the industrial age. With little support from outside, they remain a vanguard, as it were, waiting to join the movement for radical—rather than incremental—change.

Parents: Among parents, too, there are unmistakable signs of disaffection with the old coalition. Many support the tiny but growing number of charter schools, magnet schools and other limited experiments within the existing public education system. Others are hiring private tutors or sending their children to after-school programs like the *juku* in Japan. "Tutoring," reports National Public Radio, "is now becoming so pervasive it is arguably changing the face of American education." Nor is tutoring limited by geography. NPR notes, "Teachers in India are tutoring American children in math over the Internet."

Other parents, having entirely given up on the old system, are teaching their children at home—and not just for religious reasons. The Web offers them more than a million listings and descriptions of home-teaching aids.

The more out of sync the failing industrial-age school system becomes with the needs of a knowledge-based economy, the more likely it is that parental protest will assume increasingly muscular forms. Angry and empowered by the Internet, activist parents can be expected to reach far beyond neighborhood parent-teacher associations and organize themselves into local, national and even global movements to demand completely new educational models, methods, content and institutions.

Students: Children didn't wield enough power in centuries past to matter much in the movement to create mass education. Today they can help bring it down. They already are waging anarchic war against the system. Their revolt takes two forms, one outside the classroom, the other within it.

Kids have always rebelled against schools, but in the past they did not have access to cell phones, computers, Ecstasy, porn or the Internet. Nor, as they grew up, did they face an economy that needed their brains, rather than their muscles. Today many, if not most, students know in their gut that today's schools are preparing them for yesterday instead of tomorrow.

The first, all-too-familiar form of rebellion consists of dropping out—and stiffing us with the bill. In a striking manifesto called *Leaving School: Finding Education,* two professors of education, Jon Wiles at the University of North Florida and John Lundt at the University of Montana, calculate that 30 percent of students in grades nine through twelve drop out of American schools— after costing $50,000 to $75,000 each—even with underpaid teachers. Once out, many join what a century ago was called the *lumpen* proletariat, or underclass, made up of street people, criminals, drug pushers, the mentally ill or unemployable.

The other rebellion takes place inside the classroom. Attacking the root assumptions of factory-style schools, Wiles and Lundt question whether education should continue to be compulsory. So, undoubtedly, do many teachers who are forced to serve as jailers faced every day with the equivalent of a riot in the cell block as their pupils fight any semblance of discipline.

Teachers cannot defend against the plague of media violence. They cannot defend against the worship of celebrities, including sports figures who cheat with drugs, lie to their spouses, get drunk, beat people up and have to be defended against rape charges. Nor can they, or parents, easily defend against pedophiles trawling the Web for unsuspecting kids. Some schools are so racked with violence—against teachers as well as pupils—that their hallways require police patrols.

Young people have always educated—and miseducated themselves. Today, however, they do so with the dubious help of the new media. Games and cell phones are hidden behind open textbooks. Text messages fly back and forth even as the teacher drones on.

It is as though, while teachers incarcerate kids in classrooms, their ears, eyes and minds escape to rove the cyberuniverse. From a very young age, they are aware that no teacher and no school can make available even the tiniest fraction of the data, information, knowledge—and fun—available online. They know that in one universe they are prisoners. In the other, free.

Business: So long as the schools continued, generation after generation, to supply companies with a workforce pre-disciplined for factory life, the coalition in support of industrial-age schools remained firm. But from the mid-twentieth century on, as the new wealth system began to spread, new, different job skills became necessary—skills the broad base of existing schools could not provide. The gap widened so dramatically that by the 1990s the business press was filled with articles about it and, in 2005, Bill Gates finally laid it on the line:

> *America's high schools are obsolete. By obsolete, I don't just mean that our high schools are broken, flawed, and under-funded. . . . By obsolete, I mean that our high schools—even when they're working exactly as designed—cannot teach our kids what they need to know today. . . . This isn't an accident or a flaw in the system; it is the system.*

This clarion call for replacing, not simply reforming, education was significant not just because it verified what we and other critics have been saying but because it marked a clear breakaway of knowledge-based businesses from the old coalition that has kept the factory-model school in place.

The interests of Second and Third Wave business are now diverging. For the first time in a century or more, it may be possible for angry parents, frustrated teachers, skill-hungry businesses, classroom innovators, online educators, game designers and kids themselves to form a new coalition with the power not merely to reform but to replace assembly-line education.

THE NEXT STEP

The energy system, transportation infrastructure and schools are not the only institutions in which advance is held back by residual industrial interests.

Defenders of yesterday's way of doing things still sit in the boardrooms of great corporations. Others populate political parties. And some, typically found lunching in university faculty clubs, hammer out ideological rationales for the others. Overt or covert wave conflict can now be found in almost every institution in America as those institutions become ever shakier, de-synchronized, dysfunctional—and headed for implosion.

There is, moreover, a lesson here for the outside world looking in—and for all countries making the transition to knowledge-intensive economies. The unprecedented transition from muscles to mind, from smokestacks to soft-ware, is not just a matter of technology. All the high-speed technological advances of recent decades and the even more amazing things scientists are discovering today are the easy part of a revolution that encompasses every aspect of life.

Unless institutional change keeps pace, de-synchronization will tear the American laboratory apart and leave tomorrow to . . . China? Europe? Islam?

And that takes us "Outside America."

CHAPTER 48

OUTSIDE AMERICA

C onduct a poll around the globe, and you'll find a vast number of people who believe that America's great wealth has been squeezed or stolen from the world's poor. This assumption can often be found behind the slogans chanted by anti-American and anti-globalization protestors. But the same questionable premise also lies behind a recent torrent of seemingly scholarly books and articles claiming that the United States is the new Rome—the latest example of classical imperialism—or that it is, as the Chinese prefer to put it, the new hegemon.

The problem with these analogies is that they don't fit the twenty-first century model of the United States. If America is such a rich and powerful hegemon, how come nearly 40 percent of U.S. Treasury bonds were owned by foreigners in 2004? Was that the case when Rome ruled much of the world, or when England did?

Why hasn't the United States sent permanent settlers to the various countries that it presumably dominates? Rome did. The Spaniards did. The British, French, Germans and Italians did, all across Africa. The Japanese did in Asia. Exactly what American university trains an elite class of colonial administrators to spend their lives ruling over remote regions, as Oxford and Cambridge did? And where is there a clamor among Americans for a long-term military occupation of another country?

The United States is powerful and surely makes its weight felt around the world. But there's something wrong about the way America—and the world—is pictured and understood here. Critics are still thinking in terms of the agrarian and industrial past. With the increase of knowledge-intensivity, the entire global game has different rules and different players. And so has the future of wealth.

THE OLD GAME

In the industrial past, Britain, with an empire "on which the sun never set," might buy cotton at depressed prices from one of its backward, agrarian colonies—Egypt, say. It could ship the cotton to factories in Leeds or Lancaster, turn the cotton into clothes, then send these higher-value-added goods right back and sell them to Egyptians at artificially high prices. The resultant "superprofits" were returned to England, where they helped finance additional factories. Britain's great navy, troops and administrators protected its colonial markets from mutiny within and competition without.

Of course, this caricatures a far more complex process. But a key to the imperial game was to keep the advanced technology of the time—textile factories, for example—in Leeds or Lancaster.

Today, by contrast, as advanced economies become more knowledge-based, factories count for less. What increasingly matters is the knowledge on which they depend. Knowledge, however, doesn't stay put, as the growing worldwide theft of intellectual property shows. And America, at least for now, is losing the fight to protect it.

Nor is all economically valuable knowledge technological. Thus Alain Minc, the controversial former chairman of *Le Monde,* tears apart the view that the United States is anything like the Rome or Great Britain of the past. It is not an imperial power but, as he puts it, the first "world country." And the mission of its universities, unlike that of Oxford and Cambridge, is not to train a national elite. It is, in his words, to transmit knowledge that will mold "the future leaders of the world."

Writing shortly before the post-9/11 tightening of U.S. immigration controls, Minc points out that in the previous fifty years the number of foreign students in the United States multiplied seventeen times. He might have added that an increasing percentage of these now return home armed with the latest scientific and technological knowledge in fields as advanced as large-scale network integration, nanotechnology and genetics—not exactly what imperialists and neocolonialists were known for in the past.

AN "UNSORDID ACT"

World War II saw the beginning of the end of classical industrial-age colonialism.

Having culminated in 1945, that war is fast fading from memory, but it may help put today's world in perspective to note that nothing since then can remotely compare with the destruction it caused—or the economic changes to which it led.

World War II casualties suffered by more than two dozen countries, including the United States, totaled at least 50 million. Take a deep breath to absorb that number. It is as though 170 tsunamis equal in force to the one that devastated Southeast Asia in 2004 had all hit the world within six years. Or a tsunami roughly every two weeks for six years.

Russia—then still the Soviet Union—alone lost at least 21 million people. Germany, defeated, lost more than 5 million, not counting the additional millions murdered in Hitler's death camps. Many of Western Europe's industries were destroyed. War's end saw hunger and chaos across much of Europe. At the opposite end of the world, Japan lost about 2.5 million before its surrender. In Japan, too, key industries such as coal, iron, steel and fertilizer were reduced to rubble.

In all these regions it was as if the industrial revolution had been rolled back in time. Mass destruction had smashed the means of mass production.

In contrast to the other major warring nations, the United States lost fewer than 300,000 troops and virtually no civilians. Its infrastructure was not bombed, which left it at war's end the only industrialized nation with a fully functioning economy and no significant competition.

Three years after the shooting stopped, the United States—today's so-called imperial power—did a very strange thing.

Rather than demanding reparations from Germany and literally carting off any of its remaining factory equipment, railcars and industrial machinery, as Soviet Russia did, and rather than reveling in the weakness of its competitors, the United States launched what came to be known as the Marshall Plan. Under its aegis, the United States, in four short years, pumped $13 billion into Europe—including $1.5 billion to West Germany—to reconstruct production capabilities, strengthen currencies and get trade moving again.

Japan, under other programs, received $1.9 billion in U.S. aid, 59 percent for food and 27 percent in the form of industrial supplies and transportation gear.

Winston Churchill, Britain's great wartime leader, called the Marshall Plan the "most unsordid act in history." Yet these programs of support for allies and enemies alike were hardly charitable. They were part of a long-term U.S. economic strategy that worked.

The Marshall Plan helped restore markets for U.S. goods. It helped prevent the reversion of Germany to Nazism. And above all, U.S. aid saved Western Europe and Japan from falling into the icy grip of the Soviet Union. It put them both back in business. It was, in retrospect, one of the smartest investments in history.

As for imperialism, by war's end Moscow had gained military and political control of all the Eastern European countries. In each it implanted troops and Communist puppet regimes, and it threatened to do the same in Western Europe where Soviet-supported Communist parties, especially in France and Italy, claimed broad popular support.

In doing so, the Soviets had created a vast region—stretching from Vladivostok all the way to Berlin—whose centrally planned economies, with inconvertible currencies and many other barriers, deliberately split 10 percent of the world population away from the rest of the world economy.

By 1949, China had joined the Communist bloc. That cut another 22 percent of the world's people out of the larger global economy. By the mid-1950s, as the wealth revolution began, fully a third of the world's people were largely off-limits to the rest of the planet in terms of trade and finance.

At the same time, Africa, Latin America and South Asia were utterly impoverished, with some regions going through the turbulent, often violent process of decolonization as their European masters pulled out.

In the early 1950s, therefore, the United States alone, with just 6 percent of the world's people, was turning out nearly 30 percent of global GDP, and fully half its manufacturing. And it faced little competition.

BACKLASH AND BEWILDERMENT

Today that world is economically unrecognizable. Global output soared from $5.3 trillion in 1950 (in 1990 international dollars) to $51 trillion by 2004. And America's role in the international money economy has changed dramatically.

As Europe, China and other regions have recovered over the years, they have become powerful competitors. As a result, the United States, instead of turning out 30 percent of global output in the early 1950s, has seen its share drop to 21.5 percent. In short, in relative terms, America commands far less of the global economy than it once did. The United States has been in *relative* decline for a half century.

Yet, if we look in absolute terms, we find a very different picture. From the mid-1950s, America's absolute wealth—admittedly measured in conventional and inadequate economic metrics—has soared. The roughly $1.7 trillion it produced in 1952 (in adjusted dollars) had ballooned to $11 trillion by 2004.

Though figures on the contribution of knowledge-based technologies, processes, organization and culture are "soft" and controversial, the United States could not have sustained its competitive position in the world—militarily as well as economically—if it had remained solely an industrial power. Nor would it face the backlash and incomprehension that confronts it today.

By increasing the role of knowledge in business and the economy, the United States is simultaneously underlining the importance of culture and, implicitly, calling attention to the fact that some cultures are more conducive to productivity than others.

And that takes us to a related accusation against the United States—the charge of "cultural imperialism" and the economics behind it. Re-globalization brings different cultures into closer and sometimes hostile contact. Moreover, people everywhere are complaining about homogenization—that everywhere one goes one sees the same Wal-Marts, the same McDonald'ses, the same Hollywood films and so on. Is this just America forcing its way down everyone's throat, as its critics insist? Or is something else happening here?

REVERSING HOMOGENEITY

The answer, as we've seen, is that there are two Americas. It is yesterday's mass-production America, not tomorrow's de-massified America, that we see reflected in the drive toward homogeneity.

Mass production, as we've noted, provides economies of scale to those who make or sell the same one-size-fits-all product over and over again, with as little change as possible. The reason is that altering a traditional assembly-line product is inordinately expensive. Thousands of workers may be forced to stand around and wait as the line is retooled—while the clock ticks and overhead costs continue to pile up.

By contrast, to change a product on a "smart" assembly line may require little more than a few new lines of software code. All the worker may have to do is push a button. The result has been to make variety cheap, as seen in the tremendous diversity of brands, types, models, sizes and materials on store shelves.

In short, as the costs of customization decline toward zero, and as people become more individuated, the drive toward uniformity will be replaced by its opposite—increasing diversity.

Because waves of change overlap and, even in the United States, the revolutionary wealth system is not yet fully developed, the United States still exports and advertises mass products and services. But increasingly it is shifting to mass customization on its way to fully de-massified output designed for increasingly individual customers.

Once upon a time a coffee shop offered only one or a few choices. Starbucks outlets may look homogeneous, but they now provide customers with dozens of possible blends and varieties.

Nike allows online customers to design their own sneakers, choosing among thousands of color combinations and adding their name or other words to the design.

Enjoy M&M's? You can now go online and put a short phrase on one side of your candy's shell.

Even the staid U.S. Post Office has experimented with allowing customers to put their own choice of a picture on the stamps they purchase—their baby's face, for example.

All these are halting steps toward truly personalized production—the opposite of the homogenization offered by industrial-era companies.

A particularly interesting case is that of Spider-Man. When the American comic book based on that superhero was licensed for publication in India, the central characters and their backgrounds were altered to accommodate the religious sensitivities of Indian audiences.

The hero was renamed so that Peter Parker of New York became Pavitr Prabhakar of Mumbai. But the more important change lay in the explanation of how Pavitr supposedly got his superhuman powers.

While in the American version Peter's capacities are enhanced by radio-active means, in India he is super-empowered by religious means. Says *Newsweek:* "The hero gets his powers from a yogi who performs a ritual on him . . . and the villain is a demon from the Hindu pantheon of gods."

In short, cultural homogenization is the message of a fast-fading, mass-production America. Heterogeneity, de-massification and personalization are the messages of a fast-rising new America that both needs and breeds diversity. And not just in goods and comic books.

Third Wave media also improve access to an endless diversity of ideas, values, lifestyles and points of view, including every conceivable political ideology and cultural variant. That is why China, for example, despite its twin-track strategy, is still censoring and manipulating what most of its citizens can receive on the Internet.

The serious question today is not how much homogeneity the United States produces but how much heterogeneity other governments, cultures and religions suppress.

The United States may currently be the world's sole superpower. But it faces constraints and complexities no previous superpower confronted—or imagined.

Acting in its own perceived—and often misperceived—self-interest, the United States has, with the rise of revolutionary wealth, helped form a new, multi-level global order very different from the one its last-generation leaders anticipated.

Start with the world's new, unseen and unprecedented game of games.

CHAPTER 49

THE UNSEEN GAME
OF GAMES

The future of revolutionary wealth in our pockets and on the planet will be determined not just by the interplay of markets. Who gets what and who makes what have never, except occasionally in theory, been determined by markets alone. Wealth everywhere is shaped by power, culture, politics and the state. At the world level in recent centuries, nations have been the primary actors.

In the years ahead, nations will still form new economic blocs, play currency games, impose tariffs and grant subsidies (increasingly cloaked in environmental, cultural and other justifications). They will continue to blame unemployment on unfair competition from other countries. They will demand so-called "level playing fields." They will make all the noise. And they will, of course, tax their citizens.

Rising powers such as India, China and Brazil will demand to be treated like Great Powers in such international institutions as the WTO, the IMF, the World Bank and the Bank for International Settlements (BIS), organizations whose decisions affect trade, currencies, credit, bank reserves and a host of other wealth variables.

But while nations will compete ever-more-fiercely on familiar territory— what we might call the nation-state game board—they will all be playing a losing game. For whether national governments like it or not, power is leaching away from all of them. The great powers are increasingly less great. And that goes for America as well.

NEO-GAMES

The reason is that nations and states are no longer the only powerful pieces in a new meta-game made up of many different sub-games linked interactively and played simultaneously. Neo-chess on one level. Neo-poker or neo-backgammon or neo-EverQuest on others. The players compete under non-linear rules that change after—or during—every move.

Corporations have been playing multinational chess for a long time and have wielded disproportionate influence at the international level. Today, because they are increasingly global, major corporations and financial institutions shift pieces around on their own game board and are less and less accountable to their nation of origin.

When Microsoft, Citigroup, Toyota, Royal Dutch/Shell, Philips or Samsung talks, national governments listen. But it isn't only national games and corporate games (or the interactions between them) that count. Nations and businesses alike now need to deal with the fast-growing community of NGOs and other rising forces.

NO LONGER HUMAN?

Many NGOs battle corporations such as Monsanto, Shell Oil and McDonald's. As we've seen, they fight free trade and re-globalization. They march for peace. They campaign to save whales and trees. In doing so, they make daily headlines.

Less visible but more numerous and, in aggregate, far more influential are countless other NGOs like worldwide business associations, professional groups, sports clubs, scientific organizations and other entities. Most focus on highly specialized issues of concern to various industries and groups ranging from custom brokers and matrimonial lawyers to geneticists, notaries, plastics distributors, chefs, models and textile designers.

Some NGOs defend producers' interests. Others defend consumers. Still others organize or represent prosumers—like the groups that coordinated thousands of volunteers from all over the world to aid the victims of the great tsunami of December 2004.

Taken together, armed with computers, Internet access and the latest communications equipment and supported by lawyers, doctors, scientists and other professionals, NGOs form a fast-growing cross-border force with which nations and corporations both will be increasingly compelled to share power.

Moreover, the proliferation of NGOs is just beginning. This is so, first, because the Internet, the Web, mobile phones and improved connectivity make it easier and cheaper for people to identify common goals or grievances, to find one another, link up and organize. Second, because the speedup of change brings new opportunities and fears. Before stem cells were identified, for instance, no one set up an NGO to support stem-cell research—or to suppress it. Today there are many NGOs for both purposes.

TOMORROW'S NGOS

Many NGOs that still operate at local and national levels can be expected before long to make their presence felt at the global level—just as environmentalists, feminists and civil rights organizations began locally, then moved up to the national scale before placing their issues on the world agenda.

Today, for example, the rights of homosexuals are fiercely contested inside many nations. As sex ratios change in many countries, with male babies outnumbering baby girls—120:100 in China, for example—the shortage of women is likely to promote male homosexuality, leading writer Mark Steyn to ask, tongue in cheek, whether China is "planning on becoming the first gay superpower since Sparta." In country after country, gays will exit the closet and, whether overtly or covertly, organize politically, as they already have in North America and Europe. They will then elevate the demand for gay rights, including the legalization of gay marriage, to the global stage.

Struggles over a raft of twenty-first-century moral issues will also give birth to entirely new NGOs.

They will arise to gain support for research into "nano-diseases" or to fight "nano-pollution." As the neurosciences advance, NGOs will fight for or against the neuro-manipulation of human intelligence.

When humans are eventually cloned—as is likely, despite attempts to ban it—we may see global movements organized to deny or protect the rights of clones.

Tomorrow we will have many more powerful ways to alter both bodies and brains with the help of genetics and science generally. Just as academic, economic, political and other boundaries are breaking down, so, too, are the boundaries that define what it means to be human.

How much can we alter a body—chemically, biologically, genetically or mechanically—before it is no longer "human" enough to merit equal treatment with humans? Tomorrow NGOs will battle globally over what separates a human from a "transhuman" and what rights each should have.

So profound are the moral issues that will soon face us, and so emotive, that we can easily picture them giving rise to new fanatic movements and becoming yet another source of global terror.

Collectively, even now, NGOs form a pot of boiling passions, ideas, early warnings and proposed social innovations, good and bad. They are already

able to organize and act more rapidly than governments and their bureaucracies (another important example of de-synchronization). What they do will
have enormous, largely unexpected impacts on the production and distribution
of wealth in the global economy.

And that leads us to what might be regarded as the biggest NGOs of all:
Religions.

RELIGIO-ECONOMICS

While the rate of increase in global population is slowing, the rates of growth
claimed for the world's two biggest religions—Christianity and Islam—are
escalating. Both will be influenced by technology and the radical redistribution of world wealth in the decades to come.

The connection between religion and money currently receiving the most
attention has had to do with the costs of terrorism. Osama bin Laden boasted
that the 9/11 attacks by his Muslim extremists cost the U.S. economy more
than $1 trillion. But bin Laden, it turns out, needs a better accountant.

The total depends on what is included. But no reputable studies came close
to bin Laden's number. It is true, as pointed out in a report prepared for the
U.S. Congress, that "aftershocks" were felt in "foreign equity markets, in
tourism and travel, in consumer attitudes, and in temporary capital flight."

But it requires Enron's accounting to approach bin Laden's fantasy figure,
especially since experience teaches us that, as in the case of disasters, many
costs are recouped when reconstruction begins. Money is simply rechanneled
from one part of the economy to another.

According to the same report to Congress, 9/11 and the later bombings in
Bali and Madrid were grandiosely aimed at partly "taking down the global
economic system." If so, the costs, even including "subsequent economic
effects," were "small when compared with global GDP." Minute would be a
more accurate term.

That is why bin Laden's Al Qaeda and other terror groups will do anything
to acquire weapons of mass destruction and why they need to be stopped at all
costs.

But even if theo-terrorism were to magically vanish, religion will have
substantial impacts on the global economy in decades to come.

GOD ON THE MOVE

The United States, termed "infidel" by Muslim extremists and "overreligious"
by Europeans, faces a world that, instead of moving toward secularism as it
did during the industrial age, seems to be reversing direction.

David B. Barrett and Todd Johnson, co-editors of the *World Christian Encyclopedia,* forecast that today's 2 billion Christians will become 2.6 billion by 2025—an overall increase of roughly 30 percent. But Islam is growing much faster. From 553 million in 1970, it shot up to 1.2 billion in 2001 and is heading, we're told, toward a grand total of 1.8 billion by 2025—a rise of 50 percent in a quarter century.

While religious statistics are no better than economic data, their general direction is clear. The numbers, moreover, are far more dramatic when we look at where all these additional Christians and Muslims are—and where they are soon likely to be.

In both we are seeing an important geographical—that is, spatial—shift. Since the mid-1950s, according to Philip Jenkins, author of "The Next Christianity," "the critical centers of the Christian world have moved decisively to Africa and to Latin America and to Asia," each of which has many more Christians today than North America. We have already commented on the rapid growth of Christianity in China.

The growth and spatial relocation of religion on the planet is a giant historical event—and it will, at least in part, shape and be shaped by the coming transfers of wealth around the world.

In Europe the number of Muslims has doubled in the past twenty years, largely because of immigration, and the growth of Islam there is expected to outpace the growth of Christianity. In fact, though little recognized, today fully a third of all the world's Muslims live as ethno-cultural minorities in non-Muslim countries, increasingly distanced from Islam's geographical center.

They include a floating, on-the-move population of middle-class Muslim intellectuals, businesspeople, engineers and professors who may work and live in a sequence of different countries as they pursue the job market.

Olivier Roy of the School of Advanced Studies in Social Sciences in Paris contends that world Islam will be increasingly influenced in terms of ideas, politics, lifestyle, culture, identity—and, one might add, attitudes toward capitalism, markets and business—by what he calls Islam's "de-territorialized" millions, largely based in Europe.

While this is happening in the West, the Muslim population is growing most quickly in the East—in an awakening Asia, where, especially in Malaysia and Indonesia, a more moderate form of Islam has prevailed than that found in Iran and the Arab countries.

Together, these eastward and westward shifts could pull the balance of religious and cultural influence within Islam away from the Middle East. That dominance, while rooted in Mecca and the annual hajj that brings millions of Muslims from everywhere to Muhammad's birthplace, has in fact long been bolted into place by money.

For centuries, the power of Muslims in the world economy resulted from the Middle East's strategic, high-value-added location as the main transit point for trade between Asia and Europe. It lost that financial advantage when, using advanced navigation and maritime knowledge, European and other traders began avoiding the Middle East and sailing around the southern tip of Africa.

Today the Middle East once more faces the loss of its most crucial source of wealth—and the financial, cultural and religious influence that comes with it. That source is, of course, oil.

THE END OF PETRO-POWER

The economic ascent of China, India and, less noticeably, Brazil helped drive oil prices to record levels in 2005; prices were twice as high as in 2002. That makes alternatives to oil more competitive. It also calls into question how long present oil reserves can last. No one can predict when the last barrel of crude will be pumped, but we already find planners in the big auto and oil companies preparing strategies for transition to a post-petroleum economy. General Motors hopes to be the first company to sell one million hydrogen-based fuel-cell cars. And if not GM, why not Toyota? Or China's own up-and-coming auto industry?

Unless governments in the Middle East start now to plan for post-oil, knowledge-intensive service economies, the exit of huge amounts of wealth from the region could well spark even more terror as poverty and hopelessness deepen.

Every fuel-cell car introduced elsewhere in the world, every nuclear plant, every solar panel, every windmill, every new source and form of non-oil energy will hasten the demise of the existing business—and religious—elites in the Middle East.

Such a collapse could erode Saudi financial resources and further under-mine its influence within world Islam—shifting the balance between Shia, Sunni and other groups.

The Saudi regime's vast petro-riches have been used to promote Wahabism, a particularly stringent brand of Islam, all over the world. The funds could have been used to educate the younger generation of Muslims in economically valuable skills.

Instead, they have funded strictly religious schools that produced the Taliban in Afghanistan and jobless, hopeless, angry youth across much of the globe, including terrorists now trying to overthrow the Saudi regime itself.

To many outsiders, it appears that Islam is already at war with itself. In that war, the enemy is not an anti-Islamic, imperial United States or some other non-Islamic nation—or the West. It is the greed, provincialism and myopia with which the leaders of so many Middle East nations have ruled for so long, and their failure to use oil money to ride the Third Wave to a better future.

UTOPIA PAST

What might have been—and what could still give hope to the world's dispirited Muslim youth—is suggested in one paragraph by economist Rima Khalaf Hunaidi, former deputy prime minister of Jordan, now director of the U.N. Development Program's Regional Bureau for Arab States:

"Knowledge increasingly defines the line between wealth and poverty, between capability and powerlessness and between human fulfillment and frustration. A country able to mobilize and diffuse knowledge can rapidly raise its level of development, help all its citizens to grow and flourish and take its proper place on the 21st Century global stage."

What follows is a twelve-page executive summary of a book-length 2003 report on "building a knowledge society" in the Arab world. Prepared by more than thirty Muslim scholars and policy analysts and sponsored by the Arab Fund for Economic and Social Development and the U.N. Development Program, the document holds out hope for a renaissance in the Arab world based on five principles, summarized by Hunaidi:

- Freedom of opinion, expression and association
- Quality education . . . available to all
- Embedding science in Arab society . . . and joining the information revolution decisively
- Shifting rapidly toward knowledge-based and higher-value-added production
- Developing an enlightened Arab knowledge model that encourages . . . critical thinking, problem solving and creativity, while promoting the Arabic language, cultural diversity and openness to other cultures

The summary looks unblinkingly at the Arab world and reports that "a large part of Arab economic activity is concentrated on primary commodities, as in agriculture, which remains largely traditional" while "at the same time, the share of the capital goods industry and of industries embodying higher technology continues to shrink.

"Access to digital media is . . . among the lowest in the world," both in terms of computers per population and Internet access.

Scientific R&D figures are equally telling. The number of scientists and engineers in R&D in the Arab world per million people is approximately a

third that of the world rate, according to the report. And while Arabs constitute 5 percent of world population, Arab countries publish only 1.1 percent of
its books.

A key point made by the team is the degree to which Islam, at least in the
Arab world, cuts itself off from the ideas, knowledge and innovative thinking
in the rest of the world.

Ahmad Kamal Aboulmagd, professor of public law at Cairo University
and an adviser to the report team, underlines the point, saying that Muslim
identity does not mean "isolation from the rest of mankind, inward-looking in
a closed circuit, surrounded by a wall without doors."

Tracing the history of Arab cultural interaction with the outside world, the
report declares: "Openness, interaction, assimilation, absorption, revision,
criticism, and examination cannot but stimulate creative knowledge production in Arab societies."

Contrast that with the Islamist vision of yesterday imposed on tomorrow.

In terms of the deep fundamentals of time, space and, above all, knowledge, therefore, Islamic terrorists promise murder to the outside world—and
nothing but misery within their own.

We have devoted more space here to Islam and the Middle East and their
lost opportunities because of current urgencies, but Africa and Latin America,
too, must face the future. They seethe with wave conflicts over land ownership, urban poverty, agribusiness, indigenous tribes, ethnicity and the environment, intensified and complicated by racism and narco-terrorism. The United
States has been so preoccupied with the Middle East that it has paid too little
attention to these other volcanic rumbles—especially those in an angry South
America about to erupt.

THE FRAGILITY OF POWER

Tomorrow's inevitable crises will occur on each of the "game boards"
described earlier, against the background of what we've called the great non-
linear, ever-more-complex, ever-interacting and accelerating "meta-game."

This means that even the shrewdest *national* strategy of China or the
United States—or any state—can be blunted, reversed or made irrelevant if it
fails to take into account the neo-games being played by NGOs, religions and
other participants in the greater meta-game. Much of America's trouble in
Iraq can be traced to its overemphasis on the role of nation-states and its
underestimate of the role played by non-national forces like anti-war NGOs,
religious sects and tribal groupings.

In tomorrow's new game the United States, like every nation, will continue
to look after its own perceived economic self-interest (or that of its influential

elites). But as this great meta-game plays out, how long will—or can—the United States remain the world's dominant economic power?

All dominance is temporary, and China is breathing hard. Washington itself is split between those resigned to the idea that China will, in a few decades, lead the world economically and those committed, at all costs, to maintaining America's leadership. Here, too, American policy overemphasizes nation-states rather than NGOs, religions and other players.

But this division is too simple. A more important question is to what degree does America's fragile wealth depend on economic dominance? The Marshall Plan experience suggested, as we've seen, that it was possible for the U.S. percentage of world GDP—its heft in the global economy—to shrink, while its citizens' wealth actually increased. Is that still true? If so, how?

If America is, as charged, an imperialist power, greedily enriching itself at the expense of others, how much of its growth and net worth is actually a consequence of its "imperial" policies? Does anyone know? Many imperialists in the past have actually lost money in the deal. Conversely, how much of America's wealth is a result of the work, creativity and fast-accumulating knowledge of its producers and prosumers?

How will the U.S. economy—and, indeed, the relative positions of all countries—change when prosuming and producivity are fully taken into account, as will inevitably be the case? What new forms of money, what future payment systems, what new financial institutions, will be needed to incorporate these changes?

Will the United States become wealthier by continuing to spread the latest technologies, advanced management models and media to other countries—or will they flow in the reverse direction? Will outsourcing R&D and high-end tasks to India and other countries permit those countries to leapfrog the United States? Could the United States prevent that even if it chose to? The ongoing theft of intellectual property by China and other countries suggests otherwise. Revolutionary wealth is no longer an exclusive American possession. It is a global fact of life.

How, then, would the present trisection—division of the world into three different wealth systems—change if the leading edge came from Asia rather than America? And would the world's poorest regions really fare any better?

Global dominance, however, is a matter not just of wealth but of security, values, human rights, cultural and moral independence and influence. What would the world—including its economy—look like if China were dominant; or a Europe led by France and Germany; or a resurgent India, Russia or anyone else?

Many pundits today call for a new global "balance of power." But would a so-called multipolar world, divided into competing alliances or regional blocs, really be economically better off and more peaceful than a unipolar world led or dominated by one country or region? The historical evidence has the scholars hopelessly divided. But even if they weren't, how relevant is past experience to the nonlinear, meta-game future?

Balance implies equilibrium, and just how "equilibrial" is the world economy? We should all by now have learned from complexity theory that equilibrium is no more the natural state of affairs than disequilibrium and chaos. Can the balance-of-power diplomacy that worked for Prince Metternich in the nineteenth century work in the twenty-first?

A balance of power in his time referred to nations. A balance of power in the future, if attainable at all for lengthy periods, would have to balance non–nation-state forces as well—including corporations and NGOs—including religions.

The great Austrian diplomat also lived at a time when new technologies were making headlines and the industrial revolution was still spreading in Europe. But the pace of "modernization" was glacial by today's standard. It left time for people and institutions to adapt. Revolutionary wealth doesn't.

America cannot control the most powerful economic, political, cultural and religious changes rushing toward us today. At best it can try, while transforming its own economy and internal institutions, to head off external threats and reduce some of the common dangers that confront us all.

THE NANO-NOW

Conspiracy theories picture cabals of American capitalists hatching strategies to take over the world and control the economic destiny of the planet. The reality is that the United States lacks anything even approximating a coherent or long-term strategy for dealing with a world divided—for the first time—into three different wealth systems. So does everyone else.

America's intense focus on the immediate reflects the culture of impatient Americans—children of the "Now Generation" as Pepsi ads once put it. When the cola company used that slogan, "now" lasted longer. In today's multitasking, on-the-fly generation, now itself has become a nano now.

Thus, in the United States, Hollywood and the other media glamorize heroes who "shoot from the hip" rather than those who think ahead and plan. Watching a car chase on the screen is a lot more visually exciting than watching people think.

When American politicians do, on rare occasions, refer to problems in the long-term future, they typically refer to individual institutions or narrowly specific programs rather than to systemic issues. And when they do look beyond one term of office, the opposition derides them as wooly-headed, dreamy and unrealistic. As a key official in Washington—who does think about big problems decades ahead—told us with sorrow, "Congress thinks a one- or two-year budget is a strategy."

One White House national security adviser was even heard to say he had no time for strategy, and that strategy is only a label pinned on actions after they have already been taken.

This focus on the immediate is present in business as well. In recent years, management gurus have told business leaders that things are moving too fast for companies to bother with strategy. What is needed, these experts tell us, is not strategy but agility. If companies and countries are just adaptive enough, flexible enough and quick enough, they don't need strategy.

Agility is, of course, absolutely vital. But agility without strategy is reactive. It merely subordinates a person, a company or a country, for that matter, to someone else's strategy—or simply to chance.

Strategies, like the humans who produce them, are always faulty. And they must obviously be flexible, subject to rapid reformulation. Indeed, smart strategies must take into account not just the speed of change today but its further acceleration tomorrow.

Admittedly, all this is easy to say and extremely hard to do. Yet simply substituting agility for strategy is like rushing madly to the nearest airport and letting the pushing and shoving crowd carry us along to whatever gate it chooses. This is perfectly acceptable if we don't care where we end up—in Texas, Tokyo or Tehran, with our luggage, no doubt, in Timbuktu.

But, in fact, we do care. And we must. Because tomorrow will belong to those who do—inside or outside America.

CHAPTER 50

EPILOGUE:
THE PROLOGUE IS PAST

W axing pessimistic is one of the easiest ways to masquerade as
wise. And there is plenty to be pessimistic about. But permanent
pessimism is a substitute for thought.

"No pessimist ever discovered the secrets of the stars, or sailed to an
uncharted land, or opened a new heaven to the human spirit," wrote Helen
Keller, the remarkable blind and deaf author who traveled to thirty-nine countries, wrote eleven books, inspired two Oscar-winning movies and fought for
the rights of the sightless until she died at eighty-seven.

Dwight Eisenhower, who orchestrated the Allied landing at Normandy in
World War II and went on to become the thirty-fourth president of the United
States, put it more bluntly: "Pessimism never won any battle."

As we move deeper into the twenty-first century, the list of potential horrors is seemingly endless: War between China and the United States; a 1930s-
style global crash that throws millions into the streets and wipes out decades
of economic advance; terrorist attacks unleashing nuclear weapons, anthrax,
chlorine gas or a cyber-assault on critical business and government computer
networks; disastrous water shortages from Mexico City and Iran to South
Africa; armed battles between rival NGOs; new diseases at the nano level; the
spread of mind-control technologies; the death of privacy; intensified religious fanaticism and violence; human cloning; combinations and convergences of these—and that's before we even get to earthquakes, tsunamis,
deforestation and global warming.

All of these are worth worrying about. But much of today's pessimism is
fashionable—exactly as it was when the industrial revolution was sweeping
over Europe and horrifying its opponents in the early to mid-1800s.

From their fear and rage against modernity, with its growing secularism and rationality, came the romantic pessimism expressed in the poetry of Lord Byron and Heinrich Heine, the music of Richard Wagner and Schopenhauer's philosophy of *pessimismus*. Not to forget the anarchist philosopher Max Stirner, who translated Adam Smith into German and was, if anyone, an expert on pessimism. Stirner's mother was insane. His first wife died giving birth to a stillborn baby. He invested a subsequent wife's fortune and lost it. At which point, he lost her as well.

THE NOSTALGIA BRIGADE

Watching a new civilization encroach on an old one inescapably calls for comparisons between the two. Those who have benefited from the past, or who have come to terms with it, form a nostalgia brigade, praising or romanticizing yesterday and contrasting it with the as-yet-ill-formed, incomplete tomorrow.

Suffering from the death of the familiar, future-shocked by the pace of change, millions in the West are watching the remnants of their industrial economies decay.

Worried about jobs and watching Asia rise, they—especially the young—are bombarded by dystopian images of the future in films, TV series, games and online messages. Media-manufactured stars are presented as role models in the form of street-corner thugs, room-wrecking musicians and drugged-up athletes. They hear religious assurances that the end is nigh. And they are showered by apocalyptic messages from a vast, once-progressive environmental movement whose dominant slogan has become "Just say no."

Yet the period ahead is about to explode with surprises of all kinds that will escape the either-or dichotomy of good versus bad. And the biggest surprise of all may be that the revolutionary wealth system and civilization described in these pages will, despite everything, open enormous opportunities for billions of us to live better, healthier, longer and more socially useful lives.

We have emphasized that the emerging wealth system cannot be understood within the framework of conventional economics, and that, to even glimpse its future, we need to look at the deep fundamentals that lie behind all wealth creation from the ancient past to today—and tomorrow.

As we've seen, these include types of work, divisions of labor, exchange systems, energy supplies, a particular family structure and a characteristic physical environment. But the deep fundamentals most unexamined, yet among the most relevant to our future, are time, space and knowledge—each of which could easily justify a library of its own.

It is clear that the everyday sound-bite economics that is the subject of so much chatter in Econo-Land focuses on only a tiny fraction of economic reality. Indeed, given the constraints of a single book, even our attempt to expand the common view of what is involved in wealth creation provides a far-from-complete picture.

We have shown why millions today feel excruciatingly time-squeezed both at work and at home—how we are irregularizing our daily schedules and how companies steal our time and impose on us an unpaid "third job." We've seen how we are changing the rates at which items are put up for sale and then withdrawn. And we've shown how, by synchronizing some of our activities, we necessarily de-synchronize others at unknown cost. We are revolutionizing the time component of wealth.

That revolution is paralleled by dramatic shifts in the spatial location of wealth and of the enterprises and technologies that produce it. And we've seen why, even if all of today's anti-globalists packed their knapsacks and went home, we could expect economic integration to slow while other dimensions of global integration speed up—another case of de-synchronization as changes in time and space intersect.

Only when all these changes are viewed against the backdrop of revolution in the knowledge system, however, can we glimpse the full transformatory power of what is happening today. These developments don't affect just the economy, and businesses can't just install a "knowledge-management system" and move on.

Today's changes affect how we all make decisions, right down to the very truth and/or lies on which we base them. We are living through a period when our long-standing criteria for separating truth from falsehood are themselves under fire. And the branch of knowledge most necessary for economic advance—science—is under widespread attack.

Science, as suggested earlier, is in more trouble than most suspect. It is in a crisis that goes far beyond immediate issues like the decline in financing for basic research. Science survives by the grace of its host culture. And that culture is turning hostile, as seen in the growing attack on evolution by creationists (a battle once thought to have ended with the Scopes trial in 1925) and the so-called intelligent-design movement.

Science now faces a blinding dust storm of subjectivism—fed by fading postmodernism and flourishing New Age "spiritualism." Its influence is also undercut by cases of corruption linking scientists to pharmaceutical firms and other industries, by repeated media portrayals of scientists as evil, by fear of oncoming biological breakthroughs that threaten traditional definitions of humanity.

More important, scientific method itself is under attack by "truth managers" who prefer decisions based on other criteria, from mystical revelation to political or religious authority. The ongoing battle over truth is part of the transformation in our relationships to the deep fundamental of knowledge.

A PROSUMER PATHWAY?

It is against these revolutionary changes in our uses of time, space and knowledge that another unanticipated historical event is unfolding—the resurgence, as we've seen, of what we have termed prosuming.

We know that in ancient times our ancestors fed, clothed and sheltered themselves long before the invention of money. They produced what they needed to consume. We also know that gradually, over the millennia, people prosumed less and relied more on money and markets. The common assumption of those who bothered to think about this was that prosuming would continue to diminish—that people creating unpaid value outside the market would shrivel into irrelevancy.

Yet exactly the opposite is happening. While shrinking in its First Wave forms, prosuming is rapidly expanding in new, Third Wave ways. It is producing more economic value, feeding more "free lunch" into the money economy and doing so through more channels. It is actually increasing productivity in the money sector and, as the World Wide Web and Linux have shown, it is challenging some of the biggest and most powerful governments and corporations in the world.

Prosuming could even, ultimately, transform the ways in which we deal with problems like unemployment. Since the Great Depression of the 1930s and the rise of Keynesian economics, part of the textbook solution for unemployment has been the injection of public funds into the money economy to stimulate consumer demand, and, through that, make jobs. The reasonable assumption was that if a million workers were out of jobs, the creation of a million jobs would solve the problem.

In a knowledge-intensive economy, however, that assumption is false. First, the United States and other countries no longer even know how many unemployed there are, or what that term means when so many people combine their "job" with self-employment and/or create unpaid value by prosuming.

More important, even creating five million jobs can't solve the problem if the one million jobless workers lack the particular knowledge or skill sets required by the new labor market. The problem of unemployment thus becomes qualitative rather than merely quantitative. Nor is conventional retraining as useful as it sounds, since, by the time new skills are learned, the economy's knowledge requirements may well have shifted again. In short, unemployment in knowledge economies is different from that in assembly-line economies. It is structural.

The largely overlooked reality is that even the unemployed are employed. They are busy, as all of us are, creating unpaid value. This is yet another reason to reexamine the entire relationship of the money and non-money sectors of the wealth system—the two lobes, as it were, of the brain-based economies of tomorrow.

New, more powerful technologies will increase prosumer productivity. How can that be used more effectively to stimulate the money economy? Are there better ways to channel value back and forth between these two parts of the wealth system? Are Linux and the Web the only models? Are there ways to remunerate the unremunerated for their contributions—perhaps with computer-aided, multi-participant barter systems or even new "para-currencies" of one kind or another?

PESSIMIST-IN-CHIEF

New problems require thinking beyond the edges of the known, and no problem needs new thinking more than the ever-worsening global energy crisis.

Today it is clear that our existing energy system is heading toward a climactic crash, not merely because of the amount of energy required but because of its centralized infrastructures and overconcentrated ownership. Both of these were, and perhaps are still, appropriate for industrial economies. But they are decidedly inappropriate for dispersed knowledge-intensive economies increasingly based on intangibility.

The economic rise of countries such as China and India heightens demand for energy at a time when it costs more and more to extract crude oil from the earth, when growing reliance on fossil fuel exacerbates ecological problems and when oil comes from some of the most politically unstable regions on the planet.

At the beginning of the twenty-first century, approximately 400 quadrillion Btu of energy per year were bought and sold in world energy markets. They mainly came from oil, natural gas, coal and nuclear sources, with oil the dominant source, providing approximately 40 percent of the total. The U.S. Department of Energy in 2004 forecast that by 2025 the total would climb to 623 quadrillion Btu, a rise of 54 percent.

Despite this increase in demand, the DoE assured us that fossil-fuel prices are "projected to remain relatively low" and that alternative energy sources "are not expected to become competitive" unless government policies to reduce greenhouse-gas emissions, as called for under the Kyoto Protocol, are implemented—at which time "nuclear power and renewable energy sources such as hydroelectricity, geothermal, biomass, solar and wind power could become more attractive." In short, expect nothing too exciting.

Contrast this with the forecast of pessimist-in-chief Matthew R. Simmons, an influential energy-industry investment banker. Simmons, using oil as a proxy for the energy picture as a whole, tells us that many of the world's most important oil fields are in "serious decline," that we cannot trust the industry's estimates of underground reserves and that finding new oil is more and more expensive.

Add the fact that tankers, refineries, drilling rigs and people are all "nearing 100 percent capacity," he says, and this is a problem that "will take a decade(s?) to correct." Worse yet, he notes, oil companies and electric utilities, like other industries that have shifted to just-in-time operations, have minimized their backup supplies, setting the stage for catastrophe.

As we've shown elsewhere, the energy crisis is, at least in part, a radical consequence of de-synchronization at work—the rise of Asian demand coming much faster than the industry and the market anticipated. That helps explain why there may not be enough new tankers built in time, enough refineries or enough inventory stored for emergencies.

Having made his compelling case, Simmons steps back from doomsday, saying, more cheerfully, that "man's creativity seems at its best at times of great crisis."

But none of these projections takes adequate account of many possible developments that could change the picture for better or worse: Social upheavals and economic slowdowns in China, India or both; regional epidemics causing massive population declines; Chinese control of the Malacca Strait and sea lanes by which oil reaches Asia from the Middle East; or little-noticed technological changes that may well reduce energy requirements—for example, the continued miniaturization of products, reducing weight, transport and storage requirements.

Even more important is the approaching demise of the internal combustion engine and its replacement by hydrogen-powered fuel cells. Says Robert Walker, former chairman of the U.S. House of Representatives Committee on Science, "Within a few years we'll see a million fuel-cell cars on the roads in China, where they don't have as big a legacy gasoline distribution system as we do. We'll have cars whose 110-kilowatt fuel cells can also serve as an auxiliary power source. So, in rural areas, where there is no electricity, you can drive to a village, plug it into the car, and provide energy for fuel cells or other purposes." Clearly, while there will be many false steps and failures along the way, we are edging out of the fossil-fuel era.

MOON POWER

Now for even better news. We have not run out of energy sources. Energy can be harvested from innumerable sources, including some that at first glance seem outlandish—as the steam engine did in its early days. Clunky and no doubt expensive by the standards of the time, it was designed to increase energy supply by helping to pump water out of coal mines.

Craig Venter, the man who led the successful private effort to decode the human genome, is working toward the creation of artificial organisms that can clean up pollution—and create energy. "Biology," he says, "can change our dependency on fossil fuels." He is not alone. Stanford professors and graduate students are also pursuing the biological production of hydrogen from genetically engineered bacteria. Entrepreneur Howard Berke's team is working to develop a material as thin as plastic wrap to directly convert sunlight into electricity capable of recharging cell phones, GPS and other devices.

Others are taking advantage of waves and tides to pull energy out of the oceans. The La Rance tidal-power station in France turns out 240 megawatts of power. Other tidal systems are used in Norway, Canada, Russia and China. In addition, every day the sun transfers the thermal-energy equivalent of 250 billion barrels of oil to the oceans, and we already have technologies that can convert it to electricity.

Farther out in both time and space is another potentially huge source of energy—the moon. It turns out that the moon is rich in helium-3—and helium-3, if combined with the hydrogen isotope deuterium, can turn out what Lawrence Taylor, a director of Tennessee University's Planetary Geosciences Institute, calls "awesome amounts of energy."

Indeed, Taylor adds, "just 25 tonnes of helium, which can be transported on a space shuttle, is enough to provide electricity for the U.S. for one full year." No less an authority than Abdul Kalam, the president of India and a space scientist, tells us that "the moon contains 10 times more energy in the form of helium-3 than all the fossil fuels on the earth."

Add to these a long list of other potential sources, and it becomes clear that there is no absolute shortage of energy available to the human race. What we need are new, creative ways to tap that supply. And today there are more scientists, engineers, inventors and sources of finance and venture capital than at any time in history.

We are also likely to see the de-massification process at work as the world energy system assumes a new structure more compatible with the needs of advanced knowledge-based economies. This suggests a multiplication of energy sources so that the system is no longer overwhelmingly dependent on coal, oil and gas. It means more different sources and more different technologies matched by more different players and producers—including prosumers who, with their fuel cells or wind towers or other personal technologies, will increasingly meet their own power needs.

The central question, then, is not *whether* we will overcome the energy disaster heading toward us but how soon. And that will depend in good measure on the outcome of wave conflict between vested interests still benefiting from our industrial-era energy system and the pioneers researching, designing and fighting for breakthrough alternatives.

Faced with this battle, we should not let the pessimists' warnings narrow our views of the possible. It helps to remember an earlier crisis that also involved energy—in this case nuclear.

In August 1945, the entire world shook when two atomic bombs—the worst weapons ever seen—were dropped on Japan, bringing World War II to a fiery end. These weapons of mass destruction perfectly paralleled the mass production of the industrial age. Yet, miraculously, for the next half century no atomic weapon has been exploded in combat anywhere. Today we worry about nuclear proliferation and fear that terrorists may acquire one or more of these bombs. These are realistic worries. But the danger does not even approach that which existed when the United States and the Soviet Union aimed literally thousands of missiles with atomic warheads at each other with triggers set to go off instantly.

HOPE FOR THE HUMAN RACE?

Not all cultures place a premium on life itself, let alone on longevity. Millions dance with death every day in their religion or local belief system. Reincarnation awaits. Virgins await. Heaven awaits.

Nevertheless, for those who highly value life in this world, the last century, as we've seen, has been extraordinary. Despite the fact that population has more than doubled, life expectancy at birth in the world—including the "poor world"—shot up 42 percent between 1950–55 and 2000–2005.

Even in poor countries, the average baby can now expect to live sixty-four years. This is still a far shorter life span than a rich-world baby can expect. But the direction and speed of change are hardly a cause for pessimism. The remaining difference is a good reason for commitment to eliminate the difference.

One reason today's baby—rich or poor—has a better chance to survive and live longer is safer drinking water. In just the twelve years between 1990 and 2002, according to the United Nations, more than a billion people have gained access to clean water. That, frightfully, leaves out 17 percent of the human race. But here, too, the news is good and provides a good reason for action—not for easy, immobilizing pessimism.

Nor are longer life spans resulting in increased poverty. The U.N. issues powerful statistics underlining the horrors of poverty in today's world. But the U.N. Development Program itself reminds us that "the proportion of humankind living in poverty has fallen faster in the past 50 years than in the previous 500 years."

We certainly cannot attribute all this gain in well-being to the rise of the Third Wave in the same half century. Correlation is not necessarily a cause. But some things clearly do point to a connection. First, as we saw earlier, was the inadvertent trickle-down effect as America, and later Japan, Taiwan and South Korea, shipped their low-value-added work to China and other predominantly agrarian countries, creating hundreds of millions of jobs in the process.

Poor-world gains also reflect, at least in part, the tremendous expansion of humanity's knowledge base during the last half-century, as the revolutionary wealth system spread from the United States outward—diffusing new ideas about agriculture, nutrition, prenatal care and disease detection and prevention, as well as technology.

In the rich world, knowledge-intensive economies have brought with them a strange phenomenon: Millions of middle-class mind workers who jog for miles every day or work out in gyms or at home, sweating and grinding and panting as they go, singing praises to physical exertion but forgetting one important fact—they live under economic conditions that grant them a choice of exertions, unlike most of the world's muscle workers, whether peasants or factory laborers, who have little choice and must sweat for survival.

Anyone who has slaved for years in the fields at the mercy of weather and a landowner, or who has been an appendage to an assembly line, knows how inhumane these forms of work can be. The shift toward knowledge work and advanced services, even at its worst, is an early liberating step toward a better future.

FROM PICOS TO YOCTOS

One could list any number of additional advances in health care and many other fields as further evidence that things are actually getting better for more people. But when future generations look back at today they may most value the extraordinary discoveries about the world that we, the first generation since the dawn of the knowledge economy, are making.

Thus, the last half century has seen a profound reconceptualization of humanity's place in the universe.

Since the first satellite was shot into the heavens in 1957, astrophysicists have had access to massive amounts of new data with which to confirm or disconfirm earlier theories of the cosmos. And most of the new data have supported the finding that the universe began with a big bang 13.7 billion years ago—an estimate experts believe is subject to an error rate of only 0.2 billion years.

Like all scientific findings, this one may be revised in light of new evidence. But so far, many different experiments have corroborated one another—and the big bang concept. The universe did not, as many still believe, come into being roughly six thousand years ago, and it is not static. Like everything in it, including us humans, it, too, is subject to change. Not only is there no life without change; there is no universe.

Even while some scientists have been expanding our conception of the cosmos, others have been probing smaller and smaller bits and pieces of it and putting that knowledge to practical use. Thus we have the current breakthroughs at the nano level. Nanotechnology promises to do a wide range of things previously far beyond our reach—from the creation of new construction materials to precision drug delivery and diagnosis and the replacement of silicon-based chips.

Thus, the coming leap to nanoproduction and nanoproducts—the source of so much stock-market excitement today—needs to be seen as only one step toward the manipulation of even tinier phenomena in the future. Still a long way off, these next steps may eventually make possible the creation of wealth at smaller and smaller levels, from those measured not just in nanos but in picos, femtos, attos and zeptos to, who knows, eventually yoctos—a yocto being the term for 0.000,000,000,000,000,000,000,001 of a meter.

What is so exciting about going to the nano level—grossly large by comparison with these—is that as we move down in scale, things are not only smaller but stranger and stranger. They behave differently. And if nanotechnology promises new cures for disease, imagine what the move to even smaller scales can do—negatively as well as positively.

At the scale of both the most minute phenomena and of the cosmos itself, we, in this generation, have learned more about nature and our species than all our ancestors combined.

We have taken up the ringing challenge Francis Bacon set out for humanity in 1603—not to create some "particular invention, however useful," but to succeed in "kindling a light in nature, a light which should in its very rising touch and illuminate all the border-regions that confine upon the circle of our present knowledge."

Having generated more new data, information and knowledge than all our ancestors combined, we have organized it differently, distributed it differently and combined and recombined it in new and more transient patterns. We have also created entire new cyberworlds in which ideas, magnificent and terrifying alike, bounce off one another like trillions of intelligent Ping-Pong balls.

We will, within the foreseeable future, through a combination of neuroscience, cybernetics and media manipulation, create far more realistic sensory, sensual and other virtual experiences. We will simulate future events, personal or otherwise, in the digital world before participating in them "live." And we will interact virtually or in the flesh with people from all over the planet. Criminals may have a field day. But so will saints.

Finally, we stand now at the time when even words like *live* and *dead* or *human* and *inhuman* may be redefined in the light of the new potentials open to our species, both on the Earth and in colonies in space. In short, nobody is promising utopia. The revolution now under way won't put an end to war, terrorism or disease. It cannot guarantee perfect ecological balance.

But it does promise that our children will live in an exciting world radically different from ours, with its own benefits and dangers and challenges. We cannot say whether this emerging world will be mostly "good" or mostly "evil," because the very definitions of these terms will change, and it is not we but our children and their children who will do the judging, according to their own values.

Living at the dawn of this century, we are direct or indirect participants in the design of a new civilization with a revolutionary wealth system at its core. Will this process complete itself—or will the still incomplete wealth revolution come to a crashing halt?

The history of the industrial revolution provides a clue.

Between the mid-1600s, when it started, and the mid-1950s, when the knowledge economy first began to overlap and supersede it, the world went through countless upheavals. Wars on end. Civil Wars in England. The Swedish invasion of Poland. The Turkish-Venetian war. The Portuguese-Dutch war in Brazil. All these and more in the single decade starting in 1650.

Later came Queen Anne's wars against the Spaniards, the French and Indian wars, the Cambodian war of succession and on and on—all before we even get to the American and the French revolutions, Napoleon's sweep across Europe, the American Civil War, World War I, the Russian Revolution and, worst of all, World War II.

These conflicts were interspersed with flu epidemics; stock-market crashes; the decline of the large, multigenerational family; economic depressions; corruption scandals; regime changes; the introduction of the camera, electricity, the automobile, the airplane, movies and radio; and a succession of schools of art in the West, from Pre-Raphaelitism and romanticism to impressionism, futurism, surrealism and cubism.

Yet through all these changes and upheavals, one thing stands out. Nothing, not all of them together, stopped the forward advance of the industrial revolution and the spread of the new wealth system it brought. Nothing.

The reason was that the Second Wave was not just a matter of technology or economics. It originated out of social and political and philosophical forces as well, and out of wave conflict in which the holdover elites of the agrarian age gradually yielded to the forces of the new.

The Second Wave led to econocentrism: The idea that culture, religion and the arts, were all of secondary importance and—according to Marx—were determined by economics.

But Third Wave revolutionary wealth is increasingly based on knowledge—and puts economics back in its place as part of a larger system, bringing, for better and worse, issues like cultural identity, religion and morality back toward center stage.

These issues should now be seen as part of a feedback process with the economy, rather than subordinate to it. The Third Wave revolution wears the face of technology because the technologies that come with it are so spectacular. But, like industrialization or "modernization," it is an all-encompassing change of civilization. And despite stock-market swings and other distractions, revolutionary wealth will continue its inexorable advance across much of the world.

As tomorrow's economy and society take form, all of us—individuals, companies, organizations and governments alike—now face the wildest, fastest ride into the future of any generation.

It is, when all is said, a fantastic moment to be alive.

Welcome to the rest of the twenty-first century!

NOTES

Bracketed [/] numbers indicate sources listed in the bibliography.

1. SPEARHEADING WEALTH

p. 3   Street gangs: "4 Presidents Seek Help in Gang Battle," by Chris Kraul, Robert Lopez and Rich Connell, *Los Angeles Times,* April 2, 2005, p. A3.

3   Teen terrorists: "Europe's Boys of Jihad," by Sebastian Rotella, *Los Angeles Times,* April 2, 2005, p. A1.

3   Prince Harry: "Jewish Groups, British Lawmakers Criticize Prince Harry's Nazi Costume," by Robert Barr, Associated Press, January 13, 2005.

4   Pillow mobs: "When Feathers Fly," by Liat Collins, *Jerusalem Post,* March 18, 2005, p. 44.

4   Virtual assets: "The Virtual Market," by L. A. Lorek, *San Antonio Express-News,* April 5, 2005, p. E1.

4   Trade deficit: "Fed Fears Inflation, but Still 'Measured,'" by Christina Wise, *Investor's Business Daily,* April 13, 2005, p. A1.

4   German unemployment: "France and Germany Dogged by Joblessness," by Mark Landler, *New York Times,* April 1, 2005, p. C4.

6   White collar/blue collar: "Employed Persons, by Major Occupation Group and Sex: Annual Averages, 1947–1962," a study by the U.S. Department of Labor included as Table A-7 in *Manpower Report of the President,* transmitted to the U.S. Congress in March 1963.

6   Computers migrate to civilian sector: "Computers: History and Development," *Jones Telecommunications & Multimedia Encyclopedia,* www.digitalcentury.com/encyclo/update/comp_hd.html.

6   Knowledge study: see Machlup, [157], pp. 394–397.

7   Stratocaster: "50 Years o Perfection: Design and History of Electric Guitars," by Tom Wheeler, *Guitar Player,* . anuary 1, 2004, p. 54.

7   NOW: "1966 Statement of Purpose" of the National Organization for Women, www.now.org/purpose66.htm.

7   ARPANET: "E-Mail Delivers," by Monty Phan, *Newsday,* October 17, 2001, p. C8.

8   Independent contractors: "Working, but Not 'Employed,'" by Robert Reich, *New York Times,* January 9, 2001.

8   Riki Anne Wilchins: "Spotlighting Issues of Gender, from Pronouns to Murder," by Carey Goldberg, *New York Times,* June 11, 1999, p. B2.

9   Total number of PCs: "PCs In-Use Surpassed 820M in 2004," *Computer Industry Almanac,* www.c-I-a.com/pr0305.htm.

9   Chips and transistors: Doug Andrey, principal analyst for the Semiconductor Industry Association, in correspondence to the authors, April 7, 2005.

9   HP's switches: "Hewlett Takes a Step Forward in the World of Tiny Chips," by John Markoff, *New York Times,* September 10, 2002, p. C1.

9   Earth Simulator: "On Top When It Comes to the Crunch," by Michiyo Nakamoto, *Financial Times,* September 16, 2002. Also, "Top 500 List" (of fastest computers), University of Mannheim and University of Tennessee, www.top500.org/list/2002/11/.

9   Lawrence Livermore: "a New Arms Race to Build the World's Mightiest Computer," by John Markoff, *New York Times,* August 19, 2005, p. C2.

9   Petaflops: "IBM Plans a Computer That Will Set Power Record," by John Markoff, *New York Times,* November 19, 2002, p. C10.

9   Worldwide Internet users, Brazil users: "Internet Usage Statistics—The Big Picture," Internet World Stats, December 31, 2005, www.internetworldstats.com/stats.htm. Also, "Internet Indicators," International Telecommunication Union, 2004, www.itu.int/ITU-D/ict/statistics/at_glance/Internet04.pdf.

9   Mobile phone subscribers: "2006: The Year of the Must-Have Phone of the Future," by Audrey Stuart, Agence France Presse, January 23, 2006. Also, "Mobile Cellular," International Telecommunication Union, 2004, www.itu.int/ITU-D/ict/statistics/at_glance/cellular04.pdf.

9   Chinese on the Internet: "Watch the Chinese Change Faster Than Others," by T. K. Chang, quoting Nicholas Negroponte in the *International Herald Tribune,* June 21, 2000.

9   Korean Internet cafés: "Starcraft Game Captures South Korea's Recession-Hit Youth," by Ahn Mi-young of Deutsche Presse-Agentur, April 20, 1999. Also, "Korea's PC 'Bangs' Are the New Place to Socialize," by Michael Baker, *Christian Science Monitor,* May 3, 2000, p. 9.

9   Software exporters: "Costa Rica Brews a New Blend of Java," by Peter Bate of the Inter-American Development Bank, 1999, from the IADB Web site @ www.iadb.org/idbamerica/Archive/stories/1999/eng/e1099fl.htm. Also, "Mr. Freeze: Iceland Moves Out into the Light as Its New President Goes High Tech," by Alex Grove, *Red Herring,* August, 1997. Also, "The Next India? Egypt's Software Dream," by the International Telecommunication Union, December, 2000, www.itu.int/ITU-D/cs/letters/egypt.html.

9   Vietnam exports: "Software Mission to Japan," *Vietnam Investment Review,* September 23, 2002.

9   I.T. firms in Recife: "Reinventing Recife as Tech Harbor," by Paulo Rebelo, *Wired,* January 18, 2002, www.wired.com/news/print/0,1294,49649,00.html.

9   High-tech in Africa: "CTs in Africa: A Status Report," by the United Nations Information and Communication Technologies Task Force, cited in the Inter Press Service article "Internet Use Growing, but Still Lags in Africa," by Thalif Deen, September 30, 2002.

10 I.T. spending: "Digital Planet 2004: The Global Information Economy," World Information Technology and Services Alliance citing research by Global Insight, www.witsa.org/digitalplanet.

10 I.T. companies: "A Growing Technology Ecosystem," Microsoft Corp., April 23, 2002, www.microsoft.com/issues/essays/2002/04-23ecosystem.asp.

10 Dark matter: "It's Dark Out There," by Hazel Muir, *New Scientist,* June 1, 2002, p. 14.

10 Anti-hydrogen: "European Scientists Produce—and Measure—Atoms of Antihydrogen," by Naomi Koppel, Associated Press, October 29, 2002. Also, "Anti-hydrogen Rivals Enter the Stretch," *Science,* November 15, 2002, p. 1327.

10 Roche ad: *Science,* September 6, 2002.

11 AB Applied Biosystems ad: Ibid.

11 Laser speeds: "Strobe Light Breaks the Attosecond Barrier," by Robert F. Service, *Science,* June 1, 2001, p. 1627.

11 Lasetron: "Lasetron to Produce Zeptosecond Flashes," by Philip Ball, *Nature,* February 5, 2002.

11 Time travel: "When Traveling Through Time, Pack Information," by Tom Siegfried, *Dallas Morning News,* September 17, 2001, p. 2C.

11 Cyborgs: "The Bionic Man," by William Underhill, *Newsweek,* October 7, 2002, p. 61.

11 Near-immortality: "As Life Spans Stretch, New Thoughts Arise on Age-Old Issues of Aging," by John Fauber, *Milwaukee Journal,* April 16, 2002, p. 1G.

11 Antigravity devices: *Melbourne Age,* reviewing *The Hunt for Zero Point,* [55], on October 8, 2002, p.5.

12 American humbug: "No Free Lunch," *Investors Chronicle,* March 22, 2002, p. 122.

2. THE CHILD OF DESIRE

13 "accumulation of possibilities": "La riqueza como problema," by Gabriel Zaid, *Reforma,* April 25, 1999, p. A26.

14 Deng: "To Get Rich Is Glorious," by Tim Healy and David Hsieh, *Asia Week,* March 7, 1997. Also, "The Economy's Long March," by Steve Schifferes, British Broadcasting Corp., September 29, 1999, http://news.bbc.co.uk/1/hi/specialreport1999/09/china.

15 U.S. ad spending: "Crowned at Last," *The Economist,* April 2, 2005, p. 4.

15 Europe ad spending: "The Online Advertising Landscape, Europe," by Chris Lake, from the DoubleClick Web site, 2005, www.doubleclick.com/us/knowledge_central/documents/TREND_REPORTS/europe_online.pdf.

15 Japan ad spending. "Ad Spending Up 3% in 2004: Dentsu," *Japan Times,* February 18, 2005.

3. WAVES OF WEALTH

19 Overweight/undernourished people: "It's a Fat, Fat, Fat World," *CBS News,* citing the findings of a World Health Organization task force, May 15, 2002, www.cbsnews.com/stories/2002/05/health/main509230.shtml. Also, "The State of Food Insecurity in the World: 2002," Food and Agriculture Organization, http://www.fao.org/documents/show_cdr.asp?url_file=/docrep/005/y7352e/y7352e00.htm.

20 Agricultural beginnings: "Einkorn's Debut," by Mark Rose, *Archaeology,* January/February, 1998. Also, "Location, Location, Location: The First Farmers," by Jared Diamond, *Science,* November 14, 1997, p. 1243.

20 Peasant prosperity zone: "The Expansion of Technology 500–1500," by Lynn White in *The Fontana Economic History of Europe* (London, 1972), cited in Cipolla, [50], p. 138.

20 Frequency of famines: "Medieval Europe: Crisis and Renewal," by Teofilo F. Ruiz, audiotape of Lecture 5: "Hunger," lecture series from the Teaching Company (Chantilly, Va., 1997).

20 Famine and daily life, satirical play: Camporesi, [41], pp. 38, 47, 56.

20 Deaths in cities: Richard S. Dunn, *The Age of Religious Wars* (New York: W. W. Norton & Co., 1997).

22 OECD member population: "World Development Indicators Database," World Bank, August, 2002, http://www.worldbank.org/data/databytopic/POP.pdf.

4. DEEP FUNDAMENTALS

24 GM chief economist: "Economists See Better Times Coming in '03," by John Gallagher, *Detroit Free Press,* November 22, 2002.

24 Time Warner Telecom chairman: "Time Warner Telecom Announces Third Quarter 2002 Results," PR Newswire, October 30, 2002.

24 Time Warner Telecom stock decline: "Historical Prices for Time Warner Telecom (TWTC)," Yahoo Finance, December 11, 2002, http:table.finance.yahoo.com/d?a=9&b =30&c=2001&d=9&e=30&f=2002&g=w&s=twtc.

24 Credit Suisse First Boston economist: "Russia Says It Can Service Foreign Debt," by Robert Cottrell and Arkady Ostrovsky, *Financial Times,* February 21, 2002, p. 30.

24 Chinese export market: "China Predicts 7% Year 2000 Growth, Deflation to End," by William J. McMahon, *China Online News,* January 5, 2000.

25 Brent Moulton: "A Clearer View of the Economy: The Commerce Department Answers Its Critics," by Louis Uchitelle, *New York Times,* October 29, 1999, p. C1.

26 Central banks: "Credibility Test," by Mervyn King, *Financial Times,* August 30, 1999, p. 12.

27 Litigation consultant: "Experts and Consultants," HGExperts.com, www.hgexperts .com/listing/Experts-Failure-Analysis.asp.

27 Post-harvest horticulturalists: "Horticultural Crops," by Fu Wen Liu, from the Food and Fertilizer Technology Center, www.agnet.org/library/article/eb465b.html.

27 Productive powers of labor: Smith, [247], p. 3.

5. THE CLASH OF SPEEDS

31 Law of congruence: Heidi Toffler has suggested that if the dominant form of organization in the public sector is sufficiently incongruent with that in the private sector, the incompatibility will create inefficiencies in both.

32 Taylorism: The application of supposedly "scientific" methods to achieve maximum worker efficiency, often criticized for subjecting workers to inhuman speed-up and turning them into adjuncts of the machine. Named after Frederick Winslow Taylor (1856–1915). Sometimes called "Fordism" after Henry Ford, Kanigel, [134], p. 7.

34 American's family: *America's Families and Living Arrangements,* U.S. Census Bureau, June 2001, p. 2.

36 Union membership in 1955: *2001 World Almanac* (Mahwah, N.J.: World Almanac Books, 2001), p. 171.

36 Union membership today: "Union Members in 2004," U.S. Bureau of Labor Statistics, www.bls.gov/news.release/union2.nro.htm.

36 Airport runways: "Airport Runway Construction Challenges," U.S. House Subcommittee on Aviation, for its hearing May 24, 2001, www.house.gov/transportation/aviation/ 05-24-01/05-24-01memo.html.

36 Highway projects: "Increasing Program Delivery Costs," American Association of State Highway and Transportation Officials, 2002, http://transportation.org/bottomline/ highways07.html.

36 $400 billion in education costs: "Revenues and Expenditures for Public Elementary and Secondary Education: School Year 1999–2000," National Center for Education Statistics, www.nces.ed.gov/pubs2002/quarterly/summer/3-7.asp.

37 Larry Summers: "U.S. Will Endorse European Nominee to Lead the I.M.F.," by David E. Sanger and Joseph Kahn, *New York Times,* March, 14, 2000, p. A1.

38 Digital time clash: The file-sharing software and technology that led to a crisis in the music industry stemmed from technology developed in the late 1980s. In 2005, the U.S. Supreme Court ruled that companies whose products promote illicit file swapping can be sued, leading *The New York Times* to conclude that each new court victory by the industry "arrives years behind the next digital innovation." See "The Imps of File Sharing May Lose in Court, but They Are Winning in the Marketplace," by Tom Zeller, Jr., *New York Times,* July 4, 2005, p. C3.

38 Time collision: "A Megadeal in PC-Land Now?" by Robert X. Cringely, *New York Times,* November 24, 1998.

39 Social Security benefits: "Clinton Signs Law That Removes Social Security Earnings Penalty," by Kathleen Pender, *San Francisco Chronicle,* April 8, 2000, p. A1. Also, "Social Security Earnings Limit Removed," by Thomas Burke, U.S. Bureau of Labor Statistics, *Compensation and Working Conditions* 5, no. 2 (Summer 2000).

39 Headline: "Flash! The Great Depression Is Over," by Steve Forbes, *Forbes,* April 3, 2000, p. 39.

39 Origins of telecom law: "Regulators' New Role in Competitive Utilities," by Kriss Sjoblom and Richard S. Davis, *Seattle Post-Intelligencer,* July 29, 1997, p. A11.

39 Glass-Steagall: "Year in Review: Looking for Someone or Something to Blame," by Dean Anason, Matthias Rieker, Rob Blackwell, Rob Garver, Barbara Rehm and Jennifer Kingson, *American Banker,* December 5, 2002, p. 19A. Also, "Bear Tracks," by Tom Walker, *Atlanta Journal and Constitution,* November 17, 2002, p. 1G.

39 Stock and securities law: "Securities Law: An Overview," Cornell University Legal Information Institute, www.law.cornell.edu/topics/securities/html.

39 Mutual funds: Table: "Total Industry Net Assets, Number of Funds, and Shareholder Accounts," Investment Company Institute, 2003, www.ici.org/pdf/02fb_datasec1.pdf.

39 Original fund law, difference in asset value: "The Forties," Investment Company Institute, 2003, www.ici.org/60year/1940s.html. Mutual funds in 1940 are obtained from the ICI table of industry assets and funds.

39 Power blackout: "Two Years After the Lights Went Out," by Thomas Homer-Dixon, *New York Times,* August 13, 2005.

6. THE SYNCHRONIZATION INDUSTRY

41 Ancient synchrony: McNeill, [174], pp. 27, 30.

41 Seasonal cycles: see Wolters, [288], p. 182.

42 Entrainment: McGrath, [172], pp. 44–45.

42 Neurons: "Listening In on the Brain," *Science,* vol. 280, April 17, 1998, p. 376.

43 "Balanced Growth" economists: Kornai, [140], pp. 56–57.

43 Joseph Schumpeter: "Feeding the Flames: What Every Manager Needs to Know About Creative Destruction," by Russ Mitchell, *Business 2.0,* May 2001.

44 Japanese management: Monden, [181].

44 MRP and JIT manufacturing: Giffi, [109], pp. 138, 215, 228–229.

44 JIT and Toyota: Ibid., pp. 136–137. The authors' conclusions are drawn in part from research by Michael A. Cusumano reported in his work "Manufacturing Innovations: Lessons from the Japanese Auto Industry," *Sloan Management Review* 30 (Fall 1988), pp. 29–39.

44 NCMS study: Ibid., referring to a study by Roger W. Schmenner as found in "The Merit of Making Things Fast," *Sloan Management Review* 30 (Fall 1998), pp. 11–17.

44 Jim Champy and Michal Hammer: Hammer, [118], pp. 150–153.

45 Enterprise resource planning: "Baan Looks to Climb Out of Trough," by Joris Evers, *InfoWorld Daily News,* December 2, 2002. Also, "Enterprise Resource Planning," Bearing Point, 2003, www.kpmgconsulting.com/solutions/enterprise_solutions/erp_solutions.html.

45 Supply chain performance: "Synchronized Supply Chains: The New Frontier," by David Anderson and Hau Lee, *Achieving Supply Chain Excellence Through Technology,* April 15, 1999, published by Montgomery Research, Inc., from the ASCET Web site, www.ascet.com/documents/asp?dID=198.

45   Recycled autos: "Industry Faces Heavy Costs for Recycling," by Vanessa Houlder, *Financial Times,* May 27, 2003, p. 11.

45   Recycled ink cartridges: "Refillers Sue Lexmark Over Ink Cartridge Recycling Plan," by Joe Ward, *Louisville Courier-Journal,* September 7, 2001, p. 1C.

7. THE ARRYTHMIC ECONOMY

48   AOL Time Warner: "Who's Afraid of AOL Time Warner?" *The Economist,* January 26, 2002.

48   Siemens CEO: "Race to Renew a Corporate Culture," by Christopher Parkes, *Financial Times,* November 11, 1994. Siemens sold Nixdorf five years later to Kohlberg Kravis Roberts & Co.

48   California developer: Interview with the authors in Los Angeles, 2001.

49   New residential construction costs: "Annual Value of Construction Put in Place in the United States 1993–2004," U.S. Census Bureau, www.census.gov/const/www/c30index.html.

49   Typical cost of low-income unit: "Public Housing Project Detailed," by Nathan Gorenstein, *Philadelphia Inquirer,* November 10, 2001, p. B1.

50   Firms decline to bid: "U.S. Congress Asserts Oversight," by Gopal Ratnam, *Defense News,* November 25, 2002, p.1.

50   Contractors and regulations: "DoD Criticized for Relying on One-Bid Contracts," by Katy Saldarini, *Government Executive,* March, 2000, www.207.27.3.29/dailyfed/0300/032200k1.htm.

50   Defense Department time conflicts: Margiotta, [165], p. 50.

50   Unregulated computer industry: "FCC Gets a Clear Signal," an editorial in the *Orange County Register,* December 1, 1999, p. B10. Also, the "The Emergence of a Networked World," Global Internet Project, www.gip.org/publications/papers/gip2h.asp.

50   Telecom regulation, impact on development: "The Cost of Telecommunications Regulation," National Center for Policy Analysis, November 19, 2002, citing Robert W. Campbell of the Brookings Institute in "A Somewhat Better Connection," from *Regulation* 25 no. 2 (Summer 2002), pp. 22–28, www.ncpa.org/iss/reg/2002/pd111902d.html. Also, "FCC Gets a Clear Signal," *Orange County Register,* citing National Economic Research Associates, December 1, 1999, p. B10.

50   Chip vs. network speeds: "The Time Is Now: Bust Up the Box," by John Markoff, *New York Times,* October 5, 2005, p. G1.

51   Naito and ATMs, early bank closings: "Banks Focus on Retail Services, Keep Cash Machines Open Later," by Masato Ishizawa, *Nikkei Weekly,* October 20, 1997, p. 1.

51   Japanese ATMs, 24-hour service: "Making News in Japan with 24-Hour ATMs," by Andrew Raskin, *Bank Technology News International,* January, 1998.

51   UFJ: "UFJ to Introduce 24-Hour ATMs," *Nikkei Weekly,* August 25, 2003.

8. THE NEW TIMESCAPE

52   American Airline flight: "Critically Ill Passengers on Two Flights Saved by Airline's Pioneering Efforts," by John Crewdson of the *Chicago Tribune,* reprinted in the *Buffalo News,* November 22, 1998, p. 18A.

53   Time and God: Le Goff, [147], p. 51.

53   Labor productivity measurement: "Productivity and Costs: People Are Asking . . ." U.S. Bureau of Labor Statistics, www.bls.gov/lpc/peoplebox.htm.

54   New vocabulary: (Twitch Speed): "Today's Free Agents Work at Twitch Speed: A Buzzword Glossary," by Hal Lancaster, *Wall Street Journal,* October 7, 1998, p. B1;

(Hurry Sickness): "Hurry Sickness Can Be Cured," by Philip Chard, *Milwaukee Journal Sentinel,* November 26, 2002, p. 1F; (Time Deepening and Time Famine): "Old Father Time Becomes a Terror," by Richard Tomkins, *Financial Times,* March 20–21, 1999; (Internet Time): "A Quicker Pace Means No Peace in the Valley," by John Markoff, *New York Times,* quoting Andy Grove of Intel. June 3, 1996, p. C1; (Digital Time): "Are You on Digital Time?" by Alan M. Webber, *Fast Company,* February, 1999, p. 114.

54   Rushaholics: "Curse of the Rushaholics," by Anastasia Stephens, *Evening Standard* (London), April 30, 2002, p. 23.

54   Attention deficit disorder: "Medication and Therapy Help Hyperactive Children," by Dr. Hank Clever, *St. Louis Post-Dispatch,* April 22, 2002, p. 9.

54   Young multitaskers: "Understanding Digital Kids," by Ian Jukes and Anita Dosai, Info-SavvyGroup, June, 2004, www.thecommittedsardine.net/infosavvy/education/handouts/it.pdf.

54   Speed dating: "Minute Mates," by Linda Wertheimer, *Dallas Morning News,* December 8, 2000, p. 1C; and SpeedDating Web site, www.aish.com/speeddating/.

54   India speed-dating: "Speed Dating Makes Inroads in India," *National Public Radio,* October 18, 2005.

54   Speed networking: "A Warm Welcome at Your City Club," by Tom Braithwaite, *Financial Times,* December 5, 2005, p. 14.

54   Page-load impatience: "Site Unseen: The Brand Suffers—The Cost of Downtime," by Tim Wilson, citing a report by Zona Research, *Internet Week,* August 2, 1999.

54   Mini-novels: "Make Short Work of a Novel," by Michelle Zhang, *Shanghai Daily,* September 15, 2005, p. 17.

55   TV visuals: "Hollywood Disinformation," by Joseph D. Duffy, *New Perspectives Quarterly,* Fall 1998, p. 14.

55   NextCard: "The Information Gold Mine," by Heather Green, *Business Week,* July 26, 1999.

55   Millisecond trades: "EBS Live Speeds Up Data System," by Jennifer Hughes, *Financial Times,* February 2, 2004, p. 28.

56   Free-agent workers: Pink, [211], pp. 34–35. Also, interview with authors on July 4, 2000.

56   Free-time periods: "Transforming the Future: Rethinking Time for the New Millennium," by Bill Martin and Sandra Mason, *Foresight,* February 1999, p. 51.

57   Short-form TV: Interview with the authors in Los Angeles, January 29, 2000.

57   *Friends* and *SNL:* "Must-win TV Comes to Thursdays," by Lauren Hunter, Cable News Network, February 7, 2001, www.cnn.com/2001/SHOWBIZ/TV/0207/friends.survivor. The *Friends* and *Saturday Night Live* episodes first aired following the Super Bowl on January 28, 2001.

57   One-minute movies: "NBC Is Hoping Short Movies Keep Viewers from Zapping," by Bill Carter, *New York Times,* August 4, 2003, p. C1.

57   Betsy Frank: "Investors May Have Repudiated the Internet, but Consumers Have Not," by Amy Harmon and Felicity Barringer, *New York Times,* July 22, 2002, p. C2.

57   Appointment-based TV: "Coming Soon to TV Land," by John Markoff, *New York Times,* January 7, 2006, p. C1.

57   John Moody: "The News Business: Stop Press," *The Economist,* July 4, 1998, p. 17.

57   Family rituals: "Rethinking the Rat Race," by Diane Brady, *Business Week,* August 26, 2002.

58   TiVo: "Podcasting: The New Broadcasting Model," by John Jerney, *Daily Yomiuri,* December 14, 2004, p. 13.

58   "Americanization" of Europe: Alvin Toffler, *Future Shock* (New York: Random House, 1970).

58   Günter Biere: "Berlin Journal: Skirmish in the Store Wars—The Souvenir Caper," by Roger Cohen, *New York Times,* August 6, 1999, p. A4.

58   Japan's late-night stores and sales: "Night and Day" and "Trend to Longer Hours Certain to Continue," by Nami M. Abe, *Nikkei Weekly,* September 30, 2002, pp. 2, 3.

59   Conectiva and others: "ICT in Curitiba," ITC Parana, www.investict.com/br/englishversion/englishversion/ccmodelo/textog.htm. Also, "Conectiva, Inc.," Intel, www.intel.com/capital/portfolio/companies/conectiva.htm.

59   Curitiba: "Reclaiming Cities for the Next Few Centuries," by Hardev Kaur, *New Straits Times Management Times,* December 27, 2002.

59   "24-Hour Street": "Brazil's Clean and Green City," by Allen Chesney, *Chattanooga Free Press,* September 13, 1998, p. K1.

59   Sweden extends hours: "Stock Exchanges: Open All Night," by Dean Foust, *Business Week,* June 14, 1999.

60   Temporary store: "A Store Made for Right Now: You Shop Until It's Dropped," by Cathy Horyn, *New York Times,* February 17, 2004, p. A1.

9. THE GREAT CIRCLE

63   China's technology in 1500: "The Historical Significance of China's Entry to the WTO," by Jeffrey D. Sachs, 2000, from the Project Syndicate, www.project-syndicate.org/article_print_text?mid=299&lang=1.

63   Asia's economic output in 1500, later decline: Maddison, [158], p. 142. Maddison notes that, despite huge increases in Asia's population, its share of world output slowly declined to less than 20 percent in 1950.

63   Zheng He: Levathes, [149].

64   Shift of wealth: The macro shift of world wealth westward toward Asia in the past half century was paralleled *inside* the United States. In 1950 nine out of the ten biggest American cities were concentrated on the East Coast and in the Midwest. By 2004, only three remained among the top ten. Fully seven were now found west of Texas. Detroit, symbol of mass production of tangible goods, had dropped off the list and been replaced by San Jose, California, the urban area adjacent to Silicon Valley, the symbol of intangible output. See "Top Ten Cities," maps in *New York Times,* June 30, 2005, p. A19.

64   Henry Luce: "Luce's Values—Then and Now," by Walter Isaacson, *Time,* March 9, 1998, p. 195. Also, "Another 'American Century'?" by William Pfaff, *International Herald Tribune,* January 3, 2000, p. 8.

64   FDI in China: "New Wave of Foreign Investors Needed," by Cary Huang, *South China Morning Post,* March 22, 2005, p. 7.

64   Miraculous torrent: "China's Foreign Investment Set for Record High in 2002," Xinhua News Agency, July 17, 2002.

64   FDI in 2003: "China Tops U.S. in Investment Table," British Broadcasting Corp., June 28, 2004, http://news/bbc.co.uk/2/hi/business/3846439/stm.

64   FDI in 2005: "U.S. to Remain Top Investment Destination for Foreign Firms," by Andrew C. Schneider, *Kiplinger Business Forecasts,* March 3, 2005.

64   U.S. investments in China: *China's Economic Conditions,* by Wayne M. Morrison of the Congressional Research Office, January 24, 2005, p. 5.

64–65   Imports from China: *Foreign Trade Statistics—Trade with China: 2003,* U.S. Census Bureau, www.census.gov/foreign-trade/balance/c5700.html.

65   China's exports: "Rank Order—Exports," *World Factbook,* www.cia.gov/cia/publications/factbook/rankorder/2078rank.html.

65   Aggregate of China, Asia, Europe: "Field Listing—GDP," *World Factbook,* www.odci.gov/cia/publications/factbook/2001.html.

65   World of 2050: "Asia," by Robert Manning, 2000, on the Council on Foreign Relations Web site @ www.foreignpolicy2000.org/library/issuebriefs/IBAsia.html.

10. HIGHER-VALUE-ADDED PLACES

66   Placelessness: Examples of these characterizations can be found in "Life Beyond Modems," by James Coates and Jon Van, *Chicago Tribune,* March 17, 1997, p. C1. Also, "Embedding the Internet," by Deborah Estrin, Ramesh Govindan and John Heidemann in *Communications of the Association for Computer Machinery,* May 1, 2000, p. 38.

66   Irrelevant locations: Knoke, [139], p. 8.

67   Poorest city: "Beneath Cleveland's Bright Façade, America's Poorest City," by Milan Simonich, *Pittsburgh Post-Gazette,* September 26, 2004, p. A1.

67   Guangdong a decade ago, Pearl River Delta: "World Watch: Asia—Poised for Growth," by Mark Graham, Industryweek.com, October 16, 2000, www.industryweek.com/CurrentArticles/asp/articles.asp?ArticleID=918.

67   Millions to Guangdong: "China's Young, Restless Seeking Future," by Jennifer Lin, Knight-Ridder Newspapers, published in the *Pittsburgh Post-Gazette,* September 26, 1999, p. A17.

67   Millions of jobs: "Completing the Jigsaw," by Duncan Hughes, *South China Morning Post,* October 29, 1994, p. 23.

67   Guangdong GDP: "FDI in China and Regional Development from Institutional Reforms to Agglomeration Economies Perspective," a paper by Chyau Tuan and F. Y. Ng for the First International Conference on Nation States and Economic Policy: Conflict and Cooperation, organized by the Japan Economic Association, November 30, December 1, 2002, Academic Society HomeVillage of Japan, www.soc.nii.ac.jp/jepa/abst/10.pdf.

67   High-tech sector: "On Changes of Economic Position of Coastal Prosperous Provinces," by Ma Chunhui, China Development Institute, June 30, 2003, www.cdi.com.cn/publication/pdf/cdireview_200302_machh.pdf.

68   Region-states: Ohmae, [200]. Also, "Putting Global Logic First," by Kenichi Ohmae, *Harvard Business Review,* January-February, 1995, p. 120.

68   Dalian: Ohmae, [198], p. 8.

68   Cross-borders in Eastern Europe: "Territoriality of Topocratic Cross-Border Networks," by Jussi S. Jauhiainen, University of Tartu, Estonia, www.ut.ee/SOPL/english/border/jj.htm.

68   Tumen River: "Tumen River Project Hopes to Gain Japan's Participation," Associated Press, April 6, 2001.

68   Pacific powerhouse: "A Lateral Piece of Logic," by Tyler Brule, *Financial Times,* October 30, 2004, p. 22.

68   Mexico signs NAFTA: "Mexico's China Obsession," by Scott Johnson, *Newsweek,* November 4, 2002, p. 48.

69   Border plants, jobs: "First Decline Seen for Border Factories," by Chris Kraul, *Chicago Tribune,* October 9, 2001, Business Section, p. 2.

69   Mexico's lost jobs: "Free Trade's Faded Dream," by Susan Ferriss of Cox News Service, published in the *Edmonton Journal,* November 23, 2003, p. D4.

69   Bustamante and Plantronics: "The China Challenge," by Dean Calbreath and Diane Lindquist, Copley News Service, September 2, 2002.

70   Indiana ad, old factors: "The New State Economy Index," by Robert D. Atkinson with assistance from Rick Coduri, Progressive Policy Institute, June 10, 2002, www.ppionline.org/ppi_ci.cfm?knlgAreaID=87&subsecID=205&contentID=896.

70   Indiana's goals today: "Break Away Growth: Economic Strategy Revealed," Indiana Economic Development Council, www.iedc.org/growth/index.html.

70   Phoenix: "Best Cities to Start and Grow a Company," *Inc.,* December 2000, p. 45.

70   South Dakota: "Small Business Survival Index 2002," by Raymond J. Keating, Small Business Survival Committee, July 2002, pp. 6–7.

71   Nevada: "Best and Worst States to Run a Small Biz," by Phillip Harper, citing reports released in July 2002, www.bcentral.com/articles/harper/141.asp.

71   Airworld: "Terminal Leave," by Greg Lindsay, *Advertising Age,* October 17, 2005, p. 12.

11. SPATIAL REACH

73   Enciso and World Cup: Interview with the authors on March 27, 2003.

73   World Cup attendance: "World Cup Had Mixed Impact on Economy; Government Reports," *Japan Economic Newswire,* July 11, 2002. Also, "232,800 Foreigners Visit Korea for World Cup," *Asia Pulse,* August 6, 2002.

73   Chuang Tzu: Waley, [274], p. 223.

73   International travel: "Surge Una Nueva Especialidad," by Alejandro Lepetic, *Corporate Traveler,* June–July–August 1997, p. 45.

74   1650 population: *World Almanac 1996* (Mahwah, N.J.: World Almanac Books, 1996), p. 553.

74   Americans' annual mileage: "Annual Vehicle Distance Traveled in Miles and Related Data—1998," U.S. Department of Transportation, www.bts.gov/ntl/query.html?qt= average+miles+per+year&search.x=6&search.y=2.

74   Average commute: "The Cost of Traffic Congestion in Colorado," The Road Information Program, citing findings of the U.S. Department of Transportation, May, 2002, http:// 216.239.39.100/search?q=cache:6EMUcR_24cIC:www.tripnet.org/ColoradoCongestion StudyMay2002.PDF+average+daily+commute+miles&hl=en&ie=UTF-8.

74   Peasant travel: Hale, [116], p. 32.

74   Multinational product inputs: "Scouring the Planet for Braniacs," by Pete Engardio, *Business Week,* October 11, 2004, p. 100.

75   Shintaro Ishihara: "Tokyo Story: Shintaro Ishihara's Flamboyant Nationalism Appeals to Many Japanese Voters," by John Nathan, *New Yorker,* April 9, 2001, p. 108; and Holstein, [127], p. 165.

76   Cross-border money and dollarization: Cohen, [53], pp. 1, 4, 94.

76   Panama and Ecuador: "Noboa: Dollar Has Been Good Thing for Ecuador," by Andres Oppenheimer, *Miami Herald,* October 13, 2002, p. HW8.

76   East Timor, Russia, former republics, Romania, Turkey, Vietnam: "Unstable Exchange Rate System Hurting Emerging Markets," *Asia Pulse,* January 8, 2003.

76   Argentina and others: U.S. Senate, Joint Economic Committee Staff Report, January, 2000, http://216.239.57.100/search?q=cache:IqBkEsZNHmMC:www.usinfo.org.sv/ IRChomepage/Dollarization.ppt+mexico+and+%22u.s.+dollar%22+and+unofficial+ currency&hl=en&ie=UTF-8.

76   Dollars held overseas: "The Location of U.S. Currency: How Much Is Abroad?" by Richard D. Porter and Ruth A. Judson, *Federal Reserve Bulletin 82,* October 1996, pp. 883–903.

76   Introduction of the euro: The future of the dollar, in terms of both its value and its use outside the United States, was, according to some analysts, placed in doubt by the replacement of twelve national currencies by the euro. Some leading financial economists forecast that the euro would replace the dollar as the world's most important currency. See "EMU and the Euro: An American Perspective," by Harvard professor Jeffrey A. Frankel, June 28, 2000, ww.fondazione.lucchini.it/pdf/frankellast.pdf. In

2005, the growth of U.S. trade and fiscal deficits and the decline of the dollar led to widespread speculation that China, Japan and other nations might dump their dollar holdings and switch to the euro. This was followed, instead, by the worst crisis in the E.U.'s history: the angry rejection of its proposed constitution by voters in France and the Netherlands, putting the future of the euro—and the E.U. itself—in doubt.

76   Mark in Balkans: "German Currency Leaves Its Mark Across the Balkans," by Lucian Kim, *Christian Science Monitor,* March 2, 2000, p. 8.

76   Franc in Africa: "Europe's Funny Money," by Martin Walker, United Press International, August 8, 2001.

76   Swiss franc in Liechtenstein: "Information About Liechtenstein and Links to Related Sites," Liechtenstein Permanent Mission to the United Nations, www.un.int/liechtenstein/info.htm.

76   Rupee in Bhutan: "Crowning Glory," by Daniel Baer, *Sydney Morning Herald,* September 28, 2002, Travel section, p. 7.

76   Krone in Greenland: "History and Adventure Kept on Ice in Greenland," by Jane M. Olsen, Associated Press, August 18, 2003.

76   Foreign currency in eighteen countries: "Monetary Policy in Dollarized Economies," by Tomas J. T. Balino, Adam Bennett and Eduardo Borensztein, International Monetary Fund, 1999, www.imf.org/external/pubs/nft/op/171.

77   Monetary spaces, seigniorage and markets: Cohen, [53], pp. 5, 92.

12. AN UNREADY WORLD

78   World Exhibition and *Le Figaro*: British Broadcasting Corporation: "Back to the Future: 1900," British Broadcasting Corp., www.bbc.co.uk/hi/english/static/specialreport/1999/12/99/backtothefuture/1900/stm.

78   Foreign trade: Antoni Estevadeordal, Brian Frantz, and Alan M. Taylor, "The Rise and Fall of World Trade, 1870–1939," a working paper for the National Bureau of Economic Research, November 2002, http://papers.nber.org/papers/.

78   Colonies in Asia, Africa: Edelstein, [81], pp. 35–37.

79   People in Open-economies: "A Tilt in the Right Direction," by Simon Kuper, *Financial Times,* January 30, 1998, published in an FT Survey on International Youth, p.1.

79   Chile and Argentina: "Letter from Chile," by Jimmy Langman, *The Nation,* December 16, 2002. Also, "Argentina Hopes to Attract Foreign Investment," Agence France Presse, January 20, 2003. Also, "Nervous Investors Watch Brazil Election," by James Cox, *USA Today,* October 4, 2002, p. 1B.

79   Microcredit: "Global Poverty: There's No Panacea, but Here Are Strategies That Work," by Pete Engardio, *Business Week,* Special Report, October 14, 2002, p. 108.

79   Earth's surface area: "Moon ABCs Fact Sheet," chart accompanying a Web section on the Lunar Prospector project, National Aeronautics and Space Administration, http://lunar.arc.nasa.gov/education/activities/active9.

80   Equity markets: "Single Market for Equities: Regulations Must Be Reformed to Encourage a Truly Pan-European Stock Market," by Stanislas Yassukovich, *Financial Times,* January 26, 1998, p. 16.

80   Costs of Evian, ketchup: "Hurdles Ahead," chart accompanying the article "Europe Sees Progress Falter in Face of Red Tape and Protectionism," *Financial Times,* Tuesday, January 14, 2003, p. 3.

80   Access to capital: "The International Financial System: Exploring Concepts," by Zanny Minton Beddoes, *Foreign Policy,* Fall, 1999, p. 16.

80   Multinationals and subsidiaries: Union of International Associations, [268], Item D3003.

80   Foreign currency deposits: "Experts Question Roving Flow of Global Capital," by Nicholas D. Kristof, *New York Times,* September 20, 1998, p. A18.

80   FDI and cross-border debt: "World Total Direct Foreign Investment," report issued by the Milken Institute in conjunction with its Global Conference held April 22–24, 2002, in Los Angeles, p. II-32.

80   World trade: "Global Financial Profile," United Nations Panel on Refinancing for Development, June 2001, www.un.org/reports/financing/profile/htm.

80   Kearney report, economic integration: "Measuring Globalization: Who's Up; Who's Down," *Foreign Policy,* January/February 2003, pp. 60–72.

81   Globalized vices: "Globalization," CSPAN transcript of Babbit's remarks, March 1, 2001.

81   Drug trafficking, illegal economy: "The Five Wars of Globalization," by Moisés Naím, citing the 1999 "Human Development Report" by the United Nations, *Foreign Policy,* January/February 2003, p. 30.

81   Sex-slave smugglers, Bucharest: "A Smuggler's Paradise," by David Binder, MSNBC, www.msnbc.com/news/667792.asp?cp1=1, quoting the Albanian Interior Ministry.

81   UNICEF report: "U.N. Children's Fund Says Millions of Children Bought and Sold as Sex Slaves," by Edith M. Lederer, Associated Press, December 12, 2001.

81   Yellow dust: "Dust Plagues Korea for Second Day," by Byun Tae-kyung, *Korea Herald,* April 10, 2002.

81–82 Indonesian fires: "2002: A Bleak Year for the Environment," by Agus P. Sari, *Jakarta Post,* December 28, 2002.

82   Cyanide spill: "Little Cyanide Peril Is Seen for Danube; Tributary Badly Polluted, but Scientists Minimize Danger to Humans," by Peter S. Green, *International Herald Tribune,* February 15, 2000, p. 1.

82   Joining the E.U.: "Benefits and Costs of EU Enlargement for Present Members, First-Round Candidates and Other Associated Countries," by Andras Inotai, a paper prepared for the Annual Bank Conference on Development Economics-Europe, Paris, June 21–23, 1999, World Bank, www.worldbank.org/research/abcde/eu/inotai.pdf.

82   Print articles on globalization: "Is It Globaloney?" by Karen Lowry Miller, *Newsweek,* December 16, 2002, p. 43.

82   Chinese out of poverty: "Enter the Dragon," *The Economist,* March 10, 2001, Special Section.

13. THRUST REVERSERS

84   Clinton: "Clinton Hails Globalization's Gains," by Alvin Powell, *Harvard University Gazette,* November 19, 2001, www.news.harvard.edu/gazette/2001/11.29/09-clinton.html.

84   Washington consensus: "Doubts Inside the Barricades—The IMF," *The Economist,* September 28, 2002, Special Report.

84   Security forces: "Stormy History of Anti-Globalization Protests," Agence France Presse, July 23, 2001.

85   Protesters meet leaders: "From the Streets to the Inner Sanctum," by Evelyn Iritani, *Los Angeles Times,* February 20, 2005, p. C1.

85   AIDS protests: "AIDS Activists Resume a Get-Tough Campaign," by Fred Tasker, *Miami Herald,* July 13, 2002, p. A1.

85   Child labor: "As Attacks Grow Against Globalization, Protesters Resist Labels That Define Them," by Alessandra Rizzo, Associated Press, July 17, 2001.

85   Tobacco: "Challenging Corporate Abuse, Building Grassroots Power," Infact, www
     .infact.org/homepg~2.html.

85   Prisoners' rights: California Prison Focus and other groups, www.prisons.org.

86   Argentina collapse: "Argentina's Crisis: It's Not Just Money," by Larry Rohter, *New
     York Times,* January 13, 2002, p. D4. Also, "Uruguay Plans to Float Its Currency on
     World Markets," by Thomas Cattan, *Financial Times,* June 21, 2002, p. 8.

86   Asian crash and global meltdown. "Point—Possibly," by Cesar Bacani, *Asiaweek,*
     October 9, 1998, p. 58. Also, "Asia Rebounds Against Odds From Crisis," by Stephen
     Seawright, *South China Morning Post,* January 1, 2000, p. 5.

86   *Titanic:* "Cheap Rivets Blamed for Sinking of Titanic," by Peter Conradi, *Sunday Times*
     (London), February 1, 1998.

86   "Circuit breakers": "SEC Approves Stock Exchange Circuit Breakers," Investment
     Company Institute, April 16, 1998, www.ici.org/issues/mrkt/arc-nasd/98_circuit
     _approve.html. Also, "SEC Revises Rules to Halt Market Drop," Bloomberg News, in
     the *Dallas Morning News,* April 11, 1998, p. 1F.

86   Trading collars: "NYSE Sets New Levels for 'Circuit Breakers,'" by David Wells,
     Bloomberg News, in the *Milwaukee Journal Sentinel,* March 31, 2003, p. 2D.

86   Measures in India: "New Circuit Breaker System on SES From Monday," *Business
     Line,* a publication of the Hindu of India group, March 29, 2002.

86   Circuit breakers in Taiwan: "Taiwan's Investors React Cautiously to New Stock Trad-
     ing System," *Taiwan Economic News,* July 2, 2002.

86   Export overload: "A Big Threat to Asia's Export-Driven Economies," by David Bar-
     boza, *New York Times,* March 21, 2003, p. W1.

87   China tries to reduce exports: "Beijing Seeks Ways to Boost Domestic Demand," by
     Peggy Sito, *South China Morning Post,* October 23, 2001, p. 4.

87   U.S. and world demand: "U.S. Economic Slowdown Is Easing Its Way Around Globe,"
     by Evelyn Iritani and Thomas S. Mulligan, *Los Angeles Times,* January 11, 2001, p. A1.

87   Zambian copper: "Zambia: Transforming a Copper-Dependent Economy," by Allan
     Peters, Inter Press Service, October 21, 2002.

87   Nigeria's oil: "Civilian Rule Brings Oil Money—but Little Progress—to a Corner of
     Nigeria's Delta," by Glenn McKenzie, Associated Press, August 11, 2002.

87   Saudi revenues: "A Test for the House of Saud," by Stanley Reed, *Business Week,* No-
     vember 26, 2001, p. 42.

87   Arab oil: "Gulf Leaders to Review IMF Call for Taxes as Oil Income Dwindles,"
     Agence France Presse, December 30, 2001.

87   Angolan oil: "2002–2003/Economy: Prospects Mixed for Southern Africa," by
     Anthony Stoppard, Inter Press Service, December 30, 2002.

87   Venezuelan oil: "Venezuelan Oil Output Climbs as Strike Against Chavez Shows Signs
     of Waning," by Fabiola Sanchez, Associated Press, January 28, 2003.

87   Russia's revenues: "Putting OPEC over a Barrel: Russia's Oil Plan Could Push West-
     ern Pump Prices Down," by Sharon LaFraniere, *Washington Post,* March 16, 2002,
     p. E1.

87   Mercosur and East Asian blocs: "Toward an East Asian Economic Community," by Ari
     A. Perdana, *Jakarta Post,* February 18, 2003.

14. THE SPACE DRIVE

90   ATM, phones: "The ABCs of GPS," by Glen Gibbons, *IPI Global Journalist,* Fourth
     Quarter 2002, p. 3.

90 Dialysis: "A New Commitment to Space," by Bill Nelson, *Washington Post,* February 2, 2003, p. B7.

90 Pacemakers: "NASA Plans to Show You How Space Program Helps You Live," by Will Hoover, *Honolulu Advertiser,* April 4, 2001, p. 1F.

90 GPS development, costs: "Location, Location, Location," *Red Herring,* October 17, 2005, p. 30.

90 $100 billion industry, revenue growth: "2001–2002 Satellite Industry Indicators Survey," conducted for the Satellite Industry Association by the Futron Corp., www.sia.org/satelliteinfo.htm.

90 Space-industry stocks: "Market Focus," by Anthony L. Velocci Jr., *Aviation Week & Space Technology,* June 10, 2002, p. 8. Also, "Space Shuttle Loss Hurts Lockheed, Other NASA Stocks," by Robert Little, *Baltimore Sun,* February 4, 2003, p. 1D.

91 Ukraine and Brazil: "Partnership with Ukraine to Use Alcantara Rocket Base," *Gazeta Mercantil,* September 20, 2002.

91 Alcantara launch site: "Columbia Disaster Could Push Brazil to Rethink Its Space Program," by Bernd Radowitz, Associated Press, February 2, 2003.

91 Equity firms: "Private Equity Firms Make a Bet on Satellite Companies," by Ken Belson, *New York Times,* April 18, 2005, p. C1.

91 MAP: "Mapping Alliance Program Provides Earth Imagery and Information Products to Markets Worldwide," a Space Imaging news release, November 19, 1996, www.spaceimaging.com/newsroom/1996_mapping_alliance.htm.

91 "Weather futures": "More Companies Try to Bet on Forecasting Weather," by Del Jones, *USA Today,* March 3, 2003, p. 1B.

91 Weather variations: "LIFFE to Launch Weather Futures Contracts," an exchange news release, November 23, 2001, Weather Risk, www.wrm.de/cgi-bin/wrm.pl?read=83.

91 Weather risk: "Atmospheric Research: Understanding Atmospheric Events to Save Lives and Property Worldwide," U.S. National Oceanic and Atmospheric Administration, January, 2001, www.oar.noaa.gov/organization/backgrounders/atmosphere.html.

91 U.S. economy: "Economy—United States, 2001 Est.," *World Factbook 2002,* www.bondtalk.com/factbook2002/geos/us.html.

91 Dialysis patients: "A Better Option for Dialysis Patients," by Linda Marsa, *Los Angeles Times,* February 3, 2003, p. F1. Also, "Spinoffs from the Space Program," National Aeronautics and Space Administration, March, 2000, www.hq.nasa.gov/office/pao/facts/HTML/FS-012-HQ.html.

91 StelSys: "StelSys Set to Score a First in Space," by Julie Bell, *Baltimore Sun,* May 30, 2002, p. 1C.

91–92 NASA health benefits: (Brain tumors) "Space Technology Helps Advance Cancer Treatment," by Susan James, *Florida Today,* May 22, 2002, News, p. 1; (Blindness) British Broadcasting Corp., "NASA Laser Could Reverse Blindness," British Broadcasting Corp., July 10, 2002, http://news.bbc.co.uk/1/hi/health/2119537.stm; (Osteoporosis and heart pump) "Shuttles Are Known Best for Exploration, but Researchers Say They Do Plenty of Good on Earth," by Jeff Donn, Associated Press, February 6, 2003.

92 Heart disease costs: "Heart Disease and Stroke Statistics—2003 Update," American Heart Association, www.americanheart.org/presenter.jhtml?identifier=3000090.

92 "Bioreactor": "Zero-Gravity Experiments Continue at Station," by Eric Schmidt, *Denver Post,* February 6, 2003, p. B2.

92 Engineered hearts: "Growing Demand for Spare Hi-Tech Hearts," by Dawn Stover, *Melbourne Sunday Herald Sun,* November 19, 2000, p. L1. Also, "Patches for a Broken Heart," National Aeronautics and Space Administration, February 14, 2002, http://science.nasa.gov/headlines/y2002/14feb_heart.htm.

92 Diabetes costs: "Health, Financial Costs Related to Diabetes Soar," by Patrick O'Neill, citing results of an American Diabetes Association study of 2002 costs, Portland *Oregonian,* February 28, 2003, p. D1.

92 SPOT-4: "Satellite Instruments," European Ozone Research Coordinating Unit at Cambridge University, www.ozone-sec.ch.cam.ac.uk/VINTERSOL/Planning%20Document/Satelliteinst.html.

92 Forest fires: "POAM III Observes Forest Fire Emissions in the Stratosphere," *2001 NRL Review,* a publication of the U.S. Naval Research Laboratory, with reference to J. Hornstein, et al., 2001, p. 82.

92 Brazil-NASA project: "Ecological, Global Change Studies in the Amazon Rainforest," National Aeronautics and Space Administration, June, 2000, http://earthobservatory .nasa.gov:81/Newsroom/Campaigns/LBAFacility.html.

92 Polar ice: "Ice, Cloud and Land Elevation Satellite (ICESat)," National Aeronautics and Space Administration, http://icesat.gsfc.nasa.gov/.

92 Satellite projects: (Water utilization) "Mojave Desert's Surface Drop Linked to Century of Groundwater Use," Associated Press, February 24, 2003; (Fisheries) "Ocean Scientists Study Mysterious Zones Near Pacific Shore," by David Perlman, *San Francisco Chronicle,* February 16, 2003, p. A6; (Estuaries) "Satellites Cull Secrets from Lake Sediments," *New Orleans Times-Picayune,* November 28, 2002, p. 18; (El Niño) "Weak El Niño Means Less Snow in West," by Lee Bowman, Scripps Howard News Service, March 6, 2003.

92 Space-shuttle images: "Shuttle's Cameras Offer New Views of the World," by Warren E. Leary, *New York Times,* January 29, 2002, p. F5. Also, "Ancient City of Angkor Wat Yields New Secrets," by Alexandra Witze, *Dallas Morning News,* June 8, 1998.

93 NAVSTAR: "Fact Sheet—NAVSTAR Global Positioning System," U.S. Air Force, May 2002, http://131.84.1.31/news/factsheets/NAVSTARGlobalPositioningSy.html.

93 Europe's GPS: "Galileo Cleared to Take On GPS," from Bloomberg News, in the *Montreal Gazette,* June 28, 2005, p. B7.

93 Shipping containers: "U.S. Customs Inspectors Deployed to Seaports of Rotterdam in ontainer Security Initiative," U.S. Mission to the European Union, August 26, 2002, www.useu.be/Categories/Justice%20and%20Home%20Affairs/Aug2602Customs RotterdamContainerSecurity.html.

93 Cargo inspections: "Devices to Secure Ship Containers; New Locks Allow Tracking and Can Even Call Security," by Eli Sanders, *Boston Globe,* February 6, 2003, p. A3.

93 Tracking systems: "Move Over Bar Codes: Here Come the RFIDs," by Teresa F. Lindeman, *Pittsburgh Post-Gazette,* February 27, 2005, p. A1.

94 Airport capacity: "FAA's Garvey Sees Grim Future for Air Travel," by Jon Hilkevitch, *Chicago Tribune,* April 30, 2001, Metro, p. 1.

94 GPS increases capacity: "How to Fix the Air-Traffic Mess," by Cait Murphy with Alynda Wheat, *Fortune,* June 25, 2001, p. 116.

94 Lower GPS costs: "Technology That Watches Over Us: Satellite-Based Air Traffic Control," by Geoff Nairn, *Financial Times,* October 9, 2002, FT Report, Business of Space, p. 3.

94 Global Differential GPS: "NASA Navigation Work Yields Science, Civil, Commerce Benefits," Jet Propulsion Laboratory, October 14, 2002, www.jpl.nasa.gov/releases/2002/release_2002_191.cfm.

94 Midwest Research study: "Reach for the Stars," by Rahul Jacob, *Fortune,* September 25, 1989, p. 6.

94 Chase study: "Space Program Pays Big Tax Refund," by former astronaut Jim Lovell, Knight Ridder/Tribune News Service, April 19, 1999. Also, "Space: Investing in the Future," by Robert Sherman Wolff, *Christian Science Monitor,* October 28, 1981, p. 23.

94   Algeria, Pakistan, Nigeria, small satellites: "Military and Industry Strive to Profit from Space," by Fiona Harvey, *Financial Times,* December 27, 2002, p. 8.

95   Nations with space programs: "3rd World Sets Sights on Space," by Peter Pae, *Los Angeles Times,* October 14, 2003, p. A1.

95   Companies competing: "Commercial Space Travel Has Become a Reality with SpaceShipOne," *Omaha World-Herald,* October 8, 2004, p. B6.

95   Ansari X Prize: "SpaceShipOne Wins $10 Million Ansari X Prize in Historic 2nd Trip to Space," by Leonard Davis, Space.com, www.space.com/missionlaunches/xprize2_success_041004.html.

95   Mars landing and Internet: Statement to the authors on May 26, 2004.

15. THE EDGE OF KNOWLEDGE

99   Binh: "Vietnam's Women of War," by David Lamb, *Los Angeles Times,* January 10, 2003, p. A1.

99   Raseikina: "GM Stakes Out Russian Frontier," by Daniel Howes, *Edmonton Sun,* June 29, 2001, p. DR14.

100 Knowledge components: It is sometimes suggested that "wisdom" is a fourth, higher category. But because there is almost zero agreement as to what wisdom might be, we will treat it here as a subset of knowledge, a decision some will no doubt find unwise.

101 Start of Yahoo!: "Building a Better Engine," by Dawn C. Chmielewski, *Orange County Register,* May 9, 2000, p. G8.

101 Smith and FedEx: "Capitalists of the World, Innovate!" by Polly LaBarre, *Fast Company,* February 1999, p. 76. Also, "The Essence of Entrepreneurial Success," by Richard L. Osborne, *Management Decision,* 33 (1995), no. 7, pp. 4–9.

101 Toshiba: "World's Smallest Hard Drive Less Than an Inch Long," *Chicago Sun-Times,* March 17, 2004, p. 6.

101 Nanoscale storage: "Nano Memories Roll Past Flash Densities," by Nicolas Mokhoff, *Electronic Engineering Times,* July 1, 2002, p. 24.

102 Lockheed Martin and Boeing: "Lockheed Sues Boeing in an Escalating Feud," by Peter Pae, *Los Angeles Times,* June 11, 2003, p. C1.

102 Value of physical vs. informational goods: Boisot, [23], p. 83.

16. TOMORROW'S "OIL"

104 Oil industry: "Energy Story, Chapter Eight: Fossil Fuels—Coal, Oil and Natural Gas," California Energy Commission, April 22, 2002, www.energyquest.ca.gov/story/chapter08.html.

105 Manufacturing, information, professional workers: "The American Work Force," chart accompanying article by Peter Francese, *American Demographics,* February 2002.

105 Computers in trucks: "Keeping Trucks on Track," by Thomas W. Gerdel, *Plain Dealer* (Cleveland), October 20, 2002. p. G1.

107 Early societies: Ochoa, [193], p. 1. Also, "New Find Shows Early Toolmakers Smarter Than Previously Thought," by Peter Svensson, Associated Press, citing a study published that week in *Nature,* May 6, 1999.

107 First pictographs: "Paintings in Italian Cave May Be Oldest Yet," by Michael Balter, *Science,* October 20, 2000, p. 419.

108 Annual "knowledge" storage: "How Much Information? 2003," Senior Researchers Peter Lyman and Hal R. Varian, University of California–Berkeley School of Information Management and Systems, October 27, 2003, www.sims.berkeley.edu/research/projects/how-much-info-2003/.

108   ASK: The term Aggregate Knowledge Supply refers only to human data, information and knowledge, as do references here and elsewhere to the concept of a "global brain." But humans are not the only species dependent on knowledge. Animals, too, store, process and communicate their own knowledge about the world we and they live in. Some day, we can speculate, the collective knowledge of the animal kingdom may be integrated with that of humans and yield insights no human cultures alone could generate, vastly, therefore, expanding ASK.

109   Information and knowledge, memorization: Michael Lesk. "How Much Information Is There in the World?," a 1997 technical paper, www.lesk.com/mlesk/ksg97/ksg.html.

109   "Total memory": Ibid., extrapolating on research by T. K. Landauer published as "How Much Do People Remember? Some Estimates of the Quantity of Learned Information in Long-Term Memory" in *Cognitive Science,* October–December 1986, pp. 477–493.

110   Woolfson quote: Woolfson, [290], p. 80.

17. THE OBSOLEDGE TRAP

112   Aristotle on eels: Cerf, [43], citing Aristotle's *Spurious and Dubious Works,* p. 303.

112   Indian Ocean: "Monsoons, Mude and Gold," *Saudi Aramco World,* July–August, 2005, p. 10.

112   Porphyry: Garnsey, [100], p. 88.

112   Saint Isadore: Cerf, [43], citing White, [282], p. 303.

112   Da Vinci: *The Notebooks of Leonardo Da Vinci,* Edward MacCurdy, ed. (Old Saybrook, Conn.: Konecky & Konecky, 2003), p. 1075.

112   Toxic tomatoes, eater: "Let Them Eat Caju," *New Scientist,* September 2, 2000, p. 3.

112   Jupiter in 1892, Barnard: *The World Almanac: The Complete 1968 Original and Selections from 25, 50 and 100 Years Ago* (New York: Pharos Books, 1992), p. 213.

112   Jupiter in 2003: "Studying Moons Helps Fill Out Picture of Solar System," by Alexandra Witze, *Dallas Morning News,* May 19, 2003, p. E1.

112   Planet count: "9 Planets? 12? What's a Planet, Anyway?" by Dennis Overbye, *New York Times,* October 4, 2005, p. F1.

112   Air purity: "Impure Air Not Unhealthful If Stirred and Cooled," *New York Times,* September 22, 1912, p. 38, quoting L. Erskine Hill.

113   CERN meeting: "Minutes of the 57th Meeting Held on 11 September 2002," Advisory Committee of CERN Users, http://ep-div.web.cern.ch/ep-div/ACCU/Minutes/Previousminutes/Minutes57.pdf.

114   Harrington: "Harrington Like a Machine," by Art Spander, *Daily Telegraph* (London), June 13, 2003, p. 2.

114   Horseless carriages: "First Cross-Country Drive Propelled Auto Age," by Mike Toner, *Atlanta Journal-Constitution,* May 19, 2003, p. 1A.

18. THE QUESNAY FACTOR

115   Bush and CEA, press spokesman: "White House Forecasts Often Miss the Mark," by Dana Milbank, *Washington Post,* February 24, 2004, p. A1.

116   Long-Term Capital Management: "From Jones to LTCM: A Short (-Selling) History," by Sharon Reier, *International Herald Tribune,* December 2, 2000, p. 16. Also, "When Theory Met Reality: Teachings of Two Nobelists also Proved Their Undoing," by Gretchen Morgenson and Michael M. Weinstein, *New York Times,* November 14, 1998, p. A1.

116   Russian economy: "By Putting Too Much Faith in One Team of Reformers, America Only Added to Russia's Economic Mess," by Andrew Nagorski, *Newsweek,* December 7, 1998, p. 41.

116   IMF and Asian crisis: "The Asian Financial Crisis: Hindsight, Insight, Foresight," by Wing Thye Woo, *ASEAN Economic Bulletin,* published by the Institute of Southeast Asian Studies, August 1, 2000, Vol. 17, no. 2, p. 113. Also, "'Solution' Leaves Legacy of Bitterness: The IMF in Indonesia," by Alan Beattie and Tom McCawley, *Financial Times,* August 9, 2002, p. 5.

116   Indonesian violence: "Retailers Still Remember May Tragedy Five Years Later," by Arya Abhiseka, *Jakarta Post,* May 13, 2003.

116   "Hall of shame": "Dismal Prophets," *Financial Times,* December 31, 2001, p. 12.

116   Consensus forecasts: "Economic Forecasts Shift in the Wind," by Guy Boulton, *Milwaukee Journal Sentinel,* June 11, 2001, p. D1.

116   *Wall Street Journal* report: "Economic Forecasts Usually Wrong," by Bruce Bartlett, National Center for Policy Analysis, www.ncpa.org/iss/eco/2002/pd010202a.html, citing an article published January 2, 2001, in the *Wall Street Journal.*

116   IMF on foreign economists: "Conference Examines U.S. Economic Uncertainties, Exchange Rate Choices, and Globalization" www.imf.org/external/pubs/ft/survey/2001/012201.pdf, citing Prakash Loungani of the IMF's External Relations Department, in comments at the January 5–7, 2001, conference of the American Economic Association. Also, Bartlett, "Economic Forecasts Usually Wrong."

116   IMF and Thailand: "The Disinformation Gap," by David J. Rothkopf, *Foreign Policy* (March 22, 1999), no. 114, p. 82.

117   Inadequate data: Employment data become harder to collect and interpret when a "job" is not a job because so many people are now self-employed, employed part-time or, for that matter, part-time employers themselves, all at the same time. Rust-belt statistics yield more and more obsoledge. But once a certain set of data has been collected for long periods, economists and statisticians dislike changing or redefining the set because it makes comparisons over time difficult.

118   Robert Solow: "The Fruits of Fieldwork," *The Economist,* August 17, 2002.

118   Jeffrey Eisenach: Interviews with the authors, June 2005.

119   Psychologists, anthropologists: The belated shift toward a more interdisciplinary economics introduces refreshing, previously unasked questions and insights. But there remains another border to be breached. Most mainstream or Western economists have yet to reach out for, and perhaps test, insights from Asian, Middle Eastern and other non-Western cultures and economics.

120   Quesnay's life: "Francois Quesnay: His Life, His Work, His Legacy," by Benoit Delzelle, 2002, http://bdelzelle.free.fr/quesnay.pdf. Also, Staley, [252], pp. 32–37. Also, Loebl, [155], pp. 16–19. Also, Clough, [51], pp. 358, 517.

121   Quesnay on sterile class: Clough, [51], p. 517.

19. FILTERING TRUTH

124   Intelligence committee: "Experts: Unreliable Data, Belief in WMD Led to Mistakes in Iraq," by Matt Kelley, Associated Press, October 7, 2004.

124   Iraqi defectors: "The Conflict in Iraq; Suspicion of Chalabi Deception Intensifies," by Bob Drogin, *Los Angeles Times,* May 23, 2004, p. A1.

125   Warren Buffett: "Invest in Warren Buffett's Market-Beating Stock," by Fiona McGoran, *Sunday Times* (London), March 30, 2003, Business and Money, p. 17.

125   Ali al-Sistani: "A Formidable Muslim Bloc Emerges," by William O. Beeman, *Los Angeles Times,* May 27, 2003. p. B13.

125   Papal infallibility: Eric O. Hansen, *The Catholic Church in World Politics* (Princeton, N.J.: Princeton University Press, 1987), p. 34.

125   CBS: "CBS Must Regain Courage in Wake of Rather Report," by David Shaw, *Los Angeles Times,* October 10, 2004, p. E18.

125   *New York Times:* "Mutiny at the Times," by James Poniewozik, *Time,* June 16, 2003, p. 48.

125   *Le Monde:* "Le Monde at War," by Jo Johnson, *Financial Times,* May 10, 2003, Weekend Magazine, p. 24.

125   Richard Gere: "A Tough Time to Talk of Peace," by Barbara Crossette, *New York Times,* February 12, 2002, p. B1.

125   Barbra Streisand: "Hollywood Goes to War," by Julian Coman, *Sunday Telegraph* (London), October 6, 2002, p. 27.

125   Welch, now retired: "Welch Asks GE to Cut His Package," by Andrew Hill, *Financial Times,* September 17, 2002, p. 1.

126   Presumptive authority: "The Birth of the Modern Mind: An Intellectual History of the 17th and 18th Century," Alan Kors, an audiotape lecture series from the Teaching Company (Chantilly, Va., 1998).

127   Science inherently antifanatic: Scientists win prizes for *disconfirming* earlier findings. Writes physicist Lawrence M. Kraus in the *New York Times,* April 22, 2003, p. D3: "Proving one's colleagues (and oneself) wrong is one of the great pleasures of scientific progress."

127   Method of discovery: Needham, [187], p. 122.

127   Francis Bacon: Pyenson, [218], pp. 3, 77–78.

127   Scientific pursuit: ". . . And Still We Evolve," a liberal studies handbook prepared by Ian Johnston for Malaspina University-College in British Columbia, Canada, May 2000, Section 1, p. 1, http://malaspina.edu/~johnstoi/darwin/sect1.htm.

128   Doctors in commercials: "Drug Firm Pulls TV Ad Amid Debate," by Bruce Japsen, *Chicago Tribune,* April 19, 2005, p. C1.

128   Dole, Armstrong: "Celebrity Plugs for Antidepressants Raise Questions," by Ed Silverman of the *Newark Star-Ledger,* on the Newhouse News Service, August 19, 2004.

128–9   Gain concept: Loebl, [155], pp. 23–25.

20. TRASHING THE LAB

130   Number of scientists growing: "Scientists and Engineers: Crisis, What Crisis?" by Mario Cervantes, OECD Observer, January 2004, www.oecdobserver.org/news/printpage.php/aid/1160/Scientists_and_engineers.html.

130   U.S. spending for R&D: "R&D Expenditures," table 4-1, "Science and Engineering Indicators, 2004," National Science Foundation, www.nsf.gov/statistics/infbrief/nsf04307.

130   Foreign researchers in U.S.: "Science and Engineering Indicators—2002 Overview," National Science Foundation, www.nsf.gov/sbe/srs/seind02/c0/c0s1.htm.

130   IBM R&D, patents, licensing income: "IBM Is Patent King Again," *The Economist,* February 19, 2005.

130   Horn: "Research Chief Is Thinker AND Doer," by Therese Poletti of Knight-Ridder Newspapers, published in the *Seattle Times,* April 4, 2005, p. C3.

130–31   IBM's income: "Financial Information, 2004," from IBM's Web site, www.ibm.com/investor/financials/index.phtml

131   Technical progress: Gary Bachula, in testimony before the Technology Subcommittee of the U.S. House of Representatives, February 11, 1999, www.house.gov/science/bachula021199.htm.

131   National Science Foundation report: "Strong R&D Spending Buttresses U.S. Economic Growth, Report Shows," National Science Foundation, April 30, 2002, www.nsf.gov/od/lpa/news/02/pr00228.htm.

131   Razor blades: "Terror Tactics," by Nell Boyce, *New Scientist,* November 6, 1999, p. 55.

131   Morrissey: "Morrissey Supports Animal Rights Violence," by Jason Allardyce, *Sunday Times* (London), January 15, 2006, p. 7.

131   Other violence: "Violence in the Name of Mercy," by Mark Lowey, *Calgary Herald,* March 21, 1992, p. B4.

131   Scientists and corporations: Rampton, [220]. Cozy financial links between government scientists and pharmaceutical and biomedical firms have drawn congressional scrutiny and criticism. In 2004, Republican Senator Arlen Spector told officials of the National Institutes of Health that "there are really major problems here."

132   Cause to be cautious: There are good reasons to be careful in the application of potentially powerful new scientific advances. But a "precautionary principle" that demands 100 percent risk-free science and technology is a formula not for the preservation of nature but for the most *unnatural* and impossible stasis. As we noted in *Future Shock* in 1970: "The incipient worldwide movement for control of technology . . . must not be permitted to fall into the hands of irresponsible technophobes, nihilists and Rousseauian romantics. . . . Reckless attempts to halt technology will produce results quite as destructive as reckless attempts to advance it."

132   "Franken-foods": "Europe Shows Little Taste for U.S. Biotech Crops," by Greg Burns, *Chicago Tribune,* October 30, 2002, Business, p. 1.

132   Protectionism in Europe: "Agriculture Impasse 'Threatens Doha,'" by Frances Williams, *Financial Times,* February 28, 2003, p. 8.

132   Zimbabwe: "Starved for Food, Zimbabwe Rejects U.S. Biotech Corn," by Rich Weiss, *Washington Post,* July 31, 2002, p. A12.

132   James Morris: "Zambia Turns Away GM Food Aid for Its Starving," by James Lamont, *Financial Times,* August 19, 2002, p. 4.

132   Monsanto: "Monsanto Struggles Even as It Dominates," by David Barboza, *New York Times,* May 31, 2003, p. C1. Also, "Predictable Surprises: The Disasters You Should Have Seen Coming," by Michael D. Watkins and Max H. Bazerman, *Harvard Business Review,* March 2003, p. 72. Also, "Sowing Disaster?" by Mark Shapiro, *The Nation* 275 (October 28, 2002), no. 14, p. 11.

132   Seed fire: "Letter Claims Responsibility for Monsanto Fire, ANSA Says," Associated Press, April 5, 2001. Also, "Arsonists Burn Monsanto Depot in Italy," Associated Press, in the *St. Louis Post-Dispatch,* April 4, 2001, p. C2.

132   Prince Charles interview: "Respect for the Earth, A Royal View," part of the Reith Lecture Series 2000, British Broadcasting Corp., http://news.bbc.co.uk/hi/english/static/events/reith_2000/lecture6.stm.

132   Charles on scientific tyranny: "Prince Charles Urges 'Materialistic' West to Seek Guidance from Islam," by Kate Watson-Smyth, *Guardian* (London), December 14, 1996, p. 4.

132   Creationists: "Not Just in Kansas Anymore: Opposition to the Teaching of Evolution," by Eugenie C. Scott, *Science* 288 (May 5, 2000), no. 5467, p. 813.

133   Unabomber: Chase, [48], pp. 18, 21, 84, 87–88. Letters were sent to the *New York Times, Washington Post* and *Penthouse.*

133   Richard Gosden: "Academics Fear Exodus in 'Anti-Science' Backlash," by David Pilling and Sheila Jones, *Financial Times,* September 24, 1999, p. 11.

133 Astrology Ph.D.: "ET in the Sorbonne," by Eric Hoogcarspel and Jan Willem Nien-huys, *Skepter,* June 2001, www.skepsis.nl/doctorteissier.html. Also, "An Academic Dis-pute That Is Out of This World," by Magnus Linklater, *The Times* (London), August 16, 2001.

133 Political war on science: "A Vast Conspiracy," by Adam Keiper reviewing *The Republi-can War on Science,* by Chris Mooney (New York: Basic Books, 2005), *National Re-view,* October 10, 2005, p. 48.

134 Institutions lag science fraud: "Global Trend; More Science, More Fraud," by Lawrence K. Altman and William J. Broad, *New York Times,* December 20, 2005, p. D1.

134 Confine new science: "Biotechnology: Mary Shelley or Galileo Galilei?" by Philip Stott in the *ACU Bulletin,* Issue 144, published by the Association of Commonwealth Universities in London. June 2000, www.acu.ac.uk/yearbook/144-stott.html.

134 Drug research and poor: "Hale and Healthy," *The Economist,* April 16, 2005.

134 Gender bias in research, feminists: Harding, [120] and [121].

134 Animal testing: "The Fur and the Fury," by Rose Palazzolo, *ABC News,* April 12, 2000, http://abcnews.go.com/sections/living/DailyNews/cosmetictesting0000412.html.

134 New weapons: "300 March on LANL" (Los Alamos National Laboratory), by Ian Hoff-man, *Albuquerque Journal,* August 10, 2000, p. 1.

135 New Age wholesalers, posters: *The New Age Wholesale Directory, 2003 Edition,* and *Your Own New Age Poster Store . . . for Only $40 Bucks!,* both at www.newagereseller .com.

135 *New York* cover: "Psychic New York: The City's Supernatural Superstars," *New York,* April 21, 2003.

135 New Age beliefs: Hanegraaff, [119], pp. 23–27, 125, 265, 271, 341, 517.

135 Origins of postmodernism: "Moral Relativity Is a Hot Topic? True. Absolutely," by Edward Rothstein, *New York Times,* July 13, 2002, p. B7.

135 Postmodernism and business: (Knowledge management) "Post Modern Knowledge Management and Social Enterprise Blogging," by Luigi Canali De Rossi, MasterMind Explorer Review, February 7, 2003, www.masternewmedia.com/issue25/post _modern_knowledge_management.htm; (SMEs) "Advanced Business Communica-tions in Europe," European Commission's research and innovation information Web site, www.cordis.lu/infowin/acts/ienm/products/ti/toc.htm; (Brunel) Brunel Univer-sity School of Business and Management, www.brunel.ac.uk/dept/sbm/postgraduate/ index.shtml?2; (Simon Fraser) Simon Fraser University, www.bus.sfu.ca/courses/ bus303/; (Las Vegas) "Background Ideas for Deconstructing Las Vegas," by David M. Boje, August 29, 1999, from the New Mexico State University Web site, http:// cbae.nmsu.edu/~dboje/postmodvegas.html.

136 Ecology and religion: "Environmental Colonialism," by Robert H. Nelson, *The Inde-pendent Review,* Summer 2003, Vol. 8, no. 1, p. 65.

136 Anti-science groups: While individual antiscience movements may start from different premises, use their own specialized jargons and pursue different tactical agendas, they often swap ideas, stereotypes and mischaracterizations of both scientists and science.

137 Baltimore on secrecy: "Baltimore Discusses Science, Community," by Eun J. Lee, *The Tech,* Massachusetts Institute of Technology 122 (February 22, 2002), no. 6.

137 Baltimore on knowledge: "Scientists in the Age of Terror and Knowledge-Based Economies," by David Baltimore, *New Perspectives Quarterly,* March 18, 2002, www .digitalnpq.org/global_services/nobel%20laureates/03-18-03.html.

137 Relinquishing research: "Why the Future Doesn't Need Us," by Bill Joy, *Wired,* April, 2000, www.wired.com/wired/archive/8.04/joypr.html.

138 Scientific disaster: Rees, [222], pp. 1–4, 127–129.

21. THE TRUTH MANAGERS

141 Bloggers: "The Young Stir Up a News Storm," by Brendan O'Neill, *Sunday Times* (London), June 5, 2005, p. 12.

141 Celebrity politicians: "Lights! Camera! Reactionaries!," by Jack Mathews, New York *Daily News,* September 5, 2004, Sunday Now, p. 4.

141 Amateur moviemakers: "The DVD: Democratizing Video Distribution," by Elaine Dutka, *Los Angeles Times,* June 21, 2005, p. E5.

141 Bloggers: Following the principle that "If you can't beat them, join them," some newspapers are experimenting with "participatory journalism" by inviting readers to add their thoughts to an unedited Web site, to rewrite staff-written stories and add them to a site created by the newspaper for that purpose, or to write and publish their own articles subject to editing by professionals.

141 Catholic church: "Sex Abuse Scandal Dominates Meeting of U.S. Catholic Bishops," by Janice D'Arcy, *Baltimore Sun,* June 17, 2005, p. A8.

142 End of Enlightenment: Many intellectuals in the West today welcome all too glibly the approaching end of the Enlightenment era. They attack the weaknesses of determinism, mechanism and linear thinking. But they often forget that the Enlightenment also introduced or spread the key ideals behind what we now, with all its faults, call democracy. These include the concept of individual human rights protected by the state, the separation of powers, religious tolerance, due process in the courts and the recognition that widespread access to knowledge is a precondition for the development and survival of democracy. Before those of us who enjoy these benefits shut the door on the Enlightenment, we had better make sure we don't turn off the lights that it turned on.

22. CODA: CONVERGENCE

146 Al-Farabi: "Abu Al-Nasr Al-Farabi," Trinity College in Hartford, Conn., www .trincollege.edu/depts/phil/philo/phils/muslim/farabi.html.

146 Europe and Al-Farabi: "The Arab Forebears of the European Renaissance," an interview with Alain de Libera in UNESCO's *Courier* magazine, February 1997.

146 *Trivium* and *quadrivium:* "A New Trivium and Quadrivium," George Bugliarello, Polytechnic University of New York, November 8, 2001, www.poly.edu/news/speech/ newTQ.cjm.

147 Beer, diapers and Pop-Tarts: "Fishing for Data," by Peter N. Spotts, *Christian Science Monitor,* November 27, 2002, p. 18. The article refers to a supermarket that used its database to learn that men who bought beer in advance of televised football games were also likely to buy diapers, presumably at the behest of their wives. The store then relocated its diaper supplies next to its beer cases. Similarly, "What They Know About You," by Constance L. Hays, *New York Times,* Sunday, November 14, 2004, p. C1, reports that marketers mined databases to learn that sales of Pop-Tarts increased by seven times just ahead of an impending hurricane.

147 Salmonella: "Genetic Fingerprinting Finds Unexpected Sources of Food Poisoning," by Daniel Q. Haney, Associated Press, October 16, 2000.

147 Mangos: Ibid., citing Robert V. Tauxe, chief of food-borne diseases at the Centers for Disease Control and Prevention.

23. THE HIDDEN HALF

151   Subsistence population: "A Hopeful Way Out of Poverty," by Shashi Tharoor, *International Herald Tribune,* July 5, 2002, p. 6. Also, "World Bank Finds Global Poverty Down by Half Since 1981," U.N. Wire, April 23, 2004.

152   Total annual output: "Bush Tax-Cut Plan Is a Drop in the World's Bucket," by Eric Pfanner, *International Herald Tribune,* January 10, 2003, p. 11.

153   Our term *prosumer* was first used in *The Third Wave* (New York: William Morrow, 1980, hardcover; and Bantam Books, 1981, paperback). See especially chapter 3, "The Invisible Wedge" for its impact on gender, personality and society.

154   Sharon Bates: "Devoted Mother in Line for Top Award," *Derby* (UK) *Daily Telegraph,* March 4, 2003, p. 12.

154   Enki Tan: Meanwhile his wife, Cheri Nursalim, began setting up a branch of the United in Diversity Foundation to provide follow-up help with relief, reconstruction and education in Aceh.

154   Twenty-eight countries: "A Resort for Volunteers," by Kultida Samabuddhi, *Bangkok Post,* March 28, 2005.

154   Bruce Lampard: "Doctors Learn Cultural Sensitivity in Far-Off Trouble Spots," by Joseph Kim, *Toronto Star,* February 8, 2003, p. Z29.

154   Marta Garcia: Interviews with the authors, May 2005.

154   Katsuo Sakakibara: "Volunteer Activities Work Wonders," *Nikkei Weekly,* July 23, 2001.

155   "socially cohesive": "Will the Real Economy Please Stand Up?" by Hazel Henderson, *Christian Science Monitor,* May 3, 1982, p. 23. In the same article, Henderson noted that: "Such nonmarket, socially cohesive work, as well as the vital caring and parenting of children, still comprises over 50 percent of all the world's real economic activity— even in industrial societies."

155   Japan Ministry statement: "Social Structure Must Change Ahead of Population Decline," by Noriko Sakakibara, *Daily Yomiuri,* August 6, 2005, p. 4.

155   Family meal, halved living standard: "Cost of Family Breakdown," by Stein Ringen, *Financial Times,* September 23, 1996, p. 18.

155   Marxist reproduction: Karl Marx, *Capital* (New York: International Publishers Co., 1939), p. 578.

157   Books: Henderson, [124]; Cahn, [39]; Glazer, [110].

157   Nonworking time: Becker, [15], pp. 90–114. This chapter is a reprint of Becker's "A Theory of the Allocation of Time," first published in *Economic Journal* 75 (September 1965), no. 299, pp. 493–517.

157   Calculating prosuming value: "Clustering and Dependencies in Free/Open Source Software Development," by Rishab Aiyer Ghosh, from the First Monday Web site @ http://firstmonday.org/issues/issue8_4/ghosh/index.html.

158–9   In partial recognition that prosumers generate wealth, the Venezuelan Constitution adopted in 1999 includes the following clause: "The State recognizes work at home as an economic activity that creates added value and produces social welfare and wealth. Housewives are entitled to Social Security in accordance with law." Chapter V, Social and Family Rights, Article 88.

24. THE HEALTH PROSUMERS

160   Hospital infections: "Stricter Antibiotics Use Urged," by M. A. J. McKenna, *Atlanta Journal-Constitution,* March 27, 2002, p. 4A.

160   Medical errors: "To Err Is Human: Building a Safer Health System," Institute of Medicine, a panel of the National Academy of Sciences, November 1999.

160 Rising health costs: "OECD Data Show Health Expenditures at an All-Time High," Organization for Economic Cooperation and Development, June 23, 2003. Also see Table 1. www.oecd.org/document/39/0,2340,en_2649_33929_2789735_1_1_1_1,00.html.

160 Aging populations: "Population Ageing: A Public Health Challenge," World Health Organization, September, 1998, www.who.int/inf-fs/en/fact135.html.

161 Sanitation improvement and disease eradication: "Control of Infectious Diseases in the U.S.," an article in the Centers for Disease Control and Prevention's *Morbidity and Mortality Weekly Report* 48 (July 30, 1999), no. 29, p. 621. Also from the CDC, "Achievements in Public Health, 1900–1999: Control of Infectious Diseases," July 30, 1999, www.cdc.gov/od/oc/media/mmwrnews/n990730.htm#mmwr1.

161 Communicable diseases: "Trends in Infectious Disease Mortality in the United States During the 20th Century," by Gregory L. Armstrong, Laura A. Conn and Robert W. Pinner, *Journal of the American Medical Association* 281 (January 6, 1999), no. 1 @ http://jama.ama-assn.org/cgi/content/abstract/281/1/61. Also, "Achievements in Public Health, 1900–1999: Control of Infectious Diseases," Centers for Disease Control and Prevention, July 30, 1999, www.cdc.gov/od/oc/media/mmwrnews/n990730.htm#mmwr1.

161 Main killer diseases today: "Leading Causes of Death," Centers for Disease Control and Prevention, U.S. statistics, 2000, www.cdc.gov/ncha/fastats/lcod.htm. Also, "Advances Begin to Tame Cancer," by Raja Mishra, *Boston Globe,* July 6, 2003, p. A1. Also, "Campaign Publicizes Obesity, Cancer Link," by Andre Picard, *Toronto Globe and Mail,* March 5, 2003, p. A2.

161 Populations over sixty and eighty, life expectancies, aging in Europe and Japan: "Population Ageing: A Public Health Challenge," World Health Organization, September 1998, www.who.int/inf-fs/en/fact135.html.

162 Health spending and GDP: "Total Expenditure on Health—% of Gross Domestic Product," Organization for Economic Cooperation and Development, www.oecd.org/dataoecd/44/18/35044277.xls.

162 Congressional Budget Office cost estimate, expenses underestimated: "The 2030 Problem: Caring for Aging Baby Boomers," by James R. Knickman and Emily K. Snell, *Health Services Research,* a journal from the American College of Healthcare Executives 37 (August 1, 2002), no. 4, p. 849.

162 Alzheimer's: "Alzheimer's in the Living Room," by Jane Gross, *New York Times,* September 16, 2004, p. A1.

163 Prescriptions: "Age Wave Holds Promise of Boom Times," by Richard Monks, *Chain Drug Review,* November 11, 2002, p. 33.

163 Comparative medical costs: "Aging Issues Move Mainstream," by Judith G. Dausch, *Journal of the American Dietetic Association* 103 (June 1, 2003), no. 6, p. 683.

164 *ER* and HPV: "TV Remains Dominant Source for Americans on Medical Information," by M. E. Malone, *Boston Globe,* March 12, 2002, p. C1.

164 TV documentary: "U.S. TV Documentary Program Awarded Japan Prize," Japan Economic Newswire, November 14, 2001.

164 Chinese television: "China's Millions Learning AIDS Prevention from TV," Xinhua News Agency, December 2, 2002. Also, "Chinese TV Series to Promote Sex Education," Xinhua News Agency, February 24, 2003.

164 Drug ads on TV: "Pharmaceutical Makers and Ad Agencies Fight to Preserve Campaigns for Prescription Drugs," by Stuart Elliott, *New York Times,* July 12, 2002, p. C2.

165 Levin on self-care: "What's Up, Doc?" by Alexandra Greeley, *The World and I,* November, 1987, www.worldandi.com/specialreport/1987/november/Sa13142.htm.

165 Home care in 1965: "From the Golden Age to the Crackdown Age," by Tom Gray, *HomeCare,* October 1, 2001, http://homecaremag.com/ar/medical_golden_age_crackdown/index.htm.

165   Diabetes products: "Report Predicts Double-Digit Growth for Diabetes Management Market," *HomeCare,* June 1, 2002, www.homecaremag.com/ar/medical_report _predicts_doubledigit/index.htm.

166   Home test kits: "Medical Testing at Home," by Mary Carmichael, *Newsweek,* May 19, 2003, p. 67. Also, "BioSafe PSA4 Prostate Cancer Screening Test," Craig Medical Distribution Inc., www.craigmedical.com/psa4_home.htm.

166   Supply catalog: FlagHouse catalog, Winter 1999–2000.

166   More home tests: (Kits for women) "FemaleCheck," Medical Home Products, Inc., www.medicalhomeproducts.com/product_info.php?cPath=29&products_id=30; (Colon cancer) "EZ Detect Colon Cancer Test," AbDiagnostics, www.homehealthtesting .com/coloncancertests.htm; (Osteoporosis) "OsteoCheck," BodyBalance, www .bodybalance.com/osteo/solution.html.

166   Home care systems and devices, T-shirt: "Emerging Trends in Medical Device Techology: Home Is Where the Heart Monitor Is," by Carol Lewis, in the Food and Drug Administration's *Consumer* magazine, May–June 2001, www.fda.gov/fdac/features/ 2001/301_home.html.

166   Home CAT scans: "Tech 2010: The Bathroom Where You Can Give Yourself a Daily Brain Scan," by Margaret Talbot, *New York Times,* June 11, 2000, p. F81.

167   Teaching health care: Lowell Levin, in an interview entitled "Power to the Patient," Health World Online, www.healthy.net/asp/templates/interview.asp?PageType=Interview &ID=263.

167   Game for diabetic children: Vikram Sheel Kumar, correspondence with the authors, December 10, 2001. The project is called DiaBetNet, with details as of February 27, 2003, available on the Verizon Web site, http:news/verizonwireless.com/news/ 2003/02/pr2003-02-27b.html.

25. OUR THIRD JOB

169   Canceled checks and employees: "Bank of America to Cut Up to 6.7% of Work Force, or 10,000 Jobs," by Diana B. Henriques, *New York Times,* July 29, 2000, p. C1.

169   ATM transactions: "ATM Fact Sheet," American Bankers Association, www.aba.com/ aba/pdf/commtools/atmfactsheet.pdf.

169   Global ATM transactions: "Cash Withdrawals: New Tower Group Analysis Finds Erosion in Return on Investment with ATMs," *Credit Union Journal,* December 2, 2002, p. 8.

169   Online stock traders: "Half of American Households Own Equities," Investment Company Institute and the Securities Industry Association, September 27, 2002, www .sia.com/press/html/pr_equity_ownership.html.

169   Online travel: "Travel Industry Sees Huge Rise in Trips Planned Online," by Karen Harrell, *Pensacola News Journal,* January 2, 2003, p. 2B.

169   Total online purchases: "2002 E-Commerce Holiday Wrap-Up," by Robin Greenspan, reporting the results of a BizRate market survey, January 3, 2003, from eCommerce-guide.com, http://ecommerce.internet.com/research/stats/article/0,,10371 _1563551,00.html.

169   General Electric: "General Electric's Spin Machine," by Mark Roberti, *Industry Standard,* January 22–29, 2001, p. 79.

170   Dohton Bori: "Originality Propels Growth at Start-Ups," *Nikkei Weekly,* November 18, 2002.

170   Clarence Saunders: "This Little Piggly Is Coming to Town," by Jenni Smith, *Dallas Morning News,* October 12, 2001, p. 5N.

170   Self-scan markets: "Now, Harried Shoppers Can Take Control at Supermarkets," by Lorrie Grant, *USA Today,* June 7, 2001, p. 1A.

170   No discount: "Short-Changed by Self-Service," by Donald L. Potter, *Los Angeles Times,* June 8, 2002, p. B23.

171   Amazon.com: "Reviewer Fills the Web Page for Amazon.com Book Sales," by Don O'Briant, *New Orleans Times-Picayune,* July 16, 2000, p. B4. For an example, see www .amazon.com/exec/obidos/ASIN/B000001VVY/qid=1060196237/sr=2-1/ref=sr_2_1/ 104-9500253-2764735.

171   Cartoon: *Dilbert,* by Scott Adams, April 27, 2003, distributed by United Feature Syndicate.

26. THE COMING PROSUMER EXPLOSION

172   Home Depot: "About the Home Depot," "Investor Relations" and "Corporate Overview," www.homedepot.com.

172   U.S. D-I-Y market: "Do It Yourself; What Drives Us to Take on Those Jobs?" by T. J. Becker, citing the Home Improvement Research Institute, *Chicago Tribune,* May 25, 2003, p. C1.

172   D-I-Y in Japan: "Japan," *Export America,* a magazine from U.S. Department of Commerce, www.ita.doc.gov/exportamerica/GlobalNewsLine/gnl_0103.

172   D-I-Y in Germany: "DIY Industry in 2002: Developments on the Overall German Market," Bundesverband der Deutschen Heimwerker-, Bau- und Gartenfachmärkte (BHB), March 9, 2003, www.textkonzept.com/bhb/Pmeng-PW03-trends.htm.

172   D-I-Y in Europe: "Report: Single Women World's Biggest Buyers," Reuters, published in *Newsday,* August 2, 2000, p. A50.

173   BBC programs: "Change Rooms at Your Peril," by Mark Keenan, *Sunday Times* (London), February 23, 2003, Features, Eire Ireland Home, p. 37.

173   Home improvement on U.S. TV: "The Fix Is On," by Gary Dymski, *Newsday,* November 14, 2002, p. B18.

173   Outside the U.S.: "About Us," Home and Garden Television, www.hgtv.com/hgtv/ about_us.

173   Appliance-repair sites: "This Week's Topic: Fixing It Yourself," by David Hayes, *Kansas City Star,* June 8, 2003, p. I16

173   Sears: "Parts to Fix All Major Brands No Matter Where You Bought Them," Sears, Roebuck and Co., www3.sears.com/intro.shtml.

173   Auto parts sales: "Odland's DIY Sales Initiatives Revitalize AutoZone," *Aftermarket Business,* December 1, 2001, Vol. 111, no. 12, p. 10.

173   U.S. gardening: "NGA Announces Lawn & Garden Statistics for 2002," National Gardening Association, www.nationalgardening.com/RSRCH/feature/asp.

173   Gardening in Britain: "Bloomin' Marvelous Business," by Helen Gibson, *Time International,* May 27, 2002, p. 54.

173   German gardening: "Gardening Industry in Germany," by Charles Pattinson, Trade Partners UK, from the British Government Web site, www.tradepartners.gov.uk/ recreation/germany2/profile/overview.shtml.

173   Gardening in Japan: "Business and Management Information," Nikkei Business Publications, www.nikkeibp.co.uk/pages/info_busandman.htm. Also, "Growing Popularity: The Burgeoning Gardening Boom," *Trends in Japan,* July 14, 1997, JapanEcho, www .jinjapan.org/trends98/honbun/njt970714. html.

173   Sewing: "Sewing: 30 Million Women Can't Be Wrong," by Mitchell Owens, referring to a report from the American Home Sewing and Craft Association, *New York Times,* March 2, 1997, p. A39.

173   Home dry cleaning: "How Home Dry Cleaning Works," by Ann Meeker-O'Connell, from the HowStuff Works Web site, www.howstuffworks.com/home-dry-cleaning.htm.

174 Digital tools: "Everyone's a Star.Com," by Romesh Ratnesar and Joel Stein, *Time*, March 27, 2000, p. 68.

175 Don Davidson: "Don Q. Davidson: Woodworking Hobby Becomes Family Business," an article on CareerJournal.com from *The Wall Street Journal*, 2000, and www .2young2retire.com/davidson.htm.

175 Neil Planick: "Hobby Becomes Business After Unexpected Layoff," by Tom Koch, *Inside Collin County Business*, July 1999.

175 Famous Amos cookies: "Amos, Wally," from A&E Television's Biography.com Web site, http://search.biography.com/print_record.pl?id=23645 Also, "Wally Amos: 'Turning Lemons into Lemonade',", Sterling International, www.sterlingspeakers.com/ amos.htm. Also, the Wally Amos Web site, www.wallyamos.com/about/about.html.

176 Computer gaming industry: "Computer Games and the Military: Two Views," by J. C. Herz and Michael R. Macedonia, *Defense Horizons*, April 2002, p. 2.

176 Computer gaming revenues: "Industry Structure: Computer Games," Department of Innovation, Industry and Regional Development for the state of Victoria, Australia, May 22, 2003, http://invest.vic.gov.au/Industry+Sectors/IT+and+Communications/ Industry+Structure:+Computer+Games.htm.

176 Torvalds, open code, support: "Open Source Drops Its Geeky Image and Adopts a Hard-Nosed Business Edge," by Colin Barker, *Computing*, April 10, 2003, p. 26. Also, "Linus Torvalds: A Humble Clark Kent of the Linux World," by Robert Thompson, *National Post* (Canada), May 18, 2000, p C3.

177 Linux in American companies: "Liberty, Technology, Duty," by Edward Rothstein, *New York Times*, May 8, 2004, p. B9.

177 Linux in China, India, Asia: "HP Launches Linux PCs, Asia Spurning Microsoft," by Peter Morris, *Asia Times*, March 19, 2004, www.atimes.com/atimes/China/ FC19Ad05.html.

177 Linux in Brazil: "Free Software's Biggest and Best Friend," by Todd Benson, *New York Times*, March 29, 2005, p. C1.

177 Investments, governments: "U.S. Government Agencies Turn to Linux," by Lisa Pickoff-White of United Press International, April 11, 2005, from the MacNewsWorld Web site, www.macnewsworld.com/story/42048.html.

177 Delegates urged: "U.N. Meeting Debates Software for Poor Nations," by Jennifer L. Schenker, *New York Times*, December 11, 2003, p. C4.

177 Other open-source programming: Linux is not the only example of prosuming programmers. According to *The Economist*, 800 volunteers from around the world—many working for such companies as Sun and Google—have, in their free time, developed Firefox, a Web browser that, like Linux, is based on open source and has already captured 8–10 percent of the global market. "Firefox Swings to the Rescue," *The Economist*, December 17, 2005, p. 64.

178 Web origins: Berners-Lee, [19], pp. 4–5.

178 Three billion Web sites: "Google Gamers' Word Pairings a Creative Addiction," by Barbara Feder Ostrov, *San Jose Mercury News*, May 31, 2003.

178 Total Web sites: Estimates of the total number of sites on the Web vary widely. Some estimates are as high as eight billion sites, as reported in "Google Insiders Sell $2.9 Billion," by Dan Lee, *San Jose Mercury News*, August 1, 2005, p. PT2.

178 Blogs: "Crashing the Blog Party," by Renee Tawa, *Los Angeles Times*, September 12, 2002, p. E1.

27. MORE "FREE LUNCH"

180   *Shobodan:* "Cold Water Thrown on Burning Ambition," by Tom Westin, *Daily Yomiuri,*
      April 5, 2002, p. 7.

180   Volunteer firefighters around the world: (Austria and Germany) "How to Run a
      Fire Service," *The Economist,* November 30, 2002; (Canada) Red Deer Volunteer
      Fire Department, www.reddeercountyfirefighters.com/mission.htm; (Finland) World
      FireDepartments.com, www.worldfiredepartments.com/International/finland.htm; (Italy)
      National Association of Voluntary Firefighters, www2.commune.bologna.it/bologna/
      assnvfv/maine.htm; (South Africa) "Volunteer Emergency Services," Station 15, Johan-
      nesburg, www.station15.org/za/get_content.php/public_home.htm; (Portugal) "Huge
      Fire Brought Under Control in Northern Portugal," by Daniel Silva, Agence France
      Presse, August 1, 2003.

180   Volunteers in U.S.: "A Nation of Volunteers," *The Economist,* February 23, 2002.

181   Hours and money value of volunteering: "Giving and Volunteering in the United States—
      2001," Independent Sector, www.independentsector.org/PDFs/GV01keyfind.pdf.

181   Great Hanshin earthquake: "Foreign Ships, Good Times Returning to Kobe Port," *Daily
      Yomiuri,* January 29, 2003, p. 25.

181   Kobe quake volunteers: "Japan's NGO Activities and the Public Support System," by
      Mitsuhiro Saotome of the Japanese Ministry of Foreign Affairs, 1997, from the Global
      Development Research Center Web site, www.gdrc.org/ngo/jp-ngoactivities.html.

181   South Korean volunteers: "World Volunteers, Recipient Nations Gather in Seoul for
      Biennial," *Korea Herald,* November 8, 2002.

181   Volunteer projects in Korea: (Typhoon relief) "Volunteers Give Ray of Hope to
      Despairing Flood Victims," *Korea Times,* September 9, 2002; (Home-building) "Habi-
      tat for Humanity Korea Gearing Up for a Busy Summer," *Korea Times,* May 15, 2003;
      (North Koreans) "Students Crossing the Korean Divide," by Barbara Demick, *Los
      Angeles Times,* August 24, 2002, p. A7. Also, "Fleeing to Culture Shock," by Barbara
      Demick, *Los Angeles Times,* March 12, 2002, p. A1.

181   Cancer care in Italy: "Volunteerism in Italy," by Claude Fusco Karmann, July 2000,
      Education Development Center, Inc., www2.edc.org/lastacts/archives/archivesJuly00/
      intlpersp.asp.

181   Floods in Germany: "Aid Floods In on a Wave of German Generosity," by Haig Si-
      monian, Bettina Wassener and Hugh Williamson, *Financial Times,* August 26, 2002,
      p. 5.

181   San Francisco earthquake: Japan Emergency Team, www.jhelp.com/en/jet.html.

182   Dying horses: "Mugabe Land Grab Leaves Horses to Starve," by Jenny Booth, *London
      Sunday Telegraph,* October, 2002, p. 21.

182   Red Cross/Crescent: "National Volunteer Week Advertising Feature: Join Red Cross
      Global Network," *Adelaide* (Australia) *Advertiser,* May 13, 2003, p. 49.

182   Tsunami aid: "United Nations Warns of Cash Shortage for Long-Term Tsunami Recon-
      struction Efforts," by Chris Brummitt, Associated Press, February 8, 2005.

182   Hot line: "Tsunami Volunteer Hotline Closes After 10,000 Calls," Australian Volunteers
      International, April 1, 2005, www.australianvolunteers.com/news/media/press/3378.

182   Flood of volunteers: "Tsunami Volunteers: Too Much of a Good Thing?" NetAid,
      www.netaid.gao.org/world_schoolhouse/actions/asia_crisis/.

182   Priestley, Fermat, Franklin: "Beating the Pros to the Punch," by K. C. Cole, *Los Angeles
      Times,* March 11, 1998, p. A1. Also, *The Columbia Encyclopedia,* 3rd ed.

182   Volunteer environmental studies: "Web Sites Let Public Join in Research Studies," by
      Donna Milmore, *Boston Globe,* December 12, 1999, p. H5.

182 Seismic volunteers: "Local Folks Equipped to Monitor Quakes," Philippine Department of Science and Technology, 2002, www.dost.gov.ph/media/article.php?sid=257.

183 Moonwatch: "After All These Years, Fred Whipple's Still Fascinated by Dirty Snowballs," by David L. Chandler, *Boston Globe,* October 28, 1996, p. C1.

183 Amateur astronomers: Hayes, [123].

183 Brigadier General Worden: "Better Asteroid Detection Needed, Experts Tell House Panel," by Robert S. Boyd, *San Jose Mercury News,* October 4, 2002. Also, "Asteroid Threat Discussed by U.S. Congress," by Keith Cowing, October 4, 2002, SpaceRef .com, www.spaceref.com/news/viewnews.html?id=509.

183 Richard Nugent: "Amateur Astronomy Section—Interview 2," an interview with Nugent conducted by *Astronomy Today*'s Lydia Lousteaux, from the Web site, www .astronomytoday.com/astronomy/interview2.html.

184 Kasnoff and Gedye, SETI deep-sky survey: "SETI@home," from the Planetary Society Web site, www.planetary.org/htm/UPDATES/seti/SETi@home/default.html.

184 SETI computers: "Supercomputing '@Home' Is Paying Off," by George Johnson, *New York Times,* April 23, 2002, p. F1.

185 Oxford and others: "Grid Computing: Thousands of Computers Linked in New Infotech Leap," by William Ickes, Agence France Presse, February 16, 2003. Also, "Getting More from a PC's Spare Time," by Joan Oleck, *New York Times,* September 11, 2003, p. G5.

185 Anthrax letters: "Reponse to Terror," by Megan Garvey, *Los Angeles Times,* January 31, 2002, p. A1.

185 Anthrax screening project: "Anthrax Screensaver Finds Promising New Drugs," *New Scientist,* February 19, 2002, www.newscientist.com/news/news.jsp?id=ns99991953. Also, "Anthrax Screening Project Completes In-Silico Screening in 24 Days," *TB and Outbreaks Week,* April 9, 2002, p. 12. Also, "Anthrax Research Project Completed; Check Your Country's Stats," United Devices, April 7, 2002, http://members.ud.com.

185 Distributed computing: "Sun Stroke," *The Economist,* Technology Quarterly, March 16, 2002. Also, "Girding for Grids," by Rob Fixmer, *Interactive Week,* January 7, 2002, p. 41. Also, "Grid Computing," by M. Mitchell Waldrop, *Technology Review,* May 2002, p. 31.

186 U.S. senior volunteers: "Retirees Rocking Old Roles," by Walt Duka and Trish Nicholson, December 2002, from the AARP Web site, www.aarp.org/bulletin/departments/ 2002/life/1205_life_1.html.

186 Japanese seniors: "Older Volunteers Offer Valuable Skills," *Nikkei Weekly,* January 28, 2002. Also, "Life: Silver Workers Still Sparkle," by Jeff Horwich, *Asahi Shimbun,* October 31, 1999.

28. THE MUSIC STORM

187 Hippiedom: Abbie Hoffman, *Steal This Book* (New York: Grove Press, 1971).

188 Napster users: "There's Still Hope for Napster Despite Stream of Troubles," by Jefferson Graham, *USA Today,* May 23, 2001, p. 3D.

188 Shawn Fanning: "Meet the Napster," by Karl Taro Greenfeld, with Chris Taylor and David E. Thigpen, *Time,* October 2, 2000, p. 60. Also, Fattah, [87], pp. 4–8.

188 Napster downloads: "Napster Tones Down the Downloads," by Ronna Abramson, citing the online music research firm Webnoize, *Industry Standard,* May 1, 2001.

188 David Benveniste: "Now Fans Call the Tune," by Geoff Boucher, *Los Angeles Times,* August 3, 2003, p. E1.

188   Kazaa: "Skype Is 2nd Jackpot for Scandanavian Duo," by Ivar Ekman, *International Herald Tribune,* September 13, 2005, p. 8.

188   Powell: "Catch Us If You Can," by Daniel Roth, *Fortune,* February 9, 2004, p. 64.

189   Today a trickle: "Wind Power Generates Income," by James R. Healey, *USA Today,* August 16, 2002, p. 1B. Also, "Business Forum: Regenerating History," by David Morris, *Minneapolis Star Tribune,* April 28, 2002, p. 8D.

189   Federal energy policy: "Wind Energy Program," U.S. Department of Energy, www.eren.doe.gov/wind/web.html.

190   Fuel-cell R&D: "Fuel Cells Vs. the Grid," by David H. Freeman, *Technology Review,* January/February 2002, p. 42.

190   Energy visionaries: "Conversations: Amory Lovins," by Jim Motavalli, *E:The Environmental Magazine,* March–April 2000, www.emagazine.com/march-april_2000/0300conversations.html.

191   Stereolithography: "Look and Feel," by David C. Churbuck, *Forbes,* November 9, 1992, p. 292.

191   Fabbers are based: "How It Works: If You Behave Yourself, I'll Print You a Toy," by Peter Wayner, *New York Times,* May 29, 2003, p. G8.

191   Penske Racing: "Penske, 3D Join Forces for Parts," *Los Angeles Daily News,* January 19, 2002, p. SC9.

191   Fabbing uses and products: "Future Tech: Behold, the 3-D Fax!" by Brad Lemley, *Discover,* February, 2000, www.discover.com/feb_00/feat3dfax.html.

191   Companies: "Application Solutions," 3D Systems, www.3dsystems.com/appsolutions/atwork_listing.asp.

191   Desktop fabrication, current research, ferrari.fab: "Napster Fabbing: Internet Delivery of Physical Products," a presentation by Marshall Burns and James Howison for the February 16, 2001, O'Reilly Peer-to-Peer Conference in San Francisco, from the Ennex Corp., www.ennex.com/publish/200102-Napster/index.asp.

191   Desktop fabrication may have a dark side, as well. Could "fabbers" be used to turn out illegal handguns, or anonymous cell phones?

191–92   Pictures on toast: "Microfinance, Microfab," by Neil Gershenfeld, *Forbes,* April 25, 2005, p. 32.

192   Fabrication inevitable, Watson forecast: Gershenfeld, [105], p. 63.

192   PCs: "PCs in Use Surpassed 820M in 2004," *Computer Industry Almanac,* March 9, 2005, www.c-i-a.com/pr0305.htm.

192   Nanotechnology: Drexler, [76].

193   Nanoproducts: "Could Tiny Machines Rule the World?" by Michael Crichton, *Parade,* November 24, 2002.

29. THE "PRODUCIVITY" HORMONE

195   PCs in the United States: "Internet Indicators," International Telecommunication Union, March 15, 2005, www.itu.int/ITU-D/ict/statistics/.

195   PC users: "153 Million U.S. Net Users and Counting," by Stefanie Olsen, March 28, 2003, CNET News.com, http://zdnet.com.com/2100-1104-994418.html.

195   Early PCs: "What Ever Happened to . . . Kit Computers?" by Stan Velt, *Computer Shopper* 14 (April 1994), no. 4, p. 595.

195   Radio Shack and TRS-80s: "Recalling What Tandy Meant to an Industry," by Cathy Taylor, *Orange County Register,* May 27, 1993, p. C1.

196   Systems operator: "At Home with Ubiquitous Computing," by W. Keith Edwards and Rebecca E. Grinter, 2001, www.grinter.org/ubicomp.pdf.

196   Sarvodaya Camp: Interview with Sugata Mitra in New Delhi. Also see "Rajender Ban
       Gaya Netizen," by Parul Chandra, *Times of India,* May 12, 1999. Also, "A Lesson in
       Computer Literacy from India's Poorest Kids," an interview with Sugata Mitra by
       Thane Peterson, March 2, 2000, *Business Week,* www.businessweek.com/bwdaily/
       dnflash/mar2000/nf00302b.htm.

197   Peer teaching: Though it is unlikely to have been measured, it is reasonable to assume
       that the speed with which the children learned was accelerated by the transfer of know-
       how among them, so that as one child learned, he showed others what to do. Each
       learner, in short, served as a temporary "micro-guru." Similar informal teaching and
       learning run through daily life in the economy and the larger society. We have few if any
       data about the impact of this process on either. We cannot assume that everything can
       be self-taught, or that self-appointed "gurus" can replace instructors and teachers of
       advanced skills. But it is unlikely that the money economy could function without the
       ongoing transfer of a great deal of unnoticed, unpaid for and unmeasured "microlearn-
       ing." To speak of a knowledge economy and ignore this form of round-the-clock teach-
       ing and learning in the society is the equivalent of going to the Louvre, focusing on a
       single hair on Mona Lisa's head and never noticing the smile.

30. CODA: INVISIBLE CHANNELS

199   Cuba Gooding Jr.: *Jerry Maguire* (Tristar, 1996). Also, "50 Greatest Sports Movies,"
       Sports Illustrated, August 4, 2003, p. 62.

199   Tom Robbins: Des MacHale, *Wit* (Boulder, Co.: Roberts Rinehart, 1998), p. 9.

199   The contributions of prosumers to the money economy raise a host of fascinating ques-
       tions. Should prosumers be paid in money for their currently unpaid efforts? Does this
       threaten to reduce all human interactions to the cash nexus? And if prosumers should be
       monetarily rewarded, where is a line to be drawn? For example, "Pass me the fork—I'll
       pay a quarter"? Or "I'm forgoing a salary of, say, $75,000 a year to stay home and raise
       a child. Shouldn't I be paid for doing that?" Should prosumers get "frequent service
       points" exchangeable for airline tickets, computers, tax rebates or, for that matter, face-
       lifts if what they do is producive—i.e., contributes to productivity in the money econ-
       omy? Seemingly far-fetched questions like these are likely to get serious attention
       tomorrow as the prosumer economy explodes and prosuming is recognized as a vital
       part of revolutionary wealth.

31. THE GOSPEL OF CHANGE

205   U.S. doctorates to foreign-born: "S&E Degrees Earned by Foreign Students Within
       Each Field, by Level: 1998–1999," chart (2–20), National Science Foundation *Science
       & Engineering Indicators, 2002,* www.nsf.gov/sbe/srs/seind02/c2/fig02-20.htm.

205   Graying of NASA: "Chief Says NASA Losing Skilled Workers; Experienced Staff Is
       Retiring Faster Than Recruits Hired," by Patty Reinert, *Houston Chronicle,* March 7,
       2003, p. A10.

205   Centers of technology-based activity: "The Graying of NASA," by Shirley Ann Jack-
       son, release from the Office of the President, Rensselaer Polytechnic Institute, in
       Research USA, April 28, 2003.

205   U.S. R&D budget: *Science and Engineering Indicators, 2002,* "U.S. and International
       Research and Development: Funds and Alliances"; also appendix table 4–40, National
       Science Foundation, www.nsf.gov/sbe/srs/seind02/c4/c4s4.htm#c4s-411.

205–6   Nobel Prizes: A compilation of laureates from the Nobel Foundation's Web site, www .nobel.se/.

206   U.S. cultural exports: "American Pop Penetrates Worldwide," by Paul Farhi and Megan Rosenfeld, *Washington Post,* October 25, 1998, p. A1. Also, "Creative Destruction" by Tyler Cowen, *Milken Institute Review,* third quarter, 2003.

206   Dumb: *Dumb and Dumber* (New Line Cinema, 1994).

206   "no education": This was the studio's promotion line for the film *School of Rock* (Paramount, 2003), as noted in "High Decibel," by Kenneth Turan, *Los Angeles Times,* October 3, 2003, p. E1.

207   Studio ownership, multinational filmmaking: Tyler Cowen, *Creative Destruction: How Globalization Is Changing the World's Cultures* (Princeton, N.J.: Princeton University Press, 2002).

207   Timbuktu: Interview with authors on September 3, 2002.

209   Heraclitus: Heraclitus, *Fragments* (circa 500 BC). Referenced by Richard Geldard, in *Remembering Heraclitus* (Great Barrington, Mass.: Lindisfarne, 2000), p. 158.

32. IMPLOSION

211   Nuclear families: "The Traditional US Family Increasingly Less Common," by Jean-Michel Stoullig, citing U.S. Census Bureau data, Agence France Presse, May 15, 2001.

211   Single-parent, no-parent homes: "A Healthy Shot in the Arm for Marriage," by Darryl E. Owens, citing the Census Bureau, *Orlando Sentinel,* July 20, 2003, p. F1.

211   U.S. elderly: "Seniors' Health: Living Alone," Aetna InteliHealth, referencing the U.S. Department of Health and Human Services, November 14, 2001, www.intelihealth.com/ IH/ihtIH/WSIHW000/22030/22031/337761.html?d=dmtContent.

211   U.S. divorce rate: "Hitch Switch," by Matthew Grimm, *American Demographics,* November 1, 2003, p. 9.

211   "Rehearsal marriage": "Starter Marriages." ABC News, January 25, 2002, http:// abcnews.go.com/sections/GMA/GoodMorningAmerica/GMA020125Feature _starter_marriage.html.

212   School enrollment in U.S.: "School Enrollment 2000," U.S. Census Bureau, www .census.gov/prod/2003pubs/c2kbr-26.pdf.

212   U.S. school spending: "Revenues and Expenditures for Public Elementary and Secondary Education: School Year 1999–2000," National Center for Education Statistics, www.nces.ed.gov/pubs2002/quarterly/summer/3–7.asp.

212   Students and reading: "Are Middle and High School Students Reading to Learn or Learning to Read?" by Joan Kuersten, citing a 1998 report from the National Assessment of Educational Progress, National Parent Teacher Association, www.pta.org/ parentinvolvement/parenttalk/read.asp.

212   Student math skills: "Can't Read, Can't Count," by Rodger Doyle, *Scientific American,* October 2001, www.sciam.com/article.cfm?articleID=0002514E-D727-1C6E-84A9809 EC588EF21.

212   Pacific Ocean: "Young Americans Flunk Geography, According to National Geographic Quiz Survey," by Paul Recer, Associated Press, November 20, 2002.

212   D.C. schools: "Revenues and Expenditures for Public Elementary and Secondary Education: School Year 1999–2000," National Center for Education Statistics, www .nces.ed.gov/pubs2002/quarterly/summer/3–7.asp.

212   D.C. test scores: "D.C. Rates Poorly in Reading, Writing," by Justin Blum, *Washington Post,* July 23, 2003, p. B5.

212 Enron: "Enron Bankruptcy Examiner Also Lays Much Blame with Banks," by Matthew Goldstein, TheStreet.com, July 28, 2003, www.thestreet.com/markets/matthewgoldstein/10104107.html.

213 Accounting scandals: "The Corporate Scandal Sheet," by Penelope Patsuris, *Forbes,* August 26, 2002, www.forbes.com/2002/07/25/accountingtracker.html. Also, "Annus Horribilis: Corporate Scandals, Lingering Recession Made 2002 Truly Horrible Year," by Verne Kopytoff, *San Francisco Chronicle,* December 29, 2002, p. G1. Also, "The Fires That Won't Go Out," by Janice Revell with Doris Burke, *Fortune,* October 13, 2003, p. 139. Also, "Third Former Rite-Aid Exec Pleads Guilty," by Mark Scolforo, Associated Press, June 26, 2003.

213 Satirists: "Remaining U.S. CEOs Make a Break for It," SatireWire, June, 2002, www.satirewire.com/news/june02/ceonistas.shtml.

213 Costs of scandals: "Corporate Scandals Cost More than $200 Billion, Report Says." By Marcy Gordon, referring to a study by the "No More Enrons" Coalition, Associated Press, October 17, 2002.

213 Health spending in U.S., Haiti: "Human Development Indicators 2003," United Nations Development Program, listing PPP expenditures by country for 2000, www.undp.org/hdr2003/indicator/indic_59_1_1.html.

213 Uninsured Americans: "Number of Uninsured Rose Dramatically Last Year, Figures Show," by Tony Pugh, citing a U.S. Census Bureau report, Knight Ridder/Tribune News Service, September 30, 2003.

213 Medical errors: "To Err Is Human: Building a Safer Health System," Institute of Medicine, a panel of the National Academy of Sciences. November 1999.

213 Alzheimer's: "Statement of Sheldon Goldberg, CEO and President of the Alzheimer's Association," to the House Appropriations Subcommittee on Labor, HHS and Education, Federal Document Clearing House, May 7, 2003.

214 Treasury Secretary John Snow: "Pension Funds and Stocks: A Longtime Alliance at Risk," by Mary Williams Walsh, *International Herald Tribune,* July 29, 2003, p. 12.

214 Train wreck: "Tripping Over Pension Shortfalls," by David Henry, *Business Week,* May 14, 2003.

214 Pension shortfall, PBGC: "U.S. Pension Agency Says It May Need a Bailout," by Kathy M. Kristof, *Los Angeles Times,* October 15, 2003, p. C1.

214 United Way: "United Way to Delay Severance Deal," by Jacqueline L. Salmon, *Washington Post,* September 28, 2002, p. B1.

214 Red Cross: "American Red Cross Faces New Disaster," by Jacqueline L. Salmon, *Washington Post,* May 19, 2003, p. A8.

214 Media scandals: "Yet Another Wake-Up Call," by Michael Getler, *Washington Post,* May 22, 2005, p. B6.

215 Newspaper ills: "Black and White and Read by Fewer," by James Rainey, *Los Angeles Times,* October 10, 2005, p. C5.

215 U.S. intelligence and 9/11: "U.S. Intelligence Bobbled 9/11 Clues," CBS News, reporting on a just-released congressional investigation into the incident, September 19, 2002, www.cbsnews.com/stories/2002/09/18/national/main522460.shtml. Also, "Missed Clues, but Old Battle," by Peter Grier, *Christian Science Monitor,* May 20, 2002, p. 1.

215 California recall election: "Voter Guide: Candidate Close-Ups," *Los Angeles Times,* September 28, 2003, p. S4. Also: "Schwarzenegger Sworn In as Governor of California," by Mary Anne Ostrom and Ann E. Marimow, *San Jose Mercury News,* November 19, 2003.

216 Japan's divorce rate: "Divorces Hit All-Time High in Japan as Stigma Against Breaking Up Fades," by Gary Shaefer, Associated Press, September 17, 2003.

216   Marriage in Japan: "The Land of Parasite Singles," by Phillip Longman, *Business 2.0,* September 2003, p. 105.

216   Korea's divorce rate: "Divorce in South Korea: Striking a New Attitude," by Norimitsu Onishi, *New York Times,* September 21, 2003, p. A19.

216   Britain's families: "Married Homes Are Now the Exception," by Alexandra Frean, *The Times* (London), February 14, 2003, p. 5.

216   Japan's classrooms: "'Classroom Collapse' Gripping Schools Nationwide," by Tomoko Otake, *Japan Times,* March 28, 2002. Also, "Educators Try to Tame Japan's Blackboard Jungles," by Howard W. French, *New York Times,* September 23, 2002, p. A6.

216   Bad loans in Japan: "Seven Major Banks Post Losses for Second Straight Year," *Daily Yomiuri,* May 27, 2003, p. 1.

216   Tokyo power company: "TEPCO Reveals Cover-Ups, Resignations," Asahi News Service, September 18, 2002.

216   Corporate scandals in Japan: "Japanese Companies Forced to Bolster Corporate Governance," Foreign Press Center of Japan, September 19, 2002, www.fpcj.jp/e/shiryo/jb/0233.html. Also, "Nissho Iwai Hid Y1.8 Billion," *Daily Yomiuri,* July 26, 2005, p. 2.

216   Tokyo Stock Exchange crises: "Mizuho Announces Steps to Prevent Stock Trade Blunders," Asia Pulse, January 23, 2006. Also, "Tokyo Bourse to Review Trading System Following Computer Glitches," Associated Press, January 31, 2006.

217   Daewoo: "Daewoo Corruption Scandal Deepens," British Broadcasting Corp., February 2, 2001, http://news.bbc.co.uk/2/hi/business/1149061.stm.

217   Hyundai: "Curse of the Korean Kennedys," by Richard Lloyd Parry, *The Times* (London), August 14, 2003.

217   SK: "SK Chief Gets Three-Year Prison Term for Financial Irregularities," by Jae-Suk Yoo, Associated Press, June 13, 2003.

217   Parmalat: "Parmalat Chief Admits Diverting Funds," from Reuters, published in the *Los Angeles Times,* December 30, 2003, p. C3.

217   Crédit Lyonnais: "Federal Reserve Fines French Bank $100 Million," by Lisa Girion, *Los Angeles Times,* December 19, 2003, p. C2.

217   Skandia: "Skandia Sues Ex-Executives Over Bonuses," by Christopher Brown-Humes, *Financial Times,* December 31, 2003, p. 20.

217   Elf: "France Probes 'Misuse of Funds' in Gas Project," by Paul Betts and Michael Peel, *Financial Times,* October 13, 2003, p. 6.

217   Royal Dutch/Shell: "Will Shell Change Its Retail Course?" by Christopher O'Leary, *Investment Dealers Digest,* May 3, 2004.

217   British Council on Health system: "Is the NHS Falling Apart?" British Council, http://elt.britcoun.org.pl/h_nhs.htm.

217   German health service: "Schröder's Little Win," by Peter Schneider, *New York Times,* September 25, 2002, p. A21.

217   Sweden: "Swedish Health System Feels the Economic Pinch," by Nicholas George and Nicholas Timmins, *Financial Times,* November 28, 2003, p. 20.

217   Japan's health system: "Blueprint for Health Care Reform," *Mainichi Daily News* (Tokyo), March 31, 2003, p. 2.

217   France's pensions: "The Crumbling Pillars of Old Age," *The Economist,* September 27, 2003, p. 69.

217   European retirees: "Europe Faces a Retiree Crisis," by Gene Koretz, *Business Week,* May 15, 2000, p. 38.

217   Pensions in Japan: "Social Security on the Edge: Sweeping Reform of Pension System Needed," by Kenji Uchida, *Daily Yomiuri,* May 20, 2002, p. 1.

217 Korea's pensions: "Thoughts of the Times: National Pension Crisis," by Harry Ha, *Korea Times,* August 19, 1999, www.koreatimes.co.kr/14_8/199908/t485139.htm.

217 Siemens: "Nest Eggs Without the Yolk," *The Economist,* Special Report, May 10, 2003.

217 *Le Monde:* "Le Monde Dismisses Author of Critical Book," by Jo Johnson, *Financial Times,* October 1, 2003, p. 2.

217 *Le Figaro:* "In France, a Newspaper Editor's Legal Woes Are Minor News," by Angela Doland, Associated Press, June 26, 2003.

217 *Asahi:* "Asahi's Bungled Story," *Asahi Shimbun,* September 2, 2005.

217 War Child: "Pavarotti Charity Cash Was Spent on TV Film," by Maurice Chittenden, *Sunday Times* (London), January 14, 2001. Also, "Stars Quit Charity in Corruption Scandal," by David Hencke, *Guardian* (London), January 10, 2001, www.guardian.co.uk/uk_news/story/0,3604,420167,00.html.

218 oil-for-food: "Texas Businessman Indicted in U.N. Oil-for-Food Probe," by Phil Hirschkorn, Cable News Network, April 14, 2005, www.cnn.com/2005/LAW/04/14/oilfood.indictment.

218 Annan: "Annan Cleared Over Oil-for-Food," British Broadcasting Corp., March 29, 2005, http://news.bbc.co.uk/1/hi/world/americas/4391031.stm. Also "Annan's Post at the U.N. May Be at Risk, Officials Fear," by Warren Hoge and Judith Miller, *New York Times,* December 4, 2004, p. A3.

218 Peacekeepers: "Explicit Photos Fan U.N. Sex Scandal," by Maggie Farley, *Los Angeles Times,* February 12, 2005, p. A4.

218 Terminal crisis: "The Struggle for Iraq," by Felicity Barringer, *New York Times,* September 24, 2003, p. A13.

218 World Bank: "Who's Minding the Bank?" by Stephen Fidler, *Foreign Policy,* September 1, 2001, p. 40.

33. CORRODING THE WIRES

220 World falling into decay: Alexis de Tocqueville, *Democracy in America,* bk. 4, chap. 8.

220 Franklin murder: "Sniper Spree Suspects to First Stand Trial in Virginia," by Curt Anderson, Associated Press, November 8, 2002. Also, "FBI Analyst Survived Cancer to Fall to Sniper's Bullet in Virginia," by Justin Bergman, Associated Press, November 8, 2002. Also, "The Making of a Murder Spree," *U.S. News & World Report,* November 4, 2002, p. 22.

220 Rapid Start: "FBI Technology Shortcomings Hamper Sniper Investigation," by Shane Harris, *Government Executive,* October 23, 2002, www.govexec.com/dailyfed/1002/102302h1.htm.

220 Timothy McVeigh: "Oklahomans Remember Bombing of Federal Building," by Jack Douglas Jr., Knight Ridder/Tribune News Service, in the *Fort Worth Star-Telegram,* April 20, 2002.

220 FBI computer overhaul, system status: "FBI Technology Upgrade More Than a Year Away," by Brian Friel, *Government Executive,* June 21, 2002, www.govexec.com/dailyfed/0602/062102b1.htm.

221 Hauled over political coals: "F.B.I. May Scrap Vital Overhaul for Computers," by Eric Lichtblau, *New York Times,* January 14, 2005, p. A1.

221 Louis Freeh: "Analysis: 'Patterns of Global Terrorism' Report," *Washington Post,* quoting National War College Prof. Melvin Goodman, May 22, 2002, http://discuss.washingtonpost.com/wp-srv/zforum/02/nation_goodman052202.htm.

221 Sniper laptop: "Prosecution Wraps Up Its Capital Case Against Muhammad," by Stephen Kiehl, *Baltimore Sun,* November 11, 2003, p. 1A.

221 Robert Hanssen: "FBI Ignored Warning Signs About Hanssen," by Barbara Bradley, National Public Radio's *Morning Edition,* April 4, 2002.

221 Franklin's FBI job: "Capsules of Individuals in the Sniper Shootings Case," Associated Press, October 11, 2003.

221 Postal facility: "Tests Point to Domestic Source Behind Anthrax Letter Attacks," by Scott Shane, citing U.S. Rep. Rush D. Holt (D-N.J.), *Baltimore Sun,* April 11, 2003, p. 1A.

221 Slammer virus: "Slow Slammer Response Points to NIPC Woes," by Paul Roberts, IDG News Service, January 28, 2003, from the Network World Fusion Web site, www.nwfusion.com/news/2003/0128slowslamm.html.

221 Hijacker visas: Gerald Posner, *Why America Slept* (New York: Random House, 2003), p. 169.

221 State Department: "Inside the Committee That Runs the World," by David J. Rothkopf, *Foreign Policy,* March/April 2005, p. 34.

222 Avian pandemic: According to former U.S. Speaker of the House Newt Gingrich, "federal, state and local governments will need to act with the speed and agility of the information age. Unfortunately, our government cannot operate at anything approaching this level." See "To Fight the Flu, Change How Government Works," by Newt Gingrich and Robert Egge, *New York Times,* November 6, 2005.

223 Sony shares: "Out of the Shadows," by Jim Frederick, *Time International,* March 21, 2005, p. 18.

223 Greenpeace: "About Us," www.greenpeace.org/international_en/aboutus/.

223 Oxfam: "About Us: Organisation of Oxfam GB," www.oxfam.org.uk/about_us/organisation.htm.

34. COMPLEXORAMA

225 Ohio U. graduates: "School of Recreation and Sports Sciences, Sports Administration and Facility Management: Overview," Ohio University, @ www.ohiou.edu/sportadmin/overview.htm.

225 Cape Town cricket: "Aspects of Sports Engineering," by A. T. Sayers, University of Cape Town, www2.mech.kth.se~erik1/sports.html.

225 Sports software: "Introduction to Sports Scheduling," FriarTuck, July 11, 2003, www.friartuck.net/solution/spors/htm.

226 Snobs: "Condescension, or by Another Name, Snobbery," by Alan Riding in his review of Epstein, [84], *New York Times,* August 21, 2002, p. E7.

226 Passat: "Arnold's VW Swan Song," by Mae Anderson, *Adweek,* September 26, 2005.

226 Astronomically rising complexity: Gates, [103].

226 Banking in Germany: "The First Directorate: Banking Supervision," Federal Financial Supervisory Authority, www.bafin.de/english/bafin_e.htm.

226 Basel II: "Asia Faces a Stark Choice," by Tom Holland and Joel Bagiole, *Far Eastern Economic Review,* September 25, 2003, www.feer.com/articles/2003/0309_25/p050money.html.

226 U.N. trade conference: "International Investment Instruments: A Compendium, Vol. XIV," United Nations Conference on Trade and Development, January 3, 2005, www.unctad.org/Templates/webflyer.asp?docid=5889&intItemID=2323&lang=1.

227 Software: "Everyone's a Programmer," by Claire Tristram, *Technology Review,* November 2003, p. 36.

227 Microsoft code: "Microsoft's Midlife Crisis," by Victoria Murphy, *Forbes,* October 3, 2005, p. 88.

227   I.T. complexity: "Ross: Systems Complexity Threatens Security," by William Jackson, *Government Computer News,* April 5, 2002, www.gcn.com/vol1_no1/daily-updates/18337-1.html.

227   Cato on tax code: "Simplifying Federal Taxes: The Advantage of Consumption-Based Taxation," by Chris Edwards, *Policy Analysis* (October 17, 2001), no. 416, pp. 1–2.

227   Low U.S. savings rate: "Key Reason USA Doesn't Save: Too Much of a Hassle," *USA Today,* January 4, 2002, p. 12A.

227   Demand for accountants: "Accounting Major," University of Scranton, http://matrix.scranton.edu/academics/ac_factsheet_accounting.shtml.

227   Accounting complexity: "Accounting: Facts and Trends," Careers in Accounting, www.careers-in-accounting.com/acfacts.htm.

227   Medical specialties, trials: "Enabling Prospective Health Care," by David M. Lawrence, 2002, from the Web site for the 2002 Duke University Private Sector Conference, http://conferences.mc.duke.edu/2002dpsc.nsf/contentsnum/af.

228   Complexity and Europe: "Managing Complexity: The New Challenge," European Commission's Innovation and SMEs Programme, published in its *Innovation & Transfer Technology* newsletter, May 2002, and www.cordis.lu/itt/itt-en/02-3/innov03.htm.

228   State solutions: "Can France Be Reformed?" by Wendy Thomson of the British Prime Minister's Office of Public Services Reform, in a speech for the Economist Conference in Paris, January 29–30, 2003.

228   University complexity: "Internationalism and Globalization: The Rising Complexity of the Policy Field HE," by Karola Kampf, Center for Higher Education Policy Studies at Twente University, the Netherlands, www.utwente.nl/cheps/documenten/susukampf.pdf.

228   World problems: Union of International Associations, [267], p. 30.

35. THE SEPULVEDA SOLUTION

230   Car wash: Sepulveda West Car Wash, 2001 S. Sepulveda Blvd., Los Angeles, CA 90025.

230   World's biggest company: "Ma Who? AT&T Loses a Familiar Name," *Time,* August 15, 1983, p. 45.

230   Bell Labs: "Bell Labs' Nobel Legacy," Lucent Technologies, October 1998, www.belllabs.com/news/1998/october/20/4.html.

230   A million employees, AT&T breakup: "Breaking Up Is Hard to Do," by John S. DeMott, *Time,* January 16, 1984, p. 52.

231   Acquired by SBC: "Telecom Mergers Could Result in Vigorous Rivalry," by Jon Van, *Chicago Tribune,* June 8, 2005.

231   "Education presidents": (Clinton) "The Second Term: Education," by Allison Mitchell, *New York Times,* February 5, 1997, p. A21; (Bush Sr.) "Bush Urges 'Education Renaissance,'" from the *Washington Post,* published in the *Toronto Star,* April 19, 1991, p. A21.

231   Bush and education: "Agreement on $26.5B Education Bill," by Elaine S. Povich, *Newsday,* December 12, 2001, p. A13.

231   Bush and school testing: "Bush Pumps Up Educators About Reforms, Funds," by Sabrina Eaton, *Plain Dealer* (Cleveland), January 10, 2002, p. A2.

231   Department of Homeland Security: "Major Management Challenges and Program Risks: Department of Homeland Security," General Accounting Office, *Reports & Testimony* 2003 (February 1, 2003), no. 2.

232   U.N. sham transformation: "Annan Urges World Leaders to Push for Expanding Secu-

rity Council to Reflect New Realities," by Ranjan Roy, Associated Press, September 24, 2003.

232   Security Council structure: "Security Council," Charter of the United Nations, chap. V, art. 23 and 27, www.un.org/aboutun/charter/. In 1971, the General Assembly voted to transfer China's permanent seat on the Security Council from the Taiwan government to the government in Bejing.

233   IBM service revenues: "Consolidated Statement of Earnings, 2004," www.ibm.com/annualreport/2004/annual/cfs_earnings.shtml.

233   IBM services employees: "IBM Global Services," www-306.ibm.com/employment/us/div_glbsvcs.shtml.

233   Kodak's move to digital: "Kodak's Photo Op," by Daniel Eisenberg, *Time,* April 30, 2001, p. 46. Also, "Can Celluloid Survive?" by Stephen Williams, *Newsday,* July 9, 2003, p. B8.

233   Kodak's digital success: "Kodak Gains on Sony in U.S. Digital Camera Market," by Ben Dobbin, Associated Press, November 19, 2004.

233   Bratton becomes NYPD chief: "For Los Angeles's New Police Chief, a New World," by Charlie LeDuff, *New York Times,* December 6, 2002, p. A20.

233   NYPD police force: "Chief Bratton Takes on L.A.," by Heather Mac Donald, *City Journal of New York,* Autumn 2003, p. 30.

233   CompStat: "CompStat's Driving Force," by Jim McKay, *Government Technology,* November, 2003, www.govtech.net/magazine/story.php?id=75047. Also, "CompStat: From Humble Beginnings," by Tom Steinert-Threlkeld, *Baseline,* September 9, 2002, from the Ziff-Davis Web site, www.baselinemag.com/article2/0,3959,1152597,00.asp.

233   "Broken windows" policy: "LAPD Tests New Policing Strategy," by Richard Winton and Kristina Sauerwein, *Los Angeles Times,* February 2, 2003, p. B1.

233   NYC crime rate: "Chief Bratton Takes on L.A.," by Mac Donald.

233   Crime rate in LA: "LA's Major Crime Rate Dips 14 Percent in 2005," Associated Press, January 6, 2006.

233   Crime statistics: Like economic data, crime statistics leave much to be desired. No doubt, they have been improved since Albert D. Biderman, in the mid-1960s, analyzed FBI data showing that "serious crime" was increasing every year. The definition of a serious crime was one that involved $50 or more. Biderman's conclusion: the "rising crime" data reflected two seldom-noted factors: inflation had sent the price of many things into the above-$50 range and affluence meant that more people had more valuable things worth stealing. Albert D. Biderman, "Social Indicators and Goals," chap. 2 in *Social Indicators,* ed. Raymond A. Bauer (Cambridge, Mass.: MIT Press, 1966). In addition, crime rates don't just depend on what police do, but on the size of the teenage population, economic conditions and other factors.

234   Steam engine: (Newcomen) "And the Credit Goes To," by Gerard J. Holtzmann, *Inc.,* September 2000, p. 176; (Savery) "Harnessing the Void," by Robert O. Woods, *Mechanical Engineering* 125 (December, 2003), no. 12, p. 38; (Other inventors) *"Encyclopaedia Brittanica's* Great Inventions," from its *2003 Almanac,* http://corporate.britannica.com/press/inventions.html.

234   First LLC: "LLC History," Limited Liability Company Reporter, www.llc-reporter.com/16.htm.

234   London map: "Fire Insurance Plans of B.C. Cities: Introduction, History," University of British Columbia, www.library.ubc.ca/spcoll/fireins/intro.htm.

235   Yunus, collection problems: "Opportunity Knocks With Microfinance," by Carl Mortished, *The Times* (London), February 8, 2002.

235   Cosigners: "Here's a Business Plan to Fight Poverty," by Peter Carbonara, *Fast Company,* December/January 1998, p. 58.

235   Grameen loans, loans to women: "Grameen Bank at a Glance," March 2005, www
      .grameen-info.org/bank/GBGlance.htm.

235   Other countries, foundation: Grameen Foundation USA. "Who We Are," Grameen
      Foundation, November, 2003, www.gfusa.org/.

235   Repayment rate: "Small Loans, Big Gains," *Boston Globe,* November 19, 2002, p. A22.

235   Trump, NGOs, MicroRate, Von Stauffenberg: "Doing Good by Doing Well," *U.S.
      Bunker* 113 (August, 2003), no. 8, p. 46.

235   Shopkeepers: "Grameen Bank, Which Pioneered Loans for the Poor, Has Hit a Repay-
      ment Snag," by Daniel Pearl and Michael Phillips, *Wall Street Journal,* November 27,
      2001, cited in "Social Entrepreneurship in Developing Countries," by Sara Foryt, an
      article on the United Nations Environment Program Financial Initiatives http://
      unepfi.net/venture/svcdn.pdf.

236   Search engines: "Searches per Day," by Danny Sullivan, 2003, Search Engine Watch,
      http://searchenginewatch.com/reports/print.php/34701_2156461.

236   Person to Person: "Welfare Model Serves Providers, Not the Clients," by Vern Hughes,
      Australian Financial Review, November 7, 2003, p. 83.

237   University of Berlin: "History of Humboldt-Universität," Berlin University, www
      .hu-berlin.de/hu/geschichte/hubdt_e.html. Also, "The European Office in Berlin: What
      We Do," Johns Hopkins University, www.jhu.edu/~europe/whatwedo.html.

238   In addressing new problems, we should not be limited to previous institutional struc-
      tures, such as bureaucracies or networks. There are infinte ways to organize human
      activities. For examples, see our book *Powershift,* Chapter 17.

238   Social invention curricula: "How to Save the World? Treat It Like a Business," by
      Emily Eakin, *New York Times,* December 20, 2003, p. B7.

238   Foundation awards: Examples include the Social Innovations Awards offered by the
      Institute for Social Invention in London (www.globalideasbank.org/Awards2003.html)
      and the Australian Competition for Social Inventions (www.globalideasbank.org/reinv/
      RIS-253.html).

238   Business-model patents: "Skyrocketing Method Patents Stifling Innovation, Say Crit-
      ics," by Justin Pope, Associated Press, November 27, 2003.

36. CODA: AFTER DECADENCE

240   Relative cost of food: "Food CPI, Prices and Expenditures: Expenditures as a Share of
      Disposable Income," Economic Research Service of the U.S. Department of Agricul-
      ture, www.ers.usda.gov/Briefing/CPIFoodAndExpenditures/Data/table7.htm.

240   Clothing expenditures: "Consumer Dominance Hits a 54-Year High," a chart accompa-
      nying an article by Floyd Norris, *New York Times,* December 1, 2003, p. C2.

240   Home ownership in 1950: "Historical Census of Housing Tables: Ownership Rates,"
      U.S. Census Bureau, www.census.gov/hhes/www/housing/census/historic/ownrate.html.

240   Home ownership today: "Homes for the Holidays," by Daniela Deane, citing figures
      from the U.S. Commerce Department, *Washington Post,* December 20, 2003, p. F1.

240   Second homes: Easterbrook, [79], p. 6.

240   Life expectancy in America: "U.S. Life Expectancy Hits New High," by Laura Meckler,
      referring to report released by the U.S. Department of Health and Human Services,
      Associated Press, September 13, 2002.

241   Companies want to be loved: "Macho Business Muscle Gives Itself a Feminine
      Makeover," by Richard Tomkins, *Financial Times,* May 17, 2005, p. 8.

242   Boxers: "Fixin' for Trouble," by Tim Smith, New York *Daily News,* September 21,
      2003, p. 72.

242   Black Sox: "Fade to 'Black,'" by Pat Rooney, *Rocky Mountain News,* July 14, 2003, p. H8.

242   Olympics and drugs: "Sports and Drugs," by Ron Kroichick, *San Francisco Chronicle,* December 29, 2003, p. C1.

242   Olympics and bribery: "Salt Lake Looks to Olympic Effect," by Matthew Garrahan, *Financial Times,* February 8, 2002, p. 7.

242   Little League: "The Enron-ing of Little League," by Blake Miller, *Philadelphia,* September 2003.

242   Athletes' arrests, team owner: "Blood Sport," by Hugo Lindgren, *New York Times Magazine,* August 31, 2003, p. 13. Also, "When Pros Turn Cons," by John Gibeaut, *American Bar Association Journal,* July 2000. Also, "Victim's Mother Wins Judgment Against Carruth, Other Defendants," Associated Press, October 15, 2003.

242   Extremes: (Sports) Extreme Sports Channel Web site, www.extreme.com/misc/index.php; (Software) Daniel H. Steinberg and Daniel W. Palmer, *Extreme Software Engineering: A Hands-On Approach* (Englewood Cliffs, N.J.: Prentice Hall, 2004); (Mountain biking) "Sites for Sore Thighs," by Tarquin Cooper, *Daily Telegraph* (London), March 16, 2002, p. 22; (Fashion) "Automatic Innovator," an interview with Karl Lagerfeld in *WWD,* November 17, 2003, p. 12; (Makovers) "Nip, Tuck Trend Goes Mainstream," by Sheri Hall, *Detroit News,* March 28, 2004, p. 1A; (Pumpkin carving) The ExtremePumpkins.com, www.extremepumpkins.com; (Elvis) "Extreme Elvis," www.extremeelvis.com/index_main.htm; (Porn sites) Google search for "extreme fetish," www.google.com/search?hl=en&ie=UTF-8&oe=UTF-8&q=extreme+fetish+&btnG=Google+ Search.

242   Spa: "Gucci Cucci," *BlackBook,* Fall 2003, p. 60.

242   Abercrombie: "Sexy Ads: What Exactly Are They Selling to Kids?" by Allie Shah, *Minneapolis Star Tribune,* December 23, 2003, p. 1A.

242   Sweepstakes: Vegas.com Skyroller Sweepstakes promotion, October 5, 2003, *Los Angeles Times.*

242   Grand Theft Auto: "Violent Video Game Has Parents, Experts Concerned About Children Who Play It," by James A. Fussell of the Knight Ridder/Tribune News Service, reprinted in the *Kansas City Star* on February 26, 2003.

242   Rappers: "Worth a Second Act?" by Geoff Boucher, *Montreal Gazette,* December 12, 2002, p. D1. Also, "Rap at the Crossroads," by Alec Foege, *Playboy,* January 1998, p. 62.

242–3   Cannibal, law on cannibalism: "Germans Get a Look at the Dark Side of Cyberspace," by Jeffrey Fleishman, *Los Angeles Times,* December 31, 2003, p. A3.

243   Misfits: "Re: The Misfits Issue," *BlackBook'*s response to a reader's letter, Fall 2003, p. 50.

243   Rap groups' new image: "Sweeten the Image: Hold the Bling-Bling," by Lola Ogunnaike, *New York Times,* January 12, 2004, p. E1. Also, "Pop and Jazz Guide," *New York Times,* February 21, 2003, p. E35.

244   EHarmony: "The Internet Battle of the Sexes," by Anna Kuchment, *Newsweek,* Issues 2004, December 22, 2003, p. 58. Also, "Love.com," by Anna Muirine, *U.S. News & World Report,* September 29, 2003, p. 52. Also, eHarmony @ www.eharmony.com.

244   Online groups: "Meetup Organizes Local Interest Groups," from the meetup.com Web site, www.meetup.com.

244   Starbucks and Borders: "Working Hard for the Money—Over Latte," by Catherine Donaldson-Evans, Fox News, March 29, 2002, www.foxnews.com/story/0,2933,49057,00.html.

244   Coffee with WiFi: "Zip to the Net with WI-FI," by Stan Choe, *Charlotte Observer,* December 9, 2002, p. 10D.

245   Book program: "Parton's Imagination Library Delivers Millionth Book," Associated Press, December 13, 2003.

245   Book program in 2004: "Year in Review, 2004," from the Imagination Library Web site, www.imaginationlibrary.com/news.php.

245   Homeschooling: "Homeschooling in the United States: 1999," National Center for Education Statistics, http://nces.ed.gov/pubs2001/HomeSchool/.

245   Online tools: "Web Resources for Home-Schooling," by Irene E. McDermott, *Searcher,* September 1, 2003, p. 27.

245   Charter schools: "The Case Against Charter Schools," by Bruno V. Manno, *School Administrator,* May, 2001, www.aasa.org/publications/sa/2001_05/2001_manno.htm.

245   CART: "School Profile: The Center for Advanced Research and Technology," Center on Education and Work, University of Wisconsin–Madison, 2002, www.cew.wisc.edu/charterSchools/profilecart.asp.

245   Ultrasonic cane: "High-Tech High," by James Hattori, Cable News Network, February 17, 2001, www.cnn.com/2001/TECH/science/02/17/index.cart/.

246   AIDS vaccine, U.S. research: "Can He Find a Cure?" by Geoffrey Cowley, *Newsweek,* June 11, 2001, p. 39.

246   Business schools: "How to Save the World? Treat It Like a Business," by Emily Eakin, *New York Times,* December 20, 2003, p. B7.

246   Incubator: "'Going to Scale' and the Social Benefit Entrepreneur," by Patrick Guerra and James L. Koch, *STS Nexus,* a publication by Santa Clara University, Fall 2003, p. 7.

246   World Economic Forum: "Seeking Common Ground," by Arlene Getz, *Newsweek Online,* January 24, 2003.

247   Fanatics: "Hezbollah Branches Out to Win Support," by Robert Collier, *San Francisco Chronicle,* March 13, 2003, p. A8. Also, "A Nation Challenged: The Money Trail," by Joseph Kahn and Patrick E. Tyler, *New York Times,* November 3, 2001, p. B1.

247   Homelessness: The homeless fall between cracks in the system, and rich countries could surely do better by them. But putting homelessness in historical perspective, the Nobel economist Robert Fogel reminds us that "down to the middle of the 19th century between 10 and 20 percent of the population in Britain and on the Continent were homeless persons that officials classified as vagrants and paupers." The major cities of the United States, at about the same time, were little different. By contrast, Fogel adds, "when we speak of homelessness in the United States today, we are talking about rates below 0.4 percent of the population." Fogel, [93].

247   Cassandra-like forecasts: "A Century of Change: The U.S. Labor Force, 1950–2000," by Mitra Toossi, U.S. Bureau of Labor Statistics, www.bls.gov/opub/mlr/2002/05/art2exc.htm.

247   U.S jobless vs. Europe: "U.S. Labor Market Performance in International Perspective," by Constance Sorrentino and Joyanna Moy, *Monthly Labor Review,* June 2002, p. 15.

248   U.S. water pollution: "Environmental Protection Agency: Budget, Fiscal Year 2004," Environmental Protection Agency, in conjunction with the Office of Management and Budget, www.whitehouse.gov/omb/budget/fy2004/epa.html.

248   Air pollution in the United States: "Air Trends: 2002 Highlights," U.S. Environmental Protection Agency, www.epa.gov/airtrends/highlights.html.

248   Kyoto: "Sparks Fly at Summit; Bush Stands Alone Against Treaty on Climate," by Bennett Roth, *Houston Chronicle,* July 22, 2001, p. A1. Also, "Europe Turns Its Anger Against Bush," by Martin Fletcher and Giles Whittell, *The Times* (London), June 15, 2001. Also: "Bush admits Human Role in Climate Change" by Caroline Daniel and Fiona Harvey, *Financial Times,* July 7, 2005, p. 3.

37. CAPITALISM'S END GAME

253-4   Property definition: *New Oxford American Dictionary* (New York: Oxford University Press, 2001), p. 1366.

254   Intangible property, capital-poor countries: De Soto, [69], pp. 4–6.

255   Google: "Internet Giant Google Shares Trade Higher in Debut," by Matthew Fordahl, Associated Press, August 20, 2004.

255   Intangibles and market value: "Trying to Grasp the Intangible," by Thomas A. Stewart, referring to a Brookings Institution study by economist Margaret Blair, *Fortune,* October 2, 1995, p. 157.

255   Innovation and intangibility: "Intangible Assets: An Interview with Baruch Lev," by Heather Baukney, *CIO,* March 15, 2001, from the IT World Web site, www .itworld.com/Man/2698/CIO010315lev/.

256   Declining fractions of spending: "Understanding the Evolution of U.S. Manufacturing," testimony by Robert Hall before the U.S. Senate Finance Committee, July 8, 2003, http://finance.senate.gov/hearings/testimony/2003test/070803rhtest.pdf.

257   Product piracy: "2004 Special 301 Report," Office of the U.S. Trade Representative, www.ustr.gov/reports/2004–301/special301.htm.

257   Volokh: Interview with the authors in Los Angeles, June 2004.

257   Barlow: "Fair Use Under Assault," by Steve Gillmor, *InfoWorld,* January 24, 2003, www.infoworld.com/article/03/01/24/030124hnbarlow_1.html.

257   Composers and royalties: "The Economy of Ideas," by John Perry Barlow, *Wired,* March 1994, from the Massachusetts Institute of Technology Web site, www.swiss .ai.mit.edu/6805/articles/int-prop/barlow-economy-of-ideas.html.

257   New life-forms: "Can You Patent a Mouse—or an Engineered Fish?" by Tracey Tyler, *Toronto Star,* May 19, 2002, p. A1.

38. CONVERTING CAPITAL

259   Darrow: "Go Directly to Jail, Do Not Pass Go, Do Not Collect Forty Billion Dollars," by Bill Hartson, *The Independent* (London), November 17, 1995, Life section, p. 4.

259   Monopoly statistics: "History of Monopoly," Hasbro Inc., www.hasbro.com/monopoly/ pl/page.history/dn/default.cfm.

259   1920s Wall Street: Chernow, [49], p. 41.

259   Stock ownership in 1950s: "Today in NYSE History—June 26, 1962," New York Stock Exchange, www.nyse.com/about/TodayInNYSE.html.

259   1970 stock ownership: "Small Investors Take a Fresh Look at Stocks," *U.S. News & World Report,* October 19, 1981, p. 93.

260   Ford family ownership, shareholders today: "Learn About Ford—An American Legend," Ford Motor Co., www.ford.ca/english/LearnAbout/NewsReleases/pr20030520 _2.asp.

260   Ford goes public: "Wall Street Party to Mark 40 Years of Ford on the Floor," by Alan L. Adler, *Detroit Free Press,* January 17, 1996, p. 1E.

260   American workers: "Reforms Could Embolden Employees," by James Flanigan, *Los Angeles Times,* July 28, 2002, p. C1.

260   U.S. Home ownership: "Homes for the Holidays," by Daniela Deane, *Washington Post,* December 20, 2003, p. F1.

260   Mortgage debt: "Cheap Loans Are Under Fire," by Tom Petruno, *Los Angeles Times,* September 18, 2005, p. C1.

260   Credit cards and consumer debt: "Most of Us Still Afloat," by Scott Burns, *Dallas Morning News,* March 6, 2005, p. D1.

260   Stock ownership in China: "Small Is Not Beautiful When It Comes to China's Inviting Stock Market," by Stephen Green, Japanese Institute of Global Communications, republishing an article from the May 12, 2003, edition of the *South China Morning Post*, from the institute's Web site, www.glocom.org/special_topics/asia_rep/20030512_asia_s16/.

261   Market democratization: "The Democratization of America's Capital Markets," by John V. Duca, *Economic and Financial Review*, Second Quarter 2001, pp. 10–19.

262   Google founders, IPO strategy: "Searching for a $2.7 Billion Result, Google Files IPO Plan," by Dan Thanh Dang, *Baltimore Sun*, April 30, 2004, p. 1A.

262   Google's IPO plan: "A Cartel-Buster," *The Economist*, May 8, 2004.

262   Google share price: "You, the Next Google Millionaire?" by Walter Updegrave, CNN/Money, April 26, 2004, http://money.cnn.com/2004/04/26/pf/expert/ask_expert/. By mid-2005, less than a year after its initial offering, Google stock had tripled.

262   Tickers on TV: "Hanging on Every Word," by Mark Jurkowitz, *Boston Globe*, August 4, 2002, p. E1.

263   CNN and outsourcing: "An Economist's Ill-Advised Moment of Truth," by Gerard Baker, *Financial Times*, February 19, 2004, p. 17.

263   Bush and cable networks: "Bush's Economic Address, Suffering Slings and (Down) Arrows," by Howard Kurtz, *Washington Post*, July 22, 2002, p. C1.

263   Yago: Interview with the authors, May 24, 2004. Also, Yago, [291].

264   Indonesia rates: "Indonesia—Economy," exchangerate.com, www.exchangerate.com/country_info.html?cont=All&cid=110&action=Submit.

39. IMPOSSIBLE MARKETS

266   Village or manor labor: Crone, [60], pp. 22, 27.

266   First bank: (Chengdu) "A Famous Cultural City," China Travel Service, www.cts.com.cn/esite/chengducity/cultural.htm; (Pingyao) "Pingyao Ancient Town," Regent Tours, www.regenttour.com/chinaplanner/pingyao/pingyao-glance.htm; (Banca Monte dei Paschi) National Italian American Foundation, www.floria-publications.com/italy/italian_culture/.

266   Cities in 1800, 1900: "From Rio to Johannesburg: Urban Governance—Thinking Globally, Acting Locally," by Molly O'Meara Sheehan, citing Chandler, [45], August 29, 2002, from the WorldWatch Institute Web site, www.worldwatch.org/press/news/2002/08/29/. Also, "Political Disorganization and Problems of Scale," by Norman Gall, Fernand Braudel Institute of World Economics, paper no. 28, www.braudel.org.br/paping28a.htm.

267   Penny press: Stephens, [254], pp. 204–206.

267   First department store, Cast Iron Palace: "The Department Store," University of San Diego History Department, January 9, 2004, http://history.sandiego.edu/gen/soc/shoppingcenter4.html.

267   First catalog: "1872 Montgomery Ward—First Mail-Order House," Chicago Public Library, www.chipublib.org/004chicago/timeline/mtgmryward.html.

268   Airline-ticket prices: "The New Realities of Dynamic Pricing," by Ajit Kambil and Vipul Agrawal, *Outlook* (Accenture, 2001), no. 2, p. 15.

269   Priceline: "Sites to Behold," by Michael Shapiro, *Washington Post*, September 15, 2000, p. E4.

269   Velvet painting: Banner advertisement for Western Union Auction Payments, www.auctionpayments.com/.

269   End of mass market: "Profits in the Age of an 'Audience of One,'" by Simon London and Tim Burt, *Financial Times*, April 16, 2004, p. 10.

270   Toyotas: "Camry Facts," Toyota Motor Corp., http://pressroom.toyota.com/mediakit/camry/factsheet2.html.

270   DaimlerChrysler: "Prowler Will Die Along with Plymouth Line," *Detroit Free Press,* December 20, 2001, p. G1.

272   Idaho baby: "Toddler Who Beat Death Still in Critical Condition," Associated Press, May 29, 2004.

272   B2C online sales: "Internet Marketing: An Overview," by Jianwei Hou and Cesar Rego of the University of Mississippi, citing estimates from eMarketer, 2002, p. 11, http://faculty.bus.olemiss.edu/crego/papers/hces0802.pdf.

272   Commerce Dept. figure: "A Perfect Market," by Paul Markille, *The Economist,* May 15, 2004.

272   Aeroxchange founders: "Aeroxchange History," 2004, www.aeroxchange.com/custom/public/corp_info/history.htm.

272   Aeroxchange operations: "Slow Exchange," by Peter Conway, *Airline Business,* October 1, 2003, p. 56.

272   Industry exchanges: (Restaurants) "Restaurant B2B," from the Business.com Web site, www.business.com/directory/food_and_beverage/restaurants_and_foodservice/b2b_markets/; (All others) "B2B Exchange Survivors," by Steve Ulfelder, *Computerworld,* February 2, 2004, www.computerworld.com/softwaretopics/erp/story/0,10801,89568,00.html.

272   Business-to-business e-commerce: "Worldwide B2B E-Commerce to Surpass $1T in 2003," eMarketer, www.emarketer.com/eStatDatabase/ArticlePreview.aspx?1002129.

40. RUNNING TOMORROW'S MONEY

273   Picard: "Out of Our Imagination," by Lanny Floyd, *IEEE Industry Applications,* quoting from the film *Star Trek: First Contact* (Paramount, 1996), January/February 2003, p. 8.

274   Cashiers: "Cashiers," U.S. Bureau of Labor Statistics, 2002 figure, www.bls.gov/oco/ocos116.htm.

274   Accountants: "About IFAC," International Federation of Accountants, 2004, www.ifac.org/About/.

274   Jonathan's: "From Coffee Houses to Computer Screens," by Clare Stewart, *The Times* (London), November 13, 1999.

275   2002 U.S. finance workforce: "National Employment: Financial Activities" and "Labor Force Statistics: Civilian Labor Force," U.S. Bureau of Labor Statistics, 2002, http://data.bls.gov/servlet/SurveyOutputServlet.

275   U.K. finance workers: "Industries and Sectors: Financial/Overview," U.K. Department of Trade and Tourism, 2000, www.dti.gov.uk/sectors_financial.html.

275   $195 billion: "XML Authoring in the Financial Services Industry," by Max Dunn, *XML Journal* 6 (June 1, 2003), no. 4, p. 6.

275   Top I.T. spender: "Financial Firms and Tech Spending," *Wall Street & Technology,* referring to a study by Forrester Research, September 1, 2002, p. 10.

275   I.T. spending vs. GDPs: "Rank Order—GDP," *World Factbook 2001,* www.odci.gov/cia/publications/factbook/rankorder/2001rank.html.

275   Computerized speculation: "Day Trading, Take 2," by David Landis, *Kiplinger's Personal Finance,* April 2004.

275   Unrecognizable market, foreign exchange trading: "Where Money Talks Very Loudly," by Jennifer Hughes, *Financial Times,* May 27, 2004, Special Report: Foreign Exchange, p. 1.

275   Compared with NYSE: "2003 Year-End Review and Statistics," New York Stock Exchange, www.nyse.com/press/1072870219900.html.

276   Stock exchange photography: Interview with the authors, June 5, 2004.

276   Pacific exchange: "Online Pacific Exchange Is Thriving," by Carolyn Said, *San Francisco Chronicle,* January 24, 2004, p. I1.

276   Archipelago and NYSE: "Big Board Seat Prices Rises to $3.6 Million," Bloomberg News, published in the *New York Times,* December 21, 2005, p. C1.

277   Money terms: "Monetary Trends—Definitions," Federal Reserve Bank of St. Louis, http://research.stlouisfed.org/publications/mt/notes.pdf.

277   Wildcat currencies: Galbraith, [97], p. 92. Also: "History of Money," *Newshour with Jim Lehrer,* from the Public Broadcasting Corp. Web site @ www.pbs.org/newshour/on2/money/history.html.

277   Yen: "A Look Back on Long, Complex History of Yen, Dollar," by Hiroshi Ota, *Daily Yomiuri,* April 28, 1999, p. 11.

277   Mark: "Europe's National Currencies," by Jonathan Williams and Andrew Meadows, *History Today* 52 (January 1, 2002), no. 1, p. 19.

277   China's currencies: "A Global History of Currency: China," Global Financial Data, Inc., www.globalfindata.com/gh/69.html.

277   Renminbi: "Mao to Star as China Launches New Yuan Notes for 50th Anniversary," Agence France Presse, July 2, 1999.

278   National card forerunner, card spending vs. cash: "J. P. Williams, 88, Bank Card Creator, Dies," by Douglas Martin, *New York Times,* November 21, 2003, p. C11.

278   Credit cards in use: "Doors Close, a Window Opens," by Joseph Mallia, citing cardweb.com, *Newsday,* March 8, 2004, p. A17.

278   Only for other flights: "History of Frequent Flyer Programs," by Randy Petersen, Webflyer.com, May 2001, www.webflyer.com/company/press_room/facts_and_stats/history.php.

278   Nontransferable: "Dealing in the Airline 'Gray' Market," by Carole Gould, *New York Times,* June 1, 1986, p. C13.

278   Family members and friends: "Buying and Selling Airline Miles," by Rudy Maxa, Awardtraveler.com, www.awardtraveler.com/articles.asp?articleno=27.

278   Merchandise: (Hockey tickets and health club) "Your Miles Are Good for More Than Flights," by Ted Reed, *Charlotte Observer,* November 10, 2003, p. D7; (All others) "Making the Most of Your Flier Miles," by Toddi Gutner, *Business Week,* June 2, 2003, p. 100.

278   Cash for points: "How to Whittle Down a Mountain of Frequent-Flier Miles," by Sam Ali, Newhouse News Service, June 15, 2004.

279   Muslim credit card: "The Very Model of a Modern Moslem State," by James Kynge, *Financial Times,* April 26, 1997, p. 1.

279   Boycotts: (Nike) "Free Speech or False Advertising?" by Stanley Holmes, *Business Week,* April 28, 2003, p. 69; (Shell) "U.N. Report on Nigerian Human Rights Calls for Investigation of Shell," Sierra Club, www.sierraclub.org/human-rights/nigeria/releases/boycott.asp; (Gap) "Businesses Decide to Tackle Problem of Being American," by Carl Weiser, Gannett News Service, February 23, 2004.

279   Paying via cell phones: "No Cash or Card? Pay by Phone," by Jane Croft, *Financial Times,* October 23, 2003, p. 16.

279   Banks and Visa, Nordea exec.: "Mobile Phone Plan May Hasten Cashless Society," by James Mackintosh, *Financial Times,* June 28, 2001, p. 9.

279   Finger ID: "JCB Makes Biometric and Mobile Breakthroughs," *Electronic Payments International,* February 13, 2004, p. 4.

279 Other biometrics: "Biometrics Come to Life," by Orla O'Sullivan, *ABA Banking Journal*, January 1997, p. 31.

280 Card alternatives, Gage: "Will That Be Cash, Fingerprint or Cellphone?" by Kevin Maney, *USA Today*, November 17, 2003, p. 1E.

280 Sony currency: "Sony Lab Proposes Corporate E-Currency," *Nikkei Weekly*, October 27, 2003.

281–2 Distressed economies: (Southeast Asia) "Bartering Gains Currency in Hard-Hit Southeast Asia," by Darren McDermott and S. Karene Witcher, *Wall Street Journal*, April 7, 1998; (South America) "Where to Swap till You Drop," by Hector Tobar, *Los Angeles Times*, May 6, 2002, p. A1; (Russia) "Fissure Finance," a review of the book *Money Unmade: Barter and the Fate of Russian Capitalism*, by David M. Woodruff (Ithaca, N.Y.: Cornell University Press, 1999), in *The Economist*, September 18, 1999, p. 5.

282 Companies using barter: "Seven Ways to Barter Smarter," by Carrie Coolidge, *Forbes*, May 21, 2004, www.forbes.com/2004/05/21/cz_cc_0521bartertips_print.html.

282 Grain bartering: "For Wary Argentines, the Crops Are Cash," by Leslie Moore, *New York Times*, December 1, 2002, p. C6.

282 Bombers for gas: "Kiev to Pay Russian Debts with Bombers," by Charles Clover, *Financial Times*, August 9, 1999, p. 3.

282 Russian vodka, alpaca to zinc: "Fair Trade," by Cullen Murphy, *Atlantic Monthly*, February 1996, vol. 277, no. 2, pp. 16–18.

282 Bernard Lietaer: "Bernard Lietaer Urges the Growth of New Currency," *Bank Technology News* 17 (July 2004), no. 7, p. 32. Also, "Co-Creator of the Euro Offers Terra," by Aldo Svaldi, *Denver Post*, October 24, 2003, p. C1.

282 International countertrade, its extent and volatility, supra-national currency: "The Terra Project," by Bernard Lietaer, October, 2003, from the DaVinci Institute, www.futureofmoneysummit.com/terra-project.php.

283 Massive barter economy: "The Original Meaning of Trade Meets the Future in Barter," by Bob Meyer, BarterNews, 1999, www.barternews.com/worldtrade.htm.

283 Ithaca program: "'Conway Hours' Add Local Focus to Buying," by Michelle Hillen, *Arkansas Democrat-Gazette*, November 29, 2003, p. 17.

283 Bartered hours: Cahn, [39].

41. THE OLD FUTURE OF POVERTY

287 Total foreign aid: Easterly, [80], p. 33.

288 Foreign aid successes: "Africa's Suffering Is Bush's Shame," by Jeffrey Sachs, *Los Angeles Times*, June 12, 2005.

288 World population in poverty, poverty in Asia: "Global Poverty Down by Half Since 1981, But Progress Uneven as Economic Growth Eludes Many Countries," World Bank, April 23, 2004, www.worldbank.org.cn/English/content/776w62628918.shtml.

288 World population in 1650: "Historical Estimates of World Population," U.S. Census Bureau, April 30, 2004, www.census.gov/ipc/www/worldhis.html.

288 Beauvaisis: Braudel, [31], p. 52.

288 French diet in eighteenth century: Fogel, [93].

288 Twice as rich: Parente, [205], pp. 11–12.

290 Poverty in Asia: "Global Poverty Down by Half Since 1981, but Progress Uneven as Economic Growth Eludes Many Countries," World Bank, April 23, 2004, http://web.worldbank.org/WBSITE/EXTERNAL/NEWS/0,,contentMDK:20194973~menuPK:34463~pagePK:64003015~piPK:64003012~theSitePK:4607,00.html.

290 Juran and Deming: "Quality Put into Practice," by Morgan Witzel, *Financial Times*,

August 13, 2003, p. 11. Also, "History's Hidden Turning Points," by Daniel J. Boorstin with Gerald Parshall, *U.S. News & World Report,* April 22, 1991, p. 52. Also, "American Guru Who Taught Importance of Quality Control Is About to Turn 100," by Richard Lee, *Stamford Advocate,* May 7, 2004.

290   Car quality: "Hyundai Joins Toyota, Honda Atop Quality List," MSNBC, April 28, 2004, www.msnbc.msn.com/id/4854302/.

290   Engelberger and Devol: "The First Robot—Unimate," Robotics Research Group at the University of Texas, www.robotics.utexas.edu/rrg/learn_more/history/.

290   Asimov: Isaac Asimov, *I, Robot* (New York: Gnome Press, 1950).

290   GM's first robot: "RIA Chooses 2003 Engelberger Winners," *Assembly* 46 (August 1, 2003), no. 9, p. 12.

290   Engelberger on Japan: "1961: A Peep Into the Automated Future," by Paul Mickle, *Trenton Trentonian,* from the Web site, www.capitalcentury.com/1961.htm.

291   Cars and robots: "The Rapid Expansion of Motorization (1965–1975)," Japanese Automobile Manufacturers Association, www.japanauto.com/about/industry8.htm.

291   Japan's robot industry: "Electronics Manufacturing and Assembly in Japan," by John A. Kukowski and William R. Boulton, Japanese Technology Evaluation Center, February 1995, from the World Technology Evaluation Center Web site, www.wtec.org/loyola/ep/c5s1.htm.

291   Toyota sales in 1957 and 2002, production in U.S.: "About Toyota: Operations—Sales & Service," Toyota Motor Corp., www.toyota.com/about/operations/sales-service/.

291   Best-selling import: "Toyota on Verge of 10%; Product Blitz Sends U.S. Market Share Toward Statistical Milestone," by Mark Rechtin and Harry Stoffer, *Automotive News,* December 11, 2000, p. 1.

291   IBM rival: Vogel, [273], p. 12.

291   Semiconductors from Japan: "Scott and Bill Went Up the Hill," by John Carey, *Business Week,* March 16, 1998, p. 26.

292   Japan displaced U.S.: "Japan—Foreign Relations: Other Asia-Pacific Countries," Library of Congress, Federal Research Division, http://countrystudies.us/japan/134.htm.

292   Japan's FDI to Asia: (1980–1985) "Japanese Foreign Direct Investment in Asia: Its Impact on Export Expansion and Technology Acquisition of the Host Economies," by Shujiro Urata, Japan Center for Economic Research and Waseda University, March 1998, www.jcer.or.jp/eng/pdf/discussion53.pdf. Also: (1986–2000) "Patterns and Strategies of Foreign Direct Investment: The Case of Japanese Firms," by Kang H. Park, *Applied Economics* 35 (November 10, 2003), no. 16, p. 1739.

292   Shifting Asian workforce: (1970) *1972 New York Times Almanac* (New York: New York Times, 1971); (2000) *2004 New York Times Almanac* (New York: Penguin, 2003).

292–3   "Leakage": Easterly, [80], pp. 145–148.

293   Recipient countries: "Data on Poverty: Social Indicators," World Bank, August 2, 2002, www.worldbank.org/poverty/data/trends/mort.htm. Also, "Population Size and Growth," Figure 3, "Average Annual Rates of Population Growth of World Regions: 1950–2020," U.S. Census Bureau, www.census.gov/ipc/prod/wp96/wp96005.pdf.

293   Food production and calories: "Crop Scientists Seek a New Revolution," by Charles C. Mann, *Science* 283 (January 15, 1999), no. 5400, p. 310.

293   East Asian income increase: "The Poverty of Nations," by Martin Wolf, *Financial Times,* August 20, 1996, p. 12.

294   Poverty in China and India: "Global Poverty Monitoring," World Bank, www.worldbank.org/research/povmonitor/.

42. TWIN TRACKS TO TOMORROW

295 *The Third Wave* and China: The influence of *The Third Wave* on Chinese reformist leaders has been widely cited by scholars. Jing Li of the Institute of Modern History noted that "in the 1980s, the Chinese intelligentsia, eager to foster liberal change, came to focus on certain works which they interpreted and expounded in close connection to the ongoing events in China: Alvin Toffler, Thomas Kuhn, Milton Friedman, Samuel Huntington . . . and Max Weber." Hong Kong author Han Shi included *The Third Wave* among "Thirty-Three Books That Changed China." And M. J. Sullivan has observed in *World Affairs* (Fall 1994) that Zhao "was known for quoting various Western studies, such as [those by] Alvin Toffler, to justify his reform policies."

295 Astronaut: "Shenzhou Soars," by Craig Covault, *Aviation Week & Space Technology* 159 (October 20, 2003), no. 16, p. 22.

295 Biotech in China, Beijing Genomics Center: "China's Biotech Is Starting to Bloom," by David Stipp, *Fortune,* September 2, 2002, p. 126.

295 China's mobile-phone subscribers: "China Cell Phone Market at 377M Users," Associated Press, October 26, 2005.

295 China's Internet users: "Number of Chinese Internet Users Tops 110 Million," by Sumner Lemon of the IDG News Service, January 18, 2006, from the InfoWorld Web site, www.infoworld.com/article/06/01/18/74273_HNchinesenetusers_1.html.

295 Technical standards: "Fast Gaining in Technology, China Poses Trade Worries," by Steve Lohr, *New York Times,* January 13, 2004, p. C1.

295 Stem-cell research in China: "An Embryonic Nation," by Xiangzhong Yang, *Nature,* March 11, 2004, www.nature.com/cgi-taf/DynaPage.taf?file=/nature/journal/v428/n6979/full/428210a_fs.html.

296 Dalian: "Doing Our Homework," by Thomas L. Friedman, *New York Times,* June 24, 2004, p. A23.

296 Science and engineering degrees: "High Tech in China," by Bruce Einhorn, with Ben Elgin, Cliff Edwards, Linda Himelstein and Otis Port, *Business Week,* October 28, 2004, p. 80.

296 Scientists return home: "China Tries to Woo Its Tech Talent Back Home," by Rone Tempest, *Los Angeles Times,* November 25, 2002, p. B1. Also, "Biotech's Yin and Yang," *The Economist,* December 14, 2002.

296 R&D labs: "Let a Thousand Ideas Flower," by Chris Buckley, *New York Times,* September 13, 2004, p. C1.

296 China's digital exports: "Digital Dragon," *The Economist,* December 17, 2005, p. 58.

296 China's problems and antipoverty programs: "Transition of China's Northeast: The Need for Combining Regional and National Policies," by François Bourguignon, in remarks at the seminar "A Development Strategy for Northeast China," December 3-4, 2003, Shenyang, China, on World Bank Web site, www.worldbank.org.cn/English/content/fb-shenyang.pdf.

296 Poorest Chinese: "Enter the Dragon," *The Economist,* March 10, 2001.

297 Kalam's background: "The Political Ascent of an Indian Missile Man," by Pallava Bagla, *Science* 297 (July 26, 2002), no. 5581, p. 503.

297 India 2020: Kalam, [133].

297 India lags behind China: "China Key to Our Fortunes," by Geoffrey Newman, *The Australian,* May 7, 2004, p. 4.

297 India's outsourcing income: "India's Software Exports at $12.5 Billion Despite Outsourcing Backlash," by S. Srinivasan, Associated Press, June 3, 2004.

298 Outsourcing's reverse effect: "Indian City Rides Tech Euphoria," by David Streitfeld, *Los Angeles Times,* June 30, 2004, p. A1.

298 Chief minister: "Interview: Buddhadeb Bhattacherjee," by Joanna Slater, *Far Eastern Economic Review,* April 28, 2004, p. 38.

298 Calcutta and IBM: "Calcutta on a Roll," by Joanna Slater, *Far Eastern Economic Review,* April 28, 2004, p. 36.

298 Karnataka: "The Digital Village," by Manjeet Kripalani, *BusinessWeek,* June 28, 2004, p. 60.

298 Internet kiosks: "Plan to Connect Rural India to the Internet," by John Markoff, *New York Times,* June 16, 2005, p. C17.

299 India's space program, telelinked clinics, Space Research Organization: "Technology for the People: A Future in the Making," by Dinesh C. Sharma, *Futures* 36 (August/September 2004), nos. 6–7, pp. 734, 740.

299 Biotech in India: "Biotechnology: India Emerging as a Partner of Choice," by K. T. Jagannathan, *The Hindu,* June 9, 2004. Also, "Biotech: India Right on Track," *Financial Express,* June 9, 2004. Even as India began opening up and moving toward a knowledge-based economy, it has also raised more than 100 million people out of dire poverty. See "Amid Disaster, New Confidence" by Fareed Zakaria, *Business Week,* January 15, p.35.

300 Top biotech investor: "Singapore Is Asia's Top Investor in Biotech Sector," *Asia Pacific Business,* citing a report in the June 2002 issue of *Asia Private Equity Review* 6, no. 10, from the Web site www.asiabiotech.com.sg/readmore/vol06/0615/singapore.html.

300 Malaysia 2020: "Malaysian Premier Mahathir Maintains 2020 Vision," Agence France Presse, January 10, 2000.

300 Companies in Malaysia: "Malaysian Cybercity a Go," Reuters, July 8, 1999, from the *Wired* Web site, www.wired.com/news/business/0,1367,20628,00.html.

300 Malaysia's changing exports: "Background on Malaysia," U.S. Department of State, Bureau of East Asian and Pacific Affairs, August 2004, www.state.gov/r/pa/ei/bgn/2777.htm. A personal note is due here: Mahathir was a visionary leader, and I—along with a long list of others, including Bill Gates, Larry Ellison, Kenichi Ohmae and Masayoshi Son—had been asked to serve on the international advisory board of the Malaysian Multi-Media Super-Corridor, an attempt to create a Malaysian Silicon Valley. But Mahathir was not above jailing his own former protégé and handpicked deputy prime minister, Anwar Ibrahim, when the two fell out over how to cope with corruption, the 1997–98 economic crisis and control of UMNO, the political coalition that put them both in office. Thrown in prison with Anwar was his speechwriter, Munawar Anees, who earlier had introduced me to both Anwar and Mahathir. Anwar and Anees were both physically abused in prison. On learning of the arrests, I immediately faxed Mahathir, calling for their release, exchanged correspondence with him and, in October 1998, wrote a column in their defense for the *International Herald Tribune.*—Alvin Toffler.

300 South Korea's Kim Dae-jung: "Asia's Rising Star: Nanotech," by Jayanthi Iyengar, *Asia Times,* April 21, 2004, http://atimes01.atimes.com/atimes/Asian_Economy/FD21Dko1.html.

300 Abdullah: "Jordan's King Lays Cornerstone for School Modeled After Deerfield Academy," by Fadi Khalil, Associated Press, July 22, 2004.

301 AIDS deaths: "AIDS Epidemic in Sub-Saharan Africa" and "AIDS Epidemic in Asia," United Nations Program on HIV/AIDS, *UNAIDS 2004 Report on the Global AIDS Epidemic,* www.unaids.org/bangkok2004/factsheets.html.

43. CRACKING POVERTY'S CORE

303 Brute labor: Patricia Crone notes that "the average world farmer is still incapable of feeding more than five people, but the average farmer of Western Europe feeds twenty while his counterpart in the USA feeds almost sixty" [60].

304 Moore: "The Promise of Food Security," by David Lague, *Far Eastern Economic Review,* April 4, 2002, p. 34.

304 Nutrients, pesticides, arid and cold, higher yields: "21st Century Agriculture: A Critical Role for Science and Technology," U.S. Department of Agriculture, June 2003, www .usda.gov/news/pdf/agst21stcentury.pdf.

304 Fertilizer: "Debate Grows Over Biotech Food," by Justin Gillis, *Washington Post,* November 30, 2003, p. A1.

304 Drought-resistant: "Can Bio-Crops Really End World Hunger?" by Margarette Driscoll, *Sunday Times* (London), June 20, 2003.

304 Lower costs: "An Environmental-Economic Assessment of Genetic Modification of Agricultural Crops," by J. C. J. M. van den Berg and J. M. Holley, *Futures* 34 (November/December 2002), nos. 9–10.

304 GM crops today: "Narrow Path for New Biotech Food Crops," by Andrew Pollack, *New York Times,* May 20, 2004, p. C1.

304 India DBT, cholera and rabies: "Technologies for the People: A Future in the Making," by Dinesh C. Sharma, *Futures* 36 (August/September 2004), nos. 6–7, p. 741.

304 Poor-world crops: "New GM Crops Research Project on the Anvil," Press Trust of India, December 18, 2003.

305 China and Monsanto, soybean imports: "China Urged to Step Up GM Efforts," by Jia Hepeng, Science and Development Network, March 5, 2004, www.scidev.net/ dossiers/index.cfm?fuseaction=dossierReadItem&type=1&itemid=1264&language=1& dossier=6.

305 China's agriculture biotech: "Plant Biotechnology in China," by Jikun Huang, Scott Rozelle, Carl Pray and Qinfang Wang, *Science,* January 25, 2002, p. 674.

305 Fuzzy factors: "Super Organics," by Richard Manning, *Wired,* May 2004, www .wired.com/wired/archive/12.05/food.html. Also see Manning, [162].

305 Hepatitis B deaths: "WHO Calls for More International Aid to Pay for Vaccination Programmes," *Pharmaceutical Journal* 269 (November 23, 2002), no. 7225, p. 733.

305 Hepatitis B carriers: "General Information," from the Hepatitis B Foundation, www .hepb.org/05-0230.hepb.

305 Vaccine costs, Cornell: "Food for the Future," by Gregg Easterbrook, *New York Times,* November 19, 1999, p. A35.

305 Tomatoes: "Transgenic Plants for the Future," Colorado State University's *Agronomy News* 21 (Autumn 2001), no. 5, www.colostate.edu/Depts/SoilCrop/extension/ Newsletters/2001/guAutumn01.htm.

305 Potatoes: "The Push for Edible Vaccines," by Rob Wherry, *Forbes,* January 20, 2003, p. 110.

305 "Golden rice": "How Science Can Save the World's Poor," by Dick Taverne, *Guardian,* (London) March 3, 2004, p. 24.

305 Diarrhea: "Biotech Crops as 'Health Food'?" by Wyatt Andrews, *CBS News,* October 9, 2000, www.cbsnews.com/stories/2002/01/31/health/main326711.shtml.

305 Cystic fibrosis: "Feed Corn, Meet 'Pharma' Corn," by Rachel Brand, *Rocky Mountain News,* March 13, 2004, p. 1C.

306 Custom seeds: "Technology Grows Many Seed Options," by Anne Fitzgerald, *Des Moines Register,* June 6, 2004, p. 1M.

306 Age of Oil: ARCO Chairman and CEO Michael Bowlin, quoted in ibid., p. 1.

306   Agriculture, genes and petroleum, 280 million tons: "From Petro to Agro: Seeds of a New Economy," by Robert E. Armstrong, *Defense Horizons,* October, 2002, pp. 1, 2.

306   Current biomass uses: "Vision for Bioenergy and Biomass Products in the United States," U.S. Department of Energy, October 2002, www.eere.energy.gov/biomass/publications.html?print.

306–7 Eden Project: "Green Giant," by Ian Wylie, *Fast Company,* June 2002, p. 64.

307   Handheld receivers: "Precision Farming Tools: Global Positioning System (GPS)," by Robert Grisso, Richard Oderwald, Mark Alley and Conrad Heatwole, Virginia Polytechnic Institute, July 2003, www.ext.vt.edu/pubs/bse/442-503/442-503.html.

307   Satellites: "Lost? Hiding? Your Cellphone Is Keeping Tabs," by Amy Harmon, *New York Times,* December 21, 2003, p. A1.

307   Reduce water needs: National Research Council, *Biobased Industrial Products: Priorities for Research and Commercialization* (Washington, D.C.: National Academy Press, 1999), cited in Armstrong, "From Petro to Agro," p. 4.

308   Wang Shiwu: "Internet Changes Chinese Farmers' Life," Xinhua News Agency, June 9, 2001.

308   Farmers online: "Narrowing China's Digital Divide," by Kaiser Kuo, *AsiaInc.,* May 2004, www.asia-inc.com/May04/narrowing_may.htm.

308   Chinese villages online: "41% of Villages in China Connected to Internet," Xinhua News Agency, June 15, 2004.

309   Joshi: "Transforming Agri-Business the E-Way," by Meera Shenoy, *Business India,* June 24, 2002.

309   E-*choupal* operations: "What Works: ITC's E-Choupal and Profitable Rural Transformation," by Kuttayan Annamalai and Sachin Rao, World Resources Institute, August 2003, http://povertyprofit.wri.org/pdfs/echoupal_case.pdf.

310   Dolly: "Dolly the Sheep Dies Young," British Broadcasting Corp., February 14, 2003, http://news.bbc.co.uk/1/hi/sci/tech/2764039.stm.

310   Dead cow: "University of Georgia Clones Calf from Dead Animal," by Rebecca McCarthy, *Atlanta Journal-Constitution,* April 26, 2002.

310   Snuppy: "Seoul Stem Cell Scandal Remains Murky," *Nikkei Weekly,* January 16, 2006.

311   Water purifier: "Inventors Develop James Bond Gadgets for War," by Kristel Halter, Columbia University News Service, February 16, 2004, www.jrn.columbia.edu/studentwork/cns/2004-02-16/516.asp.

311   Crop sensors: "Psst. This Is Your Sensor. Your Grapes Are Thirsty," by Barnaby J. Feder, *New York Times,* July 26, 2004, p. C2.

311   Tissue sensors, nanotech monitors, airborne spores, magnetics: "A Compendium of DARPA Programs," Defense Advanced Research Projects Agency, a division of the U.S. Defense Department, April 2002, pp. 13, 55, 58, 60, www.darpa.mil/body/newsitems/darpa_fact.html.

312   "Let's Get Real": " 'Going to Scale' and the Social Benefit Entrepreneur," by Patrick Guerra and James L. Koch, *STS Nexus* 4 (Fall 2003), no. 1, p. 7.

312   Bill Gates: "Gates Rejects Idea of E-Utopia," by Dan Richman, *Seattle Post-Intelligencer,* October 19, 2000, p. A1.

312   Sachs: "Technological Solutions, Not Political Changes, Key to Ending African Poverty," by Jeffrey D. Sachs, Project Syndicate, published in *Daily Yomiuri,* January 27, 2006.

314   Rural electricity: "World Energy Outlook 2002: Energy and Poverty," International Energy Agency, chapter 13, p. 5.

314   China's reactor construction: "Nuclear Plants to Ease Power Shortages," China *People's Daily,* May 26, 2004, http://english.people.com.cn/200405/26/eng20040526_144420.html.

314 Three Gorges: "After Years of Weighing Pros and Cons, China Is Now All for Nuclear Energy," by Peter Harmsen, Agence France Presse, July 29, 2004.

314 Rural electricity in India: "Full Rural Electrification Only by 2012," Winrock International India, reporting on Planning Commission Working Group conclusions to the Power Ministry regarding the country's 10th Plan (2002–2007), June 2002, www .renewingindia.org/news1/news_archive/jun/news1_june_ruralelec.html.

44. CHINA'S NEXT SURPRISE?

319 U.S. trade, Asia's influence: "America Must Not Leave Asia in a Trade Blind Spot," by Max Baucus, *Financial Times,* December 13, 2004, p. 17.

320 Third-largest trader: "China Surpasses Japan to Become the World's Third-Largest Trader," by Chi Hung Kwan, Research Institute of Economy, Trade and Industry (Japan), March 23, 2004, www.rieti.go.jp/en/china/04032301.html.

320 China's foreign-currency reserves: "The Mainland Is No Longer Cheering the Influx of Foreign Funds," by Mark O'Neill, *South China Morning Post,* November 10, 2004, p. 14.

320 World's reserves: "Is the Dollar's Role as the World's Reserve Currency Drawing to a Close?" *The Economist,* November 23, 2004.

320 U.S. Treasuries: "Treasuries Fall on Report China Cuts Back on U.S. Debt Holdings," Bloomberg News Service, November 26, 2004, http://quote.bloomberg.com/apps/ news?pid=10000006&sid=a747P240y4uU&refer=home.

320 "Catching up with the West": "Zhao Urges 'Revolution' for Economy as China Tries to Catch Up with the West," by Daniel Southerland of the *Washington Post,* reprinted in the *Toronto Star,* October 26, 1987, p. A1.

321 Competitive speed: "The China Price," by Pete Engardio and Dexter Roberts, *Business Week,* December 6, 2004, p. 102.

321 Robert Fonow: "Beyond the Mainland: Chinese Telecommunications Expansion," by Robert C. Fonow, *Defense Horizons,* July 2003, no. 29, pp. 2–3.

321 Change in China: Stille, [255], pp. 48 and 58, cited in Matthew Brown, "Can the Past and the Future Coexist?" *Independent Review* 8 (Winter 2004), no. 3, pp. 439–444.

321 Asia free-trade zone: "East Asia Nations Make Headway in Trade Talks," *People's Daily,* July 21, 2003, http://english.people.com.cn/200307/21/eng20030721_120717.shtml.

322 Cheap Chinese goods: (Mexico) "Mexico Losing NAFTA Advantage," by John Lyons, *Milwaukee Journal Sentinel,* November 27, 2003, p. D1; (Colombia) "Latin American Countries Lose Business, and Jobs, as a Huge Wave of Low-Cost Goods Floods Markets," *Miami Herald,* December 7, 2003, p. L1; (Indonesia) "More Risks Ahead for Textile Industry," by Bill Guerin, *Asia Times,* 2004, www.atimes.com/atimes/ Southeast_Asia/FH03A304.html.

322 Lenovo: "Big Blue's Bold Step into China," by Steve Hamm, with Pete Engardio and Frederik Balfour, *Business Week,* December 9, 2004.

322 Huawei: "Huawei: More Than a Local Hero," by Bruce Einhorn, *BusinessWeek,* October 11, 2004, p. 180.

322 China's foreign businesses: "China's Outward Investments Hit $33.4 Billion by End of 2003," Japan Economic Newswire, citing a report from China's Ministry of Commerce and National Bureau of Statistics, September 7, 2004.

322 China's FDI: "Outward FDI Tops US$33bn," by Olivia Chung, *Hong Kong Standard,* October 7, 2004, www.thestandard.com.hk/stdn/std/China/FJ07Ad01.html.

322 South American investments: "Beijing Bolsters Economic Ties with Eager Latin America," by Gary Marx, *Chicago Tribune,* December 20, 2004, p. 4.

322   Taiwan's U.S. backing, Beijing's threat of force: "Dangerous Straits," by Melinda Liu, *Newsweek,* June 28, 2004, p. 32.

322   China's military budget: "FY 2004 Report to Congress on PRC Military Power," U.S. Department of Defense, www.dod.gov/pubs/d20040528PRC.pdf.

323   China's military capacities: "China Reshaping Military to Toughen Its Muscle in the Region," by Craig S. Smith, *New York Times,* October 16, 2002, p. A12. Also, "Unmanned Tactical Aircraft: China Is Pursuing," by Roxana Tiron, *National Defense* 88 (May 1, 2004), no. 606, p. 34.

323   Nuclear missiles: "US Missiles: China's View," by James Miles, British Broadcasting Corp., July 6, 2000, http://news.bbc.co.uk/2/hi/asia-pacific/822277.stm.

323   Maritime strategy: "Chinese Sea Power Is on the Rise," by Hideaki Kaneda, *Taipei Times,* September 14, 2005, p. 8.

323   R&D spending in China: "20% R&D Expenditure Increase in 1002," Chinese Ministry of Science and Technology, October 20, 2004, www.most.gov.cn/English/newletter/q382.htm.

323   U.S. R&D: "R&D Budget and Policy Program," Table I-11, American Association for the Advancement of Science, citing data from the National Science Foundation, 2004, www.aaas.org/spp/rd/guitotal.htm.

323   Von Zedtwitz: "Let a Thousand Ideas Flower: China Is a New Hotbed of Research," by Chris Buckley, *New York Times,* September 13, 2004, p. C1.

323–4   Technology transfer: "U.S. Commercial Technology Transfers to the People's Republic of China," U.S. Bureau of Export Administration, 1999, www.bis.doc.gov/defenseindustrialbaseprograms/OSIES/DefMarketResearchRpts/techtransfer2prc.html.

324   MBA programs: "But Can You Teach It?" *The Economist,* Special Report, May 22, 2004.

324   MBA partnerships: "Your Guide to MBA and EMBA Courses on the Mainland," *South China Morning Post,* November 6, 2004, p. 50.

324   Foreigners in China: "Foreigners Living in South China's Shenzhen Increasing," *People's Daily,* December 4, 2001, http://english.people.com.cn/200112/06/eng2001 1206_86062.shtml.

324   Most pessimistic: Table of contents in Chang, [46].

325   Mao's China, peasants and industrialization: "Sharing Economic Fruits with 900 Million Farmers," by Qiao Tianbi, *China Today,* May 2005, p. 14.

325   "City-first" policy, Sichuan strike, China's dilemma: "In China, Stresses Spill Over into Riots," by Robert Marquand, *Christian Science Monitor,* November 22, 2004, p. 1.

325   Chinese peasants: "Exercising Government Power in the Interests of the People," Xinhua News Service, October 6, 2004.

325   Land losses: "Farmers Being Moved Aside by China's Real Estate Boom," by Jim Yardley, *New York Times,* December 8, 2004, p. A1.

325–6   Enclosure Acts: Porter, [213], p. 308–309. Also "Agricultural Enclosures: The Major Phase, 1760 Onwards," *Literary Encyclopedia,* www.litencyc.com/php/stopics .php?rec=true&UID=1472.

326   Peasant benefits: In late 2005 China announced an experimental program to grant to peasants in eleven provinces the same medical, housing, education and other benefits available to urban residents. See "China to Drop Urbanite-Peasant Legal Differences," by Joseph Kahn, *New York Times,* November 3, 2005, p. A8.

326   Two-class system: "Amid China's Boom, No Helping Hand for Young Qingming," by Joseph Kahn and Jim Yardley, *New York Times,* August 1, 2004, p. A1.

326   Peasants financing urban boom: "China's Strength Begins at Home," by Yasheng Huang, *Financial Times,* June 2, 2005.

326   China's development options: "China's Heavy Industry Delusions," by Wu Jinglian, *Far Eastern Economic Review,* July–August 2005, p. 56.

326   Protest issues: "China Crushes Peasant Protest, Turning 3 Friends into Enemies," by Joseph Kahn, *New York Times,* October 13, 2004, p. A1.

326   Protests across China: "The Cauldron Boils," *The Economist,* October 1, 2005, p. 38.

326   87,000 protests: "Pace and Scope of Protest in China Accelerated in '05," by Joseph Kahn, *New York Times,* January 20, 2006. P. A1.

326   Other rallies and strikes: "Repression in China Worsens Workers Protests," Human Rights Watch, August 2, 2002, www.hrw.org/press/2002/08/china080202.htm.

326   Dongzhou: "China Blames 'Instigators' in Deadly Siege," by Peter Enav, Associated Press, December 10, 2005.

327   PLA and infowar: "Like Adding Wings to the Tiger: Chinese Information War Theory and Practice," by Timothy L. Thomas, also citing Wei Jincheng, "New Form of People's Warfare," and Wang Xiaodong, "Special Means of Warfare in the Information Age: Strategic Information Warfare," Foreign Military Studies Office, 2000, http://fmso.leavenworth.army.mil/fmsopubs/issues/chinaiw.htm.

328   Falun Gong: Schechter, [242]. Regarding demons, "Faithful Follow Falun Gong," by Brian Jackson, *Chicago Sun-Times,* February 27, 2000, p. 33.

328–9   Mao's peasant revolution: Solomon, [249], pp. 190–198, 213–214.

329   Rapidly growing Christianity: "China Opens Door to Christianity—Of a Patriotic Sort," by Robert Marquand, *Christian Science Monitor,* March 8, 2004, p. 1.

329   Religious practitioners: "For Beijing, Fear Grows as Spirituality Blooms," by Howard W. French, *International Herald Tribune,* September 16, 2005.

329   Countryside cults: "Violence Taints Religion's Solace for China's Poor," by Joseph Kahn, *New York Times,* November 25, 2004, p. A1.

330   Taiping Rebellion: Spence, [250], pp. 170–178.

330   Rebellion casualities: "Taiping Rebellion," *Encyclopaedia Brittanica,* www .brittanica.com/ebi/article-92277247.

330   Great Leap and Cultural Revolution: "The Inhuman Touch," by Richard McGregor, *Financial Times,* reviewing Chang [47], June 18, 2005, p. 29.

330   Fixed-asset investments: "Implication of Opening Up China to Economic Development," Table 1: "Share of China's FDI in Fixed Asset Investment, 1992–2002," by Zhang Xiaoji, Research and Information System for the Non-Aligned and Other Developing Nations, www.ris.org.in/DRC_Report.pdf.

330   Muslim northwest: "One Nation—Divided," by Matthew Forney with Mark Thompson, *Time International,* March 25, 2002, p. 38.

45. JAPAN'S NEXT BAMBOO RING

332   Hayato Ikeda: "Will Fatal Flaws Eventually Doom the Alliance?" by Michael Hirsh, Associated Press, January 5, 1992.

333   Crash contradictions: Ohmae, [199], pp. 12–15.

333   Property prices: "The Measure of One's Worth: Real Estate," by John Dodd, *Japan Inc.,* December 2003, www.japaninc.net/article.php?articleID=1247.

333   Nonperforming loans, shrinking factory output, exports: "Japan's Phoenix Economy," by Richard Katz, *Foreign Affairs,* January/February 2003, p. 114.

334   Japan at forefront: (Fuel cells) "Fuel-Cell Nation," by Irene M. Kunii, *BusinessWeek,* October 6, 2003, p. 26; (Alternative energy) "Japan: Environmental Issue," U.S. Department of Energy, January 2004, www.eia.doe.gov/emeu/cabs/japanenv.html; (Digital electronics) "Japan's Sun Rises Again," by Michael Kanellos, CNET News, December 6, 2004, http://ecoustics-cnet.com.com/Japans+tech+industry+banks+on+

cool+factor/2009-1041_3-5471753.html?tag=jp.toc; (Robots) "Making Robots More Like People," by Byron Spice, *Pittsburgh Post-Gazette,* June 18, 2001, p. A8; (Artificial blood) "Artificial Blood Ready for Testing in People," by Leo Lewis, *The Times* (London), May 15, 2004, p. 11; (Glycobiology) "The History of Glycobiology in Japan," by Akira Kobata, *Glycobiology,* May 25, 2001, Vol. 11, no. 8; (Gaming devices) "Sony Ready to Battle Nintendo in Game Arena," by Levi Buchanan, *Chicago Tribune,* January 6, 2005, p. C1.

334   Japan and nanotech: "Japan's Sun Rises Again," by Michael Kanellos, citing the National Science Foundation, CNET News, December 6, 2004, http://ecoustics-cnet .com.com/Japans+tech+industry+banks+on+cool+factor/2009-1041_3-5471753.html? tag=jp.toc.

334   Services imports: "Services Balances," Keizai Koho Center, the Japan Institute for Social and Economic Affairs, citing data from the Bank of Japan, www.kkc-usa.org/ index.cfm/2487.

334   *Economist:* "Dead Firms Walking—Japan's Service Economy," *The Economist,* Special Report, September 25, 2004.

335   Japan's wave confict: The Livedoor scandal in 2006, by contrast, was not so polite. It was accompanied by one suicide and the jailing of Livedoor President Takafumi Horie on charges of financial skullduggery. Rightly or wrongly, it was seen by many as an attack by the industrial "old guard"—read Second Wave—on a flamboyant young entrepreneur who symbolized the Third Wave.

335   Lifetime employment: Fingleton, [91], pp. 204–212.

335   *Keiretsu* system: Holstein, [127], pp. 199–208.

336   *Keiretsu*s on decline: "Keiretsu Dynasties Give Way," by Michael Kanellos, CNET News, December 7, 2004, http://news.com.com/Keiretsu+dynasties+give+way+to+ global+changes/2009-1041_3-5471874.html.

336   Mitsubishi: "Mitsubishi Moves to Reinstate Closed Supplier Group," by James B. Treece, *Automotive News,* October 18, 2004, p. 6.

336   Venture capital, loans: "The Challenge of Entrepreneurship in a Developed Economy: The Problematic Case of Japan," by Marilyn M. Helms, *Journal of Developmental Entrepreneuring* 8 (December 1, 2003), no. 3, p. 247.

336   Keidanren: "Rakuten Allowed to Join Keidanren," *Japan Times,* November 17, 2004.

336   U.S. Entrepreneurs: "Global Entrepreneurship Monitor, 2000," by Paul D. Reynolds, S. Michael Camp, William D. Bygrave and Erkko Autio, cited in "From Keiretsu to Startups: Japan's Push for High Tech Entrepreneurship," by Henry S. Rowen and A. Maria Toyoda, Asia/Pacific Research Center, October 2002, p. 9.

336–7   Lack of new products: "From Keiretsu to Startups: Japan's Push for High Tech Entrepreneurship," by Rowen and Toyoda.

337   Joint enterprises, university startups, annual new businesses: "VC Funding Gets Scholarly," *Red Herring,* also citing *Nikkei Weekly,* December 15, 2004, www .redherring.com/Article.aspx?a=11047&hed=VC+funding+gets+scholarly&sector= Capital&subsector=VentureCapital.

337   Silicon Valley and universities: "The Heart of Silicon Valley," by James Aley, *Fortune,* July 7, 1997, p. 66.

338   Division of labor by gender, women in management: "Lifting Women's Job Status," by Hiroku Hanai, *Japan Times,* July 26, 2004.

338   Unmarried rate, Christmas cakes: "Japanese Women Staying Single by Droves as Gender Schism Grows in Nation's Culture," by Yuri Kageyama, Associated Press, November 15, 2004.

338   Fewer babies, City of Ota: "Fathers Will Be Forced to Mind Baby," by Leo Lewis, *The Times* (London), December 3, 2004.

339   Women in workforce: "Statistical Handbook of Japan: The Labor Force," Statistics Bureau of Japan's Ministry of Internal Affairs and Communications, www.stat.go.jp/english/data/handbook/c12cont.htm.

339   Women's earned income. "Human Development Indicators—2004," table 25, United Nations Development Program, http://hdr.undp.org/statistics/data/pdf/hdr04_table _25.pdf.

339   Mandatory retirement age: "Mandatory Retirement," Japan Aging Research Center, www.jarc.net/aging/04dec/page2.shtml.

340   Life expectancy in Japan, healthy elderly: "Old, but Not Retiring," by Anthony Faiola, *Washington Post,* October 27, 2004, p. A1.

339–40   Oldest population: "The Dilemma Posed by Japan's Population Decline," by Julian Chapple, Electronic Journal of Contemporary Japanese Studies, October 18, 2004, www.japanesestudies.org.uk/discussionpapers/Chapple.html.

340   American retirees, Mexico: "Retiring Abroad a Tantalizing Dream for Boomers," by Dave Carpenter, Associated Press, July 30, 2002.

340   Guadalajara rentals: "La Vida Cheapo," by Bary Golson, *AARP,* March/April 2004, www.aarpmagazine.org/travel/Articles/a2004-01-21-mag-mexico.html.

340   British retirees abroad: "More Retirees Will Quit UK to Live Abroad," by Nicky Burridge, citing a report carried out with the Centre of Future Studies, Press Association, November 17, 2003.

340   Akira Nihei and his wife: "A Retirement Home in the Sun Begins to Appeal to Japanese," by Miki Tanikawa, *International Herald Tribune,* May 29, 2004, Special Report, p. 15.

342   Koizumi: "Koizumi's LDP Wins Big, *Japan Times,* September 12, 2005, p. 1.

342   Courtis: Interview with the authors, October 2005.

342–3   Japanese investment in China: "Foreign Direct Investment," Japan's Ministry of Finance, www.mof.go.jp/english/e1c008.htm.

343   China's exports to Japan, share: "Japanese Capital and Jobs Flowing to China," by Ken Belson, *New York Times,* February 17, 2004, p. C1.

343   Companies in China: (GM) "Our Plants: China," General Motors, www.gm.com/company/gmability/environment/plants/plant_list/plant_db/asia-pacific/china.html; (Intel, Anheuser-Busch) "Foreign Investments in China," U.S. China Business Council, 2004, www.uschina.org/statistics/fdi_2004.html; (BMW, Siemens, BASF) "Foreign Direct Investments in China—Good Prospects for German Companies?" Deutsche Bank Research, August 24, 2004.

46. EUROPE'S LOST MESSAGE

344   Xavier: Debray, [67].

345   Trade since 1985: "U.S. Aggregate Foreign Trade Data, 2003 & Prior Years," U.S. Department of Commerce's International Trade Administration, www.ita.doc.gov/td/industry/otea/usfth/.

345   E.U. import restrictions: (GM foods, bananas) "Euro Clash," by Tim Reason, *CFO,* May 2004; (Honey, roller skates, nuclear reactors) "EU Opens New Front in Trade War," British Broadcasting Corp., March 1, 2004, http://news.bbc.co.uk/2/hi/business/3521731.stm.

345   Microsoft, merger, duties, all-time low: "Euro Clash," by Tim Reason, *CFO.*

345   Arms sales ban: "House Urges EU to Maintain Arms Embargo," by Jim Abrams, Associated Press, February 2, 2005.

345   Sale on hold: "Booming China Promises Peace and Goodwill," by Justin McCurry and Jonathan Watts, *Guardian* (London), December 23, 2005, p. 12.

346   Europe's advanced sectors: (Mobile phones) "Mobile Cellular Subscribers Per 100 People, 2003," International Telecommunication Union www.itu.int/ITU-D/ict/statis tics/at_glance/cellular03.pdf; (Airbus) "Boeing Roars Ahead," by Stanley Holmes with Carol Matlack, *Business Week,* November 7, 2005, p. 44; (Grid computing) "Europe Exceeds U.S. in Refining Grid Computing," by John Markoff and Jennifer L. Schenker, *New York Times,* November 10, 2003, p. C1; (Satellite launches) "Arianespace at Europe's Spaceport," European Space Agency, May 12, 2004, www.esa.int/ SPECIALS/Launchers_Europe_s_Spaceport/ASE7EOI4HNC_0.htm; (GPS) "Europe's New Air War," by Oliver Morton. August 2002 *Wired,* www.wired.com/wired/archive/ 10.08/airwar.html.

346   Berners-Lee, more time and energy: "Playing to Win," by Viktor Mayer-Schoenberger, *The Parliament,* reprinted November 17, 2003, on the Harvard Web site, www.ksg .harvard.edu/news/opeds/2003/mayer_schoenberger_playing_win_pm_ 1103.htm.

346   Torvalds: "Tech's Great Inventor? Europe," by David Kirkpatrick, *Fortune,* July 9, 2001, p. 132.

346   Saturn's moon: "Landing on Titan Triumph for US and Europe," by Clive Cookson, *Financial Times,* January 15, 2005, p. 3.

346   E.U. harmonizing: (Taxes) "EU Law + Policy Overview: Value Added Tax," European Union, http://europa.eu.int/eur-lex/pri/en/oj/dat/2003/l_066/l_06620030311en002600 35.pdf; (Motorcycles) "Ban on Big Motorcycles for Younger Novice Riders," by Ben Webster, *The Times* (London), January 27, 2005; (Résumés) "Defining a Standard in Résumés," by Thomas Fuller, *International Herald Tribune,* December 1, 2004, p. 11; (Cosmetics) "Directive 2003/15/EC," European Parliament and EU Council, February 27, 2003, http://europa.eu.int/eur-lex/pri/en/oj/dat/2003/l_066/l_06620030311en002600 35.pdf.

346   Most stringent: "Europe's Merger Directive," *The Economist,* December 4, 2004.

346–7   Maastricht pact violators: "Accepting Reality, EU Plans Change," by Graham Bow-ley, *International Herald Tribune,* September 3, 2004, p. 1.

347   E.U. constitution vote: "In Europe, Opportunity Knocks," by Carol Matlack, *Business Week,* June 2, 2005.

347   Longer vacations: "Europe Reluctantly Deciding It Has Less Time for Time Off," by Mark Landler, *New York Times,* July 7, 2004, p. A1.

347   Shorter workweek: "EU Head Office Says Delays in Economic Reforms Harm Growth," by Paul Geitner, Associated Press, January 14, 2003.

347   "slow food" origins, in Italy: "Slower Progress: A Protest Against Fast Food in Italy Has Now Developed into a European Campaign to Keep the Quality of Small-Town Life," by Chris Arnot, *Guardian* (London), January 2, 2002, p. 9.

347   Slow-food membership and events: "The Movement," Slow Food, www.slowfood.com/ eng/sf_ita_mondo/sf_ita_mondo.lasso.

347   U.S. chapters: "Through the Looking Glass—Slowly," *Index,* November 2005, p. 24.

348   Slow Agincourt: "Here Come the Brits," by William Underhill, *Newsweek,* November 13, 2003, p. 31.

348   Slow setting up a business: "More 'Thinking Small' Policies Needed to Help SMEs," European Comission, May 27, 2002, http://dbs.cordis.lu/fep-cgi/srchidadb?ACTION= D&SESSION=148082005-1-28&DOC=1&TBL=EN_NEWS&RCN=EN_RCN_ID: 18447&CALLER=EN_NEWS.

348   Slow patents: "Coping with a Climate of Uncertainty," by Nigel Page, *Financial Times,* June 21, 2001, Survey—FT Director, p. 2.

348   Rita Villa: Interview with the authors, January 2005.

349   Defense industries and "rapid reaction" force: "U.S. Pullout Puts Pressure on Europe's Defence Plans," by Michael Thurston, Agence France Presse, August 17, 2004.

349　"Heartland": "The Geographical Pivot of History," by Halford J. Mackinder, as published in [74], p. 185.

350　E.U. as transnational organization: "The Great Powers of Europe, Redefined," by Timothy Garton Ash, *New York Times,* December 17, 2004, p. A35.

350　Landmasses: (E.U.) "European Union Data," U.S. Department of Agriculture's Foreign Agriculture Service, October 23, 2003, www.fas.usda.gov/dlp/circular/2004/04-10LP/ EUDataNotes.html; (All others) *World Almanac 2004* (New York: World Almanac Books, 2004).

350　Russia and Comparative GDPs: (E.U. and U.S.) "Country Analysis Briefs: European Union," Energy Information Administration, U.S. Department of Energy, January 2005, www.eia.doe.gov/emeu/cabs/euro.html; (All others) *World Factbook 2004,* from its Web site @ http://TheWorldFactbook.info.

350　Small countries flourish: "Software Exports in 2003," Central Bank of Iceland, June 8, 2004, www.sedlabanki.is/uploads/files/Software%20exports.pdf The same point was made at an earlier stage of the E.U. by former leader of British Labour Party Hugh Gaitskell who, in contrast with bigger-is-better claims, noted that "some of Europe's most successful economies belonged to smaller countries, such as Switzerland and Sweden, which did not have large home markets." See Booker, [24].

350　E.U. high-tech in 1997–1998, top 10 I.T. companies: "The Diffusion of Information Technology in Europe," by Harald Gruber, *EIB Papers,* a publication of the European Investment Bank 6 (2001), no. 1, pp. 151–163.

351　Software firms: "Europe's Companies Dwindle in Number, Size and Revenues," by Maija Pesola, *Financial Times,* April 6, 2005, p. 3.

351　Lisbon goal: "EU Leaders Agree to Sweeping Reforms," by Brian Groom and Peter Norman, *Financial Times,* March 25, 2000, p. 1.

351　Poland minister: "How Europe Could Grow Again," by John Rossant, *BusinessWeek,* November 17, 2003, p. 56.

351　Living standards: "Competitiveness Report 2001," European Commission, http:// europa.eu.int/comm/enterprise/library/enterprise-europe/issue6/articles/en/enterprise04 _en.htm.

351　Europe and biotech revolution?: "Navigating the Doldrums," by Ted Agres, *The Scientist,* May 12, 2003, from the BioMed Central Web site @ www.biomedcentral.com/ news/20030512/01/

351　Nanotech gap widening: "Creating New Knowledge in Nanotechnology and Turning It into Better Quality of Life, Competitiveness and Jobs," European Commission, May 12, 2004, http://europa.eu.int/rapid/pressReleasesAction.do?reference=IP/04/639 &format=HTML&aged=0&language=EN&guiLanguage=en.

351　European innovation lags: "Enterprise Europe 15: Innovation," European Commission, April–June, 2004, http://europa.eu.int/comm/enterprise/library/enterprise-europe/ issue15/articles/en/topic5.htm.

351　Schröder on "unrealistic" goal: "Schröder to Urge Economic Rethink for Europe," by Bertrand Benoit and George Parker, *Financial Times,* November 4, 2004, p. 11.

351　Prodi on big failure: "Schröder Sets Out Seven Ways to Stronger EU Internal Market," Agence France Presse, October 26, 2004.

351　Eurochambres conclusion: "EU Economy 'At Same Level as US in Late 1970s,'" by Tobias Buck, *Financial Times,* March 11, 2005, p. 8.

352　Leading industrial power: Todd, [265], p. 146.

352　Unemployment rates: "Little Sign of New Jobs Created in Europe," Associated Press, September 1, 2004.

352　Muslims in Europe: "Special Report: Struggle for the Soul of Islam," by Evan Osnos,

Chicago Tribune, December 19, 2004, p. C1. The issue has intensified since the terrorist attacks in Madrid and London.

352 Riots in Francce: "Get French or Die Trying," by Olivier Roy, *New York Times,* November 9, 2005.

352 Czech graduates: "Czech Republic," *fDI,* January 5, 2004, www.fdimagazine.com/news/categoryfront.php/id126/Czech_Republic.html.

352 Hi-tech firms in Czech Republic: "Planning an Investment in Strategic Services," PriceWaterhouseCoopers, April 2004, www.pwcglobal.com/cz/eng/ins-sol/issues/StrategicServices_DR.html.

352 Slovenia: "Slovenia," *fDI,* January 5, 2004, www.fdimagazine.com/news/category front.php/id/138/Slovenia.html.

352 Hungary and Nokia, Exxon: "Outsourcing Debate Flairs in Europe as Jobs Flow Eastward," by Paul Geitner, Associated Press, May 17, 2004.

352 Hungary's high-tech exports: "EU Spent Nearly 2% of GDP on Research and Development," Eurostat, February 25, 2004, European Union, http://europa.eu.int/comm/eurostat/Public/datashop/print-product/EN?catalogue=Eurostat&product=9-25022004 -EN-AP-EN&type=pdf.

47. INSIDE AMERICA

354 America's evolution: Dominique Moïsi quoted "An American in Paris," by Thomas L. Friedman, *New York Times,* January 20, 2005, p. A23.

355 Old elites: "The Defeat of the Elite," by Walter Wriston, *Forbes,* December 1, 1997, p. 156.

355 U.S. energy delivery: "National Energy Policy—America's Energy Infrastructure: A Comprehensive Delivery System," U.S. Department of Energy, 2001, pp. 5–7, 7–9.

356 Four million miles: Federal Highway Administration. "Public Road Length—2003," Federal Highway Administration, www.fhwa.dot.gov/policy/ohim/hs03/htm/hm12.htm.

356 Trucks and companies: "American Trucking Trends 2003," American Trucking Associations, American Transportation Research Institute, www.atri-online.org/industry/.

356 Volume of transported goods: "Truckers Needed to Keep Economy Rolling," by Barbara Hagenbaugh, *USA Today,* October 12, 2004, p. B1.

356 Trucking revenues: "American Trucking Trends 2003," American Trucking Associations, citing statistics from a Freight Transportation Forecast produced by Global Insight for the ATA.

356 Share of GDP: "U.S. Department of Transportation Adopts New UAlbany Economic Index," State University of New York, March 10, 2004, www.albany.edu/news/releases/2004/mar2004/lahiri_tsi.htm.

356 America's commuters: "Journey to Work: 2000," U.S. Census Bureau, March 2004, pp. 3, 5.

356 "Intelligent transportation" potentials: "Notes from the field," by Tod Newcombe, *Government Technology,* June 1998, www.govtech.net/magazine/gt/1998/june/notes/notes.php.

356 Clinton's highway bill: "Clinton Signs $203 Billion Highway Bill," Cable News Network, June 9, 1998, www.cnn.com/ALLPOLITICS/1998/06/09/highway/.

356 Intelligent systems allocation: "Federal Funding for ITS Programs," table in "The Smart Highway: Still a Less Traveled Road," by Tod Newcombe, *Government Technology,* June 2000, www.govtech.net/magazine/gt/2000/june/highway.php.

356 Superhighway: "New Push for Info Superhighway," by Jube Shriver Jr., *Los Angeles Times,* December 27, 1994, p. D1.

357 Stock options: "Silicon Valley Loses Fight on Stock Options," by Tom Abate, *San Francisco Chronicle*, December 17, 2004.

357 School enrollment: "Enrollment in Education Institutions . . . Fall 1980 to Fall 2005," National Center for Education Statistics, http://nces.ed.gov//programs/digest/do3/tables/pdf/table2.pdf.

358 "Industrial disclipline," immigrants and education: Cremin, [58], p. 351.

359 Education apparatus: "At Long Last a Break in the Clouds," by Ken Robinson, *Times Educational Supplement*, March 12, 2004, p. 23. See also [229].

360 Pervasive tutoring: "Growth Spurt: The Rise of Tutoring in America," by Margot Adler, National Public Radio's *Morning Edition*, June 6, 2005, www.npr.org/templates/story/story.php?storyId=4676496.

360 Tutoring from India: "Internet Tutors from India Aid U.S. Kids with Math," by Philip Reeves, National Public Radio's *All Things Considered*, February 12, 2005, from its Web site @ www.npr.org/templates/story/story.php?storyId=4497026.

360 Current state of education: Wiles, [283], pp. iii, 4–6, 8–9, 181, 211–212.

361 High schools obsolete: Remarks by Bill Gates at the National Education Summit on High Schools, February 26, 2005, Gates Foundation, www.gatesfoundation.org/MediaCenter/Speeches/BillgSpeeches/.

48. OUTSIDE AMERICA

363 Bond ownership: "The Overstretch Myth," by David H. Levy and Stuart S. Brown, *Foreign Affairs*, March/April 2005, http://www.foreignaffairs.org/20050301facomment84201/david-h-levey-stuart-s-brown/the-overstretch-myth.html.

364 Colonial markets: McNeill, [175], pp. 147–158.

364 U.S. not imperialist: Minc, [180], pp. 21, 22, 26–28.

365 World War II deaths: Casualty figures that include civilians are difficult to collect in wartime and are often imprecise. International aggregates are even less precise. See "From Depression to Enormous Wealth; War Turned Impoverished U.S. into a Superpower," by Stanley Meisler, *Los Angeles Times*, August 31, 1989, p. A1.

365 Tsunami deaths: "Measuring the Tsunami's Wake," *BusinessWeek*, March 21, 2005, p. 12.

365 Soviet casualties: "Summit Realties Temper Joy in Russia," by James P. Gallagher, *Chicago Tribune*, May 10, 1995, p. 3.

365 War deaths in Germany (not including concentration camp victims): "World War II Casualties, 1939–1945," table from the Encarta Web site, http://encarta.msn.com/media_701500550_761563737_-1_1/World_War_II_Casualties_1939–45.html.

365 Japan casualties: "The Sacred and the Dead: Japanese World War II Casualties in Body and Spirit," Association for Asian Studies, prepared in conjunction with the group's annual meeting March 31–April 3, 2005, www.aasianst.org/absts/2005abst/Japan/j-31.htm.

365 U.S. losses: "Aug. 14, 1945: The Day the Fighting Stopped," by David Lamb, *Los Angeles Times*, August 14, 1995, p. A1.

365 Soviets cart off equipment: Donnelly, [73], p. 219.

365 Marshall Plan aid: "For European Recovery: The Fiftieth Anniversary of the Marshall Plan," U.S. Library of Congress, www.loc.gov/exhibits/marshall/m46.html.

365 Assistance to Japan: "Country Studies: Japan, The Economy—Patterns of Development," U.S. Library of Congress, www.country-studies.com/japan/the-economy—patterns-of-development.html.

366 Winston Churchill: "How One Man's Short, Vague Speech Shaped the World," by Rod MacLeish, *Christian Science Monitor*, June 5, 1997, p. 4.

366   Population/world percent of Soviet bloc in 1950: (World) Total Midyear Population of the World, 1950," U.S. Census Bureau, www.census.gov/ipc/www/worldpop.html; (East Germany's population in 1950) "Country Studies—Germany, Population, Historical Background," U.S. Library of Congress, www.country-studies.com/germany/population—historical-background.html; (All other countries) "Countries Ranked by Population: 1950," U.S. Census Bureau, www.census.gov/cgi-bin/ipc/idbrank.pl.

366   U.S. GDP, share of world total in early 1950s: Maddison, [160], Table 2.2a, "Shares of World GDP, 1700–1995," from the University of Groningen Web site @ www .ggdc.net/home.shtml#top

366   Manufacturing output in 1950s: "From Depression to Enormous Wealth: War Turned U.S. Into a Superpower," by Stanley Meisler, *Los Angeles Times,* August 31, 1989, p. A1.

366   World, U.S. GDP in 1950: Maddison, [159].

366   World, U.S. GDP in 2003: "Field Listing—GDP," *World Factbook,* www.odci.gov/cia/publications/factbook/fields/2001.html.

367–8   Sneakers, candy, stamps: "Cashing in on the New World of Me," by Julie Schlosser, *Fortune,* December 13, 2004, p. 244.

368   Spider-Man: "A Multicultural Web," by Jason Overdorf, *Newsweek,* July 26, 2004, p. 54.

368   Internet censorship: "Chinese Censors and Web Users Match Wits," by Howard W. French, *New York Times,* March 4, 2005, p. A10.

49. THE UNSEEN GAME OF GAMES

370   Neo-games: This complex new order, of which disorder is a necessary part, cannot be adequately described in yesterday's jargon. Lacking a new vocabulary, we fall back, even in these pages, on terms like *democracy, liberal, globalism, multipolar* and *multilateral.* But they do not do justice to the new, multi-*dimensional* reality.

370   NGO protests: (Monsanto) "Farmers, Citizens and NGOs Protest Genetically Modified Wheat at Agriculture Minister's Office," Sierra Club of Canada, December 9, 2003, www.sierraclub.ca/national/media/item.shtml?x=553; (Shell) "Oil Companies Under Fire Over Human Rights, Environment," by Coralie Schaub, Agence France Presse, April 22, 2000; (McDonald's). "Fires and Anti-Americanism Burn McDonald's," by Michelle Goldberg, *Toronto Star,* December 9, 2002, p. A1.

370   Tsunami volunteers: "Tsunami Relief Effort Still Disorganized, Report Says," by Ellen Nakashima, *Washington Post,* January 23, 2005, p. A15.

370   NGO proliferation: Twenty-five years ago, in testimony before the U.S. Senate Committee on Foreign Relations, we reported that over 3,000 NGOs were operating internationally. Today there are more than 50,000, [268] http:/www.uia.org/statistics/organizations/ytb199.php.

371   Sex ratios in China: " 'Bare Branches' and Danger in Asia," by Valerie M. Hudson and Andrea M. Den Boer, *Washington Post,* July 4, 2004, p. B7.

371   "Gay superpower": "Happy Warrior," by Mark Steyn, *National Review,* October 10, 2005, p. 60.

372   World population growth: "Lower Birth Rate, AIDS Help Slow World Population Growth," Associated Press, March 23, 2004.

372   Bin Laden: "9/11 Terrorism: Global Economic Costs," by Dick K. Nanto, citing an article from rediff.com, Congressional Research Service, October 5, 2004, p. 1.

372   Lower 9/11 estimates: "Review of Studies of the Economic Impact of the September 11, 2001, Terrorist Attacks on the World Trade Center," Government Accountability Office, May 29, 2002, www.gao.gov/new.items/d02700r.pdf.

372 "Aftershocks," grandiose plan: "9/11 Terrorism: Global Economic Costs," by Dick K. Nanto, p. 3.

373 Growth rate of Christianity, Islam by 2025: "Our Religio-Secular World," by Martin E. Marty, *Daedalus* 132 (June 22, 2003), no. 3, p. 42, citing David B. Barrett and Todd M. Johnson.

373 Shifting Christian populations: "The Next Christianity," by Philip Jenkins, *Atlantic Monthly,* October 2002, p. 53.

373 Muslims in Europe: "Islam Shaping a New Europe," by Evan Osnos, *Chicago Tribune,* December 19, 2004, Special Report, p. 1.

373 Muslims in non-Muslim societies, deterritorialization: Roy, [230], pp. 18–20.

374 Oil prices: "Oil Prices Rocket to Record Highs Near 58 Dollars," Agence France Presse, March 18, 2005.

374 Fuel cells and GM: "GM Hoping for Beijing's Help in Promoting Cars That Run on Hydrogen," by Stephanie Hoo, Associated Press, November 18, 2003.

374 Wahabism: "Iranians Recruit Suicide Brigade," by Soraya Sarhaddi Nelson of the Knight-Ridder Foreign Service, published in the *St. Paul Pioneer Press,* June 14, 2004, p. 1A.

375 Executive summary: "The Arab Human Development Report, 2003," United Nations Development Program and the Arab Fund for Economic and Social Development.

376 Arabs and books: The report pointed out that only 4.4 translations of foreign books were published per million people in the Arab world each year during the early 1980s. By contrast, the "corresponding rate for Hungary was 519 books . . . and in Spain 920 books." It argued that development would be aided if Arabs were more open to the outside world.

376 Wall without doors: "The Arab Human Development Report, 2003," p. 6.

50. EPILOGUE: THE PROLOGUE IS PAST

380 Keller on pessimism: "Thoughts on the Business of Life," *Forbes,* January 16, 1998, p. 124.

380 Eisenhower on pessimism: "Wisdom Found in Words About War," by Dennie Hall, reviewing *The Military Quotation Book* by James Charlton (New York: Thomas Dunne, 2002), *Daily Oklahoman,* March 10, 2002, Destinations, p.5.

381 Max Stirner: "Stirner's Life and Work," Stanford Encyclopedia of Philosophy, http://plato.stanford.edu/entries/max-stirner/.

382 Scopes trial: "Rhea Courthouse to Get Statue of Scopes Trial Prosecutor Bryan," Associated Press, February 25, 2005.

382 "Intelligent design": "Not Intelligent, and Surely Not Science," by Michael Shermer, *Los Angeles Times,* March 30, 2005, p. B11.

384 Energy consumption in 2001, oil's share, consumption in 2025: "International Energy Outlook 2004," U.S. Department of Energy, www.eia.doe.gov/oiaf/ieo/world.html.

384–5 Oil declines: "Energy: A Global Overview," by Matthew R. Simmons, presentation for the Stanford GSB Global Conference, November 10, 2004.

385 Robert Walker on fuel-cell power: Interview with the authors, June 7, 2005.

386 Craig Venter: "Scientists Use DNA to Make Virus," British Broadcasting Corp., November 13, 2003, http://newsvote.bbc.co.uk/1/hi/sci/tech/3268259.stm.

386 Biological hydrogen: "Stanford Researchers Work to Create Fuel from Bacteria," by Rose Jenkins, *Stanford Daily,* February 8, 2005.

386 Berke: "Cheap Solar," by Brian Dumaine and Julia Boorstin, *Fortune Small Business,* February 1, 2005, p. 35.

386   La Rance, sun power: "Tidal Energy" and "Ocean Technologies," U.S. Department of Energy, February 7, 2003, www.eere.energy.gov/RE/ocean.html.

386   Other tide-based systems: "What's So Special About Norway's New Power Station?" by Tim Radford, *Guardian* (London), September 25, 2003, p. 2.

386   Taylor and Kalam on energy from moon: "Moon Gas May Solve Earth's Energy Crisis," ABC News, November 26, 2004, www.abc.net.au/news/newsitems/200411/s12522715.htm.

387   World population doubled: "Total Midyear Population for the World: 1950–2050," U.S. Census Bureau, www.census.gov/ipc/www.worldpop.html.

387   Life spans up 42 percent: "World Population Ageing: 1950–2050," U.N. Department of Economic and Social Affairs, www.un.org/esa/population/publications/world ageing19502050/.

387   Poor-country babies: "Getting Better All the Time," *The Economist*, November 10, 2001, p. 3.

387   Safer water: "A Billion Thirsts Quenched," *The Economist*, August 28, 2004.

388   50 vs. 500 years: "Facts and Figures on Poverty," U.N. Development Program, www .undp.org/teams/english/facts.htm.

388   Age of universe: Singh, [246], p. 482.

389   Six thousand years ago: "God or Science?" by Mark Sappenfield and Mary Beth McCauley, *Christian Science Monitor*, November 23, 2004, p. 11.

389   Nanotech applications: "Nanotechnology Size Matters," by Jim Akin, *PC*, July 13, 2004, p. 134. Also, "The Business of Nanotech," by Stephen Baker and Adam Aston, *BusinessWeek*, February 14, 2005, p. 67.

389   International System units: "Prefixes of the SI," University of Exeter Centre for Innovation in Mathematics Teaching, www.ex.ac.uk/cimt/dictunit/dictunit.htm.

389   Francis Bacon: Henry, [125], p. 1.

390   Wars: Brownstone, [33].

BIBLIOGRAPHY

[1]   Aaron, Henry J., and William B. Schwartz, eds. *Coping with Methuselah.* Washington, D.C.: Brookings Institution Press, 2004.

[2]   Adams, James. *The Financing of Terror.* London: New English Library, 1986.

[3]   Aikman, David. *Jesus in Beijing.* Washington, D.C.: Regnery, 2003.

[4]   Al-Harran, Saad Abdul Sattar. *Islamic Finance.* Selangor Darul Ehsan, Malaysia: Pelanduk Publications, 1993.

[5]   Alckaly, Roger. *The New Economy.* New York: Farrar, Straus & Giroux, 2003.

[6]   Amsden, Alice H. *The Rise of "The Rest."* New York: Oxford University Press, 2001.

[7]   Applebaum, Herbert. *Work in Non-Market & Transitional Societies.* Albany: State University of New York Press, 1984.

[8]   Attali, Jacques, and Marc Guillaume. *L'anti-economique.* Paris: Presses Universitaires de France, 1974.

[9]   Bai, Chong-En, and Chi-Wa Yuen. *Technology and the New Economy.* Cambridge, Mass.: MIT Press, 2002.

[10]   Bakar, Osman. *Classification of Knowledge in Islam.* Kuala Lumpur: Institute for Policy Research, 1992.

[11]   Baxter, Brian. *Ecologism.* Edinburgh: Edinburgh University Press, 1999.

[12]   Beaud, Michel. *A History of Capitalism.* New York: Monthly Review Press, 2001.

[13]   Becker, Gary S. *A Treatise on the Family.* Cambridge, Mass.: Harvard University Press, 1993.

[14]   ———. *Human Capital.* Chicago: University of Chicago Press, 1983.

[15]   ———. *The Economic Approach to Human Behavior.* Chicago: University of Chicago Press, 1976.

[16]   Becker, Gary S., and Guity Nashat Becker. *The Economics of Life.* New York: McGraw-Hill, 1996.

[17]   Becker, Jasper. *The Chinese.* London: John Murray, 2000.

[18]   Beinin, Joel. *Workers and Peasants in the Modern Middle East.* Cambridge: Cambridge University Press, 2001.

[19]   Berners-Lee, Tim. *Weaving the Web: The Past, the Present and Future of the World Wide Web.* London: Orion Business Books, 1999.

[20]   Blair, Margaret M., and Steven M. H. Wallman. *Unseen Wealth: Report of Brookings Task Force on Intangibles.* Washington, D.C.: Brookings Institution Press, 2001.

[21]   Blake, Robert. *Disraeli.* New York: St. Martin's Press, 1967.

[22]   Boden, Mark, and Ian Miles. *Services and the Knowledge-Based Economy.* London: Continuum, 2000.

[23]   Boisot, Max H. *Knowledge Assets.* Oxford: Oxford University Press, 1999.

[24]   Booker, Christopher, and Richard North. *The Great Deception.* London: Continuum, 2005.

[25]   Booth, Ken. *Strategy and Ethnocentrism.* London: Croom Helm, 1979.

[26]   Boserup, Esther. *Women's Role in Economic Development*. New York: St. Martin's Press, 1970.

[27]   Boulding, Kenneth E. *Beyond Economics*. Ann Arbor: University of Michigan Press, 1970.

[28]   Brahm, Laurence J. *Zhong Nan Hai*. Hong Kong: Naga, 1998.

[29]   Brandt, Barbara. *Whole Life Economics*. Gabriola Island, Canada: New Society Publishers, 1995.

[30]   Brass, Tom. *Peasants, Populism and Post-Modernism*. London: Frank Cass, 2000.

[31]   Braudel, Fernand. *Capitalism and Material Life 1400–1800*. New York: Harper Colophon, 1975.

[32]   Brown, Michael Barratt. *The Economics of Imperialism*. Middlesex, England: Penguin Books, 1976.

[33]   Brownstone, David, and Irene Franck. *Timelines of War*. New York: Little, Brown, 1994.

[34]   Bryson, John R., et al., eds. *Knowledge, Space, Economy*. London: Routledge, 2000.

[35]   Burggraf, Shirley P. *The Feminine Economy & Economic Man*. Reading, Mass.: Addison-Wesley, 1997.

[36]   Burns, Scott. *Home, Inc*. New York: Doubleday, 1975.

[37]   Burns, Tom. *Industrial Man*. Middlesex, England: Penguin Books, 1973.

[38]   Cahn, Edgar. *Service Credits: A New Currency for the Welfare State*. London: London School of Economics Press, 1986.

[39]   Cahn, Edgar, and Jonathan Rowe. *Time Dollars*. Emmaus, Pa.: Rodale Press, 1992.

[40]   Camerer, Colin, et al., eds. *Advances in Behavioral Economics*. New York: Russell Sage Foundation, 2004.

[41]   Camporesi, Piero. *Bread of Dreams*. Chicago: University of Chicago Press, 1989.

[42]   Center for Medieval and Renaissance Studies, University of California Los Angeles. *The Dawn of Modern Banking*. New Haven: Yale University Press, 1979.

[43]   Cerf, Christopher, and Victor Navasky. *The Experts Speak*. New York: Pantheon, 1984.

[44]   Chancellor, Edward. *Devil Take the Hindmost*. New York: Farrar, Straus & Giroux, 1999.

[45]   Chandler, Tertius. *Four Thousand Years of Urban Growth*. Lewiston, N.Y.: Edwin Mellen Press, 1987.

[46]   Chang, Gordon G. *The Coming Collapse of China*. New York: Random House, 2001.

[47]   Chang, Jung, and Jon Halliday. *Mao: The Unknown Story*. New York: Alfred A. Knopf, 2005.

[48]   Chase, Alston. *Harvard and the Unabomber*. New York: W. W. Norton, 2003.

[49]   Chernow, Ron. *The Death of the Banker*. New York: Vintage, 1997.

[50]   Cipolla, Carlo M. *Before the Industrial Revolution: European Society and Economy, 1000–1700*. New York: W. W. Norton, 1994.

[51]   Clough, Shepard Bancroft, and Charles Woolsey Cole. *Economic History of Europe*. Boston: D. C. Heath, 1947.

[52]   Cohen, Benjamin J. *The Future of Money*. Princeton, N.J.: Princeton University Press, 2004.

[53]   ———. *The Geography of Money*. Ithaca, N.Y.: Cornell University Press, 1998.

[54]   Cohen, Stephen P. *India—Emerging Power*. Washington, D.C.: Brookings Institution Press, 2001.

[55]   Cook, Nick. *The Hunt for Zero Point*. New York: Broadway Books, 2002.

[56]   Cornish, Edward, ed. *Futuring*. Bethesda, Md.: World Future Society, 2004.

[57]   Cox, W. Michael, and Richard Alm. *Myths of Rich and Poor*. New York: Basic Books, 1999.

[58]   Cremin, Lawrence A. *American Education: The National Experience 1783–1876.* New York: Harper Colophon, 1982.

[59]   Crockett, Andrew. *Money.* London: Thomas Nelson & Sons, 1973.

[60]   Crone, Patricia. *Pre-Industrial Societies: Anatomy of the Pre-Modern World.* Oxford: One World Publications, 1989.

[61]   Crook, Nigel, ed. *The Transmission of Knowledge in South Asia.* Delhi: Oxford University Press, 1996.

[62]   Curtin, Philip D. *Cross-Cultural Trade in World History.* London: Cambridge University Press, 1984.

[63]   Czeschin, Robert W. *The Last Wave.* Boca Raton, Fla.: Shot Tower Books, 1994.

[64]   Dattel, Eugene R. *The Sun That Never Rose.* Chicago: Probus, 1994.

[65]   Davis, Jim, Thomas Hirschl, and Michael Stack, eds. *Cutting Edge.* London: Verso, 1997.

[66]   Deane, Phyllis. *The Evolution of Economic Ideas.* Cambridge: Cambridge University Press, 1979.

[67]   Debray, Régis. *Empire 2.0: A Modest Proposal for a United States of the West.* Berkeley, Calif.: North Atlantic Books, 2004.

[68]   Delamaide, Darrell. *The New Superregions of Europe.* New York: Dutton, 1994.

[69]   De Soto, Hernando. *The Mystery of Capital: Why Capitalism Triumphs in the West and Fails Everywhere Else.* New York: Basic Books, 2000.

[70]   ———. *The Other Path.* New York: HarperCollins, 1989.

[71]   De Villiers, Marq. *Water.* Boston: Houghton Mifflin, 2000.

[72]   Devlin, Keith. *Goodbye, Descartes.* New York: John Wiley & Sons, 1997.

[73]   Donnelly, Desmond. *Struggle for the World.* New York: St. Martin's Press, 1965.

[74]   Dorpalen, Andreas. *The World of General Haushofer.* Port Washington, N.Y.: Kennikat Press, 1942.

[75]   Downs, Ray F., ed. *Japan Yesterday and Today.* New York: Bantam Pathfinder, 1970.

[76]   Drexler, Eric K., and Chris Peterson, with Gayle Pergamit, *Unbounding the Future.* New York: William Morrow, 1991.

[77]   Dukes, Paul. *The Superpowers.* London: Routledge, 2000.

[78]   Dunbar, Nicholas. *Inventing Money.* Chichester, England: John Wiley & Sons, 2000.

[79]   Easterbrook, Gregg. *The Progress Paradox.* New York: Random House, 2003.

[80]   Easterly, William. *The Elusive Quest for Growth.* Cambridge, Mass.: MIT Press, 2002.

[81]   Edelstein, Michael. *Overseas Investment in the Age of High Imperialism.* New York: Columbia University Press, 1982.

[82]   Edvinsson, Leif, and Michael S. Malone. *Intellectual Capital.* New York: HarperCollins, 1997.

[83]   Emmott, Bill. *The Sun Also Sets.* New York: Times Books, 1989.

[84]   Epstein, Joseph. *Snobbery: The American Version.* New York: Houghton Mifflin, 2002.

[85]   Evans, Philip, and Thomas S. Wurster. *Blown to Bits.* Boston: Harvard Business School Press, 2000.

[86]   Everard, Jerry. *Virtual States.* London: Routledge, 2000.

[87]   Fattah, Hassan M. *P2P: How Peer-to-Peer Technology Is Revolutionizing the Way We Do Business.* Chicago: Dearborn, 2002.

[88]   Feigenbaum, Edward, et al. *The Rise of the Expert Company.* New York: Times Books, 1988.

[89]   Ferguson, Niall. *The Cash Nexus.* New York: Basic Books, 2001.

[90]   Fernandez-Armesto, Felipe. *Millennium: A History of the Last Thousand Years.* New York: Charles Scribner's Sons, 1995.

[91]   Fingleton, Eamonn. *Blindside: Why Japan Is Still on Track to Overtake the U.S. by the Year 2000*. New York: Houghton Mifflin, 1995.

[92]   Fishman, Ted C. *China, Inc.* New York: Charles Scribner's Sons, 2005.

[93]   Fogel, Robert W. *The Escape from Hunger and Premature Death 1700–2100*. Cambridge: Cambridge University Press, 2004.

[94]   ———. *The Fourth Great Awakening*. Chicago: University of Chicago Press, 2000.

[95]   Frowen, Stephen F., ed. *Unknowledge and Choice in Economics*. London: Macmillan Press, 1990.

[96]   Fuwei, Shen. *Cultural Flow Between China and the Outside World Throughout History*. Beijing: Foreign Languages Press, 1996.

[97]   Galbraith, John Kenneth. *Economics in Perspective*. Boston: Houghton Mifflin, 1987.

[98]   ———. *Money*. Boston: Houghton Mifflin, 1975.

[99]   Gardels, Nathan, ed. *The Changing Global Order: World Leaders Reflect*. Oxford: Basil Blackwell, 1997.

[100]   Garnsey, Peter. *Food and Society in Ancient Antiquity*. Cambridge: Cambridge University Press, 1999.

[101]   Garraty, John A. *Unemployment in History*. New York: Harper & Row, 1978.

[102]   Garreau, Joel. *Radical Evolution*. New York: Doubleday, 2005.

[103]   Gates, Bill. *Business @ the Speed of Thought: Succeeding in the Digital Economy*. New York: Warner Books, 2000.

[104]   Geerken, Michael, and Walter R. Gove. *At Home and at Work*. Beverly Hills, Calif.: Sage Publications, 1983.

[105]   Gershenfeld, Neil. *FAB*. New York: Basic Books, 2005.

[106]   ———. *When Things Start to Think*. New York: Henry Holt, 1999.

[107]   Ghazali, Aidit, and Syed Omar, eds. *Readings in the Concept and Methodology of Islamic Economics*. Selangor Darul Ehsan, Malaysia: Pelanduk Publications, 1996.

[108]   Giarini, Orio, and Walter R. Stahel. *The Limits to Certainty*. Dordrecht, Netherlands: Kluwer Academic Publishers, 1993.

[109]   Giffi, Craig, Aleda V. Roth and Gregory M. Seal, National Center for Manufacturing Sciences. *Competing in World-Class Manufacturing: America's 21st Century Challenge*. Homewood, Ill.: Business One Irwin, 1990.

[110]   Gingrich, Newt. *Winning the Future*. Washington, D.C.: Regnery, 2005.

[111]   Glazer, Nona Y. *Women's Paid and Unpaid Labor*. Philadelphia: Temple University Press, 1993.

[112]   Good, H. G. *A History of Western Education*. New York: Macmillan, 1947.

[113]   Goodstein, David. *Out of Gas*. New York: W. W. Norton, 2004.

[114]   Government Accountability Office. *Informing Our Nation: Improving How to Understand and Assess the USA's Position and Progress*. Washington, D.C.: U.S. Government Accountability Office, 2001.

[115]   Group of Thirty. *Global Institutions, National Supervision and Systemic Risk*. Washington, D.C.: Group of Thirty, 1997.

[116]   Hale, J. R. *Renaissance Europe 1480–1520*. London: William Collins, 1971.

[117]   Hamid, Ahmad Sarji Abdul. *Malaysia's Vision 2020*. Selangor Darul Ehsan, Malaysia: Pelanuk Publications, 1995.

[118]   Hammer, Michael, and James Champy. *Reengineering the Corporation: A Manifesto for Business Revolution*. New York: HarperBusiness, 1993.

[119]   Hanegraaff, Wouter J. *New Age Religion and Western Culture*. Albany: State University of New York Press, 1998.

[120]   Harding, Sandra. *Whose Science? Whose Knowledge?* Ithaca, N.Y.: Cornell University Press, 1991.

[121]   ———. *The Science Question in Feminism.* Ithaca, N.Y.: Cornell University Press, 1986.

[122]   Harrison, Lawence E., and Samuel P. Huntington, eds. *Culture Matters.* New York: Basic Books, 2000.

[123]   Hayes, E. N. *Trackers of the Skies.* Cambridge, Mass.: Doyle, 1968.

[124]   Henderson, Hazel. *Paradigms in Progress.* Indianapolis: Knowledge Systems, 1991.

[125]   Henry, John. *Knowledge Is Power.* Cambridge: Icon Books, 2003.

[126]   Herbolzheimer, Emil, et al. *Innovating Proposals for Rethinking the Economy.* Barcelona: Fundacion Jaume Provenca, 1995.

[127]   Holstein, William J. *The Japanese Power Game.* New York: Charles Scribner's Sons, 1990.

[128]   Hope, Jeremy, and Tony Hope. *Competing in the Third Wave.* Boston: Harvard Business School Press, 1997.

[129]   Hourani, Albert. *A History of the Arab People.* New York: Warner Books, 1992.

[130]   Hutchings, Graham. *Modern China.* Cambridge, Mass.: Harvard University Press, 2001.

[131]   Iqbal, Muzaffar. *Islam and Science.* Aldershot, England: Ashgate, 2002.

[132]   Joshi, Akshay. *Information Age and India.* New Delhi: Institute for Defense Studies and Analyses, 2001.

[133]   Kalam, A. P. J. Abdul, with Y. S. Rajan. *India 2020: A Vision for the New Millennium* New York: Viking Press, 1998.

[134]   Kanigel, Robert. *The One Best Way.* New York: Viking Press, 1997.

[135]   Kepel, Gilles. *The War for Muslim Minds.* Cambridge, Mass.: Harvard University Press, 2004.

[136]   ———. *Jihad.* Cambridge, Mass.: Harvard University Press, 2003.

[137]   ———. *Allah in the West.* Stanford, Calif.: Stanford University Press, 1997.

[138]   Klare, Michael T. *Resource Wars.* New York: Owl Books, 2002.

[139]   Knoke, William. *Bold New World.* New York: Kodansha, 1996.

[140]   Kornai, Janos. *Rush Versus Harmonic Growth.* Amsterdam: North Holland, 1972.

[141]   Kuhn, Robert Lawrence. *The Man Who Changed China.* New York: Crown, 2004.

[142]   Kuhn, Thomas S. *The Structure of Scientific Revolutions.* Chicago: University of Chicago Press, 1996.

[143]   Kuran, Timur. *Islam & Mammon: The Economic Predicaments of Islamism.* Princeton, N.J.: Princeton University Press, 2004.

[144]   Kurtzman, Joel. *The Death of Money.* New York: Simon & Schuster, 1993.

[145]   Lal, Deepak. *The Poverty of "Development Economics."* Cambridge, Mass.: MIT Press, 2000.

[146]   Laulan, Yves Marie. *La planète balkanisée.* Paris: Economica, 1991.

[147]   Le Goff, Jacques. *Time, Work & Culture in the Middle Ages.* Trans. Arthur Goldhammer. Chicago: University of Chicago Press, 1980.

[148]   Lev, Baruch. *Intangibles: Management, Measurement, and Reporting.* Washington, D.C.: Brookings Institution, 2001.

[149]   Levathes, Louise. *When China Ruled the Seas.* New York: Oxford University Press, 1996.

[150]   Levitt, Steven D., and Stephen J. Dubner. *Freakonomics.* New York: William Morrow, 2005.

[151]   Levy, Frank, and Richard J. Murnane. *The New Division of Labor.* New York: Russell Sage Foundation, 2004.

[152]   Levy, Pierre. *Collective Intelligence.* New York: Plenum Trade, 1997.

[153]   Lewis, Alan, Paul Webley, and Adrian Furnham. *The New Economic Mind: The Social Psychology of Economic Behavior.* London: Harvester/Wheatsheaf, 1995.

[154]   Lipnack, Jessica, and Jeffrey Stamps. *The Age of the Network.* Essex Junction, Vt.: Oliver Wight, 1994.

[155]   Loebl, Eugen. *Humanomics.* New York: Random House, 1976.

[156]   Lowy, Michael, and Robert Sayre. *Romanticism Against the Tide of Modernity.* Durham, N.C.: Duke University Press, 2001.

[157]   Machlup, Fritz. *The Production and Distribution of Knowledge in the United States.* Princeton, N.J.: Princeton University Press, 1962.

[158]   Maddison, Angus. *The World Economy, 1950–2001.* Paris: Organization for Economic Cooperation and Development, 2004.

[159]   ———. *The World Economy.* Paris: Organization for Economic Cooperation and Development, 2001.

[160]   ———. *Chinese Economic Performance in the Long Run.* Paris: Organization for Economic Cooperation and Development, 1998.

[161]   Malos, Ellen. *The Politics of Housework.* London: Allison & Busby, 1982.

[162]   Manning, Richard. *Against the Grain: How Agriculture Has Hijacked Civilization.* New York: Farrar, Straus & Giroux, 2004.

[163]   Mansell, Robin, and Uta Wehn, eds. *Knowledge Societies.* New York: Oxford University Press, 1998.

[164]   Mansfield, Edward D. *Power, Trade, and War.* Princeton, N.J.: Princeton University Press, 1994.

[165]   Margiotta, Franklin D., and Ralph Sanders. *Technology, Strategy and National Security.* Washington, D.C.: National Defense University Press, 1985.

[166]   Marx, Karl. *Pre-Capitalist Economic Formations.* New York: International, 1971.

[167]   ———. *Selected Writings in Sociology and Social Philosophy.* New York: McGraw-Hill, 1964.

[168]   Mau, Bruce. *Massive Change.* London: Phaidon Press, 2004.

[169]   Mawdudi, Mawlana. *The Revivalist Movement in Islam.* Kuala Lumpur: Other Press, 2002.

[170]   May, Jon, and Nigel Thrift. *Timespace.* London: Routledge, 2001.

[171]   Mayer, Arno J. *The Persistence of the Old Regime.* New York: Pantheon Books, 1981.

[172]   McGrath, Joseph E., and Janice R. Kelly. *Time and Human Interaction.* New York: Guilford Press, 1986.

[173]   McKnight, Lee W., and Joseph Bailey, eds. *Internet Economics.* Cambridge, Mass.: MIT Press, 1997.

[174]   McNeill, William H. *Keeping Together in Time.* Cambridge, Mass.: Harvard University Press, 1995.

[175]   ———. *The Pursuit of Power.* Chicago: University of Chicago Press, 1982.

[176]   Mead, Walter Russell. *Mortal Splendor: An American Empire in Transition.* Boston: Houghton Mifflin, 1987.

[177]   Menzies, Gavin. *1421: The Year China Discovered America.* New York: Perennial, 2004.

[178]   Meulders, Daniele, Olivier Plasman and Robert Plasman. *Atypical Employment in the EC.* Aldershot, England: Ashgate, 1994.

[179]   Miller, Daniel. *Acknowledging Consumption.* London: Routledge, 1995.

[180]   Minc, Alain. *Ce monde qui vient.* Paris: Bernard Grasset, 2004.

[181]   Monden, Yasuhiro, Rinya Shibakawa, Satora Takayanagi and Teruya Nagao. *Innovations in Management: The Japanese Corporation.* Atlanta: Industrial Engineering and Management Press, 1985.

[182] Mosher, Steven W. *Hegemon: China's Plan to Dominate the World.* San Francisco: Encounter Books, 2000.

[183] Murakami, Yasuke. *An Anti-Classical Poliical-Economic Analysis.* Stanford, Calif.: Stanford Univesity Pess, 1996.

[184] Napoleoni, Loretta. *Modern Jihad: Tracing the Dollars Behind the Terror Networks.* London: Pluto Press, 2003.

[185] Nathan, John. *Japan Unbound.* Boston: Houghton Mifflin, 2004.

[186] National Commission on Terrorist Attacks. *The 9/11 Commission Report.* New York: W. W. Norton, 2004.

[187] Needham, Joseph. *Science in Traditional China.* Cambridge, Mass.: Harvard University Press, 1981.

[188] Nef, John U. *The Conquest of the Material World.* Cleveland: Meridian Books, 1967.

[189] Nelson, Robert H. *Economics as Religion.* University Park: Pennsylvania State University Press, 2001.

[190] Nisbett, Richard E. *The Geography of Thought.* New York: Free Press, 2003.

[191] Nonaka, Ikujiro, and Hirotaka Takeuchi. *The Knowledge-Creating Company.* New York: Oxford University Press, 1995.

[192] Nye, David E. *Electrifying America.* Cambridge, Mass.: MIT Press, 1992.

[193] Ochoa, George, and Melinda Corey. *The Timeline Book of Science.* New York: Ballantine Books, 1995.

[194] Odescalchi, Edmond. *The Third Crown: A Study in World Government Exercised by the Popes.* Oxford: University Press of America, 1997.

[195] O'Driscoll, Gerald P., Jr., and Mario J. Rizzo. *The Economics of Time and Ignorance.* Oxford: Basil Blackwell, 1985.

[196] Office of International Affairs. *Marshaling Technology for Development: Proceedings of a Symposium.* Washington, D.C.: National Academies Press, 1995.

[197] O'Hanlon, Michael, and Mike Mochizuki. *Crisis on the Korean Peninsula.* New York: McGraw-Hill, 2003.

[198] Ohmae, Kenichi. *The Next Global Stage.* Upper Saddle River, N.J.: Wharton School Publishing, 2005.

[199] ———. *The Invisible Continent.* London: Nicholas Brealey, 2001.

[200] ———. *End of the Nation State: The Rise of Regional Economies.* New York: Free Press, 1995.

[201] Ormerod, Paul. *The Death of Economics.* New York: John Wiley & Sons, 1997.

[202] Packard, Vance. *The Hidden Persuaders.* New York: Pocket Books, 1958.

[203] Paine, Lynn Sharp. *Value Shift.* New York: McGraw-Hill, 2003.

[204] Parry, Jonathan, and Maurice Bloch, eds. *Money and the Morality of Exchange.* New York: Cambridge University Press, 1989.

[205] Parente, Stephen L., and Edward C. Prescott. *Barriers to Riches.* Cambridge, Mass.: MIT Press, 2002.

[206] Pasinetti, Luigi L. *Lectures on the Theory of Production.* London: Macmillan, 1978.

[207] Perelman, Lewis J. *School's Out.* New York: Avon Books, 1992.

[208] Pillsbury, Michael, ed. *Chinese Views of Future Warfare.* Washington, D.C.: National Defense Univesity Press, 1997.

[209] Pine, Joseph, II, and James H. Gilmore. *The Experience Economy.* Boston: Harvard Business School Press, 1999.

[210] Pink, Daniel H. *A Whole New Mind.* Riverhead, N.Y.: Penguin Books, 2005.

[211] ———. *Free Agent Nation.* New York: Warner Books, 2001.

[212] Polanyi, Karl. *The Great Transformation.* Boston: Beacon Press, 1971.

[213] Porter, Roy. *The Creation of the Modern World.* New York: W. W. Norton, 2000.

[214]   Posner, Richard A. *Catastrophe.* New York: Oxford University Press, 2004.

[215]   Prahalad, C. K. *The Fortune at the Bottom of the Pyramid.* Upper Saddle River, N.J.: Wharton School Publishing, 2005.

[216]   Price, Colin. *Time, Discounting & Value.* Oxford: Basil Blackwell, 1993.

[217]   Putti, Joseph M. *Management—Asian Context.* Singapore: McGraw-Hill, 1991.

[218]   Pyenson, Lewis, and Susan Sheets-Pyenson. *Servants of Nature: A History of Scientific Institutions, Enterprises and Sensibilities.* New York: W. W. Norton, 1999.

[219]   Quinn, James Brian. *Intelligent Enterprise.* New York: Free Press, 1992.

[220]   Rampton, Sheldon, and John Staub. *Trust Us, We're Experts! How Industry Manipulates Science and Gambles with Your Future.* New York: Tarcher/Putnam, 2002.

[221]   Rees, Dai, and Steven Rose, eds. *The New Brain Sciences.* Cambridge: Cambridge University Press, 2004.

[222]   Rees, Martin. *Our Final Hour.* New York: Basic Books, 2003.

[223]   Revel, Jean-François. *Anti-Americanism.* San Francisco: Encounter Books, 2000.

[224]   Reynolds, Christopher. *Global Logic.* Singapore: Prentice Hall, 2002.

[225]   Rheinbold, Howard. *Smart Mobs: The Next Social Revolution.* New York: Perseus, 2002.

[226]   Riessman, Frank, and David Carroll. *Redefining Self-Help.* San Francisco: Jossey-Bass, 1995.

[227]   Roberts, Paul. *The End of Oil.* Boston: Houghton Mifflin, 2004.

[228]   Robinson, Alan G., and Dean M. Schroeder. *Ideas Are Free.* San Francisco: Berrett-Koehler, 2004.

[229]   Robinson, Ken. *Out of Our Minds: Learning to Be Creative.* Indianapolis: Capstone/Wiley, 2001.

[230]   Roy, Olivier. *Globalized Islam: The Search for a New Ummah.* New York: Columbia University Press, 2004.

[231]   Roderick, Jack. *Crude Dreams.* Seattle: Epicenter Press, 1997.

[232]   Rodinson, Maxime. *Islam and Capitalism.* New York: Pantheon Books, 1973.

[233]   Rosenblatt, Roger, ed. *Consuming Desires.* Washington, D.C.: Island Press, 1999.

[234]   Rostow, W. W. *The Stages of Economic Growth.* Cambridge: Cambridge University Press, 1971.

[235]   Roy, Olivier. *Globalized Islam.* New York: Columbia University Press, 2004.

[236]   Rueschemeyer, Dietrich. *Power and the Division of Labor.* Cambridge: Polity Press, 1986.

[237]   Ryan, Michael P. *Knowledge Diplomacy.* Washington, D.C.: Brookings Institution Press, 1998.

[238]   Sakaiya, Taichi. *What Is Japan?* New York, Kodansha America, 1995.

[239]   ———. *The Knowledge-Value Revolution.* Tokyo: Kodansha International, 1985.

[240]   Sanders, T. Irene. *Strategic Thinking and the New Science.* New York: Free Press, 1998.

[241]   Sardar, Ziauddin. *Desperately Seeking Paradise.* London: Granta Books, 2004.

[242]   Schechter, Danny. *Falun Gong's Challenge to China.* New York: Akashic Books, 2001.

[243]   Schofield, Robert E. *The Lunar Society of Birmingham.* Oxford: Clarendon Press, 1963.

[244]   Shourie, Arun. *The World of Fatwas.* New Delhi: Rupa, 2002.

[245]   Simmons, Matthew R. *Twilight in the Desert.* Hoboken, N.J.: John Wiley & Sons, 2005.

[246]   Singh, Simon. *Big Bang: The Origin of the Universe.* New York: Fourth Estate, 2004.

[247]   Smith, Adam. *The Wealth of Nations.* New York: Modern Library, 1965.

[248] Solomon, Lewis D. *Rethinking Our Centralized Monetary System*. Westport, Conn.: Praeger, 1996.

[249] Solomon, Richard H. *Mao's Revolution and the Chinese Political Culture*. Berkeley: University of California Press, 1971.

[250] Spence, Jonathan D. *God's Chinese Son*. New York: W. W. Norton, 1996.

[251] ———. *The Search for Modern China*. New York: W. W. Norton, 1990.

[252] Staley, Charles E. *A History of Economic Thought: From Aristotle to Arrow*. Cambridge, Mass.: Basil Blackwell, 1989.

[253] Steidl, Rose E., and Esther Crew Bratton. *Work in the Home*. New York: John Wiley & Sons, 1968.

[254] Stephens, Mitchell. *A History of News*. New York: Viking Press, 1988.

[255] Stille, Alexander. *The Future of the Past*. New York: Farrar, Straus & Giroux, 2002.

[256] Sveiby, Karl Erik. *The New Organizational Wealth*. San Francisco: Berrett-Koehler, 1997.

[257] Swedberg, Richard. *Economics and Sociology*. Princeton, N.J.: Princeton University Press, 1990.

[258] Tapscott, Don, et al. *Digital Capital*. Boston: Harvard Business School Press, 2000.

[259] Taverne, Dick. *March of Unreason*. Oxford: Oxford University Press, 2005.

[260] Tawney, R. H. *Religion and the Rise of Capitalism*. New York: New American Library, 1954.

[261] Tay, Simon S. C., ed. *Pacific Asia 2022*. Tokyo: Japan Center for International Exchange, 2005.

[262] Thapar, Romila, ed. *India: Another Millennium?* New Delhi: Penguin Books India, 2000.

[263] Thompson, E. P. *The Making of the English Working Class*. New York: Vintage, 1963.

[264] Thompson, Laurence G., trans. *Ta T'ung Shu: The One-World Philosophy of K'ang Yu-wei*. London: Allen & Unwin, 1958.

[265] Todd, Emmanuel. *After the Empire: The Breakdown of the American Order*. New York: Columbia University Press, 2003.

[266] Turner, Howard R. *Science in Medieval Islam*. Austin: University of Texas Press, 1995.

[267] Union of International Associations. *Encyclopedia of World Problems and Human Potential*. 4th ed. Vol.1, *World Problems*. London: K. G. Saur, 1994.

[268] ———. *Encyclopedia of World Problems and Human Potential*. 4th ed. Vol. 2, *Human Potential*. Munich: K. G. Saur, 1995.

[269] Valenze, Deborah. *The First Industrial Woman*. New York: Oxford University Press, 1995.

[270] Van Kooten, G. Cornelis, and Erwin H. Bulte. *The Economics of Nature*. Malden, Mass.: Basil Blackwell, 2000.

[271] Van Wolferen, Karel. *The Enigma of Japanese Power*. New York: Alfred A. Knopf, 1989.

[272] Vickers, Douglas. *Economics and the Antagonism of Time*. Ann Arbor: University of Michigan Press, 1997.

[273] Vogel, Ezra F. *Japan as No. 1*. Rutland, Vt.: Charles E. Tuttle, 1980.

[274] Waley, Arthur. *Three Ways of Thought in Ancient China*. London: George Allen & Unwin, 1946.

[275] Wallach, Lori, and Michelle Sforza. *Whose Trade Organization?* Washington, D.C.: Public Citizen Foundation, 1999.

[276] Warden, John, III, and Leland A. Russell. *Winning in Fast Time*. Montomery, Ala.: Venturist, 2002.

[277]   Warsh, David. *The Idea of Economic Complexity.* New York: Viking Press, 1984.

[278]   Warwick, David R. *Ending Cash.* Santa Rosa, Calif.: Vision Books International, 1997.

[279]   Weatherford, Jack. *The History of Money.* New York: Crown, 1997.

[280]   Weber, Max. *Economy and Society.* Berkeley: University of California Press, 1978.

[281]   Wen, Sayling, and Tsai Chih-Chung. *Taiwan Experience.* Taipei: Locus, 1998.

[282]   White, Andrew Dickson. *A History of the Warfare of Science with Theology in Christendom.* Amherst, N.Y.: Prometheus, 1993.

[283]   Wiles, Jon, and John Lundt. *Leaving School: Finding Education.* St. Augustine, Fla.: Matanzas Press, 2004.

[284]   Williams, Ann, and G. H. Martin, eds. *Domesday Book.* New York: Penguin Books, 1992.

[285]   Wolf, Charles, Jr., et al. *Fault Lines in China's Economic Terrain.* Santa Monica, Calif.: RAND, 2003.

[286]   Wolf, Michael J. *The Entertainment Economy.* New York: Times Books, 1999.

[287]   Wolin, Richard. *The Seduction of Unreason.* Princeton, N.J.: Princeton University Press, 2004.

[288]   Wolters, Willem. *Locating Southeast Asia.* Singapore: Singapore University Press, 2005.

[289]   Woo, Henry K. H. *The Unseen Dimensions of Wealth.* Fremont, Calif.: Victoria Press, 1984.

[290]   Woolfson, Adrian. *Life Without Genes.* London: Flamingo, 2000.

[291]   Yago, Glenn, and Susanne Trimbath. *Beyond Junk Bonds: Expanding High Yield Markets.* New York: Oxford University Press, 2003.

[292]   Zelizer, Viviana A. *The Social Meaning of Money.* New York: Basic Books, 1994.

ACKNOWLEDGMENTS

Many people have contributed to making this book possible and deserve recognition. Reversing the usual pecking order in literary acknowledgments, let's begin at home, where, in fact, this book has been written, and check in as well at the office we maintain nearby.

We need to thank Linda Paul who, with the help of Carol Simmons, has overseen our ever-expanding research files, neatly sorted into thousands of distinct categories. For decades Linda has known where everything is, why the computers break down, how to get us on the right flights on short notice, how to talk sweetly to strangers—and, especially, how to laugh out loud.

Alicia Garcia, meanwhile, has kept our home offices—and our home—shipshape and stood with us during the worst days of our daughter's fatal illness. She is smart, kind and utterly reliable.

At home and in our travels around the globe, we have met with and learned from many thoughtful people to whom we are grateful. They include:

Paul Romer, professor of economics at the Stanford Graduate School of Business, who gave hours of his time at a restaurant in Silicon Valley to help us understand key economic implications of a knowledge-based economy.

William Easterly, author of *The Elusive Quest for Growth,* codirector of the Development Research Institute at New York University, and formerly of the World Bank, for his ideas about the role of knowledge and incentives in battling poverty.

Financial economists Glenn Yago and Susanne Trimbath of the Milken Institute, with whom we spent an afternoon exploring the less obvious relationships of time to money.

Professor emeritus Michael D. Intriligator, UCLA's renaissance econometrician, whose interests range from modeling health and water resources to nuclear nonproliferation and the transition of Russia from communism to a quasi-market economy.

Special thanks are due Jeffrey Eisenach, who co-chairs a team of fifty economists as chairman at CapAnalysis, LLC, in Washington, and who administered first aid when he thought we needed it, firing off late-night e-mails that actually, on occasion, changed our minds.

We wish to remember, as well, the late Ilya Prigogine, Nobel Prize winner in physical chemistry and one of the founders of complexity theory, whose conversations with us deepened our understanding of chaos and order—both of which underlie wealth.

Our conversations in Mexico with Carlos Slim and his family expanded our understanding not merely of the business and economics of Mexico and Latin America but of far broader topics as well. At dinner with him, one is just as likely to run into Carlos Fuentes and Gabriel García Márquez as Bill Clinton and Magic Johnson.

To Newt Gingrich, former speaker of the U.S. House of Representatives, with whom we have debated, argued, screamed and laughed over the years. Whatever our political disagreements, we never spent an hour with him without learning something new. That's a good mind to be around, especially when we disagree. And we are grateful.

Similarly, we owe thanks to Lee Kwan Yew, founding father and former prime minister of Singapore, who helped awaken all of Asia to its economic potentials. As a senior statesman and long-range thinker, he has shared with us his thoughts about the future of Asia.

And to Richard Danzig, former U.S. secretary of the navy, who asked us to accompany him to China for discussions with businessmen in Shanghai and meetings with admirals of the Chinese navy.

To Cherie Nursalim and Enki Tan for their valuable briefings about the current changes across Asia—and for opening Asian hearts to us.

Thanks are due to the late Sayling Wen of Inventec in Taiwan, who fought to narrow the digital divide in China, all the way from Beijing to Yellow Sheep River, among the poorest of all its regions.

Closer to home, we thank our friends Bob and Pam Weingarten, for unhesitating straight talk, for correcting errors before they found their way into text and for their enthusiasm and years of encouragement as the chapters were written.

We're deeply grateful to Emmy-winner Al Burton and Sally, with whom we discussed this book as it progressed, for their Friday-night ideas about the media, popular culture, politics and the "next big thing"—and for just being there for us always, including during the very worst of times.

And to Matt Fong, former Treasurer of the state of California, for great Chinese dinners and insights into public finance.

To Wictor and Eva Osiatynski. Wictor, an eminent constitutional scholar and author, is professor of law and sociology at Central European University and has taught at the University of Chicago Law School. Eva and Wictor are both international leaders in the battle against alcoholism, which has frequently overlooked economic impacts on productivity, crime, policing and family life.

Thanks are owed, as well, to our editor at Knopf, Ash Green, who deserves a Nobel Prize for patience and who helped keep the manuscript on course when we threatened to veer off in unrelated directions.

To Tim Knowlton, Dave Barbor and Grace Wherry, old friends at Curtis Brown Ltd., our longtime literary agency, who have always been a pleasure to deal with. All writers should be so lucky.

To Bill Leigh, Wes Neff and Larry Leson, and the rest of the people who either are or were at the Leigh Bureau and who have sent us on speaking tours around the world more times than we can recall. This has given us the opportunity to meet not only many of the thinkers and doers who are creating the revolutionary wealth system but intelligent, question-asking audiences from many different cultures. These travels helped shape our lives.

We thank Nathan Gardels, editor of our monthly column, whose brain is bigger than his Rolodex, which is the size of Mount Rushmore.

Last, special thanks are owed to our colleagues at Toffler Associates (TA). To Tom Johnson, for his invaluable critiques of the ongoing manuscript, his sense of humor no matter what, his daily check on our progress and for gently—but continuously—pressuring us to hurry up. A warm friend for decades, Tom is co-founder and a partner in TA, which would never have raised anchor or continued on course without his remarkable seamanship. We owe special thanks, too, to Dick Szafranski, whose intellectual curiosity and razor-sharp insights always stir fresh ideas. Our gratitude goes as well to Deb Westphal, who helped create GPS and who, among many other things, tutors us on everything at or above low-Earth orbit. And to Aaron Schulman, who combines lofty brainpower and feet firmly planted on the ground. And not least to Jae Engelbrecht, who once decades ago showed up with a set of mind-stretching questions and hasn't stopped doing so.

In addition, thanks are due all the TA colleagues who responded to our occasional questions and who organized and participated in the TA dinners at which we spoke but, more important, at which we listened to very smart people. Thanks, too, for fond memories of Bonnie O'Gorman, whose recent death affected us all.

There have, of course, been many, many others, too numerous to list here but remembered with gratitude, who over more than a decade have contributed useful data, information and knowledge, giving us face time and answering our e-mails and phone calls.

Add to them the unknown thousands who have collectively fed our image of the changing world—hundreds of authors, academics who share their ideas online and the hardworking, much-maligned, underpaid and largely un-bylined reporters who every day, working on short deadlines, cover business news, economic-policy issues and related matters, as they pound out on their keyboards what has been called "the first draft of history."

Many of them make occasional mistakes, as we no doubt also do in these pages. Certainly, no manuscript of this length can be 100 percent error-free. Unfortunately, there is no one else we can blame. The clichéd *mea culpa* found in acknowledgments is, alas, true: Authors are ultimately responsible for every word to which they affix their names. Any errors and shortcomings, therefore, are all ours.

INDEX

AARP, 186
AB Applied Biosystems, 11
Abdullah, King of Jordan, 300
Abercrombie & Fitch, 242
Aboulmagd, Ahmad Kamal, 376
Accenture, 45, 296, 352
Aceh, Indonesia, 154
Adelphia Communications, 124, 212
Advanstar Communications, 93
Advertising Age, 71
Aeon Maxvalue, 58
Aeroxchange, 272
Afghanistan, 185, 319
Africa, 69, 209, 363, 366, 376
    AIDS in, 69, 301
    as Christian center, 373
    decolonization of, 78
    electricity in, 314
    poverty in, 288
    Third Wave wealth in, 319
After the Empire (Todd), 351–2
Against the Grain (Manning), 305
Agency for International Development, U.S.,
    81
Agincourt, 348
aging societies, 339–41
agriculture, 67, 225, 308–10, 311
    cloning and, 310
    hyper-, 5, 314–16
    invention of, 19–20
    knowledge and, 271, 315
    Quesnay on, 121
    subsidies for, 301
    Third Wave knowledge-based, 302,
    309–10
    see also genetically modified foods;
    wealth system, first
AIDS, xiii, 3, 69, 85, 185, 296, 299
Airbus, 191, 346

Air Force, U.S., 92–3
airlines, 272
airline tickets, 278
Air New Zealand, 272
air pollution, 82
"Airworld," 71
Albania, 81
Alcantara Launch Center, 91
Alcatel Space, 90
Alfred P. Murrah Federal Office Building,
    220
Algeria, 94
Alliance & Leicester International, 340
All Nippon, 272
Al Qaeda, 93, 232, 372
Altair 8800, 195
Alzheimer's disease, 162, 213
"amateur," 182–3
Amazon.com, 171, 236
Amazon region, 92
American Association for Homecare,
    165
American Association for the Advancement
    of Science, 205
American Education (Cremin), 358
Americanization, 58
American Revolution, 390
American Telephone and Telegraph (AT&T),
    230–1
Amos, Wally, 175
analogies, rate of change and, 114
Anderson, David L., 45
Anderson Consulting, 45
Anees, Munawar, 440*n*
Angkor Wat, 92
Angola, 87
Anheuser-Busch, 343
Anhui Province, China, 308
Annamalai, Kuttayan, 309

Annan, Kofi, 218, 232
Anne, Queen of England, 390
Anonymous (rapper), 243
Ansari X Prize, 95
anthrax, 185, 221
anti-globalist, 82, 84, 363
anti-science, 131–8, 142, 304, 352, 413n
Antone, Tom, 165
Anwar Ibrahim, 440n
AOL Time Warner, 48
Arab Fund for Economic and Social
    Development, 375
Arab Malaysian Bank, 279
Archipelago, 276
Argentina
    capitalism in, 79
    Chinese investments in, 322
    currency in, 75, 76
    financial crisis in, 86, 282
Aristotle, 13, 112
Armed Forces Journal International, 50
Armenia, 76
Armstrong, Lance, 128
Armstrong, Robert E., 306
ARPANET, 7
Arthur Anderson, 213
Ash, Timothy Garton, 349–50
Asia, 72, 77, 95, 290, 300, 374, 385
    AIDS in, 301
    as Christian center, 373
    decolonization of, 78
    electricity in, 314
    financial crisis in, xiii, 85–6, 264, 276,
        282, 324, 440n
    as former world leader, 63–4
    Hepatitis B in, 305
    poverty in, 288
    Third Wave wealth in, 319
Asia-Pacific Research Center, 336–7
Asimov, Isaac, 290
Atkinson, Robert D., 71
ATMs, 90, 169
atomic bombs, 387
Atta, Mohamed, 221
auctions, 269
"Audience of One, The" (*Financial Times*),
    269
Aunt Jemima, 128
Australia, volunteer work in, 182
authority, 125–6, 127, 140, 141
Automated Case Support System, 220

Automotive Aftermarket Industry
    Association, 173
Azerbaijan, 76

Babbitt, Harriet, 81
Bachula, Gary, 131
Bacon, Francis, 127, 389
balanced growth, 43
balance of power, 378
Bali, 372
Balkans, 76
Baltimore, David, 137
Banca Monte dei Paschi, 266
Bank for International Settlements (BIS),
    226, 369
Bank of America, 169
Bank of England, 283
banks, banking, 238, 266, 277–80
Barcelona, 84
Barclays, 279
Barlow, John Perry, 257
Barnard, E. E., 112
Barrett, David B., 373
Barry, Nancy, 235
barter, 282–3, 384
Basel, 226
Basel II, 226
BASF, 343
Bates, Sharon, 154
Bauhaus, 172
bauxite, 87
BBC, 24, 173
bCentral.com, 71
Becker, Gary, 156, 157
Beddoes, Zanny Minton, 80
Beijing, 323
Beijing Genomics Center, 295
Bell, Alexander Graham, 234
Bell Labs, 230
Benveniste, David, 188
Berke, Howard, 386
Berkley, Seth, 246
Berlin, 266
Berlin, University of, 237
Bernardino of Siena, 53
Berners-Lee, Tim, 178, 346
Bettiford, Rosalyn, 180
Bhutan, 76
Bible, 125
Biderman, Albert D., 429n
Bill of Rights, 347

bin Laden, Osama, 372
bio-economies, 306–7
biomedical firms, 411n
biotechnology, 132, 304–7, 310
 in China, 295, 304–5
 Europe and, 351
 in India, 299, 304
Bird & Bird, 348
bisection, 325–7, 332
BlackBook, 243
blackout (2003), 39
bloggers, 141, 413n
Bloomberg, 24
Blue Chip Consensus Forecast on Economic
 Growth, 116
BMW, 343
BNP Paribas, 279
Boeing, 90, 102, 191, 346
Boisot, Max, 102–3
Bolivia, 76
Bolsa, 263
Bolshevik revolution, 78
Bolton, William R., 291
bonds, 261
Bon Marché, 267
Borders, 244
Bowie, David, 217
Brando, Marlon, 7
Bratton, William J., 233–4
Braudel, Fernand, 288
Brazil, 9, 92, 232, 350
 Linux in, 177
 oil prices driven by, 374
 Portuguese-Dutch war in, 390
 as rising power, 369
 in space "club," 91
 trisected wealth system of, 22, 325, 332
Bread of Dreams (Camporesi), 21
Bristol-Myers Squibb, 128
British Empire, 363, 364
British Royal Society, 133
broadband communication, 300
Brookings Institution, 255
Budapest, 352
Buenos Aires, 84
Buffett, Warren, 125, 263
bureaucracy, 31–2, 222, 237, 430n
 governmental, 36
Bureau of Economic Analysis, U.S., 25
Bureau of Labor Statistics, U.S., 53, 227
Burger King, 274

Burns, Marshall, 191, 192
Burton, Al, 57
Bush, George W., 115, 125, 133, 215, 231,
 263
BusinessWeek, 57, 74, 214, 217, 321
Bustamante, Alejandro, 68, 69
Byron, George Gordon, Lord, 381

Cahn, Edgar, 157, 283
California/Berkeley, University of, 108
California Institute of Technology, 112
Calogero, Francesco, 138
Cambodia, 390
Cambridge University, 161–2, 363, 364
Camporesi, Piero, 20–1
Canada
 NAFTA and, 68–9
 tidal system in, 386
cancer, 185
CapAnalysis, 118
Cape Town, University of, 225
capital, 253, 254, 263–4
 intangible, 254–7, 268
capitalism, 21, 79, 249, 253–84
 investments and, 259–64
 markets and, 265–72
 property and, 253–8
"capitalists," 259
"captains of industry," 259
Carnival Cruise Lines, 282
Case Western Reserve, 67
Cassidy, Robert B., 321
Cast Iron Palace, 267
Castro, Fidel, 344
Cato Institute, 227
CBS News, 125, 215
Center for Advanced Research and
 Technology, 245–6
Center for Technology and National Security
 Policy, 306
Center for the Study of Popular Television,
 263
Centers for Disease Control and Prevention,
 U.S., 147, 160
centralization, 346
CERN (Center for European Nuclear
 Research), 113, 178
CFO, 345
Chain Drug Review, 163
Champy, Jim, 44
Chang, Gordon G., 324

Changing Rooms (TV shows), 173
Channel Tunnel, 348
Chaplin, Charlie, 53
Chapple, Julian, 339
charities, 181–2
  scandals of, 214, 217
Charles, Prince of Wales, 132
charter schools, 245
Chart House restaurant, 278
Chase Econometrics, 94
Chernow, Ron, 259
Chile, capitalism in, 79
China, 40, 71, 293, 301, 319–31, 345, 355,
    369, 374, 380, 384, 385
  AIDS in, 164, 296
  American investments in, 64–5
  in ancient times, 52
  biotechnology in, 295, 304–5
  bureaucracies in, 31
  Communist takeover of, 78, 366
  corporate research in, 323
  Cultural Revolution in, 143, 330
  exporters in, 24, 321, 322, 343
  FDIs in, 64
  as former world power, 63–4
  globalization and, 82, 87
  India vs., 297
  Internet in, 308–9, 327, 328, 368
  Japanese reliance on, 75, 342–3
  as key economy, 31
  Linux in, 177
  market socialism in, 79
  monetary chaos in, 277
  as next superpower, 4, 332, 377
  nuclear arms of, 323
  old banks in, 266
  prosumerism in, 160
  protests in, 326
  Quesnay on, 120
  real estate bubble in, 333
  recent growth of, xiii, 14, 64–5
  scientists from, 130, 295
  sex ratio in, 371
  Third Wave in, 295, 439n
  tidal system in, 386
  trisected wealth system in, 22, 325–9, 332
  twin-track development in, 294, 295–6,
    314–15, 328, 368
  wealth relocation in, 144
  in World War II, 232
  "yellow dust" from, 81

China Central Television, 177
China Development Institute, 67
China Great Wall Industry Corporation, 90
China Today, 326
Chinese, as Internet language, 9
chits, 283
choupal, 309
Christensen, Steve, xv-xvi
Christianity, 329, 372–3
"Christmas Cakes," 338
chronomics, 43–4
Chuang-tzu, 73
Churchill, Winston, 365
CIA, 223
Citigroup, 370
cittàslow, 347
civil rights movement, 7
civil societies, 34
Civil War, U.S., 38, 327, 390
Cleveland, Ohio, 67
climate change, 82, 185
Clinton, Bill, xiii, 37, 356
  globalization preached by, 84
  surreal politics and, 215
cloning, xiii, 11, 310, 371
"Closing Bell, The" (photographic series),
    276
CNBC, 24
CNN, 24, 263
cobalt, 87
Coca-Cola, 67
cocoa, 87
Coduri, Rick, 71
coffee, 87
Cohen, Benjamin J., 76–7
Cold War, 319
Colombia, 81
Coming Collapse of China (Chang), 324
Commerce Department, U.S., 91, 272
commodities, 270
communication satellites, 90
communications system, 357
communism, 22
Communist Party, China, 260, 277, 328, 330
Communist Party, France, 366
Communist Party, India, 298
Communist Party, Italy, 366
Communist Party, U.S.S.R., 32
commuting, 356
companies, 33–4, 255–6, 348–9
  see also corporations

Compaq, 351
Competing in World-Class Manufacturing, 44
Completely Bare Spa, 242
Complexorama, 224, 225–9
CompStat, 233
Computer Associates, 350
computer industry, 50
computers, 9–10, 195–7, 350
　see also Internet; Microsoft; World Wide Web
concentration, 346
Conectiva, 59
Confucius, 112, 121
Congress, U.S., xv, 38, 39, 49, 372, 379
Congressional Budget Office, U.S., 162
Congress Party, India, 298
consensus, 123–4, 127, 141
consistency, 124–5, 127
constitution, E.U., proposed, 4, 347
Constitution, Japanese, 342
Constitution, U.S., 347
Controlled Biological and Biomimetic Systems, 311
Cook, Trevor, 348
copper, 87
copyrights, 256–7
Cornell University, 305
corporations, 35, 241, 255, 378
　bonds issued by, 261
　limited liability, 234
　media, 257
　multinational chess played by, 370
　scandals of, 31–2, 124–5, 212–13, 216–17
　transatlantic differences in rules for, 348–9
　see also companies
Costa Rica, 9, 161
cost-of-living index, 119
cotton, 364
Council of Economic Advisors, 115
Council on Foreign Relations, 65, 333
counterglobalists, 84–5
counterrevolutionaries, 355
Courtis, Kenneth, 330, 342
Creating a New Civilization (Toffler and Toffler), xvi
credit cards, 278, 279–80
Crédit Lyonnais, 217
Credit Suisse First Boston, 24

Cremin, Lawrence A., 358
crime, 89, 233–4, 429*n*
Cringley, Robert X., 38
Crone, Patricia, 266
Crossing Over (TV show), 133
cultural imperialism, 367
Cultural Revolution, 143, 330
Curitiba, 59
currency, 75–7, 276, 282–4
　see also specific currencies
Cusumano, Michael, 397*n*
CVS, 278
cystic fibrosis, 305
Czech Republic, 352

Daewoo, 217
Daguerre, Louis-Jacques-Mandé, 234
Daily Yomiuri, 217
DaimlerChrysler, 270
dark matter, 10
Darrow, Charles, 259
Darwin, Charles, 132
Davidson, Don, 175
Davis, Gray, 215
Davos, 77, 84, 246
DAX, 263
Dean, James, 7
Death of the Banker, The (Chernow), 259
Death Row, 242
debit cards, 280–1
Debray, Régis, 344
debt relief, 314
de C***, Xavier, 344
deep fundamentals, 24–8, 90, 229, 231, 232, 267, 271, 319, 346
　in China, 321
　definition of, 143
　Econo-Land and, 263
　knowledge as, 99–100, 104, 114, 122, 148, 177, 198, 249, 321, 350–2, 355, 376, 381, 382
　space as, 63, 68, 82, 90–5, 148, 198, 222–3, 249, 315, 321, 322, 349–50, 354–5, 376, 381
　time as, 46, 82, 114, 148, 168, 198, 222, 249, 315, 321, 347–9, 350, 354, 376, 381
　in U.S., 254–5
　war against science and, 130
　work as, 26–7, 143
　see also knowledge; space; time

Defense Department, U.S., 7, 49–50, 90, 311
Defense Horizons (Herz and Macedonia), 176
de Gaulle, Charles, 332
de-globalization, 78, 83, 88–9, 95, 144, 198
Dell Computer, 128, 296
de-marketization, 270
de-massification, 268, 346, 386
Deming, W. Edwards, 290
democracy, 84, 139, 206, 208, 247
Democratic Party, U.S., 263
Deng Xiaoping, 14, 295, 323
Denmark, 76, 352
    Iraq intelligence of, 124
Department of Human Services, Australia, 236
deregulation, 84
Descartes, René, 21
desertification, 82
de Soto, Hernando, 254
de-synchronization, 40, 46–51, 52, 144, 198, 222, 229, 264, 276, 348, 382
    in Asia, 87
    failures of, 31–2
    ignorance of, 41, 46
    in Japan, 51
    need for, 43–4
    paradox of, 45
    time tax and, 49
    in U.S., 357
    see also synchronization
Deutsche Bank, 279
deutschemarks, 76, 277
Development Program, U.S., 375
Development Program's Regional Bureau for Arab States, U.S., 375
Devol, George C., 290
diabetes, 92, 167
Diderot, Denis, 120
Digital Planet 2004, 10
Dilbert (cartoon), 171
Discover, 191
Discovery Health Channel, 164
division of labor, 26–7
divorce, 211, 216
D-I-Y companies, 172–3, 174
DIY Network, 173
Dohton Bori restaurant chain, 170
Dole, Bob, 128
dollars, U.S., 75–6
Dolly (cloned sheep), xiii, 310

Dosaj, Anita, 54
Dow Jones index, 86
Drexler, K. Eric, 192
drugs, illegal, 81, 93, 145
Dubai, 275
Duca, John C., 261
Dudden, Ian, 91
Dunn, Richard S., 20
durability, 126, 127, 141

EADS/Astrium, 90
Earhart, Amelia, 122
Earth Simulator, 9
Easterly, William, 292–3
eBay, 3, 236, 268
e-choupal, 309
ecology
    eco-extremists, 132
    eco-missionaries, 46–8
"ecology of time," 46–8
e-commerce, 272
Econo-Land, 262–3, 332, 381
Economic and Financial Review, 261
economics, as exact science, 102–3, 147
Economist, 334, 346
economists
    challenges to, 118–19, 410*n*
    predictions of, 115–17
economy, 276, 301
    agrarian, 41–2, 99
    arrhythmic, 46–51
    balanced growth in, 43
    black, 152
    E.U., 351
    fundamentals of, 24–8
    future of, 31, 39–40
    "hidden," *see* prosumers, prosumption
    high-speed changes in, 222, 267
    industrial, 42, 99
    integration of, 289
    "new," *see* economy, knowledge
    in 1950's U.S., 355
    "rival," 99
    of Soviet Union, 32–3
    see also de-synchronization; synchronization
economy, knowledge, 69, 88, 206, 249, 315, 334
    law of obsoledge and, 114
    transition to, xiii, 6–7, 64, 70, 208, 240
    in U.S., xiii, 247, 355–6

see also knowledge; wealth system, knowledge-based
Ecuador, 306
Eden Project, 306–7
Edison, Thomas, 234
education, 4, 195, 218, 231, 313, 358–62
  Gates on, 361
  industrialism and, 35, 55, 314, 358, 359
  in Japan, 216, 360
  in U.S., 36–7, 212, 245–6, 357–8, 360
Edwards, W. Keith, 196
Egypt, 9, 364
eHarmony, 244
Eisenbach, Jeffrey, 118–19
Eisenhower, Dwight D., 380
elections, U.S., 2000, 38
electricity, 314
electronics, 350–1
Elf, 217
Ellison, Larry, 440*n*
embryonic stem-cell research, 295
Enciso, Hugo, 73
Enclosure Acts, 325
Encyclopedia of World Problems and Human Potential, 228
Encyclopédie (Diderot), 120
Endangered Species Act, 136
Endeavor, 92
"End of Mass Market, The" (*Financial Times*), 269
energy, 143, 314, 334, 362, 385–6
Energy Department, U.S., 189, 384
Engelberger, Joseph F., 290–1
England
  Civil Wars in, 390
  gardening in, 173
  Iraq intelligence of, 124
  post-imperial nostalgia in, 128
  see also United Kingdom
Enlightenment, 21, 63, 126, 139, 142, 414*n*
Ennex Corporation, 191
Enquire, 178
Enron, 31–2, 124, 212–13, 372
enterprise resource planning (ERP), 45
environment, 143
environmentalism, 131, 136
Environmental Protection Agency, U.S., 248
Epstein, Joseph, 226
ER (TV show), 164
Ericsson, 350
Ernst & Young, 299

ERP (enterprise resource planning), 45
ESADE (La Escuela Superior de Administación y Dirección de Empresas), 102
euro, xiii, 75, 76, 277, 282, 346, 402*n*
Eurobond, 275
Eurochambres, 351
Europe, 231, 344–53, 355, 366, 374, 377
  advertising in, 15
  agricultural subsidies in, 301
  corporate scandals in, 217
  eco-extremism in, 132
  electronic components produced by, 350–1
  exporters in, 321
  in feudal times, 52–3
  as "oldest" part of world, 162
  Second Wave strategy proposed by, 289
  sham transformations in, 232
  social security in, 339
  technology in, 351
  U.S. growing apart from, 345–51
European Commission, 348
European Union (E.U.), 40, 87, 210, 228–9, 350
  bisected wealth system in, 332
  bureaucracy and, 232
  computers produced by, 350
  constitution of, 347
  currency of, *see* euro
  expansion of, 4
  GDP of, 65
  genetically modified food banned by, 345
  as key economy, 31
  proposed military force of, 349
Evening Standard, 54
Evian, 80
evolution, 132, 382
exports, 321, 322, 334
External Trade Organization, 336
ExxonMobil, 352

fabbers, 191–2
Falun Gong, 133, 328, 330
families, 211, 216, 218, 241, 313, 338
famines, 20–1
Famous Amos, 175, 189
Fanning, Shawn, 188
Farabi, Abu Nasr al-, 146
Fast Company, 306–7
(FDI) foreign direct investment, 64

Federal Bureau of Investigation (FBI), 220–1, 223
Federal Emergency Management Act, 221
Federal Express, 101, 168–9
Federal Financial Supervisory Board, 226
Federal Reserve, U.S., 26, 41, 76, 116, 260, 263, 277
Federal Reserve Bank of Dallas, 261
feminism, 131–2
Fermat, Pierre de, 182
feudalism, 31, 266
Figaro, Le (Paris), 78, 217
films, 206, 367, 378, 390
Filo, David, 101
Financial Accounting Standards Board (Fazbee), 357
financial meltdown, 214
Financial Times, 48, 54, 68, 80, 116, 241, 269, 275–6, 352
Finland, 275, 350
    Evian prices in, 80
First Wave, *see* wealth system, first
FlagHouse, 166
Flanigan, James, 260
flash markets, 267–8
flash mobs, 4
flexible fungibility, 278–83
float, disappearance of, 281
Fogel, Robert, 288, 432n
Fonow, Robert C., 321
Food and Agriculture Organization, 287
Food and Drug Administration, U.S., 36, 164, 166
Forbes, 39, 192, 282
Ford, Edsel, 260
Ford, Henry, 260
Ford Motor Company, 260, 282
foreign direct investment (FDI), 64
Foreign Policy, 80, 81
Foresight (Martin and Mason), 56
Foresight Institute, 192
Fortune, 70, 188, 213, 282
Fortune 500, 280
Fox News, 57
France, 65, 80, 84, 243, 288, 344, 347, 377
    bureaucracies in, 31
    Communist Party in, 366
    corporate scandal in, 217
    E.U. constitution rejected by, 4, 347
    Evian prices in, 80
    fast food in, 58

health expenditures in, 162
    as Imperial power, 363
    Iraq intelligence of, 124
    old people in, 162
    pensions in, 217
    post-imperial nostalgia in, 128
    riots in, 352
    satellite-launch business, 346
    tidal system in, 386
    volunteer work in, 185
    in World War II, 232
francs, French, 76
francs, Swiss, 76
Frank, Betsy, 57
Frankfurt, 275
Franklin, Benjamin, 182
Franklin, Linda, 220–1
Franklin, Ted, 220
Free Agent Nation (Pink), 56
free agents, 56
Freeh, Louis, 221
free trade, 84, 208
French and Indian wars, 390
French Revolution, 390
Friedman, Milton, 102, 439n
Friedman, Thomas, 296
FTSE, 263
Fujitsu, 291, 351
fundamentals, 143, 147
    of economy, 24–8, 198
    see also deep fundamentals
Futures, 299
Future Shock (Toffler and Toffler), xv, 11, 54, 59, 187, 412n

Gage, John, 280
Gaitskell, Hugh, 449
Galileo Galilei, 93
Garcia, Marta, 154
Gates, Bill, 226, 312, 361, 440n
Gaye, Marvin, 175
gay rights movement, 7
Gedye, David, 184
GenderPAC, 8
General Electric, 169, 282, 296, 345
General Motors, 24, 214, 290, 343
genetically modified (GM) foods, 132, 304–7
Genoa, 84
genocide, 89, 145
Geography of Money, The (Cohen), 76

Georgia, 76
Gere, Richard, 125
Germany, 65, 80, 226, 232, 277, 320, 377
  cannibal in, 242–3
  corporate research in, 323
  corporate scandal in, 217
  currency of, 75, 76
  gardening in, 173
  health expenditures in, 162
  Heinz prices in, 80
  home improvement in, 172
  as imperial power, 363
  Iraq intelligence of, 124
  Maastricht Treaty and, 346–7
  old people in, 162
  pensions in, 217
  sales regulations in, 58
  unemployment in, 4
  volunteer work, 181, 185
  in World War II, 232
  World War II casualties of, 365
Gershenfeld, Neil, 192
Gesellschaft mit beschrankter Haftung, 234
Ghosh, Rishab Aiyer, 158
Gibbons, Glen, 93
giggle anchors, 8
Glass-Steagall Act (1934), 39
Glazer, Nona Y., 157
globalization, 77, 78, 81–3, 181, 198, 208, 345, 354
  index of, 80
  protests against, 84–5
  weighing negatives of, 82
  Weingarten on, 79
Global Positioning System (GPS), 90, 93–4, 307, 346, 386
  NAVSTAR, 93
Global Social Benefit Incubator, 246
global warming, 82
Goldman Sachs, 330, 342
Gooding, Cuba, Jr., 199
Google, 236, 255, 262, 264
Gosden, Richard, 133
Gospel of Change, 205–10
Government Technology, 356
Grameen Bank, 235–6
Grand Exhibition, 78
Grand Theft Auto: Vice City (online game), 242
Grateful Dead, 257

Great Depression, 38, 78, 253, 281, 383
Great Hanshin Earthquake, 181
Great Leap Forward, 330
Greece, 81, 84
Greenland, 76
Greenpeace, 223, 304
Greenspan, Alan, 263
Grinter, Rebecca E., 196
Grossman, Marc, 221
Ground Force (TV show), 173
Guangdong, 67, 69
Guevera, Che, 344
Guinness World Records, 101

Habitat for Humanity, 181
Hall, Robert E., 256
Hammer, Michael, 44
Hanegraaff, Wouter, 135
Hang Seng, 263
Han Shi, 439n
Hanssen, Robert, 221
Harley-Davidson, 44
Harrington, Padraig, 114
Harry, Prince of England, 3
Hayes, E. Nelson, 183
health care, 91, 160–7, 217, 218, 228
  in U.S., 213, 216
Heine, Heinrich, 381
Heinz ketchup, 80
Henderson, Hazel, 154–5, 157
hepatitis B, 305
Heraclitus, 209–10
Herz, J. C., 176
Heston, Charlton, 126
heterogeneity, 368
Hewlett-Packard, 9, 351
HGTV, 173
high-value-added places, 66–72, 256
Hill, L. Erskine, 112
Hilton, 278
Hindus, 299–300
Hitachi, 291, 351
Hitler, Adolf, 365
Hoffman, Abbie, 187
Home Depot, 172, 274
Homeland Security Department, U.S., 231–2, 236
homelessness, 247, 432n
Homer-Dixon, Thomas, 39
homogeneity, 367–8
Honda, 290

Honeywell, 345
Hong Kong, 67, 86, 275
Hong Xiuquan, 330
Horn, Paul, 130
Horwood, Richard, 234
House Committee on Science, U.S., 183, 385
Houston Medical (TV show), 164
How Can I Tell You This (sex-education series), 164
Howison, James, 191, 192
HP, 296
Huang, Yasheng, 326
Huawei, 322
Hughes, Vern, 236
Hu Jintao, 322, 325
Hull, Charles, 191
human genome, xiii, 134, 386
Hunaidi, Rima Khalaf, 375
Hungary, 82, 352
hunter-gatherer societies, 19, 41, 111
Huntington, Samuel, 439*n*
Hu Yaobang, 295
Hyderabad, 84
hyper-agriculture, 5, 314–16
Hyundai, 216

I, Robot (Asimov), 290
IBM, 44, 130–1, 192, 233, 234, 269, 280, 291, 298, 322, 336, 351, 352
Iceland, 9
Ikeda, Hayato, 332
Imagination Library, 245
Immigration and Naturalization Service, U.S., 221
Inc., 70
Incas, 120
Independent Sector, 180–1
India, 14, 40, 232, 293, 301, 369, 374, 377, 384, 385, 386
    agronomy in, 309–10
    biotechnology in, 299, 304
    China vs., 297
    currency of, 76
    decolonization of, 78
    electricity in, 314
    Huawei in, 322
    Internet in, 196–7, 298, 309–10, 313
    Linux in, 177
    outsourcing to, 263, 309
    prosumerism in, 160

    scientists from, 130
    Spider-Man in, 368
    trisected wealth system of, 22, 325, 332
    twin-track development in, 294, 296, 297–300, 315
    vaccine-laden food research in, 305
    violence in, 327
    wealth relocation in, 144
"India—Giant or Pygmy?" (New Delhi conference), 297
Indiana, 70, 71
Indian Department of Biotechnology, 304
Indian Space Research Organization, 299
India 2020–A Vision for the New Millennium, 297
Indonesia, 81–2, 264, 292
industrialism, 21–3, 208, 211, 225, 248, 266, 314, 316
    in China, 295, 326
    criticism of, 294
    education and, 358, 359
    in Japan, 336
    knowledge and, 271
    in U.S., 355, 372
    see also wealth system, second
industrial revolution, xiv, 7, 8, 10, 21, 53, 126, 238, 289, 390–1
    democracy and, 139
    economists in, 117
    markets and, 266–7
    wealth-poverty gap and, 303
    see also wealth system, second
industrial robot, 290–1
industry bias, 326
Industry Week, 67
information, 100, 102, 268
InfoSavvy Group, 54
Innovations in Management: The Japanese Corporation, 44
Inotai, András, 82
Institute for Advanced Study, 266
Institute for World Economics, 82
Institute of Industrial Engineering, 44
insurance, fire, 234
Insurance Regulatory and Development Authority, India, 299
intangibility, 70, 254–7, 268
Intangibles (Lev), 255
Intel, 50, 185, 300, 322, 343
intellectual property, 187, 377
intelligent-design movement, 382

"intelligent transportation," 356
Intelsat, 91
InterContinental Hotels, 278
intergovernmental organizations (IGOs), 37, 218
International AIDS Vaccine Initiative (IAVA), 246
International Herald Tribune, 347
International Monetary Fund, 37, 76, 116–17, 218, 234, 369
  poverty and, 287
Internet, 7, 9–10, 24, 35, 38, 54, 83, 91, 118, 122, 123, 133, 137, 171, 177–8, 196–7, 201, 214, 246, 255, 308–9, 310, 313
  barter conducted over, 283
  in China, 295, 308–9, 327, 328
  in India, 196–7, 298, 309–10, 313
  investing over, 262–3
  knowledge and, 104
  matchmaking on, 244
  medical information on, 164
  music and, 188–9
  NGOs and, 370
  SETI and, 184–5
  space called into question by, 66
  "wealth" on, 265
  Yahoo!, 101
Intersputnik, 90
investments, 259–64
Invisible Continent, The (Ohmae), 333
iPods, 200
Iran, 128, 247, 380
Iraq, 124, 215, 218, 376
Iraq War, xiii, 345
Ireland, 80, 350
Isadore of Seville, Saint, 112
Ishihara, Shintaro, 75
Islam, 299–300, 372–6
Israel, 81, 350
I.T., 45, 47, 51, 70, 153, 177, 227, 255, 261, 275, 297, 298, 300, 309, 312, 321, 346
  in Europe, 351, 352
  in Japan, 334, 337, 339
Italy, 65
  Communist Party in, 366
  corporate scandal in, 217
  ex trade in, 81
  Heinz prices in, 80
  as imperial power, 363
  Iraq intelligence of, 124
  "slow food" movement in, 347

  volunteer work in, 181
  in World War, II, 232
ITC, 309
Iwai, Nissho, 216

Jackson, Michael, 124
Jackson, Shirley Ann, 205
Jamaica, 161
Japan, 22, 40, 51, 64, 65, 73, 164, 231, 232, 320, 332–43, 350, 355, 388
  advertising in, 15
  atomic bombs dropped on, 387
  bureaucracies in, 31
  China attacked by, 331
  computers produced by, 350
  corporate research in, 323
  corporate scandals in, 216
  currency of, 76, 277
  education in, 216, 360
  electronic components produced by, 350–1
  emergency services in, 181
  exporters in, 321, 334
  gardening in, 173
  globalization of, 80
  health care in, 160
  health expenditures in, 162
  home improvement in, 172
  as imperial power, 363
  JCB in, 279
  as key economy, 31
  Linux and, 177
  marriage and divorce in, 216
  nanotechnology in, 351
  old people in, 162
  Pearl Harbor attack of, 64
  pensions in, 217
  post-World War II development of, 290–2
  prosumerism in, 160, 339
  retirement in, 339–42
  science emphasized in, 128
  sex trade in, 81
  24/7 retailers in, 58
  volunteer work in, 180, 181, 186
  women in, 338–9
  in World War II, 232
  World War II casualties of, 365
Japan, Bank of, 41
Japan as No.1, 291
Japan Emergency Team, 181–2
Japanese Evaluation Center, 291

Japan Times, 216, 339
Jauhiainen, Jussi, 68
JCB, 279
Jenkins, Philip, 373
Jerry Maguire (film), 199
Jet Propulsion Lab, 94
Jiang Zemin, 325
Jing Li, 439*n*
JIT (just-in-time) principle, 44, 333
jobs, future of, 26–7
Joffe, Adrian, 60
Johnson, Todd, 373
Johnson Space Center Astronomical Society, 183
Johnston, Ian, 127
Jonathan's Coffee House, 274
Joshi, Shashank, 309
Joslin Diabetes Center, 167
Journal of the American Dietetic Association, 163
Joy, Bill, 137–8
Jukes, Ian, 54
juku, 360
Juran, Joseph, 290
just-in-time (JIT) principle, 44, 333

Kaczynski, Ted, 133
Kaiser Permanente, 227
Kalam, A. P. J. Abdul, 297, 386
Kampf, Karola, 228
kanban (just-in-time principle), 44, 333
Kandarian, Steven, 214
Kaneda, Hideaki, 323
Kanniainen, Liisa, 279
Kant, Immanuel, 112
Kasnoff, Craig, 184
Katrina, Hurricane, xiii, 32, 181
Kawakubo, Rei, 60
Kawasaki, 278
Kazaa, 188
Kearney, A. T., 80
keiretsu, 335–6
Keller, Helen, 380
Kelly, Maggie, 348
Kennedy, John F., assassination of, 143
Kentucky Fried Chicken, 122
Keynes, John Maynard, 102, 117, 324, 383
Kim Dae-jung, 300
King, Mervyn, 26, 283
KLM Royal Dutch, 272
Kmart, 93

Knickman, James R., 162
Knoke, William, 66
knowledge, 6, 99–148, 225, 289, 310, 332, 357, 364, 388
    Aggregate Supply of (ASK), 108
    cultural, 106, 107–8
    as deep fundamental, 99–100, 104, 114, 122, 148, 177, 198, 249, 321, 350–1, 355, 376, 381, 382
    definition of, 100, 271
    economy and, 104–5, 118
    future of, 109–10
    individual humans and, 106–7
    oil vs., 104–5
    scientific, 10
    six filters for, 123–8
    undepleteable character of, 117, 119, 120, 256
    U.S. dominance and, 205–6
    see also economy, knowledge; obsoledge; science; technology; wealth system, knowledge based
knowledge market, 271
Kodak, 233, 234
Koizumi, Junichiro, 342
Komatsu, Sakyo, 341
Koran, 125
Korea Times, 217
Kors, Alan, 126
krone, 76
K-tools, 10–11
Kukowski, John A., 291
Kumar, Vikram S., 167
Kuwait, 87
Kyoto Protocol, 248, 384
Kyoto Sangyo University, 340

labor unions, 35–6
Ladies' Home Journal, 175
Lampard, Bruce, 154
Lang, Fritz, 53
language, 156
Latin America, 209, 366, 376
    as Christian center, 373
    electricity in, 314
    poverty in, 288
    Third Wave wealth in, 319
law, 38
Law of Congruence, 31
    definition of, 396*n*
law of obsoledge, 114

Lawrence, David M., 227
Lawrence Livermore National Laboratory, 9
League of Nations, 37
leakage, 293
Leaving School: Finding Education (Wiles and Lundt), 360
Lee, Hau, 45
Lee Kwan Yew, 300
Le Goff, Jacques, 53
Leninism, 32
Lenovo, 322
Leonardo da Vinci, 112, 122
Leontief, Wassily, 120
leprosy, 288
Lerner, Jaime, 59
Lesk, Michael, E., 109
Lev, Baruch, 255
Levathes, Louise, 63
Levin, Lowell, 165, 167
Liberal Democratic Party, Japan, 290, 342
liberalization, 84, 208
Library of Congress Country Studies, 292
Liechtenstein, 76
Lietaer, Bernard, 282
Life Without Genes (Woolfson), 109–10
Lindsay, Greg, 71
Linnaeus, Carolus, 112
Linux operating system, 59, 176–7, 346, 383, 384
Lisbon, 351
Lisbon Agenda, 351
Lockheed Martin Corporation, 102
Loebl, Eugen, 128
Logica, 352
London, 266
London International Financial Futures and Options Exchange (LIFFE), 91
London Stock Market, 274
Long Term Capital Management, 116
Longul, Wally, 338
Los Angeles, Calif., 230, 234
Los Angeles Times, 215, 242, 298
Louis XV, King of France, 120
Lovins, Amory, 190
Lovins, Hunter, 190
Luce, Henry, 64
Lufthansa, 272
Lundt, John, 360

Maastricht Treaty, 346–47
Ma Bell, 230

Macao, 67
Macedonia, Michael R., 176
Machlup, Fritz, 6
Mack, Connie, 37–8
Mackinder, Halford, 349
Madhya Pradesh, India, 309
Madrid, 372
Magna Blast!, 75
Mahathir Mohamad, 300, 440n
Malacca Strait, 385
Malaysia, 82, 86, 161, 292, 300, 334, 340, 440n
Malaysian Multi-Media Super Corridor, 440n
Manchu Dynasty, 330
Manchurian Candidate, The (film), 139
M&M's, 368
Manning, Richard, 305
Manning, Robert, 65
manufacturing
    in South Korea, 105
    in U.S., 105
Mao Zedong, 325, 328
Mapping Alliance Program (MAP), 91
Marconi, Guglielmo, 234
markets, 253, 264, 265–72, 308
Marriott, 282
Marshall Plan, 365, 377
Martin, Bill, 56
Maruetsu supermarkets, 58
Marx, Karl, 102, 117, 260
Marxism, 31, 133, 295, 329
Mason, Sandra, 56
massification, 346
material requirements planning (MRP), 44
Matshushita, 351
Matsushita, 75, 130
Mattel, 191
maximization, 346
Max Plank Institute, 161–2
Mayer-Schoenberger, Viktor, 348
McDonald's, 274, 367, 370
McKinsey & Co., 226
McNeill, William, 41
McVeigh, Timothy, 220
MDs (TV show), 164
media, 217–18, 257, 267, 269, 360
Media Lab, 192
MedTech, 165
meetup.com, 244
Meiji restoration, 277, 327

Mercosur, 87
mergers, 47–8
Metropolis (Lang), 53
Metternich, Prince, 378
Mexico, 71, 84
  financial crisis in, 85
  NAFTA and, 68–9
  retired Americans in, 340
  scientists from, 130
  trisected wealth system of, 325, 332
Mexico City, 380
microfinance, 235
MicroRate, 236
Microsoft, 38, 50, 71, 185, 227, 296, 300,
    322, 350, 370
Middle East, 6, 209, 374–5, 385
  Japanese reliance on, 75
  scientists from, 130, 375
Midwest Research Institute, 94
Million, Les (film), 281
Minc, Alain, 364
Ministry of Science and Technology, China,
    308–9
Minix, 176
Mitra, Sugata, 196–7
Mitsubishi, 291
Mitsubishi Motors, 67, 216
Mitsui, 216
Modern Times (Chaplin), 53
Moïsi, Dominique, 354
Monde, Le (Paris), 125, 217, 364
money, 13–14, 253, 264, 273–84
  see also currency; para-money
Money, 14
Monopoly, 259
Monsanto Corporation, 132, 304, 370
Montana, University of, 360
Moody, John, 57
moon landing, 143
Moonwatch, 183
Moore, Patrick, 304
Morita, Akio, 56
Morley, Robert, 290
Morris, James, 132
Morse, Samuel, 234
Motorola, 44, 191, 351
Moulton, Brent, 25
MRP (material requirements planning), 44
MTV, 55
Mueller, Robert, 220
multipolar world, 377–8

Murder, Inc., 242
Muslims, 299–300, 372–6
Mussolini, Benito, 33
mutual funds, 234–5
Myanmar, 323
Mystery of Capital, The (de Soto), 254

NAFTA (North American Free Trade
    Agreement), 68–9
Naím, Moisés, 81
Naito, Minoru, 51
nanodevices, 311
nanoproducts, 88
nanotechnology, 10, 192–3, 300, 311, 334,
    351, 389
Napoleon I, Emperor of the French, 390
Napster, 188–9
NASA (National Aeronautics and Space
    Administration), 91–2, 94–5, 205, 346
NASDAQ, 263
National Academy of Science, U.S., 137
National Center for Manufacturing Sciences,
    44
National Committee on Science and
    Technology, Korea, 300
National Defense University, 306
National Foreign Trade Council, 345
National Foundation for Cancer Research,
    185
National Guard, 125
National Health Service, U.K., 217
National Information Assurance Partnership,
    227
National Institute of Health, 411*n*
National Organization for Women (NOW), 7
National Public Radio, 360
National Research Council, 307
National Science Board, 205
National Science Foundation, U.S., 109, 131
NATO (North Atlantic Treaty Organization),
    349
Naval Research Laboratory, U.S., 92
NAVSTAR Global Positioning System, 93
  see also global positioning system
    (GPS)
NEC, 351
NEC computers, 75
Needham, Joseph, 127
Neil's Wheels Model Car Speedway, 175
Nelson, Robert N., 136
neo-games, 370, 452*n*

Nestlé, 67
Netherlands, 80
   E.U. constitution rejected by, 4, 347
Nevada, 71
New Age, 132, 134–5
New Age Religion and Western Culture
   (Hanegraaff), 135
Newcomen, Thomas, 234
New Delhi, 54
newly industrialized countries (NICs), 64
Newman, Ryan, 191
New Orleans, La., 221
New Skies, 91
Newsweek, 82, 368
Newton, Isaac, 21, 102, 146
New York, 135
New York Police Department (NYPD), 233,
   234
New York Stock Exchange, 86, 263, 275,
   276
New York Times, 8, 37, 125, 215, 216, 296,
   326, 329, 396n
New York Times Magazine, 166
New Zealand, 84
NextCards, 55
"Next Christianity, The" (Jenkins), 373
Next Global Stage, The, 68
Nguyen Thi Binh, 99
NICs (newly industrialized countries), 64
Nieman Marcus, 278
Nigeria, 87, 94
Nihei, Akira, 340–1
Nihon Keizai Shimbun, 51
Nike, 367
Nikkei, 263
Nikkei Weekly, 337
Nippon Meat Packers, 216
Nissan, 290
Nissan SUVs, 75
Nobel Prizes, 205–6
Noguchi, Tomoo, 59
Nokia, 350, 352
nongovernmental organizations (NGOs), 34,
   94, 157, 181, 182, 223, 228, 232,
   235–6, 238, 245, 246, 287, 289, 315,
   352, 370–2, 376, 378, 380
Nordea, 279
North American Free Trade Agreement
   (NAFTA), 68–9
North Atlantic Treaty Organization (NATO),
   349

North Florida, University of, 360
North Korea, 181, 247
Northwest Airlines, 272
Norway, tidal system in, 386
Novell, 350
NTT, 300
Nugent, Richard, 183

Obi, 172
obsoledge, 111–14, 115, 122, 130, 141, 145,
   163, 198, 223, 410n
   definition of, 111, 122, 271
   law of, 114
Office Depot, 274
Office Max, 274
Office of Public Reform, 228
Official Development Assistance, 341
Ohmae, Kenichi, 68, 333, 440n
oil, xiii, 87, 88, 374, 384–5
   vs. knowledge, 104–5
Olympia, 352
Olympics, 242
Oman, 87
Omohundro, John, 41–2
Opinión, La (Los Angeles), 73
Oracle software, 45, 255, 350
O'Reilly, Sharon, 165
Organization for Economic Cooperation and
   Development, 22, 162
Our Final Hour (Rees), 138
Out of Our Minds: Learning to Be Creative
   (Robinson), 359
outsourcing, 69, 263, 309
Owest, 213
Oxfam, 223
Oxford University, 185, 350, 363, 364
ozone depletion, 82

Pacific Stock Exchange, 276
Pakistan, 94, 299, 319
Palo Alto Research Center, 196
PanAmSat, 91
Panay, 41–2
Paracel Islands, 323
Paradigms in Progress (Henderson), 157
para-money (para-currency), 278–83, 384
Paris, 266
Parker Brothers, 259
Parliament Magazine, 348
Parmalat, 217
Parton, Dolly, 245

Patent Office, U.S., 238
patents, 238, 256, 348
Pavarotti, Luciano, 217
peer teaching, 194–7, 422n
Pension Benefit Guaranty Corporation, 214
pensions, 214, 216, 217, 218
Penske Racing, 191
Pentagon, see Defense Department, U.S.
People's Liberation Army, 327
PeopleSoft, 45
Pepsi-Cola, 282, 378
Person to Person, 236
Peru, 76
pesos, Argentine, 75
Pet Psychic (TV show), 133
pharmaceutical firms, 257, 411n
Philippines, 182, 292
Philips, 280, 370
Phoenix, Ariz., 70
Phoenix Assurance Company, 234
Physicians' Desk Reference, 164
Pinheiro, Mariana Pimenta, 154
Pink, Daniel H., 56
Pitsilis, Emmanuel, 226
Planetary Geoscience Institute, 386
Planetary Society, 184
Planick, Neil, 175
Plantronics, 69
Plato, 112
POAM III, 92
Poetics (Aristotle), 112
Point and Click Appliance Repair, 173
Poland, Sweden's invasion of, 390
polio, 288
pollution, 144–5, 248
Pompadour, Madame de, 120
pop culture, 206–7
Porphyry, 112
Pôrto Alegre, Brazil, 77, 84
Portuguese-Dutch war, 390
postmodernism, 135–6
"Post-Modern SMEs," 135
Post Office, U.S., 368
Potter, Donald, 170
poverty, 194, 287–316
    in China, 295–6, 297, 303
    in India, 296, 297–300, 303
Powell, Michael, 188
Powershift (Toffler and Toffler), 253
Praktiker, 172
Presley, Elvis, 7, 122

Priceline, 269
Priestley, Joseph, 182
Princeton University, 266
privatization, 84
Procter & Gamble, 67
Prodi, Roman, 351
producivity, 194–7, 377
    definition of, 194
production, 267–8, 370
Progressive Policy Institute, 71
property, 253–8
Prosumer Economy, 152–4
prosumers, prosumption, 5, 151–201, 265,
        283, 339, 377, 383, 386, 422n-3n
    definition of, 153, 155
    D-I-Yers as, 173
    of the elderly, 341
    energy and, 189–90
    health care and, 165–7
    hobbies and, 175–6
    industries launched by, 176
    NGOs and, 370
    producivity provided by, 194–7
    third job and, 169–70
    in Venezuelan Constitution, 415n
    volunteer work and, 182, 184, 185,
        200
    World Wide Web and, 178
Protestantism, 14
Ptolemy, 112
Public Utilities Regulatory Policy Act
        (1978), 189
Putin, Vladimir, 33
Pythagoras, 112

Qinghua University, 323
quadrivium, 146
Quaker Oats, 128
Qualcom, 322
quantum theory, 102–3
Quesnay, François, 120–1

Radio Shack, 195
Raffaele, Paul, 207–8
Rao, Sachin, 309
rap groups, 242, 243–4
Rapid Start, 220
Raseikina, Tatiana, 99
Reagan, Ronald, 355
reality TV, 4
Red Crescent, 182

Red Cross, 182
  American, 214
Reengineering the Corporation (Champy and Hammer), 44
Rees, Martin, 138
Regional Cancer Center, 299
re-globalization, 69, 79–80, 83, 85–9, 95, 144–5, 181, 218, 229, 367
Reich, Robert, 8
Reinsch, William A., 345
relativity, theory of, 102–3
religion, 131, 140, 372–4, 378
renminbi yuan, 277
RepairClinic.com, 173
Republic (Plato), 112
Republican Party, U.S., 116
"Respect for the Earth" (lecture), 132
Reuters, 24
revelation, 126, 127, 141
revolutionary wealth, *see* wealth, revolutionary
revolutions, xiii, 7–8
Ricardo, David, 102, 117
Ringen, Stein, 155, 157
Rita, Hurricane, 181
Rite Aid, 213
river blindness, 288
robber barons, 259
Robbins, Tom, 199
Robert Wood Johnson Foundation, 162
Robinson, Ken, 359
Roche Applied Science, 10
rock 'n' roll, 7
Rocky Mountain Institute, 190
Roman Empire, 363, 364
Romania, 76, 81, 82
Ross, Diana, 175
Ross, Ron S., 227
Rowen, Henry S., 336–7
Roy, Olivier, 373
Royal Dutch/Shell, 217, 370
Rudgley, Mervyn, 191
Ruiz, Teofilo, 20
rupee, 76
Russia, 22, 24, 87, 282, 349, 350, 377
  financial crisis in, 85, 282
  foreign investment in, 79
  tidal system in, 386
  in World War II, 232
Russian Revolution, 328, 390
Rwanda, 288

Sakakibara, Katsuo, 154
Samsung, 370
sanchalak, 309
San Francisco, earthquake in, 181–2
SAP, 45, 296
SARS, xiii, 141, 296
Satellite Industry Association, 90
Saudi Arabia, 87, 247, 306, 374
Saunders, Clarence, 170
Savery, Thomas, 234
SBC Communication, 231
School of Advanced Studies in Social Sciences, 373
School of Information Management and Systems, 108
School of Information Management Services, 108
Schopenhauer, Arthur, 381
Schriever Air Force Base, 92–3
Schröder, Gerhard, 351
Schumpeter, Joseph, 43, 117
Schwarzenegger, Arnold, 215
science, 126–8, 129, 130–1, 141–2, 146–7, 382, 388–9, 411n
  in Middle East, 130, 375
  movements against, 131–8
  religion and, 131, 140
  see also biotechnology; technology
Science, 42–3, 305
Scientific-Atlanta, 321
scientific knowledge, 10
Scopes trial, 382
Scotland, 182
Scrubs (TV show), 164
Search for Extraterrestrial Intelligence (SETI), 184–5, 189
Sears, 93, 173
Seattle, Wash., 84
Second Wave, *see* wealth system, second
Securities and Exchange Commission, U.S., 31
Sen, Amartya, 156
Senate Intelligence Committee, U.S., 124
sensor technology, 311
Seoul, South Korea, 81
September 11, 2001, terrorist attacks of, xiii, 32, 93, 215, 231, 319, 372
Sepulveda Boulevard, 230
Sepulveda solution, 230–9
Seven Doorways to Money, 151–2
7-Eleven, 274

sex trade, 81, 145
Shanghai, 275
Sharma, Dinesh C., 299
Shehhi, Marwan al-, 221
Shell Oil, 370
shift of wealth, 63–4, 400n
shobodan, 180
Shum, Harry, 296
Siemens, 217, 322, 343, 351
Siemens Nixdorf, 48
Sikorski, Radek, 351
Simmons, Matthew R., 384–5
Simon and Garfunkel, 175
Singapore, 65, 80, 82, 86, 275, 300, 340, 350
Singh, Rajnath, 304
Sistani, Ali al-, 125
SK, 217
Skandia, 217
Skype, 188
Slammer virus, 221
slavery, 89, 266
Slovenia, 352
"slow food" movement, 347
Small Business Survival Committee, 70–1
smallpox, 185, 287
Smit, Tim, 306–7
Smith, Adam, 27, 102, 381
Smith, Fred, 101
Smithsonian Astrophysical Observatory, 183
Snell, Emily K., 162
Snow Brand Food, 216
Social Security, 39, 339–40, 415n
Socrates, 121
software, 350, 351
    see also Microsoft
Sol-20, 195
Solow, Robert, 118
Son, Masayoshi, 440n
Sony, 222–3, 280, 291, 296
Sony PlayStations, 75
Sorbonne, 133
South Africa, 182, 380
South America
    capitalism in, 79
    Chinese investments in, 322
South Asia, 366
South Dakota, 70–1
South Korea, 22, 64, 65, 73, 80, 86, 292,
    300, 320, 350, 388
    bisected wealth system in, 332
    cell phone-credit cards in, 279

corporate scandals in, 217
divorce rates in, 216
exporters in, 321, 334
health expenditures in, 162
Linux and, 177
pensions in, 217
prosumerism in, 160
volunteer work in, 181, 185
Soviet Union, 32–3, 290, 346, 365–6, 387
    Second Wave strategy proposed by, 289
    World War II casualties of, 365
space, 63–95, 382
    as deep fundamental, 63, 68, 82, 90–5,
        148, 198, 222–3, 249, 315, 321, 322,
        349–50, 354–5, 376, 381
    high-value-added places and, 66–72, 256
    outer, 90–5
    spatial relations, 74–5
SpaceShipOne, 95
Spain, 65, 352, 363
    Iraq intelligence of, 124
    old people in, 162
    Queen Anne's wars against, 390
Spector, Arlen, 411n
speed dating, 54
Spider-Man, 368
sports, 225, 241–2
SPOT-4, 92
Spratley Islands, 323
Sprint Japan, 321
Sputnik, 6, 95, 183
Sri Lanka, 161
standardization, 346
Stanford University, 337
Starbucks, 244, 367
Starscan, 183
Star Trek: First Contact (film), 273
State Department, U.S., 221
State New Economy Index, 71
Steal This Book (Hoffman), 187
steam engine, 312
StelSys, 91
stem-cell research, 11
stereolithography, 191
Steyn, Mark, 371
Stille, Alexander, 321
Stirner, Max, 381
stock markets, 274–5
Stolichnaya vodka, 282
Stoppard, Tom, 217
Stott, Philip, 134

stovepipes, 223
Streisand, Barbra, 125
sugar, 87
Sullivan, M. J., 439*n*
Summers, Larry, 37
Sun Microsystems, 280
Supreme Court, U.S., 396*n*
Surrey Satellite Technology, 94
Sutton, Willie, 198–9
Sweden, 22, 80, 350
    corporate scandal in, 217
    Huawei in, 322
    Iraq intelligence of, 124
    Poland invaded by, 390
Sweeting, Martin, 94
Switzerland, 76, 80, 182, 340
Symantec, 350
synchronization, 32–3, 40, 144, 382
    "ecology of time" and, 46
    in history, 41–2
    ignorance of, 41, 46
    in Japan, 51
    need for, 43–5
    of neurons, 42–3
    paradox of, 45
    three "giant leaps forward" of, 44–5
    see also de-synchronization

Tableau Économique (Quesnay), 120
Taiping Rebellion, 330
Taiwan, 65, 86, 292, 299, 320, 322, 329,
    334, 345, 388
Tan, Enki, 154
Target, 93
Tattini, Eugene, 95
taxes
    in China, 326
    hidden, 273–4
taxes, time, 48–50
Taylor, Lawrence, 386
Taylorism, 32, 396*n*
technology, 10–12, 34, 95, 143, 233, 289,
    301, 310–12, 313–15, 366
    in China, 323–4
    see also biotechnology; nanotechnology;
    science
Technology Review, 227
Telecom, 300
telecommunications, 39, 50, 321, 334, 336,
    350
television shows, 56–7, 206

Tennessee University, 386
Terra Project, 283–4
terrorism, 88, 89, 145, 231–2, 247, 319, 372
    see also Al Qaeda; September 11, 2001,
    terrorist attacks of
Tesco Europe, 278
Texas, University of, 340
Texas Instruments, 191
Thailand, 116, 292, 323, 328
think tanks, 237, 238
third jobs, 5, 168–71, 172, 382
    definition of, 168–9
Third Wave, *see* wealth system, third
Third Wave, The (Toffler and Toffler), 153,
    165, 295, 439*n*
Thompson, Robert, 263
3D Systems, 190–1
Three Gorges Dam, 314
Tiananmen Square, 326, 328
Tighe, Michael, 52
Tijuana, 69
Timbuktu, 207–8
time, 31–60
    Americanization and, 58
    as deep fundamental, 46, 82, 114, 148,
        168, 198, 222, 249, 315, 321, 347–9,
        350, 354, 376, 381
    hourly wages and, 52–3
    regularity of, 55–6
    speed and, 31–40
    24/7 future and, 58–9
    youth and, 54–5
Time, 64, 174
Time Dollars (Cahn), 157, 283
Times (London), 12, 216
time tax, 48–50
Time Warner Telecom, 24
Titan, probe on, 346
Tocqueville, Alexis de, 220
Todd, Emmanuel, 352
Togliatti, Russia, 99
Tokyo, xiii, 275
Tokyo Electric Power Co., 216
Tokyo Sowa Bank, 51
Tokyo University, 337
Tomkins, Richard, 241
Torvalds, Linus, 176–7, 178, 346
Toshiba, 101, 291, 351
Toyoda, A. Maria, 336–7
Toyota, 44, 270, 282, 290, 291, 370, 374
trachoma, 288

Trackers of the Skies (Hayes), 183
trade, foreign, 78
trademarks, 256
transportation, in U.S., 356–7, 362
Transportation Department, U.S., 356
Trauma: Life in the E.R. (TV show), 164
Treasuries, U.S., 320, 363
Treaty of Mutual Cooperation and Security,
    343
trickle-down economics, 293, 388
Trimbath, Susanne, 264
trisection, 325–9, 332
trivium, 146
TRS-80, 195
tsunami (2004), xiii
Tupperware, 191
Turgot, Baron de, 120
Turkey, 19–20, 76, 81
Turkish-Venetian war, 390
"24 Hour Street," 59
twin-track development, 295–302, 314–15,
    328, 368
Tyco, 125, 213

Ubar, 92
UBS, 279
UFJ, 51
Ukraine, 76, 282
  in space "club," 91
UMNO, 440*n*
Unbounding the Future (Drexler), 192
U.N. Conference on Trade and Develop-
    ment, 322
unemployment, 247, 383
  in China, 326
  in Germany, 4
UNICEF, 81
Unimation, 290
unions, 27, 358–9
United Arab Emirates, 87
United Devices, 185
United Kingdom, 65, 348
  corporate research in, 323
  Enclosure Acts in, 325
  families in, 216
  finance in, 275
  health expenditures in, 162
  home improvement in, 173
  Huawei in, 322
  in World War, II, 232
  see also England

United Nations, 37, 85, 234, 315, 387–8
  corruption at, 218
  drugs business estimates from, 81
  poverty and, 287
  Second Wave strategy proposed by, 289
  sham transformations in, 232
United Nations Conference on Trade and
    Development, 226–7
United Nations Development Program,
    387–8
United Press International, 177
United States, 354–62, 369, 376–7, 380
  advertising in, 15
  agricultural subsidies in, 301
  bisected wealth system in, 332
  bureaucracies in, 31, 231–2
  Chinese competition with, 320
  Chinese imports in, 87
  Chinese investments of, 64–5
  Chinese nuclear arms and, 323
  in Cold War, 387
  communications system of, 357
  computers produced by, 350
  corporate research in, 323
  education in, 36–7, 212, 245–6, 357–8,
    360
  electronic components produced by,
    350–1
  Europe growing apart from, 345–51
  exporters from, 343
  as FDI recipient, 64
  GDP of, 65, 356
  globalization of, 80
  Gospel of Change in, 205–10
  hatred of, 5–6
  health care in, 160, 162
  hepatitis inoculations in, 305
  home improvement in, 172
  Huawei in, 322
  innovation in, 71, 238, 247, 260
  Iraq War and, 124
  Japanese reliance on, 75
  as key economy, 31, 64, 198, 260
  knowledge-based wealth system in, 290
  NAFTA and, 68–9
  nanotechnology in, 351
  September 11 attacks' effect on economy
    of, 372
  outsourcing from, 263, 309
  past empires vs., 363–4
  post-World War II production in, 79

proposed European confederation with, 344

prosumerism in, 160, 377

relative vs. absolute wealth in, 366–7

residential construction in, 49

Second Wave strategy proposed by, 289

social security in, 339

speed of, 347–9

standard of living, in, 240

trade deficit of, 4

transportation system in, 356–7

trickle-down effect and, 388

volunteer work in, 180–1, 185, 186

wave conflict in, 355–6, 359

wealth promoted in, 14–15

weather risk in, 91

workers as "owners" in, 260

in World War II, 232, 365

United Way, 214

Universal Postal Union, 37

universities, 228

UNIX, 176

urbanization, 266–7

USA Today, 215, 227

utility bills, 281

values, 240–9

Vatican, 125

Vegas.com, 242

Venezuela, 81, 87, 415*n*

Venter, Craig, 386

venture capital, 154, 336, 337

Viagra, 128, 354

Vietnam, 9, 76, 99

Vietnam War, 7, 143

Villa, Rita, 348–9

Visa, 279

Vista software, 227

Voice over Internet Protocol (VoIP), 188–9, 200

Volkswagen, 217

Volokh, Eugene, 257

volunteer work, 154, 180–6, 200, 246

von Stauffenberg, Damian, 236

von Zedtwitz, Maximilian, 323

wage labor, 266

Wagner, Richard, 381

Walker, Robert, 385

Wallace, Rusty, 191

Wall Street Journal, 14, 116, 235

Wal-Mart, 93, 274, 367

Walras, Léon, 117

Wang Shiwu, 308

war, as de-globalizer, 88

War and Anti-War (Toffler and Toffler), xvi

War Child UK, 217

Ward, Aaron Montgomery, 267

Warner, David, 340

Washington, D.C., 84, 220

Washington Concensus, 84

Washington Post, 115, 212

water-supply shortages, 82

Watson, Thomas, 192, 336

wave conflict, 325–6, 327–8, 342, 355–7, 359

wave policy, 325

wealth, xiii, 3, 13–15, 178, 198

definition of, 14, 19

future of, 5, 13, 145, 343, 363

Internet hits of, 265

knowledge and, 70, 105, 108

mobility of, 63–65

outer space and, 90–5

prosumer economy and money economy as, 5

Quesnay on, 121

"third world" relocation of, 144

time and, 53–8

wealth, revolutionary, xiii, 68, 108–9, 118, 119, 159, 201, 229, 248, 316, 352, 381

future of, 141–2, 369

poverty and, 287

in U.S., 354, 367

see also deep fundamentals

wealth revolution, 3, 12, 95, 119–20, 198, 277, 301, 357, 366

anti-Americanism and, 6

key forces behind, 144–5

roots of, 6–7

see also deep fundamentals

wealth system, first, 19–21, 22–3, 193, 300, 329, 383

see also agriculture

wealth system, knowledge-based, 55, 117, 225, 232, 249, 267, 270–2, 277, 290, 300, 302, 320, 323, 335, 346, 351, 363, 382, 383, 384

in India, 298

in Japan, 335

property called into doubt by, 254

see also economy, knowledge; knowledge

wealth system, second, 21–3, 53, 63–4, 140, 163, 209, 211, 257, 266, 289, 300, 302, 319, 335, 361, 390–1
  in China, 294, 314, 326, 329
  in India, 294
  in U.S., 355, 356
  see also industrialism; industrial revolution
wealth system, third, 22–3, 53, 64, 67, 163, 193, 208–9, 257, 272, 284, 287, 289, 300, 303, 319, 320, 335, 361, 368, 383, 388, 391
  in China, 194, 295, 314, 327, 329
  in Europe, 352
  in Japan, 335, 336
  Middle East and, 375
  in U.S., 355, 356
  see also wealth system, knowledge-based
wealth systems, 19, 174–5, 198–9, 218, 225
  Anti-Americanism and, 5–6
  irregularities of, 57–8
  payment and, 281
  speed and, 55
weapons of mass destruction, 372
Weaving the Web (Berners-Lee), 178
Weber, Max, 439*n*
Weingarten, R. I., 79
Weingarten, Robert, 276
Welch, Jack, 126
Western Union, 269
Whipple, Fred, 183
White, Lynn, 20
Whitehall Financial Group, 79
White House Economic Advisory Policy Board, 355
White House Office of Management and Budget, 118
Whitney, Eli, 234
Wilchins, Riki Anne, 8
Wiles, Jon, 360
Windows software, 50, 227, 345
Winston Cup series, 191
WIPO (World Intellectual Property Organization), 37, 257–8
Wolters, Willem, 42
Woman's Day, 175
women, in Japan, 338–9

Women's Paid and Unpaid Labor (Glazer), 157
women's rights movement, 7
Women's World Banking, 235
Woolfson, Adrian, 109–10
Worden, Simon "Pete," 183
work, 26–7, 218
World Affairs, 439
World & I, The, 165
World Bank, 218, 292, 298, 369
  on China, 296
  poverty and, 287–8, 296
World Christian Encyclopedia, 373
WorldCom, 124, 213
World Economic Forum, 246
World Food Program, U.N., 132
World Health Organization, 161, 162
World Intellectual Property Organization (WIPO), 37, 257–8
World Resources Institute, 309
World Trade Center, 93, 322
World Trade Organization, 37, 218, 369
World War I, 78, 319, 390
World War II, 64, 78, 319, 364–5, 390
World Wide Web, 177–8, 269, 330, 346, 370, 383, 384
  see also Internet
Wriston, Walter, 355
writing, invention of, 107–8

Xena, 112
Xerox, 213
Xinhua news service, 64, 308, 328

Yago, Glenn, 263
Yahoo!, 101, 236
Yang, Jerry, 101
yen, 76, 277
Yunus, Muhammad, 235

Zaid, Gabriel, 13
Zambia, 87
Zhao Ziyang, 295, 330, 439*n*
Zheng He, 63
Zhou Yongkang, 326
Zimbabwe, 132, 182
Zurich, 275

A NOTE ABOUT THE AUTHORS

Alvin Toffler and Heidi Toffler are founders of Toffler Associates and write and lecture widely about emerging global trends in science, economics and social dynamics. They are the authors of such classics as *Future Shock* and *The Third Wave,* as well as *Powershift, War and Anti-War* and, most recently, *Creating a New Civilization.*

The Tofflers work on identifying the newest forces behind change, synthesizing them and setting them into a coherent intellectual framework. In their early years, they spent half a decade as blue-collar workers in heavy industry, later putting that practical experience to use by writing about the nature of work and the contrast between manual and mental labor. Both the Tofflers are Distinguished Adjunct Professors at the National Defense University in Washington and honorary co-chairs of the U.S. Committee for the United Nations Development Fund for Women. They have worked together as an intellectual team since their marriage more than fifty years ago.

A NOTE ON THE TYPE

The text of this book was set in a typeface called Times New Roman, designed by Stanley Morison (1889–1967) for *The Times* (London) and first introduced by that newspaper in 1932. Among typographers and designers of the twentieth century, Stanley Morison was a strong forming influence—as a typographical adviser to the Monotype Corporation, as a director of two distinguished publishing houses, and as a writer of sensibility, erudition, and keen practical sense.

Composed by Stratford Publishing Services,
Brattleboro, Vermont
Printed and bound by Berryville Graphics,
Berryville, Virginia